Seeking
and
Resisting
Compliance

In memory of Robert Thomas Wilson

Steven R. Wilson
Purdue University

Seeking
and
Resisting
Compliance

Why People Say
What They Do
When Trying to
Influence Others

SAGE Publications
International Educational and Professional Publisher
Thousand Oaks ▪ London ▪ New Delhi

For information:

Sage Publications, Inc.
2455 Teller Road
Thousand Oaks, California 91320
E-mail: order@sagepub.com

Sage Publications Ltd.
6 Bonhill Street
London EC2A 4PU
United Kingdom

Sage Publications India Pvt. Ltd.
M-32 Market
Greater Kailash I
New Delhi 110 048 India

Printed in the United States of America

Library of Congress Cataloging-in-Publication Data

Wilson, Steven R.
  Seeking and resisting compliance : why people say what they do when trying to influence others / Steven R. Wilson.
        p. cm.
Includes bibliographical references and index.
  ISBN 0-7619-0522-7 -- ISBN 0-7619-0523-5 (pbk.)
  1. Persuasion (Psychology) 2. Influence (Psychology)
  3. Communication--Psychological aspects. I. Title.
  BF637.P4 .W55 2002
  153.8′52--dc211

                                      2001007983

02 03 04 05 10 9 8 7 6 5 4 3 2 1

Acquiring Editor:	Margaret H. Seawell
Editorial Assistant:	Alicia Carter
Production Editor:	Claudia A. Hoffman
Copy Editor:	Judy Selhorst
Indexer:	Molly Hall

Contents

Preface   vii
Acknowledgments   xi

Introduction

1. What Is Persuasive Message Production?   1
   What Is Compliance Gaining?   4
   On the Ethics of Seeking Compliance   8
   What Is Message Production?   13
   Persuasive Message Production: Three Themes   15
   Summary   16

Part I. Describing Influence Interactions   19

2. The Traditional Approach to Message Analysis:
   Nominal-Level Strategies   21
   The Task of Describing Influence Interactions   24
   Nominal-Level Typologies of Influence Strategies   27
   Evaluation of Nominal-Level Typologies   39
   Summary   44

3. Alternative Approaches to Message Analysis:
   Themes, Dimensions, and Temporal Characteristics   47
   Nominal-Level Content Themes in Influence Messages   48
   Dimensions of Influence Behavior   56
   Temporal Characteristics of Influence Interactions   69
   Summary   79

Part II. Metaphors for Studying Persuasive Message Production   83

4. The First Generation: Persuasive Message
   Production as Strategy Selection   85
   The Compliance-Gaining Tradition   86
   The Constructivist Tradition   115
   From Strategy Repertoires to Goal Pursuit   128
   Summary   130

5. The Second Generation: Persuasive Message
   Production as Goal Pursuit   133
     Conceptualizing Goals   134
     Defining the Situation: Research on Influence Goals 139
     Multiple Goals as Constraints: Research on Secondary Goals 144
     Forming Interaction Goals: The Cognitive Rules Model 168
     Evaluating the Utility of a Goals Perspective   173
     Summary   179

Part III. Theories of Goal Pursuit   **181**

6. Discourse Perspectives on Persuasive Message Production   183
     Questions Posed by Discourse Scholars   185
     Background Concepts and Assumptions   187
     Obstacles to Compliance: Attribution and
     Speech Act Theories   201
     Threats to Face: Politeness and Message
     Design Logic Theories   218
     Summary   239

7. Cognitive Perspectives on Persuasive Message Production   241
     Cognitive Theories: Key Concepts and Assumptions   246
     Plans and Planning for Communication   249
     Action Assembly Theory   280
     Summary   287

Part IV. Studying Persuasive Message Production in Context   **291**

8. Producing Persuasive Messages in Context: Two Case Studies   293
     Case 1: Persuasive Message Production and
     Child Physical Abuse   297
     Case 2: Persuasive Message Production and
     Upward Influence in Organizations   310
     Summary   336

Conclusion

9. The Future of Theory and Research on Persuasive
   Message Production   341
     Persuasive Message Production: Three Challenges   342
     Summary   348

References   349
Author Index   377
Subject Index   386
About the Author   393

Preface

In this book, I review the literatures on seeking and resisting compliance from a message production perspective. The primary issue addressed here is captured by the following questions: When we want to convince another person to do something, why do we say what we do? Consciously or unconsciously, how do we decide what to say as an influence interaction unfolds? To address these questions, I integrate the research tradition on "compliance gaining" with emerging theories of "message production." This integration, which I refer to as *persuasive message production*, is tempered by a healthy respect for the interactive nature of seeking and resisting compliance. Examples of compliance-gaining interactions, from both my research and my personal life, are scattered throughout the book.

There are four major sections in this book, sandwiched between introductory and concluding chapters. Chapter 1 describes the scope and themes of the book. For readers new to this area, it should help clarify exactly what the book is about. The chapters that make up Part I then address four different approaches to the description of interpersonal influence interactions. Before one can discuss theories of message production, one needs to clarify exactly which features of influence messages and interactions one hopes to explain. In Chapter 2, I address the traditional approach of analyzing message strategies, and in Chapter 3, I discuss the three alternative approaches of analyzing message themes, behavioral dimensions, and temporal characteristics.

The chapters in Part II describe two metaphors that have dominated the study of persuasive message production. Historically, issues concerning message production have been phrased as questions about "strategy selection." In Chapter 4, I review two research traditions that provide the genesis for contemporary theories of persuasive message production: the compliance-gaining literature associated with the late Gerald Miller and his colleagues at Michigan State University, and the early constructivist tradition associated with Jesse Delia and his colleagues at the University of Illinois. Both traditions imply a "strategy-selection" metaphor of message production. More recently, issues concerning message production have been phrased as questions about "goal pursuit." In Chapter 5, I describe a "second generation" of scholarship, which has moved toward studying the production of influence messages as a goal-driven process. I discuss how researchers today are grappling with the issues of conceptualizing, measuring, and modeling interaction goals.

The chapters in Part III survey theoretical perspectives on how individuals pursue influence goals. In Chapter 6, I review discourse perspectives, provide background material about pragmatics and conversation analyses, and then review work on two topics with special relevance to persuasive message production: obstacles to compliance (as framed by attribution and speech act theories) and threats to "face" (as framed by politeness and message design logic theories). These approaches highlight the pragmatic knowledge individuals need to seek/resist compliance, as well as the unfolding sequential structure of influence interactions. In Chapter 7, I discuss cognitive perspectives on the pursuit of influence goals and review theories of plans/planning and action assembly theory. These approaches present detailed assumptions about the knowledge structures and psychological processes that underlie persuasive message production.

In Chapter 8, the sole chapter in Part IV, I address persuasive message production within two specific relational and institutional contexts. Specifically, I discuss research exploring (a) how physically abusive versus nonmaltreating parents seek to regulate perceived misbehavior by their children and (b) how employees attempt to influence members at higher levels in the formal hierarchy of their work organizations. In each case, I draw on the theories reviewed in Parts II and III for insights into how individuals seek/resist compliance within these particular contexts.

In Chapter 9, I summarize the themes that run throughout the book and then ponder future challenges and prospects for theories of persuasive message production. These challenges include whether comprehensive theories of persuasive message production can be developed as well as whether emotional processes can be incorporated into such theories.

As the above description of this book's organization makes clear, I do not devote specific chapters to issues of culture, development, or gender. Instead, I pose questions about how children acquire knowledge and skill at seeking/resisting compliance and about how influence interactions vary across cultures and genders throughout several chapters.

I have been motivated to write this book by four interrelated goals. First, I want to highlight the pervasive, potentially complex, and important role of interpersonal influence episodes in our personal and professional lives. At present, no single-authored text focuses solely on how individuals produce messages within influence interactions. This omission is a noteworthy one.

Interpersonal influence episodes have real consequences—in some cases because it matters whether we are successful at seeking and/or resisting compliance, and in others because seeking and resisting compliance themselves play important roles in (re)defining our relationships.

My second goal is to provide theoretical grounding for the literatures on seeking and resisting compliance. People seek and resist compliance in a host of relational, institutional, and cultural contexts; thus literatures on compliance-gaining and -resisting strategies have sprung up in many different disciplines and specialties. Unfortunately, these specific literatures often are isolated from work on interpersonal influence in other contexts, as well as from broader theories that might guide the work. I hope to breathe new life into the literatures on seeking and resisting compliance by reframing them from a message production perspective. I show how theories from communication, psychology, and sociolinguistics can be used to guide theoretical choices about how to describe influence messages and interactions, explain regularities in how we seek and resist compliance, and offer suggestions for reframing problematic or dysfunctional interactions.

My third goal is to draw links between communication and cognitive processes during influence interactions. The compliance-gaining literature often is criticized for being "one-sided." Compliance-gaining interactions are interactive and incremental (Sanders & Fitch, 2001), and yet scholars often study acts of seeking or resisting compliance as if these acts were performed in isolation. The literature on message production also has been criticized for being too "individualistic," in the sense of focusing on only one participant in a dialogue. In this book I attempt to address such criticisms by focusing on the interdependent nature of seeking and resisting compliance. I describe the emergent nature of both participants' perceptions, emotions, and goals as influence interactions unfold.

Fourth and finally, I want to show that work on persuasive message production can speak to issues of larger societal import. In Chapter 8, I discuss how theory and research in this area can offer insights about parenting and child abuse as well as about upward influence and mobility in the workplace, illustrating how research on interpersonal communication can play a role in helping us to address issues that our society has identified as important challenges.

Given these four goals, this volume can be useful as a supplemental text for graduate- or bridge-level courses on persuasion and social influence. It also can function as a primary text for special-topics courses on interpersonal influence or message production. The book presumes no prior background in these areas, only basic familiarity with the goals and methods of social science. If you are a seasoned colleague who shares my interests in compliance gaining and message production, I hope that this book stimulates your thinking. If you are a newer colleague, I hope that it helps you analyze interpersonal influence episodes in your own life.

Acknowledgments

This book has been more than 5 years in the making, and I am indebted to many people who have helped me initiate and complete the project. I have been blessed with a number of talented teachers who have shaped my thinking about persuasive message production, as well as about conducting and evaluating communication research more generally. Brant Burleson, Linda Putnam, John Greene, Dale Hample, and Vince Follert have been especially important in this regard.

I am indebted to many colleagues, including Jim Dillard, Frank Boster, Mike Roloff, Charles Berger, and Barb O'Keefe, who have contributed many of the concepts and theories discussed in this book and discussed them with me along the way. I am indebted also to Joel Milner and Ellen Whipple, two colleagues from other disciplines who have helped me appreciate the relevance of communication theory for understanding family violence. I am especially grateful to dozens of students who have read, and provided feedback on, parts of this book. My thanks to participants in graduate seminars at Northern Illinois University, Northwestern University, and Purdue University.

Margaret Seawell, executive editor at Sage Publications, has been especially patient as I have set writing this book aside at various points and then returned to it. She and others at Sage have been instrumental in helping me complete the project.

My family has been extremely supportive throughout the writing process. My mother, Marilyn, has made many trips to our home and folded endless baskets of laundry to give me time to write. She and my father, Robert, to whom this book is dedicated, both were educators. My parents instilled in me the values of hard work, personal confidence, and regard for others. My sister, Sheryl, and her family graciously allowed me to live with them for two nights a week during a year when I completed several chapters.

My own children—Brendan (and his wife Ashley), Sheridan, Ashlee, Lisette, Annie, and Robyn—have provided much fodder for this book. They have taught me a great deal about seeking and resisting compliance. I hope they can laugh when reading about our lives together in the pages of this book. My greatest debt is to my wife and partner, Patrice Buzzanell. She has listened politely on countless occasions when I talked about the book, encouraged me to do what it took to finish it, and spent endless weekends giving me the chance to do so. I could not have completed this project without her support. Finally, I must say thanks to Christopher and Teddy Buzzanell, who have kept my ego in check and taught me that one can be adored simply for being (well, for being a terrier).

1

What Is Persuasive Message Production?

Looking Ahead . . .

This chapter previews the nature and scope of the book. Initially, the chapter analyzes an example to show what types of questions are posed by scholars interested in persuasive message production. Then the terms compliance gaining and message production are defined and the ethics of seeking compliance are considered. Finally, a rationale for integrating the literatures on compliance gaining and message production is provided, and three themes running throughout the book are discussed.

Imagine yourself in the following hypothetical situation: You've known your friend, Pat, for 6 months. Two weeks ago, you lent Pat $50 with the understanding that you would get your money back in a week. Now it is a week past the agreed-upon time, and you've yet to receive your money. Your own bank account is smaller than you would like it to be. You want Pat to repay your $50. You speak to Pat.

What, if anything, would you say to Pat? Several colleagues and I asked undergraduate students at two large, midwestern universities how they would handle this situation (Wilson, Aleman, & Leatham, 1998). Most of our participants (95%) answered that, if this were a real situation, they would confront Pat and talk to him or her. When asked to write out, word for word, what they believed they would say, four participants wrote the following messages:

Participant 237: Hey Pat, I was wondering if you could possibly pay me the $50 you owe me, because I have to put it into my account as soon as possible. If you don't have the whole amount, could you pay me half?

Participant 257: Hey Pat, what's up? Listen, I know you've been short on cash lately, but I think if I'm nice enough to lend you money, you should be nice enough to pay it back to me on time. You said that you would pay me back in a week and it's been over a week. I would really appreciate it if you would get the money back to me soon because I'm running pretty low on funds.

Participant 100: "Hey Pat, can I borrow $50?" If he didn't get the clue then I would say, "I could really use that $50 you owe me."

Participant 312: Pat, I was just wondering when you would be able to pay me back my $50. I really need the money back. I wouldn't be hounding you about it but it's a pretty large sum and I really need it.

These four written messages raise a number of questions about why individuals say what they do as they seek compliance. To begin with, the four messages contain some striking similarities. Notice, for example, that all four participants mention that Pat owes them money:

Participant 237: I was wondering if you could possibly pay me the $50 *you owe me.*

Participant 257: You said that you would *pay me back in a week* and *it's been over a week.*

Participant 100: I could really use that $50 *you owe me.*

Participant 312: I was just wondering when you would be able to *pay me back my* $50.

As a second example, notice that all four participants also mention that they need their money:

Participant 237: I have to put it into my account as soon as possible.

Participant 257: I'm running pretty low on funds.

Participant 100: I could really use that $50.

Participant 312: I really need the money back.

Why do all four participants mention that Pat owes them money and explain that they need this money? Perhaps the participants simply are repeating information mentioned in our description of the hypothetical scenario. After all, the scenario states that "you've yet to receive your money" and that "your bank account is smaller than you would like it to be." Although at first glance this seems like an obvious answer, notice that these four participants do not repeat other information mentioned in the scenario. Not one participant includes the information that he or she has known Pat for 6 months in the message. So we are back to the same question: Why would all four participants choose to mention some pieces of information from the scenario but decide not to mention others? Are concepts such as "need" (i.e., the participant needs money now) and "obligation" (i.e., Pat owes the participant money and thus is obligated to repay the loan) especially relevant for understanding what people say during influence interactions (i.e., for understanding the production of *persuasive* messages)?

Aside from these similarities, we also can ask questions about differences across the four messages. For example, notice how each participant phrases his or her actual request for the money. Participants 237 and 312 both ask questions about Pat's ability to repay the money (i.e., the question "I was wondering"). In contrast, Participant 100 simply states a need for the money, and Participant 257 states a desire to receive the money (i.e., the phrase "I would really appreciate it"). Why do the four participants phrase their requests for the money in these ways? Are there common ways of phrasing requests? Do most individuals alter how they phrase requests depending on particular situations?

As a second example of differences, notice how each participant attempts to induce Pat to pay back the loan. Although all four explain that they need the money, they differ in what else they include in their messages. Participant 237 offers a bargain: If Pat can't pay back the full amount at this time, then perhaps Pat can at least pay back half now. Participant 257 argues that those who borrow money are responsible for repaying on time, perhaps as an attempt to make Pat feel guilty (i.e., "if I'm nice enough," then "you should be nice enough"). Participant 100 initially asks to borrow the same amount of money that Pat owes, apparently as an attempt to remind Pat about the loan without explicitly asking for repayment. Finally, Participant 312 mentions the size of the loan (i.e., "it's a pretty large sum"), perhaps both to justify seeking compliance and to provide Pat an additional rationale for repaying the money. Why do the four participants attempt to induce Pat to repay the loan in different ways? Are there common "strategies" for seeking another person's compliance? Do most individuals alter their choice of strategies depending on particular situations?

In the preceding paragraphs about the "repay loan" scenario, I have posed a number of questions about persuasive message production. Persuasive message production is concerned with why individuals say what they do as they seek to exert and/or resist influence in everyday life. This volume provides an introduction to theory and research about persuasive message production. As the title *Seeking and Resisting Compliance* suggests, this book integrates the literatures on compliance gaining and message production. Hence I begin by defining and describing these two areas of research. I then discuss three themes that run throughout various chapters.

What Is Compliance Gaining?

The term *compliance gaining* refers to any interaction in which a message source attempts to induce a target individual to perform some desired behavior that the target otherwise might not perform (see Wheeless, Barraclough, & Stewart, 1983). Consider the following examples of compliance-gaining episodes from a typical day in my own life:

7:00 A.M.: The alarm goes off. I grumble "morning" to my partner and get up to shower and dress. Before reaching the shower, I hear my 17-year-old stepdaughter playing music loudly as she gets ready for school. Afraid that she will wake up her younger sisters, *I ask her to turn the music down* (seeking compliance).

7:15 A.M.: After finishing my shower, I go to wake up my two youngest daughters. The 9-year-old says she does not want to get up. *I offer to carry her to the bathroom if she will get out of bed* (seeking compliance). The 6-year-old *asks if she can wear a dress to school* (seeking compliance). *I tell her no, explain that I don't want her to get a nice dress dirty* (resisting compliance), and *suggest that she wear one of her favorite T-shirts instead* (seeking compliance).

7:20 A.M.: My 17-year-old stepdaughter starts to leave for school. I ask her if she has eaten breakfast. She *says that she doesn't have time* (resisting compliance). *I tell her to take something to eat while she drives to school and remind her that she is supposed to eat breakfast every day* (seeking compliance).

8:20 A.M.: After getting my youngest daughters on the school bus, I drive to school. Just before my first class, *a student asks if she can take the upcoming exam a day early. She explains that she already has two other exams on the day my exam is scheduled* (seeking compliance). *I tell her that I may not have the exam ready a day early, but that she can take it a day later than it is scheduled if that will help* (resisting compliance, proposing an alternative).

10:30 A.M.: During a discussion in my office, a first-semester master's student asks whether I would recommend that she complete a master's thesis or take additional classes and complete the nonthesis track. When I ask about her plans after graduation, she indicates that she hopes to go on to a doctoral program and earn her Ph.D. I list several advantages and disadvantages of the thesis and nonthesis tracks, and then *explain that, in my opinion, students who want to go on to a doctoral program should complete a thesis in order to obtain hands-on research experience* (seeking compliance).

1:00 P.M.: During a meeting of the search committee for a faculty position in the area of public relations (PR), three colleagues and I discuss how to word the job advertisement. Although the person being hired will replace a former colleague whose degree was in journalism, *I advocate defining the PR position broadly with regard to type of degree and background in order to attract the largest possible pool of good candidates* (seeking compliance).

2:30 P.M.: I check my e-mail and find a message from a colleague at another university who is the editor of a scholarly journal. She reminds me that I am late returning my review of a manuscript submitted to her journal for consideration. *She asks if I can complete the review and fax it to her by the end of the week* (seeking compliance). I agree to do so.

2:45 P.M.: I telephone my spouse, and we discuss how to coordinate the evening's activities—my older stepdaughter has swim team practice, and my younger daughters have Brownies and a "Japanese fun" class. Given all the planned activities, *I suggest that we order pizza for dinner* (seeking compliance). *My wife says that she is tired of pizza* (resisting compliance) and *offers to cook spaghetti for dinner if I will pick up sauce at the store on my way home* (seeking compliance).

3:00 P.M.: I drive to the dentist for my 6-month checkup. *My dentist warns that if I don't start flossing regularly, soon I will need an expensive and time-consuming treatment for receding gums* (seeking compliance).

5:00 P.M.: After picking up my youngest daughter from Brownies, we walk out to our Chevy Suburban to head home. She runs ahead of me. *I shout for her to stop at the curb, in case there is moving traffic in the parking lot* (seeking compliance).

5:45 P.M.: During a phone conversation, I ask my 20-year-old stepdaughter how she is doing in her college classes. She reveals that she is getting a D in biology. When asked if she has turned in all of her homework, she admits that she has forgotten to turn in several assignments. I ask if she still likes her major, and she replies, "Sort of." *I offer to pay for a tutor if she needs help and tell her that I am going to be very upset if she fails to turn in any more assignments this semester* (seeking compliance).

5:50 P.M.: My 17-year-old stepdaughter *asks if she can drive this Friday to visit a friend in Illinois* (seeking compliance). *I tell her that I'm not thrilled with her driving through Chicago traffic during rush hour* (resisting compliance), but say *that I'd be willing to let her go if she left Saturday morning and returned before dark on Sunday* (proposing alternative).

6:05 P.M.: I receive a telephone call from a representative of the phone company MCI. He asks why I recently switched from MCI to another company for my long-distance phone service. *The representative then offers me a certificate for $75 in free calls if I will come back to MCI* (seeking compliance).

9:30 P.M.: We finally finish with activities and homework and put our younger daughters to bed. My spouse and I begin talking about where we would like to be in our careers 5 years in the future. *She says that she'd like to be on the East Coast, closer to her family. I reply that we have moved several times in recent years, and that our children would find it difficult to move again* (resisting compliance). *My spouse says that her mother is already in her 80s, and she wishes they could talk more often* (seeking compliance).

Seeking and resisting compliance are common activities.[1] Indeed, I suspect that, like me, you participate in multiple compliance-gaining episodes each day. Compliance gaining can involve requests with important implications, such as my spouse's desire that we look for jobs in a different region of the country. Compliance gaining also can involve seemingly more trivial requests, such as my telling my stepdaughter to turn down her music in the morning. Compliance-gaining episodes can involve requests to perform actions at the present time, such as my suggestion that my 6-year-old daughter wear one of her favorite T-shirts to school on this particular day rather than a dress. They also can involve requests to perform actions in the future, such as my advice to a new graduate student that she complete a master's thesis at the end of her course work. Attempts to gain our compliance often come from message sources that we know well (e.g., my spouse), but they also come from sources that are acquaintances (e.g., my colleague the journal editor, my dentist) and even strangers (e.g., the MCI representative). As these examples illustrate, message sources use a variety of techniques, including explanations, bargains, and warnings, to seek target persons' compliance. Message targets may comply almost immediately with sources' requests, may offer alternatives to requests, or may refuse to comply at all. In sum, seeking compliance involves an attempt by a message source to alter a target's behavior. Of course, message sources at times also wish to change targets' attitudes and beliefs, and not just targets' behavior. I hope that my stepdaughter not only will turn in her college biology assignments but also will continue to enjoy the subject matter.[2]

Compliance gaining falls within the domain of "persuasion" or "social influence," yet the study of compliance gaining differs in two respects from the scholarship reported in the traditional persuasion literature (Miller & Burgoon, 1978). First, persuasion scholars traditionally have focused on public and mass communication contexts, whereas compliance gaining focuses on influence within *interpersonal contexts*. Rather than examining political campaigns and product advertisements, this volume explores how individuals seek and resist compliance during conversations with friends, family members, and coworkers.

A second difference is that persuasion scholars traditionally have focused on message effects, whereas researchers who study compliance gaining focus on message *choices*. Persuasion researchers have investigated the use of fear appeals, one-sided versus two-sided arguments, and other message factors that affect audiences' attitudes (see Eagly & Chaiken, 1993; D. J. O'Keefe, 1990; Perloff, 1993; Stiff, 1994). Even when focusing on interpersonal contexts, persuasion scholars often have investigated questions about message effects. A number of studies, for example, have explored the "foot-in-the-door" technique, in which a message source strategically makes a larger request (e.g., asking for a monetary donation) only after convincing the target to comply with a smaller initial request (e.g., signing a petition; see Cialdini, 1993).

In contrast to this focus on the outcomes of messages, compliance-gaining scholars have investigated why individuals choose one approach over others in seeking/resisting compliance in the first place. Researchers have explored questions such as the following: Why do individuals sometimes say what they want explicitly, but at other times only hint about what they want? Why do individuals sometimes simply make a request or say no, whereas at other times they provide reasons for making/refusing requests (e.g., Dillard, Segrin, & Harden, 1989; Wilson & Kunkel, 2000)?

Although the traditional persuasion and compliance-gaining literatures differ in focus, they inform each other. Questions about message effects and message choices are complementary. Even if we know how parents can persuade their children to study or how dentists can convince patients to floss their teeth (message effects), we also need to understand why parents and dentists do not always use the most effective persuasive strategies (message choices).[3]

Compliance gaining is an important area of study for three reasons. First, compliance-gaining interactions can have important pragmatic outcomes. When I ask my children not to get into a friend's automobile if that friend has been drinking alcohol, for example, at some point their lives literally may depend on the effectiveness of my influence attempt. Second, compliance-gaining interactions are likely to offer insights about communication in close relationships, because individuals who are "close" frequently seek and resist each other's compliance on a wide range of topics (Kelley et al., 1983). For example, episodes of child physical abuse often arise from parents' ineffective attempts to gain their children's compliance (Cerezo, 1997; Wilson, 1999). Third and finally, compliance-gaining interactions often contain interesting individual, situational, and cultural variations. Different people often approach the "same" compliance-gaining situation in distinct ways, and most of us recognize that different situations call for different approaches (Craig, Tracy, & Spisak, 1986; B. J. O'Keefe, 1990).

Given these three reasons, it is not surprising that compliance gaining has captured the attention of scholars in communication and related fields. In this book, I present reviews of studies that have examined how individuals seek and/or resist compliance in general, as well as within particular contexts, such as parent-child, employee-supervisor, and physician-patient relationships. Prior to doing so, I discuss the ethics of seeking compliance.

On the Ethics of Seeking Compliance

Ethical issues "focus on value judgments concerning degrees of right and wrong, goodness and badness, in human conduct" (Johannesen, 1995, p. 28). Given that seeking compliance always involves an attempt to modify a target individual's behavior, ethical questions naturally can be raised about both the means used to seek compliance and the goals or ends being sought.

ETHICAL JUDGMENTS ABOUT
MEANS OF SEEKING COMPLIANCE

People can seek compliance in a variety of ways, some of which may be ethically questionable. For example, is a message source ever justified in using lies or deception to gain a target's compliance? Imagine that I am scheduled to teach a graduate course in persuasion, but my course is in danger of being canceled due to low enrollment. A student who is considering taking my course discloses that she always has been afraid of giving public speeches. She inquires whether I will be teaching concrete techniques for coping with speech anxiety. If my graduate course in persuasion has a theoretical rather than a skills-based focus, am I justified in lying about what I will cover so that this student will enroll? Such conduct on my part surely would be unethical. As a second example, is a message source ever justified in using threats to gain compliance? If my graduate course in persuasion has low enrollment, is it ethical for me to tell one of my graduate advisees that I will make it very difficult for him to complete his master's thesis unless he enrolls in my course? Again, most people would object to such a use of threats and coercion.

Although we may be able to reach agreement about the ethics of compliance-seeking techniques in some cases, other situations are less clear-cut. Is deception unethical when it is motivated by a genuine desire to avoid unnecessarily hurting a message target's feelings? Imagine that my 9-year-old daughter comes to breakfast in a striped shirt, checked shorts, and argyle socks. I suggest that she change clothes before going to school. When she asks why, am I ethically compelled to be honest and inform my daughter that her peers will make fun of her for lacking fashion sense? Is it unethical for me to suggest that it is too cold for shorts, even if that is not my real concern, and propose that a pair of blue jeans would be a better choice given the weather? According to many scholars, the admonition that one should always be "honest and open" reflects a particular ideological and cultural view. These scholars argue that ambiguity, and in some cases deception, is useful, and its employment responsible, within close relationships (e.g., Bavelas, Black, Chovil, & Mullett, 1990; Bochner, 1984; Parks, 1982, 1995).

As a second example of the complexity of making ethical judgments, consider the distinction between "pure" persuasion and coercion. Imagine that I suggest to one of my graduate advisees that a course in persuasion, such as the one I teach, would be useful to her, given her interests in advertising. I also stress, however, that ultimately the choice regarding which class to take is her own. Even if I am totally sincere about these statements, could my advisee still feel pressure to enroll in my class simply because she likes and respects me? Compliance-seeking messages frequently contain a mix of "classically rational" and "reward/punishment-based" appeals (see, e.g., Wilson, Whipple, & Grau, 1996), and the line between choice and obligation, as well as that between persuasion and coercion, often is difficult to define clearly (Roloff, Janiszewski, McGrath, Burns, & Manrai, 1988; Simons, 1974).

The point of the preceding discussion is not to argue that ethical judgments are totally subjective, and hence not worth discussing. In many cases people can reach consensus about the ethics of techniques for seeking compliance. Even in more difficult cases, individuals can clarify the standards underlying their own judgments while also acknowledging the possibility of other standards and of views different from their own (Johannesen, 1996, pp. 17-19).

ETHICAL JUDGMENTS ABOUT
THE GOAL OF SEEKING COMPLIANCE

Aside from ethical judgments about specific means of seeking compliance, questions can be raised about whether seeking compliance, using any means, is an ethical end. In day-to-day life, the term *compliance* often has negative connotations, bringing to mind acquiescence, control, and manipulation. Consistent with these views, some humanistic and feminist scholars raise ethical objections to attempts to seek compliance in most, if not all, situations.

Carl Rogers (1957), the well-known psychotherapist, asserts that three qualities are necessary and sufficient to promote therapeutic growth. Through *empathy*, a therapist attempts to take the client's perspective and understand the client's views and emotions about the world. When in *congruence*, a therapist is in touch with his or her own internal experiences and is genuine about sharing those experiences with the client. Finally, the therapist expresses *unconditional positive regard* by communicating a nonjudgmental attitude and by treating the client as an intrinsically valuable person. Although the therapist may offer reactions to the client's behavior, he or she avoids questioning the client's fundamental worth or imposing external value standards on the client. According to Rogers, a therapist who displays these three qualities need not attempt to bring about specific changes in the client's behavior; rather, the client changes from within as he or she experiences the therapist's empathy, congruence, and unconditional positive regard. Indeed, Rogers (1975) expresses strong disdain for directive forms of therapy such as behavior modification: "A technological society has been delighted to have found a technology by which a man's behavior can be shaped, even without his own knowledge or approval, towards goals selected by the therapist, or by society" (p. 3).

Outside of the context of therapy, Rogers (1980) also raises questions about individuals' attempting to influence others and champions positive regard as an ethical ideal for everyday behavior:

> So often, even with our children, we love them to control them rather than loving them because we appreciate them. One of the most satisfying feelings I know— and also one of the most growth-promoting experiences for the other person— comes from appreciating this individual in the same way that I appreciate a sunset. . . .When I look at a sunset as I did the other evening, I don't find myself saying, "Soften the orange a little on the right hand corner, and put a bit more purple along the base, and use a little more pink in the cloud color." . . . I don't *try* to control a sunset. I watch it with awe as it unfolds. I like myself best when I can appreciate my staff member, my son, my daughter, my grandchildren, in this same way. (pp. 22-23)

Foss and Griffin (1995), in a feminist critique of rhetorical theories, voice concerns about seeking compliance similar to those of Rogers. Although feminist scholars work from a variety of perspectives, Foss and Griffin argue that feminists are united in a commitment to three basic values: (a) creating relationships of equality, as opposed to domination and elitism; (b) recognizing the uniqueness and immanent value of all living beings; and (c) promoting a self-determination that treats individuals as authorities on their own lives, with the right to make their own choices. According to Foss and Griffin, attempting to change another person's behavior runs contrary to these basic feminist values. Commenting on the value of equality, they argue that efforts to change others always are motivated by a desire to control and dominate:

> Even in cases where the strategies used are less coercive, rhetors who convince others to adapt their viewpoints exert control over part of those others' lives. A student who tells another student that she ought to take a particular course, for example, controls or influences the nature of another's life, if only for a few minutes, if the other enrolls in the course or even considers enrolling in it. (p. 3)

With regard to individuals' immanent value and right to self-determination, they go on to say:

> The act of changing others . . . also devalues the lives and perspectives of those others. The belief systems and behaviors others have created for living in the world are considered by rhetors to be inadequate or inappropriate and thus in need of change. . . . Audience members are assumed to be naive and less expert than the rhetor if their views differ from the rhetor's own. (p. 3)

As an alternative to traditional theories, Foss and Griffin (1995) propose an "invitational" rhetoric based on feminist values. The goal of invitational rhetoric is understanding rather than change: The rhetor invites the audience to enter the rhetor's world and see it as the rhetor does, while simultaneously being open to and validating perspectives different from the rhetor's own. The rhetor does not analyze his or her audience in terms of obstacles to gaining compliance, but rather for obstacles to creating understanding. Change may result from invitational rhetoric, but "change is not its purpose. . . . In the traditional model, change is defined as a shift in the audience in the direction requested by the rhetor. . . . In invitational rhetoric, change occurs in the audience or rhetor or both as a result of new understanding" (p. 6).[4]

Although a detailed critique of humanistic and feminist perspectives is beyond the scope of this book, I do not agree that attempting to seek compliance is inherently unethical. Seeking compliance can be defended as an ethical pursuit on at least two grounds. One problem with the views just described is that they are based on the oversimplified notion that seeking compliance and communicating positive regard are antagonistic or opposite aims. Dialectical perspectives challenge the notion that seeking change and communicating acceptance are antithetical (Baxter & Montgomery, 1996; Rawlins, 1992).[5] People can offer advice to their friends, family members, and colleagues out of concern for the other persons' well-being rather than out of a desire to control or dominate. Evaluation and acceptance, rather than being polar opposites, are both necessary in close relationships. As one example, Rawlins (1992) notes that close friends recognize each other's immanent value but also risk offering candid advice aimed at keeping each other honest about themselves. Based on detailed interviews with adult friends, Rawlins concludes:

> Individuals often want and need to feel accepted, valued, and confirmed as worthwhile people, both in their role-related capacities and for their intrinsic qualities transcending specific social functions. . . . Meanwhile, their responses [also] evidence considerable need for someone they trusted to honestly appraise and perceptively counsel them about various matters, including work-related problems and decisions, relationships with spouses, and doubts and frustrations in raising children. (p. 196)

Seeking and resisting compliance, then, are not antithetical to creating close, caring, and genuine relationships; rather, they are fundamental to the processes by which close relationships are created and sustained. Asking favors, offering advice, proposing joint activities, and negotiating obligations are day-to-day enactments of a close relationship (Dillard, 1989). Some scholars go so far as to define "close relationships" as those in which the participants frequently seek each other's compliance about a range of topics (Kelley et al., 1983). Although defining close relationships solely in terms of influence may be too narrow, it is also true that "any analysis of interpersonal behavior that ignores either the function of influence or the function of affection will necessarily be too limiting" (Bochner, 1984, p. 571).

A second problem is that Rogers's (1980) as well as Foss and Griffin's (1995) argument that seeking compliance is unethical is based on a cultural view of the independent self that, although valued by middle-class European Americans, is not universally shared. Independent views of self, common in the United States and other Western, developed nations, define individuals as autonomous agents who possess enduring psychological qualities that remain constant across situations and relationships (see Markus & Kitayama, 1991). In contrast, interdependent views of self, common in many African, Asian, and South American nations, define persons in terms of their connections to others and emphasize the fluid and situated nature of "one's selves." To argue that seeking a target individual's compliance devalues that individual's beliefs and choices is to assume that the most important qualities of "the self" are the individual's own autonomy and unique worldview. Such an argument makes much less sense from the frame of reference of the interdependent self. Fitch (1994), in a cross-cultural comparison of compliance gaining in the United States and Colombia, explains how different views of the self lead to different evaluations of seeking compliance. Specifically, the Colombian perspective of

> helping people by telling others what to do reflects a sharply distinctive view of personhood and a substantially different meaning for intimacy and power, than does "empowering" them to "make their own decisions." In this view, relationships rather than individuals are the locus of social action. Words give voice, often ineffectually, to the rights and obligations attendant upon those relationships, rather than posing a potentially ominous threat to the self-esteem and autonomy of the hearer. (p. 197)

In sum, seeking compliance is not an inherently unethical end. Rogers (1980) and Foss and Griffin (1995) do well in challenging us to consider our motives for seeking compliance. Seeking compliance, however, is not antithetical to communicating positive regard and caring. In some circumstances and cultures, seeking compliance may communicate these very qualities.

THE ROLE OF ETHICS IN THIS BOOK

This book is devoted primarily to the traditional social scientific goals of predicting and explaining how people seek and resist compliance. Despite this focus, ethical issues do enter into the discussion at both descriptive and normative levels. At a descriptive level, people decide how to seek compliance, in part, based on their ethical judgments about specific means of exerting influence. Hunter and Boster's (1978, 1987) "ethical-threshold model," which I discuss in Chapter 4, claims that people decide on how to seek compliance based on whether they feel justified in creating negative emotional reactions within message targets in particular situations. Hample and Dallinger's (1987a) work on cognitive editing, which I address in Chapter 5, proposes that people decide what *not* to say when seeking and resisting compliance, in part, based on their internal value standards. At a normative level, in the chapters that follow I occasionally consider how we ought to study persuasive message production. As one example, in Chapter 5, I examine whether treating the goal of exerting influence as "primary" and the goal of maintaining relationships as "secondary" is an inherently masculine view that devalues alternative understandings of communication.

What Is Message Production?

Aside from addressing the topics of seeking and resisting compliance, in this book I also review theory and research on *message production*. Message production scholars explore the internal, psychological processes involved in generating verbal and/or nonverbal messages (Greene, 1997a; Littlejohn, 2002; Wilson, Greene, & Dillard, 2000). Researchers in this area ask questions such as the following:

- What types of goals do individuals commonly pursue during conversation? How does an individual decide which of these goals actually to pursue in a specific conversation?
- What types of knowledge do individuals possess about potential means for accomplishing their social goals?
- How do individuals recall knowledge about social goals during interaction, integrate it with other knowledge about what they view as appropriate and relevant topics for conversation, and translate it into action?
- How do individuals generate messages when they have the opportunity to plan what they will say in advance? What occurs when they have to figure out what to say on the spot?
- How do individuals typically react when initially they do not succeed at accomplishing their social goals? When are they likely to persist in trying to accomplish their goals, and when are they likely to give up? How do individuals typically adjust, or not adjust, their initial attempts to accomplish their goals in the face of obstacles and resistance?
- What occurs when individuals' ideas about how to accomplish particular social goals seem to run contrary to their ideas about how to accomplish other goals? How do individuals manage multiple and competing goals in their messages?
- Are individuals consciously aware of how they decide what to say during conversation? Of which decisions are they typically aware, and which typically occur with little awareness? In what situations are people more or less aware of their message choices?
- What roles do arousal and emotion play during message production? How do they affect individuals' interpretations of particular situations? Their own social goals and expectations? Their attempts to accomplish social goals?

Message production is a relatively new area of research. Twenty years ago, most scholars would not have recognized the term. To my knowledge, O'Keefe and Delia (1982) were the first communication scholars to use it, in a chapter that analyzed individual differences in social cognition and multiple-goal messages. By the late 1980s, however, scholarly journals were devoting special issues to the topic (see Cody & Greene, 1985; "Cognition in Message Processing," 1989). Littlejohn began including a chapter on message production in the fourth edition of his well-known text *Theories of Human Communication* (1992). Several book-length treatments of the topic are also now available (e.g., Berger, 1997; Dillard, 1990b; Greene, 1997a).

In this book, I focus on how individuals produce messages during influence interactions, rather than write in general terms about message production. In part, my decision to focus on seeking/resisting compliance reflects the current state of the message production literature. Although scholars have investigated how individuals generate messages to seek information (e.g., Waldron, 1990), communicate criticism or rejection (e.g., Greene & Lindsey, 1989), and comfort distressed others (e.g., Burleson, 1985), the largest body of research has investigated how individuals produce messages to exert and resist influence (see Dillard, 1990b; Seibold, Cantrill, & Meyers, 1994). I want to emphasize, however, that my decision to integrate the compliance-gaining and message production literatures is deliberate. In my opinion, the most useful explanations of message production will be developed at multiple levels of abstraction. To develop compelling explanations, we need to integrate general theories of psychological and interactional processes, analyses of specific message functions such as seeking and resisting compliance, and analyses of particular relational, institutional, and cultural contexts. We need to understand what is unique about the production of *persuasive* messages, as opposed to messages designed to comfort a distressed friend, make a good first impression with a potential employer, or account for a problematic behavior. We saw hints of this in the example at the beginning of this chapter, where the concepts of "need" and "obligation" figured prominently in what students saw as relevant when they were attempting to persuade a hypothetical friend to repay a loan. I explore this theme further in Chapter 6, where I discuss discourse perspectives on persuasive message production. We also need to understand what is unique about a physician who attempts to convince a patient with chronic back pain to make long-term lifestyle changes, as opposed to a student who attempts to convince a friend to repay an overdue loan. I explore seeking and resisting compliance within specific relational and institutional contexts in Chapter 8. I then return to the theme of integrating general process theories with analyses of specific communicative functions and contexts in the final chapter of this book.

Persuasive Message Production: Three Themes

In this book I do not present a single "grand theory" of persuasive message production; rather, three themes lend the book coherence. First, persuasive message production is seen as a goal-oriented activity. Early work on persuasive message production was guided by a "strategy-selection" metaphor; that is, it was assumed that individuals selected methods for seeking/resisting compliance from their repertoires of message strategies (see Seibold, Cantrill, & Meyers, 1985). Contemporary theories of persuasive message production are guided by a metaphor of "goal pursuit"; that is, it is assumed that individuals understand situations in terms of influence goals, generate messages to accomplish goals, rely on knowledge about means for accomplishing goals, and edit messages based on what is relevant and appropriate for accomplishing goals (see Wilson, 1997).

This goal-pursuit metaphor of message production is not without its critics, who charge that (a) the psychological processes linking goals to action are unclear, (b) goals may be useful for explaining monologues but not dialogues, (c) empirical measures of goals have unknown validity, (d) a focus on goals implies that individuals pay conscious attention to most of what they say, (e) a focus on goals reduces the social to the psychological, and (e) a focus on goals represents an ideological position that is individualist, Western, and politically conservative (e.g., Bavelas, 1991; Donohue, 1990; Lannamann, 1991; Shepherd, 1998). I address several such criticisms in this book; for example, in Chapter 5, I discuss procedures for assessing interaction goals, as well as ideological assumptions underlying the goal-pursuit metaphor. Readers must judge whether progress is being made in addressing these criticisms, as well as whether these criticisms can be addressed at all within a goal-pursuit metaphor.

A second theme running throughout this book is that persuasive message production needs to be explained within interactive contexts. This means that we need to analyze both sides of influence interactions: how message sources seek compliance and how targets resist and/or comply. It also means that we need to analyze how influence interactions unfold over time and how they are structured. Finally, it means that theories of persuasive message production should be plausible given the constraints of conversation. These constraints include that individuals are faced with multiple demands on their attention during conversation and that they often must make decisions about what to say in a matter of seconds. I return to these issues in Chapter 9.

A third and final theme in this book is that various theoretical perspectives offer insights about persuasive message production. Message production is a thriving, interdisciplinary area of research. In the chapters that follow, I review the work of scholars in cognitive science, communication, philosophy, psychology, sociolinguistics, and other fields who have stimulated thinking about how individuals produce messages within influence interactions.

Summary

The study of persuasive message production is concerned with why individuals say what they do as they seek and/or resist compliance in everyday life. I began this chapter with a hypothetical situation in which a friend was overdue repaying a loan, to illustrate the types of questions posed by persuasive message production scholars. Following this, I defined the terms *compliance gaining* and *message production* and then considered the ethics of compliance gaining. Finally, I provided a rationale for integrating these two research literatures and described the three themes that run throughout this book: (a) Persuasive message production is a goal-oriented activity; (b) persuasive message production should be explained within interactive contexts; and (c) multiple theories offer insights into persuasive message production.

Notes

1. The body of writings on research into how message sources seek to alter target persons' behavior has been labeled the *compliance-gaining literature*, even though the word *gaining* might be taken to imply that the sources' attempts to encourage compliance ultimately will be successful (Sanders & Fitch, 2001). To remain consistent with prior literature, I describe episodes in which message sources seek behavior change by targets as *compliance-gaining interactions*. In contrast, I describe message sources' attempts to induce target compliance as behaviors that *seek* compliance. Thus I discuss *compliance-seeking* and *compliance-resisting* strategies as parts of compliance-gaining interactions.

2. The term *compliance* in this book's title refers to the goal that defines the interaction, that is, a message source's desire to alter a target individual's behavior. In many cases the source also hopes to alter the target's attitudes and/or beliefs, perhaps so that the target will continue wanting to comply in the future. My use of the term *compliance* thus is broader than that applied by Kelman (1958, 1961), who limits it to instances in which a target individual, under pressure from another person, performs behaviors in public without any accompanying internalized attitude change. A message source may seek a target's compliance without regard for whether the target wants to comply or believes in complying; however, sources often use "classically rational" arguments to promote "internalization" and/or appeals to targets' social connections to promote "identification" during their attempts to seek compliance.

3. I use the terms *interpersonal influence* and *influence interaction* more narrowly than do other authors (e.g., Cialdini, 1993). My focus is on message choices rather than on message effects; thus I use *interpersonal influence* synonymously with the study of how people decide what to say when seeking and/or resisting influence in their personal or professional relationships. My focus also is on *intentional* attempts to influence other persons, thus cases of "unintended influence" and "self-persuasion" are beyond the scope of this book.

4. Near the end of their article, Foss and Griffin (1995) acknowledge that their conception of rhetoric is "not meant as an ideal for which rhetors should strive" and may not be useful in all situations (p. 17). They also state that speakers should be skilled in various rhetorics, including persuasion. Such qualifications, however, seem to run contrary to their blanket indictment of persuasion as being based on patriarchal, and unethical, values.

5. Aside from dialectics, some feminist perspectives also challenge the assertion that seeking compliance must be motivated by a desire to control. Commenting on a feminine view of communication competence, Shepherd (1992) argues that requesting a favor could be seen "as a way of enacting a relational bond. . . . favors [can be] requested not because of a personal desire to have something granted but because of a relational desire to signal, establish and/or foster interdependence" (p. 211).

Part I

*Describing Influence
Interactions*

2

The Traditional Approach to Message Analysis

Nominal-Level Strategies

Looking Ahead . . .

This chapter discusses how to analyze influence interactions. It starts with an example in which one individual (Kathy) attempts to convince another (Lisa) to honor her commitment to participate in a research experiment. The example is used to show that many different features of influence interactions may capture our attention and provide insight into why people seek and resist compliance as they do. After making this point, the chapter reviews what has become the "traditional" approach to analyzing influence interactions: developing and applying typologies of nominal-level strategies. Key terms are defined, three specific typologies of compliance-seeking/resisting strategies are introduced, and potential limitations of this approach to message analysis are discussed.

EXAMPLE 2.1

((phone rings))

| 01 | Lisa: | Hello |
| 02 | Kathy: | Hi, is Lisa there? |

03	Lisa:	This is
04	Kathy:	Hi, this is Kathy calling from the Department of
05		Communications, and I am just calling to remind you
06		that you have an extra credit experiment due tomorrow.
07	Lisa:	What time is it at?
08	Kathy:	It's at 3:00
09	Lisa:	I've made other plans
10	Kathy:	Oh, well you signed up for it
11	Lisa:	Yea, but
12	Kathy:	((interrupts)) And you're gonna get two bonus
13		points
14	Lisa:	Yea, but I invited friends out for happy hour at that
15		time though
16	Kathy:	Well, uh ((chuckle)) you're only gonna be here for
17		half an hour ((laugh))
18		You could go after that
19	Lisa:	I know but we don't get a chance to get together very
20		often, so we're all pretty excited
21	Kathy:	Well you are gonna get two bonus points
22	Lisa:	Yea, I understand that, but we made other plans
23	Kathy:	But you already signed up for this
24	Lisa:	Ya but, I'm gonna, I'm really excited about this
25	Kathy:	Well just meet them half an hour later. Happy hour
26		doesn't start till 4:00
27	Lisa:	No it doesn't
28	Kathy:	What happy hour, are you gonna to have your own
29		happy hour?
30	Lisa:	No, we're going to Rick's. It starts at 3:00
31	Kathy:	Well, you could just jog over there after and meet
32		them. Cuz your partner's gonna lose out also
33	Lisa:	Oh really?
34	Kathy:	Uh huh
35	Lisa:	Well ((pause)) I know but I've already made plans
36		with them also
37	Kathy:	((interrupts)) All right then
38	Lisa:	Ok. Bye bye
39	Kathy:	Thank you

(Wilson, Cruz, Marshall, & Rao, 1993, pp. 371-372)

Communication scholars frequently conduct research with samples of college undergraduates. Undergraduates often constitute appropriate samples for observing communication phenomena, especially those phenomena salient to young adults as well as those that occur in similar fashion regardless of the people involved. It is also true, however, that we study college undergraduates because they are an accessible group and can often can be induced to participate in our research without monetary compensation.

One potential hazard of conducting research with college undergraduates is that students sometimes agree to participate but then fail to show up for a study at the appointed time. From a student perspective, this is easy to understand. Undergraduate students typically sign up to participate simply to earn extra course credit. They sometimes must complete dull tasks during communication studies, and they often leave afterward without understanding why they did what they did. Students also are busy with school and work demands, hence it makes sense that they often change their minds after signing up to participate in research projects.

Several colleagues and I saw this state of affairs as an opportunity to study how individuals seek compliance (Wilson et al., 1993). Participants in our research were undergraduates who signed up for an out-of-class study on interpersonal persuasion. When they arrived, we told them a story about a different study being conducted by another professor, whom we'll call Professor Jones. Specifically, our participants were told:

> Professor Jones wants to study initial conversations between individuals from different backgrounds. To do this, Professor Jones has given a questionnaire about people's backgrounds to students in an introductory communication class. Based on their answers, Professor Jones has established pairs of unacquainted students who come from different backgrounds. He then has scheduled these pairs of students to arrive at a communication laboratory at a specific time to engage in a "get-acquainted" conversation. The problem is that many of Professor Jones's students are failing to show up at the communication laboratory. Aside from inconveniencing Professor Jones, students who do not show up also prevent their partners (i.e., the other students with whom they have been paired) from completing the study.

What did this have to do with our own study? After telling this story, we gave each of our own participants a list of the names of 20 undergraduate students who supposedly had signed up for Professor Jones's experiment. We asked each participant to telephone these 20 students and remind them about the time and place of their own experiment. We told our participants that if any of the students had changed their minds about coming, the participants should try to persuade them to honor their promises to complete Professor Jones's study. We told our participants to use their own judgment about what to say and about how long to persist in trying to persuade Professor Jones's students to show up. Hence each of our participants made 20 telephone calls; all calls were audio-taped and transcribed for analysis.

As you probably have guessed, our story about Professor Jones's study on initial interactions was fictitious. Our participants actually were telephoning 20 "confederates," each of whom was working with us. Of each participant's 20 phone calls, 10 were answered by confederates who were instructed simply to say yes, they would show up for Professor Jones's study as promised. One call always went to a wrong number, and a second always went to someone we knew was not there to receive the call. The remaining 8 calls were answered by confederates who were trained to say no, they would not show up. When prompted, each of the confederates provided a different reason why he or she had changed his or her mind about participating in Professor Jones's study.[1] In the telephone call shown in Example 2.1, "Lisa" is a confederate who tells "Kathy" that she will not show up because she has made plans to go to happy hour instead.

The conversation in Example 2.1 offers a useful illustration of how the same influence interaction can be described using many different approaches. In the following section, I use this conversation to show both the complexity and the importance of describing influence interactions.

The Task of Describing Influence Interactions

MULTIPLE APPROACHES TO
DESCRIBING THE KATHY-LISA CONVERSATION

Let's say that we want to analyze the conversation between Lisa and Kathy as an interpersonal influence episode. To analyze the conversation, what would we look at? Clearly, there are many possible answers to this question. As one approach, we could analyze how Lisa and Kathy try to influence each other. Focusing on Kathy, we might notice that she stresses how Lisa can help herself by showing up for Professor Jones's study. Kathy calls the study an "extra credit experiment" (see line 06) and emphasizes that Lisa will earn "two bonus points" (lines 12 and 21). Kathy also argues that Lisa has an obligation to parti-cipate because Lisa "signed up" for Professor Jones's study (lines 10 and 23). If we focus on Lisa rather than Kathy, we could analyze how Lisa tries to resist Kathy's request. Lisa justifies backing out by stressing how excited she is about meeting her friends at happy hour, especially since she rarely gets to see her friends (see lines 19-20, 24).

As a second approach, we could look at the topics Kathy and Lisa talk about. In lines 04-05, Kathy talks about "calling from the Department of Communications" and says she is calling to remind Lisa about the experiment. In line 30, Lisa talks about "going to Rick's" and about happy hour starting at 3:00. We might ask why Kathy and Lisa talk about these topics, and whether certain topics occur repeatedly in these telephone calls.

A third approach would be to analyze general qualities of Kathy's and Lisa's behavior. For example, we could ask whether Kathy exerts strong pressure on Lisa to comply with her request, as opposed to letting Lisa back out on her promise easily. There are several signs that Kathy exerts strong pressure: She interrupts and begins arguing why Lisa should comply before Lisa has an opportunity to disclose the specific reason she is backing out (lines 10 and 12); she stresses that Lisa is obligated to comply (lines 10 and 23); she suggests ways that Lisa could participate in the experiment and still attend happy hour, rather than simply accepting the obstacle Lisa poses (lines 25 and 31); and she emphasizes that Lisa's decision not to show up will hurt Lisa's partner (line 32). As a complementary question, we could ask whether Lisa is firm in resisting Kathy's request. This question might draw our attention to the fact that Lisa repeats her statement that she has "made other plans" three times (lines 09, 22, and 35).

A fourth approach would be to analyze the order in which Kathy and Lisa perform actions over time. If we focus on Kathy, we might notice that early in the conversation she stresses how Lisa can help herself by completing the experiment (line 12), whereas later in the conversation she emphasizes how Lisa will hurt her partner by not showing up (line 32). We might investigate whether individuals typically save particular arguments until after they have encountered firm resistance to their initial influence attempts. In addition to focusing on Kathy and Lisa as individuals, we could analyze their joint sequences of action over time. When Kathy asks whether Lisa still plans to participate, for example, notice that Lisa does not respond immediately with either yes or no, but rather asks the time of her appointment (line 07). After Kathy says that the appointment is at 3:00, Lisa then answers no to the question Kathy originally posed (by saying that she has made other plans). We could examine whether sequences such as request-question-answer-agreement/ refusal (e.g., lines 04-09) occur frequently during influence interactions.

In sum, we could analyze what Kathy and Lisa do, what they talk about, whether their behavior has general qualities, or what they say and do over time. Moreover, these four approaches are not the only ways in which we might analyze the Kathy-Lisa conversation. For example, we have not looked so far at the nonverbal elements of the interaction. Put simply, an influence interaction is not amenable to only one description; rather, such an interaction can be described using many different approaches to message analysis.

THE SIGNIFICANCE OF MESSAGE ANALYSIS

What does all this have to do with persuasive message production? As I explained in Chapter 1, theories of persuasive message production are designed to explain why people say what they do during influence interactions. But in order to explain why people say what they do, we need conceptual schemes or vocabularies for describing what people say. Because many questions can be posed about influence interactions, we can choose among many different conceptual schemes or vocabularies. We must not make our choice of a scheme for analyzing messages arbitrarily or mindlessly, because different conceptual schemes will focus our attention on different features of influence interactions. As Greene (1995a) explains:

> Communicative behavior lends itself to multiple, only partially overlapping conceptual schemes, each of which serves to illuminate a portion of the properties of a given message (and then only to the satisfaction of some). Hence, each conceptual scheme provides a perspective that emphasizes some details while leaving us blind to others. (p. 51)

Because there are numerous options, we need to think carefully about how we want to analyze influence interactions.

In the past, the most common approach researchers have used to describe influence interactions has been to develop typologies of message strategies. In the remainder of this chapter, I explore the strengths and limitations of this "traditional" type of message analysis. I then discuss three alternatives to this traditional approach in Chapter 3. Throughout both chapters, I emphasize that one's choice of a conceptual vocabulary for describing influence interactions should be tied to one's theory about how people produce influence messages (and vice versa). Describing what people say during influence interactions and explaining why they say what they do are interrelated tasks.

Before I present a discussion of nominal-level influence strategies, let me clarify two points about the material on message analysis in this chapter and Chapter 3. First, my concern in these chapters is with descriptions of people's overt *behavior* during influence interactions. Communication theories often make reference to nonbehavioral concepts, such as attitudes, emotions, and ideologies, to help explain behavior (Chaffee, 1991). As you will see, theories of persuasive message production are no exception. In these chapters, however, I focus on schemes for describing the observable behaviors that people use to seek and/or resist compliance. A second point is that in these chapters I focus on *describing* influence behaviors. In order to build empirical theories of persuasive message production, we need to develop clear verbal descriptions of concepts (conceptual definitions) as well as reliable and valid measures of those concepts (operational definitions; Chaffee, 1991). In these two chapters, I evaluate the utility of various ways of describing influence interactions. Questions about methods for eliciting and collecting data are addressed in Chapter 4.

Nominal-Level Typologies of Influence Strategies

The most popular approach to describing influence attempts has been to analyze the types of strategies that individuals use to seek/resist compliance. In this section, I define the key terms *"strategy, typology,* and *nominal-level measurement;* describe three widely used typologies; and clarify limitations of nominal-level strategy typologies.

WHAT IS A STRATEGY?

In this book, I use the term *strategy* to refer to an abstract category of behaviors that share a common feature or quality and that appear to pursue a goal.[2] Any strategy is an "abstract act type" because it is defined by attributes or features common to a group of concrete utterances. For example, "threats" can be defined as the category of utterances in which a speaker states or implies that he or she personally will create negative consequences unless a target complies (e.g., Schenck-Hamlin, Wiseman, & Georgacarakos, 1982). Of course, there are many ways to phrase a threat. If my daughter refuses to share her new toy with a friend, I could say, "Robyn, either share your toy or I'm going to put it away," or "Robyn, either share your toy or else," or even "Robyn, what happened last time when you refused to share your toys?"

I refer to the concrete verbal and nonverbal behaviors that instantiate a strategy as an *utterance.* An utterance comprises the particular words, spoken or written, that carry out a specific message strategy. The phrase "Robyn, either share your toy or else" is an utterance instantiating the compliance-seeking strategy of threat. Within face-to-face interaction, an utterance may be a single conversational turn, part of a turn, or several successive turns. Within a written message, an utterance may be a sentence, part of a sentence, or several successive sentences. Using this terminology, all three of the utterances suggested above are examples of the compliance-seeking strategy of threat.

These three utterances differ in several respects, but they share a common form that distinguishes them from utterances that are not threats. For example, a "warning" can be defined as any utterance in which the speaker says that a third party or the nature of things (rather than the speaker him- or herself) will create negative consequences unless the target complies (Schenck-Hamlin et al., 1982). If her older sister, Sheridan, says, "Robyn, you'd better share your toy or Dad will take it away," then Sheridan has warned, rather than threatened, Robyn.

Describing an utterance as a strategy implies that it serves a function and can be understood as a means for accomplishing a goal (Kellermann, 1992). Compliance-seeking strategies are abstract act types used by message sources in attempting to alter targets' behavior, whereas compliance-resisting strategies are abstract act types used by targets who wish to avoid complying with message sources' requests. Describing compliance-seeking messages as strategies, however, should not be taken to imply that speakers typically think a great deal about how to exert/resist influence during conversation. Message sources may plan more or less in advance and think more or less about what to say during interaction itself, depending on many factors, such as whether their request is important, whether they expect the target to comply, whether they are self- or other-focused, and whether their culture values advance planning (Cai, 1994; Cegala & Waldron, 1992; Dillard, Segrin, & Harden, 1989). But in many cases, influence behaviors are "intentional and monitored while still occurring outside awareness" (Kellermann, 1992, p. 293).

WHAT IS A NOMINAL-LEVEL STRATEGY TYPOLOGY?

A *strategy typology* is a list of abstract act types that a message source could use to accomplish a specific function. Typologies are systems for categorizing and measuring the various strategies present within influence interactions. Numerous typologies of compliance-seeking and -resisting strategies have been developed; for example, Kellermann and Cole (1994) have identified 74 distinct typologies of compliance-seeking strategies. Aside from seeking/resisting compliance, researchers have developed typologies of strategies for a variety of other communication functions, including strategies for accounting for poor performance; comforting distressed others; initiating, maintaining, and terminating relationships; managing conflict; and reducing embarrassment (see Cody & McLaughlin, 1990; Daly & Wiemann, 1994).

The majority of typologies of influence strategies are *nominal-level* category schemes. A nominal-level typology is one in which (a) all of the utterances assigned to some strategy category are alike with respect to some attribute or feature, (b) strategy categories in the typology are not designed to vary from "most to least" or "low to high" with respect to any attribute or dimension, and hence (c) the numerical value assigned to each strategy category is arbitrary, reflecting only the presence or absence of the defining attribute or feature (Kerlinger, 1973; Nunnally, 1967). Imagine a system that classifies students in a college of communication arts and sciences according to academic major using the following categories: 1 = communication, 2 = telecommunications, 3 = advertising, 4 = journalism, and 5 = speech and audiology sciences. Students assigned to each category are alike with regard to their topic of study, but the five categories are not ordered from low to high on any dimension. In the same way, utterances assigned to each category in a nominal-level strategy typology are alike with regard to a specific feature, but categories are not ordered intentionally along any conceptual dimension.

Most typologies of influence strategies intend to be *mutually exclusive* and *exhaustive*. A typology is mutually exclusive when each utterance can be assigned to only one strategy category, and hence no utterance falls into two or more categories. A typology is exhaustive when each and every utterance being studied can be classified within one of the strategy categories (Krippendorff, 1980).

Having defined these key terms, I turn now to describing three widely used nominal-level typologies of influence strategies.

THREE NOMINAL-LEVEL TYPOLOGIES

Marwell and Schmitt's Typology of Compliance-Seeking Strategies

Analyses of power and influence have a long history in the social sciences (see Berger, 1994). Despite this, sociologists Marwell and Schmitt (1967) observed that scholars up to the time of their research had paid very little attention to the range of strategies individuals might use to exert control. After reviewing theoretical writings about power by a variety of social theorists, Marwell and Schmitt proposed a list of 16 specific compliance-seeking strategies.[3] Their definitions of these strategies are shown in Table 2.1, along with examples from a situation in which you (a parent) are trying to convince your high school-age son, Dick, to spend more time studying.

Aside from compiling their strategy typology, Marwell and Schmitt (1967) wanted to group strategies in a fashion that would aid scholars in predicting their use. They believed that trying to predict people's use of 16 different strategies was too large a task; in their words, it was "a task for a science of immense power" (p. 351). Hence Marwell and Schmitt also wanted to identify "clusters" of strategies that would covary in terms of perceived likelihood of use. As they put it, "We might aspire to predict the differential use of behaviors from among meaningful groupings" (p. 351).

Table 2.1   Marwell and Schmitt's (1967) 16 Compliance-Seeking Strategies With
Examples From a Hypothetical Family Situation

Strategy	Definition/Example
1. Promise	If you comply, I will reward you. *Example:* You offer to increase Dick's allowance if he increases his studying.
2. Threat	If you do not comply, I will punish you. *Example:* You threaten to forbid Dick the use of the car if he does not increase his studying.
3. Expertise (positive)	If you comply you will be rewarded because of "the nature of things." *Example:* You point out to Dick that if he gets good grades he will be able to get into a good college and get a good job.
4. Expertise (negative)	If you do not comply you will be punished because of "the nature of things." *Example:* You point out to Dick that if he does not get good grades he will not be able to get into a good college or get a good job.
5. Liking	Actor is friendly and helpful to get the target in a "good frame of mind" so that he will comply with a request. *Example:* You try to be as friendly and pleasant as possible to get Dick in the "right frame of mind" before asking him to study.
6. Pregiving	Actor rewards the target before requesting compliance. *Example:* You raise Dick's allowance and tell him you now expect him to study.
7. Aversive stimulation	Actor continuously punishes target, making cessation contingent upon compliance. *Example:* You forbid Dick the use of the car and tell him he will not be allowed to drive until he studies more.
8. Debt	You owe me compliance because of past favors. *Example:* You point out that you have sacrificed and saved to pay for Dick's education and that he owes it to you to get good enough grades to get into a good college.
9. Moral appeal	You are immoral if you do not comply. *Example:* You tell Dick that it is morally wrong for anyone not to get as good grades as he can and that he should study more.
10. Self-feeling (positive)	You will feel better about yourself if you comply. *Example:* You tell Dick he will feel proud if he gets himself to study more.

(Continued)

Table 2.1 (Continued)

Strategy	Definition/Example
11. Self-feeling (negative)	You will feel worse about yourself if you do not comply. *Example:* You tell Dick he will feel ashamed of himself if he gets bad grades.
12. Altercasting (positive)	A person with "good" qualities would comply. *Example:* You tell Dick that since he is a mature and intelligent boy he naturally will want to study more and get good grades.
13. Altercasting (negative)	Only a person with "bad" qualities would not comply. *Example:* You tell Dick that only someone very childish does not study as he should.
14. Altruism	I need your compliance very badly, so do it for me. *Example:* You tell Dick that you really want very badly for him to get into a good college and that you wish he would study more as a personal favor to you.
15. Esteem (positive)	People you value will think better of you if you comply. *Example:* You tell Dick that the whole family will be very proud of him if he gets good grades.
16. Esteem (negative)	People you value will think worse of you if you do not comply. *Example:* You tell Dick that the whole family will be very disappointed (in him) if he gets poor grades.

SOURCE: From "Dimensions of Compliance-Gaining Behavior: An Empirical Analysis," by G. Marwell & D. R. Schmitt, 1967, *Sociometry, 30*, pp. 357-358. Copyright 1967 by the American Sociological Association. Reprinted with permission.

To accomplish this task, Marwell and Schmitt created a questionnaire containing four compliance-gaining scenarios—involving a work situation, a family situation, a sales situation, and a roommate situation—along with examples of the 16 strategies written for each situation (see Table 2.1 for the family situation). After reading each situation, Marwell and Schmitt's study participants (undergraduates) rated their likelihood of using each of the 16 compliance-seeking strategies on a 6-point scale with the endpoints *definitely would use* and *definitely would not use*. Respondents' ratings for each of the 16 strategies were summed across the four scenarios, after which these summed scores were subjected to a factor analysis.[4]

Results from this analysis revealed that perceived use scores for the 16 compliance-seeking strategies loaded onto five factors: (a) rewarding strategies (e.g., pregiving, liking), (b) punishing strategies (e.g., threat, aversive stimulation), (c) expertise strategies (e.g., positive and negative expertise), (d) strategies that activate impersonal commitments (e.g., positive and negative altercasting), and (e) strategies that activate personal commitments (e.g., negative esteem, debt). Given that each of these five factors represents a group of strategies, I will refer to each one as a *strategy cluster*. A second-order factor analysis revealed that the rewarding, expertise, and impersonal commitments strategy clusters loaded together, as did the punishing and personal commitment clusters. Based on this, Marwell and Schmitt (1967) concluded that the first three strategy clusters represent "socially acceptable" strategies, whereas the last two clusters represent "socially unacceptable" strategies.

Researchers have used Marwell and Schmitt's typology frequently to investigate how college students, parents, environmentalists, managers, and physicians select/reject compliance-seeking strategies (e.g., Baglan, Lalumia, & Bayless, 1986; Burgoon et al., 1990; deTurck & Miller, 1983; Hample & Dallinger, 1987a; Lamude, Daniels, & White, 1987; Lustig & King, 1980; Miller, Boster, Roloff, & Seibold, 1977; Roloff & Barnicott, 1978; Sillars, 1980). Some researchers have analyzed each of the 16 compliance-seeking strategies as separate dependent variables, whereas others have analyzed smaller numbers of strategy clusters.[5]

Schenck-Hamlin et al.'s Typology of Compliance-Seeking Strategies

Not all scholars have been satisfied with Marwell and Schmitt's (1967) category system. In the early 1980s, Schenck-Hamlin et al. (1982; Wiseman & Schenck-Hamlin, 1981) raised two criticisms of the Marwell and Schmitt typology. First, they questioned whether the typology provided a representative or exhaustive list of the strategies available for seeking compliance; for example, they claimed that strategies such as "hinting" and "nagging" are missing from Marwell and Schmitt's typology. Second, they argued that the conceptual dimensions differentiating and interconnecting the 16 strategies in Marwell and Schmitt's typology had not been specified clearly. Because Marwell and Schmitt did not begin with an analysis of the properties of influence messages, their typology was an ad hoc list that failed to measure any specific feature of compliance-seeking messages clearly (see also Clark & Delia, 1979).

In response to these limitations, Schenck-Hamlin et al. (1982) aimed to develop an exhaustive typology of compliance-seeking strategies and to ascertain the minimal number of message features needed to distinguish and classify these strategies. They pursued these goals in two phases. In the first, they developed their own typology of compliance-seeking strategies. Rather than surveying theoretical writings about power, Schenck-Hamlin et al. argued that an exhaustive typology was more likely to be derived "inductively" from examples of compliance-seeking messages written by everyday actors (see also Wiseman &

Schenck-Hamlin, 1981). Hence they presented 221 college students with 10 hypothetical situations involving a student who was trying to influence a roommate in various ways. Each student was asked to pick 3 of the 10 situations that he or she could imagine most easily and to write down exactly what he or she would say to the roommate in each situation. Each student also wrote an essay on "how I get others to do what I want them to do" in general. After reading these materials, Schenck-Hamlin et al. developed a list of 14 compliance-seeking strategies that captured most of the attempted means of persuasion in the students' written materials. Definitions of these 14 strategies are shown in Table 2.2, along with examples from a hypothetical situation in which you (a college student) try to persuade your roommate to turn down the volume on a stereo.

Despite the claimed advantage of an "inductive" approach, other scholars have pointed out that a comparison of Schenck-Hamlin's typology with the earlier Marwell and Schmitt category system "reveals more similarities than dissimilarities" (Boster, Stiff, & Reynolds, 1985, p. 178). Based on conceptual definitions for each strategy category, I compare the two typologies in Table 2.3, which shows that they do contain substantial overlap. "Direct request," "hinting," and "deceit" are missing from Marwell and Schmitt's system, but the remaining 11 Schenck-Hamlin et al. categories appear to have one or more counterparts in the Marwell and Schmitt typology.[6]

Aside from developing a typology, Schenck-Hamlin et al. (1982) also wanted to ascertain the number of message features researchers would need to distinguish among compliance-seeking strategies. In the second phase of their work, they argued that 13 of the 14 strategies could be differentiated based on the answers to four questions: (a) Does the strategy reveal the actor's intent to alter the target's behavior explicitly or only implicitly? (b) Is the strategy based on sanctions (rewards/punishments) or other means of inducement? (c) Is the message source, the target, or a third party responsible for creating the consequences of (non)compliance? and (d) Does the strategy focus on the past, present, or future? Put differently, Schenck-Hamlin et al. argued that explicitness, type of inducement, locus of control, and temporal sequence are "distinctive features," because each compliance-seeking strategy differs from every other with respect to at least one of these four features. Because "deceit" could not be distinguished from the remaining strategies using these features, they also argued that deceit is better conceptualized as a dimension along which any strategy could vary (i.e., truthful-misleading) rather than as a separate strategy category itself.

Researchers have used Schenck-Hamlin et al.'s (1982) typology frequently to investigate people's choice of compliance-seeking strategies (e.g., Burleson et al., 1988, Study 2; Dillard et al., 1989; Neuliep, 1986; Tracy, Craig, Smith, & Spisak, 1984). In most studies, each of the 14 strategies has been analyzed as a separate dependent variable.

Table 2.2   Schenck-Hamlin et al.'s (1982) 14 Compliance-Seeking Strategies
With Examples From a Hypothetical Stereo Situation

Strategy	Definition/Example
1. Ingratiating	Actor offers goods, sentiments, or services before making the request. Includes gift giving, love, affection, or favor doing. *Example:* I would be nice and polite to my roommate, then ask him or her to turn off the stereo.
2. Promise	Actor offers goods, sentiments, or services in exchange for compliance. Includes bribes, trades, compromises, and logrolling. *Example:* I would promise to do a favor for my roommate in the future if he or she will turn the stereo down now.
3. Debt	Actor recalls obligations owed him or her as a way of inducing the target to comply. Past debts include favors and loans. *Example:* I would recall past favors I've done for my roommate and say that he or she owes me a few hours of quiet.
4. Esteem	Target's compliance will result in an automatic increase in self-worth, such as feeling powerful, ethical, or competent. *Example:* I would tell my roommate that it would be very thoughtful of him or her to turn the stereo down.
5. Allurement	Target's reward for complying arises from persons or conditions other than the actor. Includes pleasing third parties. *Example:* I would tell my roommate that our apartment will be a more comfortable place for us to study if the stereo is turned down.
6. Aversive stimulation	Actor continuously punishes the target, making cessation contingent on the target complying. Includes pouting, crying, acting angry, "the silent treatment," and ridicule. *Example:* I would act irritated toward my roommate until he or she turns off the stereo.
7. Threat	Actor proposes actions that will have negative consequences for the target if he or she does not comply. Includes threats of firing, violence, and breaking off a relationship. *Example:* I would tell my roommate to turn off the stereo now or I will not cooperate when he or she wants to study.
8. Guilt	Target's failure to comply will result in an automatic decrease in self-worth, such as feeling inept, irresponsible, or unethical. *Example:* I would tell my roommate that it is inconsiderate of him or her to play the stereo while people are trying to study.

(Continued)

Table 2.2 (Continued)

Strategy	Definition/Example
9. Warning	Target's punishment for not complying arises from persons or conditions other than the actor. Includes upsetting third parties. *Example:* I would tell my roommate that our neighbors will complain if he or she does not turn the stereo down.
10. Altruism	Actor requests that the target engage in behavior that will help the actor rather than the target. Target may feel helpful by complying. *Example:* I would ask my roommate to turn down the stereo for my sake.
11. Direct request	Actor simply asks the target to comply. Actor does not provide the motivation or inducement for complying; the target must infer it. Includes recommendations and commands. *Example:* I would simply ask my roommate to turn off the stereo.
12. Explanation	Actor offers reasons the target should comply. May include the actor's credibility as well as references to shared values or observable evidence. *Example:* I would explain to my roommate that the stereo's volume is too loud to study by.
13. Hinting	Actor represents the situational context in such a way that the target is led to conclude the desired action/response. The desired response is not stated directly. *Example:* I would drop subtle hints about how hard it is to study.
14. Deceit	Actor gains the target's compliance by intentionally misrepresenting characteristics or consequences of the desired response. Includes false reasons or rewards. *Example:* I would lie, implying that our neighbors had complained about the loud stereo.

SOURCE: From "A Model of Properties of Compliance-Gaining Strategies," by W. J. Schenck-Hamlin, R. L. Wiseman, & G. N. Georgacarakos, 1982, *Communication Quarterly, 30,* pp. 94-95. Copyright 1982 by the Eastern Communication Association. Adapted with permission.

McLaughlin et al.'s Typology of Compliance-Resisting Strategies

Studying compliance gaining as an interactive phenomenon requires the study of both participants in influence episodes. Despite this, as McLaughlin, Cody, and Robey (1980) pointed out, early research on compliance gaining

Table 2.3   A Comparison of Two Typologies of Compliance-Seeking Strategies

Schenck-Hamlin et al. (1982)	Marwell and Schmitt (1967)
Ingratiation	Liking, Pregiving
Promise	Promise
Debt	Debt
Esteem	Positive self-feeling, positive esteem
Allurement	Positive esteem
Aversive stimulation	Aversive stimulation
Threat	Threat
Guilt	Negative self-feeling, moral appeal?
Warning	Negative esteem, negative expertise
Altruism	Altruism
Direct request	—
Explanation	Positive/negative expertise? moral appeal?
Hinting	—
Deceit	—

NOTE: Question marks in this table denote instances in which a Marwell and Schmitt strategy may or may not overlap with a Schenck-Hamlin et al. strategy, depending on the specific phrasing (see note 6 at the end of this chapter).

was "one-sided, focusing only on the potential persuader . . . as an active element in the interpersonal persuasive attempt; yet the recipient of a particular compliance-gaining message (the target) may, for whatever reason, choose to resist compliance" (p. 14). To gain a more complete picture of interpersonal influence, McLaughlin et al. proposed a nominal-level typology of strategies for resisting compliance. After examining existing typologies of compliance-seeking strategies, they initially proposed five broad clusters of compliance-resisting strategies. First, *nonnegotiation strategies* occur when the target overtly declines to comply with the source's request in a straightforward and unapologetic fashion. Second, *identity management* strategies are those in which the target refuses the request indirectly, by manipulating one or both of the parties' self-images. Third, *justification strategies* occur when the target justifies his or her unwillingness to comply on the basis of potential positive/negative outcomes for one or both parties. Fourth are *negotiation strategies*, in which the target proposes an alternative behavior to that requested by the source. Fifth, *emotional appeals* involve the target's appealing to the message source's affect.

McLaughlin et al. (1980) undertook a three-step procedure to assess the representativeness and exhaustiveness of their five strategy clusters. In the first step, 108 undergraduates each read eight different hypothetical scenarios and wrote out exactly what they would say to resist compliance in each situation. Each student was asked to imagine, for example, that his or her fiancée/fiancé wanted to convince him or her to postpone the wedding, that his or her roommate wanted the student to clean up his or her half of the room, and that a coworker wanted the student to cut down on smoking while at work. Students wrote what they would say in response after the message sources had sought their compliance with direct requests (e.g., "I would like for us to postpone our wedding").

In the second step, McLaughlin et al. coded messages written in response to four of these influence situations "for every distinctive occurrence of one of the five [strategy clusters]" (p. 23). Using this procedure, they identified a total of 21 commonly used compliance-resisting strategies and then grouped these strategies within the five original strategy clusters (nonnegotiation, identity management, justification, negotiation, and emotional appeals). Between 3 and 10 strategies fell into each strategy cluster.

In the third step, McLaughlin et al. asked a new group of 230 undergraduates to read the same eight hypothetical scenarios and then rate how likely they would be to use each of the 21 individual compliance-resisting strategies in that situation on a 9-point scale ranging from *extremely unlikely to use* to *extremely likely to use*. Likelihood-of-use ratings for the 21 compliance-resisting strategies were summed across situations and subjected to factor analysis (see note 4). The results were consistent with four of McLaughlin et al.'s five original strategy clusters: identity management, negotiation, nonnegotiation, and justification. However, "emotional appeal" strategies that provoked negative affect (such as anger and guilt) unexpectedly loaded with the identity management strategies, and strategies that provoked positive affect (such as happiness and pride) loaded alone. Based on these findings, O'Hair, Cody, and O'Hair (1991) reorganized the original identity management strategies and the negative emotional appeal strategies into a cluster labeled *negative identity management*, and also grouped the positive emotional appeal strategies along with several new strategies into a cluster labeled *positive identity management*. Their revised version of McLaughlin et al.'s typology of compliance-resisting strategies is shown in Table 2.4

Researchers have used the McLaughlin et al. typology to investigate how children and college students choose compliance-resisting strategies (e.g., McLaughlin et al., 1980; McQuillen, Higginbotham, & Cummings, 1984; O'Hair et al., 1991). Alberts, Miller-Rassulo, and Hecht (1991) have adapted the typology into a scheme of strategies for resisting offers to use illegal drugs. Researchers typically have analyzed 4- to 5-strategy clusters rather than individual compliance-resisting strategies as the dependent variable.

Table 2.4   A Revised Version of McLaughlin et al.'s (1980) Typology of
Compliance-Resisting Strategies

Negative identity management strategies
  1. I would point out to the person that I had never made a request like this one of him or her.
  2. I would tell him or her that no reasonable person would make the request.
  3. I would let the other person know how hurt I was that he or she made the request.
  4. I would act surprised and astonished so that he or she would feel bad about making the request.

Nonnegotiation strategies
  6. I would tell the other person that I don't want to discuss it.
  7. I would make it clear to the person that I have no obligation to go along with the request.
  8. I would simply refuse to go along with the request.
  9. I would dismiss the request by making it seem unimportant.

Negotiation strategies
  10. I would tell the person that we should have mutual talks and work it out.
  11. I would suggest to the other person that both of us should give in a little bit and reach a compromise.
  12. I would offer to make some sort of concession rather than go along with the original request.
  13. I would ask the other person to explain his or her reasons for making the request.
  14. I would suggest to the other person that he or she ought to make some sort of concession, rather than my complying with the original request.

Justification strategies
  15. I would explain to the person how he or she actually would benefit from my not complying with the request.
  16. I would explain to the person the negative consequences to me of my complying with the request.
  17. I would explain to the person how I would personally benefit from not complying with the request.

Positive identity management strategies
  18. I would try to make the other person feel good about him- or herself so that I could get out of going along with the request.
  19. I would act very nice to the person in order to avoid complying.
  20. I would appeal to the person's affect for me.

SOURCE: From "The Impact of Situational Dimensions on Compliance-Resisting Strategies: A Comparison of Methods," by M. J. O'Hair, M. J. Cody, & D. O'Hair, 1991, *Communication Quarterly, 39*, pp. 232-233. Copyright 1991 by the Eastern Communication Association. Adapted by permission.

NOTE: Four compliance-resisting strategies that each appeared to fit into more than one strategy cluster have been deleted.

Evaluation of Nominal-Level Typologies

Researchers have used nominal-level typologies of compliance-seeking/resisting strategies to conceptualize and describe interpersonal influence attempts more often than they have used any other approach. Despite this, the Marwell and Schmitt (1967), Schenck-Hamlin et al. (1982), and McLaughlin et al. (1980) category systems, as well as most other nominal-level typologies, suffer from two problems that often limit their utility: They are atheoretical, and they do not provide exhaustive lists of strategies within many situations.

LACK OF THEORETICAL GROUNDING

None of the influence typologies discussed above was designed with the intention of describing specific features or dimensions of influence messages. The lack of theoretical underpinning in these systems is evident in two respects: The strategies composing these typologies are not differentiated from each other consistently, and hence the strategies vary in unspecified ways.

Influence strategies can be defined and differentiated based on numerous features, such as their form, their content, their intended effect, their temporal sequencing, and their truth value. Unfortunately, most nominal-level typologies are atheoretical mixes that do not distinguish influence strategies systematically using one or a few message features. As Kellermann and Cole (1994) have demonstrated, "The attributes used to differentiate one strategy in a taxonomy rarely are used to differentiate others" (p. 26). They go on to explain:

> Marwell and Schmitt's (1967) [typology] has strategies defined by form (e.g., promise, threat), functions (e.g., liking), content (e.g., altruism, expertise, self-feeling, moral appeal, debt), presentation (e.g., pregiving), and continued use (e.g., aversive stimulation). Wiseman and Schenck-Hamlin's (1981) taxonomy includes strategies defined by form (e.g., warning, direct request, promise, threat), function (e.g., guilt), content (e.g., altruism, explanation, allurement, debt), presentation (e.g., ingratiation), continued use (e.g., aversive stimulation), and truth value (e.g., deceit). (p. 27)[7]

McLaughlin et al.'s (1980) typology also contains clusters of compliance-resisting strategies defined by content (e.g., positive and negative identity management, justification), sequencing (e.g., negotiation), and the refusal to engage in discussion (e.g., nonnegotiation).

One consequence of failing to design nominal-level typologies systematically is that the strategies in them vary in countless unspecified ways. Strategies in Marwell and Schmitt's (1967) typology can be differentiated on numerous grounds. For example, strategies differ in their emphasis on rewards versus punishments: Promise and positive expertise stress the benefits of complying, whereas aversive stimulation and negative esteem stress the costs of not complying. Strategies differ in terms of who controls the consequences of complying: Pregiving and threat rely on consequences controlled by the message source, whereas negative expertise and positive esteem rely on consequences controlled by other people. Strategies differ in terms of how actions are sequenced: Liking and pregiving involve performing other actions prior to making a request, whereas altruism or positive expertise may begin with the request itself. Strategies differ in whether they utilize social-normative pressure: Debt and moral appeal refer to social norms, whereas positive expertise and threat do not. Strategies differ in their form of reasoning: Positive and negative expertise provide classically "rational" arguments why the target should comply, whereas liking and negative altercasting do not. Strategies differ in their reliance on emotion: Positive self-feeling and negative esteem are designed to evoke specific emotions in the target, whereas positive and negative expertise may not be designed to do this. Strategies differ in their temporal focus: Debt focuses on prior actions, whereas positive expertise and negative esteem focus on future consequences. Using your own creativity, you undoubtedly can generate additional ways of differentiating the 14 compliance-seeking strategies.

Because nominal-level typologies are not conceptualized clearly with regard to specific message features or dimensions, it is difficult to explain why a person chooses one strategy rather than another. As D. J. O'Keefe (1990) argues, the "consequence of having such a hodgepodge of categories is that research results using such a system are very nearly uninterruptible" (p. 208). To illustrate this problem, consider a study in which Sillars (1980) used Marwell and Schmitt's typology to compare how individuals would seek compliance from a spouse versus a neighbor. Undergraduate participants reported that they were more likely to use "threat" when they imagined seeking the compliance of a neighbor rather than a spouse, but said that they were more likely to use "debt" with a spouse than with a neighbor. What accounts for differential ratings of these two strategies with neighbors versus spouses? The participants could have rated these strategies differently because calling in debts is more socially acceptable than using threats, or because debt focuses on the past whereas threats focus on the future, or because debt relies on feelings of obligation whereas threats rely on sanctions. If Marwell and Schmitt's 14 strategies were organized systematically based on a single message feature, such as temporal focus, then we could assess whether different strategies that focused on the future (e.g., positive expertise, promise, threat, warning) all were more likely to be selected with neighbors than with spouses. But because nominal-level typologies such as Marwell and Schmitt's do not systematically assess message features, one has little idea how to evaluate which interpretation of Sillars's findings is most plausible.

Of course, the influence strategies composing nominal-level typologies can be organized in a theoretical fashion to help make research findings more interpretable. For example, Wheeless, Barraclough, and Stewart (1983) argue that both the Marwell and Schmitt typology and the Schenck-Hamlin et al. typology can be grouped into three strategy clusters labeled "expectancy/consequences, relationships/identification, and values/obligations," each of which reflects a different base of power. Miller and Parks (1982) claim that compliance-seeking strategies can be classified based on two theoretical categories: whether they rely on rewards or punishments, and whether the motivation for behavior change lies within the message source (communicator onus) or the target (recipient onus). Roloff (1976) distinguishes "prosocial" strategies, in which sources attempt to gain targets' compliance by facilitating "understanding of [the targets'] attitudes and needs," from "antisocial" strategies, in which sources attempt to impose "their position on another through force and deception" (p. 181; see also Baglan et al., 1986; Burleson et al., 1988; Hunter & Boster, 1987; Marwell & Schmitt, 1967; Sorenson, Plax, & Kearney, 1989). Rather than analyzing nominal-level typologies as ad hoc lists, scholars should organize strategies based on some theoretical analysis of message features as they design and conduct research.

I should clarify two points about imposing a theoretical structure on nominal-level typologies. First, there is no objectively "best" way or only one correct way to organize influence strategies (D. J. O'Keefe, 1990). The researcher's choices should be guided by which message features are of interest. For example, if we want to explore whether managers at different levels in an organizational hierarchy rely on different power bases to exert and/or resist influence, then organizing typologies into strategy clusters reflecting power bases makes sense. If we want to know whether experienced high school teachers rely more on recipient-onus strategies than on communicator-onus strategies to deal with disruptive classroom behavior, then organizing influence strategies in terms of this conceptual distinction should be useful.

A second point is that decisions about how to organize influence strategies should be based on analyses of message features, not on the perceived likelihood that particular strategies will be used. Both Marwell and Schmitt (1967) and McLaughlin et al. (1980; O'Hair et al., 1991) attempt to group influence strategies into interpretable clusters based on factor analyses of likelihood-of-use ratings. But questions about how to organize compliance-seeking strategies and questions about whether people tend to use specific strategies together are different questions. This distinction is important, because message features can be analyzed across contexts, whereas strategy use is contextually bound (Kim & Wilson, 1994). As an example, both "promise" and "positive esteem" can be classified as reward-oriented strategies regardless of the situation, because both refer to consequences that are attractive to the message target. But whether promise and positive esteem are effective strategies for seeking compliance, and hence whether their likelihood-of-use ratings will covary, will depend heavily on the specific context.[8]

In sum, future research should organize strategies composing nominal-level typologies in a meaningful fashion. As Boster et al. (1985) have noted, describing strategies conceptually is not an end in itself. We want to specify the message features or dimensions assessed by a strategy typology clearly in order to predict variation in those features or dimensions. But unless some theoretical underpinning is imposed, research using these typologies is nearly uninterpretable.

FAILURE TO BE EXHAUSTIVE

A second problem is that nominal-level typologies do not provide an exhaustive scheme for coding influence strategies in many specific contexts. Arguing that a nominal-level coding scheme should be exhaustive could be interpreted in two ways. First, it could be taken to mean that a typology should provide an exhaustive list of every possible compliance-seeking or compliance-resisting strategy that could be used in every possible context. This is not what I mean by exhaustive. Indeed, such a requirement is "doomed to failure" (Boster et al., 1985, p. 178), because the number of strategies that might be used in every conceivable compliance-gaining situation may be infinite (D. J. O'Keefe, 1990). In a painstaking analysis, Kellermann and Cole (1994) identified 64 distinct strategies present in current compliance-seeking typologies, and even their list does not include all possible strategies (for several others, see Wilson et al., 1993). Possible means of seeking compliance, in the abstract, may be limited only by the ingenuity of everyday actors and the creativity of the scholars describing their efforts.

A second interpretation of an argument for exhaustiveness is that a typology should be able to classify every utterance that is used to seek/resist compliance during interactions situated in a particular context. When employed as coding schemes, the three typologies reviewed above often fail this more restricted sense of exhaustiveness. All three typologies were developed, implicitly or explicitly, to study influence episodes within particular relationships and/or cultures. Marwell and Schmitt (1967) developed their typology after reviewing theories of social power proposed by Western (primarily U.S.) scholars. Both Schenck-Hamlin et al. (1982) and McLaughlin et al. (1980) developed their typologies from messages written by U.S. college students in response to hypothetical scenarios. None of these typologies, nor for that matter any nominal-level typology, is likely to describe most of the "available means of persuasion" in contexts different from the ones for which they were developed, because the available means vary depending on relationships, institutions, and cultures. In addition, none of these typologies was developed with an emphasis on the interactive nature of seeking/resisting compliance; hence they all fail to capture some of the possibilities for seeking/resisting compliance as influence interactions unfold.

Social and institutional contexts may give rise to unique strategies for seeking and resisting compliance. Researchers have developed numerous nominal-level typologies of compliance-seeking/resisting strategies with the intention of analyzing influence episodes in specific contexts, such as in for-profit organizations, in the classroom, or at home. I review the research on persuasive message production within particular contexts in Chapter 8. For now, the point is that research that simply employs the Marwell and Schmitt (1967), Schenck-Hamlin et al. (1982), or McLaughlin et al. (1980) typology as a strategy list or coding scheme without attention to the particular context will overlook commonly used compliance-seeking/resisting strategies. Given that many work organizations are hierarchically structured and competitive, for example, it makes sense that employees at times appeal to superiors or form coalitions with coworkers to pressure targets to comply (Kipnis, Schmidt, & Wilkinson, 1980; Schriesheim & Hinkin, 1990). Strategies that actively enlist assistance from third parties are absent from both Marwell and Schmitt's and Schenck-Hamlin et al.'s typologies. In the classroom and at home, children often strategically "ignore" teachers and parents as a means of resisting their compliance-seeking appeals (e.g., Kearney & Plax, 1992; Kuczynski & Kochanska, 1990). Simply failing to respond is a strategy missing from McLaughlin et al.'s typology.

Cross-cultural comparisons also may reveal unique strategies. Comparisons of influence episodes across cultures represent a growing body of research (e.g., Blum-Kulka, House, & Kasper, 1989; Bresnahan, Cai, & Rivers, 1994; Burgoon, Dillard, Doran, & Miller, 1982; Fitch, 1994; Hirokawa & Miyahara, 1986; Holtgraves & Yang, 1992; Kim & Wilson, 1994; Tannen, 1981). Several studies have revealed cross-cultural differences in how individuals interpret and evaluate indirect forms of seeking/resisting compliance. For example, both Chinese (Ma, 1996) and Greek (Tannen, 1981) adults are significantly more likely than Americans to interpret unelaborated, unenthusiastic agreement with a request (e.g., "okay") as indirect resistance. Graham and Sano (1989) present anecdotal examples in which Japanese negotiators have been found to interpret postponement statements (e.g., "That's an interesting proposal, let me get back to you on it") as refusals when their American counterparts do not. Neither of these indirect forms of resistance is included in McLaughlin et al.'s (1980) typology.

Finally, examining compliance seeking and resisting as interactive phenomena may reveal unique strategies. The investigation of influence interactions is another area in which there is a growing body of literature (e.g., Applegate, 1982; Boster, Kazoleas, Levine, Rogan, & Kang, 1995; Boster, Levine, & Kazoleas, 1993; Boster & Stiff, 1984; Dillard, 1988; Dillard & Fitzpatrick, 1985; Lim, 1990; Newton & Burgoon, 1990; Scudder & Andrews, 1995; Wilson et al., 1993; Wilson, Levine, Humphreys, & Peters, 1994; Witteman & Fitzpatrick, 1986). Once influence episodes are examined beyond the initial request and response, additional options for seeking compliance become apparent. Consider the study described at the beginning of this chapter, in which undergraduates telephoned other students (actually confederates) and asked them to complete Professor Jones's research project (Wilson et al., 1993). In these telephone conversations, we found examples of only 4 of the 16 Marwell and Schmitt (1967) strategies (altruism, negative and positive expertise, and negative self-feeling),[9] and only 5 of the 14 Schenck-Hamlin et al. (1982) strategies (allurement, altruism, direct request, guilt, and warning). In addition, however, participants attempted to discover why the students had changed their minds about participating (identifying obstacles), refuted the validity of the students' reasons for backing out (denying obstacles), and suggested ways the students could still participate (suggesting plans). These "obstacle-oriented" strategies are missing from both Marwell and Schmitt's and Schenck-Hamlin et al's typologies.

In sum, the three nominal-level typologies reviewed in this section do not offer an exhaustive list of common compliance-seeking/resisting strategies within many specific contexts. Of course, researchers can adapt nominal-level typologies by adding, modifying, and deleting strategy categories depending on their purposes and the contexts of interest. Rather than applying standard category schemes mindlessly, researchers should determine whether they capture most of the "available means of persuasion" in a given context. Experience tells us this often will not be the case.

Summary

In this chapter, I have discussed the complexities of analyzing influence interactions. I began with an example that was used to show that influence interactions can be described using a variety of approaches. Following this, I presented the "traditional" approach to analyzing influence episodes: developing and applying typologies of nominal-level message strategies. I reviewed the development of three widely used typologies: Marwell and Schmitt's (1967) and Schenk-Hamlin et al.'s (1982) lists of compliance-seeking strategies as well as McLaughlin et al.'s (1980) list of compliance-resistance strategies. I closed the chapter with two recommendations for future work using this form of message analysis:

the need to organize lists of strategies based on some theoretical analysis of message features and the need to adapt strategy typologies to specific relational, institutional, cultural, and interactional contexts.

Notes

1. After our participants finished making their 20 telephone calls, we debriefed them in detail about the true purpose of the study.

2. Like any conceptual definition, these specify what I mean by the terms *strategy* and *utterance* in this book. Presenting clear conceptual definitions is important, in part, because scholars have not used the term *strategy* consistently within the compliance-gaining literature (see Greene, 1990; Kellermann & Cole, 1994). Although I limit my use of the term *strategy* to descriptions of overt behaviors, others have described people's mental representations of actions as strategies. Still others have used the term *tactic* to describe what I call strategies and *strategy* in turn to describe clusters or sequences of tactics. I attempt to avoid terminological confusion by using terms such as *strategy* consistently throughout the book.

3. Marwell and Schmitt (1967) describe their 16 abstract act types as *compliance-gaining techniques* rather than *compliance-seeking strategies*. To remain consistent with the definitions I have already introduced, I refer to their 16 act types as *compliance-seeking strategies*.

4. Factor analysis is a statistical technique designed to reduce a large number of observed variables (e.g., likelihood-of-use ratings for the 16 compliance-seeking strategies) into a smaller number of factors by combining together variables that correlate with each other and that are relatively independent from other variables (for an overview, see Tabachnick & Fidell, 1989).

5. Hunter and Boster (1987) argue that one nonlinear dimension underlies likelihood-of-use ratings for Marwell and Schmitt's strategies. Because their model of compliance-seeking strategy selection tells us more about the methodology of likelihood-of-use ratings than about the conceptual nature of Marwell and Schmitt's typology, I review the Hunter and Boster model in Chapter 4.

6. Comparison of the two typologies is muddied by the fact that neither defines strategies using a consistent set of message features (Kellermann & Cole, 1994). As an example, Marwell and Schmitt's "moral appeal" strategy is defined based on a persuasive appeal's content, whereas Wiseman and Schenck-Hamlin's "guilt" strategy is defined based on a persuasive appeal's emotional impact on the target. In some cases, compliance-gaining messages that appeal to shared morals will create guilt in the target (i.e., they are the "same" strategy), but in other circumstances moral appeals may not create guilt, or a target may feel guilty even when the persuasive appeal does not appeal to morals (i.e., they are "different" strategies). The question marks in Table 2.3 denote instances where strategies from the two typologies may or may not overlap.

7. Of the researchers who developed the three typologies reviewed earlier, only Schenck-Hamlin et al. (1982) attempted to identify a set of distinctive message features that distinguish strategies composing their category system. Because they conducted their analysis only after developing an inductive list of strategies, however, the results are still messy. Some strategy categories in their list are better conceptualized as message dimensions (something along which any strategy could vary from low to high) than as strategies. Besides "deceit," "hinting" is an example: Threats can be phrased explicitly ("Robyn, share your new toy or I'll have to take it away") or implicitly ("Robyn, what happened the last time you played with Justin?"), as can promises, debt, and other compliance-seeking strategies. Aside from questionable categories, concerns also can be raised about Schenck-Hamlin et al.'s concept of "distinctive" features. Strategies in their list can be

distinguished based on many other features as well, such as bases of social power (Wheeless et al., 1983) or types of politeness (Baxter, 1984); hence their four features are not "distinctive" in the sense of describing all possible types of variation across strategies.

8. Consider the following example: If reward versus punishment orientation is an important feature that influences whether messages are effective in one context, then perceived use ratings for promise and positive esteem may load on the same factor. In contrast, if power base is an important feature influencing whether messages are effective in a second context, then perceived use ratings for promise versus positive esteem may not load on the same factor in that second context because the two strategies rely on different bases of power. The key point is that promise and positive esteem are both reward-oriented strategies in either case, despite the different factor-analytic results.

9. We also observed a variation of Marwell and Schmitt's debt strategy, when our participants argued that the student (confederate) had signed an agreement to complete Professor Jones's study and hence had an obligation to do so.

3

Alternative Approaches to Message Analysis

Themes, Dimensions, and Temporal Characteristics

Looking Ahead . . .

The preceding chapter examined the "traditional" approach of using nominal-level typologies of message strategies to describe influence interactions. Continuing the discussion, this chapter explores three alternative approaches to describing interactions: identifying content themes, deriving message dimensions, and exploring temporal sequences. Similar to the traditional approach, each of these alternative approaches to message analysis needs to be connected to theories of persuasive message production.

In Chapter 2, we examined how influence interactions such as the "Kathy-Lisa conversation" could be described using nominal-level typologies of message strategies. Given the potential limitations of this "traditional" form of message analysis, you may have wondered what alternatives are available. In this chapter,

I present and evaluate three alternative approaches to message analysis: (a) identifying nominal-level content themes in influence messages, (b) deriving conceptual dimensions underlying influence behaviors, and (c) describing temporal characteristics of influence interactions.

Nominal-Level Content Themes in Influence Messages

As an alternative to describing influence "strategies," O'Keefe and Lambert (1995) advocate analyzing content themes within compliance-seeking/resisting messages. After defining *theme*, I describe and evaluate this second approach.

WHAT IS A THEME?

A theme can be defined as a "patterned semantic issue or locus of concern around which . . . interaction centers" (Owen, 1984, p. 274). In a study of relational communication, Owen (1984) identified themes inductively by looking for the "repetition of key words, phrases, and sentences" as well as for "the same thread of meaning even though different wording indicated such a meaning" (p. 275). Researchers have used thematic analyses to study a variety of topics, such as communication in conflict, gender, leadership, and personal relationships (e.g., Buzzanell & Burrell, 1997; Owen, 1989; Sillars, Weisberg, Burggraf, & Wilson, 1987).

Barbara O'Keefe, Bruce Lambert, and their colleagues have analyzed "patterns of repeated phrases" and "threads in meaning" within influence messages. This work is part of their larger theory of message design, which I describe in Chapters 6 and 7. What is important at this point is that their description of compliance-seeking and -resisting messages differs from work on message strategies. The term *strategy* has been defined based on the intentions, functions and effects of talk (i.e., what the message does). In contrast, O'Keefe and Lambert's (1995) thematic analysis classifies messages based on their semantic content or substance (i.e., what the message says). Although talk centering on a theme may end up serving a particular goal or function, these researchers attempt to analyze message content without regard to function. Within a compliance-gaining interaction, each person's turns at talk may contain many different and potentially unrelated themes, and different themes within the same person's talk may serve very different functions.

EXAMPLES OF THEMATIC ANALYSES

Two studies illustrate how content themes can be identified. Lambert and Gillespie (1994) identified content themes within compliance-seeking messages generated by pharmacy students in response to a hypothetical situation. They asked 85 doctor-of-pharmacy students in their third year of coursework to imagine that they were "approached by a familiar patient who is notoriously late in obtaining refill prescriptions for his antihypertensive [high blood pressure] medication. The patient complains that the medication is ineffective and expensive and that it has unpleasant side effects" (p. 314). Participants wrote out what they would say to the patient.

Lambert and Gillespie used a three-step procedure to identify content themes in these compliance-gaining messages. First, they unitized or segmented the 85 written messages into independent clauses. Each clause in a written message that contained a grammatical subject and verb was counted as a different unit. Sentences with compound predicates (e.g., "This medication lowers your blood pressure *and* makes you healthier in the long run") were treated as two separate units. Second, Lambert and Gillespie developed a classification scheme to group synonymous units. Independent clauses were treated as synonymous "if they expressed the same idea using slightly different vocabulary or using the same vocabulary with slight variations in syntax" (p. 317). The 49 substantive "idea types" identified in this second step are listed in Table 3.1.

In a third step, Lambert and Gillespie grouped the idea types based on similar meaning into 11 content themes (see Table 3.1). To assess the interrelationship among themes, they scored the number of idea types within each message that belonged to each of the 11 content themes. Correlations between frequency of occurrence for the 11 themes were not strong, ranging from only −.22 to .28. Based on this finding, they concluded that "each message, rather than being a coherent grouping of functionally similar elements, was instead a relatively fragmented collection of independently elaborated themes" (p. 318). The pharmacy students seemed to discuss individual themes independently. Knowing that a student wrote extensively about one theme would not allow us to predict accurately whether he or she elaborated other themes.

To assess the effects of theme elaboration, Lambert and Gillespie also asked patients at the ambulatory hypertension clinic of a Veterans Administration hospital to rate the overall quality and effectiveness of the written compliance-gaining messages. Frequencies of occurrence for three themes were positively associated with perceptions of message quality: doctor communication ($r = .21$), express understanding ($r = .38$), and express concern ($r = .20$).

In a second study, Saeki and O'Keefe (1994) identified content themes within "rejection" messages generated in response to a hypothetical scenario. They asked each of 124 American and 104 Japanese undergraduates to imagine that he or she was chairing the committee responsible for selecting which individuals would be invited to become new members of a student organization. As committee chair, the participant supposedly was responsible for notifying each candidate about whether his or her application had been

Table 3.1   Content Themes in Pharmacy Students' Compliance-Seeking Messages

Theme	Idea Type
1. Take medication	The medication only works when taken as directed.
	It is important to take the medication as directed.
	If you do not take the medication as directed, it will not work.
	Take the medication as directed.
	Don't stop taking the medication.
	It's up to you to take your medication.
2. Dangerous disease	It is important to control your hypertension.
	Uncontrolled hypertension has dangerous consequences.
	High blood pressure has no symptoms.
	You feel fine without the medication.
	This medication is for your high blood pressure.
3. Doctor communication	If there are problems, the doctor should be notified.
	You/I should contact your doctor.
	Tell your doctor how you feel about the side effects.
	Have you contacted your doctor lately?
	The doctor will follow up with your care.
	Get your blood pressure checked.
4. Express understanding	I understand the medication has some unpleasant side effects.
	I understand your feelings.
	Taking the medication makes you feel bad/worse.
	You do not like taking your medicine.
	Your situation is not unusual.
	The medication may not work well for you.
5. Express concern	The medication will make you healthier in the long run.
	I am concerned about your health and well-being.
	I want to help you.
	We need to work together.
	You are a regular customer.
6. Describe alternatives	A more effective alternative can be found.
	There are alternative drugs.
	A proper diet can help control your blood pressure.
	The regimen can be made easier.

(Continued)

Table 3.1 (Continued)

Theme	Idea Type
7. Be patient	Be patient so the medicine has a chance to work. The medication may take some time to work. You may not feel the medicine working. The side effects go away eventually. You'll see your blood pressure go down. Let's see how it works.
8. Cost-benefit	The medication is effective/is not ineffective. The medication is worth the cost. The medication is expensive. You may be wasting your money.
9. Describe experience	Tell me how you feel when you take the medication. Tell me how you take your medication.
10. Patient problem	You are noncompliant/overdue for a refill. Your blood pressure is not controlled.
11. Gather information	Why aren't you taking your medication? Do you have any questions? What do you think?

SOURCE: From "Patient Perceptions of Pharmacy Students' Hypertension Compliance-Gaining Messages: Effects of Message Design Logic and Content Themes," by B. L. Lambert & J. L. Gillespie, 1994, *Health Communication, 6*, pp. 319-320. Copyright 1994 by Lawrence Erlbaum Associates, Inc. Reprinted with permission.

accepted. As part of this role, each participant was asked "to notify Robin Jones of the failure of his or her application" (p. 79). Aside from varying culture, Saeki and O'Keefe wrote different versions of the scenario, manipulating whether Robin was a friend or a stranger and whether he or she was qualified or unqualified given the organization's admission standards. In each case, participants wrote exactly what they would say to Robin in their situation. After writing their messages, participants also completed single-item 7-point semantic differential scales assessing how much importance they placed on six interaction goals (e.g., justifying why Robin was rejected, protecting Robin's self-esteem) in the situation.[1]

Based on an analysis of the social implications of rejection and of serving as a spokesperson for a larger organization, Saeki and O'Keefe had anticipated that six content themes would emerge from their message data. Using the same three-step procedure as that used by Lambert and Gillespie (1994), they identified 20 different idea types, which they grouped into eight content themes (the six anticipated themes plus two others). Their idea types and themes are shown in Table 3.2. Frequency of occurrence for seven of the eight themes varied across participant culture, type of relationship, and/or candidate qualification, and different themes also were associated with the importance attributed to different interaction goals. Based on these findings, Saeki and O'Keefe (1994) concluded that "the influence of situational conditions, including communicator goals, was felt at the level of the message theme rather than the message taken as a whole" (p. 94). Put differently, these researchers feel that they learned more about how students varied their rejection messages across situations and culture by examining the elaboration of multiple themes within each message than would have occurred had they made a single, global judgment (e.g., polite versus rude) about each message.

Two points about these studies of content themes in influence episodes merit note. First, the researchers assessed content themes at a nominal level of measurement. Both Lambert and Gillespie (1994) and Saeki and O'Keefe (1994) identified themes in a sample of influence messages using inductive procedures, and their resulting lists of content themes are not intended to vary from "most to least" or "high to low" with respect to any conceptual dimension (see Tables 3.1 and 3.2). Second, content themes in principle could be identified in influence interactions. Although Lambert and Gillespie as well as Saeki and O'Keefe assess content themes within written messages generated in response to hypothetical scenarios, Bonito (2001) has used similar procedures to identify content themes within group discussions.

EVALUATION OF CONTENT THEMES

In comparison to nominal-level typologies of compliance-seeking and -resisting strategies, the analysis of content themes is a relatively new approach to describing interpersonal influence attempts. The analysis of content themes avoids at least two of the pitfalls that have beset nominal-level strategy typologies. Similar to nominal-level strategies, however, the utility of this newer approach depends on whether a theoretical underpinning can be imposed upon the content themes that emerge in any situation.

By identifying themes consistently based on semantic content, the analysis of content themes avoids one pitfall of nominal-level strategy typologies. As you will recall, most nominal-level typologies are conceptual mixtures that distinguish influence strategies based on semantic content, pragmatic form, intended

Table 3.2   Content Themes in American and Japanese Students' Rejection
Messages

Theme	Idea Type
1. Report rejection	The committee had a long discussion. You did not make it.
2. Supportive account	There were many excellent applicants. You came very close. You would make a nice addition to the honor society.
3. Critical account	There were applicants who were more qualified.
4. Encourage candidate	I encourage you to apply again next year. You would have a great shot at it. We appreciate your interest in the club.
5. Impersonal decision	We have strict guidelines that must be filled. We judged by the criteria very strictly. I hope you understand.
6. Deflect anger	I wanted you but others did not. I value our friendship. Don't let this affect our relationship. I did my best.
7. Minimize rejection	The society is a lot of crap anyway. Please, don't let this get to you.
8. Offer consolation	I'm upset you won't be in the club. Do you have time to go get a beer?

SOURCE: From "Refusals and Rejections: Designing Messages to Serve Multiple
Goals," by M. Saeki & B. J. O'Keefe, 1994, *Human Communication Research,*
21, pp. 82-83. Copyright 1994 by the International Communication Association.
Adapted by permission.

effect, temporal sequencing, and so forth. In contrast, O'Keefe, Lambert, and
colleagues identify content themes based solely on the semantic content of independent clauses, as reflected in repetitious wording and synonymous meanings.
Because they differentiate themes using a consistent set of message features,
these researchers are in a better position to specify what it is about influence
messages that varies across persons and situations. If message sources elaborate
different content themes when seeking compliance from their spouses than they
do when seeking compliance from their neighbors, for example, we know that

something about the semantic content of their compliance-gaining messages varies across the two types of relationships.

Aside from classifying messages consistently, an additional advantage of this approach is that lists of themes can be identified by a computer program rather than by human analysts. Lambert and O'Keefe have developed a computer-assisted message analysis system, called the "theme machine," that groups independent clauses into thematic categories based on the frequency of co-occurrence of individual words within clauses (Lambert, 1996b; O'Keefe, 1996).[2] Although written messages must be typeset and unitized by hand, this computer program can identify content themes present within thousands of independent clauses in seconds, whereas the same task might take human analysts weeks or even months. Bonito (2001) has shown how the program also can identify themes from written transcripts of face-to-face interactions.

By deriving themes inductively within each influence situation, the analysis of content themes also avoids a second potential pitfall of nominal-level strategy typologies: the exhaustiveness criterion. Although Saeki and O'Keefe (1994) anticipated that particular themes would occur based on the nature of the rejection situation, the list of themes in any study ultimately emerges from the sample of influence messages collected in that study. Because the researcher does not begin with a preformulated list, thematic categories do not have to be added, deleted, or modified for particular situations. Whether similar themes emerge as people seek and/or resist compliance in different situations becomes an empirical question rather than an assumption made by the researcher.

Despite these advantages, the analysis of content themes shares a similar dilemma with nominal-level strategy typologies: the need to impose an underlying theoretical structure.[3] Regardless of whether human analysts or computer programs are used, lists of themes are derived based solely on similarity of semantic content. Individual themes are neither deduced directly from nor organized around more abstract conceptual categories. Themes also are not designed to vary systematically from low to high on one or a few conceptual dimensions.

Because lists of content themes are not designed with a conceptual scheme in mind, the resulting themes can vary in countless unspecified ways. Individual themes in Lambert and Gillespie's (1994) list, for example, can be distinguished on numerous grounds. Themes differ in object of focus: Themes 1, 6, and 8 focus on the medication; theme 2 focuses on the disease; theme 3 focuses on the doctor; and themes 4, 5, 7, 9, 10, and 11 focus on the patient. Themes differ in valence: Themes 4 and 5 express positive regard for the patient, whereas theme 10 implies negative judgment. Themes differ in terms of proposed course of action: Themes 1 and 7 encourage the patient to continue the current medical treatment, whereas themes 3 and 6 imply that changes in treatment may be needed. Themes differ in orientation to feelings: Themes 4 and 5 confirm the patient's feelings, whereas theme 7 diminishes/discounts feelings. Themes differ in informational focus: Themes 1, 2, 5, 6, 7, and 8 provide information, whereas themes 9 and 11 seek information. Using your own creativity, you undoubtedly can think of several other ways to distinguish the individual themes displayed in Table 3.1.

The problem of failing to derive content themes using a conceptual scheme is that it is difficult to explain why individuals elaborate one theme rather than another. Of course, theoretical explanation for differences can be advanced after the fact. Recall that Lambert and Gillespie (1994) found that frequency of occurrence for themes 3, 4, and 5 was associated with the perceived quality of the pharmacy students' compliance-gaining messages. They claim that themes 4 and 5 are unique because they "focus on the personal relationship," "strive for cooperation and consensus," and "acknowledge the validity of the other's perspective" (p. 321). To support their claim, Lambert and Gillespie also coded each of the 85 written compliance-gaining messages at a global level for whether the message treated the situation "as an occasion to reaffirm and restructure the therapeutic relationship between pharmacist and patient" (p. 314).[4] Messages that reaffirmed and restructured the relationship at a global level were more likely to contain themes 4 and 5, and less likely to contain theme 1, than were messages that did not. Despite this evidence, however, questions still can be raised about Lambert and Gillespie's interpretation. Their interpretation does not explain why theme 3 also was associated with perceived quality, since it is not relationally focused. Their interpretation also seems to imply that theme 7 (which discounts the patient's feelings and perspective) and theme 10 (which implies negative judgment of the patient) should have been inversely associated with perceived message quality, but this was not the case.

In sum, the utility of analyzing content themes, using the procedures developed by O'Keefe, Lambert, and their colleagues, depends upon the degree to which emergent themes can be mapped directly and unambiguously onto theoretical constructs pertaining to message functions and effects after the fact. As with typologies of influence strategies, there is no single "objectively correct" way to organize content themes conceptually. Themes might be organized in terms of object focus, valence, proposed course of action, orientation to feelings, or in other ways depending on the researcher's purpose. Rather than deriving themes in a strictly inductive fashion, however, the results of studies such as Lambert and Gillespie's (1994) and Saeki and O'Keefe's (1994) might be easier to interpret if the researchers had derived content themes from theoretical constructs or at least organized themes around constructs prior to analyzing how themes varied across relationships, situations, and cultures (for an example, see Sillars et al., 1987).

Dimensions of Influence Behavior

Aside from nominal-level strategy typologies and content themes, scholars have described how influence interactions vary along conceptual dimensions. In this section, I define *conceptual dimension* and *ordinal-level measurement*, describe inductive and deductive procedures for deriving conceptual dimensions, and evaluate this third approach for describing influence episodes.

WHAT IS A CONCEPTUAL DIMENSION?

A conceptual dimension is an abstract continuum along which objects, people, or events can be placed. Analyzing dimensions of influence behavior assumes an ordinal level of measurement, in which "a set of objects or people is ordered from 'most' to 'least' with respect to a given attribute" (Nunnally, 1967, p. 12). For example, a group of children could be rank ordered from tallest to shortest with regard to the quality or continuum of height. A sample of compliance-seeking/resisting messages could be ordered along numerous conceptual dimensions, such as directness, dominance, listener adaptedness, and social appropriateness.[5]

Three points regarding the analysis of influence interactions along conceptual dimensions should be clarified. First, conceptual dimensions can be analyzed at either global or local units of analysis. Imagine that we want to assess people's degree of social appropriateness as they seek or resist compliance during interaction. Using a global index, we could ask raters to judge how appropriate each person's compliance-seeking/resisting behavior was in general over an entire conversation. Using a local index, we instead could ask raters to judge the appropriateness of every separate turn at talk and then perhaps compute an average level of appropriateness for each person's compliance-seeking/resisting behavior across all of his or her conversational turns (or across different "phases" of the interaction). Using either procedure, message sources can be rank ordered from "most" to "least" in terms of social appropriateness.

A second clarification is that one can analyze conceptual dimensions either with or without first classifying messages as strategies. Scholars have developed many typologies of influence strategies designed to vary from high to low along conceptual dimensions. For example, Blum-Kulka, House, and Kasper (1989) as well as Kim and Wilson (1994) classify requests into one of three strategy clusters varying from low to high in terms of "directness," or the degree to which a request makes the speaker's intent explicit. Consider a situation in which you must ask a friend to repay an overdue loan. The most indirect request strategies are hints, in which the speaker's intent must be inferred from the context (e.g., "Gee, I seem to have run out of cash"). Query strategies, which pose questions about the target's ability or willingness to comply, are moderately direct (e.g., "Could you repay the loan?" or "Would you mind repaying the loan?"). Direct-statement strategies are most to the point (e.g., "I'm asking you to repay the loan," or "Please repay the loan"). Using this strategy typology, requests first could be classified as hints, queries, or direct statements, and then assigned a score for degree of directness (hint = 1, query = 2, direct statement = 3). Using a different approach, however, coders could simply rate each request in a sample of influence messages for directness along a 1 to 5 scale (on which 1 = *very indirect* and 5 = *very direct*) without classifying requests into the strategy categories of hint, query, or direct statement at all.

A third clarification is that conceptual dimensions can be identified inductively or deductively. Inductive approaches seek to describe the perceptual dimensions along which everyday actors distinguish influence messages. Deductive approaches define conceptual dimensions in terms of one or more constructs deemed important within a theory. Both approaches have been used to derive conceptual dimensions.

DERIVING CONCEPTUAL DIMENSIONS INDUCTIVELY

To my knowledge, four studies have attempted to identify the perceived dimensions along which individuals naturally distinguish compliance-seeking messages (Cody, McLaughlin, & Jordan, 1980; Falbo, 1977; Falbo & Peplau, 1980; Wiseman & Schenck-Hamlin, 1981).[6] As an example, Wiseman and Schenck-Hamlin (1981) had 254 undergraduate students read one of two hypothetical compliance-gaining situations involving a roommate. Half of the sample imagined trying to convince the roommate not to invite a third party to move in with them indefinitely, and the other half imagined trying to convince the roommate to turn off the stereo so that they could study for a midterm exam. For each situation, the researchers had written 14 messages (i.e., utterances), each illustrating 1 of the 14 compliance-seeking strategies in Schenck-Hamlin, Wiseman, and Georgacarakos's (1982) typology. They had pretested these messages to assure that each was seen as a representative example of the intended strategy category. The 14 messages from the stereo situation appear in Table 2.2 in Chapter 2.

After reading the hypothetical compliance-seeking scenario as well as the 14 strategy labels and sample messages for that scenario, each participant completed a "paired-comparison" task, rating how similar each of the 14 strategies was with every other strategy on a 10-point scale. For example, participants were asked to "rate the similarity of 'debt' and 'ingratiation' where zero means they are identical and nine means they are [very] different" (Wiseman & Schenck-Hamlin, 1981, p. 262). The researchers subjected the ratings from this paired-comparison task to multidimensional scaling to identify the number of perceptual dimensions that participants used to make their similarity judgments.[7] After participants had finished making similarity ratings for every strategy pair, they then evaluated each of the 14 strategies individually on unidimensional scales measuring whether that strategy revealed the message source's intent explicitly/implicitly, manipulated rewards/punishments, dominated the target/treated the target as an equal, and presented a(n) reasonable/ unreasonable rationale. The researchers used these unidimensional ratings to help interpret the nature or content of the perceptual dimensions that emerged from the multidimensional scaling procedure.

Wiseman and Schenck-Hamlin (1981) concluded that participants distinguished compliance-seeking messages in both situations along four dimensions. Dimension 1 reflected the *directness/explicitness* of the influence message. Strategies that made the source's intent explicit in the message itself, such as "direct request" and "explanation," fell high on this dimension, whereas "hinting" fell low. Dimension 2 captured whether a strategy *manipulated rewards/punishments*. Reward-based strategies such as "promise," "ingratiation," and "esteem" fell at one end of this dimension, and punishment-based strategies such as "aversive stimulation," "threat," and "warning" fell at the other. Dimension 3 reflected the *locus of control* regarding behavior change. Strategies in which the message source controlled sanctions, such as "promise," "debt," and "aversive stimulation," fell at one end of this dimension. Strategies in which the locus of control resided in the target and/or the context, such as "esteem," "allurement," and "explanation," fell at the other end. Dimension 4 appeared to tap the *explicitness of the rationale* for compliance. Strategies that offered overt reasons the target should comply, such as "explanation" and "deceit," fell high on this dimension, whereas strategies that contained implicit or unstated reasons, such as "direct request" and "guilt," fell low.

Dillard, Wilson, Tusing, and Kinney (1997) report a detailed comparison of the four studies that have used multidimensional scaling to describe the perceived dimensions of compliance-gaining messages (Cody et al., 1980; Falbo, 1977; Falbo & Peplau, 1980; Wiseman & Schenck-Hamlin, 1981). Information on the number of judges and stimulus messages from these four studies appears in Table 3.3. The sizable range for numbers of judges reflects the fact that Cody et al. (1980) and Wiseman and Schenck-Hamlin (1981) collected similarity ratings from large samples of undergraduates, whereas Falbo (1977; Falbo & Peplau, 1980) had small numbers of "expert" raters (social psychology faculty and graduate students) make similarity judgments.

Despite procedural differences, Dillard et al. (1997) argue that three conceptual dimensions emerged consistently in these studies: (a) *explicitness*, or the degree to which the message source makes his or her intentions apparent to the target; (b) *dominance*, or the degree to which the message source's behavior

Table 3.3   Perceived Dimensions of Compliance-Seeking Messages:
A Summary of Four Studies

	Number of		Dimensions Reported		
Study	Judges	Stimuli	Explicitness	Dominance	Argument
Cody et al. (1980)					
Best friend scenario	121	68	Direct vs. manipulation	—	Direct/rationale vs. coercive
Barking dog scenario	119	72	—	Cooperation vs. negative consequences	Direct/rationale vs. inaction
Antique scenario[a]	97	65	—	Strong vs. weak	—
Falbo (1977)	8	16	Direct vs. indirect	—	Rationale vs. nonrationale
Falbo & Peplau (1980)	9	13	Directness	Bilateral vs. unilateral	—
Wiseman & Schenck-Hamlin (1981)[b]	254	28	Directness	Manipulation of rewards	Explicitness of rationale

SOURCE: J. P. Dillard, S. R. Wilson, K. J. Tusing, & T. A. Kinney, "Politeness Judgments in Personal Relationships," *Journal of Language and Social Psychology, 16,* p. 300. Copyright © 1997 by Sage Publications, Inc. Reprinted by permission of Sage Publications, Inc.

a. Cody et al. (1980) also report an inaction versus manipulation dimension for this scenario that has no obvious parallels in the other studies.

b. Wiseman and Schenck-Hamlin (1981) also report a locus-of-control dimension that has no obvious parallels in the other studies.

implies that he or she has power over the target; and (c) *argument,* or the degree to which the message source offers explicit reasons the target should comply with his or her request (regardless of the quality of those reasons). Each of the four studies identified at least two of these three dimensions, and no dimension beyond these three has been identified consistently (see Table 3.3). We should be cautious about generalizing these findings too far, however, because the participants in the four studies are highly homogeneous with regard to ethnic and cultural background.

In sum, research suggests that white, middle-class Americans often rely on explicitness, dominance, and argument to distinguish and evaluate compliance-seeking strategies. I should clarify, however, that explicitness, dominance, and argument are not the only dimensions—or necessarily even the most useful dimensions—for describing influence interactions. Theories of persuasive message production are designed to predict and explain why individuals say what they do as they seek or resist compliance. Given these scholarly goals, the utility of any conceptual dimension depends on how/why we expect individuals to differ during influence interactions.[8] As you will see, several theories discussed in this book do focus our attention on explicitness, dominance, and argument. Brown and Levinson's (1978) politeness theory (see Chapter 6), for instance, predicts that explicitness will vary depending on the size of the request being made as well as the nature of the message source–target relationship. But other theories presented here focus our attention on different conceptual dimensions. For example, the "constructivist" perspective (see Chapter 4) predicts that as children mature, they become increasingly skilled at adapting their compliance-gaining appeals to the unique perspective of the message target. To test this theory, we obviously need to describe whether influence messages vary along the dimension of "listener adaptedness." Describing influence messages along the dimensions of explicitness, dominance, and argument would not allow us to assess whether messages actually change in the predicted fashion as children mature. Aside from the three inductively derived dimensions, then, theories of persuasive message production direct attention to other dimensions of influence interactions.

DERIVING CONCEPTUAL DIMENSIONS DEDUCTIVELY

The "Constructivist" Analysis of Listener Adaptation

Ruth Anne Clark, Jesse Delia, and their colleagues' work on "listener adaptation" represents one of the best-known examples of a theoretically derived conceptual scheme for describing influence interactions. I describe their "constructivist" perspective on persuasive message production in Chapter 4. At this point, it is sufficient to say that Clark and Delia (1976) expected children's compliance-seeking messages to vary systematically as children grew older. With maturation, children become more adept at distinguishing different message targets, taking the perspective of particular targets, and inferring targets' feelings and motivations. Given these developments, Clark and Delia expected that children also would produce increasingly "listener-adapted" persuasive messages as they matured. Listener-adapted persuasive messages are those in which the message source adapts his or her request and supporting arguments to the wants and needs of the message target. Aside from children, adults with well-developed social-perception skills also might be expected to produce compliance-gaining appeals that are better adapted than those of adults whose social-perception skills are poorly developed.

In their initial study, Clark and Delia (1976) interviewed individually 29 boys and 29 girls ranging from second through ninth grade. They asked each child to speak aloud exactly what he or she would say in three hypothetical influence situations: trying to persuade the child's parents to buy something the child wanted, trying to persuade the child's mother to let the child have a large overnight party, and trying to persuade a woman the child does not know to keep a lost puppy the child had found near the woman's house. After each child had finished his or her response to each situation, the interviewer asked the child to imagine that the target looked like he or she was about to say no, and then instructed the child to say anything else that might persuade the target to comply. The children's responses were audiotaped and transcribed for analysis.

Clark and Delia divided each message into a major request plus one or more supporting arguments. They coded the child's request and his or her supporting arguments separately, using four-level hierarchical schemes ordered in terms of increasing perspective-taking skill. For *requests themselves*, messages without an explicit request were coded at Level 0, those with an unelaborated request or statement of desire (e.g., "Will you keep this dog?") were coded at Level 1, those with a request phrased to forestall counterarguments (e.g., "Will you keep this dog just until tomorrow when I can try to find its owner?") were coded at Level 2, and those phrased to acknowledge the desires of the target (e.g., "Since we both want this puppy to have a good home, would you like to keep him?") were coded at Level 3. For *supporting materials*, messages without any support for the request were coded at Level 0, those that demonstrated a need for the request (e.g., "The puppy looks skinny") were coded at Level 1, those that dealt with counterarguments (e.g., "It doesn't cost much to feed a dog, if you buy the big bags of food") were coded at Level 2, and those that supplied advantages to the target (e.g., "If I were you and I lived alone, I'd like a good watchdog like this one") were coded at Level 3.

For each situation, the children were assigned scores for the highest-level request and supporting argument that was present in each of their messages. Scores on the two measures were combined into a total score for each situation (range = 2 to 8 points). Clark and Delia argue that these highest-level scores tap children's ability to generate listener-adapted messages, because one must identify information about the other's needs and wants in order to anticipate counterarguments or describe advantages to the other.

Mean scores for level of listener adaptation within the three compliance-seeking situations and across situations appear in Table 3.4. As predicted, the children produced increasingly adapted compliance-seeking appeals as grade level increased. Means scores across the three situations suggest that major jumps in listener adaptedness occurred between third and – fourth grades and between eighth and ninth grades. Children of all ages on average also produced more adapted appeals in response to the "lost puppy" situation than they did for the present and party situations. Finally, the children also included a larger

Table 3.4 Mean Scores for Highest-Level Strategy in Three Compliance-Gaining Situations

	Compliance-Gaining Situation			
Grade Level	Present	Party	Puppy	Mean
Second ($N = 6$; med. age = 7-0)	1.00	1.08	2.33	1.47
Third ($N = 6$; med. age = 8-3)	1.38	1.50	1.88	1.58
Fourth ($N = 9$; med. age = 9-4)	2.75	2.33	3.58	2.89
Fifth ($N = 7$; med. age = 10-5)	2.55	3.15	3.55	3.08
Sixth ($N = 12$; med. age = 11-5)	2.67	2.67	4.08	3.14
Seventh ($N = 5$; med. age = 12-1)	2.42	2.00	4.42	2.94
Eighth ($N = 9$; med. age = 13-1)	2.82	3.00	3.00	2.94
Ninth ($N = 4$; med. age = 14-1)	4.75	4.50	4.75	4.67

SOURCE: From "The Development of Functional Persuasive Skills in Childhood and Early Adolescence," by R. A. Clark & J. G. Delia, 1976, *Child Development, 47*, p. 1011. Copyright 1976 by the Society for Research in Child Development. Adapted by permission.

number of supporting arguments, and more arguments from different levels in the hierarchical coding scheme, as grade level increased.

In a subsequent study, Delia, Kline, and Burleson (1979) elaborated and refined Clark and Delia's four-level coding scheme to provide a more precise description of how listener adaptation varies across a broad age range of children. Participants in their study, who ranged from kindergarten to twelfth grade, spoke aloud exactly what they would say in the "overnight party" and "lost puppy" hypothetical compliance-gaining scenarios. The researchers developed a nine-level hierarchical coding system, composed of three major strategy levels with three subdivisions within each major level, to assess degree of listener adaptation in these messages. Requests and supporting arguments were not scored separately. Definitions for each strategy level and example messages from the "lost puppy" situation appear in Table 3.5. Strategies scored at Levels 0-2 show little recognition that the target's perspective might differ from the source's own perspective. Children at this level simply asked or pleaded. Strategies scored at Levels 3-5 show implicit adaptation to the target's perspective, for instance, by anticipating and refuting potential objections that might be raised by the target. Strategies scored at Levels 6-8 show explicit adaptation to the target's perspective, for example, by arguing that the requested course of action is in the target's own best interest. Coders scored the highest-level strategy present in each participant's oral response to both hypothetical scenarios. Once again, listener adaptation increased with grade level. Children at all grades also used more adapted strategies in response to the "puppy" situation than to the "party" situation. Several differences between the "puppy"

Table 3.5   Delia et al.'s (1979) Nine-Level Hierarchical Scheme for Coding the Listener-Adaptedness of Compliance-Seeking Appeals, With Examples From the Lost Puppy Situation

Level	Definition/Example

Major Level I: Strategies with no discernible recognition of and adaptation to the target's perspective

1. Level 0   No statement of desire or request; no response given

2. Level 1   Unelaborated request
Example: Could you please take care of this puppy?

3. Level 2   Unelaborated statement of personal desire or need; includes pleas, begging, or a repeated statement of the request
Example: Could you please, please keep this dog—oh please don't say no.

Major Level II: Strategies that display implicit recognition of and adaptation to the target's perspective

4. Level 3   Elaboration of the necessity, desirability, or usefulness of the persuasive request, from the perspective of the message source or a third party
Example: This dog is really skinny and he doesn't have anyplace to go.

5. Level 4   Elaboration of the source's or the persuasive object's need plus minimal dealing with anticipated counterarguments
Example: This is a lost puppy. Could you maybe keep it for a day or two cause I can't keep it at my house?

6. Level 5   Elaborated acknowledgment of and dealing with multiple anticipated counterarguments
Example: It's big enough to stay outside and you only have to feed him and water him and that doesn't take all day.

Major Level III: Strategies that display explicit recognition of and adaptation to the target's perspective

7. Level 6   Truncated efforts to demonstrate relevant consequences to the target of accepting (or rejecting) the persuasive request, such as a general advantage to anyone granting this request
Example: You know, a dog's a good playmate for kids.

8. Level 7   Elaboration of specific consequences of accepting (or rejecting) the persuasive request for the target
Example: You need a watchdog around here because there have been some break-ins around here. This dog might be able to help you.

(Continued)

Table 3.5 (Continued)

Level	Definition/Example
9. Level 8	Demonstrable attempts by the persuader to take the target's perspective in articulating an advantage; attempts to lead the target to assume the perspective of the persuader, another person, or the persuasive object
	Example: If you were out in the cold and everything, wouldn't you want somebody to come and pick you up and give you a home? That's what this puppy wants.

SOURCE: From "The Development of Persuasive Communication Strategies in Kindergartners Through Twelfth-Graders," by J. G. Delia, S. L. Kline, & B. R. Burleson, 1979, *Communication Monographs, 46,* pp. 248-249. Copyright 1979 by the Speech Communication Association. Reprinted with permission.

and "party" situations may explain this latter finding, such as that in the former situation the request is larger, more altruistic, and has less direct benefit for the child (self), as well as that the target is less familiar (Delia et al., 1979).

In addition to seeking compliance, messages that resist compliance also can be conceptualized along the dimension of listener adaptedness. McQuillen (1984, 1986) investigated the degree to which first, fourth, and tenth graders adapted their reasons for refusing requests to the wants and needs of the message source. Each child, interviewed individually, spoke aloud what he or she would say in each of three compliance-resisting situations: (a) the child's mother had asked him or her to help clean up the kitchen, (b) the child's best friend had asked him or her to watch a different TV show, and (c) the child's younger sibling had asked the child to tell the sibling a story. For each situation, one-third of the children were told that the message source had used the compliance-gaining strategy of simple request (e.g., "I'd like you to help me clean up the kitchen. Will you help me clean up the kitchen?"), one-third were told that the source had used a promise strategy (e.g., "If you help me clean up the kitchen, I'll let you stay up/out an hour later tonight"), and one-third were told that the source had used an altruism/debt strategy (e.g., "You should help me clean up the kitchen because it's your turn to help around the house"). McQuillen's experimental design included two between-groups factors (child's grade level and type of compliance-gaining strategy) and one repeated-measures factor (type of message source who made the request).

McQuillen coded the children's compliance-resisting messages for the highest-level strategy generated in each of the three situations, using a modified version of Delia et al.'s (1979) nine-level hierarchical coding system. Definitions for each of McQuillen's strategy levels and example messages from the "tell story" scenario appear in Table 3.6. Compliance-resisting strategies at

Table 3.6   McQuillen's (1984) Nine-Level Hierarchical Scheme for Coding the
Listener Adaptedness of Compliance-Resisting Appeals, With
Examples From the "Tell Story" Situation

Level	Definition/Example

Major Level I: Strategies with no discernible recognition of and adaptation to the
source's perspective

1. Level 0   No statement of desire or resistance; no response given

2. Level 1   Unelaborated resistance
Example: No, I won't read you a story.

3. Level 2   Unelaborated statement of personal need or desire; includes pleas
and begging
Example: I don't want to read you a story.

Major Level II: Strategies that display implicit recognition of and adaptation to the
source's perspective

4. Level 3   Elaboration of the necessity, desirability, or usefulness of resisting
the request, from the perspective of the message target or a third
party
Example: I can't read a story to you because I have to study for a test.

5. Level 4   Elaboration of the target's needs while focusing on a single
perspective; includes references to the negative consequences of
compliance, positive consequences of noncompliance, or norms
Example: I have to practice (instead of reading a story to you) so I
can make the team.

6. Level 5   Elaboration of the target's needs while focusing on multiple
perspectives
Example: I can't read you a story because I have to go to the game.
I'm the star, and if I don't go they may lose.

Major Level III: Strategies that display explicit recognition of and adaptation to the
source's perspective

7. Level 6   Target attempts to coordinate multiple perspectives; includes
exchanges, compromises, and third-party solutions
Example: If you let me go to the game (instead of reading you a
story now), I'll read you two stories tomorrow.

8. Level 7   Elaboration of specific consequences of rejecting the persuasive
request for someone with characteristics of the source
Example: You need your sleep to be bright and chipper in school
tomorrow. So, I shouldn't tell you a story tonight.

9. Level 8   Leading the source to take the target's perspective
Example: If you had to play in a big game, you wouldn't want to be
late because you were telling somebody a story.

SOURCE: From *An Investigation of Compliance-Resisting Behaviors in First-,
Fourth-, and Tenth-Grade Children,* by J. S. McQuillen. Unpublished doctoral
dissertation, University of Oklahoma, 1984, pp. 161-163.

the upper end of this coding hierarchy explicitly recognize and adapt to the message source's perspective, by offering bargains or compromises that meet part of both parties' interests, by showing how the reasons for rejecting the request are deemed important by the source, or by asking the source to take the psychological perspective of the target.

As predicted, both fourth and tenth graders' compliance-resisting messages were significantly more listener adapted than were messages produced by first graders. Tenth graders also were more likely than either first or fourth graders to vary their degree of listener adaptation depending both on who had made the request (mother, best friend, younger sibling) and on what type of compliance-gaining strategy the source had used (direct request, promise, altruism/debt).

Other Conceptually Derived Dimensions

Aside from these studies on listener adaptation, researchers also have described influence interactions using many other conceptual dimensions. Table 3.7 lists and defines nine different conceptual dimensions and cites representative studies that have examined each dimension. This list is intended simply to indicate the variety of conceptual dimensions that have been investigated; it is by no means exhaustive.

EVALUATION OF CONCEPTUAL DIMENSIONS

In comparison to nominal-level strategy typologies and content themes, describing behaviors along conceptual dimensions may be better suited for drawing clear, unambiguous inferences about influence interactions. Assuming that concepts are defined precisely and measured validly, scholars who assess conceptual dimensions can infer what it is about compliance-seeking/resisting messages that varies across persons and situations. After reading Clark and Delia's (1976) study, for example, we know that children's grade level is associated with the degree of listener adaptation present in their compliance-gaining appeals. We do not have to ask questions such as "Why did ninth graders use strategy X more frequently than fourth graders?" or "Why did ninth graders elaborate content theme Y more than did fourth graders?" after the fact in order to interpret which quality of compliance-gaining behavior is being assessed. We still need to explain why grade level is associated with listener adaptation, but, by specifying this conceptual dimension in advance, we are in a better position—we know what needs to be explained.

Despite this advantage of a priori dimension specification, describing influence interactions along conceptual dimensions has potential limitations. One

Table 3.7   Examples of Conceptual Dimensions Assessed in Persuasive Message Production Research

Conceptual Dimension	Definition	Representative Studies
Elaboration	Number of reasons/strategies given to justify a request/refusal	Applegate (1982) (cs) Boster et al. (1993) (cs) Dillard et al. (1989) (cs) Kline & Floyd (1990) (cr) Roloff et al. (1988) (cs)
Strategic diversity	Number of distinct strategies used to seek/resist compliance	Boster et al. (1993) (cs) Wilson et al. (1993) (cs)
Directness	Degree to which the speaker reveals his or her intent in the message	Bresnahan et al. (1994) (cr) Dillard et al. (1989) (cs) Kim & Wilson (1994) (cs)
Pressure	Degree of force used to seek/resist compliance, constrain other	Clark (1979) (cs) Leichty & Applegate (1991)(cs) Lim (1990) (cr)
Obstacle orientation	Degree to which speaker addresses obstacles to compliance raised by the target	Wilson et al. (1993) (cs)
Social appropriateness	Degree to which strategy is polite, considerate	Burleson et al. (1988) (cs) Waltman (1995) (cs)
Verbal aggressiveness	Degree to which strategy attacks other's self-concept/feelings	Burgoon et al. (1991) (cs) Lim (1990) (cs)
Face support	Degree to which speaker supports other's desires for inclusion/respect while seeking/resisting compliance	Fairhurst et al. (1984) (cs) Lim & Bowers (1991) (cs) Newton & Burgoon (1990) (b)
Goal integration	Degree to which message simultaneously pursues seeking/resisting compliance along with other goals	Bingham & Burleson (1989)(cr) Kline & Floyd (1990) (cr) O'Keefe (1988) (cs) O'Keefe & Shepherd (1987) (b)

NOTE: (cs) = compliance seeking, (cr) = compliance resisting, and (b) = both.

of these is that conceptual dimensions will be chosen in haphazard fashion rather than derived from theories of persuasive message production. Compliance-seeking/resisting behaviors can be arrayed along a large, perhaps infinite, number of conceptual dimensions (D. J. O'Keefe, 1990; see Table 3.7). But as Kellermann and Cole (1994) warn:

Differences between compliance-gaining messages must *relate systematically* to differences in other variables (i.e., other message, situational, relational, cultural variables and so on) to be theoretically meaningful. . . . Put simply, not all differences are created equal; some are theoretically meaningful and others are not. (p. 48)

As with message strategies, there is no one "correct" or "best" set of conceptual dimensions. Clark and Delia (1976) found listener adaptedness to be a useful dimension for distinguishing the compliance-seeking appeals of younger and older children, but do not expect that listener adaptedness, or any other conceptual dimension, will be useful for answering all research questions. Using Kellermann and Cole's (1994) language, the same conceptual dimension may be "meaningful" within one theoretical perspective but meaningless within another. As you read this book, notice how different theories of persuasive message production draw our attention to different dimensions of influence interactions. Continually ask yourself, Why did the researchers assess these conceptual dimensions and not others?

A second limitation of describing compliance-seeking/resisting behaviors along conceptual dimensions is that often it produces only a very global characterization of an entire influence interaction. To understand this limitation, recall the study described at the beginning of Chapter 2, in which participants such as "Kathy" tried to convince confederates such as "Lisa" to fulfill their agreements to complete an experiment (Wilson, Cruz, Marshall, & Rao, 1993). Kathy and the other participants each telephoned several different targets, each of whom gave a different reason for failing to complete the experiment. Based on attribution theory (discussed in Chapter 7), we expected that the participants would use socially inappropriate compliance-seeking strategies such as "warning," "guilt," and "debt" more often when responding to some types of reasons (e.g., Lisa wants to go to happy hour at the time of the experiment) than when responding to others (e.g., Lisa got scheduled to work at that time by her boss). To test this reasoning, my colleagues and I analyzed the percentage of compliance-seeking strategies in each telephone call that were socially inappropriate (i.e., number of inappropriate strategies divided by total number of strategies). Notice, however, that this procedure provides only a very global description of the compliance-seeking behavior in each telephone call. By using this procedure we could determine whether participants used a larger percentage of socially inappropriate compliance-seeking strategies in some telephone calls than in others. However, we could not determine whether participants as a group tended to begin with socially appropriate strategies and then shift to inappropriate strategies after they encountered resistance, or whether the rate at which participants might have used increasingly inappropriate strategies varied across different telephone calls. To address these latter two questions, we need to move beyond making single, global judgments about influence interactions and analyze what happens as interactions unfold over time.

Temporal Characteristics of Influence Interactions

The final approach to describing influence interactions invites us to examine how compliance-seeking/resisting strategies, content themes, and/or dimensions of influence behavior vary over time. In reality, the "temporal characteristics" approach is not an alternative to the "message strategy," "content theme," and "conceptual dimension" approaches to message analysis, but a way of elaborating and enriching them.[9] In this section, I define five types of temporal characteristics, describe research examining each characteristic, and evaluate this final approach for analyzing influence episodes.

WHAT ARE TEMPORAL CHARACTERISTICS?

Compliance-gaining interactions occur at specific points in time, unfold over time, and can recur over the same topic at different points in time. Temporal characteristics focus attention on how individuals seek/resist compliance over time, as well as how they reference time within compliance-gaining/resisting messages. Drawing on the work of Werner and Baxter (1994), I have identified five temporal qualities of compliance-interactions: First, questions of *salience* ask whether interaction focuses on the past, present, or future; second, questions of *frequency* ask how often a phenomenon occurs over time; third, questions of *duration* pertain to how long a phenomenon tends to occur; fourth, questions of *sequence* ask whether there is an order to unfolding events; and fifth, questions of *pace* ask how rapidly events unfold.[10]

We can analyze each temporal characteristic by focusing on individuals or dyads. We can assess duration, for example, by investigating how long individuals persist at seeking compliance or how long compliance-gaining episodes between dyads tend to last. Regarding sequence, we can assess whether persons use compliance-seeking strategies in a predictable order. At a dyadic level, we can assess whether specific compliance-resisting strategies tend to be used in response to particular compliance-seeking strategies.

Although research on persuasive message production often has neglected temporal characteristics, some studies have explored questions about the salience, frequency, duration, sequence, and pace of influence interactions.

EXAMPLES OF RESEARCH ON TEMPORAL CHARACTERISTICS

Research questions concerning five temporal characteristics, along with a sampling of studies that have investigated these questions, are summarized in Table 3.8.

Questions of Salience

Compliance-seeking strategies can be distinguished in terms of temporal focus (Schenck-Hamlin et al., 1982). Some strategies reference prior events (e.g., debt), others mention current circumstances (e.g., altruism), and others highlight future consequences (e.g., warning). Aside from individual strategies, compliance-gaining appeals as a whole may focus on the past, present, or future. In her theory of message design logics, Barbara O'Keefe (1988, 1990) identifies three distinct sets of beliefs about the functions and coherence of communication. I review O'Keefe's theory of message design logics in Chapter 5; at this point, it is sufficient to note that individuals with different design logics tend to impose different temporal foci on events.

The messages in Examples 3.1 and 3.2 display different message design logics. Both were written by college undergraduates in response to the same hypothetical scenario. These undergraduates imagined that they were working with a group of students on a class project, and that they had been assigned the role of group leader. Their task was to deal with another group member, named Ron, who had failed to attend group meetings and complete his work:

EXAMPLE 3.1

Ron, I can't believe you haven't finished your research. You have been inconsiderate to the group all along. Several members even suggested that you be taken out of the group but we decided to give you a chance. Now what are we supposed to do? It was your responsibility and you backed out. I'm afraid that I'm going to have to tell the T.A. that you haven't done your share. I will be so mad at you if we get a bad grade on this—I need an A in this course. (quoted in B. J. O'Keefe, 1990, p. 95)

EXAMPLE 3.2

Well, Ron, it's due next week and we have to get it all to the typist. OK, if it's not done it's not. Tell you what. Why don't you jot down your main ideas so that we can include them in the introduction and conclusion. Also, tell me when you think your section should come in the whole project. Then get it to my apartment by 10:00 the next day because I have to get it to the typist by 2:00. Is this okay? (quoted in B. J. O'Keefe, 1990, p. 97).

Table 3.8   Examples of Temporal Characteristics Assessed in Persuasive Message Production Research

Research Question	Representative Studies
Salience	
1. Do individual compliance-seeking strategies focus on the past, present, or future?	Schenck-Hamlin et al. (1982) (cs)
2. Do compliance-seeking messages, as a whole, focus on the past, present, or future?	O'Keefe (1988) (cs) O'Keefe & McCornack (1987) (cs)
Frequency	
1. How frequently do individuals seek/resist compliance?	Cody et al. (1994) (cs) Oldershaw et al. (1989) (b)
2. How frequently do compliance-gaining episodes about the same topic recur?	Wilson & Kang, 1991
Duration	
1. How long do individuals persist at seeking compliance?	Boster et al. (1993) (cs) Wilson et al. (1993, 1994, 1996) (cs)
2. How long do individuals take to start speaking? How long do individuals pause?	Berger et al. (1989) (cs) Greene et al. (1990) (cs) Greene & Lindsey (1989) (cr)
Sequence	
1. How do individuals' subsequent compliance-seeking strategies differ from their initial strategies?	deTurck (1985) (cs) Roloff et al. (1988) (cs)
2. What types of joint action sequences emerge around requests/refusals?	Rule et al. (1985) (cs) Beach & Dunning (1982) (b) Jacobs & Jackson (1983) (b) Sanders & Fitch (2001) (b)
Pace	
1. At what rate do individuals increase the level of aggressiveness in their compliance-seeking messages?	Lim (1990) (cs)

NOTE: (cs) = compliance seeking, (cr) = compliance resisting, and (b) = both.

These two messages differ in several respects, including temporal focus. Five of the seven sentences in Example 3.1 describe and evaluate Ron's past performance. In contrast, more than half of Example 3.2 outlines future plans and deadlines. In sum, individuals who possess different message design logics have distinct notions about what material from the past, present, and future is relevant to express during a compliance-gaining interaction.

Questions of Frequency

Questions of frequency pertain to how often individuals seek/resist compliance in everyday life. Available data suggest that individuals seek/resist compliance quite often within personal relationships. In one study, 60 college students kept diaries in which they recorded information about the persons they tried to influence during a 12-week period (Cody, Canary, & Smith, 1994). The students described the participants, topics, and outcomes of each episode. Teaching assistants examined the diaries every 2 weeks. By the end of the 12 weeks, the 60 diaries contained more than 3,000 entries describing compliance-gaining episodes. Frequent targets for students included friends, parents, siblings, bureaucrats (such as financial aid officers), and roommates.

Scholars interested in parent-child communication have explored frequency data in detail. A large body of research has compared compliance-gaining episodes between parents and children in physically abusive versus non-abusive families (see Wilson, 1999). I describe the differences between physically abusive and nonabusive parents' compliance-seeking behaviors in Chapter 9; what is important at this point, however, is that compliance-seeking and -resisting behaviors occur frequently even within nonabusive families. As one example, Oldershaw, Walters, and Hall (1989) compared compliance-gaining episodes between 73 physically abusive and 43 demographically matched nonabusive comparison mothers and their children (mean child age = 45 months; range = 18-94 months; 50% female). Mother-child dyads were videotaped for 40 minutes in a playroom setting, during which they engaged in a mealtime, free play, and cleanup activity. Comparison families, who were enlisted for the study through day-care centers or newspaper ads, had no documented histories of physical abuse. During the recorded parent-child interactions, the physically abusive mothers on average issued 120 requests and commands per hour to their children. The physically abused children failed to comply with 44% of their mothers' requests. Although the nonabusive comparison mothers were somewhat less intrusive, they still used an average of 75 requests and commands per hour, and their children did not comply with 35% of these requests.

A related question concerns how frequently people seek/resist compliance about the same topic over time. When the parties share an ongoing relationship, compliance-gaining interactions often recur about the same topics (Cronen, Pearce, & Snavely, 1979; Trapp & Hoff, 1985; Wilson & Kang, 1991). In one study, a colleague and I asked 216 undergraduates to recall a real-life situation in which someone had failed to do something he or she was obligated to do (Wilson & Kang, 1991). One-half of the sample recalled a situation in which they had to convince another person to fulfill an obligation, and the other half recalled a situation in which someone else had to convince them to fulfill an obligation. Most participants recalled situations involving friends, family members, dating partners, and roommates (67% had known the other individual for a year or longer). Although 71% of participants reported that the target complied—either immediately or eventually—with the message source's request, 69% indicated that the two parties had discussed the same topic at least once before, and 41% reported that the same topic recurred at least once again afterward. The latter figure may underestimate the actual frequency of recurrence, as 44% of the sample described an interaction that had occurred within the preceding week.

Questions of Duration

Questions of duration concern the length of compliance-gaining episodes. Several studies have explored the message source's persistence, or the degree to which the source continues seeking compliance after encountering resistance from a message target. Recall the study described at the beginning of Chapter 2, in which participants such as "Kathy" tried to convince other students (actually confederates such as "Lisa") to fulfill their agreements to complete an experiment. In that study, persistence within each telephone call was scored higher when participants spoke for a longer amount of time, used a larger number of compliance-seeking strategies, and used a larger variety of strategies (Wilson et al., 1993). Researchers have also assessed persistence by asking individuals whether they would persist with hypothetical targets (Cody et al., 1994; Wilson, Whipple, & Grau, 1996), by counting the number of compliance-seeking strategies individuals used after a target's initial refusal (Roloff & Janiszewski, 1989; Roloff, Janiszewski, McGrath, Burns, & Manrai, 1988), and by counting the number of additional message targets individuals tried to persuade after they failed to persuade their first target (C. A. Anderson, 1983; Anderson & Jennings, 1980). Results from these studies show that individuals vary the degree to which they persist in seeking compliance depending on several factors, including the size of their initial request (Roloff et al., 1988), their reasons for requesting (Cody et al., 1994; Roloff & Janiszewski, 1989; Wilson et al., 1996), the target's reasons for refusing (Wilson et al., 1993; Wilson, Levine, Humphreys, & Peters, 1994), and the degree of intimacy and power shared between the source and target (Boster, Kazoleas, Levine, Rogan, & Kang, 1995; Roloff & Janiszewski, 1989; Roloff et al., 1988). Individuals also differ in their general likelihood of persisting depending on their personalities (Boster, Levine, & Kazoleas, 1993; Humphreys & Wilson, 1996) and their cognitive styles (C. A. Anderson, 1983; Anderson & Jennings, 1980). To my knowledge, no study has explored message targets' persistence in resisting compliance-gaining attempts.

Questions of duration also have been posed about the paraverbal features of compliance-seeking messages. Cognitive theories of persuasive message production (discussed in Chapter 7) make assumptions about the mental processes that are involved as individuals decide what to say to exert influence. As you will see, these theories predict that deciding what to say requires more cognitive effort in some situations than in others, and that having to exert cognitive effort should be evident in paraverbal features of speech such as greater hesitations and pauses. Hence studies of persuasive message production have examined how long individuals take to start speaking, how many silent and filled ("uhh," "ahh") pauses occur, the duration of long silent pauses, how many false starts occur, and at what speed individuals speak (e.g., Berger, Karol, & Jordan, 1989; Greene & Lindsey, 1989; Meyer, 1992).

Questions of Sequence

Questions about the ordering of events during influence interactions have focused on both individuals and dyads. Several studies have explored how individuals' subsequent compliance-seeking strategies, after they encounter initial resistance from message targets, differ from their initial strategies (e.g., Bisanz & Rule, 1989; deTurck, 1985, 1987; Hample & Dallinger, 1998; Pruitt, Parker, & Mikolic, 1997; Roloff & Janiszewski, 1989; Roloff et al., 1988; Rule & Bisanz, 1987; Wilson et al., 1994, 1996). Most of these studies have investigated what Hample and Dallinger (1998) label the *rebuff hypothesis*, which predicts that "when an initial message is rebuffed, follow-up persuasive messages are ruder, more aggressive, and more forceful than the first one" (p. 305). Based on this hypothesis, individuals would be expected to initiate compliance-seeking attempts using highly appropriate strategies such as "direct request" and "positive expertise," then respond to initial resistance from a target with moderately appropriate strategies such as "promise" or "positive esteem," then respond to additional resistance with somewhat inappropriate strategies such as "debt" or "guilt," and finally resort to highly inappropriate strategies such as "threat," "aversive stimulation," or even physical aggression if they believed the situation warranted such action.[11]

Although a good deal of support has been obtained for the rebuff hypothesis (e.g., deTurck, 1985, 1987; Pruitt et al., 1997; Rule & Bisanz, 1987; Wilson et al., 1996; for a review, see Hample & Dallinger, 1998), it also is clear that message sources do not always use socially inappropriate strategies after encountering resistance to a request. For example, the validity of the rebuff hypothesis appears to depend on relational intimacy, although research findings have been complex. DeTurck (1985) found that college students reported being more likely to use socially inappropriate compliance-seeking strategies after encountering resistance from a nonintimate target, but more likely to use both appropriate and inappropriate strategies after encountering resistance from an intimate target. In contrast, Roloff et al. (1988) found that students were less polite when they continued to seek compliance from either a friend or an acquaintance who initially had refused to do them a favor, but were no less polite when they continued to seek compliance from a stranger. Several procedural differences may explain the seemingly inconsistent findings from these two studies, including that the participants imagined making different types of requests (see Roloff & Janiszewski, 1989).

Aside from moderating factors, questions can be raised about whether the rebuff hypothesis would hold up during naturalistic influence interactions. In most of the studies just reviewed, participants simply were asked to imagine that the target said no to their initial request. Participants were not told how or why the target said no, despite the fact that an individual's choice of subsequent compliance-seeking strategies is likely to be based in part on the reasons the target is refusing (Ifert & Roloff, 1996; Wilson et al., 1993) and the target's nonverbal style when refusing (Lim, 1990). In sum, we need to know a great deal more about how individuals sequence compliance-seeking messages with regard to social appropriateness. Research also could explore how persons alter their compliance-gaining messages along other conceptual dimensions (e.g., indirect–direct, unelaborated–elaborated) over time.

Questions of sequence also have focused on how two individuals jointly construct recognizable patterns of talk. In Chapter 6, where I review research that has been conducted on pragmatics and conversation analysis, I describe several action sequences that can emerge during naturalistic influence interactions. One set of sequences starts with a "prerequest," in which a speaker inquires about the status of the other party or the situation prior to making a request (Beach & Dunning, 1982; Jacobs & Jackson, 1983; Nofsinger, 1991). Consider the following four examples:

EXAMPLE 3.3

1	B:	Uh, are you gonna have access to the car about five thirty
2		or six today?
3	E:	Uh:: yeah, I think so. Why?
4	B:	Cause I'm gonna need a ride down to . . .

(Nofsinger, 1991, p. 56)

EXAMPLE 3.4

(C is standing in the hallway of the speech department, holding the hand of his 15-month-old son, Curtis)

1   C: Hey, Debbie. Are you going to be free from 1:30 to 2:30?

2   D: Yeah. I think so. You want me to watch him?

3   C: Yeah.

4   D: I'd love to. It'd be a pleasure.

5   C: Okay. Thanks. I'll bring him around then.

(Jacobs & Jackson, 1983, p. 299)

Example 3.5

1   A: How's your budget this month?

2   B: Empty!

3   A: You're not the only one.

(Beach & Dunning, 1982, p. 174)

Example 3.6

1   A: Are you close to the 'fridge, honey?

2   B: You know I am. Get it yourself for a change . . .

(Beach & Dunning, 1982, p. 180)

In all four examples, the message source initially asks about the target's schedule, location, or access to resources at a particular time. In each case, the target recognizes that the source's question is setting up some type of action to follow. In Example 3.3, for instance, notice how E responds with the question "Why [are you asking]?" at the end of line 3. Because both parties implicitly understand the functions of prerequests, several different sequences can unfold: The source can go ahead with a request after verifying the target's ability to comply (Example 3.3), the target can anticipate the source's upcoming request and voluntarily offer to comply (Example 3.4), the target can signal his or her inability to comply and short-circuit the upcoming request (Example 3.5), or the target can anticipate and refuse the upcoming request before it is made (Example 3.6). As we will see in Chapter 6, participants jointly construct many recognizable action sequences during influence episodes based on their implicit understandings of conversational moves.

Questions of Pace

Questions of pace ask about the rate at which compliance-seeking/resisting behaviors change over time. Lim (1990) has conducted one of the few studies to date examining the pace of influence interactions. Upon arriving at a communication laboratory, 76 college undergraduates individually were given instructions asking them to imagine they were involved in a group research project worth two-thirds of the grade in an important class. Part of each group member's grade was to be determined by peer evaluation. Each participant was told that one member of his or her group was doing work so poor that it jeopardized the entire group's grade. Hence the participant's task was

> to persuade this member to find more relevant evidence to the three points of the opening chapter and rewrite the chapter as thoroughly as possible. Since you are certain that the group grade will be very bad unless this one member does his/her part again, you would not give up asking him/her to re-do his/her part of the project even if he/she resists your persuasive attempts. (Lim, 1990, p. 179)

As the participant was reading these instructions, another student arrived at the laboratory and was given instructions to play the role of the group member who had done poor work. In reality, this second student was always one of six confederates who were working with the experimenter.

The confederates had been trained to enact one of four styles of resistance, which varied along the conceptual dimensions of strong–weak and friendly-unfriendly. Confederates enacting strong resistance consistently used a non-negotiation strategy; for example, they said phrases such as "I can't do it again" or "I don't want to talk about it" every time a participant asked them to redo their work. Those enacting weak resistance instead used a negotiation strategy. Although they never complied completely, they offered compromises such as "If you promise to help me, I'll think about doing it again" or "Since I am so busy, I can do only a part of it; I can't do the whole thing again" when a participant asked them to redo their work. Confederates enacting unfriendly resistance disagreed with whatever the participant said, provided negative feedback such as head shaking, avoided the use of in-group pronouns such as *we* and *us,* and claimed that their work was not bad. Those enacting friendly resistance agreed with whatever the participant said as long as doing so did not imply compliance, acknowledged that other group members had done a good job on their parts of the project, and showed solidarity by using in-group pronouns and positive feedback such has "um hum."

After both parties understood the instructions, they role-played a conversation in which the participant tried to persuade the other student (confederate) to redo his or her work. The confederate enacted one of the four styles of resistance—strong/unfriendly, strong/friendly, weak/unfriendly, or weak/friendly—throughout the conversation. The conversations, which were audiotaped, were stopped after 5 minutes. The recordings were divided into 1-minute intervals, and three coders rated the degree to which participants used verbally aggressive compliance-seeking messages (i.e., messages that attacked the target's self-concept) during each 1-minute interval of the conversation (i.e., the first minute, the second minute, and so forth).

Based on the norm of reciprocity, Lim (1990) predicted that participants on average would use more verbally aggressive messages when seeking compliance from unfriendly targets than they would when seeking compliance from friendly targets. With regard to pace, Lim also predicted that participants would resort to verbally aggressive compliance-seeking messages sooner in the face of strong resistance than when they encountered weak resistance. When participants encountered strong resistance from the start, Lim reasoned, they would infer quickly that the target had no intention of complying with the request. Because they were frustrated about getting a poor group grade, participants in this condition would resort quickly to verbally aggressive messages. When the target offered weak resistance, however, participants initially might infer that the target eventually would comply if they continued giving reasons the work needed to be redone. Only over time would these participants realize that the target was not going to comply totally with their request. Hence they should resort to verbally aggressive messages later in the interaction.

The results of the experiment were consistent with both predictions. Participants on average were more verbally aggressive with unfriendly targets than with friendly targets. Participants also resorted to verbally aggressive strategies sooner when faced with strong rather than weak resistance to their request. Participants who met strong resistance became aggressive more quickly and continued increasing their aggressiveness over time. In contrast, those who met weak resistance became aggressive more slowly over time, as periods of increase were balanced by periods of leveling off. Lim's (1990) results illustrate the "transactional" nature of influence interactions by showing that "persuaders base their strategy not only on situations and their personal preferences, but also on the responses issued by receivers" (p. 185).

EVALUATION OF TEMPORAL CHARACTERISTICS

A focus on temporal characteristics represents an important addition to the first three approaches to describing influence interactions. As the research examples presented above show, temporal characteristics are not an alternative to descriptions of influence interactions based in nominal-level strategy typologies, nominal-level content themes, or dimensions of influence behaviors, but a way of elaborating those descriptions. Because they extend the approaches discussed previously, however, descriptions of temporal characteristics are subject to many of the same potential problems as those approaches.

Specifically, both the choices of temporal characteristics and the descriptions of these characteristics need to be grounded in theory.

Decisions about which temporal characteristics to investigate should be grounded in theories of persuasive message production rather than made haphazardly. Similar to nominal-level strategies or behavioral dimensions, the number of temporal characteristics that could be examined is quite large (perhaps infinite). No single temporal characteristic is likely to be useful for all research questions and theoretical explanations. As one example, O'Keefe (1988) reasoned that temporal focus on the past, present, and future was a useful way of differentiating individuals with different beliefs about communication, whereas Wilson et al. (1993) reasoned that persistence at seeking compliance was a useful way of distinguishing how the same individual would respond to multiple targets who disclosed different reasons for not complying. It is not clear, however, that the opposite would hold true. Compliance-seeking persistence may not be useful for differentiating individuals with distinct beliefs about communication, just as temporal focus may not capture how the same individual responds to multiple targets who disclose different reasons for not complying. Unless connected to theories of persuasive message production, decisions about which temporal characteristics to investigate are bound to seem arbitrary.

Like the selection of temporal characteristics, decisions about how to define and describe these characteristics also should be theoretically grounded. To understand this point, reconsider Sillars's (1980) comparison of how individuals sought compliance from a spouse versus a neighbor. In that study, undergraduate participants rated their use of "threat" as more likely when they imagined seeking the compliance of a neighbor rather than a spouse, but rated their use of "debt" as more likely with a spouse than with a neighbor. We had difficulty interpreting this finding because each of the strategies in Marwell and Schmitt's (1967) typology differs from other strategies in countless unspecified ways. Now imagine that Sillars had investigated strategy sequences. For example, individuals might be more likely to use "threat" before "debt" when seeking compliance from a neighbor, whereas they might be more likely to use "debt" before "threat" when seeking compliance from a spouse. Would this result be any easier to interpret than Sillars's original finding? As you can see, exploring temporal characteristics still requires theoretically grounded descriptions of the properties of influence messages.

Summary

In this chapter I have discussed alternatives to the "traditional" approach of describing influence interactions using typologies of nominal-level message strategies. I have presented and evaluated three alternative approaches: nominal-level content themes, dimensions of influence behavior, and temporal characteristics of influence interactions. Each approach gives rise to a set of choices about how to conceptualize influence messages and interactions. Each approach can be useful, provided that conceptual choices are tied to theories of persuasive message production.

Notes

1. Strictly speaking, Saeki and O'Keefe (1994) did not study a compliance-resisting situation, given that participants rejected Robin's application for membership rather than a request. "Rejections" and "refusals" of requests nevertheless are similar in several respects. For example, participants in both Saeki and O'Keefe's and McLaughlin, Cody, and Robey's (1980) studies often felt the need to justify their actions.

2. For a detailed description of the procedures for this semiautomated content analysis system, see Lambert (1996b).

3. B. J. O'Keefe, Lambert, and colleagues' approach to analyzing content themes certainly contains implicit theoretical assumptions about describing influence episodes. For example, the authors assume that an analysis of semantic content will provide important insights about persuasive message production and effects, and that semantic themes can be mapped onto theoretical constructs pertaining to message functions and effects. The particular list of content themes that emerges from a sample of influence episodes, however, is neither derived from a conceptual scheme nor intended to vary systematically along a conceptual dimension.

4. Messages that "reaffirm and restructure the therapeutic relationship" are examples of O'Keefe's (1988, 1990) rhetorical message design logic, whereas those that do not are examples of the expressive or conventional design logic. I introduce the topic of message design logics in Chapter 6.

5. I will avoid the issue of whether conceptual dimensions actually assess influence behaviors at an ordinal, interval, or ratio level of measurement entirely (see Nunnally, 1967). My only intention is to distinguish conceptual schemes that imply a rank ordering of influence behaviors from those that do not.

6. To my knowledge, no study has explored the perceptual dimensions along which everyday actors distinguish compliance-resisting appeals.

7. Multidimensional scaling attempts to identify the structure in a set of distance ratings between objects. Multidimensional scaling often is applied to research participants' subjective ratings of (dis)similarity between objects (e.g., compliance-seeking strategies). Each strategy is assigned a specific location in a conceptual space (in most cases, a 2- to 3-dimensional space) such that the distances between points in space capture participants' similarity ratings as closely as possible.

8. If our goal were to describe the "interpretive schemes" that everyday actors use to make sense of influence interactions, then explicitness, dominance, and argument might well be the most useful conceptual dimensions. As D. J. O'Keefe (1993) has argued, the goals of interpretive and traditional social scientific studies of persuasion, although often complementary, nevertheless do differ in important respects.

9. Most research exploring influence strategy sequences has been quantitative in nature. Scholars have (a) analyzed change in participants' likelihood-of-use ratings for preformulated compliance-seeking strategies made in response to a hypothetical scenario, where participants made initial ratings, imagined that the message target said no to their first appeal, and then made

ratings again (e.g., deTurck, 1985; Hample & Dallinger, 1998); (b) content analyzed change in the strategies participants included in their written responses to a hypothetical scenario, where participants wrote out what they would say initially, imagined the target said no, and then wrote a second message (e.g., Roloff et al., 1988; Wilson et al., 1996); and (c) content analyzed change in the compliance-seeking or resisting strategies that participants enacted over time in laboratory situations, where participants attempted to persuade or resist confederates who were trained to display specific responses (e.g., Lim, 1990; Pruitt et al., 1997; Wilson et al., 1993). In addition to these quantitative studies, a growing number of "qualitative" investigations of compliance-gaining episodes are being published in the "conversation-analytic" (e.g., Pudlinski, 1998; Sanders & Fitch, 2001) and "ethnography of communication" (e.g., Fitch, 1994; Goldsmith & Fitch, 1997) traditions. Rather than categorizing message strategies, themes, or dimensions over time, these scholars employ alternative descriptive vocabularies with different assumptions to explore temporal features of influence interactions. I review qualitative studies as part of Chapter 6, where I explore discourse perspectives on persuasive message production.

10. I have modified Werner and Baxter's (1994) list of temporal characteristics in two respects. First, I have subdivided what they call "scale" into the separate categories of frequency and duration. Second, I have deleted what they call "amplitude," which "refers to the degree or intensity of partners' subjective experiences and objective behaviors" (pp. 327-328). For influence interactions, questions about amplitude might explore how much pressure individuals exert to seek/resist compliance or how much anxiety they experience during compliance-gaining episodes. As these examples illustrate, questions about amplitude are not inherently temporal in nature. Although these questions could be studied over time, they also could be assessed along conceptual dimensions for the interaction as a whole. Because they are not inherently temporal, I do not include questions about amplitude in this section.

11. Aside from the rebuff hypothesis, a large body of research has examined whether individuals are more successful at gaining compliance when they sequence multiple requests in strategic fashion (e.g., the "foot-in-the-door" and "door-in-the face" techniques; for reviews, see Seibold, Cantrill, & Meyers, 1994; Stiff, 1994). Although these techniques have been observed occasionally during relatively unconstrained influence interactions (e.g., Boster et al., 1995), for the most part they have been investigated in highly scripted studies where message sources make multiple requests in a totally preplanned sequence. Given my focus on persuasive message production during naturalistic influence interactions, I have chosen not to review this literature.

Part II

*Metaphors for Studying
Persuasive Message Production*

4

The First Generation

Persuasive Message Production as Strategy Selection

Looking Ahead . . .

This chapter argues that contemporary theory and research on persuasive message production have emerged from earlier programs of research on "compliance gaining" and "constructivism." Both of these earlier research traditions were guided, implicitly, by a "strategy-selection" metaphor for persuasive message production. After reviewing these two research traditions, the chapter argues that the metaphor guiding contemporary work on persuasive message production has shifted from "strategy selection" to "goal pursuit."

Come back with me to 1982, the year I entered graduate school at Indiana University. Ronald Reagan was in the first term of his presidency, and the Hoosier men's basketball team (led by Isiah Thomas) had recently won the NCAA national championship. Imagine I had asked my professors and classmates at Indiana University, "What do you think about work on persuasive message production?" They likely would have stared blankly at me, given that message production was not yet a recognizable area of study. But what if I had phrased my question differently, saying, "I'm interested in how people decide what to say when exerting influence in everyday life. Is there any work relevant to this topic?" In response to that question, my professors and classmates almost certainly would have mentioned two programs of research that were being pursued vigorously in 1982: work on "compliance gaining," initiated by Gerald Miller and his colleagues at Michigan State University, and work on the "constructivist" perspective on communication associated with Jesse Delia and his colleagues at the University of Illinois.

In this chapter, I argue that contemporary theory and research on persuasive message production have their genesis in these two research programs. Although Miller and his associates did not intend to construct a theory of message production (Boster, 1990, 1995; Miller, 1990), questions arising from their work on seeking compliance provided strong impetus for such theories. Delia and his associates did develop a rudimentary theory of message production, the limits of which have provided important insights for contemporary theories. For each of these two traditions, I describe a pioneering study, summarize subsequent research, evaluate theoretical and methodological limitations, and highlight contributions to current thinking about message production.

Although different in many respects, the programs of research on compliance gaining and constructivism both contained an implicit "strategy-selection" metaphor for persuasive message production. As you will see, these research traditions both assumed that people have "repertoires" of potential compliance-seeking and -resisting strategies at their disposal (although the sizes of these repertoires might vary across individuals), and both sought to identify individual and situational variables that could predict people's choice of strategies from their repertoires (see B. J. O'Keefe, 1990; Seibold, Cantrill, & Meyers, 1985). Both traditions were in their heyday during the late 1970s to early 1980s and then came under substantial attack and/or were redefined by the late 1980s. After describing each tradition, I show how the metaphor guiding contemporary work on persuasive message production has shifted from "strategy selection" to "goal pursuit."

The Compliance-Gaining Tradition

THE MBRS STUDY

As defined in Chapter 1, seeking compliance involves attempts by a message source to induce a target individual to perform a desired action that the target otherwise might not have performed. Gerald Miller, Franklin Boster, Michael

Roloff, and David Seibold (1977) conducted the pioneering investigation of how people select compliance-seeking strategies. The "MBRS study," as it has become known, was designed to test ideas found in Miller and Steinberg's innovative interpersonal communication textbook, *Between People* (1975). According to Miller and Steinberg, individuals want to maintain control over their social environments and hence acquire sets of message strategies for influencing others. During influence interactions, individuals make predictions about the probable outcomes of their using various compliance-seeking strategies. When the parties share an *interpersonal* relationship (i.e., know each other well), a message source can rely primarily on "psychological-level knowledge"— that is, information about how the message target is unique or different from others—in order to predict how the target will react to alternative strategies. In contrast, when the parties have a *noninterpersonal* relationship (i.e., do not know each other well), a message source must rely primarily on sociological- and cultural-level knowledge—that is, information about how the target is similar to others, such as group stereotypes or cultural norms for interaction— to predict the target's reactions. Drawing on these ideas, Miller et al. (1977) identified three primary questions for research on seeking compliance:

RQ1. What are the compliance-seeking strategies available to potential persuaders and how can these strategies be grouped and classified most usefully?

RQ2. How is the choice of compliance-seeking strategies influenced by certain situational differences associated with the persuasive transaction?

RQ3. How do relevant individual differences of potential persuaders affect the choice of compliance-seeking strategies? (p. 38)

As an initial investigation, the MBRS study dealt primarily with RQ1 and RQ2. Research participants came from several backgrounds, including 75 undergraduate students from a large midwestern university, 76 part-time students from a community college (most of whom worked full-time in a variety of occupations), and 17 career U.S. Army recruiters enrolled in extension classes of a midwestern liberal arts college. Participants each read four different hypothetical compliance-gaining scenarios that were designed to manipulate two situational variables: (a) whether the message source-target relationship was *interpersonal/noninterpersonal* and (b) whether the request had *short-term/long-term relational consequences*. When responding to the interpersonal scenarios, participants imagined seeking compliance from a long-term romantic partner. When responding to the noninterpersonal scenarios, they imagined seeking compliance from a used-car salesperson and a neighbor with whom they had made only limited contact. Regardless of the type of relationship, participants in the long-term consequences conditions imagined making requests that could alter their current relationship with the target substantially. In the short-term consequences scenarios, they imagined making requests that were unlikely to affect the relationship. The four scenarios used in the MBRS study appear in Table 4.1.

To assess people's choice of strategies, the MBRS study drew on Marwell and Schmitt's (1967) nominal-level typology of 16 compliance-seeking strategies (for a detailed discussion, see Chapter 2). The researchers created 16 concrete messages (i.e., utterances), illustrating each of the 16 compliance-seeking strategies, for each of the four scenarios. After reading each scenario, participants rated how likely they would be to use each of the 16 messages written for that situation on an 8-point Likert scale ranging from *extremely unlikely* to *extremely likely*. The researchers analyzed whether participants' likelihood-of-use ratings for each compliance-seeking strategy varied significantly across the four situations (RQ2) as well as whether different strategies tended to cluster together within different situations (RQ1).

Results from the MBRS study can be grouped into three general findings. First, participants' likelihood-of-use ratings for each of the 16 compliance-seeking strategies did vary significantly across the four situations (RQ1).[1] As one example, participants reported that they would be more likely to use the compliance-seeking strategy of "positive expertise" when responding to the two situations in which they shared a noninterpersonal relationship with the message target than in the two interpersonal situations.

To highlight how strategies varied across situations, Miller et al. (1977) displayed compliance-seeking strategies that were "likely to be used" (which the researchers arbitrarily designated as those strategies with a mean likelihood-of-use rating of greater than 5.00 on the 8-point scale) and strategies that were "unlikely to be used" (i.e., those with a mean likelihood-of-use rating of less than 3.00) within each of the four situations. Their results are reprinted in Table 4.2. Inspection of the table reveals that participants rated a larger number of compliance-seeking strategies as likely to be used, and a smaller number as unlikely to be used, in the noninterpersonal situations as opposed to the interpersonal situations. To explain this finding, Miller et al. speculated that participants were more uncertain about which strategies would be effective in the noninterpersonal situations because they lacked information about the message target as a unique individual, and hence they tended to "grab at any strategic straw which promises to produce some measure of control over an uncertain environment" (p. 49).

A second major finding was that the number and composition of compliance-seeking strategy clusters varied across situations (RQ2). Rather than replicating the five clusters of compliance-seeking strategies identified by Marwell and Schmitt (1967), the MBRS study found between one and three

Table 4.1   Four Hypothetical Compliance-Gaining Scenarios From the MBRS Study

Noninterpersonal; short-term consequences situation: The car that you presently own is beginning to require large maintenance costs, and you would like to trade it on a new car. You are interested in getting the best deal that you can on a new Chevrolet. You want Mr. Buckley, the Chevrolet dealer, with whom you are only slightly acquainted, to give you $1,000, as a trade-in, for your old car. How likely would you be to employ each of the following strategies in order to get a $1,000 trade-in on your old car?

Noninterpersonal; long-term consequences situation: You have been living six months in a house that you have purchased. You learn that your next-door neighbors (the Smiths—people with whom you have had only limited contact since moving in) plan to cut down a large shade tree that stands near your property in order to construct their new two-car garage. However, in the long run, the loss of the shade tree will adversely affect the beauty of your home, your comfort, and perhaps the value of your home. How likely would you be to employ each of the following strategies in order to get the Smiths to leave the tree standing?

Interpersonal; short-term consequences situation: You have been carrying on a close relationship with a woman (man) for the past two years. On this particular evening an old acquaintance unexpectedly passes through town. You want to visit with your acquaintance, but you have already promised to go to the movies with your friend and she (he) has made it clear that she (he) is counting on it very much. How likely would you be to employ each of the following strategies in order to get your friend to allow you to visit your acquaintance?

Interpersonal; long-term consequences situation: You have been carrying on a close relationship with a woman (man) for the past two years. You have recently received two employment offers: one in the immediate vicinity and one in the Southwest United States, over 1,000 miles away. Although both of you wish to stay together and to continue the relationship, you find the latter position much more challenging and attractive while she (he) wants you to take the local position so that she (he) can remain close to friends and relatives. How likely would you be to employ each of the following strategies in order to get your friend to accompany you to the job in the Southwest U.S.?

SOURCE: From "Compliance-Gaining Message Strategies: A Typology and Some Findings Concerning Effects of Situational Differences," by G. R. Miller, F. J. Boster, M. E. Roloff, & D. Seibold, 1977, *Communication Monographs, 44,* pp. 43-44. Copyright 1977 by the Speech Communication Association. Reprinted with permission.

strategy clusters within each of the four situations. The strategies composing each cluster also differed depending on the specific situation. For instance, "promise" and "debt" fell into the same cluster in the noninterpersonal, long-term consequences situation but fell into different clusters in the interpersonal, short-term consequences situation.

Table 4.2   Compliance-Seeking Strategies Rated as Likely and Unlikely to Be Used in the MBRS (1977) Study

Type of Strategy	Short-Term Consequences	Long-Term Consequences
Interpersonal situations		
Likely strategies	Altruism ($M = 5.95$)	Threat ($M = 5.88$)
	Altercasting + ($M = 5.81$)	Altercasting + ($M = 5.82$)
	Liking ($M = 5.29$)	Liking ($M = 5.45$)
		Promise ($M = 5.28$)
Unlikely strategies	Moral appeal ($M = 2.42$)	Esteem − ($M = 2.17$)
	Aversive stimulation ($M = 2.42$)	Self-feeling − ($M = 2.25$)
	Esteem − ($M = 2.45$)	Aversive stimulation ($M = 2.51$)
	Threat ($M = 2.51$)	Debt ($M = 2.74$)
	Pregiving ($M = 2.85$)	Esteem + ($M = 2.94$)
Noninterpersonal situations		
Likely strategies	Threat ($M = 5.83$)	Expertise + ($M = 6.15$)
	Promise ($M = 5.79$)	Expertise − ($M = 5.86$)
	Liking ($M = 5.62$)	Altruism ($M = 5.52$)
	Expertise + ($M = 5.36$)	Promise ($M = 5.23$)
		Liking ($M = 5.21$)
		Debt ($M = 5.17$)
		Altercasting + ($M = 5.08$)
Unlikely strategies	Moral appeal ($M = 2.98$)	Aversive stimulation ($M = 2.28$)

SOURCE: From "Compliance-Gaining Message Strategies: A Typology and Some Findings Concerning Effects of Situational Differences," by G. R. Miller, F. J. Boster, M. E. Roloff, & D. Seibold, 1977, *Communication Monographs, 44,* p. 45. Copyright 1977 by the Speech Communication Association. Reprinted with permission.

Despite this variation in strategies across situations, a third major finding was that participants in general rated "prosocial" or "socially appropriate" compliance-seeking strategies such as altruism, positive altercasting, and liking as likely to be used and "antisocial" or "socially inappropriate" strategies such as aversive stimulation, moral appeal, and negative esteem as unlikely to be used. With a few exceptions, the "likely" strategies in Table 4.2 are socially appropriate (i.e., they appeal to rewards or positive emotions) and the "unlikely" strategies are socially inappropriate (i.e., they appeal to sanctions or negative emotions). This third finding is reminiscent of Marwell and Schmitt (1967), who collapsed their 16 compliance-seeking strategies into two second-order factors labeled "socially acceptable" and "socially unacceptable" strategies.

The MBRS study is important for several reasons. Miller et al. (1977) delineated a specific research agenda (i.e., RQ1-3) that expanded the study of persuasion from public and mass communication contexts into the then relatively new area of interpersonal communication (see Miller & Burgoon, 1978). Their study also provided a methodological exemplar for pursuing this research agenda, by (a) using hypothetical scenarios to manipulate situational variables and (b) having participants provide likelihood-of-use ratings for lists of preformulated compliance-seeking strategies. This latter practice has come to be known as the *strategy-selection procedure*.

Following its publication, the MBRS study spurred a large body of research on how people choose compliance-seeking strategies (for reviews, see Boster, 1995; Burgoon, 1994; Seibold et al., 1985; Wheeless, Barraclough, & Stewart, 1983; Wilson, 1997).[2] As I described in Chapter 2, scholars developed and debated the utility of several different nominal-level typologies of compliance-seeking (e.g., Boster, Stiff, & Reynolds, 1985; Cody, McLaughlin, & Jordan, 1980; Schenk-Hamlin, Wiseman, & Georgacarakos, 1982) and compliance-resisting strategies (e.g., McLaughlin, Cody, & Robey, 1980). Scholars also explored whether a host of situational and individual-difference variables predicted people's choice of strategies. Finally, two explanatory models were proposed to account for why people select specific compliance-seeking strategies. I describe these two explanatory models below and then review research on individual/situational predictors of strategy choice.

EXPLANATIONS FOR STRATEGY CHOICE

A Subjective Expected Utility Model

Although the MBRS study showed that people's choice of compliance-seeking strategies vary across situations, it provided less information about *why* people choose different strategies with different targets. According to Sillars (1980), to address the "why" question, "we need to consider people's perceptions of the strategies" (p. 265). Sillars proposes applying a *subjective expected utility* (SEU) model to explain people's choice of compliance-seeking strategies.

SEU models assume that individuals, when faced with alternative actions, will choose the alternative they perceive to have the highest probability of creating desirable outcomes. When choosing compliance-seeking strategies, Sillars (1980) argues, individuals consider the value of two outcomes: the importance of gaining the target's compliance in this situation (labeled "compliance value") and the importance of maintaining a good relationship with the target over the long run (labeled "relational value"). Thus the process of selecting compliance-seeking strategies can be modeled with Equation 4.1:

$$L = p_1 CV + (p_2 RR - p_3 RC),$$

[4.1]

where L = the likelihood of using a particular strategy in this situation; CV = the perceived value of gaining compliance in this situation; RR = the perceived rewards to the relationship from seeking compliance in this situation; RC = the perceived cost to the relationship from seeking compliance in this situation; and p_1-p_3 = the probability that CV, RR, and RC will occur if the strategy is used in this situation.

Notice that the three terms on the right side of Equation 4.1 are multiplicative (e.g., p_1 and CV are multiplied together). What this means, in practical terms, is that an individual is unlikely to select a specific compliance-gaining strategy if either (a) that strategy, on balance, is likely to produce outcomes perceived as costly or trivial (i.e., RC is seen as large relative to CV and RR) or (b) that strategy, in principle, could produce beneficial outcomes but the likelihood of this occurring is seen as low (i.e., p_1 or p_2 are small).

Sillars's (1980) SEU model suggests several explanations for why message sources might vary their compliance-seeking strategies across situations where they share an interpersonal versus noninterpersonal relationship with the target. In general, individuals should place greater value on maintaining interpersonal relationships than they place on noninterpersonal relationships. They also may place different value on gaining a familiar versus unfamiliar target's compliance. Finally, the perceived probability that the same strategy will be effective at gaining compliance or will create relational costs (as opposed to rewards) may vary across interpersonal versus noninterpersonal situations.[3]

To test this reasoning, Sillars (1980) had 148 undergraduate students read one of two hypothetical compliance-seeking scenarios and complete a three-step procedure. Participants in the *noninterpersonal condition* read the "shade tree" situation (i.e., the noninterpersonal, long-term consequences scenario from the MBRS study; see Table 4.1). Participants in the *interpersonal condition* instead read a variation of the same scenario in which their own spouse was planning to cut down a large tree on their property.[4] After reading the scenario, participants first rated how important it was to gain compliance (CV), to improve the relationship (RR), and to avoid damaging the relationship (RR) in their situation. Second, participants made judgments about how likely they were to use each of Marwell and Schmitt's (1967) 16 compliance-seeking strategies in that situation. Third and finally, participants evaluated the probability that each of the 16 strategies would gain compliance (p_1) and benefit/damage the relationship (p_2 and p_3).

Using a statistical technique called multiple regression analysis, Sillars (1980) reached two conclusions. First, the SEU model did a good job of predicting participants' likelihood of using most compliance-seeking strategies. For 9 of the 16 strategies, the variables on the right side of Equation 4.1 accounted for more than 40% of the variance in likelihood-of-use ratings. The model did the poorest job of predicting participants' ratings for aversive stimulation and threat, the two strategies rated least likely to be used. Second, the model helped explain why participants chose different compliance-seeking strategies in the interpersonal versus the noninterpersonal scenario (likelihood-of-use ratings for 5 of the 16 strategies differed significantly at $p < .05$, although most effect sizes were small). For example, "reward" or "personal commitment" strategies were seen as more persuasive in the interpersonal scenario, and most strategies were seen as more likely to create relational costs in the noninterpersonal scenario.

An Ethical Threshold Model

Hunter and Boster (1978, 1987) present a different explanation for how people select compliance-seeking strategies. According to these authors, attempts to persuade produce emotional reactions in message targets (e.g., anger, resentment, gratitude) that vary in part depending on the types of message strategies used. One might expect that the strategy of "threat," for example, often would be more likely to produce negative emotions in targets than "positive expertise." Thus compliance-seeking messages can be arrayed along a dimension from those likely to produce positive feelings in the target (e.g., prosocial or appropriate strategies) to those likely to produce negative feelings in the target (i.e., antisocial or inappropriate strategies).

Hunter and Boster (1987) argue that for each individual, there is a point on this continuum that divides "those compliance-gaining messages that produce acceptable emotional responses in the listener and those messages that produce unacceptable ones" (p. 65). This point, called the *ethical threshold*, measures "how negative an emotional response the persuader is willing to produce in the listener to gain the listener's compliance" (p. 65). An important point is that ethical thresholds vary across both persons and situations. Some message sources, in general, are more willing than others to create negative emotions (or are less aware that they have created negative emotions) within targets to gain compliance. Across different situations, the same message source also may be more or less willing to create negative emotions to gain compliance, depending on the importance of his or her request as well as his or her relationship with the message target. The degree to which a message source is willing to risk creating negative emotions in a target, then, is a function of both the message source and the situation. When the ethical threshold is very high, a message source is *unwilling* to use most potential compliance-seeking strategies in a particular situation (i.e., he or she gives most strategies low likelihood-of-use ratings). When the threshold is low, a source is *willing* to use virtually any strategy in a situation (i.e., he or she gives most strategies high likelihood-of-use ratings).

Aside from providing an explanation for how individuals evaluate compliance-seeking strategies, Hunter and Boster's (1978, 1987) model has two related implications for how we think about likelihood-of-use ratings. First, Hunter and Boster argue that only a single dimension (i.e., the emotional impact on the target), and not multiple dimensions, underlies individuals' likelihood-of-use ratings. Prior studies using factor analysis had found that individual compliance-seeking strategies fell into three to eight strategy clusters (e.g., Marwell & Schmitt, 1967; Miller et al., 1977; Roloff & Barnicott, 1978, 1979). Based on a complex set of statistical procedures, Hunter and Boster (1987) argue that these prior studies had produced misleading results.[5]

Second, Hunter and Boster (1987) claim that an individual's likelihood-of-use ratings for a typology of compliance-seeking strategies should all be added together to form a single dependent variable. This single summed score represents the individual's ethical threshold, or his or her willingness to use a wide range of strategies—including antisocial strategies—in that situation. Hunter and Boster's practice of summing likelihood-of-use ratings for multiple strategies into a single total score obviously changes our conception of what the strategy-selection procedure actually measures. When Miller et al. (1977) had participants make likelihood-of-use ratings for 16 different compliance-seeking strategies, they presumably thought that those ratings would predict whether participants actually would use each of those 16 strategies in a similar "real" situation. In contrast, Hunter and Boster argue that participants' likelihood-of-use ratings for 16 strategies predict only whether individuals in general are willing to use antisocial strategies in a real situation, and not which specific prosocial or antisocial strategies they will use. I review evidence concerning the validity of both positions later in this chapter.

Although different in several respects, the SEU and ethical threshold models both imply that people's choice of compliance-seeking strategies should be affected by situational and individual-difference variables. I next turn to research that has sought to identify situational and individual-difference predictors of compliance-seeking strategy choice.

THE SEARCH FOR PREDICTORS
OF COMPLIANCE-SEEKING STRATEGY CHOICE

Identifying Situational Dimensions

People make numerous types of requests of friends, family members, and coworkers. How do people distinguish among these compliance-gaining situations? In the first study to investigate this issue, Cody and McLaughlin (1980) argue that compliance-gaining situations are perceived to vary along multiple dimensions, which might or might not include the two situational factors (i.e., interpersonal/noninterpersonal relationships and consequences) in the MBRS study.

In order to identify the perceived dimensions of compliance-gaining situations, Cody and McLaughlin (1980) initially had undergraduate students generate a "population" of 87 situations that the students experienced with some frequency. The researchers randomly selected three different sets of 12 situations from this larger population. Following this, participants in a different sample of 197 undergraduates each made paired-comparison judgments for one of the three sets of 12 compliance-gaining situations. Participants judged how similar each situation was to every other situation using an 11-point scale ranging from 1 = *the two situations are exactly alike* to 11 = *the two situations are totally different* (p. 137). Cody and McLaughlin conducted multidimensional scaling (MDS) separately on all three sets of similarity judgments. After completing the paired-comparison task, participants also rated their 12 situations along 23 Likert scales. The researchers used these Likert scale ratings to help interpret and label dimensions that emerged from the MDS.

Based on the MDS results, Cody and McLaughlin concluded that individuals distinguish compliance-gaining situations along six dimensions. *Intimacy*, similar to the distinction between interpersonal and noninterpersonal relationships, asks whether the source-target relationship is close or superficial. *Dominance* taps the degree to which the message source controls, as opposed to being controlled by, the target. *Personal benefits* assesses the degree to which the message source will gain personally if the target complies with his or her request. *Resistance* taps how much the message source expects the target to resist complying with his or her request. *Rights* concerns whether the message source believes that he or she is justified in making this request. Finally, *consequences* involves the degree to which the request could affect the message source-target relationship in the long run. Cody and McLaughlin (1980; Cody, Woefel, & Jordan, 1983) have developed questionnaire items that measure each of these six perceived situational dimensions, a sampling of which appears in Table 4.3.

Table 4.3   Questionnaire Items Measuring Six Perceived Dimensions of
             Compliance-Gaining Situations

Item	Factor

Intimacy

1. This situation involves a superficial relationship.—This situation involves an intimate relationship.
2. This situation involves a personally meaningless relationship.—This situation involves a personally meaningful relationship.

Dominance

3. The person in a situation like this situation usually dominates me.—The person in a situation like this situation usually does not dominate me.
4. I am usually submissive to the person in a situation like this one.—I am not usually submissive to the person in a situation like this one.

Personal Benefits

5. I personally do not gain if successful in this situation.—I personally gain if successful in this situation.
6. It would not be to my personal advantage if I were successful in this situation.—It would be to my personal advantage if I were successful in this situation.

Resistance

7. I could talk the person in this situation into doing this very easily.—I could not talk the person in this situation into doing this very easily.
8. I think the person in this situation would be very agreeable to this persuasion.—I do not think that the person in this situation would be very agreeable to this persuasion.

Rights

9. I have no justification for making this request.—I have every justification for making this request.
10. I do not have a right to make this request.—I have a right to make this request.

Consequences

11. This persuasion does not have future consequences for the relationship between the person in the situation and myself.—This persuasion has future consequences for the relationship between the person in the situation and myself.
12. This persuasion does not have long-term consequences for the relationship between the person in the situation and myself.—This persuasion does have long-term consequences for the relationship between the person in the situation and myself.

SOURCE: From "Perceptions of Compliance-Gaining Situations: A Dimensional Analysis," by M. J. Cody & M. L. McLaughlin, 1980, *Communication Monographs*, 47, p. 143. Copyright 1980 by the Speech Communication Association. Adapted by permission.

Although Cody and McLaughlin's (1980) work represents the most comprehensive scheme for classifying compliance-gaining situations, others have modified or added to their list of perceived dimensions. Using similar procedures, Hertzog and Bradac (1984) replicate most of Cody and McLaughlin's (1980) six dimensions but also report evidence for a gender relevant/irrelevant dimension (i.e., whether the sex of the participants is seen as important or relevant to the interaction).[6] Other scholars distinguish between self (personal) and other (target) benefits, because either party or both parties may gain from compliance with a request (e.g., Boster & Stiff, 1984; Dillard & Burgoon, 1985). Finally, some scholars break the multidimensional construct of "intimacy" into subdimensions such as interdependence versus affection, because message sources and targets may know each other well and influence each other frequently without necessarily liking one another (e.g., Burgoon & Hale, 1984; Kelley et al., 1983).

Testing Situational Predictors

Drawing on Cody and McLaughlin's (1980) work, a number of researchers have investigated whether the compliance-seeking strategies that people choose differ across situations that vary along single dimensions such as intimacy (e.g., Cody, McLaughlin, & Schneider, 1981; Miller, 1982; Sillars, 1980; Tracy, Craig, Smith, & Spisak, 1984), dominance (e.g., Miller, 1982; Tracy et al., 1984), self- and/or other-benefit (Boster & Stiff, 1984; Clark, 1979), and relational consequences (e.g., Cody et al., 1981; Lustig & King, 1980). Complementary studies have examined whether people's ratings of compliance-resisting strategies vary along single dimensions such as intimacy (Bresnahan, Cai, & Rivers, 1994; McLaughlin et al., 1980; O'Hair, Cody, & O'Hair, 1991), dominance (Bresnahan et al., 1994; McQuillen, Higginbotham, & Cummings, 1984), relational consequences of noncompliance (McLaughlin et al., 1980; O'Hair et al., 1991), and type of compliance-seeking strategy employed by the source (McLaughlin et al., 1980; McQuillen et al., 1984). In contrast to these studies, two articles report tests of whether a large number of situational dimensions, as a group, predict people's choice of compliance-seeking strategies (Cody et al., 1986; Dillard & Burgoon, 1985). Using diverse methods, both reach pessimistic conclusions about the predictive utility of the situational dimensions approach.

Dillard and Burgoon (1985) conducted two studies exploring the effects of multiple situational dimensions on the selection of compliance-seeking strategies. Basing their work on the ethical threshold model, they summed participants' likelihood-of-use ratings across the 16 Marwell and Schmitt (1967) compliance-seeking strategies into a single total score, which they interpret as a measure of how willing participants were to use verbally aggressive messages to gain compliance. In Study 1, college undergraduates responded to two hypothetical compliance-gaining scenarios in which they imagined trying to convince their teenage son to study more often and trying to persuade their best friend to repay on overdue loan. After reading each scenario, participants indicated whether they were willing to use each of the 16 compliance-seeking strategies and then rated the scenario for seven perceptual dimensions: intimacy, dominance, self-benefit, other-benefit, rights, resistance, and consequences. Using multiple regression analysis, Dillard and Burgoon assessed whether participants' perceptions of the seven situational dimensions predicted their summed likelihood-of-use scores separately within each scenario. Participants who perceived greater intimacy were less willing to be verbally aggressive in both scenarios. Perceived self-benefit was positively associated with verbal aggressiveness in the "repay loan" (but not the "study more") scenario, whereas perceived right to persuade was positively associated with aggressiveness in the "study more" (but not the "repay loan") scenario. Although statistically significant, none of these three situational dimensions was a strong predictor of summed use scores (in the "repay loan" situation, $R^2 = .10$ for the two significant dimensions; in the "study more" situation, $R^2 = .06$ for the two significant dimensions). The remaining five situational dimensions failed to predict summed use scores in either scenario.

In Study 2, participants in a different sample of 268 undergraduates recalled a recent real-life situation in which they had tried to gain someone else's compliance. Participants rated how willing they would have been to use each of the 16 Marwell and Schmitt (1967) strategies in their situations, after which they rated their situations along the same seven situational dimensions. In this study, perceived dominance, self-benefit, and other-benefit all were positively associated with verbal aggressiveness, although the size of these associations was small ($R^2 = .06$ for all three dimensions). The remaining dimensions were not significant predictors of summed use scores. Dillard and Burgoon (1985) conclude, "Across the two studies the effects attributable to the situation were relatively few in number and small in size. . . . At no time did even a majority of situational dimensions, much less all of them, function as significant predictors" (p. 301).

Cody et al. (1986) also assessed the effects of multiple situational dimensions on choice of compliance-seeking strategies. To ensure a broad sample of realistic situations, they initially collected 42 hypothetical compliance-gaining scenarios from prior research. After reading 1 of these 42 scenarios, each of 1,064 undergraduate students recalled a compliance-gaining episode from his or her own life that was similar to that scenario. For example, participants who read the hypothetical scenario "Persuade your landlord to repair the plumbing" recalled real-life episodes "that dealt with landlords and plumbing, repairing windows, repairing air conditioning units, cleaning carpets, installing deadbolt locks, and the like" (p. 398). Participants initially rated their recalled scenarios on scales measuring the six situational dimensions identified by Cody and McLaughlin (1980; see Table 4.3). After this, they wrote essays describing how they went about trying to persuade the targets in their situations. Coders then classified the first compliance-seeking strategy present in each written message into one of seven categories: supporting evidence, self-benefit requests, other-benefit requests, empathic understanding, exchange, face maintenance, and distributive strategies.

Using a statistical technique called logistic regression analysis, Cody et al. (1986) tested whether ratings of the six situational dimensions were sufficient to predict whether participants would (or would not) use each of the seven compliance-seeking strategies. In addition to examining the six situational dimensions individually, they examined interactions between situational dimensions. For example, they assessed not only whether perceived intimacy in general predicted if participants initially would (or would not) use supporting evidence, but also whether intimacy was a better predictor of supporting evidence when anticipated resistance by the target was high rather than low (or vice versa). This study generated findings that are too numerous to summarize here, but Cody et al. concluded in general that situational dimensions, even in combination, did not adequately account for whether participants chose specific compliance-seeking strategies. They state bluntly that situational "perceptions do not, in concert, predict selection of strategies" (p. 416).

Personality Attributes as Predictors

In addition to situational variation, researchers have investigated stable individual differences in people's choice of compliance-seeking strategies. Table 4.4 summarizes the methods used in and the results from 13 studies that have examined the predictive utility of nine different personality attributes. The major conclusion arising from this research is that personality attributes, in and of themselves, are at best modest predictors of strategy choice. Several reliable predictors have been identified. For example, four studies using varied methods have documented significant positive associations between dogmatism and people's willingness to use "aggressive" or "antisocial" compliance-seeking strategies (Boster & Levine, 1988; Boster & Stiff, 1984; Dillard & Burgoon, 1985; Roloff & Barnicott, 1979). In all four studies, however, dogmatism accounted for only 1-9% of the variance in people's aggressiveness (see Table 4.4). Inspection of Table 4.4 suggests that the effects of personality attributes have been especially small in studies using the "strategy-selection" methodology. To complicate matters further, the effects of one personality attribute on people's choice of strategies can differ depending on levels of a second attribute

Table 4.4 A Sampling of Research on Individual Differences in Compliance-Seeking Strategy Choice

Personality Variable/Study	Method	Dependent Variable	Summary of Key Findings
Argumentativeness (Arg.)			
Boster & Levine (1988)	Selection	Summed use scores	$\beta = .09$ and $.19$ in 2 situations
Boster et al. (1993)	Interactive	Strategy diversity & persistence	$r = .35$ w/diversity for persist, effects of Arg. depend on VA
Communication apprehension (CA)			
Lustig & King (1980)	Selection	Individual strategies	No significant effects for CA
Communication motives			
Javidi et al. (1994)	Construction	Individual strategies	Motive to control best predictor
Dogmatism			
Boster & Levine (1988)	Selection	Summed use scores	$\beta = .13$ and $.21$ in 2 situations
Boster & Stiff (1984)	Interactive	No. of requests for self/other	$\beta = .15$ for self; $\beta = .01$ for other
Dillard & Burgoon (1985, Study 2)	Recall	Summed use scores	$r = .14$
Roloff & Barnicott (1979)	Selection	Strategy clusters	$r = .29$ w/prosocial; $r = .22$ w/psy. force; $r = .19$ w/punish
Locus of control			
Canary et al. (1986)	Recall	Individual strategies	12 of 40 differences statistically significant; no estimates of effect size
Lamude et al. (1987)	Selection	Individual strategies	Significant difference on 3 of 10 strategies; small effects ($r^2 = .03-.06$)

Personality Variable/Study	Method	Dependent Variable	Summary of Key Findings
Self-monitoring (SM)			
Smith et al. (1990, Study 1)	Selection	Individual strategies	Effects of SM depend on participant sex, $r < .30$
Machiavellianism/negativism			
Boster & Levine (1988)	Selection	Summed use scores	$\beta = .23$ and $.13$ in 2 situations
Boster & Stiff (1984)	Interactive	No. of requests for self/other	$\beta = -.26$ for self $\beta = -.15$ for other
Roloff & Barnicott (1978)	Selection	Strategy clusters	$r = .21$ w/prosocial $r = .34$ w/psy. force $r = .10$ w/punish
Need for social approval			
Boster et al. (1985)	Selection	Summed use scores	$r = .05$ and $-.04$ for two typologies
Burleson et al. (1988, Studies 1-2)	Selection	Individual strategies	Significant r for only 9 of 30 strategies, most $< .30$
Verbal aggressiveness (VA)			
Boster & Levine (1988)	Selection	Summed use scores	$\beta = .20$ and $-.06$ in 2 situations
Boster et al. (1993)	Interactive	Strategy diversity & persistence	$r = -.12$ w/diversity for persist, effects of VA depend on Arg.

NOTE: Selection = likelihood-of-use ratings for preformulated strategies in hypothetical situations; construction = content analysis of written strategies in hypothetical situations; recall = ratings for preformulated strategies in recalled situations; interactive = content analysis of strategies in role-play or naturalistic interactions.

(e.g., Boster, Levine, & Kazoleas, 1993; Smith, Cody, LoVette, & Canary, 1990) or on the type of compliance-gaining situation under investigation (e.g., Boster & Levine, 1988; Javidi, Jordan, & Carlone, 1994; Lamude, Daniels, & White, 1987).

Sex and Gender Differences

Sex is a biological classification; the term refers to whether an individual is biologically and genetically male or female. *Gender* is socially constructed; it is based in a person's view of him- or herself as possessing those qualities that society deems to be masculine, feminine, or both. Gender may be described as the ways in which a culture invests "biological sex with social significance" (Wood, 1999, p. 22).

Many researchers have investigated whether males and females, in personal and professional relationships, differ in their choice of compliance-seeking and -resisting strategies (e.g., Belk et al., 1988; Bisanz & Rule, 1989; Bresnahan et al., 1994; Burgoon, Dillard, Koper, & Doran, 1984; Dallinger & Hample, 1989; deTurck, 1985, 1987; Falbo & Peplau, 1980; Harper & Hirokawa, 1988; Hirokawa, Kodama, & Harper, 1990; Hirokawa, Mickey, & Miura, 1991; Howard, Blumstein, & Schwartz, 1986; Offermann & Kearney, 1988; Offermann & Schrier, 1985; Schlueter, Barge, & Blankenship, 1990; Smith et al., 1990; Sprowl, 1986; Sullivan, Albrecht, & Taylor, 1990; for a review, see Carli, 1999). Most researchers have explored sex differences, although the rationales they have employed for anticipating sex differences typically have been drawn from societal gender expectations. Only a few studies have assessed psychological gender directly (e.g., Howard et al., 1986).

Two large-scale investigations offer a representative picture of the findings on sex differences. In the first study, Dallinger and Hample (1994) conducted a secondary analysis of sex differences in data from several earlier investigations (e.g., Dallinger & Hample, 1989; Hample & Dallinger, 1987a, 1987b). In these prior studies, a total of 1,471 college students (838 male, 633 female) had read one of several hypothetical compliance-gaining scenarios. Participants then had decided whether they would use (i.e., endorse) or would not use (i.e., reject) 48 concrete messages, which the authors had generated by writing 3 examples for each of the 16 Marwell and Schmitt (1967) compliance-seeking strategies, in that situation. The main focus of these prior studies had been on the reasons participants rejected potential compliance-seeking strategies, and I review these findings in Chapter 5. In their secondary analysis, however, Dallinger and Hample also examined whether males and females differ in their willingness to use particular compliance-seeking strategies, as well as in the total number of strategies they endorse.

With this large sample, Dallinger and Hample (1994) detected significant sex differences for 10 of the 16 compliance-seeking strategies. Males were more likely than females to endorse threat, negative expertise, positive expertise, negative altercasting, negative esteem, aversive stimulation, debt, liking, and pregiving. Females were more likely than males to endorse altruism. The size of these sex differences, however, was extremely small (rs ranged from .05 to .11). In sum, Dallinger and Hample found a slight tendency for males to endorse a larger number of compliance-seeking strategies, and especially aggressive strategies, compared with females. But this tendency was slight; indeed, biological sex accounted for only 1% of the variance in whether participants endorsed or rejected specific compliance-seeking strategies.

In the second large-scale study, Krone, Allen, and Ludlum (1994) conducted a meta-analysis of sex differences in managers' choice of compliance-seeking strategies. Meta-analysis is a set of techniques for statistically summarizing and synthesizing results from multiple individual studies.[7] Krone et al. identified 10 prior studies that had compared male and female managers' use of compliance-seeking strategies and that had reported sufficient statistical information for meta-analysis. More than 2,000 individuals from a variety of organizations had participated in the 10 original studies. The original studies had used several different data collection methods, including having managers rate preformulated strategies for likelihood of use (e.g., Offermann & Schrier, 1985), having managers write out what they believed they would say in hypothetical scenarios (e.g., Harper & Hirokawa, 1988), and having undergraduate students enact organizational simulations (e.g., Instone, Major, & Bunker, 1983). Because the original studies had employed different nominal-level typologies, Krone et al. recoded compliance-seeking strategies from the 10 studies into four clusters: reward strategies (e.g., promise, positive self-esteem), punishing strategies (e.g., threat, warning), persuasion strategies (rational explanation, negotiation), and altruism strategies (e.g., requests for favors, appeals to duty).

Krone et al.'s meta-analysis revealed small sex differences for two of the four strategy clusters. Male managers were significantly more likely than females to use both reward and punishment strategies; however, biological sex accounted for only 1% of the variance in use of both strategy clusters (average $r = .038$ and .066, respectively, across the 10 studies). Males and females did not differ significantly in their use of persuasion and altruism strategies.

Dallinger and Hample's (1994) and Krone et al.'s (1994) large-scale investigations suggest that males and females are much more similar than different in their choice of compliance-seeking strategies. Caution is warranted regarding this conclusion, however, because traditional studies often have (a) failed to specify exactly what feature of compliance-seeking messages should differ by sex (see below), (b) used biological sex as a marker for psychological gender, and (c) relied on data collection methods that are insensitive to individual differences (see below). Sex differences in compliance-seeking strategies also may vary in size depending on other factors, such as the relative power of male and female message sources (Hirokawa et al., 1990) and the type and perceived legitimacy of the request being made (Harper & Hirokawa, 1988; Hirokawa et al., 1991; Schlueter et al., 1990). Moreover, people may *expect* women and men to use different compliance-seeking strategies, even when in reality sex differences typically are small. Gendered expectations about appropriate behavior can mean that perceivers evaluate women more negatively than men for using "aggressive" (i.e., stereotypically masculine) compliance-seeking strategies (Burgoon, Birk, & Hall, 1991; Carli, 1999).

I have now reviewed research examining both situational and individual-difference predictors of compliance-seeking strategies. Although a large body of research has explored these questions, on the whole these studies have failed to identify many strong predictors of people's strategic choices. This failure suggests that traditional compliance-gaining studies may suffer both theoretical and methodological shortcomings.

CRITICISMS OF THE COMPLIANCE-GAINING LITERATURE

By the late 1980s, the traditional compliance-gaining literature had come under attack (see Miller, Boster, Roloff, & Seibold, 1987; D. J. O'Keefe, 1990). Critics claimed that compliance-gaining research was atheoretical, and they questioned the validity of typical research methods.

Conceptual Criticisms

Compliance-gaining research has been criticized as being atheoretical on two grounds. First, the vast majority of studies have failed to specify which particular feature of compliance-seeking messages they hope to predict/explain. Put differently, these studies have not specified the dependent variable clearly. D. J. O'Keefe (1990) illustrates the problem with an example:

> Consider a research question such as "Does the intimacy of the relationship between the interactants influence the compliance-gaining message produced?" Though at first glance this may seem like a perfectly sensible question, a closer look will reveal that it is not sufficiently carefully put. After all, compliance-gaining messages in intimate and nonintimate relationships might be very similar in some ways, but very different in others; relational intimacy might influence some aspects of compliance-gaining behavior, but be unrelated to other facets. (p. 203)

Many compliance-gaining studies suffer from this problem. In research on intimacy, for example, participants often have selected compliance-seeking strategies from nominal-level typologies (e.g., Cody et al., 1981, 1986; Levine & Wheeless, 1990; Miller et al., 1977; Miller, 1982; Sillars, 1980). As described in Chapter 2, the categories composing nominal-level typologies vary in countless unspecified ways, including the degree to which strategies are prosocial/ antisocial, direct/indirect, elaborated/unelaborated, listener-adapted/egocentric, and so forth. Hence it is not clear whether researchers anticipated that the compliance-seeking messages within intimate versus nonintimate relationships would differ in these or other respects. Many studies examining personality attributes or sex differences also have failed to specify the dependent variable clearly.

A second problem is that researchers have investigated situational and individual predictors of compliance-gaining strategy choice in ad hoc fashion, with relative lack of regard for developing theory that could account for results across studies (Boster, 1995). Consider the lengthy list of personality attributes summarized in Table 4.4. Researchers often begin with hunches rather than theoretical rationales for why particular attributes, such as "locus of control," might predict particular (and often unspecified) features of compliance-seeking messages. These hunches typically are specific to the personality attributes under investigation, and hence do not contribute to the development of theory that can predict and explain how a wide range of individual-difference and situational variables affect what people say when seeking compliance.

These two criticisms may seem overly harsh, especially given that I have reviewed theoretical models of compliance-gaining strategy choice. The SEU model (Sillars, 1980), however, fails to specify exactly which feature of compliance-gaining messages it is designed to explain. This is an important limitation, because different concepts may be needed to explain different message qualities. For example, "compliance value" and "relational rewards/ costs" may help explain whether people use prosocial as opposed to antisocial appeals in their compliance-seeking messages, but perhaps not whether they use listener-adapted as opposed to egocentric appeals. In addition, the SEU model underestimates the number of factors that affect message choices. Aside from "compliance value" and "relational rewards/costs," people's decisions about what to say, and what not to say, during influence interactions are affected by goals such as being true to themselves, saying things that are relevant, and maintaining comfortable levels of arousal (Dillard, Segrin, & Harden, 1989; Hample & Dallinger, 1987a; Kim & Wilson, 1994; O'Keefe & Shepherd, 1987; Smith, 1984). Perhaps for these reasons, the SEU model has generated little compliance-gaining research.

The ethical threshold model (Hunter & Boster, 1978, 1987) fares better with regard to the two aforementioned criticisms. It is designed to explain the degree to which people will use compliance-seeking messages that create negative emotional responses in the target. It also suggests both individual-difference (e.g., verbal aggressiveness) and situational (e.g., self/other-benefit) factors that should affect this quality of compliance-gaining messages. Despite this, the model has several shortcomings as an explanation for why people say what they do when attempting to exert influence. Perhaps most important, Hunter and Boster (1987) proposed the ethical threshold model to explain data generated by the strategy-selection procedure. To the degree that people's behavior during influence interactions deviates from their responses to this procedure (see the methodological criticisms below), the ethical threshold model will make inaccurate assumptions. One example of this problem is Hunter and Boster's (1987) assumption that people choose compliance-seeking strategies based solely on the anticipated emotional reactions of the target; target emotional response is the *single* antecedent variable to message choice (p. 65). This assumption is too restrictive when people seek compliance during interaction, where message choices typically reflect *multiple* goals (Dillard et al., 1989; Hample & Dallinger, 1987a; O'Keefe & Shepherd, 1987; Tracy et al., 1984).[8] As a theory of persuasive message production, the ethical threshold model may have limited utility.

Methodological Criticisms

Aside from these conceptual challenges, the research methods used in most compliance-gaining studies also have been criticized for lacking predictive/external validity as well as replicability (see Miller et al., 1987; D. J. O'Keefe, 1990). Methodological criticisms center on (a) the predictive validity of the strategy-selection procedure, (b) the problem of generalizing about abstract message strategies from single messages, and (c) the limits of hypothetical scenarios. I address questions about the predictive validity and limits of the strategy-construction procedure later in this chapter.

Predictive validity of the strategy-selection procedure. In the majority of studies in the "compliance-gaining" tradition, participants have made likelihood-of-use ratings for preformulated lists of message strategies. Critics of this "strategy-selection" procedure charge that it presents participants with a variety of message strategies, some of which participants might not consider or even be capable of enacting during interaction. Critics also stress that the method encourages participants to compare strategies along salient dimensions such as social appropriateness, and hence results in participants as a group overselecting prosocial and underselecting antisocial strategies (e.g., Burke, 1989; Burke & Clark, 1982; Clark, 1979; Neuliep, 1986; O'Hair et al., 1991; Waltman & Burleson, 1997a).

Extending these criticisms, Burleson et al. (1988) claim that the strategy-selection procedure is contaminated by an "item desirability bias":

> Instruments contaminated by this . . . bias unintentionally make the social appro-priateness of item content quite salient to all persons completing the question-naire. Consequently, an instrument affected by the item desirability bias results in persons uniformly reporting their perceptions of an item's desirability or social appropriateness rather than directly responding to the content of an item (e.g., rather than reporting the actual likelihood of using a particular compliance-gaining strategy described in an item). (p. 438)

Burleson et al. argue that individuals, as a group, agree that certain compliance-seeking strategies (e.g., altruism, positive expertise) are more socially appropri-ate or desirable than other strategies (e.g., threat, negative self-feeling).[9] Given this, if people's likelihood-of-use ratings simply reflect the social appropriateness of compliance-seeking strategies, then one group's likelihood-of-use ratings for a list of strategies should be predictable from a *different* group's appropriateness ratings of those same strategies.

Burleson et al. (1988) report multiple studies testing this prediction. In Study 1, a group of undergraduates (Group 1) read four different compliance-gaining scenarios drawn from earlier research. Paired with each scenario was a list of 16 concrete compliance-seeking messages that illustrated each of the 16 Marwell and Schmitt (1967) strategies in that situation. Students in Group 1 rated how likely they would be to use each compliance-seeking strategy in each situation. A different group of students (Group 2) read the same four scenarios and the same 16 compliance-seeking strategies for each situation. Rather than making likelihood-of-use ratings, however, students in Group 2 rated the social appro-priateness of each strategy in each situation on four semantic differential scales (polite–impolite, considerate–inconsiderate, socially appropriate–socially inap-propriate, follows social expectations–violates social expectations).

Burleson et al. (1988) initially calculated Group 1's mean likelihood-of-use ratings for each of the 16 compliance-seeking strategies in each of the four situations. That is, the strategy that Group 1, on average, rated as most likely to be used in a situation received the highest mean score, the strategy rated as second most likely to be used received the second-highest mean score, and so forth. The researchers also calculated Group 2's mean social appropriateness rating for each of the 16 compliance-seeking strategies in each of the four situ-ations. The strategy that Group 2, on average, perceived as most appropriate in a situation received the highest mean score, the second most appropriate strategy received the second-highest mean score, and so forth. To test their hypothesis, Burleson et al. then correlated Group 1's mean likelihood-of-use ratings for the 16 strategies with Group 2's mean social appropriateness ratings. Correlations between mean likelihood-of-use ratings and mean social appropriateness ratings within each of the four situations were $r = .71, .86, .88,$ and .85. In other words, Group 1's ratings of which of the 16 Marwell and Schmitt compliance-seeking strategies were most (and least) likely to be used could be predicted, with a very high degree of accuracy, from Group 2's ratings of which of those same strategies were most (and least) appropriate. Burleson et al. replicated this basic finding in several ways, including by showing that very similar results occurred when two different groups rated compliance-seeking strategies from Schenck-Hamlin et al.'s (1982) typology rather than Marwell and Schmitt's (1967) typology (Study 2), and when individuals rather than groups were used as the unit of analysis (Studies 3 and 4).

In a fifth study, Burleson et al. (1988) demonstrated that patterns of likelihood-of-use ratings made by participants in the MBRS study and other early investigations of seeking compliance also were predictable. Burleson et al. initially identified five prior published studies that met two criteria: each had used the Marwell and Schmitt typology, and each had reported mean likelihood-of-use ratings for the 16 strategies. None of these five studies had employed the same four hypothetical scenarios or the same concrete examples of the 16 strategies as had Burleson et al. The researchers then correlated mean likelihood-of-use ratings from the five prior studies with mean social appropriateness ratings for the 16 strategies from two different groups of students who had participated in their own studies. The resulting correlations appear in boldface type in rows 6 and 7 of Table 4.5. As is apparent, mean likelihood-of-use ratings from all five prior studies are predicted quite accurately by the mean social appropriateness ratings from Burleson et al.'s own participants. The authors conclude that, "despite differences in subjects, situations, and strategy [examples], most people respond basically the same way to preformulated lists of compliance-gaining strategies, and their responses appear to be heavily determined by the perceived appropriateness of these preformulated strategies" (p. 462).

These findings help explain, at least in part, why compliance-gaining scholars have failed to identify strong predictors of people's strategy choices. If most people, regardless of their personalities or specific situations, agree that some compliance-seeking strategies are more socially appropriate than others, and if likelihood-of-use ratings largely reflect each strategy's perceived social appropriateness, then likelihood-of-use ratings will not differ substantially across the personality attributes listed in Table 4.4 or across Cody and McLaughlin's (1980)

Table 4.5   Correlations Among Patterns of Likelihood of Use and Social
Appropriateness Ratings for Studies Using the Marwell and
Schmitt (1967) Typology

Study	1	2	3	4	5	6	7
1. Marwell & Schmitt (1967)	—						
2. Miller et al. (1977)	.63	—					
3. Lustig & King (1980)	.52	.97	—				
4. Sillars (1980)	.73	.72	.68	—			
5. Burgoon, Dillard, Koper, & Doran (1984)	.86	.49	.36	.60	—		
6. Appropriateness 1	.80	.76	.71	.93	.74	—	
7. Appropriateness 2	.79	.74	.67	.82	.75	.92	—

SOURCE: From "Item Desirability Effects in Compliance-Gaining Research: Seven
Studies Documenting Artifacts in the Strategy Selection Procedure," by B. R. Burleson,
S. R. Wilson, M. S. Waltman, E. M. Goering, T. K. Ely, & B. B. Whaley, 1988, *Human
Communication Research, 14,* p. 461. Copyright 1988 by the International
Communication Association. Reprinted with permission.

NOTE: $rs > .43, p < .05$; $rs > .57, p < .01$; $rs > .70, p < .001$. Appropriateness = social
appropriateness ratings from Burleson et al. (1988, Studies 1 and 3).

situational dimensions. Put simply, if likelihood-of-use ratings do not vary, then
they cannot covary with individual-difference or situational factors.

Burleson et al. (1988) claim that item desirability bias has stark implications
for the predictive validity of the strategy-selection procedure. Unless one
assumes that people choose initial compliance-seeking strategies during interaction based almost solely on considerations of social appropriateness, it seems
unlikely that data from the selection procedure will correspond with actual
compliance-seeking behavior. Common sense and some empirical data (e.g.,
Neuliep, 1989) suggest that people, as a group, sometimes rely primarily
on antisocial compliance-seeking strategies during interaction. Based on these
considerations, Burleson et al. (1988) recommend that scholars stop using the
strategy-selection procedure as a measure of strategy use.

As one might imagine, defenders of the strategy-selection procedure have
taken sharp exception to Burleson et al.'s conclusions (see Boster, 1988; Hunter,
1988; Kearney & Plax, 1997; Plax, Kearny, & Sorenson, 1990; Seibold, 1988;
Sorenson, Plax, & Kearney, 1989; for replies, see Burleson & Wilson, 1988;
Waltman & Burleson, 1997b). Among a host of other things, these scholars
have stressed that Burleson et al. (1988) provide no direct evidence that data
from the strategy-selection procedure failed to predict compliance-seeking
behavior. Boster (1988) states bluntly that "in all the experiments presented by

Burleson et al., there is not one measure of compliance-gaining *behavior*" (p. 173), and Seibold (1988) echoes that "in seven studies these researchers' data do not themselves offer any evidence that selection choices are unrelated to behavior" (p. 155). Given this key limitation to Burleson et al.'s research, it is important that we assess carefully any studies that directly test whether likelihood-of-use ratings predict compliance-seeking behaviors. Unfortunately, very little research has done so. To my knowledge, Dillard (1988) has conducted the only studies that address this issue directly. His findings also raise concerns about the selection procedure's predictive validity.

Dillard (1988) reports two studies examining degree of correspondence between likelihood-of-use ratings and compliance-seeking behavior. In Study 1, which examined *retrospective correspondence,* 147 undergraduates each recalled one actual recent compliance-gaining episode in which they had been the message sources. Each participant provided a written description of the interaction that had occurred. Following this, the participant read definitions and examples of Marwell and Schmitt's (1967) 16 compliance-seeking strategies and then rated how willing he or she would have been to use each of the 16 strategies in that situation. Each also reported how much the message target in the episode had resisted his or her request. Coders analyzed written interaction descriptions for how often the participants had actually used each of the same 16 strategies. Coders also rated how much pressure, in general, participants put on the message targets to comply, as well as how verbally aggressive the participants' compliance-gaining appeals had been.

In Study 2, which examined *predictive correspondence,* students from a large-lecture undergraduate class ($N = 261$) made likelihood-of-use ratings for Schenck-Hamlin et al.'s (1982) 14 compliance-seeking strategies in response to two hypothetical scenarios (situations A and B), both of which involved a close friend, lover, or spouse as the target. Two weeks later, 34 students from the same large-lecture class agreed to participate in a supposedly unrelated study on dyadic interaction. Each student agreed to bring along a close friend, lover, or spouse to serve as interaction partner. When they arrived at the lab, each student and his or her partner were videotaped while completing two matched-pair role-play compliance-gaining interactions (situations C and D).[10] The student always was assigned the role of message source in both role plays, and the partner (friend, lover, spouse) always played the target. After each role play, the student rated how much his or her partner had resisted the student's request. Videotapes of these interactions were coded for how frequently students actually used each of the 14 Schenck-Hamlin et al. strategies in each role play. Once again, coders also rated how much pressure, in general, the student put on the target to comply in each role play, as well as how verbally aggressive each student's compliance-seeking attempts had been.

In both studies, Dillard (1988) analyzed correspondence between likelihood-of-use ratings and compliance-seeking behaviors at three different levels of abstraction. At the level of *individual strategies,* Dillard examined whether participants who rated a specific compliance-seeking strategy as "likely to be used" actually performed that same strategy in their written descriptions or role plays. For example, a student who rated the "promise" strategy 5 or higher on the 7-point likelihood-of-use scale and who also used the "promise" strategy during his or her role play was counted as an instance of agreement. A student who rated "promise" 5 or higher but who did not use it during the role play, or who rated "promise" 4 or lower but who did use it, was counted as an instance of disagreement. At the level of *strategy clusters,* Dillard examined whether participants who rated strategies sharing a particular quality as "likely to be used" actually performed the same type of strategies in their written descriptions or role plays. For example, he computed correlations between each student's likelihood-of-use ratings for a cluster of three reward-based strategies (pregiving, promise, and liking) and the student's frequency of using the same three strategies. Finally, at the level of *global dimensions,* Dillard examined whether participants' summed likelihood-of-use scores for an entire list of compliance-seeking strategies predicted general qualities of their compliance-seeking appeals. For example, he computed correlations between each student's likelihood-of-use ratings for all 14 Schenck-Hamlin et al. strategies and coders' ratings of how much pressure the student actually put on the target during the role play.

At the level of individual strategies, Dillard (1988) found virtually no correspondence in either study between likelihood-of-use ratings and compliance-seeking behavior. Across the 16 specific compliance-seeking strategies in Study 1, only 3% of participants showed agreement between their likelihood-of-use ratings and written descriptions of interaction. Across the 14 specific compliance-seeking strategies in Study 2, only 10% and 13% of participants showed agreement between their likelihood-of-use ratings and actual behavior in the two role plays. Dillard found the same lack of correspondence at the level of strategy clusters. Only 3 of the 12 correlations between likelihood-of-use ratings for a strategy cluster and behaviors enacting that same strategy cluster were statistically significant, and 2 of these 3 correlations were *negative* (i.e., participants were less likely actually to perform a strategy from a cluster if they had rated strategies in that cluster as likely to be used).

At the level of global dimensions, Dillard (1988) found some, albeit limited, correspondence between likelihood-of use ratings and compliance-seeking behavior. Across the two studies, participants' summed likelihood-of-use ratings for the entire list of compliance-seeking strategies were not a reliable predictor of how much they pressured targets to comply. In contrast, participants' summed likelihood-of-use ratings were a reliable predictor of their overall level of verbal aggressiveness, but only when targets had resisted their requests. For the subset of participants who had encountered strong resistance, correlations between summed use scores and ratings of their verbal aggressiveness were $r = .30$ in the recall study and $r = .35$ in one of the two role plays (both $p < .05$). A correlation of $r = .02$ in the second role play may have reflected that very few targets offered strong resistance in that situation.[11]

These results offer a pessimistic picture regarding the predictive utility of the strategy-selection procedure. As Dillard (1988) concludes, the "message selection data, regardless of the method by which it is analyzed, exhibits a degree of correspondence to reported and/or actual compliance-gaining behavior that is less than optimal" (p. 180).

Problems with drawing generalizations about message strategies. Aside from predictive validity, critics also have questioned whether valid conclusions about compliance-seeking strategies can be drawn when each strategy is operationalized by a single message (utterance). As defined in Chapter 2, strategies are abstract act types in the sense that they summarize a feature common to many concrete messages. Concrete utterances that illustrate the same strategy are by no means necessarily identical. My stepson, Brendan, probably would hear both "I'll pay you $10.00 if you'll mow the yard today" and "If you mow the yard I'll have more time to talk with your mom about letting you go the concert" as promises. Although both enact the strategy of promise, I may not be equally willing actually to use both messages because they differ in several respects, including directness and legitimacy of the rationale. People's likelihood-of-use ratings for different concrete utterances that illustrate the same compliance-seeking strategy in the same situation typically are associated only moderately (e.g., Hample & Dallinger, 1987a; Jackson & Backus, 1982).

Given this state of affairs, conclusions about people's choice of compliance-seeking strategies need to be based on multiple examples of each strategy. As Jackson and Jacobs (1983) explain, "The use of a single message to instantiate each [strategy] category means that any difference between one [strategy] category and another may be due to individual peculiarities of the particular messages rather than to genuine categorical differences" (p. 171).[12] Unfortunately, the MBRS study and many other early investigations (e.g., Lustig & King, 1980; Roloff & Barnicott, 1978, 1979; Sillars, 1980) used only one concrete message to represent each compliance-seeking strategy. This practice raises concern about whether findings from these studies can be generalized across different messages. Results from a study by Jackson and Backus (1982) suggest that caution is warranted. These researchers performed an exact replication of the MBRS study, with the exception that they used four messages (utterances) rather than only one concrete message to illustrate each of the 16 Marwell and Schmitt compliance-seeking strategies. Whereas the MBRS study reported situational differences in people's likelihood-of-use ratings for all 16 strategies, Jackson and Backus found reliable situational differences for only 3 of the 16 strategies when each strategy was instantiated by four different messages.[13]

Limits of hypothetical scenarios. In order to study what people say when they are attempting to exert influence, researchers must utilize some method for collecting data on compliance-seeking/resisting messages. To date, they have employed a variety of data collection methods, including having message sources recall prior influence episodes (e.g., Dillard & Burgoon, 1985; Wilson & Kang, 1991), asking sources to keep diaries (e.g., Cody, Canary, & Smith, 1994), asking targets of influence attempts to report on message sources (e.g., Lamude & Scudder, 1993; Waltman, 1994), having message sources perform simulations or role plays (e.g., Applegate, 1982; Boster & Stiff, 1984; Dillard, 1988), having sources interact with confederate targets trained to resist compliance (e.g., Boster et al., 1993; Lim, 1990; Neuliep, 1989; Wilson, Cruz, Marshall, & Rao, 1993), and observing message sources during naturalistic influence episodes (e.g., Jacobs & Jackson, 1983; Sanders & Fitch, 2001). Despite this variety, most studies examining compliance-seeking/resisting messages have gathered message sources' or targets' responses to hypothetical influence scenarios (see Table 4.4).

Hypothetical scenarios have many advantages as a data collection method (see D. J. O'Keefe, 1990). First, hypothetical scenarios provide a high degree of experimental control. Researchers can design scenarios to manipulate situational dimensions of interest (e.g., dominance, rights to persuade) while holding other dimensions constant. This level of control is difficult to attain with many other methods. In one study in which college students volunteered on behalf of the American Red Cross to persuade prior donors to give blood again (Wilson, Levine, Humphreys, & Peters, 1994), for example, my colleagues and I could not control whether student callers would reach younger or older prior donors, or whether donors who refused to give blood again would provide legitimate or weak excuses.

A second advantage is that hypothetical scenarios allow the collection of data across multiple situations to enhance generalizability (Jackson & Jacobs, 1983; see note 12). Researchers who want to compare compliance-resisting messages in "interpersonal" versus "noninterpersonal" relationships, for example, can gather data using multiple scenarios that illustrate each type of relationship very quickly. In contrast, collecting naturalistic data on compliance-gaining episodes in even one specific influence situation can be very time-consuming. A third advantage is that realistic hypothetical scenarios can be written for a variety of research populations and topics. A college student can imagine how he or she would persuade another class member to do his or her part in a group project (O'Keefe, 1988), children can imagine how they would persuade their parents to let them have an overnight party (Clark & Delia, 1976), and parents can imagine how they would convince their children to stop throwing temper tantrums in the grocery store (Wilson, Whipple, & Grau, 1996). Scenarios also can be written when behavioral observation is impractical, such as in research on strategies for resisting unwanted sexual advances (Bingham & Burleson, 1989; Edgar & Fitzpatrick, 1990).

Despite these advantages, we risk developing a distorted understanding of compliance seeking and resisting by relying too heavily on hypothetical scenarios. Miller et al. (1987, pp. 103-104) summarize four key differences between responding to hypothetical scenarios and seeking compliance during naturalistic interaction:

1. Individuals may be more mindful or reflective about message choices when responding to scenarios than they typically are during interaction.

2. Individuals face less formidable information-processing demands when responding to scenarios than they face during interaction.

3. Individuals encounter fixed, static situations rather than dynamic, fluid situations when responding to scenarios rather than engaging in interaction.

4. Individuals select strategies without experiencing lived emotions when responding to scenarios rather than engaging in interaction.

Aside from these concerns about external validity, hypothetical scenarios provide little information about the interdependent, incremental nature of influence episodes (Sanders & Fitch, 2001; Wilson, Cameron, & Whipple, 1997; Wilson et al., 1994). Questions about how long compliance-gaining episodes typically last, how message sources and targets decide whether and how to persist/resist, and how both tailor their attempts to seek/resist compliance based on what the other has said (e.g., how compliance-seeking messages are modified in the face of different types of verbal/nonverbal resistance) will receive limited attention if researchers continue to rely primarily on hypothetical scenarios (see Chapter 2).

The use of hypothetical scenarios, like any data collection method, has advantages and disadvantages. As Miller et al. (1987) note: "As long as researchers are aware of the limitations of a method and that method satisfies the demands of the question, various approaches, including joint use of self-reports and actual interaction, are appropriate for studying compliance-gaining strategies" (p. 107).

SUMMARY OF THE COMPLIANCE-GAINING TRADITION

In this section I have reviewed and critiqued work on compliance gaining, one of two research traditions from which contemporary theory and research on persuasive message production has arisen. The program of research that began with the MBRS study, and reached its heyday in the early 1980s, suffers from theoretical and methodological problems that prevent us from drawing many firm conclusions about interpersonal influence. Despite these problems, research on compliance gaining has highlighted the importance of persuasion within personal relationships and initiated a "source-oriented" perspective on interpersonal influence (Miller & Burgoon, 1978). Questions arising from this research program also have stimulated the development of current theories of persuasive message production. The quest to identify situational and individual-difference predictors of compliance-seeking strategies has led scholars to begin studying the psychological processes by which people generate messages in the first place (see Berger, 1995; Wilson, 1997). Aside from the compliance-gaining literature, the program of research on constructivism also has contributed to our understanding of how people decide what to say when they are attempting to exert influence.

The Constructivist Tradition

THEORETICAL AND METHODOLOGICAL FOUNDATIONS

As a theoretical perspective, constructivism asserts that people actively interpret their environment (Delia, O'Keefe, & O'Keefe, 1982). We decide what to say based on our construal of the current situation; thus "the employment of communicative strategies depends centrally on the interpretive schemes interactants bring to bear on the world" (Delia et al., 1982, p. 151).

The constructivist analysis of interpretive schemes integrates ideas from Kelly's (1955) personal construct psychology and Werner's (1957) structural developmental theory. Drawing on Kelly, the fundamental cognitive structure is taken to be the *personal construct*. Personal constructs are bipolar dimensions (e.g., good/bad, large/small) used to anticipate, interpret, and evaluate objects and events. Werner's "orthogenetic principle" provides a way of analyzing individual differences in systems of personal constructs. According to Werner, "Wherever development occurs, it proceeds from a state of relative globality and lack of differentiation to states of increasing differentiation, articulation, and hierarchic integration" (p. 126). With regard to personal constructs, Werner's principle suggests that children, as they mature, should develop systems of constructs that are more differentiated (i.e., larger in number), more articulated (i.e., increasingly abstract), and more integrated (i.e., organized) in nature. Developmental changes in the content and structure of children's impressions of others are consistent with this claim (e.g., Biskin & Crano, 1977; Scarlett, Press, & Crockett, 1971).

Construct systems develop in a domain-specific fashion (see Burleson, 1987; Delia et al., 1982). In other words, the same individual might possess a highly developed system of *interpersonal* constructs (i.e., those used to interpret/evaluate his or her own and other people's actions) but relatively less developed systems of constructs for other domains (e.g., automobiles, music). Given this, any group of adults, or of children the same age, will contain persons with more differentiated, abstract, and organized systems of interpersonal constructs as well as persons with less differentiated, abstract, and organized systems.

Constructivist scholars have used Crockett's (1965) Role Category Questionnaire (RCQ) to measure individual differences in the development of people's interpersonal construct systems.[14] In its most common form, the RCQ asks people to describe two well-known peers, one liked and the other disliked. College students are asked to describe the two peers in writing, whereas children as well as adults less familiar with the research process are often asked to provide oral descriptions. In either case, respondents are asked to describe each peer in detail, focusing on the peer's habits, beliefs, and personality characteristics rather than his or her physical attributes. Complete instructions for eliciting descriptions of the two peers can be found in Burleson and Waltman (1988).

These open-ended descriptions can be scored for several indices of interpersonal construct system development. In the most common procedure, coders count the number of psychological or motivational attributes present in each respondent's impressions of the liked and the disliked peers. For example, a respondent who wrote, "Jim is a *smart, strong-willed* individual who *loves baseball*" would be scored as using three attributes. Burleson and Waltman (1988) describe specific rules for identifying and counting the number of relevant attributes in each impression. The total numbers of attributes in the two impressions are summed to form a global index of that respondent's *interpersonal construct system differentiation* (*construct differentiation* for short).[15]

The abstractness of interpersonal constructs also has been assessed from the RCQ (e.g., Burke & Clark, 1982; Delia, Kline, & Burleson, 1979). In these studies, coders have rated each attribute in a respondent's impression along a continuum of abstractness, where physical descriptions and social roles receive lower scores and general beliefs/attitudes and personality traits receive higher scores. Ratings are averaged across all of the attributes in a respondent's two impressions to compute a global index of *interpersonal construct system abstractness* (*construct abstractness* for short). Burleson and Waltman (1988) review substantial evidence supporting the RCQ measure's reliability as well as convergent/divergent validity. I review some criticisms of the measure below.

Constructivists assume that all social-perception processes, such as perspective taking, causal attribution, and information integration, occur through the application of interpersonal constructs. Differences in the development of people's interpersonal construct systems, therefore, should be reflected in differences in how they perform such processes. Consistent with this assumption, people's levels of construct differentiation and abstractness, as assessed by the RCQ, have been associated with their abilities to take the psychological perspective of others (e.g., Hale & Delia, 1976), alter attributions about others across different situations (e.g., Wilson, Cruz, & Kang, 1992), recognize others' affective states (e.g., Burleson, 1982), and integrate and reconcile inconsistent information about others (e.g., Nidorf & Crockett, 1965).

Aside from social-perception processes, the constructivist perspective also assumes that interpersonal construct system development should be reflected in qualities of people's persuasive messages. Ruth Anne Clark and Jesse Delia (1977) conducted the pioneering study in this area. It is to their study that I now turn.

THE CLARK AND DELIA STUDY

In the first constructivist investigation of persuasive message production, Clark and Delia (1977) examined how children acquire person-perception skills that enable them to produce "listener-adapted" persuasive messages. As defined in Chapter 3, listener-adapted messages are those in which the source adapts his or her request and supporting arguments to the wants and needs of the target (e.g., "Mom, if you get me a bike for my birthday, I could run errands to the store when you're busy") rather than simply emphasizing his or her own wants and needs (e.g., "Please, Mom, I really, really want a bike").

Clark and Delia (1977) reasoned that children must develop social-perception skills in order to produce listener-adapted persuasive messages. For example, children who can distinguish various message targets along a larger, as opposed to a smaller, number of psychological dimensions should have an advantage in identifying different ways of adapting their persuasive appeals. Children who can take the perspective of a particular message target and understand the target's point of view in a situation also should have an advantage in selecting appeals well suited for that target. Thus Clark and Delia hypothesized that the ability to adapt persuasive messages is dependent on social-perception skills.

To test this reasoning, Clark and Delia (1977) asked each of 58 children enrolled in second to ninth grade to state aloud exactly what he or she would say in response to three hypothetical persuasive scenarios. Two of the scenarios involved the child's persuading a parent (e.g., convincing the child's mother to allow the child to have an overnight birthday party), and one scenario involved the child's persuading a woman the child had not previously met to keep a lost puppy.[16] The children's open-ended responses to each situation were scored using a four-level hierarchical coding scheme, ranging from strategies indicating no awareness that the message target had a perspective distinct from the child's own to strategies that emphasized the advantages to the target of acceding to the child's request (I have described the specifics of this hierarchical coding system in detail in Chapter 3). Each child's scores were summed across the three hypothetical scenarios, so that higher scores reflected a greater tendency to produce listener-adapted appeals across situations. After finishing this persuasion task, the children also completed two measures of their social-perception skill: the two-role version of the RCQ measure and the Social Perspectives Task (Hale & Delia, 1976). The latter, which assesses a child's ability to describe and explain other people's behavior as those people would do so, served as a measure of perspective-taking skill.

Clark and Delia (1977) expected that older children would possess better-developed social-perception skills and would adapt their persuasive messages more than would younger children. After controlling for chronological age, however, Clark and Delia predicted that children's levels of social-perception skill still would be positively associated with the degree to which the children adapted their persuasive messages. The researchers expected that older children would produce more adapted persuasive messages than would younger children, due to the older children's better-developed social-perception skills.

Results from the study, shown in Table 4.6, were consistent with Clark and Delia's predictions. Children's construct differentiation, perspective-taking ability, and listener-adaptation skills all increased with age. After controlling for the effects of chronological age, however, Clark and Delia found that construct differentiation and perspective-taking skill still were associated with the degree of listener adaptation in children's persuasive messages (see the partial rs in Table 4.6). Taken together, these two indices of social-perception skill explained almost one-third of the variance in degree of listener adaptation ($R^2 = .32$) even after the effects of child's age had been statistically controlled.

Clark and Delia's (1977) study is important for several reasons. It was the first to document a relationship between interpersonal construct system development and the adaptation of persuasive messages; indeed, it was the first to link RCQ scores directly to any index of communicative behavior. Like the MBRS study, however, Clark and Delia's study also established an agenda for subsequent research. Following Clark and Delia's lead, a large number of researchers explored the relationships among construct system development,

Table 4.6   Correlations Among Age, Social-Perception Skills, and
                 Listener-Adapted Persuasive Strategies From the Clark and
                 Delia (1977) Study

	Age	Construct Differentiation	Perspective Taking
Construct differentiation	.33		
Perspective taking	.46	.48 (.39)	
Listener adaptation	.58	.53 (.45)	.64 (.51)

SOURCE: From "Cognitive Complexity, Social Perspective-Taking, and Functional Persuasive Skills in Second- to Ninth-Grade Children," by R. A. Clark & J. G. Delia, 1977, *Human Communication Research, 3,* p. 132. Copyright 1977 by the International Communication Association. Reprinted with permission.

social-perception processes, and listener-adapted persuasive messages in greater detail. Clark and Delia also provided a methodological exemplar for subsequent research by (a) gathering open-ended responses to hypothetical scenarios, (b) using a hierarchical scheme to code degree of listener adaptation, and (c) exploring both developmental trends and stable individual differences in construct differentiation and adaptation of persuasive messages (see Burleson, 1989). The practice of having participants state aloud or write out what they would say in response to hypothetical scenarios has come to be known as the *strategy-construction procedure.*

ELABORATING THE LINK BETWEEN CONSTRUCT SYSTEM DEVELOPMENT AND LISTENER ADAPTATION

Building on Clark and Delia's (1977) study, constructivist scholars generated a large body of research examining the relationship between people's interpersonal construct system development and their ability to produce listener-adapted persuasive messages. These studies elaborated Clark and Delia's work in five respects. First, scholars refined and expanded Clark and Delia's four-level hierarchical system for coding listener adaptation. As you may recall from Chapter 3, Delia et al. (1979) developed a nine-level hierarchy that captures in greater detail variations in the degree to which message sources adapt their persuasive messages to the wants/needs of targets (see Table 3.5). Others developed hierarchical systems for coding the degrees to which targets of persuasive appeals adapt their own refusal messages to the wants/needs of the sources (e.g., Kline & Floyd, 1990; McQuillen, 1984; see Table 3.6).

Second, scholars explored the relationship between individual differences in construct system development and the production of listener-adapted messages across a broad range of participants and situations. Aside from additional studies of elementary and secondary school students (e.g., Delia & Clark, 1977; Delia et al., 1979; Ritter, 1979; O'Keefe, Murphy, Meyers, & Babrow, 1989), scholars studied college students (e.g., Applegate, 1982; O'Keefe & Delia, 1979), teachers (e.g., Applegate, 1980a, 1980b), health care professionals (e.g., Kline & Ceropski, 1984), and parents (e.g., Applegate, Burke, Burleson, Delia, & Kline, 1985). The vast majority of these studies detected a moderate-level ($r = .35$ to .60) positive association between construct differentiation/abstractness and use of listener-adapted persuasive messages across age groups and situations (for a detailed review, see Burleson, 1987).[17]

Third, constructivist scholars attempted to show that interpersonal construct system development and degree of listener adaptation are not "spuriously" related. A spurious relationship exists when two variables covary only because both are caused by a third variable. For example, the number of firefighters at the scene of a fire and the amount of damage caused by the fire share a spurious positive association: Both increase with the size of the fire. Arguing against the possibility of spurious association, researchers have shown that interpersonal construct system development remains positively associated with listener adaptation in persuasive messages after many other variables are statistically controlled, including the message source's age (e.g., Delia et al., 1979; O'Keefe et al., 1989), sex (e.g., Applegate & Woods, 1991), socioeconomic status (e.g., Applegate et al., 1985), emotional empathy (e.g., Kline & Ceropski, 1984), and trait and state anxiety (e.g., Shepherd & Condra, 1988). Based on these findings, Burleson (1987) concludes, "While all possible spurious factors have not been studied, the variables most likely to produce spurious relationships between construct system properties and communicative behavior have been examined and found to exert little influence" (p. 330).

Fourth, scholars showed that interpersonal construct system development affects people's ability to produce listener-adapted messages during influence interactions. Although most researchers, following Clark and Delia (1977), used the strategy-construction procedure, a few observed face-to-face interaction (Applegate, 1980b, 1982; Kline & Ceropski, 1984; O'Keefe & Shepherd, 1987). For example, Applegate (1982) had 145 undergraduates complete measures of construct differentiation and abstractness, and then write out what they would say in response to two hypothetical persuasion scenarios. Later, 50 of these students were matched into 25 pairs of strangers and scheduled to return. When each pair arrived at the laboratory, the experimenter

> showed them a five dollar bill and told [them] that for the next ten minutes each was to persuade the other to let him/her have the five dollars using the best arguments each could muster. The students were instructed not to role play but to

provide realistic arguments showing why he/she should get the five dollars rather than the partner. The only rule was that they could not divide the money evenly. One was to get the five dollars, the other nothing. They were told that if after ten minutes neither had convinced the other, each would receive one dollar. (Applegate, 1982, p. 280)

These interactions were videotaped, and coders identified the number of arguments made by each party. Coders then scored each argument for degree of listener adaptation using Delia et al.'s (1979) nine-level hierarchical system. Participants were scored for the highest-level arguments they used during the interaction. After completing the interaction, participants also wrote down their impressions of their partners.

Several findings from Applegate's (1982) study are relevant here (see Table 4.7). As in prior research, construct differentiation and abstractness both were positively associated with the highest-level strategy that participants included in their written messages. More important, construct abstractness also was positively associated with the highest-level strategy that participants used during the influence interaction ($r = .67$). Although construct differentiation, as measured by the RCQ, was not significantly associated with listener adaptation during interaction ($r = .18$), a measure of the degree of differentiation in participants' postinteraction impressions of their partners was associated with their listener adaptation during interaction ($r = .32$). Thus the constructivist analysis of listener-adapted communication appears to provide insight into how people produce persuasive messages during interaction.

Fifth and finally, scholars sought more detailed insights into exactly how interpersonal construct system development enables people to generate listener-adapted messages. Several researchers asked participants, after they completed the strategy-construction procedure, to provide rationales for why they had said what they had in their persuasive messages (Delia et al., 1979; O'Keefe & Delia, 1979). Using these and other methods, scholars determined that persons with highly differentiated and abstract constructs, compared with those with less differentiated/abstract constructs, were more adept at (a) identifying communication-relevant differences between multiple targets in the same situation (Delia & Clark, 1977), (b) generating arguments of any kind to support their requests (Applegate, 1982; O'Keefe & Delia, 1979), (c) selecting arguments that appeal to particular message targets rather than to "anyone" (Burke & Clark, 1982; O'Keefe & Delia, 1979), and (d) anticipating potential obstacles from the targets to their requests and generating responses to them (Delia et al., 1979). In general, construct differentiation and abstractness appear to enhance people's ability to take the perspectives of their targets as they produce persuasive messages.

Table 4.7   Correlations Between Construct System Development and Persuasive
             Strategies Used Within Constructed Messages and During Interaction

Variable	1	2	3	4	5	6	7	8
1. Sex								
2. Construct differentiation	.33							
3. Construct abstractness	.40	.44						
4. Number of persuasive strategies (constructed message)	.30	.53	.39					
5. Highest-level listener-adapted strategy (constructed message)	.43	.52	.65	.54				
6. Number of persuasive strategies (interaction)	.21	.18	.43	.31	.35			
7. Highest-level listener-adapted strategy (interaction)	.38	.18	.67	.42	.37	.49		
8. Differentiation of postinteraction impression of partner	.24	.50	.43	.46	.46	.25	.32	
9. Abstractness of postinteraction impression of partner	.08	.14	.30	.34	.31	.09	.36	.30

SOURCE: From "The Impact of Construct System Development on Communication and Impression Formation in Persuasive Contexts," by J. L. Applegate, 1982, *Communication Monographs, 49*, p. 286. Copyright 1982 by the Speech Communication Association. Reprinted with permission.

As I have just illustrated, the constructivist analysis of listener-adapted communication both described and explained variations in people's persuasive messages. Unlike the compliance-gaining tradition, which failed to identify many reliable predictors of strategy choice, constructivist scholars were able to document moderate-sized associations between measures of interpersonal construct system development and listener adaptation. Their success reflects that they avoided many of the pitfalls that befell compliance-gaining researchers. Rather than relying on nominal-level strategy taxonomies that failed to operationalize any specific message quality, constructivist scholars developed hierarchical coding schemes that were designed purposefully to tap the degree to which individuals adapted their persuasive messages to their targets' perspectives. Rather than investigating situational and individual-difference variables haphazardly, these researchers proposed a theoretical account of how construct system development enables people to generate listener-adapted messages, which in turn provided a rationale for determining which developmental and individual-difference variables should be studied. Finally, constructivist scholars gathered open-ended responses to hypothetical scenarios rather than likelihood-of-use ratings for preformulated strategies, arguing that the strategy-selection procedure is insensitive to the effects of developmental and individual-differences variables on listener adaptation (e.g., Burke & Clark, 1982).

Despite these strengths, the view of persuasive message production arising from Clark and Delia's work was being criticized by the mid-1980s. Critics focused on the constructivist tradition's limits: (a) the implied constructivist view of message production and (b) the methods used to study this view.

CRITICISMS OF THE CONSTRUCTIVIST TRADITION

Conceptual Criticisms

The work of early constructivists has been criticized as providing an inadequate explanation of persuasive message production on two grounds. First, the concept of "listener adaptation" presents an oversimplified view of persuasive message production. In an influential critique of their own prior work, O'Keefe and Delia (1982) argued that early constructivist research had focused on how construct system development affects whether persuaders adapt preexisting message content to the needs and wants of specific targets. Focusing solely on listener adaptation, O'Keefe and Delia noted, oversimplifies what is involved in the production of a persuasive message:

> It is simply not plausible that messages begin as packages of potential arguments or contents; obviously, messages begin as purposes. . . . Message contents are generated in relation to purposes, both the specific purposes or [goals] that grow out of the task at hand and the generalized tacit purposes that might accompany any act of communication (such as intelligibility, efficiency, and face protection). . . . It makes no sense to suppose that messages are adapted to listeners only *after* these processes have produced a potential message. (p. 51)

To move beyond this oversimplified view, O'Keefe and Delia returned to the fundamental constructivist premise that persons act based on their construals of social situations. In a nutshell, these authors argue that social-perception skills should influence whether messages sources see interpersonal goals (e.g., not making the target defensive, presenting oneself in a favorable light) as relevant and important to pursue within influence situations. Persons with highly differentiated and abstract constructs tend to form psychologically centered impressions of others; hence O'Keefe and Delia suggest that such persons also may be more likely than those with less differentiated/abstract constructs to see interpersonal goals as relevant when seeking/resisting compliance. Following this line of thinking, they argue that construct differentiation and abstractness should be positively associated with the likelihood that people will produce persuasive messages designed to accomplish multiple (i.e., both influence and interpersonal) goals. I describe and evaluate O'Keefe and Delia's position in detail in Chapter 5. For now, the key point is that producing a persuasive message involves more than just adapting arguments to particular targets. Construct differentiation/abstractness, rather than simply affecting whether people adapt their arguments and requests/refusals to specific listeners, may also affect the goals that motivate persons to produce persuasive messages in the first place.

Aside from oversimplifying message production, the listener-adaptation account also fails to explain why people vary their persuasive messages across situations. As you will recall, people distinguish compliance-gaining situations along multiple dimensions, including features of the source-target relationship (e.g., intimacy, dominance) as well as features of the request (e.g., benefits, rights; see Cody & McLaughlin, 1980). Several studies have found that persons who are seeking or resisting compliance vary their degree of listener adaptation depending on situational dimensions (Clark & Delia, 1976; Delia et al., 1979; McQuillen, 1986). For example, children from kindergarten through high school age are more likely to use requests and arguments adapted to the wants/needs of their message targets—instead of relying solely on simple requests or egocentric arguments—when they attempt to persuade an adult stranger to keep a lost puppy than when they attempt to persuade their own parents to let them have an overnight party (Clark & Delia, 1976; Delia et al., 1979). Several explanations could account for this finding, including that (a) people feel less compelled to explain the reasons underlying their requests when they are seeking compliance from an intimate (e.g., parent) rather than a nonintimate (e.g., stranger) target (Ritter, 1979; Roloff, Janiszewski, McGrath, Burns, & Manrai, 1988); (b) people anticipate fewer objections from familiar targets than from unknown targets, and hence are less likely to address counterarguments when seeking compliance from familiar targets (Delia et al., 1979); and (c) people find it easier to generate listener-adapted arguments when making altruistic requests (i.e., helping a lost puppy) than when making requests that benefit primarily themselves (i.e., getting to have a party). Unfortunately, none of these explanations received sustained attention in early constructivist work. Research in the constructivist tradition explored how construct system development enabled people to generate listener-adapted persuasive messages across situations, but paid little attention to how situational factors themselves affect people's ability and/or motivation to produce such messages.

Methodological Criticisms

In addition to these two conceptual limits, research modeled after the Clark and Delia (1977) study has been criticized on methodological grounds.

Questions have been raised about the methods used to assess construct differentiation and abstractness (i.e., the RCQ) as well as listener adaptation (i.e., the strategy-construction procedure).

Validity of the RCQ measure. Critics and defenders have engaged in vigorous debate about the convergent, divergent, and predictive validity of the RCQ measure (e.g., Allen, Mabry, Banski, & Preiss, 1991; Beatty, 1987; Burleson, Applegate, & Delia, 1991; Burleson, Waltman, & Samter, 1987; Dallinger & Hample, 1991; for a recent review of the debate, see Gastil, 1995). Of the various criticisms, the best known charges that the RCQ actually measures people's "loquacity" rather than their construct system differentiation (Beatty & Payne, 1984, 1985; Powers, Jordan, & Street, 1979). To understand this position, recall that the most common procedure for analyzing responses to the RCQ is to count the number of attributes included in impressions of liked and disliked peers. According to the critics, people who write lengthier impressions end up receiving higher scores for numbers of constructs; hence the RCQ may be nothing more than a measure of people's propensity to produce a large "amount of verbal response to stimuli" (Beatty & Payne, 1984, p. 207).

To support the claim that the RCQ measures people's loquacity, Beatty and Payne (1984) had 51 undergraduates complete the two-role version of the RCQ as well as Hale and Delia's (1976) Social Perspectives Task (i.e., the measure of perspective taking used in Clark & Delia's 1977 study; see Table 4.6). As a measure of loquacity, Beatty and Payne counted the total number of words students used in their two written impressions. Results revealed that (a) the total number of words contained in students' RCQ responses was positively associated ($r = .53$) with the total number of constructs in their responses, and (b) the total number of words contained in students' RCQ responses also was positively associated ($r = .53$) with their scores on the Social Perspectives Task. Beatty and Payne conclude that it is plausible that the RCQ measures loquacity rather than construct differentiation.

Constructivist scholars have strongly rejected the claim that the RCQ measure actually may tap loquacity rather than construct differentiation (see Burleson, Applegate, & Neuwirth, 1981; Burleson et al., 1987). First, they charge that the critics have employed an inappropriate measure of loquacity. As Burleson et al. (1987) explain:

> Because more words are required to express more constructs, the total number of words in an impression and the number of constructs appearing in that impression are (under all normal circumstances) *necessarily related.* . . . any valid test of the relationship between "loquacity" . . . and [construct differentiation] would have to employ *independent* measures for each variable. (p. 319)

Burleson et al. (1987) argue that construct differentiation and loquacity are unrelated when both are measured independently. To support this argument, they reanalyzed data from an earlier study in which each participant first completed the RCQ measure and then later engaged in a conversation with an experimental confederate who feigned emotional distress about having been "dumped" by her boyfriend (Samter & Burleson, 1984). Participants' scores on the RCQ (i.e., the number of attributes in their two impressions) were *not* significantly associated with any measure of their loquacity during the conversation, including the total number of words they spoke, the total number of turns they took, or the average number of words they spoke per conversational turn.[18] In light of these results, it seems much less plausible that the RCQ measures loquacity.

Second, constructivists have argued that interpreting the RCQ as a measure of loquacity cannot explain findings from prior research. For example, it is not clear why people would be more likely to produce requests and arguments adapted to the perspective of a specific target simply because they talk a great deal. Scores on the RCQ also have been associated with the degree to which people vary their attributions about why other persons are not complying with their requests depending on the situation (Wilson et al., 1992; Wilson & Kang, 1991). Why would loquacity affect whether people varied their attributions across situations? As Gastil (1995) concludes, "The most powerful response to these criticisms of the RCQ is that alternative understandings of what it measures must explain all of its previous correlations. . . . If rival interpretations of the RCQ are unable to subsume available data, they are not satisfactory alternatives" (p. 89).

Predictive validity of the strategy-construction procedure. Modeled after Clark and Delia's (1977) pioneering study, most research examining listener adaptation has analyzed people's open-ended responses to hypothetical scenarios. To rationalize this practice, constructivist scholars have argued that people are less likely to report using only "socially appropriate" strategies when constructing messages rather than selecting from preformulated lists, and hence the "strategy-construction" procedure is more sensitive to the effects of individual and situational variables than is the "strategy-selection" procedure (e.g., Burke & Clark, 1982; Burleson et al., 1988; Clark, 1979). A good deal of debate has ensued over the relative merits of the strategy-construction procedure versus the strategy-selection procedure (e.g., Boster, 1988; Burke, 1989; Burleson & Wilson, 1988; Neuliep, 1986; O'Hair et al., 1991; Plax et al., 1990; Sorenson et al., 1989).

In general, the strategy-construction procedure appears to have better-established predictive validity, for a broader range of message qualities, than does the strategy-construction procedure. Both constructivist scholars

(Applegate, 1980b, 1982; Kline & Ceropski, 1984) and scholars in other disciplines (e.g., Kendall & Fischler, 1984; Selman, Schorin, Stone, & Phelps, 1983) have documented moderate degrees of convergence between people's strategy constructions and their behavior during interaction. As you will recall, Applegate (1982) had undergraduates write responses to two hypothetical persuasion scenarios and then later try to convince another student whom they did not know that they (and not the other student) should get to keep $5.00. Applegate found statistically significant, albeit only moderate, convergence between the number and adaptation of arguments in written messages versus the interactive task (see Table 4.7). Specifically, the total number of arguments that students used in their two written messages was positively associated with the number of arguments they used during interaction ($r = .31$). Students' highest-level listener-adapted strategy in their written messages also predicted the highest-level strategy they used during interaction ($r = .37$). Similarly, Kline and Ceropski (1984) report moderate convergence ($rs = .33$ and $.48$) between the level of listener adaptation displayed by medical students in their written responses to two hypothetical scenarios and in their behavior during an actual patient interview, and Kendall and Fischler (1984) report moderate convergence (several $rs = .30$ to $.55$) between both parents' and children's written responses to hypothetical interpersonal problem-solving scenarios and their problem-solving behavior during a family discussion.

These studies suggest that the strategy-construction procedure is a valid method for predicting many qualities of people's persuasive messages (e.g., number of arguments, adaptation of arguments). The strategy-selection procedure, in contrast, appears to provide valid information *only* about people's general willingness to use verbally aggressive or socially inappropriate messages to gain compliance (Burleson et al., 1988; Dillard, 1988; Hunter & Boster, 1987; see the prior subsection on the predictive validity of the strategy-selection procedure). The strategy-construction procedure appears to be a valid method for investigating a much broader set of questions than can be addressed using the strategy-selection procedure.

Despite its broader utility, it is important to stress that the strategy-construction procedure still asks people to respond to hypothetical scenarios. Hence the method provides little insight into the unfolding, interdependent nature of influence interactions (see the prior subsection on the limits of hypothetical scenarios). This limitation helps explain why the degree of convergence between the strategy-construction procedure and actual behavior during influence interactions is, at best, only moderate ($r = .30$ to $.45$). Constructivist scholars have explained the lack of strong convergence by arguing that open-ended responses to hypothetical scenarios reflect people's *ability* to generate listener-adapted persuasive messages (Applegate, 1980b; Burleson, 1987).

During actual interaction, however, respondents with the ability to produce listener-adapted appeals may not do so due to performance-inhibiting factors (e.g., exhaustion, stress). Aside from performance inhibitors, however, the lack of strong convergence also reflects that the ways in which people attempt to exert influence within interaction vary depending upon how targets behave. People may be more likely to produce listener-adapted arguments when targets refuse their initial requests using a friendly rather than an unfriendly nonverbal style (Lim, 1990). People also may be more likely to produce listener-adapted arguments if targets ask questions like "What's in it for me?" Due to researchers' heavy reliance on the strategy-construction procedure, we know little about how listener-adapted persuasive appeals are produced within the sequential context of interaction.

SUMMARY OF THE CONSTRUCTIVIST TRADITION

In this section I have reviewed and critiqued the constructivist perspective on listener-adapted persuasive communication. Building on Clark and Delia's (1977) groundbreaking study, constructivist scholars have described how persuasive messages vary in terms of a single quality (i.e., degree of listener adaptation) and have generated a theoretical rationale for how developmental and individual-difference variables affect people's ability to produce listener-adapted strategies. Although the early constructivist research program avoided several pitfalls that befell the compliance-gaining tradition, the model of message production implicit within Clark and Delia's work was overly simplistic (Burleson, 1987; O'Keefe & Delia, 1982). In an attempt to develop more plausible models, scholars have begun studying the psychological processes by which people actually generate messages in detail (e.g., O'Keefe & Lambert, 1995; Waldron & Applegate, 1994; Wilson, 1990, 1995; see also Burleson & Caplan, 1998). As with the compliance-gaining tradition, questions and insights arising from the early constructivist tradition provided an important impetus for contemporary theory and research on persuasive message production.

From Strategy Repertoires to Goal Pursuit

To this point, I have argued that the "compliance-gaining" and "constructivist" traditions represent the genesis of research on persuasive message production. Although different in many respects, the research questions and methods employed by researchers in both traditions are similar in many respects. Specifically, both compliance-gaining and constructivist scholars have (a) analyzed influence messages using strategy typologies, (b) attempted to identify individual-difference and situational predictors of strategy choice, and (c) relied heavily on responses to hypothetical scenarios. In addition to similar research questions and methods, both groups have also shared deeper implicit assumptions about the nature of message production. In their chapter on "interpersonal influence" in the first edition of the *Handbook of Interpersonal Communication*, Seibold et al. (1985) argued that the compliance-gaining and constructivist literatures both assume a highly calculated, conscious, and static view of message production in which message sources weigh the costs and benefits of a host of strategic options. Labeling this view the "strategic choice model," Seibold et al. argued that both traditions seemed to assume that message sources have the following:

1. Conscious awareness of the influence "situation"

2. Sufficient time to assess the situation rationally and consider options

3. The intention to formulate a plan designed to accomplish a well-defined outcome

4. A diverse, complex, and differentiated repertoire of strategies and tactics to draw upon

5. Sufficient awareness and individual perspective-taking ability to weigh the consequences of enacting each strategic alternative

6. An ability to choose some strategies and forgo others (p. 557)

In response to these criticisms, scholars from both the constructivist and compliance-gaining traditions turned their attention to developing more plausible models of persuasive message production. As we will see in Chapter 5, the common thread running through this newer work is the concept of "interaction goals." Within the constructivist tradition, Barbara O'Keefe has reframed the listener-adaptation model of message production by exploring how individuals (a) attempt to reconcile multiple conflicting goals within messages (O'Keefe & Delia, 1982) and (b) differ in their conceptions of how multiple conflicting goals can be resolved (O'Keefe, 1988). Within the compliance-gaining tradition, Cody and his colleagues (Canary, Cody, & Marston, 1986; Cody et al., 1994) have explored how individuals organize their knowledge about compliance-gaining situations around influence goals, and Dillard (1990a) has proposed a goal-driven model of persuasive message production. To summarize, contemporary researchers examining persuasive message production share a focus on how individuals form, alter, and pursue goals during interaction.

Summary

Contemporary theory and research on persuasive message production has emerged from earlier programs of research on "compliance-gaining" and "constructivism." Building on the work of Miller et al. (1977), compliance-gaining researchers examined situational and individual-difference variables that predict people's choice of strategies for seeking and resisting compliance. Building on Clark and Delia's (1977) study, constructivist scholars have explored developmental and individual differences in how people adapt persuasive strategies to particular message targets. Both research traditions have been guided implicitly by a "strategy-selection" metaphor for persuasive message production. After reviewing these two research traditions, I have illustrated how questions arising from both traditions spurred newer work on persuasive message production. It appears that the metaphor guiding contemporary work on persuasive message production has shifted from "strategy selection" to "goal pursuit."

Notes

1. Miller et al. (1977) conducted a one-way repeated measures analysis of variance (ANOVA) to assess whether likelihood-of-use ratings for each of the 16 compliance-seeking strategies differed significantly across the four hypothetical scenarios. Although they do not report F values, Miller et al. note that the probability levels for 15 of the 16 tests were < .0001, whereas the p level for the strategy of liking was .019 (p. 46). Miller et al. did not conduct a 2 × 2 repeated-measures ANOVA; hence it is not possible to determine whether the independent variables of interpersonal/noninterpersonal relationships and short-term/long-term consequences interacted in their effects on likelihood-of-use ratings. Miller et al. also do not report estimates of effect size.

2. As one indication of its importance, the MBRS study in 1989 received the Charles H. Woolbert Research Award from the Speech Communication Association for "Scholarship of Exceptional Originality and Influence."

3. Although Sillars (1980) does not investigate individual differences in strategy choice, these also could be explained by an SEU model. For example, individuals in general might differ in the values they place on preventing relational damage (RR), or in their judgments of the persuasive efficacy of particular strategies (p_1).

4. Sillars's (1980) manipulation of the shade-tree scenario almost certainly confounded interpersonal/noninterpersonal relationships with the message source's rights to persuade. In the interpersonal scenario, the tree is on your own (rather than your neighbor's) property. As joint owner, you have a much greater right to determine whether the tree should stand or fall in the interpersonal scenario compared with the noninterpersonal scenario.

5. In a nutshell, Hunter and Boster (1978, 1987) argue that a single dimension underlies likelihood-of-use ratings for multiple strategies, but this dimension is related in a *nonlinear* fashion to use ratings for any single strategy. In any given situation, an individual will give all of the strategies above his or her ethical threshold high scores for likelihood of use and all strategies below that threshold low scores. Increasingly appropriate strategies are *not* increasingly likely to be

used in a linear fashion; rather, strategies below the threshold are not used (regardless of their relative appropriateness to each other), and those above the threshold are used. One consequence is that likelihood-of-use scores for different strategies (especially those at opposite ends of the continuum) also are not associated in linear fashion. Because factor analysis presumes that the variables being analyzed are linearly related, Hunter and Boster (1987) argue that prior studies have produced spurious results.

6. Hertzog and Bradac (1984) identify four dimensions: resistance, values/rules, gender relevant/ irrelevant, and dominance. Resistance, however, also appears to tap variation in the degree of message source-target intimacy. The values/rules dimension appears to contrast situations having high self-benefits and low rights with situations having high other-benefits and high rights.

7. Meta-analysis involves integrating findings from multiple studies that have investigated the same variables, such as sex differences in ratings for specific compliance-seeking strategies. Each study in a meta-analysis is treated as a single participant would be in an individual study. Results from individual studies are converted to a common metric. The researcher then computes the statistics to assess the mean level of effect across studies. Such estimates of effect sizes tend to be very stable, because they are based on data from multiple studies (i.e., a large number of participants). The researcher also computes statistics to assess whether findings across studies are more variable than one would expect simply due to sampling error. When more variability exists across studies than would be expected by chance, the scholar conducting the meta-analysis can code individual studies for possible moderating variables. When less variability exists across studies than would be expected by chance, strong evidence is present for a general relationship between two variables. For more information on meta-analysis, see Hunter, Schmidt, and Jackson (1982).

8. Vinson and Biggers (1993) challenge the assumption that message choice is solely a function of the target's emotional response even with data from the strategy-selection procedure. In their study, they found that participants' own emotional responses to compliance-gaining scenarios were better predictors of the participants' willingness to use verbally aggressive strategies (i.e., their summed likelihood-of-use scores) than were participants' perceptions of the targets' likely emotional responses.

9. Notice that Hunter and Boster's (1978, 1987) ethical threshold model, when applied to compliance-seeking *strategies*, makes this same assumption.

10. The content of these two role plays was *not* identical to the content of the two hypothetical situations to which the students had responded 2 weeks earlier, because having students role-play the exact same scenarios for which they already had provided likelihood-of-use ratings would have raised obvious connections between the two phases of the study. Rather than using the same scenarios, Dillard (1988) developed matched pairs of scenarios. For example, the source in scenario A had to ask the target to run a pressing errand for him or her because the source needed to wait for an important phone call, whereas the source in matching role-play scenario C had to ask the target to drive him or her somewhere immediately rather than watching TV so that the source could complete a pressing errand. Although different in substance, scenarios A and C were rated in a pretest as not differing on any of Cody and McLaughlin's (1980) six situational dimensions. The same was true of scenarios B and D.

11. You may have noted that these results also have relevance for Hunter and Boster's (1978, 1987) ethical threshold model. Although people's summed likelihood-of-use scores correlate positively with ratings of verbal aggressiveness when seeking compliance, correlations between these two indices are not strong enough to suggest that they are alternative measures of the same construct (see Dillard, 1988, p. 179).

12. Since publication of the Jackson and Jacobs (1983) article, substantial debate has arisen over the most appropriate methods for designing and analyzing data from experiments that use multiple examples of strategy categories (see, e.g., "Colloquy on Generalization," 1988; and the special issue of *Communication Monographs*, 1989, vol. 56, no. 4). All sides, however, agree that researchers need to use multiple messages in order to draw valid generalizations about compliance-seeking strategies.

13. This subsection focuses on the problems of drawing generalizations about abstract compliance-seeking strategies from single concrete messages. However, the same concerns arise when generalizations about an abstract situational dimension, such as intimacy or relational consequences, are drawn even though only a single hypothetical scenario has been used to illustrate each level of the dimension (see Jackson & Backus, 1982; Jackson & Jacobs, 1983).

14. Although a few studies have used alternatives measures to assess particular indices of interpersonal construct system development (e.g., Applegate, 1982; O'Keefe & Delia, 1979), the vast majority have used Crockett's (1965) RCQ measure.

15. *Interpersonal construct differentiation* refers to the sheer number of interpersonal constructs that a person spontaneously uses to interpret and evaluate the actions of others. *Cognitive complexity* is a broader term that describes the overall character of a person's interpersonal construct system. Cognitively complex persons are those who possess differentiated, abstract, and integrated systems of interpersonal constructs.

16. As readers may have noticed, the study that I am describing here (Clark & Delia, 1977) is based on the same data as a study described in Chapter 2 (Clark & Delia, 1976). In their 1976 study, Clark and Delia introduced the concept of listener adaptation, explained the rationale for using a hierarchical coding scheme to tap listener adaptation, and reported how children's scores on the coding scheme increased with maturation. In their pioneering 1977 study, Clark and Delia reported how children's scores on measures of social-perception skill also increase with maturation and showed that these skills still predict children's degree of listener adaptation even after the effects of chronological age have been statistically controlled.

17. To my knowledge, only two published studies in which the researchers used procedures similar to those used by Clark and Delia (1977) have failed to detect a statistically significant relationship between interpersonal construct system development and listener-adapted persuasive communication (Hecht, Boster, & LaMer, 1989; Ritter, 1979). Burleson (1987) reviews 17 studies that detect a significant relationship.

18. As predicted, participants' RCQ scores were significantly associated with several qualitative features of their conversational behavior, such as the proportion of turns in which they tried to comfort the experimental confederate (Burleson et al., 1987).

5

The Second Generation

Persuasive Message Production
as Goal Pursuit

Looking Ahead . . .

People produce messages during influence interactions to accomplish goals. This chapter explicates the concept of goal, draws a distinction between primary and secondary goals, and discusses procedures for measuring people's goals. Following this, research on both influence (primary) and secondary goals is reviewed, and a cognitive rules model of how people form and modify goals as influence interactions unfold is described. The chapter concludes with a discussion of some criticisms of a goals perspective and a preview of the need for theories about how individuals translate goals into action.

The assumption that communicative action is strategic and goal-oriented is virtually a given starting point of communication research. (Tracy, 1991a, p. 1)

There are few properties of human communication more frequently noted than that interpersonal messages function in the service of multiple, social goals. (Greene & Lindsey, 1989, p. 120)

The notion that persons pursue multiple goals in their interactions with others has achieved the status of a truism among interpersonal-communication researchers. (Berger, 1995, p. 144)

The concept of goal has become a centerpiece in theorizing about message production. (Wilson, 1995, p. 4)

A s the above quotes make clear, communication scholars typically presume that people pursue goals during interaction. Goals have received tremendous attention from interpersonal communication researchers over the past 15 years. During the spring of 1988, just before I left graduate school to take my first faculty position, I attended the Ninth Annual Temple University Conference on Discourse Analysis. That year's conference, sponsored by Professor Karen Tracy, brought together faculty and graduate students from varied theoretical and methodological backgrounds to discuss the promise, as well as the dilemmas, of the then-emerging consensus that "communication is goal oriented." An edited book (Tracy, 1991b) and special journal issue (Tracy & Coupland, 1990) resulted from the conference. Aside from these works, both the second (Miller, Cody, & McLaughlin, 1994) and third (Berger, in press) editions of the *Handbook of Interpersonal Communication* include chapters on goals. These chapters are among only a handful that discuss "fundamental units" for studying interpersonal communication.

Contemporary theory and research on persuasive message production offer no exception to this trend. A new generation of theories about persuasive message production research has emerged, guided by the metaphor of "goal pursuit" (see Seibold, Cantrill, & Meyers, 1994; Wilson, 1997). In this chapter, I attempt to explain what all the fuss is about. In the following sections, I define the concept of goal, review research on two different types of goals, and present a cognitive rules model of how people form goals. Near the end of the chapter, I discuss some issues related to how goals are translated into action, in order to preview the content of upcoming chapters.

Conceptualizing Goals

WHAT ARE INTERACTION GOALS?

Goals are future states of affairs that individuals desire to attain or maintain (Dillard, 1997). Desired end states become *interaction goals* when individuals must communicate and coordinate with others to achieve those states (Clark & Delia, 1979). For example, my spouse and I often take turns performing certain tasks in the evening, with one of us driving our younger children to activities while the other cleans up after dinner. Getting the kitchen clean is a goal that, in principle, I can accomplish myself. Convincing my spouse on a specific evening to both drive our children and clean up, so that I can return to my office to do some work, is a goal that can be achieved only through interaction.

Although pursued through communication, interaction goals are part of the *cognitive* (i.e., mental) rather than the behavioral domain. Imagine that a stranger approaches you and asks, "Excuse me, can you tell me how to get to the library?" Even though the goal underlying this question seems obvious at first glance, literally, you can observe the stranger's behavior but you must infer his or her goal. It is possible, for instance, that the stranger is using this question as an opening line to strike up a conversation, rather than, or in addition to, as a means of obtaining directions. Goals motivate and explain behaviors, but they are not behaviors themselves. Goals and behaviors share a complex and indeterminate relationship (Craig, 1986; Tracy, 1991a).

Interaction goals are end states desired by individuals. People pursue goals in situations, but, as conceptualized here, *individuals have goals, whereas situations do not* (Benoit, 1990). People possess vast stores of knowledge about goals that typically might be pursued in situations; however, people possess those goals only when they themselves desire to reach those end states. Put differently, one may know about an interaction goal without adopting it as one's own.

In general, I assume that interaction goals are *proactive;* that is, people strive to accomplish goals (Tracy, 1989; Wilson & Putnam, 1990). As Kellermann (1992) argues:

> Communication is goal-directed. . . . We don't communicate (i.e., engage in symbolic exchange) randomly. Symbols are not selected like poker chips by reaching one's hand into a bag and drawing them out in random combinations. Symbols are selected and structured. Symbols are also not cast willy-nilly for whomever might wish to grab one going by. Even when we beam symbols into outer space in a search for extraterrestrial intelligence, these symbols are organized and transmitted for a purpose. (p. 289)

It is true that individuals at times invent goals, after the fact, to make sense of their actions (see Donohue, 1990). Even some cases of retrospective sense making, however, are motivated proactively by goals.[1] Throughout this chapter, I explore how people's actions of seeking and resisting compliance are motivated, explained, shaped, and constrained by interaction goals.

By describing interaction goals as proactive, I do *not* mean to imply (a) that people are highly conscious of their goals, (b) that people consciously plan how to accomplish goals in advance, or (c) that people's goals are static. To illustrate these points: Imagine that I receive a telephone call from a teacher saying that my stepdaughter Lisette is earning a grade of D in her English class. Given these circumstances, I might set up a time to discuss the issue with Lisette and plan the general nature of my remarks in advance. On the other hand, if Lisette shows me a D on her report card without any prior warning, I might launch into some remarks about why she needs to earn a better grade immediately, without advance planning and without much thought about exactly what I hope to accomplish. Imagine that you stop me in the middle of the conversation and ask, "What are you doing?" Regardless of whether my remarks are rehearsed or spontaneous, I would reply, "I am trying to convince Lisette that she needs to improve her performance in English." My remarks, in either case, are motivated proactively by this goal. Finally, imagine that I have made a mistake in reading the grade on Lisette's report card, such that I thought it said D when actually her grade is a B. My goals would change quickly after Lisette informs me of my mistake, but my behavior at that point still would be motivated proactively by goals (e.g., wanting to reduce my embarrassment and make amends with Lisette). As this example shows, people have greater awareness of their interaction goals under certain conditions, such as when their expectations are violated, their initial attempts to accomplish goals are thwarted, or their goals come into conflict (Motley, 1986; von Cranach, Kalbermatten, Indermuhle, & Gugler, 1982). In general, however, people often have only limited and fleeting awareness of their interaction goals (Greene, 2000; Kellermann, 1992; Wilson & Putnam, 1990).

My claims in the preceding paragraph raise questions about how inter-action goals can be measured. If an actor often has limited awareness of his or her goals, and those goals can change quickly and may be only partially evident from the actor's behavior, then how can anyone (including the actor) really know whether he or she is pursuing a goal? Researchers are using a variety of techniques to address these potential obstacles to measuring goals, including the following:

1. Inferring participants' goals from examples of their discourse, interpreted in context (e.g., O'Keefe & Shepherd, 1987; Tracy, 1991a)

2. Asking participants to write out open-ended descriptions of their goals, or to complete closed-ended rating scales evaluating the importance of various goals, within hypothetical scenarios (e.g., Kline, 1991; Wilson, 1990; Wilson, Aleman, & Leatham, 1998)

3. Asking participants to complete closed-ended rating scales evaluating the importance of various goals within episodes recalled from their own lives (e.g., Meyer, 1994a)

4. Using task instructions to manipulate the assigned importance of various goals during spoken monologues or written dialogues, and then asking participants

to complete closed-ended scales rating the importance of various goals during their performance (e.g., Greene & Lindsey, 1989; Tracy, 1984)

5. Asking participants to complete closed-ended rating scales or open-ended lists of their rationales for choosing *not* to use particular messages in hypothetical scenarios (e.g., Dillard, Segrin, & Harden, 1989; Hample & Dallinger, 1987a)

6. Asking participants to provide cued or uncued lists of their thoughts as they watch videotape of a conversation in which they have just taken part, and then content analyzing the lists of thoughts for instances of goals (e.g., Cai, 1994; Cegala & Waldron, 1992; Waldron, Cegala, Sharkey, & Teboul, 1990)

7. Asking participants to provide closed-ended ratings of the importance of various goals at multiple points in time as they watch videotape of a conversation in which they have just taken part (e.g., Waldron, 1997)

8. Asking participants to "speak aloud" everything they are thinking as they go about generating a message, or their plan for a message, and then content analyzing the spoken thoughts for instances of goals (e.g., Berger & Jordan, 1992; Daly, Weber, Vangelisti, Maxwell, & Neel, 1989)

Evidence regarding the reliability and validity of these techniques is reviewed elsewhere (Craig, 1986; Greene, 1988; Waldron & Cegala, 1992; Wilson & Putnam, 1990), hence I will not address these methods in detail here. Each has its strengths and limitations; for example, some methods are better suited for capturing how goals change quickly during conversation, whereas others are better suited for making people aware of interaction goals that typically remain implicit or tacit. Despite these differing strengths and limitations, research using a variety of these methods is providing a consistent picture of people's goals during interpersonal influence episodes.

PRIMARY AND SECONDARY GOALS

Individuals often pursue multiple goals while seeking and resisting compliance (Dillard et al., 1989; Hample & Dallinger, 1987a; Kline & Floyd, 1990; Saeki & O'Keefe, 1994; Schrader & Dillard, 1998). According to Dillard (1990a), participants define influence episodes on the basis of the goals or objectives that account for their interaction. During a compliance-gaining interaction, the message source's *primary goal* by definition is a desire to modify the target's behavior. The primary goal exerts a "push" force that motivates the message source to speak, hence it also helps explain why the interaction is taking place. The primary goal "brackets the situation. It helps segment the flow of behavior into a meaningful unit; it says what the interaction is about" (Dillard et al., 1989, p. 21). The primary goal offers a "frame" within which participants recognize "what is going on" and thus signals expectations about each party's identity, rights, and obligations (Goffman, 1959).

The following hypothetical scenarios help to illustrate the concept of primary goal:

Scenario 1: You've known your friend Chris for 3 years. Chris has spent one semester at a community college and is now thinking about quitting school and going to work full-time. In your opinion, a college education is essential for career opportunities. You believe that if Chris quits school now, he or she will never finish any more college course work. You want Chris to stay in school. You speak to Chris.

Scenario 2: You've known your friend Chris for 3 years. You are going to Florida over spring break and do not want to leave your car at the airport for a week while you are gone. You want Chris to take you to the airport for your flight, which takes off at 8:00 A.M. this Saturday morning. You'd also like Chris to pick you up when you return next week. You speak to Chris.

What is "going on" in each of these scenarios? Does it seem likely that you are about to offer Chris advice and hope that he or she will take it into consideration in the first scenario, whereas in the second you are about to ask Chris a favor and hope that he or she will grant it? Notice that in the second scenario, but not in the first, it would seem sensible for you to lead up to what you ultimately want to say to Chris by saying, "Chris, can I ask you a big favor?" Similarly, in the first scenario, but not the second, it would make sense for you to lead into your conversation with Chris by saying, "Chris, can I give you some advice?"[2] In both scenarios, the primary goal (i.e., giving advice or asking a favor) is what motivates you to seek compliance. It also provides a culturally viable explanation for why, at the moment, each interaction is taking place.

Although the primary goal defines a compliance-gaining interaction, it often is not the message source's only goal. In Scenario 1, you may want to give advice without (a) appearing to be butting into Chris's affairs, (b) making Chris defensive, and/or (c) damaging your relationship. In Scenario 2, you may want to ask your favor without (a) appearing to lack the ability to handle your own problems, (b) imposing too much on Chris, and/or (c) making Chris feel like he or she is being used. These latter concerns are *secondary goals*, or objectives "that derive from more general motivations that are recurrent in a person's life" (Dillard et al., 1989, p. 20). Whereas the primary goal exerts a "push" toward action, secondary goals exert a "pull" force that acts to "shape, and typically to constrain, the behaviors whose overriding purpose is to alter the behavior of the target" (Dillard et al., 1989, p. 21).

The labels *primary* and *secondary* have been taken to imply that the desire to seek, or resist, compliance always is more important than other goals (Shepherd, 1992, 1998), but they are not intended here in that sense.[3] In this context, *primary* and *secondary* refer to the functions and directional forces of goals, rather than to their importance. Influence goals are primary only in the sense that, for a point in time, they may frame what an interaction is about and energize the actors.

Having explicated the concepts of primary and secondary goals, I turn now to a review of research on the nature of people's influence (primary) and secondary goals.

Defining the Situation: Research on Influence Goals

A number of researchers have proposed typologies of influence goals, or lists of specific reasons individuals seek compliance. Some of these researchers have asked managers about specific goals that motivate their upward, lateral, or downward influence attempts within work organizations (e.g., Kipnis, Schmidt, & Wilkinson, 1980; Yukl & Falbe, 1990), whereas others have asked college students about specific goals that motivate influence attempts with friends, family members, classmates, and coworkers (e.g., Cody, Canary, & Smith, 1994; Rule, Bisanz, & Kohn, 1985). Although these scholars have conducted studies employing different participants, methods, stimulus materials, and relational contexts, several specific influence goals have emerged consistently. Table 5.1 provides information about eight specific influence goals that have emerged across studies.

Two typologies have been developed in studies with organizational managers. Kipnis et al. (1980) asked 165 U.S. American managers (75% male) from engineering and technical organizations to "describe an incident in which they actually succeeded in getting either their boss, a co-worker, or a subordinate to do something they wanted" (p. 441). Of this group of participants, 62 described incidents involving their bosses, 49 described incidents involving coworkers, and 54 described incidents involving subordinates. In their descriptions, participants recalled what they wanted from their targets, what they (the participants) did, whether their targets resisted, and what the participants did in response to any resistance. After reading these descriptions, Kipnis et al. proposed a list of five general categories of influence goals. Subsequent studies have used slight variations on this typology, often grouping the five or six specific influence goals into the larger categories of "personal goals" (i.e., those that benefit primarily the employee him- or herself, such as asking for a raise) versus

Table 5.1   A Comparison of Five Studies on Types of Influence Goals

Cody et al. (1994)	Dillard (1989)	Kipnis et al. (1980)	Rule et al. (1985)	Yukl et al. (1995)
Gain assistance (friend, professor)	Gain assistance	Obtain assistance	Agency/assist	Get assistance
Share activity (friend)	Share activity	—	Activity	—
Give advice (friend, parent)	Give advice (lifestyle, health)	Initiate change	Change habit (health)	Change work (procedures)
(De)Escalate relationship	Change relationship	—	Change relationship	—
Enforce obligation	—	Get others to do their jobs	—	Change work (follow rules)
Obtain permission (parent, professor)	—	—	Get permission	Get support (approval)
—	—	Obtain benefits	—	Get benefit
Elicit support for third party	—	—	Help third party	—

"organizational goals" (i.e., those that potentially benefit the larger organization, such as advocating a procedural change to improve coordination between different departments; Erez & Rim, 1982; Schmidt & Kipnis, 1984).

Based on previous research on the nature of managerial work as well as reports from 197 employed MBA students on how frequently they pursued various objectives at work, Yukl and Falbe (1990) initially proposed a typology of eight influence goals. After conducting a subsequent pilot study in which they analyzed diaries and critical incidents, Yukl, Guinan, and Sottolano (1995) further grouped Yukl and Falbe's initial typology into five categories of influence goals.

Aside from studies of organizational influence episodes, three investigations have used diverse methods to identify influence goals commonly pursued by undergraduate students. Rule et al. (1985) asked 32 male and 32 female Canadian undergraduates, "What kinds of things do people persuade ____ to do?" (p. 1129). Participants initially listed as many responses as they could when the target individuals were specified as "other people," then again when the targets were "their friends," and finally when the targets were either "their fathers" or "their enemies." Based on previous research and responses from their participants, the researchers developed a list of 12 specific influence goals.

Dillard (1989) used a three-step procedure to develop a typology of influence goals. He initially asked 152 U.S. American college undergraduates (59% female) and 49 employees of retail and service businesses (M age = 27 years; 75% female) to provide a written description "of a situation in which they tried to persuade someone to do something and to describe their goal in that influence attempt" (p. 296). Participants were instructed that the target should be someone they knew well, that the influence attempt should have involved trying to change the target's behavior, and that the situation should be one in which they were either successful (n = 87 participants) or unsuccessful (n = 104 participants) at getting the target to comply. After analyzing the goal descriptions for topical content (e.g., health matters, entertainment), structure (i.e., who benefited from the request), and clarity, three coders identified a total of 59 unique goal statements in these written descriptions.

In the second phase of Dillard's (1989) study, each participant in a sample of 100 additional undergraduates was given a deck of 59 index cards with one goal statement printed on each card. Each of these participants completed a Q-sort task in which he or she sorted the cards into piles so that all of the goal statements in each pile were alike and the statements in each pile were different from the statements in other piles. Data from the individual participants then were subjected to cluster analysis.[4] In the third phase, each of 240 additional undergraduates rated a subset of the 59 goal statements in terms of a number of dimensions along which compliance-gaining situations can differ (e.g., benefit of compliance to the message source, benefit to the target, specificity of the source's request). Dillard used these dimensional ratings to help interpret the clusters of goal statements identified in the second phase of the study. Using these procedures, Dillard developed a typology of six influence goals that are common in close, personal relationships.

Taking a different approach, Cody et al. (1994) asserted that influence goals can be thought of as different points at which the multiple dimensions of compliance-gaining situations intersect. Favors, for example, are requests that benefit primarily the message source rather than the target. Typically, we do not ask favors of complete strangers. Hence situations defined by the influence goal "obtaining a favor" should share the qualities of having high source benefits, low target benefits, and at least moderate relational intimacy. To test this reasoning, Cody et al. reanalyzed data from the Cody et al. (1986) study, in which 1,064 U.S. American undergraduates from three different universities each had recalled a compliance-gaining episode from his or her own life and then rated the situation along seven situational dimensions (e.g., rights to request, perceived resistance, source benefits). A variety of message targets were included in these recalled situations, including parents, friends, romantic partners, roommates, and professors (for more details about the Cody et al., 1986, study, see Chapter 4). After subjecting these earlier data to cluster analysis, Cody et al. (1994) proposed a typology of 12 influence goals. In some cases, the situations in each cluster were defined both by a common goal and by a common message target. For example, Cody et al.'s undergraduate participants seemed to distinguish two types of situations defined by the influence goal of giving advice: one cluster involving advice to friends and a second involving advice to parents.

To summarize, these studies have (a) included college student and non-student participants, (b) investigated episodes with a variety of targets, (c) used different stimuli to elicit data about goals, and (d) used both quantitative and qualitative methods to establish goal categories. Despite this diversity, these studies have produced a number of similar findings. In particular, eight specific influence goals have been identified in at least two of the five studies just reviewed (see Table 5.1). The influence goals of "gaining assistance" (e.g., favors) and "giving advice" emerged in all five studies. Four goals (obtain permission, enforce obligations, share activity, de/escalate relationship) appeared in three of the five studies, and the final two (obtain personal benefit, elicit support for third party) were detected in two studies. Although managers and college students in some cases report different influence goals (e.g., obtain personal benefits versus share activity), in many cases both groups report similar goals (e.g., gain assistance, enforce obligations).

The fact that these studies have produced similar findings is important for three reasons. First, these findings help explain why individuals are able to define compliance-gaining episodes in terms of underlying primary goals. In order for individuals to make sense of an unfolding compliance-gaining episode based on the influence goal, it seems necessary that at least some goals should be common within a given culture. As Dillard (1990a) explains: "It is important to emphasize that these investigations are not simply exercises in list making. Rather, illumination of the substance of goals provides some clues as to what constitutes culturally viable explanation and to the ways that compliance seekers conceive of their own actions" (p. 46).

A second, related reason these findings are important is that people appear to organize their knowledge about seeking and resisting compliance around influence goals. People not only share an understanding about which specific influence goals are common, they appear to associate a wide range of information with each influence goal. This information includes the following:

1. *Situational dimensions:* For example, the goal of asking a favor is associated with high self-benefits, low target benefits, and relational intimacy, whereas the goal of giving advice typically involves high target benefits and moderate perceived resistance (Cody et al., 1994; Dillard, 1989; Rule et al., 1985).

2. *Message targets:* For example, people typically think about pursuing the goal of seeking permission from targets such as parents and bosses rather than from friends or coworkers (Cody et al., 1994; Rule et al., 1985; Yukl et al., 1995).

3. *Threats to identity:* For example, people are more likely to worry that they could appear to be "nosy" when they pursue the goal of giving advice than when they ask a favor. In turn, people are more likely to worry that they could appear to be too "lazy" to handle their own problems when they ask a favor than when they give advice (Cai & Wilson, 2000; Wilson et al., 1998; Wilson & Kunkel, 2000).

4. *Emotions:* For example, people associate the emotion of anger more strongly with the goal of having to enforce unfulfilled obligations than with most other influence goals (Canary, Cody, & Marston, 1986; Wilson, 1990).

Given this wealth of information, several scholars suggest that persons develop "schemas" about compliance gaining that are organized around influence goals (Bisanz & Rule, 1990; Meyer, 1996, 2000; Rule et al., 1985; Smith, 1982, 1984). A *schema* is "a cognitive structure that represents knowledge about a concept or type of stimulus, including its attributes and the relations among those attributes" (Fiske & Taylor, 1991, p. 98). People develop schemas based on repeated experience, be it direct or indirect, with groups of people, objects, or events. We hold schemas about roles (e.g., professors), situations (e.g., job interviews), persons (e.g., extroverts), relationships (e.g., stages of "breaking up"), and even ourselves (see Fiske & Taylor, 1991; Smith & Wilson, 1996). In each case, our schemas represent our knowledge about attributes typically associated with particular domains of experience (e.g., many professors are absentminded; saying that you "just want to be friends" is one way of trying to redefine a romantic relationship) as well as associations among these attributes. Schemas serve numerous functions during conversation, including setting up expectations about what is and is not likely to occur, directing attention toward specific pieces of information, suggesting inferences about other persons that go beyond what we literally have observed, and helping us to integrate large amounts of information into a coherent picture (see Brewer & Nakamura, 1984; Fiske & Taylor, 1991). Like any type of generic knowledge, schemas can create perceptual problems. By relying too rigidly on schemas, we may make inaccurate inferences based on nothing that we have directly observed about other parties, fail to remember evidence contradicting our schemas, fail to modify our schemas in light of contradictory evidence, and/or communicate our expectations about others in ways that set off self-fulfilling prophecies. Despite such risks, schemas play a vital role in interpersonal communication, for without them we would perpetually be like aliens from another universe who know nothing about the circumstances of human life (Smith & Wilson, 1996).

The research reviewed above suggests that people do *not* develop a single schema for "seeking compliance." Instead, people appear to organize their knowledge about compliance gaining in a more differentiated fashion; that is, they form multiple situation schemas, each of which is defined by a specific influence goal such as wanting to "give advice," "ask a favor," or "share an activity." I address some theories linking situation schemas to what people actually say when seeking and resisting compliance in Chapter 7; here it is sufficient to note that we abstract schemas about compliance gaining based on influence goals.

A third reason studies of influence goals are important is that people vary how they seek and/or resist compliance depending on the underlying influence goal. Presumably, we organize our knowledge about compliance gaining around influence goals, in part, because we experience noticeably different interactions during episodes defined by different goals. Results from several studies using varied methods and participants support this claim. Depending on the specific influence goal, people report being more or less likely to (a) confront their targets and actually seek compliance, (b) be direct about what they want, (c) provide explicit reasons to support their requests, (d) anticipate that their targets will raise particular obstacles, (e) persist in the face of initial resistance by their targets, (f) use particular compliance-seeking strategies both before and after encountering resistance, and (g) succeed at getting their targets to comply (Cai & Wilson, 2000; Canary et al., 1986; Cody et al., 1994; Dillard, 1989; Kipnis et al., 1980; Roloff & Janiszewski, 1989; Smith, Cody, LoVette, & Canary, 1990; Wilson et al., 1998; Wilson, Anastasiou, Kim, Aleman, & Oetzel, 2000; Wilson & Kunkel, 2000; Yukl et al., 1995).

In sum, individuals share similar understandings about what are common reasons for seeking compliance. Individuals also appear to organize their own knowledge about compliance gaining around influence goals. Although people decide what to say when seeking or resisting compliance based in part on qualities of the influence goal, they also orient to other concerns during compliance-gaining interactions.

Multiple Goals as Constraints: Research on Secondary Goals

Participants define compliance-gaining interactions in terms of influence goals, but they often pursue additional objectives when seeking or resisting compliance. Four groups of scholars have explored how goals shape and constrain the ways in which individuals exert influence.

HAMPLE AND DALLINGER'S COGNITIVE EDITING STANDARDS

During a compliance-gaining interaction, participants make decisions about what to say, but also about what *not* to say, to exert influence. Dale Hample and

Judi Dallinger (1990) have conducted a program of research investigating this latter issue. As they explain:

> In the course of producing an argument, people must do two analytically distinct things. They must generate messages which might possibly be said, and then must decide whether or not to utter them. . . . Rather than studying the whole process of argument production, we have concentrated on the editing phase. By "editing," we refer to the simple decision to say or suppress a possible argument. (p. 153)

Hample and Dallinger have attempted to identify "cognitive editing standards," or grounds on which potential arguments are rejected, and have explored individual-difference factors that predict people's choice of editing standard.

Throughout their studies, Hample and Dallinger (1985, 1987a, 1987b; Dallinger & Hample, 1989, 1994) have employed a "strategy-rejection" procedure. Participants in each study have read multiple hypothetical compliance-gaining scenarios as well as lists of possible messages that might be used in each scenario (derived from Marwell & Schmitt's, 1967, typology of 16 compliance-seeking strategies; for a detailed description of this typology, see Chapter 2). Hample and Dallinger typically have written three concrete messages (utterances) to instantiate each of the 16 compliance-seeking strategies in each scenario, that is, three examples of the "positive expertise" strategy, three examples of the "promise" strategy," and so forth within each situation. In their early studies (e.g., Hample & Dallinger, 1985), participants indicated which compliance-seeking messages they would and would not be willing to use in each situation. For each rejected message, participants then wrote out why they would not be willing to use that message in the given situation. Hample and Dallinger (1990) explain their rationale for using this strategy-rejection procedure:

> We certainly do not believe that people in ordinary argumentative situations will consider more than a handful of possible arguments. . . . We felt, however, that we could not obtain plausible data simply by asking subjects to report their own suppressed arguments. People are naturally reluctant to paint themselves unattractively, and so we would not have been told about obviously stupid or offensive thoughts. And some suppressed arguments may only have flickered through consciousness or perhaps never arrived there at all; obviously these would have been unavailable for self reporting. (pp. 154-155)

Drawing upon these rationales for rejected compliance-seeking messages, Hample and Dallinger (1985) developed a category system of eight cognitive editing standards (see Table 5.2). Participants rejected messages based on *effectiveness*; that is, they perceived that some messages would not convince the

Table 5.2   Hample and Dallinger's (1990) Cognitive Editing Standards for
                   Compliance-Seeking Messages

Editing Standard	Description
1. I would use this one.	This means that you would be willing to say or do whatever is indicated. You may accept as many of the 48 messages as you wish.
2. No: This would not work.	You reject this approach because it would fail, or perhaps even backfire.
3. No: This is too negative to use.	You prefer not to use this one because it is too high pressure—a distasteful threat or bribe, perhaps.
4. No: I must treat myself positively.	You might later regret using this approach, or it doesn't match your self-image.
5. No: I must treat the other positively.	You feel that this approach might hurt the other's feelings—perhaps make him/her feel guilty or mad.
6. No: I must treat our relationship positively.	You reject this approach because it might injure the relationship between you and the other person.
7. No: This is false.	You consider that this approach is false or impossible or easily refuted.
8. No: This is irrelevant.	The approach seems irrelevant, either to you or to the other person.
9. No: Other.	You wouldn't use this approach, but for reasons other than numbers 2 through 8.

SOURCE: From "Arguers as Editors," by D. Hample & J. M. Dallinger, 1990,
Argumentation, 4, pp. 157-158. Copyright 1990 by Kluwer Academic Publishers.
Reprinted with permission.

target to comply, and might even make the target more resistant (standard 2).
Effectiveness reflects concern about accomplishing the influence, or primary,
goal. Participants also rejected messages on *principled grounds;* that is, some
persons objected to specific strategies due to the nature of those strategies
(standard 3). Participants also rejected compliance-seeking messages due to
concern for oneself (i.e., the message would project an undesirable self-image;
standard 4), *concern for the other* (i.e., the message would make the target look
or feel bad; standard 5), and *concern for the relationship* (i.e., the message might
damage the participant's relationship with the target; standard 6). Standards 4-6
all reflect "person-centered" concerns about supporting identities and relationships. Finally, participants rejected compliance-seeking messages due to concerns about *truthfulness* (i.e., the message is false or is not logical in the

situation; standard 7) and *relevance* (i.e., the message does not fit the topic or situation; standard 8). Standards 7 and 8 both reflect "discourse competence" concerns about meeting fundamental expectations for conversation (see Grice, 1975). In sum, people edit compliance-seeking messages not only out of a concern for what will and will not work, but also in light of whether the message makes sense within the situation, whether it is an appropriate or ethical form of action, and whether it will have desirable interpersonal consequences.

Aside from identifying cognitive editing standards, Hample and Dallinger (e.g., 1987a, 1987b; Dallinger & Hample, 1994) also have investigated individual differences in people's preferences for specific standards. In these studies the researchers have employed a "checklist" methodology, in which participants have been presented hypothetical compliance-gaining scenarios, lists of potential messages for each scenario, and the list of editing standards displayed in Table 5.2 Rather than writing out a rationale for each rejected compliance-seeking message, participants have selected *the single criterion* that best represents their reason for rejecting that message from the preformulated list of editing criteria. Hample and Dallinger have explored whether personality traits such as argumentativeness, construct differentiation, interpersonal orientation, self-monitoring, social desirability, and verbal aggressiveness are associated with an individual's tendency to use one editing criterion rather than another across situations (for a review, see Hample & Dallinger, 1990). For example, consider the trait "verbal aggressiveness," or the propensity to attack another party's self-concept, rather than or in addition to that party's ideas, during interpersonal disagreements (Infante & Wigley, 1986). Verbally aggressive individuals, in comparison with their less aggressive counterparts, reject fewer compliance-seeking strategies in general and rely more heavily on the editing criterion of effectiveness and less heavily on the criterion of concern about the other party when deciding what not to say in order to seek compliance (Hample & Dallinger, 1987a; see also Boster & Levine, 1988; Kosloski, Hinck, & Dailey, 1991). This finding suggests that people differ in whether they typically prioritize primary or secondary goals when seeking compliance.

Although Hample and Dallinger (1990) have concentrated on identifying individual differences in preferences for particular editing standards, a complete understanding of cognitive editing also must consider situations and relationships. As noted above, Hample and Dallinger have included multiple scenarios in their studies to assess whether the effects of personality variables generalize across situations. Given this purpose, they have not selected scenarios that differ systematically in terms of the influence goal defining the situation or the perceptual dimensions along which compliance-gaining situations can vary (Cody & McLaughlin, 1980). Nevertheless, subsidiary analyses have revealed that individuals do vary their use of specific criteria for editing compliance-seeking messages across situations and that personality traits often exert different effects on editing criteria in different situations. Main and interaction effects for situations, taken together, account for as much as 50% of the explained variance in people's use of editing criteria (Hample & Dallinger, 1990; see also Kosloski et al., 1991).

Explanations for cognitive editing also must include relational factors. Although the participants in Hample and Dallinger's research usually have been college students, in one study Hample, Dallinger, and Meyers (1989) explored how married couples edit compliance-seeking messages. Participants were 68 couples who on average had been married 21.1 years and who reported moderately high levels of marital satisfaction; each member of these 68 couples completed the strategy-rejection procedure separately. The researchers found that a married person's preference for specific editing criteria was predictable, in part, from his or her partner's preferences. For example, if partner A selected "concern for oneself" (standard 4) frequently, partner B tended not to select "concern for the other party" (standard 5) as a criterion for editing his or her messages (and vice versa). In addition, in some couples both partners selected the "other" category (standard 9) frequently, perhaps indicating that these couples had developed their own, idiosyncratic editing criteria. In sum, people's preferences for specific editing criteria appear to develop within and reflect their close personal relationships.

DILLARD'S SECONDARY GOALS

At the same time that Hample and Dallinger were developing a list of cognitive editing standards, James Dillard and his colleagues were conducting an independent series of studies to specify the content of secondary goals, or recurrent motivations in individuals' lives that shape and constrain how they seek compliance. Based on a review of the literature, Dillard et al. (1989) initially proposed a typology of four secondary goals:

1. *Identity goals:* objectives related to the self-concept, that focus on internal standards of behavior, and that derive from one's own moral standards or preferences for conduct

2. *Interaction goals:* objectives concerned with social appropriateness, such as to manage one's own public impression, to avoid threatening the other party's face, and to produce messages that are relevant and coherent

3. *Resource goals:* objectives related to increasing or maintaining valued assets, such as one's own physical or material assets as well as the rewards of participating in a relationship with the target

4. *Arousal management goals:* objectives related to maintaining a state of arousal that falls within comfortable boundaries for the individual, such as reducing excessive apprehension

Table 5.3   Dillard et al.'s (1989) Content Analysis of Reasons for Rejecting
             Compliance-Seeking Messages

Goal Category	Frequency	Proportion (%)	Exemplar Statements
Influence	865	44	It wouldn't work. It's irrelevant.
Identity	672	34	It's immoral. Not my style.
Interaction	180	9	That would make me look bad. This is inappropriate for the situation.
Resource	98	5	This would cost me our friendship. I'd suffer for it.
Arousal	8	1	This would make me apprehensive. Makes me too nervous.
Uncodable	136	7	This is stupid. You must be kidding.
Total	1,959	100	

SOURCE: From "Primary and Secondary Goals in the Production of Interpersonal
Influence Messages," by J. P. Dillard, C. Segrin, & J. M. Harden, 1989, *Communication
Monographs, 56*, p. 24. Copyright 1989 by the Speech Communication Association.
Reprinted with permission.

To evaluate their typology, Dillard et al. (1989, Study 1) used a strategy-
rejection procedure. They had each of 100 undergraduates read 2 hypothetical
compliance-gaining scenarios drawn from a larger pool of 10 scenarios. For
each scenario, participants decided whether they would (or would not) use each
of 14 messages derived from Schenck-Hamlin, Wiseman, and Georgacarakos's
(1982) typology of compliance-seeking strategies and then wrote out their reasons for each rejected message. Across situations and strategies, the 100 students
generated a total of 1,959 written reasons for rejecting specific compliance-
seeking messages. As is apparent in Table 5.3, nearly half of these reasons reflected
concern about accomplishing the influence (primary) goal, whereas most of the
remaining reasons reflected concerns about one of the four secondary goals.

In a second study, Dillard et al. (1989) generated closed-ended, Likert-type
scales to measure people's degree of concern about each of their proposed goal
categories. The researchers developed scale items by adapting the reasons for
rejecting strategies that had been written in the first study (see the "exemplar
statements" in Table 5.3). Each participant in a new sample of 604 undergraduates recalled a recent compliance-gaining episode from his or her own life and
then rated how important each goal statement was in that situation. Based on
a series of statistical analyses, Dillard et al. selected a 5-item scale to measure

the importance of the influence goal, as well as 3- to 5-item scales to measure each secondary goal. In addition, they divided the original "resource goals" category into two separate goals: relational resources versus personal resources. Table 5.4 shows a sampling of items that measure the influence goal and five secondary goals.

To examine how goals guide people's planning and action, Dillard et al. (1989) conducted yet a third study. In this study, each of 304 undergraduates recalled a recent episode from his or her own life in which he or she sought a target person's compliance, describing the interaction in response to the alternating prompts "First, you said," "Then he [or she] said," "Next, you said," and so forth. Coders then analyzed each participant's own turns from the recalled conversation, as a set, along three dimensions: (a) *explicitness,* or the degree to which the participant made his or her intentions apparent to the target; (b) *positivity,* or the degree to which the participant highlighted positive consequences if the target complied, as opposed to highlighting negative consequences if the target did not comply; and (c) *argument,* or the degree to which the participant offered explicit reasons the target should comply with his or her request, regardless of the quality of those reasons (for a discussion of these dimensions, see Chapter 3). After recalling his or her conversation, each participant also rated the degree to which he or she had thought about how to persuade the target in advance (*planning*) and had tried hard to persuade the target (*effort*). Finally, each participant completed the closed-ended goal scales shown in Table 5.4 for his or her situation.

Given the conceptual distinction between primary and secondary goals, Dillard et al. (1989) predicted that the importance of the influence goal would determine how motivated participants were to seek compliance (i.e., planning and effort), whereas secondary goals would predict how participants actually went about seeking compliance (i.e., explicitness, positivity, and argument). As the influence goal became more important, participants reported that they had planned more in advance and had exerted more effort; in addition, they included more reasons in their recalled attempts to gain compliance. Regarding secondary goals, participants were (a) less likely to be explicit about what they wanted as their concern about both identity and arousal management goals increased, (b) more likely to emphasize positive consequences as their concern about both interaction and relational goals increased and as their concern about arousal management goals decreased, and (c) more likely to provide reasons as their concern about identity goals increased and as their concern about arousal management goals decreased. Dillard et al. (1989) conclude, "While the pattern [of results] is not a perfect dichotomy, it does support our distinction between primary and secondary goals; the primary goal serves to initiate and maintain social action, while the secondary goals act as a set of boundaries which delimit verbal choices available to sources" (p. 32).

Table 5.4   Dillard et al.'s (1989) Scales for Measuring Influence and Secondary
              Goals

Goal Type	Sample Scale Items
Influence	1. It was very important for me to convince this person to do what I wanted him or her to do. 2. I really didn't care that much whether he or she did what I asked (R).
Identity	3. In this situation, I was concerned with not violating my own ethical standards. 4. I was concerned about being true to myself and my values.
Interaction	5. In this situation, I was careful to avoid saying things which were socially inappropriate. 6. I didn't want to look stupid while trying to persuade this person.
Relational resource	7. I was not willing to risk possible damage to the relationship in order to get what I wanted. 8. I didn't really care if I made the other person mad or not (R).
Personal resource	9. This person could have made things very bad for me if I kept bugging him/her. 10. I was worried about the threat to my safety if I pushed the issue.
Arousal management	11. This situation did *not* seem to be the type to make me nervous (R). 12. I was afraid of being uncomfortable or nervous.

SOURCE: From "Primary and Secondary Goals in the Production of Interpersonal Influence Messages," by J. P. Dillard, C. Segrin, & J. M. Harden, 1989, *Communication Monographs, 56,* p. 27. Copyright 1989 by the Speech Communication Association. Adapted by permission.

NOTE: Only 12 of the 25 total goal scales are shown. A 5-point Likert scale ranging from *strongly disagree* to *strongly agree* accompanied each item. (R) = an item that was reverse scored.

KELLERMANN'S AND KIM'S CONVERSATIONAL CONSTRAINTS

In a third research program, Kathy Kellermann and Min-Sun Kim both have explored constraints on strategic communication. Kellermann (1992) distinguishes *primary goals* such as seeking or resisting compliance, "that are impermanent and can be achieved at particular moments in time," from *constraints,* or "ongoing regulators of behavior" (p. 289). Kellermann has analyzed the nature of and relationships among conversational constraints with middle-class European American samples, whereas Kim has explored conversational constraints across cultures.

Explicating Two Conversational Constraints

According to Kellermann (1992; Kellermann & Park, 2001), communication is regulated by two overarching constraints: social appropriateness and efficiency. *Appropriateness* refers to whether a message is "nice, civil, pleasant, proper, and courteous" as opposed to "rude, uncivil, nasty, improper, and ill-mannered" (Kellermann & Shea, 1996, p. 161). This first constraint is reminiscent of Hample and Dallinger's (1990) "person-centered" editing criterion as well as Dillard et al.'s (1989) interaction and relational resource categories of secondary goals. *Efficiency* refers to whether a message is "direct, immediate, and to the point, wasting neither time, energy, steps, or effort" as opposed to "roundabout, indirect, and wasteful, consuming time, energy, and/or effort" (Kellermann & Shea, 1996, p. 161; see also Berger, 2000). This second constraint corresponds, loosely, to Dillard et al.'s (1989) personal resource secondary goal. Keep in mind that this second constraint is labeled *efficiency*, and not *effectiveness*. *Effectiveness* refers to whether a compliance-seeking strategy will succeed at gaining the target's compliance, whereas *efficiency* refers to the expenditure of time and/or effort that a strategy requires. Hints, for instance, are inefficient because the message target must infer the source's actual intent, but hints are seen as a very effective compliance-gaining strategy in some cultures (Kim & Wilson, 1994).

Appropriateness and efficiency are constraints in that they set limits on people's choices during compliance-gaining interactions. As Kellermann (1992) explains:

> Communication is selected, fashioned, edited, enacted, and evaluated on these grounds. . . . This is not to say that individuals always will be (or want their behavior to be) appropriate and efficient; rather, it is saying that individuals are constrained by the *level* of appropriateness and efficiency expected in particular situations (which could call for high, moderate, or low levels). (pp. 289-290)

Expectations about proper levels of appropriateness and/or efficiency during compliance-gaining episodes vary depending on many factors, including the type of influence goal being pursued (Canary et al., 1986; Wilson et al., 1998), the urgency of the requested action (Kellermann & Park, 2001), and participants' genders, cultures, and relationship (Burgoon, Birk, & Hall, 1991; Burgoon, Dillard, & Doran, 1984; Kim & Wilson, 1994; Metts, Cupach, & Imahori, 1992).

Individuals can feel pressure to meet social expectations when seeking/resisting compliance, because violating expectations can undermine one's credibility and persuasiveness (Burgoon & Burgoon, 1990). In sum, Kellermann (1992) asserts that people always orient to these two conversational constraints.

Kellermann also has explored the perceived relationship between these two conversational constraints. Kellermann and Kim (1991) argue that appropriateness and efficiency are separate dimensions, and that the relationship between them takes different forms depending on the type of primary goal that defines the interaction. According to Kellermann, however, many scholars mistakenly assume that appropriateness and efficiency form opposite ends of a single dimension (see Kellermann & Kim, 1991; Kellermann & Shea, 1996). As one example, she cites the "rebuff hypothesis," which predicts that message sources, upon encountering resistance, typically use less polite *and* more direct strategies in their subsequent compliance-gaining attempts (for a discussion of the rebuff hypothesis, see Chapter 3). If the assumption of a single dimension were correct, then knowing whether a compliance-gaining strategy is efficient also would tell us whether it is appropriate (and vice versa). Assuming a single dimension, if the strategy of "hint" is seen as inefficient, then it also would be seen as appropriate; moreover, if "hint" is seen as less efficient than the strategy of "direct request," then "hint" would also have to be more appropriate than "direct request."

To rebut such "single-dimension" thinking, Kellermann and Shea (1996) had 169 undergraduates rate the appropriateness and efficiency of five specific compliance-seeking strategies (direct request, suggestion, hint, promise, and threat). To ensure generalizability, the researchers had each participant rate one of three different sets of examples of these five strategies. Their findings indicate that U.S. American students do make separate, and largely independent, judgments about the appropriateness and efficiency of compliance-seeking strategies. For instance, these students always rated examples of the "direct request" strategy as much more efficient than examples of the "hint" strategy, and yet they rated examples of "direct request" and "hint" as almost equally appropriate. Kellermann and Shea conclude: "Compliance-gaining researchers treat nice strategies as inefficient and nasty strategies as expedient and hinge their theoretical thinking on such supposition. The available evidence suggests that this supposition is simply incorrect" (p. 157).

Although Kellermann has clarified the concept of conversational constraints, her work, like most research on persuasive message production, has been conducted exclusively with European American participants. Min-Sun Kim and her colleagues (e.g., Kim, 1994; Kim et al., 1996; Kim & Wilson, 1994) have compared the importance of appropriateness and efficiency, as well as the perceived relationship between these two constraints, across individualist and collectivist cultures.

Culture and Conversational Constraints

According to Triandis (1993), culture can be defined as "shared attitudes, beliefs, categorizations, expectations, norms, roles, self-definitions, values, and other such elements of subjective culture found among individuals whose interactions were facilitated by *shared* language, historical period, and geographic region" (p. 156). When elements of a subjective culture are organized around a theme, a cultural syndrome is present. Individualism and collectivism are examples of cultural syndromes. "In the case of individualism, the organizing theme is the centrality of the autonomous individual; in the case of collectivism, it is the centrality of the collective—family, tribe, work organization, consumer group, state, ethnic group, or religious group" (Triandis, 1993, p. 156). Thus individualist cultures emphasize autonomy and independence, self-determination, and concern for one's own interests, whereas collectivist cultures emphasize interconnectedness, conformity to group norms, relational harmony, and concern for in-group interests (see Hofstede, 1980, 2001; Hui & Triandis, 1986; Schwartz, 1990; Triandis, Bontempo, Villareal, Asia, & Lucci, 1988). Collectivist cultures place greater emphasis than do individualist cultures on status and legitimate authority, and distinguish more clearly between in-groups and out-groups (Gudykunst et al., 1992). Australia, Great Britain, and the United States are places where individualism is the predominant cultural syndrome, whereas Colombia, Japan, South Korea, and Pakistan are countries in which the cultural syndrome of collectivism is predominant (Hofstede, 1980, 2001).

As widely shared sets of beliefs and values, cultural syndromes are transmitted "through socialization, modeling, and other forms of communication from one generation to another" (Triandis, 1993, p. 156). Thus an individual's sense of self reflects, in part, the cultural syndrome into which he or she is born (Kim et al., 1996; Kitayama, Markus, Matsumoto, & Norasakkunkit, 1997; Triandis et al., 1988). According to Markus and Kitayama (1991), persons within individualist cultures tend to develop *independent* self-construals; that is, they view themselves primarily in terms of internal, psychological qualities that distinguish them from others and that remain constant across situations. In contrast, persons within collectivist cultures tend to develop *interdependent* self-construals; that is, they think of themselves primarily in terms of the social relations (e.g., family, workplace, community) of which they are a part. Interdependent self-construals do not draw sharp boundaries between self and others, and, compared with independent self-construals, they vary more in content across situations involving different relationships. Remember, independent and interdependent self-construals are qualities of individuals, whereas individualism and collectivism are cultural syndromes. Although members of individualist cultures, on average, develop more independent self-construals than do members of collectivist cultures, not every person within an individualist culture will form a highly independent sense of self (and vice versa). The predominant cultural syndrome is but one factor influencing a person's self-construal.

In a recent series of studies, Min-Sun Kim and her colleagues (Kim, 1994; Kim & Bresnahan, 1994, 1996; Kim et al., 1996; Kim & Sharkey, 1995; Kim, Sharkey, & Singelis, 1994; Kim, Shin, & Cai, 1998; Kim & Wilson, 1994) have examined similarities and differences in conversational constraints within individualist and collectivist cultures. The researchers have used similar methods throughout these studies. With one exception (Kim & Sharkey, 1995), each has compared undergraduate college students studying in the mainland United States (a predominantly individualist culture) with students studying in South Korea and/or Japan (both predominantly collectivist cultures) and Hawaii (where local culture has been influenced by both cultural syndromes). In each study, participants have read one or more hypothetical compliance-gaining situations defined by different influence goals and containing different levels of source-target dominance.

After reading one or more hypothetical scenarios, the participants have completed one of two tasks. In one set of studies (Kim, 1994; Kim & Bresnahan, 1996; Kim et al., 1994, 1996; Kim & Sharkey, 1995), participants have rated the importance of satisfying four conversational constraints in the scenario: (a) concern for clarity, (b) concern for avoiding hurting the other's feelings, (c) concern for avoiding negative evaluation by the hearer, and (d) concern for minimizing imposition. Aside from these four conversational constraints, participants also have rated the importance of being effective at accomplishing the influence (primary) goal. Table 5.5 displays the scales that have been used to measure each constraint, plus effectiveness. As is apparent, concern for clarity is synonymous with Kellermann's (1992) efficiency constraint, and each of the latter three concerns taps a more specific aspect of Kellermann's social appropriateness constraint.

In the second set of studies (Kim & Bresnahan, 1994; Kim et al., 1998; Kim & Wilson, 1994), participants have read a hypothetical scenario plus 12 different strategies for requesting compliance in that scenario. The 12 request strategies have been organized into three larger strategy clusters:

1. *Direct statements:* requests in which the message source's intent is stated explicitly (e.g., "You must repay the loan")

2. *Queries:* conventionally indirect requests, which make reference to the logical preconditions for requesting (e.g., "Could you repay the loan?")

3. *Hints:* nonconventionally indirect requests, in which the message source's intent is left implicit (e.g., "I have run out of cash")

Table 5.5   Kim's (1994) Scales for Measuring Four Conversational Constraints, Plus Effectiveness

Type of Constraint	Scale Items
Clarity	1. In this situation, it is very important to make my point as clearly and directly as possible.
	2. In this situation, I want to directly come to the point while conveying my message.
Feelings	1. In this situation, I feel it is very important to avoid hurting the other's feelings.
	2. In this situation, being considerate toward the other's feelings is a major concern to me.
Avoiding negative evaluation	1. In this situation, it is very important that the other person does not see me in a negative light.
	2. In this situation, it is very important that my message does not cause the other person to dislike me.
Avoiding imposition	1. In this situation, it is very important not to intrude on the other person.
	2. In this situation, it is very important to avoid inconveniencing the other.
Effectiveness (influence goal)	1. In this situation, it is very important to get the other person to do what I want.
	2. In this situation, making the other person comply with my request is very important.

SOURCE: From "Cross-Cultural Comparisons of the Perceived Importance of Conversational Constraints," by M. S. Kim, 1994, *Human Communication Research, 21,* p. 139. Copyright 1994 by the International Communication Association. Reprinted with permission.

NOTE: A 7-point Likert scale ranging from *strongly disagree* to *strongly agree* accompanied each item.

Participants typically have rated the degree to which each request strategy meets the four conversational constraints. For example, for the "clarity" constraint, participants were instructed, "Please rate each statement in terms of the degree to which it communicates your intention in a clear, explicit, and unambiguous manner" (Kim & Wilson, 1994, p. 221). Aside from the four conversational constraints, participants also judged the perceived effectiveness of, as well as their likelihood of using, each request strategy in the scenario.

In their earlier studies, Kim and her colleagues simply compared how students from individualist and collectivist cultures completed these tasks (Kim, 1994;

Kim & Bresnahan, 1994; Kim & Wilson, 1994). In more recent studies, however, participants also have completed scales that measure the degree to which they possess an independent and/or interdependent sense of self (Kim et al., 1994, 1996; Kim & Sharkey, 1995; Kim et al., 1998). Measures of independent and interdependent self-construals are shown in Table 5.6. By including these scales, Kim and her colleagues have been able to assess whether individuals from different countries of origin tend to possess different self-construals as well as whether individuals who possess different self-construals, whatever their countries of origin, differ in their perceptions of conversational constraints.

Five major findings about conversational constraints have emerged from Kim et al.'s research. First, similarities exist between individualist and collectivist cultures. Students from the mainland United States and South Korea, for example, rate the three clusters of request strategies quite similarly in terms of the relative degree to which they meet the four conversational constraints (Kim & Wilson, 1994). For instance, individuals from both cultures see direct statements, on average, as clearer (i.e., more efficient) than queries, which they see in turn as clearer than hints. Students from the mainland United States, Hawaii, and South Korea also do not differ in their importance ratings for effectiveness at gaining compliance (the primary goal), because all three cultures place a high degree of importance on being effective (Kim, 1994).

A second finding is that members of individualist and collectivist cultures differ dramatically in which specific request strategies they view as most effective. South Korean students, on average, rate hints as a more effective strategy for gaining compliance than queries, which they in turn rate as more effective than direct statements. Just the opposite pattern occurs for U.S. American students (Kim & Wilson, 1994). Regardless of country of origin, the degree to which students possess an independent sense of self is inversely related to the degree to which they view hints as effective means of responding to target resistance (Kim et al., 1998). Not surprisingly, then, students from South Korea and the United States also see different conversational constraints as important for being effective. For South Korean students, the degree to which a request is sensitive to the other's feelings and the degree to which it avoids creating disapproval are the two most important determinants of whether it is perceived as effective, whereas clarity and avoiding imposition are unrelated to effectiveness. For U.S American students, the degree to which a request is clear is the most important determinant of whether it is perceived as effective. Being sensitive to the other's feelings is a less important determinant, and avoiding disapproval and imposition are unrelated to effectiveness (Kim & Bresnahan, 1994).

A third finding is that members of individualist and collectivist cultures hold different perceptions of the relationships among conversational constraints. Replicating Kellermann and Shea's (1996) findings, mainland U.S. students

Table 5.6   Kim and Sharkey's (1995) Scales for Measuring Two Types of
                  Self-Construals

Scale Items	Type of Self-Construal

Independent Self

1. I don't change my opinions in conformity with those of the majority.
2. I don't support my group when they are wrong.
3. I assert my opposition when I disagree strongly with members of my group.
4. I act the same way no matter who I am with.
5. I enjoy being unique and different from others in many respects.
6. I am comfortable with being singled out for praise or rewards.
7. Speaking up in a work/task group is not a problem for me.
8. I value being in good health above everything.

Interdependent Self

1. I will sacrifice my self-interest for the benefit of the group I am in.
2. I act as fellow group members would prefer.
3. I stick with my group even through difficult times.
4. It is important for me to maintain harmony with my group.
5. It is important to me to respect decisions made by the group.
6. I will stay in a group if they need me, even when I am not happy with the group.
7. Even when I strongly disagree with group members, I avoid an argument.
8. I respect people who are modest about themselves.
9. I often have the feeling that my relationship with others is more important than my own accomplishments.
10. My happiness depends on the happiness of those around me.

SOURCE: From "Independent and Interdependent Construals of Self: Explaining Cultural Patterns of Interpersonal Communication in Multi-cultural Organizational Settings," by M. S. Kim & W. F. Sharkey, 1995, *Communication Quarterly, 43,* p. 38. Copyright 1995 by the Eastern Communication Association. Reprinted with permission.

NOTE: A 7-point Likert scale ranging from *strongly disagree* to *strongly agree* accompanied each item.

make separate, and only moderately related, judgments of a request strategy's appropriateness (i.e., the degree to which it avoids hurting the other's feelings, negative evaluation, and imposition) and that strategy's efficiency (i.e., the degree to which it is clear). On the other hand, students from South Korea treat appropriateness and efficiency more as a single dimension, in that their average ratings of a request strategy's appropriateness are highly predictable from their average ratings of that strategy's efficiency (Kim & Wilson, 1994).

Fourth, persons from individualist and collectivist cultures differ in the importance they place on meeting specific conversational constraints. The most striking cross-cultural differences involve clarity (i.e., efficiency). Mainland U.S. students, on average, place greater importance on being clear than do students from Hawaii, and both groups place much greater emphasis on being clear than do South Korean students (Kim, 1994). Indeed, Kim (1994) found that nation of origin accounted for almost 25% of the variance in importance ratings for clarity. South Korean students, in turn, place significantly greater emphasis on avoiding hurting the other's feelings and avoiding imposing than do students from Hawaii or the mainland United States. Cultural differences in importance ratings for these two constraints, however, are smaller than the differences for clarity. These cultural differences hold up for both female and male participants (Kim & Bresnahan, 1996).

Fifth and finally, cultural differences in importance ratings for conversational constraints are mediated, in part, by differences in self-construal. According to Kim and Sharkey (1995), different self-construals should lead individuals to prioritize different conversational constraints:

> Individuals with the predominant tendency towards independent self-construals tend to assert their needs with direct, clear, and non-ambiguous forms of communicative strategies that make the speaker's intention more or less transparent to the hearer. Such discourse functions to express or assert the individual needs of the self. . . . Unlike the self-contained and consistent independent self, the interdependent self does not exist except in relation to the actors and situations around it. . . . Thus, in choosing a communicative strategy, the person with a tendency towards interdependence will be concerned about the other's evaluation of him or her and not hurting the other's feelings. (pp. 25-26)

Kim et al. (1996) report that college students from the mainland United States ($M = 5.15$), on average, score higher on level of independent self-construal than do students from Hawaii ($M = 4.93$), Japan ($M = 4.80$), or South Korea ($M = 4.38$), although students from all four cultures differ much less in their average level of interdependent self-construal. As expected, type of self-construal predicts importance ratings for conversational constraints. Individuals with higher levels of independent self-construal, regardless of country of origin, rate efficiency (i.e., concern for clarity) as a more important constraint; those with higher levels of interdependent self-construal rate appropriateness (i.e., concerns for not hurting the other's feelings, not imposing, and avoiding negative self-evaluation) as more important (Kim et al., 1994, 1996; Kim & Sharkey, 1995). Finally, cultural differences in the importance of conversational constraints are significantly smaller once the effects of culture on self-construal have been controlled statistically (Kim et al., 1996).

In sum, the research program undertaken by Kim and her colleagues reveals several cross-cultural differences in perceived constraints during compliance-gaining episodes. The most striking difference pertains to efficiency. Persons from individualist cultures, who tend to have more independent self-construals than do persons from collectivist cultures, place greater value on being clear and direct than do persons from collectivist cultures. Persons from individualist cultures also view efficient request strategies as being an effective means for gaining compliance, whereas those from collectivist cultures view request efficiency as irrelevant to effectiveness or even counterproductive.

According to Kim (1994; Kim & Wilson, 1994), these cross-cultural differences in conversational constraints increase the possibility of misunderstanding during *intercultural* interactions. As we saw in Chapter 2, both Chinese (Ma, 1996) and Greek (Tannen, 1981) adults are significantly more likely than U.S. Americans to interpret unelaborated, unenthusiastic agreement with a request (e.g., "okay") as indirect resistance. During an intercultural compliance-gaining episode, a Chinese message target (who is likely to expect people to be sensitive to others' feelings) may be resentful if a U.S. American interprets the target's "okay" as signaling a willingness to comply. The U.S. American message source (who in turn likely expects people to "say what they mean" rather than "beating around the bush") may be frustrated when the Chinese target does not communicate reluctance to comply directly. As this example illustrates, intercultural competence requires knowledge of cultural differences in conversational constraints. Aside from cultural differences, however, individuals within a culture also differ in their propensities for recognizing and attending to multiple concerns during compliance-gaining episodes.

O'KEEFE AND DELIA'S ANALYSIS OF GOAL AND BEHAVIORAL COMPLEXITY

The research programs of Hample and Dallinger (1990), Dillard et al. (1989), and Kim (1994) all confirm that individuals frequently pursue multiple goals when seeking compliance. Why is this the case? In one attempt to address this issue, Barbara O'Keefe and Jesse Delia (1982) have analyzed the potential "complexity" of compliance-gaining situations. However, they claim that individuals also differ in their likelihood of recognizing and addressing this complexity.

At the outset, O'Keefe (1988) distinguishes two senses of the term *goal:* "goals as generalized constraints defined and activated by social structures and goals as they are recognized and pursued by individuals" (p. 82). O'Keefe's first sense of *goal* refers to general problems posed by a social situation, given its constituent features (e.g., the focal task, the participants' roles and relationship). In this sense, goals are demands implicit within the nature of social situations themselves. Goals in this sense are identified through an analysis of "the predefined activities of human cultures and the general norms of consideration, self-respect, cooperation, and so on, that govern group life" (p. 82). They are "the central elements of socially codified representations of situations" (p. 82); hence goals in this first sense exist independent of the desires of any specific individual. O'Keefe provides the following example:

> For any situation, some possible goals are intrinsically relevant and some are not. For instance, in a committee meeting any goal related to the accomplishment of committee business is naturally relevant and *a committee member can be held accountable for meeting such a goal* whether or not that particular member identifies with the committee and its objectives. (p. 82; emphasis added)

O'Keefe's second sense of the term *goal* refers to those future states of affairs that an individual wants to attain or maintain. Goals in this second sense involve an individual's mental states, and, as such, one identifies them by asking the individual what he or she is trying to accomplish and/or by inferring purpose(s) from the individual's behavior. It is in this second sense that I am using the term *goal* throughout this chapter. Hence, to avoid confusion, from this point forward I will use the term *situationally relevant objective* when referring to a goal in O'Keefe's first sense of the term, and I will limit my own use of the word *goal* to O'Keefe's second sense.[5]

Drawing upon the concept of the situationally relevant objective, O'Keefe and Delia (1982) distinguish between "complex" and "simple" communicative situations. A situation is complex when (a) its constituent features create multiple situationally relevant objectives, (b) significant obstacles to achieving those objectives are present, and/or (c) actions that accomplish one objective conflict with those that accomplish other relevant objectives. To illustrate the concept of a complex situation: Consider a pharmacist who hopes to convince a patient to continue taking her antihypertension medication regularly (Lambert & Gillespie, 1994). The patient often is late in refilling her prescription and frequently complains about the medication's side effects. In this situation, would we hold the pharmacist accountable for trying to (re)gain the patient's commitment to control her high blood pressure? Given the pharmacist's role and the patient's condition, this is one situationally relevant objective. Should the pharmacist also discuss the medication's side effects with the patient as well as acknowledge the patient's ultimate control over decisions regarding her own health? Given the patient's comments and the value placed on autonomy and personal responsibility within individualist cultures such as the United States, these also are situationally relevant objectives. All three criteria for complex situations are present in this example: (a) The pharmacist reasonably could be held accountable for meeting multiple objectives, (b) obstacles (e.g., the medication's side effects) to achieving these objectives are present, and (c) actions that help accomplish one objective (e.g., acknowledging that side effects are not uncommon) could undercut other objectives (e.g., gaining this patient's compliance).

According to O'Keefe and Delia (1982), compliance-gaining situations, by their nature, contain the potential for complexity. How many situationally relevant objectives are present in each of the following examples?

- A parent wants to advise her spouse about the best ways to get their 3-year-old daughter to "listen."
- An office manager wants to convince an employee who occasionally is 5-10 minutes late returning from lunch to arrive back at work on time.
- A college student wants to convince the person he has been seeing for 2 months that the two should stop dating and "just be friends."
- An adult son wants to convince his mother to take care of his children for 5 days while he and his spouse are away at a professional conference.

As you can see, many compliance-gaining situations, including those defined by the influence goals of giving advice (Goldsmith & Fitch, 1997), enforcing obligations (Wilson, 1990), redefining relationships (Metts, 1992), and asking favors (Tracy, Craig, Smith, & Spisak, 1984), contain potential complexity. Compliance-gaining situations also can be complex from the perspective of the message target, because the target may be accountable to multiple demands, such as opposing the request clearly, providing a rationale for refusal, and not communicating disapproval of the message source (Kline & Floyd, 1990; Metts et al., 1992; Saeki & O'Keefe, 1994).

Although compliance-gaining episodes typically contain multiple situationally relevant objectives, individuals do not always form and pursue multiple goals when seeking and resisting compliance. According to O'Keefe and Delia (1982), people with higher levels of *interpersonal construct differentiation* are more likely than their less differentiated counterparts to define compliance-gaining situations in a manner that makes salient multiple situationally relevant objectives. Highly differentiated persons, who spontaneously rely on a larger number of abstract, psychological dimensions to interpret others' actions, are more skilled at taking the perspective and inferring the affective states of others than are their less differentiated counterparts (for a detailed discussion of construct differentiation, see Chapter 4). Given these differences in person perception, O'Keefe and Delia argue that highly differentiated individuals also are more likely than less differentiated persons to form multiple interaction goals during influence episodes, as well as to use "behaviorally complex" communication strategies that address multiple goals.

O'Keefe and Delia (1982) propose three strategies for managing multiple conflicting goals. *Selection* involves giving priority to one goal, either the primary or a secondary goal, while ignoring other goals. Our pharmacist, for example, could prioritize the primary goal of gaining compliance by saying only, "Hypertension is a serious disease" and hence, "Don't stop taking the medication," with no attention to the patient's concerns about side effects or the patient's role in decision making. *Separation* involves addressing multiple goals in temporally or behaviorally distinct aspects of a message. A pharmacist who says, "I understand the medication has some unpleasant side effects," but then counsels the patient that "the medication is worth the cost" starts by addressing secondary goals, followed by the primary goal. *Integration* involves attempting to address multiple goals simultaneously. A pharmacist who says, "One of us should contact your doctor and see if a more effective alternative can be found" is trying simultaneously to keep the patient's hypertension controlled and to involve the patient in decision making about her health. Separation and integration are more "behaviorally complex" than selection in that they reflect greater concern about accomplishing multiple goals (Burleson, 1987). In a nutshell, O'Keefe and Delia (1982) predict that highly differentiated persons will use behaviorally complex strategies.

Consistent with this thinking, several studies have shown that adults high in construct differentiation are more likely than less differentiated adults to use persuasive strategies that address multiple goals when seeking or resisting compliance (Applegate & Woods, 1991; Hale, 1986; Kline, 1991; Kline & Ceropski, 1984; Kline & Floyd, 1990; Leichty & Applegate, 1991; O'Keefe, 1988; O'Keefe & Shepherd, 1987; but not Waldron & Applegate, 1994). For example, O'Keefe and Shepherd (1987) explored the effects of construct differentiation on people's goal management strategies during face-to-face persuasive interactions. Participants in their study, who were college students, individually completed a preinteraction questionnaire that assessed their attitudes about 15 policy issues, after which they filled out Crockett's (1965) Role Category Questionnaire (RCQ) measure of construct differentiation. Participants then were grouped into pairs, and each pair was informed that they would be discussing the single issue from the attitude questionnaire about which the two of them disagreed most strongly. Participants were given up to 15 minutes to discuss this issue, during which time each was to try to persuade the other party to accept his or her own position on the issue. The interactions were videotaped. After completing the interaction, each participant individually rated how much his or her own attitude on the issue had changed. Each also rated the overall quality of his or her partner's arguments as well as the extent to which the partner was persuasive, credible, likable, and skilled at argument.

Given the nature of argumentative situations, O'Keefe and Shepherd's (1987) participants had to manage potential conflict between stating clearly what they themselves believed to be true and showing respect for their partners' ideas and beliefs. For example, if party A said something about the controversial issue to which party B expressed overt disagreement, then party A was faced with formulating a response. Party A could choose to talk about party B's prior turn or to bring up something else, and whatever party A said could be heard as agreement or disagreement with party B's position. Regardless of which option party A chose, he or she could carry it out in a manner that pursued one goal or multiple goals. If party A chose to disagree explicitly with party B's prior turn, for instance, party A could do so in one of the following ways:

1. By directly criticizing party B's views with no effort to qualify or tone down the disagreement (selection)

2. By directly criticizing party B's views while also including qualifiers, apologies, or other attempts to mitigate the disagreement (separation)

3. By directly criticizing party B's views within a larger discussion of how considering the strengths and weaknesses of all positions is central to the process of argumentation, so as to depersonalize the disagreement (integration)

In contrast, if party A chose to agree explicitly with party B's prior turn, he or she could do one of the following:

1. Claim to have been persuaded on the point while giving no explanation for this change in position (selection)

2. Claim to have been persuaded while also providing a justification for this change in position (separation)

3. Claim to have been persuaded as part of a larger analysis of why being open to change is part of the argumentation process (integration)

In this fashion, O'Keefe and Shepherd (1987) coded how frequently participants used each of the three goal management strategies throughout their interactions.

During these interpersonal arguments, participants in general used the "selection" strategy most often. As predicted, however, highly differentiated participants used "behaviorally complex" strategies that addressed multiple goals more frequently than did their less differentiated counterparts. Specifically, level of construct differentiation was *not* related to frequency of use for selection strategies, was moderately related ($r = .27$) to frequencies for separation strategies, and was strongly related ($r = .61$) to frequencies for integration strategies.

Regarding message effects, goal management strategies did not predict whether participants were viewed as skilled at argument, but they did influence how much they were liked by their partners. Participants who used integration strategies frequently were liked better than those who did not, whereas those who used separation strategies actually were liked less than those who did not. Put differently, simply attempting to address multiple goals did not guarantee success. Integration strategies, however, did work better than messages that pursued only a single goal (i.e., selection), assuming that one wanted to argue about a controversial issue and still remain a likable person. In a follow-up analysis of the same data, O'Keefe and Shepherd (1989) found that whether participants were likely to use integration strategies was especially noticeable to partners who themselves were high, rather than low, in interpersonal construct differentiation (see also Bingham & Burleson, 1989, O'Keefe & McCornack, 1987; Waldron & Applegate, 1998).[6]

O'Keefe and Delia's (1982) "goal complexity/behavioral complexity" analysis has made two important contributions to the study of persuasive message production. First, it has reframed the role that person-perception skills play during message production. In the original "listener-adapted" model of message production, interpersonal construct differentiation was believed to affect people's ability to adapt their persuasive appeals to specific targets. Highly differentiated persons were seen as better able than their less differentiated counterparts to understand the message target's perspective, and hence to produce persuasive appeals that explicitly discuss the target's views (for an extended discussion of this listener-adapted model, see Chapter 4). In the "goal complexity/behavioral complexity" account, however, construct differentiation influences people's likelihood of forming and pursuing multiple goals during persuasive attempts; that is, it affects the forces that motivate and shape message production from the start. O'Keefe and Delia (1982) explain the difference between the two views of message production as follows:

> The conception of message production as involving only a set of processes for adapting messages to particular recipients is not just oversimplified, but also limits the role social cognition [e.g., construct differentiation] might be seen to play in the production of messages. ... In fact, social cognitive processes might be involved at many different stages in the process of producing a message; in particular, representations of listeners and social situations might generate the communicative intentions out of which messages originate. ...This model suggests that the primary processes in message production are the generation or reconciliation of message objectives, not taking the listener's perspective on potential messages and adjusting them. (pp. 51-52)

Although the newer "goal complexity/behavioral complexity" account offers a more detailed portrayal of message production than did the listener-adaptation model, it shares one limitation with that older model. Specifically, O'Keefe and Delia (1982) say little about situational variation in the use of behaviorally complex persuasive strategies. Leichty and Applegate (1991), for example, have shown that the effect of construct differentiation on use of multiple-goal persuasive strategies varies depending on several situational factors, such as the size of the message source's request and the degree of intimacy and power shared between the source and target. In particular, these researchers found that highly differentiated individuals did *not* use behaviorally complex persuasive strategies more often than did their less complex counterparts when the target was a stranger or when their requests were small and they had formal authority over a familiar target. O'Keefe and Delia (1982) emphasize the potential complexity of all compliance-gaining situations, even though situations defined by different influence goals appear to vary in terms of their potential complexity (Dillard & Solomon, 2000; Schrader & Dillard, 1998). O'Keefe and Delia's account, by itself, offers little insight into why the effects of construct differentiation would depend on situational factors such as request size and type or relational dominance.

Despite this shortcoming, O'Keefe and Delia's (1982) work is valuable because it highlights key components of communication competence (Wilson & Sabee, in press). Within complex compliance-gaining situations, people who address multiple goals when seeking or resisting compliance are judged, in general, as more "competent" than those whose messages address only the primary goal (Adams & Shepherd, 1996; Bingham & Burleson, 1989; Kline & Floyd, 1990; O'Keefe & McCornack, 1987; but not Waldron & Applegate, 1998). People judged as highly competent, in comparison with those judged less competent, also report having had more goal-relevant thoughts, and fewer self-focused thoughts, when asked to recall their thoughts immediately after an informal conversation (Cegala & Waldron, 1992). Based on O'Keefe and Delia's (1982) framework, communication competence seems to mean (a) being able to identify when one may be held accountable for meeting multiple objectives and (b) being able, when faced with such situations, to produce messages that coordinate seeking or resisting compliance with secondary goals (see Parks, 1995; Tracy, 1989; Wilson & Sabee, in press).

SUMMARY OF RESEARCH ON SECONDARY GOALS

In this section I have reviewed four research programs on multiple goals during compliance-gaining interactions. Three important conclusions can be drawn from these studies. First, people's attempts to seek and resist compliance are shaped and constrained by multiple goals. People decide what to say, and what not to say, during influence interactions based on concerns such as being true to themselves, looking favorable in the eyes of significant others, protecting others' self-esteem, maintaining desired relationships, meeting the norms for cooperative interaction, and not wasting time, energy, or other valued resources (Dillard et al., 1989; Hample & Dallinger, 1987a; Kim, 1994; O'Keefe & Shepherd, 1987). An individual is unlikely to have all of these goals within any specific interaction, and the goals he or she does possess typically will be prioritized such that some are more important than others (Wilson et al., 1998). Still, people's compliance-gaining messages typically reflect their concerns about multiple goals (e.g., Dillard et al., 1989).

A second conclusion is that people's concerns about multiple goals vary across individuals, situations, relationships, and cultures. Individuals differing in personality attributes such as argumentativeness or interpersonal construct differentiation place differing importance on primary and/or secondary goals (e.g., Hample & Dallinger, 1990; O'Keefe & Shepherd, 1987). Situational and relational factors such as intimacy or benefits to self also affect the importance that people place on primary and/or secondary goals (Hample & Dallinger, 1987a; Meyer, 1994a; Smith, 1982, 1984; Wilson et al., 1998). Individuals from different ethnic and cultural backgrounds also conceptualize and prioritize secondary goals differently (Cai, 1994; Kim, 1994; Tracy, 1989). Interaction goals are "heuristic" in the sense that they help explain how a host of factors affect persuasive message production.

A third conclusion is that a focus on multiple goals highlights the potential complexity of influence interactions (Dillard & Solomon, 2000; O'Keefe & Delia, 1982). Primary and secondary goals frequently conflict, such that the actions one might take to accomplish the influence goal seem to jeopardize secondary goals (and vice versa). A goals perspective highlights why interpersonal influence episodes can be complicated to manage, suggests competencies needed to manage complex episodes (O'Keefe, 1988; Tracy, 1989), and highlights how judgments about communication competence can vary across cultures (Kim, 1994).

Although the research programs reviewed in this section provide some insight into persuasive message production, they fail to address several questions about how people form and pursue goals during influence interactions. As we have seen, people prioritize influence and secondary goals differently depending on their personalities and cultural backgrounds, as well as on qualities of the specific compliance-gaining situation. What is lacking to this point, however, is an integrative framework that explains how, and in some senses why, a host of individual, cultural, and situational factors can affect people's goals. Indeed, we have not posed the basic questions of how people form interaction goals in the first place, and how people are able to do so under the time constraints and pressures of everyday conversation. To address these issues, I have presented one explicit set of assumptions about how interaction goals are formed (Wilson, 1990, 1995).

Forming Interaction Goals: The Cognitive Rules Model

The cognitive rules (CR) model assumes that people possess knowledge about a wide range of primary and secondary goals, as well as about numerous situational features relevant to each goal (Wilson, 1990, 1995). This goal-relevant knowledge is stored in an associative network model of long-term memory, composed of nodes representing concepts such as people, traits, roles, relational qualities, settings, and desired outcomes. Each cognitive rule links a node representing an interaction goal with multiple nodes representing situational features pertinent to that goal. Table 5.7 shows two hypothetical cognitive rules: one for the influence goal of giving advice and one for the goal of enforcing an unfulfilled obligation. The situational features associated with each goal in the table are taken from research on when people are likely to give advice (e.g., Goldsmith & Fitch, 1997; Rawlins, 1992) or to enforce obligations (e.g., Cody et al., 1994; Wilson & Kang, 1991). Still, the rules illustrated in Table 5.7 are hypothetical in the sense that any two individuals might associate the same goal with slightly different sets of situational features.

The CR model assumes that a spreading activation process operates on this associative memory network (Anderson, 1984). A cognitive rule is activated directly by a match between perceived features of the current situation and situational features in the rule. If I perceive that my stepdaughter is leaning toward going to work full-time rather than attending college after she graduates from high school, and furthermore believe that going to work full-time at this point is not in her best interest, then the rule for "giving advice" in Table 5.7 would receive activation. This same rule also would receive activation if I were to perceive that a work colleague whom I like needs to spend more time on a specific aspect of his job.[7] A cognitive rule also may be activated indirectly, when activation spreads from a directly stimulated node to other nodes that are associatively linked. Simply thinking about the concept of "liking" or "love," for example, should spread some activation to the first rule in Table 5.7 (as well as to many other cognitive rules that contain liking or loving as an associated situational feature). This spreading activation process is assumed to occur in "parallel," meaning that people typically compare cognitive rules to their perceptions of the current situation largely outside of consciousness, with little demand on their attentional resources. Parallel processing also means that the current situation can activate simultaneously the cognitive rules needed to form multiple goals.

Table 5.7   Hypothetical Cognitive Rules for Two Different Influence Goals

Type of Influence Goal	Situational Features Associated With Influence Goal
Give advice	Person A is about to do action X.
	X will have undesirable consequences for A.
	A would benefit more by doing Y.
	I like/love A.
	A ultimately has to decide what to do him- or herself.
Enforce an obligation	Person A promised to do action X.
	A has not done X.
	A could have done X if she or he had wanted to do so.
	I need X done.
	A has status that is less than or equal to mine.

Activation is a necessary but not sufficient condition for goal formation. The CR model assumes that cognitive rules have an activation "threshold": A goal is not formed unless a certain level of activation is received, and once that level is reached a rule is "triggered" and forms a goal (Higgins, Bargh, & Lombardi, 1985). The probability of a rule's being triggered is a function of three general criteria: fit, strength, and recency (J. R. Anderson, 1983; Greene, 1984a).

Based on the fit criterion, the probability of goal formation increases when a larger rather than a smaller number of situational conditions represented in a rule are perceived in the current situation. For example, a message source is likely to form the goal of "enforcing an obligation" when a target person of equal or lesser status knowingly fails to perform a promised action with tangible consequences for the source, but is less likely to do so when only some of these situational conditions are present (see the second rule in Table 5.7).

Aside from fit, situations also vary in ambiguity. Ambiguous situations are open to multiple plausible interpretations, and hence partially match and activate a larger number of cognitive rules than do clear situations. Consider the three versions of the "repay loan" scenario that appear in Table 5.8. In this scenario, you are asked to imagine having to persuade your friend, Chris, to pay back an overdue loan. One question that might occur to you is "Why hasn't Chris paid back the loan yet?" Indeed, you probably would try to persuade Chris in particular ways depending on your answer to this question (Wilson, 1990; Wilson, Cruz, Marshall, & Rao, 1993). In the first version of the scenario, marked "external cause," there are clear indications that Chris's failure to repay the loan on time is due to extenuating circumstances—Chris has a consistent history of repaying loans promptly, and Chris's only prior failure was due to illness. In the last version, marked "internal cause," there are clear indications that Chris's failure to repay the loan on time is intentional—Chris has a habit of paying you back late, even though he or she pays others back on time. Chris probably figures that he or she can get away with being late with you. In contrast, the question of why Chris hasn't paid you back yet is much less clear in the middle version shown in Table 5.8. In this version, Chris occasionally has been late repaying you in the past, but on the whole Chris has been about as prompt as others, and extenuating circumstances typically have been present on the occasions when Chris has been late. This middle version contains situational features associated with the judgment that "Chris hasn't paid me back yet on purpose," but also features associated with "Chris hasn't paid me back yet due to external circumstances." Hence this ambiguous version should partially match and activate cognitive rules linked to both sets of situational features.

An important assumption of the CR model is that when both degree and clarity of fit are high (e.g., the first or third scenario in Table 5.8), then situational features themselves are sufficient to trigger cognitive rules. But when fit is only moderate and ambiguity is high (e.g., the middle scenario in Table 5.8), strength and recency are more important determinants of goal formation (Srull & Wyer, 1979).

Both the *strength* and *recency* criteria relate to the accessibility of cognitive rules. Within ambiguous situations, a cognitive rule is more likely to be triggered as the strength of associations between the situational features and the desired end state represented in the rule increases. Strength of association is related directly to the frequency of prior activation of the rule. A cognitive rule that has been triggered frequently in the past becomes "chronically accessible," and hence now is triggered more easily than a rule that has been used infrequently in the past (Fazio, Sanbonmatsu, Powell, & Kardes, 1986; Higgins, King, & Marvin, 1982). Within ambiguous situations, a cognitive rule also is more likely to be triggered if that rule already has been activated by a recent event (because an activated rule takes time to dissipate). Curiously, this can occur even in cases where the recent event that spread accessibility to a cognitive rule has little to do with the topic of the current influence interaction (Higgins et al., 1985; Wilson, 1990).

In an initial experiment testing the CR model, I manipulated three experimental factors (Wilson, 1990). Each experimental factor was designed to correspond with one of the three criteria affecting the probability of goal formation (i.e., fit, frequency, and recency). Participants provided open-ended reports of their interaction goals in response to one of four hypothetical scenarios, all of which were defined by the influence goal of enforcing an obligation. The number of "supportive secondary goals" included in each list served as the primary dependent variable. Supportive secondary goals included objectives such as wanting to "maintain a good relationship with the target" and to "protect the target's self-concept."

To manipulate the *fit* criterion, I created attributionally "ambiguous" versus "clear" versions of each scenario, such as those for the "repay loan" scenario that appear in Table 5.8. I manipulated the *recency* criterion through a "relational intimacy priming task." Participants in this condition read their hypothetical compliance-gaining scenario immediately after completing a word-association task that contained terms relevant to interpersonal relationships (e.g., friends, trust, support). This priming task should have spread activation to situational features relevant to rules forming "supportive" secondary goals. Participants in a control condition read their hypothetical scenario immediately after completing a word-association task about the weather (e.g., rain, wind, clouds), which should have had little to do with the situational features relevant to supportive secondary goals. Finally, I tapped the "frequency" criterion indirectly, using Crockett's (1965) RCQ measure of interpersonal construct differentiation. Prior research suggested that highly differentiated persons should have formed supportive secondary goals spontaneously and pursued them more frequently in the past than had their less differentiated counterparts (see the discussion of the "goal complexity/behavioral complexity" account earlier in this chapter). Following this reasoning, highly differentiated participants should have possessed stronger or more accessible cognitive rules for forming supportive secondary goals. Both the relational priming manipulation and construct differentiation were predicted to influence whether participants reported supportive secondary goals in the ambiguous compliance-gaining scenarios, but not in the clear scenarios.

This initial experiment produced many findings consistent with the CR model. As predicted, the relational priming manipulation affected participants' reports of supportive secondary goals in response to the ambiguous compliance-gaining scenarios, but not in response to the clear scenarios. When the scenario was ambiguous (e.g., the middle version of the "repay loan" situation in Table 5.8), participants who had completed the "relational priming" word-association task just before reading their scenario reported, on average, 72% more supportive secondary goals in their open-ended lists than did those in the control condition, who had completed the word-association task about the weather before reading their scenario. In these ambiguous scenarios, recency of activation affected the likelihood that a cognitive rule was triggered. When the scenario was clear (e.g., the top or bottom version of the "repay loan" scenario in Table 5.8), however, participants who had just completed the relational priming word-association task did not differ from those in the control condition with regard to the number of supportive secondary goals they reported. Recency of activation did not affect the likelihood that a cognitive rule was triggered in the clear scenarios, presumably because the situational features themselves were sufficient to trigger cognitive rules in those scenarios.

Table 5.8   Clear and Ambiguous Versions of the "Repay Loan"
                   Compliance-Gaining Scenario

Clearly external cause (circumstances) version: Imagine that Chris, a friend you have
known for several years, has borrowed money from you occasionally but has
virtually always repaid you on time. In fact, you can remember only one instance
when Chris did not repay a loan on time, which occurred about a year ago when
Chris came down with a severe case of the flu. Other people have commented that,
like yourself, they can always count on Chris to return borrowed items on time.
Chris certainly repays debts as promptly as any individual to whom you have
loaned money. Last week, Chris borrowed $25 to get through till payday, which you
know was two days ago. Because of some recent expenses, your own bank balance is
now smaller than you would like it to be. You decide to talk to Chris about the loan.

Attributionally ambiguous version: Imagine that Chris, a friend you have known for
several years, has borrowed money from you in the past and occasionally not repaid
it on time. In fact, Chris sometimes seems to take longer repaying loans from you
than loans he/she has received from other people. You know of times when Chris
has had to delay repaying you because unpredictable and uncontrollable expenses
arose just before payment was due. On the whole, Chris probably repays debts
about as promptly as other individuals. Last week, Chris borrowed $25 to get
through till payday, which you know was two days ago. Because of some recent
expenses, your own bank balance is now smaller than you would like it to be.
You decide to talk to Chris about the loan.

Clearly internal cause (intentional) version: Imagine that Chris, a friend you have
known for several years, has the habit of borrowing money from you and then not
repaying it for long periods of time. In fact, it seems that Chris has been late only
when repaying money borrowed from you; that is, Chris always has repaid loans on
time whenever he/she has received the loans from individuals other than you. Chris
is the only person you can remember who has borrowed money from you and then
not repaid the debt promptly. Because of some recent expenses, your own bank
balance is now smaller than you would like it to be. You decide to talk to Chris
about the loan.

SOURCE: From "Development and Test of a Cognitive Rules Model of Interaction
Goals," by S. R. Wilson, 1990, *Communication Monographs, 57,* pp. 102-103. Copyright
1990 by the Speech Communication Association. Reprinted with permission.

In addition to these results, the initial test of the CR model also generated
several unexpected findings. Predictions from the model, in general, fared
much better for individuals high in interpersonal construct differentiation
than for less differentiated individuals. Highly differentiated participants
varied their reports of supportive secondary goals in response to the relational
intimacy priming manipulation within the ambiguous (but not the clear)
compliance-gaining scenarios. Less differentiated individuals, in contrast,

did not vary their reports of supportive secondary goals depending on the relational priming manipulation, the type of scenario they read (ambiguous versus clear), or any other experimental factor. For example, less differentiated individuals did not vary their likelihood of reporting supportive secondary goals depending on whether they had read the top, middle, or bottom version of the "repay loan" scenario in Table 5.8. This unexpected finding is difficult to reconcile with the idea that personality traits such as construct differentiation affect only the chronic accessibility of people's rules for forming supportive secondary goals. As I noted at the time:

> Such a position assumes that all message sources have the same kind of rules, but that some people have rules which simply are more accessible. However, less differentiated people failed to report more supporting goals even when the fit between rules and situational features should have been high and clear, that is, in situations where most pretest participants attributed the target's noncompliance only to extenuating circumstances. (Wilson, 1990, p. 98)

In light of such findings, I have proposed a more detailed version of the CR model that suggests multiple ways in which personality and situational factors can affect people's interaction goals (Wilson, 1995). Personality attributes and cultural orientations may be reflected in the content of cognitive rules (i.e., the specific situational features associated with goals), the structure of rules (e.g., the number of situational features associated with goals), and/or the chronic accessibility of rules (i.e., how frequently a rule has been activated in the past). Individuals high in interpersonal construct differentiation, for instance, appear to possess more elaborate, and not simply more accessible, rules for forming secondary goals than do less differentiated persons (Wilson, 1995; Wilson, Cruz, & Kang, 1992). Future research is needed to evaluate whether this revised CR model can explain how a host of individual, cultural, and situational factors affect people's interaction goals.

Evaluating the Utility of a Goals Perspective

As I have documented in this chapter, scholars who study persuasive message production have moved away from simply trying to identify personality and situational factors that predict people's choice of compliance-gaining/resisting strategies and have explored what goals motivate people to seek and resist compliance in the first place. The trend toward studying interaction goals, although widespread, is not without its critics. Some of these critics focus on the ideological assumptions underlying the concept of interaction goals, whereas others question whether interaction goals can explain the emergent nature of influence interactions.

IDEOLOGICAL CRITICISMS

The term *ideology* refers to a set of issues regarding the interrelationships among knowledge, meaning, and power (Lannamann, 1991; Parks, 1995). Ideological criticisms challenge scholars to make explicit their own underlying, taken-for-granted assumptions about individuals, relationships, and communication, and to recognize that these assumptions are not the only ways of understanding the world. Ideological criticisms draw attention to how scholars' taken-for-granted assumptions reflect the larger cultures and political systems in which they live. Ideological analyses push scholars to explore what questions about communication they typically ask (and what questions they do not ask) and how their understandings of communication may be influenced by what they typically look for (and do not look for) when conducting research.

In one such critique, Lannamann (1991) argues that the concept of "interaction goals" is central to the ideology that underlies contemporary research on interpersonal communication. According to Lannamann, most studies of interpersonal communication, including those on persuasive message production, share four ideological tendencies: (a) individualism (studies typically examine the "individual" as their unit of analysis, and thereby ignore the social origins of the self and fail to explore how individuals are constrained by power relations within the larger society), (b) subjectivism (studies rely heavily on self-report measures that capture people's subjective perceptions of interaction, and thereby fail to analyze how social and material conditions shape those perceptions), (c) intentionality (studies rely on the goals and desires of individuals to explain their behavior during interpersonal communication, and thereby ignore how individuals' goals and desires are shaped and constrained by larger social forces as well as downplay the unintended consequences of interpersonal behavior), and (d) ahistoricism (studies rely primarily on experimental rather than historical methods, and thereby reify current social practices as if they were timeless generalizations). In response to these four tendencies, Lannamann calls for research that illuminates, and challenges, how everyday interactions both reflect and are constrained by historical, societal-level values and relations of power.

Lannamann's (1991) characterization of the ideological tendencies underlying mainstream interpersonal communication research, although exaggerated, is largely accurate. As we have seen in this chapter, scholars rely heavily on goals and desires to explain what people say, and do not say, when seeking and resisting compliance. Scholars have relied heavily on various self-report procedures to identify the types of goals that individuals commonly pursue during influence interactions. And historical analyses of societal-level forces are rare. Studies comparing individualist and collectivist cultures, for instance, have examined how individuals from different countries of origin perceive and prioritize conversational constraints (Kim, 1994; Kim & Wilson, 1994), but they have ignored the historical and economic forces that helped to create those cultural syndromes (see Triandis, 1993). Research exploring whether conversational constraints are changing within different segments of collectivist cultures, such as South Korea or Japan, in response to economic and technological developments would complement current studies (see Rao, Singhal, Ren, & Zhang, 2001).

Having said this, I should also note that I believe that we can appreciate Lannamann's (1991) ideological critique without devaluing current research on persuasive message production. Individuals are not automatons who are buffeted about by historical and economic forces. Individuals do pursue goals and make choices, albeit within circumstances that are not totally of their own choosing. Rawlins (1992) puts it nicely when he writes, "The human communicator [is] an ongoing producer and product of his or her choices within an encompassing cultural matrix" (pp. 7-8). As the discussion in this chapter has shown, one promising feature of the concept of "interaction goal" is that it can highlight both choice and constraint. My main contention, throughout this book, is that we can learn a great deal about influence interactions by studying people's interaction goals. The level of the "individual" is not the only valid vantage point from which we can study influence interactions, but it is one useful vantage point (Hewes & Planalp, 1987).

In another ideological critique, Shepherd (1992, 1998) argues that the concepts of primary and secondary goals, which I have used as an organizing framework for this chapter, are part of a masculine and egoistic bias that pervades the communication discipline. Initially, Shepherd (1992) argues:

> From humanistic definitions of rhetoric in the 1930's, through social scientific conceptions of communication in the 1960's, to critical considerations of discourse in the 1990's, interaction processes have typically been characterized essentially and primarily in terms of persuasion, influence, and power. The history of communication as a field of study coalesces around this traditional conceptualization of communication as social influence. (p. 204)

Shepherd claims that this historical tradition is masculinely biased, in that it prioritizes qualities, such as "being able to get one's way" and "controlling one's environment," that stereotypically are viewed as important for men in U.S. society (see Bem, 1993; Buzzanell, 1994). This historical tradition also de-emphasizes alternative feminine views that define communication "in terms of relations, concern, caring, and responsibility, rather than influence" (Shepherd, 1992, p. 206).

According to Shepherd, the conception of influence goals as "primary" and relational concerns as "secondary" represents one example of masculine bias. Taking issue with Dillard's (1990) description of primary goals, Shepherd (1992) writes:

> Communication as the realization of a desire to influence, however, may be *an* explanation for a given interaction but it is not *the* explanation for any interaction. There is no "influence interaction," there are only interactions that we, as theorists and researchers, label. The field's masculine definitional bias has simply led to a corresponding bias in labeling. If we had long-assumed a feminine definition of communication, our collective theories and corpus of research might look very different. Goal-based approaches, for example, would probably have theorized relational desires as typically primary in communication situations, with influence conceived as a secondary, sometimes constraining concern. (pp. 210-211)

There is some merit to Shepherd's criticism here. As you will recall, studies of influence goals often have instructed women and men to describe interactions from their own lives in which they attempted to alter another person's behavior, and then classified common reasons why behavior change is sought (e.g., Dillard, 1989; Kipnis et al., 1980). Put differently, these studies have simply assumed, rather than verified, that both women and men (or feminine and masculine individuals) actually defined what was going on in their recalled interactions as "attempts to seek compliance." More recent research has found that participants in general, when asked to imagine or recall situations defined by an influence (primary) goal, often still rate one or more secondary goals as more important than gaining compliance (Schrader & Dillard, 1998; Wilson et al., 1998).

Although these points suggest that scholars should take care in studying primary/secondary goals, to my mind they do not undermine the utility of Dillard's conceptual distinction. Primary and secondary goals differ in function and directional force, but not necessarily in importance. Participants in an interaction may define it, for the moment, as one in which a message source is offering a target advice (primary) even though both participants have cross-situational concerns that are more important than giving/receiving advice (secondary goals). In addition, primary goals do not inevitably involve influence; relational desires can become primary in the sense of defining, for the moment, what is going on in an interaction (Dillard & Schrader, 1998, pp. 301-302). Participants may understand the "same" interaction to be about influence, then about relational maintenance, and then about influence again over short periods of time.

Finally, the question of whether women and men actually define interactions differently in terms of underlying goals is an *empirical* question. No study to date, to my knowledge, has addressed this question directly. Several recent findings, however, raise doubt about whether women and men differ substantially in how they frame interactions. Shepherd (1992, p. 208), drawing on Hample and Dallinger's (1987a) research on cognitive editing, claims that men in general are more likely to adopt a task orientation (emphasizing effectiveness during interaction), whereas women in general are more likely to adopt a relational orientation (emphasizing concern for others). Although it is true that Hample and Dallinger report sex differences in these cognitive editing standards, the *magnitude* of the differences is extremely small. After reanalyzing data from several early studies involving a total of 1,471 college students, Dallinger and Hample (1994) found that biological sex explained at most only 1% of the variance in people's choices of particular cognitive editing standards. In a similar vein, Kim and Bresnahan (1996) detected no significant differences in Hawaiian, Japanese, South Korean, or mainland U.S. women's and men's importance ratings for the conversational constraints of efficiency and appropriateness, either within each culture or across cultures. Findings such as these suggest that college-age women and men actually are more similar than different in how they frame interactions in terms of primary and secondary goals.

FROM GOALS TO (INTER)ACTION?

In addition to the ideological issues noted above, some critics question whether people's behavior during influence interactions can be explained in terms of goals. One group of scholars emphasizes that goals, in and of themselves, are insufficient to generate communicative *action* (Berger, 1995; Greene, 1984a; O'Keefe, 1988). Aside from goals, people also must possess "procedural knowledge" about potential means by which they might accomplish their goals (Anderson, 1985). Without procedural knowledge, we would live in a constant state of confusion, wanting things but having no idea what to say in order to achieve what we want. O'Keefe (1988) explains the necessity of procedural knowledge nicely:

> We know that messages are designed to serve goals . . . but it is transparently clear that goals alone cannot generate messages. Simply wanting some end or effect to be brought about does not specify or mark out ways of bringing about the end or effect. Therefore, a message producer must have some process or principle that is used in constructing the verbal expressions that will serve goals. (p. 96)

Thus individuals can differ not only in terms of how they weight influence and secondary goals, but in the amount and type of knowledge they possess about pursuing and coordinating multiple goals, as well as in their ability actually to put their procedural knowledge into practice. I discuss research on how people represent procedural knowledge about seeking and resisting compliance in memory, and how they translate this knowledge into action, in Chapter 7.

Other scholars argue that goals may not be well suited for explaining communicative *interaction* (for debate on this point, compare Bavelas, 1991, with Hewes & Planalp, 1987). A message source does not seek compliance in isolation, but rather during conversation with a target individual who has his or her own set of goals. Neither party may behave exactly as the other anticipates, and both will adapt what they themselves say depending on what the other says. Goals may explain how a message source and target initiate an influence interaction, but do people really continue to pursue goals as their interaction unfolds? Do conversations develop a momentum of their own, independent of the participants' goals? Can goals explain the emergent nature of influence interactions? Bavelas (1991) poses the problem in this fashion:

> The essential nature of a mental goal, however, is *monadic:* It refers to some process, disposition, or awareness in an individual. Yet, if such goals are then connected with face-to-face *interaction,* a fundamental disparity of units arises. Goals as a construct located in an individual mind might explain monologue, but even the cleverest and bravest reductionist does not have the alchemy to produce the creative spontaneity of dialogue out of two goals, in separate minds. . . . Mentally driven theories can hypothesize a start to the interaction, but they also must account for the reciprocity and accommodation that characterize face-to-face interaction. Otherwise, the goals of the two individuals would run parallel, never affecting each other. (p. 122)

The issues that Bavelas raises here are important. Identifying the content of primary and secondary goals is not an end in itself. Primary and secondary goals are useful only to the degree to which they help explain people's messages during influence interactions. It is my belief, however, that a goals perspective can account for the dynamic, emergent nature of influence interactions. Unlike static personality traits, interaction goals are dynamic forces that can change quickly over time. Using a stimulated recall method, Waldron (1997) demonstrates how participants' ratings of the importance of Dillard et al.'s (1989) five secondary goals vary dramatically on a minute-by-minute basis over the course of a 10-minute get-acquainted conversation. During an influence interaction, the message source's and target's goals may change, and new goals may emerge, whenever (a) initial attempts to seek or resist compliance are thwarted,

(b) assumptions about the other party or the situation prove false, and/or (c) one or both parties feel attacked and become defensive (Sanders, 1991; Wilson & Putnam, 1990). I review research on how people pursue both influence and secondary goals over time, in response to each others' moves and within the norms and constraints of conversation, in Chapter 6.

Despite these criticisms, most scholars continue to view persuasive message production as a goal-driven process. The "goal-pursuit" metaphor avoids many problematic assumptions implicit in the earlier metaphor of "strategy selection" (Seibold et al., 1994; Wilson, 1997). Whereas the strategy-selection metaphor implied that influence situations come predefined in a manner obvious to all, the goal-pursuit metaphor presumes that message sources and targets actively define influence situations in terms of underlying goals and recognizes that sources and targets do not always agree about "what is going on." Whereas the strategy-selection metaphor implied that message sources and targets consciously assess their motivations and strategic options, the goal-pursuit metaphor presumes that people having shifting, momentary, and often limited awareness of their primary and secondary goals. Whereas the strategy-selection metaphor presumed that people possess the ability to enact a large repertoire of compliance-seeking and -resisting strategies, the goal-pursuit metaphor suggests that people may differ in their ability to draw on strategic and pragmatic means for pursuing and coordinating multiple goals. And whereas the strategy-selection metaphor highlighted static predictors of people's initial compliance-seeking and -resisting strategies, the goal-pursuit metaphor highlights the dynamic and unfolding nature of influence interactions.

Summary

Most contemporary theories describe persuasive message production as a goal-driven process. During a compliance-gaining interaction, a message source pursues the primary goal of wanting to modify the target's behavior. This primary goal motivates the message source to speak and defines what the interaction is about. Both the message source and the target also may pursue secondary goals, or recurrent motivations that shape and constrain their attempts to seek or resist compliance. In this chapter I have reviewed research on the nature and substance of both primary (influence) and secondary goals, and I have presented a cognitive rules model of how interaction goals are formed. I have concluded the chapter by addressing some criticisms of the move toward studying goals.

Notes

1. For example, negotiators at times attempt to maintain positive impressions with their own constituents by claiming, after the fact, that serendipitous events actually were part of their plans for achieving their constituents' goals. But a negotiator's objective in such instances is not simply to make sense of prior experience; rather, it is to persuade constituents that the "sense" he or she has made is a valid interpretation of prior events. Such impression management objectives are examples of interaction goals (see Wilson & Putnam, 1990).

2. My point here is not that every friend would offer Chris advice in this situation. Some friends, despite their desire for Chris to stay in school, might feel it is not their place at that moment to offer advice. In such a case, the interaction, for the moment, would be defined by some primary goal other than giving advice. As will become clear, my point also is not that giving advice would be the friend's only goal, or even the friend's most important goal. People frequently offer advice in indirect ways, for instance, to avoid looking "too pushy" (Pudlinski, 1998). Rather, my point is that "giving advice" provides one recognizable frame for what may be about to unfold in this situation. If the friend's behavior can be construed as "giving advice," then both participants, for the moment, are likely to orient to it as such.

3. To be fair, Dillard has been somewhat vague on this point. He is clear that primary goals vary in strength across people and situations (Dillard et al., 1989, p. 20), and he has maintained that actors may understand episodes to be about influence (e.g., asking a favor) even when they rate other goals (e.g., not imposing too much on the target) as more important (Dillard & Schrader, 1998, p. 302). However, he also has written that, for researchers, the primary goal is "the chief purpose of an interaction [that] distinguishes that communication event from other areas of inquiry" (Dillard et al., 1989, p. 21), and this could be taken to mean that for a goal to be labeled as primary, it must be an actor's most important concern. In this book, I use the term *primary* to refer to the goal that, for the moment, frames the interaction; this may or may not be the goal that is most important.

4. Cluster analysis is a statistical procedure that attempts to identify relatively homogeneous groups of cases (in this instance, goal statements) based on selected characteristics (in this instance, regularities in how participants grouped goals statements into piles).

5. For discussions similar to O'Keefe's (1988) regarding the two senses of *goal*, see Craig's (1986) distinction between "functional" and "intentional" goals and Donohue's (1990) distinction between goals from "restricted" versus "generalized" subject-meaning perspectives.

6. Waldron and Applegate (1998) found that participants in face-to-face arguments who tended to use "person-centered" persuasive tactics (those that managed primary and face goals) were evaluated by their partners as more persuasive, but not more socially attractive or more competent, than participants who tended to use "position-centered" tactics (those that addressed only the primary goal).

7. As these examples illustrate, the letters A, X, and Y in Table 5.7 are variables or slots that must be filled in within the situation. These letters are typically used to refer to classes of people or actions, rather than to specific persons or actions. Over time, however, we may develop unique cognitive rules for forming goals with specific persons (e.g., our relational partners).

Part III

Theories of Goal Pursuit

Part III

Theories of God Pursuit

6

Discourse Perspectives on Persuasive Message Production

Looking Ahead . . .

This chapter reviews discourse perspectives on persuasive message production. Although diverse, these perspectives focus on how people rely on knowledge of linguistic forms and conventions when generating influence messages, and how they design messages in light of unfolding talk. The chapter opens with an example designed to illustrate some of the questions raised by discourse scholars. Following this, concepts such as conversational maxims, speech acts, and adjacency pairs are reviewed to provide readers new to the area with necessary background. The chapter then explores two concepts with special relevance for understanding persuasive message production: (a) "obstacles," analyzed from the view of speech act and attribution theories; and (b) "face," analyzed from the perspective of politeness and message design logic theories.

EXAMPLE 6.1

((Phone rings; another party answers, the caller, "Mike," asks for "Mr. Jenkins"; the other party then goes to get Mr. Jenkins.))

| 01 | Mr. J.: | Hello |
| 02 | Mike: | Hi there, Mr. Jenkins? |

03	Mr. J.:	Yeah
04	Mike:	Hi, my name is Mike and I'm calling from the
05		American Red Cross

((8 intervening turns occur, in which Mike asks for permission to audio-tape the call and verifies background information about Mr. Jenkins))

14	Mike:	I'm just calling to see if I can get you uh to set up an
15		appointment to donate blood.
16	Mr. J.:	OK
17	Mike:	At the uh Great Lakes Regional Blood Center
18	Mr. J.:	Uh huh
19	Mike:	And that's in Lansing
20	Mr. J.:	Yeah, I know, it's about three blocks from my house
21	Mike:	Oh really
22	Mr. J.:	Yeah
23	Mike:	((interrupts)) Would you, uh, help us out, and could you
24	Mr. J.:	((interrupts)) I, I, I think I can, sure, I've been,
25		I I've been a little sick there all winter there, so you
26		know, so I try to get in at least once or twice a year
27	Mike:	Yeah, well uh ah oh uh how, have you just been like
28		sick with colds?

((13 intervening lines occur in which someone else at Mr. J's house picks up the phone and accidentally interrupts the conversation))

42	Mike:	eh have you just been sick with colds?
43	Mr. J.:	Yeah, right
44	Mike:	Because, uh, the uh, what the Red Cross said is if
45		you've been sick with a cold you can donate to
46		just 24 hours after you ((pause)) begin to feel better
47	Mr. J.:	Yeah right, that's ((not intelligible)) OK, sure
48	Mike:	So you'd be interested in donating for us?
49	Mr. J.:	((interrupts)) sure

(data from Wilson, Levine, Humphreys, & Peters, 1994)

Has a volunteer from the American Red Cross ever telephoned and asked you to donate blood? In the United States today, someone requires a blood trans-fusion every 12 seconds. Aside from lifesaving transfusions, blood products such as plasma, platelets, and immune serum globulin are used to treat patients suffering from cancer, leukemia, and other life-threatening diseases (American

Red Cross, 1989). The Red Cross collects, processes, and distributes one-half of the nation's blood supply. Although the organization is constantly attempting to recruit new donors, the vast majority of individuals donating blood (78-91%) are repeat donors (Piliavin, 1990). Thus the Red Cross keeps careful records of prior donors and telephones them periodically to encourage repeat donations. Both professional and volunteer solicitors are used in this process.

Several years ago, three colleagues and I collaborated with the American Red Cross's Great Lakes Regional Blood Center in Lansing, Michigan, to study how volunteer telephone solicitors attempted to persuade prior donors to give blood again (Wilson et al., 1994). Participants in our study were college undergraduates who volunteered to work one evening as telephone solicitors on behalf of the American Red Cross. Participants initially attended a 1-hour training session conducted by the regional center's staff, at which they learned about procedures for donating blood, uses of blood products, steps for maintaining donor confidentiality, requirements for medical eligibility, and suggestions for overcoming common obstacles to donating.

After completing this training, participants returned 2 to 4 weeks later to telephone prior blood donors. Upon arrival at the communication laboratory, each volunteer received a calling list of 20 prior donors and a sheet of instructions. For each call, participants were instructed to follow a three-part sequence in which they asked for permission to audiotape the call, verified background information, and asked for an appointment. Instructions for the last step suggested the following wording: "I'm calling to see if we could schedule you to donate blood again. Can we count on you again?" Following this initial request, participants used their own judgment about whether and how to persist in seeking to convince the prior donor to comply. Our primary interests in the study were learning how college student volunteers decided whether to persist after prior donors resisted their initial requests and whether volunteers persisted differently depending on the ways in which prior donors resisted. The conversation in Example 6.1 between Mike and Mr. Jenkins provides a convenient starting point for illustrating the concerns of discourse scholars.

Questions Posed by Discourse Scholars

Discourse scholars would raise a number of very specific questions about audiotaped interactions such as that displayed in Example 6.1. These perspectives focus our attention on why Mike and Mr. Jenkins say what they do, turn by turn, as their conversation unfolds. To get a feel for this type of analysis, start by examining the form of Mike's initial request for Mr. Jenkins to donate blood again (see lines 14-15). Why does Mike phrase this initial request as he does? Couldn't he get to the point more quickly rather than being so wordy? Why include the adverb *just*, "I'm *just* calling," rather than say only "I'm calling"? Why use the phrase "to see if I can get you uh to" rather than the less tentative "to get you to"? Or for that matter, why doesn't Mike just ask, "Will you donate blood?" Do Mike's word choices have anything to do with the nature of his request? After all, he is asking Mr. Jenkins to take about 90 minutes out of his schedule, drive to the regional blood center, and donate bodily fluid. Do Mike's word choices also reflect that he is making this request of a stranger who is older than himself?

Turning to Mr. Jenkins, why does he initially say "OK" rather than "Sure" or "No, I can't" in response to Mike's initial request (see line 16)? If Mr. Jenkins isn't saying yes or no to Mike's request at this point, what is he saying? And don't people usually respond to requests by saying yes (complying) or no (refusing) in the very next turn at talk? If not, what other types of actions often follow requests?

When Mr. Jenkins, in lines 24-26, finally does give an answer to Mike's request, why doesn't he just say "Yeah" or "Sure"? In other words, why does he mention that he's been "a little sick" in the past? Is he sick at this time? And why does Mr. Jenkins tell Mike, a complete stranger, that he tries to donate blood twice a year? Similarly, why does Mike ask exactly what Mr. Jenkins means by the phrase "a little sick" in lines 27-28? Does Mike have a personal interest in Mr. Jenkins's health during the past winter? Are Mike's questions somehow related to his initial request for Mr. Jenkins to donate blood?

Finally, why does Mr. Jenkins not seem surprised to learn that an individual can donate blood only 24 hours after feeling better from a cold? Notice that he says "Yeah right" rather than "Oh really?" in line 47. But if Mr. Jenkins already understands that a cold is not a reason for failing to donate blood over a long period of time, why did he mention having been "a little sick" back in line 25?

These questions about the "Mr. Jenkins-Mike" conversation illustrate the types of issues posed by discourse perspectives on persuasive message production. The theories reviewed in this chapter come from many fields, including communication, philosophy, psycholinguistics, sociolinguistics, sociology, and social psychology.[1] Although diverse, these perspectives clarify how people use knowledge of linguistic forms and conventions when generating influence messages. Discourse scholars explore how people's attempts to seek and resist compliance are shaped and constrained by what each party already has said. They often examine how people attempt to create and sustain desired identities for themselves, as well as their interactional partners, through talk. Discourse scholars highlight patterns that occur at minute levels of talk, such as precise regularities in the ways that people word requests and responses to requests.

The remainder of this chapter is divided into three major sections. In the first, I review the basic concepts and assumptions with which readers need to be familiar in order to understand discourse perspectives. In this section I cover briefly some relevant writings on conversational maxims, speech acts, and the "conversation analysis" tradition. In the second and third main sections, I explore in more depth two concepts with special relevance for an understanding of *persuasive* message production. First, message targets often state "obstacles" when resisting message sources' influence attempt, and sources and targets may negotiate the feasibility of overcoming obstacles to compliance. "Obstacles" are analyzed using both speech act (Searle, 1969) and attribution (Weiner, 1986) theories. Second, message sources, by seeking compliance, often raise threats to face for both participants, and the forms of requests and responses are shaped in part by desires to maintain face. Threats to face are analyzed using Brown and Levinson's (1987) politeness theory and O'Keefe's (1988) theory of message design logics.

Background Concepts and Assumptions

CONVERSATIONAL MAXIMS

People often mean more than what they say. Consider the following example:

EXAMPLE 6.2

| 1 | A: | Where's Bill? |
| 2 | B: | There's a yellow VW outside Sue's house |

(Levinson, 1983, p. 102)

B's words in Example 6.2, taken literally, do not answer A's question. A asks about the location of a male named Bill, whereas B says that a specific automobile is located outside the house of a female named Sue. Despite this, we assume that B is attempting to answer A's question. In order to hear line 2 as an answer, we must infer (a) that Bill owns a yellow VW, and hence (b) that Bill may be inside, or near, Sue's house. B appears to assume that A can make these inferences.

Example 6.2 shows how we make inferences that go beyond the literal meaning of words. In some cases, however, what a speaker means has virtually no connection to what he or she says. Consider a fictional example, which could have occurred at many points as I wrote this book:

EXAMPLE **6.3**

| 1 | Friend: | So, how's your book coming? |
| 2 | Me: | It sure is starting to rain hard outside. |

My words, taken literally, do not seem even remotely related to my friend's question. What does the weather have to do with this book? Did I simply fail to hear my friend's question? Possibly, but you probably already have inferred a different meaning: I am having difficulty with the book, and I do not wish to talk about the topic at this time. How did you arrive at this inference? How is it possible for me to imply that I do not wish to talk about writing a book by talking about rain?

Paul Grice (1975), a British philosopher of language, has proposed a theory of conversational implicature to explain how speakers can infer things distinct from the conventional meaning of their words. He begins with the observation that conversation is a "cooperative" activity, meaning that it requires minimal levels of collaboration and coordination between participants. As Grice puts it:

> Our talk exchanges do not normally consist of a succession of disconnected remarks. . . . They are characteristically, to some degree at least, cooperative efforts; and each participant recognizes in them, to some extent, a common purpose or set of purposes, or at least a mutually accepted direction. This purpose or direction may be fixed from the start . . . or it may evolve during the exchange. . . . But at each stage, SOME possible conversational moves would be excluded as conversationally unsuitable. (p. 45)

Given this observation, Grice argues that conversationalists share a set of overarching assumptions about talk. Participants are expected to follow what Grice labels the "cooperative principle," namely: "Make your conversational contribution such as is required, at the stage at which it occurs, by the accepted purpose or direction of the talk exchange in which you are engaged" (p. 45). Grice has formulated four principles, or "maxims," the following of which will lead to behavior consistent with the cooperative principle. Grice's maxims of quantity, quality, relation, and manner are summarized briefly in Table 6.1.

The quantity maxim pertains to the expected amount of talk. It is violated when speakers are overinformative, as B is in Example 6.4, or underinformative, as B is in Example 6.5:

Table 6.1   Grice's (1975) Four Conversational Maxims

Maxim	Definition
Quantity	Provide the proper amount of information: 1. Say as much as is required (given the current purposes of the talk). 2. Do not say more than is required.
Quality	Try to make your contribution one that is true: 1. Do not say what you believe to be false. 2. Do not say that for which you lack adequate evidence.
Relation	Be relevant.
Manner	Be clear: 1. Avoid obscure expressions. 2. Avoid ambiguity. 3. Be brief (avoid unnecessary wordiness). 4. Be orderly.

SOURCE: From "Logic and Conversation," by H. P. Grice, in P. Cole & J. L. Morgan (Eds.), 1975, *Syntax and Semantics: Vol. 3. Speech Acts* (pp. 45-46). Efforts were made to secure permission from the copyright holder to adapt this table.

EXAMPLE 6.4

1	A:	What's up?
2	B:	Well, I got up this morning, and I was feeling pretty good, but then I went downstairs to eat breakfast, and I was out of orange juice—I hate it when that happens, and then . . .

EXAMPLE 6.5

1	A:	Do you know what time it is?
2	B:	Yes.
3		((pause))
4	A:	Well, what time is it?!

The quality maxim pertains to the sincerity of talk, such as expectations that speakers will avoid dishonesty, deception, hearsay, or gossip. The maxim of relation states that speakers should make relevant contributions given the current topic and purpose(s) of talk. This maxim seems to be violated in Example 6.6, where a psychiatrist tries to interview a patient who is being admitted to a hospital.[2]

EXAMPLE 6.6

1	Dr.:	What is your name?
2	Patient:	Well, let's say you might have thought you had
3		something from before, but
4		you haven't got it anymore.
5	Dr.:	I'm going to call you Dean.

(Labov & Fanshel, 1977, p. 2)

The maxim of manner pertains to the clarity of talk, such as expectations that speakers will avoid obscurity, ambiguity, and other factors that may hinder understanding. To sum, these four maxims "specify what participants must do in order to converse in a maximally efficient, rational, co-operative way" (Levinson, 1983, p. 102).

Now many readers will object that these maxims, although they may describe some idealized form of talk, do not accurately characterize "real" conversation. But Grice's (1975) point is different from, and more subtle than, this. Grice will readily admit that people often do not follow the four maxims, to the letter, during everyday conversation. His point is that when a speaker does not follow the maxims at a literal level, our initial impulse still is to assume that, contrary to appearances, the speaker is adhering to them at some deeper level. For instance, we assume that speaker B in Example 6.2 is being cooperative even though his response in line 2, taken literally, seems to violate the maxims of quantity and relation. Our expectations that conversation is cooperative are so strong that we look for a way of hearing B's response as an "answer," and we find it by inferring that Bill must own a yellow VW.

The strength of our expectations about cooperation creates an interesting possibility, which Grice (1975) calls "flouting" the maxims. A speaker flouts or exploits a maxim when he or she blatantly violates the principle in order to achieve some communicative purpose. In Example 6.3, for instance, I flout the maxim of relevance in line 2 by abruptly shifting the topic. In doing so, I assume that my friend will infer that my comment is "relevant" to her question in line 1 in the deeper sense that it signals that I do not wish to discuss the topic of writing a book.

Each of Grice's four maxims may be flouted strategically (see Grice, 1975, pp. 52-56; Levinson, 1983, pp. 109-113). Tautologies such as "Boys will be boys" and "If she does it, she does it" are totally noninformative at a literal level and hence violate the quantity maxim; nonetheless, they communicate meaning in terms of what they implicate. Figures of speech such as irony and metaphor often violate the quality maxim. If someone with whom we have been on close terms until now betrays an important confidence, we might say, "X is a fine friend" and mean just the opposite. Transparent questions violate the relation maxim to emphasize a point:

EXAMPLE 6.7

1 A: Are you going to the bar tonight?

2 B: Is the Pope Catholic?

(Bowers, Elliot, & Desmond, 1977, p. 236)

Finally, speakers may use excessive technical jargon intentionally, and thereby violate the maxim of manner, to create a humorous effect (e.g., Buzzanell, Burrell, Stafford, & Berkowitz, 1996).

Grice's theory of conversational implicature offers several insights about persuasive message production. The maxims are guidelines to which participants orient during compliance-gaining episodes. Consider the quantity maxim. Participants hold expectations about how many reasons a message source should provide to justify a request. Message sources often offer little or no justification when making small requests of people they know well, such as asking to borrow a pencil from a friend (Brown & Levinson, 1987; Roloff, Janiszewski, McGrath, Burns, & Manrai, 1988). Of course, a target may believe that a request needs more justification than the message source initially provides, as in the following example, which involves my stepdaughter Ashlee and me:

EXAMPLE 6.8

1 Ashlee: Can you drive me to school tomorrow?

2 Me: Why can't you take the bus?

3 Ashlee: I've got to be there early.

4 Me: Why?

5 Ashlee: Spanish club.

6 Me: Okay, when do you have to be there?

Put differently, message sources and targets jointly negotiate how much reasoning is sufficient to warrant compliance (Jackson & Jacobs, 1980).

Although participants orient to the maxims during compliance-gaining episodes, at times they also deviate from them in order to accomplish other purposes. As the discussion in the upcoming section on politeness theory shows, message sources and targets at times say more than literally needs to be said (quantity), say things with more than one plausible interpretation (manner), and so forth in order to protect the face of both parties. Grice specifies how speakers should converse in order to communicate in a maximally efficient fashion, but communicating efficiently is only one of several goals that participants typically pursue when seeking and resisting compliance (see Chapter 5). Deviations from Grice's maxims during compliance-gaining episodes often can be understood as attempts to manage multiple conflicting goals.

SPEECH ACTS

People not only "say" things with words, they also "do" things with words. People perform a variety of actions through talk, such as requesting, promising, warning, describing, and asserting. Speech act theorists have grappled with how speakers are able to make their intentions apparent through talk and how hearers are able to recognize speakers' intentions. Like the work on conversational maxims, speech act theories can be traced to the writings of two British philosophers of language, John Austin and John Searle.

According to Austin (1962), a speaker simultaneously does three things whenever she or he says something. Consider lines 14-15 from the conversation between Mike and Mr. Jenkins in Example 6.1, in which Mike says, "I'm just calling to see if I can get you uh to set up an appointment to donate blood." At one level, Mike is referring to objects and saying something about those objects. Mike talks about himself (I'm, I), Mr. Jenkins (you), appointments, donating, and blood. Austin refers to talking about topics as the *locutionary* level of a speech act.

At a second level, Mike is doing more than talking about topics. Surely we recognize that Mike is "requesting" that Mr. Jenkins set up an appointment with the Red Cross. Mike is saying something that he intends Mr. Jenkins to recognize as a request. Austin (1962) refers to the type of action performed by a statement as the *illocutionary* level of a speech act; thus Mike's phrase has the "illocutionary force" of requesting.

At yet a third level, Mike brings about certain effects in Mr. Jenkins by saying what he does. He may make Mr. Jenkins feel annoyed, pressured, or pleased to help. He may persuade, or fail to persuade, Mr. Jenkins to set up an appointment. Some of these effects may be intended by Mike, whereas others may be unforeseen and unintended. Austin refers to the range of effects brought about by a statement as the *perlocutionary* level of a speech act.

Speech act theorists focus primarily on the illocutionary level of speech acts, posing questions such as, How are we able to recognize a speaker's intentions from what he or she says? How do we know, for example, that Mike is "requesting" in lines 14-15, rather than "promising" or "warning" Mr. Jenkins? To address this issue, Searle (1969) distinguishes between regulative and constitutive rules. *Regulative rules* are social conventions that govern preexisting forms of behavior. Rules associated with table manners, such as "Don't talk with your mouth full" and "Start with the silverware on the outside," are regulative rules. These rules specify "proper" ways of eating; however, the act of eating existed prior to, and exists apart from, these cultural conventions. A regulative rule takes the form "If Y, then X," and someone violating such a rule is perceived as acting "incorrectly."

Constitutive rules are social conventions that create and define forms of behavior, such that the behavior does not exist apart from the rules. The rules for a game such as American football are constitutive rules. The concept of "touchdown" is created by the rules of football and does not exist independent of those rules; after all, could someone have scored a "touchdown" before the game of football was invented? Moreover, one can score a touchdown only by following the rules. If I run out onto the field during halftime at a Purdue University football game, pick up the ball, and cross into the opponent's end zone, have I scored six points for the Boilermakers? One would not say that I have scored a touchdown "improperly," but rather that I have not scored a touchdown at all. A constitutive rule takes the form "Doing X counts as Y." Someone who violates a constitutive rule is perceived as acting "incoherently," in the sense that it is not clear what he or she is doing (e.g., my behavior at the Purdue football game).

According to Searle (1969), any speech act is governed by a set of constitutive rules that specify the necessary and sufficient conditions for performing that speech act. Put differently, these rules specify the conditions that must exist for a behavior to "count as" performing a speech act. Searle analyzes what conditions must be assumed to exist in order for a speaker to be recognized as performing speech acts, such as requesting, promising, warning, and advising. A set of constitutive rules for requesting, adapted from Searle (1969) as well as Labov and Fanshel (1977), appears in Table 6.2.[3]

The propositional content rule sets restrictions on the content or locution of a speech act. For requests, this rule states that the source's message must refer to a present or future action to be performed by the target rather than by the source. It sounds sensible for me to ask my stepson, "Brendan, would you take out the garbage?" In contrast, it would sound odd for me to say to myself, "Steve, would you take out the garbage?" Similarly, the request "Brendan, could you take out the garbage tomorrow morning?" sounds plausible. "Brendan, could you take out the garbage last week?" makes little sense. My stepson initially might interpret this latter message as a joke, or perhaps as an indirect rebuke for his failure to take the garbage out the week before. If neither of these interpretations is plausible, however, and I repeat my request that Brendan "take out

Table 6.2   Searle's (1969) Constitutive Rules for the Speech Act of Requesting

Type of Rule	Definition
Propositional content rule	The message source refers to a present or future action to be performed by the target.
Preparatory rules	
Need for action	The message source perceives a reason the requested action needs to be performed.
Need for request	It should not be obvious that the message target already was planning to perform the requested behavior.
Ability	The message source believes that the target plausibly may be able to perform the requested action.
Willingness	The message source believes that the target plausibly may be willing to perform the requested action.
Sincerity rule	The message source sincerely wants the requested action to be performed.

SOURCE: Adapted from Searle (1969) and Labov and Fanshel (1977).

the garbage last week," Brendan might infer that I have "lost touch with reality" (i.e., I am talking without any point to my talk).

Preparatory rules, sometimes also called "felicity conditions," state restrictions about the situations that must exist in order for an individual to perform a speech act. Table 6.2 lists four preparatory rules. First, the source must perceive some reason the action needs to be performed. I would be violating this "need for action" rule if the garage door at our home was open, Brendan and I both knew this, and yet I still said, "Brendan, would you open the garage door?" Second, it should not be apparent that the target already was about to perform the requested action. I would be violating this "need for request" rule if Brendan had gone out to the garage, reached up, and put his finger on the garage door opener's button before I asked, "Brendan, would you open the garage door?"

A third preparatory rule states that the source must believe that the target plausibly can perform the requested action. I would be violating this "ability" rule if some of my papers blew under our Chevy Suburban truck and I said, "Brendan, pick up the Suburban so that I can get my papers out from underneath it without getting dirty." A fourth preparatory rule is that the source also must believe that the target plausibly is willing to perform the requested action. A source may perceive willingness because he or she believes that the target will enjoy performing the requested action, will appreciate the need to perform the requested action, or will feel a sense of obligation to help the source

(Roloff et al., 1988). My students occasionally violate this rule, as a joke, by "requesting" that I give them all A's (i.e., they are joking rather than requesting).

The sincerity rule states restrictions on the psychological state of the message source. For requests, this rule states that the message source sincerely must want the requested action to be performed. This rule helps explain why, under most conditions, we hear phrases such as "Go jump in a lake" as insults rather than as sincere requests.

So, to return to an earlier question, how do we know that Mike is "requesting" in lines 14-15 of the Example 6.1 rather than "promising" or "warning" Mr. Jenkins? How are we able to identify the illocutionary force of Mike's utterance? The answer, in part, lies in the constitutive rules listed in Table 6.2. Consistent with the propositional content rule, Mike refers to a future action, "setting up an appointment," that he hopes will be performed by Mr. Jenkins rather than himself. Mike also inquires explicitly about Mr. Jenkins's "willingness" to perform the desired action in line 14, when he says, "to see if I can get you," as well as in line 23, when he says, "Would you, uh, help us out." Mike's utterance appears to enact the necessary and sufficient conditions for performing a request.

One additional complication in interpreting the illocutionary force of Mike's utterance in lines 14-15 is that, taken literally, it does not "request" that Mr. Jenkins set up an appointment. Notice that Mike literally does not say, "I request that you set up an appointment to donate blood," or even "Please set up an appointment to donate blood." Mike literally describes his purpose as to see what he, himself, is capable of doing, as is apparent in the following fictional dialogue:

Mike:	I'm just calling to see if I can get you uh to set up an appointment to donate blood.
Mr. Jenkins:	Go ahead, see if you can get me to do that.
Mike:	OK, will you set up an appointment?
Mr. Jenkins:	Yes.

Put differently, Mike's utterance in line 12 is an indirect speech act. *Indirect speech acts* are messages that, given the circumstances, imply additional or different purposes from those conventionally associated with their linguistic form (Searle, 1975). Thus the utterance "Can you shut the door?" usually is heard as an indirect request to shut the door, rather than, or in addition to, a literal question about the target's ability to do so. We hear Mike as making an indirect request in lines 14-15 for several reasons, including that Mike inquires about Mr. Jenkins's willingness (a rule for requesting) and that Mike's call would seem odd if his sole purpose were to see what he, himself, is able to get a complete stranger to do.

Having said all this, I should add that the illocutionary force of Mike's utterance in line 12 also is apparent, in good measure, because of the larger institutional and conversational context. Mike identifies himself as "calling from the American Red Cross" in line 04, and Mr. Jenkins has donated blood with the Red Cross in the past. Indeed, Mike confirms information about the date of Mr. Jenkins's last donation in the turns immediately preceding line 12. Given this, we clearly expect a request for repeat donation to occur at some point in the call. Critics have charged that Searle's (1969) version of speech act theory pays too little attention to how the illocutionary force of an utterance is shaped by institutional roles and purposes, as well as by preceding and projected future conversational turns (Levinson, 1983; Streeck, 1980). Searle often seems to treat "context" as something "given" or already established prior to the utterance of a speech act, rather than as something created, in part, through the performance of speech acts (Streeck, 1980).

Despite these limitations, speech act theory, with its emphasis on constitutive rules, provides a useful conceptual framework for analyzing persuasive message production. By specifying the necessary and sufficient conditions for requesting, constitutive rules highlight what a speaker assumes by saying something intended to count as a request. As Searle (1969) puts it: "The preparatory conditions tell us (at least part of) what a speaker *implies* in the performance of the act. To put it generally, in the performance of any illocutionary act, the speaker implies that the preparatory conditions of the act are satisfied" (p. 65). For example, if I request that my stepson, Brendan, clean out the garage, I imply that the garage needs to be cleaned, that Brendan wasn't already going to clean the garage, and so forth (see the preparatory rules in Table 6.2). Brendan may resist my request by arguing that one of the preparatory conditions for requesting, in fact, is not satisfied. If Brendan exclaims, "It can't be dirty, I just cleaned it last week," he is saying, in effect, that there is no "need for action." As will become apparent below in the section on obstacles to compliance, speech act theory offers one framework for analyzing how targets resist message sources' requests.

In addition to highlighting obstacles to compliance, speech act theory clarifies how seeking compliance can threaten identities. By making his request in line 12, Mike presumes that Mr. Jenkins plausibly may be "willing" to donate blood (see Table 6.2). Mr. Jenkins may fear how he will appear if he says that he is not willing to do so, as giving blood generally is regarded as helping with a "good cause." Indeed, Mr. Jenkins emphasizes that he usually is willing to help and justifies why he has not been in to donate "all winter" (see lines 22-24). Alternatively, Mike may fear how he himself will appear if he assumes that Mr. Jenkins is willing to donate blood too rapidly, because he is making a large request of a complete stranger. By specifying what a speaker "implies" in requesting, the constitutive rules clarify how either party's identity can be threatened during a compliance-gaining episode (see Wilson, Aleman, & Leatham, 1998). As noted below, Brown and Levinson's (1987) politeness theory draws heavily on concepts from speech act theory.

THE CONVERSATION ANALYSIS PERSPECTIVE

Conversation analysis (CA), as a perspective on analyzing situated talk, emerged during the late 1960s and early 1970s. It is associated most closely with Harvey Sacks, Emanuel Schegloff, Gail Jefferson, and their colleagues in sociology. In the past two decades, CA has gained adherents in many disciplines (see Psathas, 1995). CA is best characterized as a set of shared commitments or "habitual ways of thinking" rather than as a set of "theoretical precepts" (Zimmerman, 1988, p. 429). These shared commitments are explored in detail elsewhere (e.g., Levinson, 1983; Nofsinger, 1991; Psathas, 1995; Zimmerman, 1988). Here I briefly explain some goals and assumptions of CA and then introduce some of the concepts associated with this perspective, such as adjacency pairs, conditional relevance, and the preference for agreement.

Goals and Assumptions of CA

CA scholars search for meaningful regularities in the structure of conversation. They attempt to identify patterns and sequences in the most minute details of everyday talk. CA researchers have documented regularities in the location of overlaps and pauses (Sacks, Schegloff, & Jefferson, 1974), the use of the interjection "oh" as opposed to "uh" (Heritage, 1984), and the placement of laughter within talk (Jefferson, 1979). We already have encountered another meaningful sequence, the "prerequest," in which a speaker inquires about the status of the other party or the situation prior to making a request (see Chapter 3, Examples 3.3-3.6). Aside from identifying meaningful regularities, CA scholars investigate how participants "do" conversation. By orienting to the details of talk, CA scholars seek to understand how participants interpret what others are doing and how they negotiate the meanings of their own actions.

CA scholars share several assumptions about studying talk (Levinson, 1983; Psathas, 1995; Zimmerman, 1988). First, they argue that conversations exhibit stable, orderly properties that are the achievements of the interactants themselves. To identify such regularities, CA scholars typically (a) videotape or audiotape a corpus of conversations; (b) transcribe those conversations in detail, using notations that mark pauses, extended vowels, rising and falling pitch, and so on; and (c) listen repeatedly to the conversations, searching for interpretable phenomena that occur across multiple conversations (see Hopper, Koch, & Mandelbaum, 1986). Second, CA scholars assume that conversation is managed locally, meaning that participants negotiate, turn by turn, whether and how much to talk, what to say and do, and so forth. Third, CA scholars advocate an inductive, data-to-theory approach. They approach conversation not with the goal of testing preexisting theories, but with an openness to discovering how participants themselves "do" talk. Because of this, CA scholars often resist theoretically grounded coding schemes and quantitative methods of interaction analysis that place talk into preformulated categories. They also seek to explain conversational regularities while resorting only to details of the talk itself and often resist discussing concepts such as interaction goals, personality traits, or "master" identities (e.g., gender, cultural, or ethnic identities) that go beyond the talk.

As this description indicates, the assumptions of conversation analysis differ in important respects from those associated with other theoretical perspectives reviewed in this book. CA scholars hesitate to make inferences about the goals underlying a speaker's actions, whereas most communication scholars take for granted that persuasive message production is goal oriented (Mandelbaum & Pomerantz, 1991; Tracy, 1991a; see Chapter 5). One can appreciate the aims and insights of CA, however, without taking all CA assumptions as one's own. Unlike traditional compliance-gaining researchers, who relied heavily on hypothetical scenarios (see Chapter 4), CA scholars analyze naturally occurring compliance-gaining episodes (e.g., Mandelbaum & Pomerantz, 1991; Sanders & Fitch, 2001). Several analytic concepts developed by CA scholars have also turned out to be useful for understanding persuasive message production. It is to these concepts that I now turn.

Analytic Concepts in CA

Schegloff and Sacks (1973) argue that the adjacency pair is a fundamental unit of conversational organization. An adjacency pair is a two-part action sequence, such as question-answer, greeting-greeting, offer-acceptance/refusal, and request-grant/refusal. Jacobs (1994) provides a succinct summary of the adjacency pair concept:

> Adjacency pairs are two turns long, having two parts said by different speakers in adjacent turns at talk. By using the first part of an adjacency pair (a "first pair part," or FPP) a speaker establishes a "next turn position" that casts the recipient into the role of respondent and structures the rank of appropriate next moves to those second pair parts (SPPs) that are congruent with the FPP. (p. 213)

By creating an expectation about what types of SPPs will follow an FPP, the concept of adjacency pairs gives a sense of coherence to the sequencing of conversation. Thus conversation might be thought of as a series of adjacency pairs: FPP1-SPP1, FPP2-SPP2, FPP3-SPP3, and so forth.

A quick peek at everyday conversation, however, reveals that the two parts of an adjacency pair do not always occur adjacently. Consider the following two examples:

EXAMPLE 6.9

FPP1	A:	May I have a bottle of Mich?
FPP2	B:	Are you twenty-one?
SPP2	A:	No
SPP1	B:	No

(Merritt, 1976, p. 333)

EXAMPLE 6.10

FPP1	A:	U:hm (.) what's the price now eh with V.A.T. [value added tax] do you know eh
FPP2	B:	Er I'll just work that out for you =
SPP2	A:	= thanks
SPP1	B:	Three pounds nineteen a tube sir

(Levinson, 1983, pp. 304-305)

Both examples contain an insertion sequence, in which one adjacency pair (FPP2-SPP2) is embedded within another (FPP1-SPP1). But if adjacency pairs do not always occur adjacently, can they still provide a sense of coherence to the sequencing of conversation?

According to Schegloff, the glue that binds the two parts of an adjacency pair together is not their adjacent location, but the concept of *conditional relevance:* "By conditional relevance of one item on another we mean: Given the first, the second is expectable; upon its occurrence it can be seen to be a second item to the first; upon its nonoccurrence it can be seen to be officially absent" (as quoted in Jacobs, 1994, p. 214). That is, when an SPP does not occur in the turn immediately following the FPP, both parties still anticipate that the SPP will occur at some future point, and both interpret subsequent utterances as relevant to the eventual performance of the SPP. This is evident in both of the prior examples. In Example 6.9, B asks a question immediately after FPP1 to determine whether the customer, A, is of legal drinking age before addressing A's initial request for a beer. In Example 6.10, B asks for time immediately after FPP1 in order to work out calculations needed to answer the customer's initial question. In both cases, the target (B) seeks more information before deciding whether, or how, to comply with the source's (A) initial request. Insertion sequences are not limited to two turns; indeed, a target may perform many actions before deciding whether to comply with a source's request (see Jacobs, 1994, pp. 214-215; Levinson, 1983, p. 305). Even in these cases, however, both parties expect that the target eventually will address the source's initial request. Given the notion of conditional relevance, the dominant adjacency pair (FPP1-SPP1) can organize extended sequences of talk.

Insertion sequences occur regularly during compliance-gaining episodes. Recall the study described at the beginning of this chapter, in which college students volunteering on behalf of the American Red Cross telephoned actual blood donors (Wilson et al., 1994). After transcribing these telephone calls, we analyzed what prior blood donors (targets) said in the conversational turn immediately following the participant's initial request to donate blood again. Slightly more than one-half (56%) of the prior donors immediately said no, whereas another 16% immediately responded with an "unconditional yes" to the participant's request. Another 12% of the prior donors immediately responded with a "conditional yes," indicating that they would be willing to comply if a stated obstacle (e.g., illness, busy schedule) could be overcome (see Example 6.1). The final 16% of the prior donors did not respond immediately with either yes or no, but instead asked questions about where and/or when they would donate (i.e., insertion sequences). In some cases, these prior donors used the participants' answers to their questions as subsequent grounds for compliance-resistance strategies, but in other cases they subsequently agreed to donate.

Aside from insertion sequences, multiple adjacency pairs can be linked in the form of presequences. A presequence is an adjacency pair that sets up, and is interpreted in light of, another adjacency pair yet to come (Beach & Dunning, 1982; Jacobs & Jackson, 1983). Examples include prerequests, preinvitations, and preannouncements. During a prerequest, the FPP typically checks on preconditions (i.e., the preparatory rules) for performing an upcoming request, such as the target's ability to comply. As I have noted in Chapter 3, both parties implicitly understand the functions of prerequests, and hence several types of sequences may unfold following their occurrence (see Chapter 3, Examples 3.3-3.6).

A final analytic concept for CA is the notion of preference organization. Of the SPPs that can coherently follow an FPP, there is usually one SPP that is preferred and one that is dispreferred. For example, the preferred SPP for a request is a grant (i.e., compliance), whereas the dispreferred SPP for a request is a refusal. CA scholars go to great lengths to emphasize that *preference* in this context is not intended to describe a psychological concept, and does not refer to the wishes of the message source or target (e.g., Levinson, 1983, p. 307; Nofsinger, 1991, pp. 71-72; but see Holtgraves, 1992, pp. 148-149). Rather, *preference* refers to structural features of the talk, in that dispreferred SPPs typically are linguistically "marked," whereas preferred SPPs typically are not. In comparison to preferred SPPs, dispreferred SPPs are more likely to (a) be preceded by pauses, (b) begin with prefaces (e.g., "Uh" or "Well"), (c) begin with token agreements before disagreements (e.g., "Yes, but . . ."), (d) include qualifiers (e.g., "I don't know for sure, but . . ."), (e) include apologies and expressions of appreciation, and (f) include accounts for why the dispreferred SPPs are being performed (see Levinson, 1983, pp. 334-335).

Research outside of the CA tradition also provides support for the claim that dispreferred SPPs tend to be linguistically marked. In the blood donation study described at the start of this chapter, for example, we found that 80% of the prior donors (i.e., targets) who said no also gave reasons why they were refusing to donate again in the turn adjacent to the participant's request (Wilson et al., 1994). In contrast, very few donors who immediately said yes gave reasons why they were willing to donate again. Similarly, in a study of responses to date requests, Folkes (1982) found that 84% of college students who recalled episodes in which they had turned down dates indicated that they gave reasons why they were saying no, whereas only 24% of students of who recalled episodes in which they said yes gave reasons why they complied.

The concept of preference organization has important implications for persuasive message production. In particular, it appears that people are *expected* to provide reasons, as well as other linguistic markers, when refusing requests (a dispreferred SPP). This expectation is not idiosyncratic or arbitrary; rather, it reflects an organizational principle that functions across a wide range of adjacency pairs. As a consequence, people may feel awkward when faced with admonitions to "just say no," because doing so violates a pervasive conversational pattern.

To this point, I have reviewed basic concepts from work on conversational maxims, speech acts, and the CA perspective. With this background completed, I turn to work on two concepts with special relevance to persuasive message production: obstacles and face.

Obstacles to Compliance: Attribution and Speech Act Theories

The CA concept of preference organization suggests that when message targets initially refuse requests, they often will mention obstacles that hinder them from complying. Obstacles are "the message recipients' beliefs that cause them to be unwilling or unable to respond immediately in the way the communicator desires" (Clark & Delia, 1979, p. 200).

Obstacles are central to any compliance-gaining episode. Message sources may anticipate potential obstacles from targets as they formulate their initial requests. Targets often will disclose obstacles as the basis for their resisting sources' requests. In Example 6.1, Mr. Jenkins states that he has been "a little sick there all winter there," which could function as an obstacle to his donating blood now. Which obstacles targets disclose are constrained, to some degree, by the form and content of sources' initial requests. Targets sometimes disclose particular obstacles even though the obstacles named are not the "real" reasons for their resistance. Both sources and targets know that this can occur, and occasionally the "actual" reason for a target's resistance itself may become a topic of discussion. After encountering obstacles, sources must choose whether or not to persist in seeking compliance, and, if they decide to persist, they must decide whether or not to address the disclosed obstacles directly (as Mike does in Example 6.1, lines 27-46). Speech act and attribution theorists have explored obstacles. In this section I examine five questions about the nature of obstacles and their roles at various points in compliance-gaining interactions.

HOW HAVE OBSTACLES BEEN DESCRIBED?

Speech act (Austin, 1962; Searle, 1969) and attribution (Heider, 1958; Weiner, 1986) theories offer different, albeit complementary, descriptions of the obstacle construct. For speech act theorists, the constitutive rules for directives offer a framework for analyzing potential obstacles to compliance. *Directives*, such as requests, recommendations, and commands, are speech acts designed to get the hearer to perform an action that he or she otherwise would not have performed (Searle, 1976). Directives are at the heart of any attempt to gain compliance, given that people seek compliance only when they presume that their targets otherwise would not have performed the desired actions (see the definition of *compliance gaining* in Chapter 1). It is true that compliance-seeking messages frequently contain speech acts in addition to directives, such as assertions or promises. Often, however, these additional acts support the logical preconditions for using directives; for example, these acts might explain why the desired action needs to be performed, why the message source cannot perform the action him- or herself, or why the target should be willing to comply (Tracy, Craig, Smith, & Spisak, 1984; see Table 6.2). It also is true that when message sources hint, they do not state directives explicitly. Even when hinting, however, message sources still adhere to the rules for directives by encouraging targets to perform behaviors that the targets otherwise did not plan to perform.

Because directives are at the heart of attempts to gain compliance, message sources adhere to the rules for directives whenever they seek compliance. Put differently, a message source, by seeking compliance, explicitly or implicitly asserts that the rules for directives are "in effect" and provide an accurate characterization of the current reality. As an example, when I ask my 9-year-old stepdaughter, Annie, to make her bed, I assert that the preconditions for making this request are met (see Table 6.2). By making my request, in other words, I assume the following: that Annie's bed currently is not made, that it needs to be made, that Annie was not about to make the bed, that Annie has the ability to make the bed at this time, that Annie is willing and/or obligated to make her bed, that I have the right to remind Annie to make her bed, and that I sincerely want the bed made.

As is apparent from this example, the message target does not always passively accept the source's "definition of the situation" (Goffman, 1959). From the perspective of speech act theory, resisting compliance means challenging the message source's definition of the situation—that is, challenging the source's assertion that the rules for directives provide an accurate characterization of the current situation. Resisting compliance means asserting that the source's request is "defective." In the "make the bed" situation, Annie might object to my request because (a) she thinks that the task of making her bed is unnecessary (there is no need for the action), (b) she already had planned to make the bed sometime later (there is no need for my request), (c) she is too busy to make the bed right now (she lacks ability), (d) she does not want to make her bed (she lacks willingness), (e) she does not have to make her bed (she is not obligated), (f) she can keep her own room any way that she wants (I have no right to make this request), or (g) she believes that I don't really care about the bed, but just want to hassle her (I lack sincerity).

During compliance-gaining episodes, the constitutive rules for directives function as *stases,* or possible points of clash in arguments about how the current situation should be defined (Jackson & Jacobs, 1980; Kline, 1979; Wilson, Kim, & Meischke, 1991/1992). As a consequence, the rules for directives should offer a comprehensive framework for analyzing obstacles to compliance, because resisting compliance means asserting that the conditions specified in one of these rules is not met in the current situation. Each of Annie's refusals in the prior example functions in this way. Indeed, a variety of specific obstacles can be analyzed using a speech act theory framework (e.g., Gibbs, 1986; Ifert & Roloff, 1994).

Attribution theory offers a second framework for describing obstacles. Attributions are personal judgments about the causes for actions or events; thus attribution theorists study how everyday actors answer "why" questions (Heider, 1958). You may make attributions about a wide variety of events, such as why you did well on a test, why a stranger bumped into you at a concert, why your romantic partner got upset during a conversation, why you received (or did not receive) a raise at work, or why a close friend or family member died at a young age. Attributions play an important role in how you interpret the meanings of events. Imagine that a stranger bumps into you as you are waiting in line to enter a movie theater. Does what is "going on" seem different if the stranger bumps into you accidentally because the theater entrance is over-crowded as opposed to if the stranger bumps into you because he or she is impatient about waiting in line? Attributions also influence your emotional reactions to events. You are likely to feel happy about having received an A on an exam regardless of whether you studied hard or whether the exam was so easy that everyone did well. Only in the former case, however, are you likely to take "pride" in how you performed on the exam (Weiner, 1986).

During a compliance-gaining interaction, a salient question can be why the target is refusing to comply immediately with the message source's request. From an attributional perspective, obstacles are causes or reasons for the target's noncompliance. Attributions are *personal* judgments, and thus message sources and targets may make different attributions about why the target is refusing to comply (Jones & Nisbett, 1972; Wilson & Kang, 1991; Wilson, Levine, Cruz, & Rao, 1997).

When we try to think about the possible causes for any specific event, the number of candidate possibilities may seem overwhelming. Consider why a student, Joan, performed poorly in delivering her first speech in a public speaking class. Perhaps Joan did not practice her speech in advance. Perhaps she picked a topic with a great deal of technical information that was difficult to explain. Perhaps Joan lacks skill at organizing her ideas clearly. Or perhaps she is very nervous about speaking in public. Perhaps Joan felt ill on the day of her speech, or was distracted because she had gotten into a fight with her boyfriend the evening before. Perhaps Joan's instructor has very high expecta-tions. Perhaps Joan was unlucky, because the best student in the class happened to be selected to speak just before she gave her own speech. Given all the pos-sible reasons for Joan's performance, how do we organize and make sense of different attributions?

In his attributional theory of motivation and emotion, Bernard Weiner (1986) argues that people distinguish causes along three basic dimensions. The first dimension, labeled *locus,* is concerned with whether the cause resides within the actor (internal) or outside of actor, in the external environment (external). Joan's anxiety about public speaking and her decision not to prac-tice in advance are examples of internal causes; her teacher's high expectations and the fight with her boyfriend are examples of external causes. The second dimension, labeled *stability,* concerns whether the cause fluctuates over time (unstable) or remains constant over time (stable). Joan's anxiety about public speaking and her teacher's high expectations are relatively stable causes; her fight with her boyfriend and her being unlucky at having the best student randomly selected to speak just before her are unstable causes (because they do not happen each time she gives a speech).[4] The third dimension, *controllability*, concerns whether the cause can be influenced by the actor and/or other parties (controllable) or whether it is beyond anyone's control (uncontrollable). Joan's decision not to practice and her instructor's high expectations are examples of controllable causes; her feeling ill and her being unlucky at having the best student randomly selected to speak just before her are uncontrollable causes. According to Weiner, locus, stability, and controllability are distinguishable on logical grounds; for example, people may succeed at a task due to internal causes that are either stable (e.g., ability) or unstable (e.g., effort). Weiner also reviews evidence that everyday actors distinguish perceived causes for interpersonal events, such as marital conflict, along these three dimensions.

By crossing the attributional dimensions of locus, stability, and controllability, we can classify eight different types of obstacles to compliance in a variety of situations. Table 6.3 lists examples of eight different types of reasons individuals may give for saying no to a date request. These data are from a study conducted by Folkes (1982), who asked each of 64 female and 64 male undergraduates to describe a recent episode in which she or he had turned down, and/or been turned down for, a date request made by someone the participant did not know well. Table 6.4 lists eight different types of reasons individuals might give for refusing to participate, after promising to do so, in a research study. My colleagues and I generated these data by asking undergraduates to list reasons a student might sign up for an out-of-class experiment but then later back out on participating (see Wilson, Cruz, Marshall, & Rao, 1993). As you will see below, message targets are not equally likely to disclose these eight types of obstacles, and message sources make choices about whether and how to persist based on the locus, stability, and controllability of the disclosed obstacles.

DO MESSAGE SOURCES ANTICIPATE OBSTACLES IN THEIR INITIAL REQUESTS?

Imagine that you want to know the time and do not happen to be wearing a watch. You approach a stranger, say, "Excuse me," and then ask for the time. There are several ways you might phrase your request, such as "Do you happen to know what time it is?" "Can you tell me the time?" or "Would you mind telling me the time?" Which of these requests would you be most likely to say in this situation? Would your choice of phrasing be completely random?

Table 6.3 Eight Reasons for Turning Down a Date Request, Varying Along Three Attributional Dimensions

Attributional Dimensions	Target's Reason for Saying No
1. Impersonal, unstable, uncontrollable	The rejecter had to study for finals.
2. Impersonal, unstable, controllable	The rejecter would rather go to a dance that night than go to the movies.
3. Impersonal, stable, uncontrollable	The rejecter was seriously involved with someone.
4. Impersonal, stable, controllable	The rejecter did not want to mess up a relationship with someone else she was dating.
5. Personal, unstable, uncontrollable	The rejected person was in a bad mood.
6. Personal, unstable, controllable	The rejected person had a lot of nerve calling up the rejecter the same night to ask her out.
7. Personal, stable, uncontrollable	The rejected person was too old for the rejecter.
8. Personal, stable, controllable	The rejecter did not agree with the rejected person's religious beliefs.

SOURCE: From "Communicating the Reasons for Social Rejection," by V. S. Folkes, 1982, *Journal of Experimental Social Psychology, 18,* p. 242. Copyright 1982 by Academic Press. Reprinted with permission.

NOTE: Personal causes referred to the rejected person (i.e., internal locus), whereas impersonal qualities related to the rejecter or the larger situation (i.e., external locus).

According to Ellen Francik and Herbert Clark (1985), speakers word requests in a predictable fashion, based on how they perceive obstacles in the situation. Francik and Clark propose an "obstacle hypothesis," which states that "speakers design requests to overcome the *greatest potential obstacle* they see to getting the information they want" (p. 560). To illustrate this hypothesis: Imagine that you want to buy a popular CD that has just been released. You drive to the store, enter, and approach a clerk. Are you likely to say, "Would you be willing to sell me the new _____ CD?" Probably not. The clerk's willingness is not at issue, given that the store's purpose is to make a profit by selling CDs. Availability is a more plausible obstacle that could prevent you from obtaining the new CD; hence you might start with a prerequest such as "Do you have the new _____ CD?" According to Francik and Clark, a speaker typically mentions what he or she perceives to be the most likely obstacle because this (a) helps the target realize what he or she needs to do in order to comply (e.g., check whether the new CD has arrived) and (b) provides the target with a plausible

Table 6.4   Eight Reasons for Refusing to Participate in a Research Study as
Promised, Varying Along Three Attributional Dimensions

Attributional Dimensions	Target's Reason for Saying No
1. Internal, stable, controllable	I always seem to volunteer whenever anyone needs help. I agreed to be a big brother/sister and will be spending that time with my little brother/sister.
2. Internal, stable, uncontrollable	I just can't do it. No matter what I do, every time I participate in one of these experiments I make a fool of myself.
3. Internal, unstable, controllable	I invited friends out to happy hour at that time, so I'm not going to be at the experiment.
4. Internal, unstable, uncontrollable	My boyfriend/girlfriend and I just had a huge fight. I'm in a bad mood and don't feel up to coming to the experiment.
5. External, stable, controllable	It's important to me to graduate in three years, so I'm taking 19 credits every term. I just don't have the time to do any extra credit.
6. External, stable, uncontrollable	I won't be there. I'm in the Marketing Club, and we meet at that time every week.
7. External, unstable, controllable	I just decided not to do it because the professor offered so little extra credit that it just isn't worth my time.
8. External, unstable, uncontrollable	I can't do it then because I have to meet with one of my professors during that time. It's the only time he can meet this week.

SOURCE: From "An Attributional Analysis of Compliance-Gaining Interactions," by S. R. Wilson, M. G. Cruz, L. J. Marshall, & N. Rao, 1993, *Communication Monographs, 60*, pp. 370-371. Copyright 1993 by the Speech Communication Association. Adapted with permission.

excuse if he or she is unable or unwilling to comply (e.g., "Sorry, we haven't received it yet").

The obstacle hypothesis has received support in several studies (Francik & Clark, 1985; Gibbs, 1986; Gibbs & Mueller, 1988; Roloff & Janiszewski, 1989). For example, Francik and Clark (1985, Experiments 1 and 2) had undergraduates listen to short tape-recorded descriptions of 24 hypothetical scenarios that contained one of three types of obstacles: (a) ability (e.g., asking someone who is not visibly wearing a watch if he or she knows the time), (b) willingness (e.g., asking someone about sensitive family information that the person may not want to reveal), or (c) memory (e.g., asking someone a question when you cannot recall whether you already have asked that person the same question at a prior time). Other versions of the scenarios did not appear to contain any obstacles (e.g., asking someone who is visibly wearing a watch if he or she knows the time). After hearing each scenario, participants stated aloud what they would say in the situation.

Francik and Clark (1985) report two main findings from this research. First, participants used more indirect requests (e.g., "Do you have any idea what time it is?") than direct requests (e.g., "What time is it?") in scenarios where obstacles were perceived as present rather than absent. Second, participants varied the forms of their indirect requests depending on the likely obstacles. Participants used the form "Do you know" when they were uncertain whether the target knew some desired information, "Did you see/hear/notice" when they were uncertain whether the target noticed and remembered the desired information, "Would you" or "Could you" when it was unclear whether the target was willing to disclose the desired information, and "Have I asked you" when they were uncertain whether they had asked about the same information at an earlier time. Consistent with the obstacle hypothesis, the participants also comprehended requests for information more quickly, and evaluated them as more appropriate, when they addressed plausible rather than implausible obstacles (Francik & Clark, 1985; Gibbs, 1986).

Francik and Clark (1985) examined only requests for information, but Michael Roloff and Chris Janiszewski (1989) have shown how the obstacle hypothesis can apply to requests for assistance as well. They distinguish two types of assistance. A request to "borrow" occurs when the message source asks the target to lend him or her a material object temporarily, promising to return that object in the same condition (e.g., you miss a class and ask to borrow another student's notes). For requests to borrow, likely obstacles include that the target may want to use the object him- or herself, may fear that the object will not be returned in a timely fashion, and/or may fear that the message source will damage the object. A request for a "favor" occurs when the source asks the target to perform some service that primarily will help the source and that will consume the target's time and/or energy (e.g., you need a ride to a location 25 minutes away and ask someone you know to drive you). For requests for favors, likely obstacles include that the target may lack time and/or energy to provide the service, may lack willingness to help, and/or may prefer to do other things with his or her time.

According to Roloff and Janiszewski (1989), the obstacle hypothesis implies that "speakers will adapt their requests to overcome potential sources of resistance

Table 6.5   Roloff and Janiszewski's (1989) Seven Types of Clauses Within
                   Request Messages

Type of Clauses	Definition/Example
Contractual clauses	Those clauses containing information about the amount, duration, or contingencies of the requested action *Example:* I will return your notes next class.
Inquiries	Those clauses in which the requester asks about the ability of the target to provide the needed assistance *Example:* Are you busy this afternoon?
Inducements	Those clauses in which the requester offers a compliment, exchange, or gratitude to the target *Example:* I will pay you for the gas.
Explanations	Those clauses in which the requester indicates why he or she needs the requested action *Example:* I have been sick.
Apologies	Those clauses in which the requester acknowledges the inappropriateness of the requested assistance *Example:* I know this is an imposition.
Introductions	Those clauses in which the requester introduces or identifies him- or herself *Example:* I live in your dorm.
Requests	Those clauses in which the requester explicitly asks for the assistance *Example:* Can you give me a ride downtown?

SOURCE: From "Overcoming Obstacles to Interpersonal Compliance: A Principle of Message Construction," by M. E. Roloff & C. A. Janiszewski, 1989, *Human Communication Research, 16,* 1989, p. 45. Copyright 1989 by the International Communication Association. Adapted with permission.

to providing each type of assistance" (p. 36). In a test of this reasoning, 120 undergraduate students wrote exactly what they would say in response to a hypothetical "request to borrow" scenario (i.e., asking to borrow either the target's class notes or $25) and a "request for a favor" scenario (i.e., asking the target either to type a paper or to provide a ride). Some students imagined that the target in both situations was another student in their class whom they considered a friend, whereas others imagined the target was an acquaintance or a stranger in their class. For each message, coders initially analyzed whether it contained one or more grammatical clauses. Clauses then were classified into one of the seven categories shown in Table 6.5. Roloff and Janiszewski developed these categories based on Brown and Levinson's (1987) types of positive and negative politeness (see below). Several categories also pertain to the constitutive rules for requests (e.g., inquiries, explanations).

Consistent with the obstacle hypothesis, participants in Roloff and Janiszewski's (1989) study varied whether they included specific types of clauses in their request messages depending on the type of assistance being sought. For example, contractual clauses occurred more frequently in "borrow" than in "favor" messages, whereas inquiries about ability and inducements occurred more often in "favor" than in "borrow" messages. These differences make sense in light of the obstacles relevant to these two types of requests: Contractual clauses assure the target that the borrowed object will be cared for and returned in a timely fashion, whereas inquiries and inducements address the target's ability and willingness to provide a favor.

To summarize, message sources do anticipate potential obstacles from targets as they design their compliance-seeking messages. Research on the obstacle hypothesis illustrates two important points about persuasive message production. First, these studies show that people often pursue interaction goals with little conscious awareness. When asking someone for the time, do you think carefully about whether to say, "Do you happen to know what time it is?" or "Can you tell me the time?" or "Would you mind telling me the time?" Despite the fact that we seem to make such requests in a mindless fashion, we alter the forms of our requests to address the most plausible obstacles that might prevent us from attaining our goals. In other words, persuasive message production can be purposive without being highly mindful (Kellermann, 1992).

A second point is that the obstacle hypothesis has received support precisely because persuasive message production is goal oriented. Message sources anticipate obstacles to compliance in their requests because doing so helps them accomplish their primary and secondary goals (Francik & Clark, 1985). In some cases, however, sources may be more likely to accomplish their goals by ignoring obstacles. As Gibbs (1986) explains:

> In other contexts, speakers . . . will design their requests without any considera-
> tion of the potential obstacles for addressees. A general making a request of a
> private is just such a case. Failure to mention an appropriate obstacle helps the
> general maintain his superior social status relative to the private. It is clear that
> speakers may satisfy many communicative goals by either highlighting or ignor-
> ing certain obstacles when formulating indirect speech acts. (p. 194)

In other words, we should not always expect speakers to address obstacles in their compliance-seeking messages. Future research might explore boundary conditions on the obstacle hypothesis.

DO TARGETS ALWAYS DISCLOSE THEIR
"REAL" REASONS FOR RESISTING COMPLIANCE?

Imagine that a person from your workplace asks you for a date (if you are in a long-term, exclusive romantic relationship, then remember a time when you dated other people). The person who has asked you out is someone you do not find physically or socially attractive. How would you go about refusing the person's date request? Would you tell the person that you simply do not feel attracted to him or her? Or would you search for another excuse, such as that you already are dating someone else. Would you use this latter excuse even if you and your current dating partner both have agreed to see other people?

Bernard Weiner, Valerie Folkes, and their colleagues have compared public and private reasons for refusing requests from an attributional perspective (Folkes, 1982; Weiner, Amirkhan, Folkes, & Verette, 1987; Weiner, Figueroa-Muñoz, & Kakihara, 1991). In the first investigation, Folkes (1982, Study 1) asked each of 64 female and 64 male undergraduates to recall a recent episode in which she or he had been rejected for a date and/or had been the rejecter of a date. Each participant was asked whether the rejecter had explained why he or she was saying no and, if so, what the rejecter's public explanation had been. As Folkes notes, this publicly stated reason may have been the real reason, may have been different from the real reason, or may have been only part of the reason the date rejecter said no. Each participant then was asked to list five "private" reasons the rejecter in his or her episode had turned down the date. Coders categorized both the public and the private reasons as (a) personal (related to the rejected person) or impersonal (related to the rejecter or situation), (b) stable or unstable, and (c) controllable or uncontrollable (see Table 6.3 for examples). Nearly two-thirds (64%) of the public reasons for refusing a date were impersonal, uncontrollable, and unstable (e.g., the rejecter had to study for final exams), whereas less than one-third (30%) of the private reasons were of this type.

Message targets at times withhold or alter their "real reasons" in a variety of situations aside from date requests. Weiner et al. (1991, Study 1) asked each of 97 undergraduate students to describe an occasion when he or she "gave an excuse to someone that was not the truth. That is, there was a real reason why something happened or failed to occur, or why you responded positively or negatively, and you withheld that reason and gave a different one" (p. 6). Each participant was asked to describe the situation, including what he or she communicated to the other person and what the real reason was that the participant withheld. Each participant also described his or her goal(s), or what he or she wanted to accomplish by giving the false excuse or reason.

Several findings from Weiner et al.'s (1991) study are of interest. First, participants had no trouble recalling recent incidents in which they had communicated false excuses. A second finding is that disclosed (false) and withheld (true) reasons differed along all three attributional dimensions. As in Folkes's (1982) earlier study, the vast majority of public reasons were external, uncontrollable, and unstable. In contrast, more than 90% of the privately withheld reasons were internal and controllable. A third finding is that participants reported that they withheld their "real" reasons to accomplish four goals; specifically, they wanted to avoid (a) complying with the other party's request, (b) hurting the other party's feelings, (c) making the other party angry, and (d) making themselves look bad. In Dillard's (1990b) terminology, targets may give false reasons for resisting compliance in order to accomplish both primary and secondary goals.

Of course, message sources realize that, at times, targets' publicly stated reasons for resisting compliance are different from their real reasons. In a study exploring this issue, Danette Ifert and Michael Roloff (1994) had undergraduate students imagine that they were going to ask a target person to loan them notes from a class as well as to type an eight-page paper for them. Students imagined that the target in both situations was either a friend or a stranger in their class. Participants initially listed all of the obstacles that would prevent the target from complying with their request or "private" reasons why the target might say no. Participants then wrote out exactly what they expected the target would say to deny their request (i.e., the target's public reasons). Coders placed both private and public reasons into one of seven categories, which were further grouped into those obstacles that primarily reflected the target's *inability* to comply (i.e., uncontrollable causes) versus those that reflected the target's *unwillingness* to comply (i.e., controllable causes). Coders also analyzed whether participants expected the target to include each private reason in his or her refusal message.

Participants from Ifert and Roloff's (1994) study expected that a target would be much more likely to disclose an "inability" obstacle than an "unwillingness" obstacle. Participants, on average, believed that message targets would mention 42% of the inability obstacles that they perceived as present in the situation, but would mention only 12% of the unwillingness obstacles. Consistent with what targets actually tend to do, message sources expected that targets would disclose uncontrollable reasons for saying no while withholding controllable reasons.

What do message sources do when they are skeptical about whether targets' public reasons for resisting compliance are the "real" reasons for the targets' resistance? In some cases, a message source simply may accept the target's public reason for saying no. If a target refuses a date request by saying that he or she "has to study for finals," the message source may accept this public explanation because pressing for the "real" reason could embarrass both parties. In other cases, however, a message source may risk pressing for the "real" reason, especially when the request is perceived to be in the target's best interest (Boster, 1995). Future research might examine when message sources and targets are likely to debate the legitimacy of public obstacles to compliance.

DOES THE NATURE OF AN INITIAL REQUEST CONSTRAIN HOW THE TARGET RESISTS COMPLIANCE?

Imagine once again that a person from your workplace asks you for a date, but you are not physically or socially attracted to the person. If the person asks, "Would you like to go see a movie Saturday night?" you might respond, "I'm sorry, but I'm busy Saturday." If the person instead asks, "Would you like to go see a movie sometime?" would you still respond, "I'm sorry, but I'm busy Saturday"? Probably not, because the person has not mentioned a specific day. Being busy on Saturday is a "relevant" obstacle to the first, but not the second, date request. To some extent, message sources can constrain which obstacles to compliance are, and are not, relevant by the phrasing of their initial requests.

According to Gaylen Paulson and Michael Roloff (1997), the form and the content of a date request both can influence the nature of a target's refusal. Table 6.6 presents six date requests that vary in form and content. Regarding request form, Paulson and Roloff argue that when a person asks a virtual stranger for a date, the source typically perceives the target's willingness to be the most plausible obstacle to compliance. In light of the obstacle hypothesis, discussed above, this means that date requests with strangers that address the target's "willingness" to comply should be perceived as more conventional, and as more appropriate or polite, than requests that address other obstacles, such as the target's "ability" to comply. In turn, both of these request forms should be perceived as more polite than requests that the source presumes will raise no obstacles, because such "obstacle-free" forms place greater constraint on the target's autonomy (see Table 6.6). Given this reasoning, Paulson and Roloff predict that date requests with strangers that address willingness obstacles will prompt more polite refusals than will requests that address ability obstacles, and that obstacle-free forms will prompt the least polite refusals.

Regarding request content, Paulson and Roloff (1997) argue that date requests can be specific or ambiguous about the proposed joint activity, participants, setting, and/or time. In particular, they predict that requests that are ambiguous with regard to time should prompt more stable refusals ("Sorry, but I'm seriously involved with someone") than requests that propose specific

Table 6.6   Paulson and Roloff's (1997) Six Examples of Date Requests

Type of Request	Example
Ability-based form	
Time specific	Could you go out with me Saturday night?
Time ambiguous	Could you go out with me sometime?
Willingness-based form	
Time specific	Would you like to go out with me Saturday night?
Time ambiguous	Would you like to go out with me sometime?
Ambiguous/obstacle-free form	
Time specific	Why don't you go out with me Saturday night?
Time ambiguous	Why don't you go out with me sometime?

SOURCE: G. D. Paulson & M. E. Roloff, "The Effect of Request Form and Content on Constructing Obstacles to Compliance," *Communication Research, 24*, p. 273. Copyright © 1997 by Sage Publications, Inc. Reprinted by permission of Sage Publications, Inc.

times, because unstable obstacles such as being "busy Saturday" are not relevant for refusing the former type of date request (see Table 6.6).

To test these hypotheses, Paulson and Roloff asked each of 65 male and 63 female undergraduates to imagine that another student in the participant's communication class, whom the participant did not know, asked the participant for a date using one of the six requests shown in Table 6.9. After reading the request, each participant was asked to imagine that for some reason he or she wanted to turn down the date. Paulson and Roloff had each participant write out exactly what he or she would say to the other person to refuse the date request and then rate both the request and his or her own refusal message in terms of perceived conventionality and politeness. Coders also analyzed whether the obstacles to compliance in participants' refusal messages were stable or unstable. The results largely supported the researchers' predictions, in that participants (a) perceived "willingness"-based date requests as more polite than "ability"-based requests, which they in turn saw as more conventional and polite than "obstacle-free" requests; (b) perceived their own refusals to be most polite when the date requester used a "willingness" form and least polite when the date requester posed no obstacles; and (c) included more stable obstacles when the date requester was ambiguous rather than specific about the proposed time for the date.

Paulson and Roloff's (1997) findings suggest that message sources should consider how they phrase important requests, because "rather small changes in wording [can] reliably influence the content of refusals" (p. 284). Asking a virtual stranger for a date without addressing potential obstacles, for example, typically is perceived as overbearing and is likely to prompt a less polite refusal than other date request forms. According to Paulson and Roloff, message sources may benefit from being either ambiguous or specific about the proposed content of their date requests, depending on the relative importance of their own primary and secondary goals.

DO MESSAGE SOURCES VARY IN WHETHER, AND HOW, THEY PERSIST IN SEEKING COMPLIANCE DEPENDING ON THE TYPES OF OBSTACLES DISCLOSED BY TARGETS?

As the examples presented throughout this text show, message targets often respond to compliance-seeking messages by asking questions or posing obstacles. Despite this, research on compliance gaining typically has examined only people's initial responses to hypothetical scenarios (see Chapter 4). Among the smaller subset of studies that have analyzed subsequent compliance-seeking strategies, many have instructed participants simply to imagine that the target said no to their initial request and then asked what participants would say or do at that point (e.g., Cody, Canary, & Smith, 1994; deTurck, 1985, 1987; Hample & Dallinger, 1998; Wilson, Whipple, & Grau, 1996). In other words, many studies have provided no information about *why* the target was saying no. To my knowledge, only two studies have investigated whether message sources vary in terms of whether, and how, they persist in seeking compliance when targets disclose different types of obstacles.

In the first study, several colleagues and I applied Weiner's (1986) attributional theory to predict whether and how message sources would persist after hearing targets disclose different reasons for their failing to honor an earlier commitment (Wilson et al., 1993). I have described the procedures for this study in detail at the beginning of Chapter 2. As you may recall, each participant was given a list of 20 students (actually confederates) who supposedly had signed up to earn extra credit by completing a study being conducted by the fictitious "Professor Jones." Participants in our study were instructed to telephone these 20 students and remind them about the time and place of their own study. If any of the 20 students had changed their minds about coming, participants were supposed to try to persuade them to honor their promise to complete their study. We told our participants to use their own judgment about what to say and how long to persist in trying to persuade Professor Jones's students to show up.

In reality, the participants telephoned 20 confederates who were working with us. Of the 20 phone calls, 10 were answered by confederates who were instructed simply to say yes, they would show up for Professor Jones's study as promised. One phone number always went to a wrong number, and another always went to someone we knew was not there to receive the call. The remaining 8 calls were answered by confederates who were trained to say no, they would not show up. When prompted, these 8 confederates all disclosed different obstacles, or reasons they had changed their minds about participating in Professor Jones's study. Developed in a pilot study, these obstacles varied in terms of Weiner's (1986) three causal dimensions of locus, stability, and controllability. Examples of all of the types of obstacles appear in Table 6.3.

Based on Weiner's (1986) theory, we reasoned that message sources would vary the degree to which they persisted, as well as their specific choices of compliance-seeking strategies, depending on the reasons the students (confederates) gave for refusing to participate in the research project as promised. According to Weiner, individuals set higher expectations and hence are more motivated to persist when they perceive that their initial failure to accomplish a goal is due to a cause that might change over time (unstable) rather than a cause that will remain constant (stable). In addition to stability, attributional theorists suggest that individuals set higher expectations and persist longer when they believe that their initial failure is due to something that can be controlled rather than something about which they are helpless (e.g., Anderson & Jennings, 1980; Dweck, 1999). Following this reasoning, we predicted that participants would persist longer with targets (confederates) who disclosed unstable, internal, and controllable reasons for refusing to participate in the study as promised than with targets who disclosed stable, external, and controllable reasons for saying no. Depending on the locus, stability, and controllability of the disclosed obstacle, we also predicted that participants would vary in terms of whether they (a) perceived the target's reason for saying no as sincere, (b) addressed that obstacle directly, and (c) used antisocial compliance-seeking strategies.

Results from the study were consistent with, albeit more complicated than, these predictions. First, participants perceived most internal causes as controllable and external causes as uncontrollable; hence we collapsed locus and controllability into a single attributional dimension. Second, the effects of locus/controllability depended on stability. In most cases, predictions regarding locus/controllability were confirmed for unstable but not for stable causes. When participants encountered targets (confederates) who disclosed unstable reasons for refusing to honor their commitment, the participants persisted longer, denied the validity of the obstacles more often, used guilt more frequently, and perceived the targets as more sincere if their reasons were "internal/controllable" rather than "external/uncontrollable." When participants encountered targets who disclosed stable reasons for refusing to honor their commitment, however, the locus/controllability of the reasons did not matter. Put differently, participants appeared to evaluate obstacles using a two-step process. Initially, they attended to stability, and they gave up seeking compliance quickly with targets who disclosed obstacles that were unlikely to change over time. In cases where the obstacles were unstable, the participants then attended to locus/controllability, choosing to persist longer at seeking compliance with targets who disclosed obstacles that were within rather than beyond the targets' control.

In the second study, Ifert and Roloff (1996) examined the joint effects of types of expressed obstacles and relational intimacy to predict whether, and how, message sources would persist in the face of resistance from targets. Participants in their study, 257 undergraduate students, wrote out exactly how they would make two requests (asking to borrow the target's class notes for two days and asking the target to type an eight-page paper on behalf of the source) of either a stranger or a friend. After writing the initial request, each participant encountered one of three types of obstacles supposedly expressed by the target: (a) unwillingness obstacles (e.g., "There's no way I would do that"), (b) inability obstacles (e.g., "I don't have notes for that day"), or (c) imposition obstacles (e.g., "I don't have time to do it"). Unwillingness and inability obstacles embody two of the preparatory rules for requests (see Table 6.2), whereas imposition obstacles express a mixture of inability and unwillingness. After reading an obstacle statement, each participant completed a measure of how much he or she would want to persist in seeking compliance, after which the participant wrote out exactly what he or she would say after encountering that obstacle. These subsequent messages were coded for the presence of (a) inquiries about why the target was refusing the request; (b) persuasion cues, or phrases that explained or justified the initial request; and (c) forgiving cues, or phrases that accepted the target's refusal gracefully.

Ifert and Roloff (1996) predicted that participants in general would show greater desire to persist after encountering resistance from intimate targets (i.e., friends) as opposed to nonintimate targets (i.e., strangers), because friends often believe that they should be able to count on each other in times of need (see Roloff et al., 1988). They also predicted that participants' desire to persist, as well as their use of specific forms of persistence, would depend on the types of obstacles disclosed by the targets. Specifically, participants were predicted to show especially high desire to persist, as well as to use more inquiries and persuasion cues and fewer forgiving cues, when intimate targets disclosed unwillingness obstacles (which are controllable) as opposed to inability obstacles (which are uncontrollable). The researchers reasoned that unwillingness obstacles are perceived as particularly unexpected and inappropriate within intimate relationships, and hence predicted that participants would feel most justified in confronting these obstacles when the target was a friend. The results were largely consistent with these predictions: Intimacy was a stronger predictor of participants' desire to persist, as well as their use of the three specific forms of persistence, when targets disclosed unwillingness as opposed to inability obstacles. Responses to imposition obstacles, in most cases, were similar to responses to unwillingness rather than inability obstacles. In sum, Ifert and Roloff's (1996) as well as Wilson et al.'s (1993) research shows that message sources vary their likelihood and means of persisting depending, in part, on the nature of the obstacles disclosed by the targets.

In this section I have addressed five questions about the role of obstacles during compliance-gaining episodes. Both speech act and attribution theories have informed research on obstacles. One research finding I have described above is that message targets sometimes withhold their "real" reasons for saying no in order to spare the sources, as well as themselves, awkwardness and embarrassment. This suggests that people design their influence messages, in part, in light of both parties' public identities, or "face." Erving Goffman (1967), the well-known symbolic interactionist, defines face as the "social value that a person effectively claims for himself by the line others assume he has taken during a particular contact. Face is an image of self delineated in terms of approved social attributes" (p. 5).

Requests and refusals project ongoing definitions of situations, in the sense that they imply that certain states of affairs exist, or should exist (Wilson et al., 1991/1992, 1998). Thus seeking and resisting compliance can raise threats to face for both parties. Perhaps not surprisingly, then, people commonly report that the desire to maintain face is one of their goals during compliance-gaining episodes (Dillard, Segrin, & Harden, 1989; Hample & Dallinger, 1987a; Kim et al., 1996; see Chapter 5). Face concerns shape the form of request and refusal messages, and individuals differ systematically in their views about possible means for balancing competing desires to seek compliance and sustain face. Face can be explored through the lenses of politeness and message design logic theories.

Threats to Face: Politeness and Message Design Logic Theories

BROWN AND LEVINSON'S POLITENESS THEORY

Basic Assumptions of Politeness Theory

Penelope Brown, an anthropologist, and Stephen C. Levinson, a linguist, developed politeness theory based on their extensive fieldwork in three diverse languages and cultures: English as spoken in Great Britain; Tamil, a dialect spoken in southern India; and Tzetal, the language of the Mayan Indians in Mexico.[5] They present politeness theory to account for "the extraordinary parallelism in the linguistic minutia of the utterances with which persons choose to express themselves in quite unrelated languages and cultures" (Brown & Levinson, 1987, p. 55). One example of this parallelism is that speakers from all three cultures often use indirect speech acts when seeking another party's compliance. Brown and Levinson show that indirect requests such as "Can you shut the door?" "Are you planning on shutting the door?" and "Did you shut the door?" occur regularly in English, Tamil, and Tzetal (p. 136).

To account for linguistic parallels across cultures, politeness theory posits that speakers in all cultures want to maintain "face." Building on Goffman (1967), Brown and Levinson divide face into two basic wants, labeled *negative* and *positive* face. *Negative face* is the desire to maintain one's own autonomy. Individuals in any culture want to be shown respect and not have their privacy and space invaded, their resources spent, and their actions restricted without cause. *Positive face* is the desire to have one's own attributes and actions approved of by significant others. Which attributes are desired and which persons are significant depend on the roles being enacted. College professors typically want students to perceive them as competent, organized, and interesting. Most parents hope that their children will view them as loving, supportive, and fair. Although desired attributes vary across roles, and cultural definitions of roles, individuals in all cultures want approval and ratification from the people they love, admire, and/or value.

Aside from maintaining one's own face, Brown and Levinson (1987) argue, relational interdependence creates motives for supporting other people's face. Face is a social commodity. Although we want to maintain face, it can be granted only by others (Goffman, 1967). A conversationalist who threatens another party's face risks retaliatory attacks on his or her own. Politeness theory thus assumes that "it is generally in everyone's best interest to maintain each other's face" (Brown & Levinson, 1987, p. 61).

Despite the interdependent nature of social relations, individuals often perform actions that threaten face. In fact, Brown and Levinson (1987, p. 65) argue that many speech acts intrinsically are face threatening, meaning that by their very nature they run contrary to the face wants of the message source or target. Politeness theory's concept of an intrinsic face-threatening act, or FTA, draws on assumptions from speech act theory discussed earlier in this chapter. To see how, consider "directives" such as requests, recommendations, and commands (Searle, 1976). Directives, like any speech act, are defined by constitutive rules or logical preconditions (see Table 6.2). Based on these defining conditions, Brown and Levinson (1987, pp. 65-66) claim that directives intrinsically threaten the target's negative face. When Mike asks Mr. Jenkins to donate blood in Example 6.1, for instance, he assumes that Mr. Jenkins (a) is unlikely to set up an appointment on his own in the near future (otherwise, Mike does not need to call Mr. Jenkins) and (b) might be willing to donate again (otherwise, Mike is wasting his time calling Mr. Jenkins). By making assumptions about what Mr. Jenkins is likely to do and what he may be willing to do, Mike constrains Mr. Jenkins's autonomy (Brown & Levinson, 1987, p. 144).

Based on the constitutive rules for various speech acts, politeness theory distinguishes between acts that threaten negative face (i.e., constrain autonomy) and those that threaten positive face (i.e., communicate disapproval). It also distinguishes between acts that primarily threaten the message target's face and those that threaten the message source's own face. Table 6.7 presents examples of speech acts that intrinsically threaten each of these four face wants. As is apparent in the table, each speech act is assumed to threaten one, and only one, type of face.[6]

Brown and Levinson's (1987) classification of directives as intrinsic FTAs has important implications for the study of compliance gaining. As I noted above in the section on obstacles to compliance, directives are at the heart of any attempt to gain compliance. Given the centrality of directives to seeking compliance, it follows that any attempt to gain compliance, by definition, places some degree of constraint on the target's negative face. Thus the message source plausibly might worry about constraining the target's autonomy within any compliance-gaining situation.

Seeking compliance is intrinsically face threatening, but not all attempts are equally face threatening. According to politeness theory, the amount of face threat created by any speech act is a linear function of three variables: (a) distance, (b) power, and (c) ranking of the degree of imposition within a culture (Brown & Levinson, 1987, p. 74). Relational *distance* is the degree of familiarity between the message source and target. Politeness theory assumes that as social distance increases, so does the magnitude or "weightiness" of face threat. Imagine that you lost your purse and/or wallet and had to ask to borrow a quarter from a complete stranger in order to make a telephone call. You might say something such as, "Excuse me, I'm sorry to bother you, but I've lost my wallet. I need to make a phone call, and I have absolutely no money. Would you happen to have a quarter?" Now imagine how you would ask your best friend for a quarter in the same situation. Can you imagine saying "Excuse me," or apologizing, or explaining in this much detail to your best friend? According to politeness theory, the same request for a quarter is more face threatening when the target is a stranger than when the target is a close friend.

Power refers to the degree of status or control the message source has in relation to the target. Politeness theory assumes that as the source's status increases relative to the target, the weightiness of any face threat decreases. All other things being equal, a sergeant in the U.S. armed forces creates a larger face

Table 6.7   Examples of Brown and Levinson's Four Types of Intrinsic
Face-Threatening Acts

Acts That Primarily Threaten	Speaker's Face	Hearer's Face
Positive face	Apologies	Criticisms
	Confessions	Insults
Negative face	Promises	Requests
	Offers	Recommendations

SOURCE: From *Politeness: Some Universals in Language Usage,* by P. Brown &
S. C. Levinson, 1987 (pp. 65-68). Copyright 1987 by Cambridge University Press.
Adapted with permission.

threat by asking for assistance from a lieutenant than by asking for assistance
from a private, because the private is obligated formally to follow most directions
from the sergeant.

Ranking refers to the extent to which a speech act, within a particular situation and cultural context, interferes with the target's desire to maintain face.
Asking to borrow $2,500 from a close friend places greater constraint on the
friend's autonomy than does asking to borrow a quarter, because the friend, by
lending the larger sum of money, may limit his or her own ability to make
desired purchases or even to pay monthly bills. Politeness theory assumes that,
in any culture, distance, power, and rank are the crucial factors determining the
weightiness of an FTA.[7]

When contemplating performing an FTA, politeness theory proposes, a
speaker chooses from five options. These five "superstrategies" are shown in
Table 6.8, along with examples from a scenario that assumes you would like to
buy a new house but are $3,000 short on the down payment. Should you ask
your parent(s) to loan you the money, realizing that it may be several years
before you can repay the loan in its entirety? After thinking about the situation, you might decide that asking to borrow $3,000 imposes too much on
your parent. In this case, you probably would choose not to do the FTA (see
superstrategy 5).

If you do decide to perform the FTA, you must choose between going on- or
off-record. Performing an FTA "on-record" means saying something that
makes your intention to ask for a loan clear, such as "Mom, can you loan me
$3,000 for my down payment on the house?" Performing an FTA "off-record"
means saying something more ambiguous, that might or might not be heard
as asking for a loan. Going off-record can be seen as a strategic violation of
Grice's (1975) maxim of manner. The example of superstrategy 4 in Table 6.8
is off-record because, as the following examples show, it plausibly might or
might not be a request for a loan:

Table 6.8   Brown and Levinson's (1987) Five Superstrategies for Doing FTAs, With Examples From a Hypothetical Loan Scenario

Superstrategy	Definition/Example
1. Do the FTA baldly, without redress.	State the FTA in the most direct, clear, and concise way possible. *Example:* Mom, loan me $3,000.
2. Do the FTA using positive politeness.	Give assurances that the message source values the target and wants what the target wants. *Example:* Mom, we're family, and we always help each other out. I know that you want me to live in a safer neighborhood. I can do that if you'll lend me $3,000 for the down payment on my house.
3. Do the FTA using negative politeness.	Give assurances that the message source respects the target's freedom and will interfere with it as little as possible. *Example:* Mom, I hate to ask you this, but is there any way that you might be able to lend me $3,000 for the down payment on my house? I'll pay you back as soon as I can.
4. Do the FTA off-record.	Do the FTA so that the message source's intent is ambiguous and so that the source can deny having performed the FTA if necessary. *Example:* I don't know how I'm going to come up with all the money for the down payment.
5. Don't do the FTA.	Choose not to perform the FTA. *Example:* Say nothing.

SOURCE: From *Politeness: Some Universals in Language Usage,* by P. Brown & S. C. Levinson, 1987 (pp. 65-68). Copyright 1987 by Cambridge University Press. Adapted with permission.

EXAMPLE 6.11

1	You:	I don't know how I'm going to come up with the money for the down payment.
2A	Parent:	How much are you short? Maybe I could help you with part of it.
2B	Parent:	Gee, honey, I'd like to help, but I don't have that kind of money right now.
2C	Parent:	Gee, honey, that must be frustrating.

The parents in lines 2A and 2B respond to line 1 as implied request, whereas the parent in line 2C responds to it only as an expression of frustration. Off-record requests are polite in the sense that they provide the message target with greater options. Rather than being forced to say either yes or no, the parent can respond to line 1 as an implied request or instead choose to hear only the literal meaning of the statement (as in line 2C). Going off-record, however, runs the risk that the parent may not even realize that a request is being made.

If you decide to perform the FTA on-record, you still must choose to do so with or without redress. Performing the FTA baldly, without redress (super-strategy 1), means doing it "in the most direct, clear, unambiguous, and concise way possible" (Brown & Levinson, 1987, p. 69). This means following Grice's (1975) maxims quite literally, by making the request as clear as possible (manner), using no more words than absolutely necessary (quantity), and so forth. Although most of us probably would not use a bald, on-record request such as the one in Table 6.8 when asking to borrow a large sum of money, we might if the request were much smaller (e.g., "Mom, loan me a dollar") or if there was an urgent need to speak efficiently (e.g., "Mom, get out!" after discovering that her house is on fire; Kellermann & Park, 2001).

Performing the FTA with redressive action means adding language to the request that attempts to minimize or counteract potential face damage. Politeness forms, in this sense, are "principled deviations" from Grice's (1975) quantity maxim, meaning that people who use them are saying more than literally is necessary in order to be polite. Two types of politeness are available. Negative politeness (superstrategy 3) offers assurances that the message source recognizes and respects the target's autonomy. The example in Table 6.8 communicates negative politeness by (a) apologizing for the intrusion ("I hate to ask you"), (b) expressing doubt about the target's ability to comply ("any way that you might be able to"), and (c) minimizing the length of the imposition ("as soon as I can"). Positive politeness (superstrategy 2) offers assurances that the message source likes and shares similar wants with the target. The example in Table 6.8 communicates positive politeness by (a) using in-group markers ("we're family"), (b) asserting common ground ("you want me to live"), and (c) providing reasons ("I can do that if").

Politeness theory assumes that each of the five superstrategies can be carried out in multiple ways. Brown and Levinson devote the bulk of the discussion in their book *Politeness: Some Universals in Language Usage* (1987) to documenting concrete linguistic strategies by which speakers of English, Tamil, and Tzetal communicate negative or positive politeness. Table 6.9 summarizes 10 linguistic strategies that speakers use to enact negative politeness. Mike uses several of these strategies in the phone call shown in Example 6.1, including

Table 6.9   Ten Linguistic Strategies for Enacting the Superstrategy of Negative Politeness

Linguistic Strategy	Definition/Example
1. Be conventionally indirect.	Use indirect request forms. *Example:* Can you do X? (versus "Do X").
2. Question, hedge.	Avoid committing to assumptions underlying the request. *Example: I was wondering* whether you might . . .
3. Be pessimistic.	Express doubt about whether the target can/will comply. *Example:* Is there any way that you could . . . ?
4. Minimize the imposition.	Downplay the size/length of the request. *Example:* I was *just* calling to see if you could . . .
5. Give deference.	Humble oneself and/or emphasize the target's status. *Example:* Excuse me, *sir,* but I wondered . . .
6. Apologize.	Indicate reluctance to infringe on the target. *Example:* I hate to ask this, but . . .
7. Impersonalize both parties.	Avoid explicitly mentioning the source and/or target. *Example:* It needs to be done (versus "*You* need to do it").
8. State a general rule.	State the request as an instance of some general rule. *Example:* Employees will wash their hands before returning to work (versus "*You* need to wash your hands . . .").
9. Nominalize.	Remove the actor from "doing" the request. *Example:* Your cooperation is urgently requested (versus "*We* urgently request your cooperation").
10. Go on record as incurring a debt.	Explicitly claim indebtedness to the message target. *Example:* I'd be eternally grateful if you could . . .

SOURCE: From *Politeness: Some Universals in Language Usage,* by P. Brown & S. C. Levinson, 1987 (pp. 129-211). Copyright 1987 by Cambridge University Press. Adapted with permission.

giving deference (line 02), being pessimistic (line 14), minimizing imposition (line 14), and using conventionally indirect requests (line 23). Brown and Levinson also document 15 linguistic strategies by which speakers in all three languages enact positive politeness. Politeness theory also assumes that negative and positive politeness are alternative ways of redressing an FTA: by using avoidance-based language to show deference and respect (negative politeness), or by using approach-based language to communicate approval (positive politeness; see Brown & Levinson, 1987, pp. 68-70).

When contemplating performing an FTA, how does a speaker choose between the five superstrategies? Politeness theory makes two important assumptions to answer this question. The first is that the five superstrategies are rank ordered from the least polite option (do the FTA baldly, without redress) to the most polite option (don't do the FTA; see Table 6.8). Brown and Levinson (1987, p. 18) argue that negative politeness (superstrategy 3) is more polite than positive politeness (superstrategy 2) because it is avoidance rather than approach based. The second assumption is that a speaker selects a superstrategy based on the perceived weightiness of the FTA. When seeking compliance, the more a potential request threatens the message target's autonomy, the more the source will want to choose a more polite (i.e., a higher numbered) superstrategy (see Table 6.8). As noted above, the message source should choose a less polite superstrategy when concerns about efficiency outweigh face concerns. A source also is likely to choose a less polite superstrategy when the degree of face threat from seeking compliance is low (e.g., the request is small, the message source has greater relative power). A speaker who uses more politeness than is necessary risks implying, by accident, that his or her request is very large. If I were to say to my stepdaughter, "Sheridan, I hate to ask you this, but is there any way you possibly might be able help your mom?" she might well think, "If Steve's being this nice about it, then Mom must want me to do something really awful." In sum, politeness theory does not assume that message sources always will be polite when seeking compliance. Rather, the theory predicts that sources will vary their levels of politeness based on the degree to which their attempts to gain compliance threaten the message targets' face. Politeness theory assumes that people are "rational" in the sense of being able to reason from goals to linguistic means for accomplishing their goals.[8]

Evaluation of Politeness Theory

Useful theories are heuristic; that is, they stimulate research and debate about issues of importance. Brown and Levinson's (1987) politeness theory fares well on this criterion. Scholars have drawn upon, extended, and modified politeness theory to pose questions about people's choice of compliance-seeking and -resisting messages across cultures, genders, and relationship types (e.g., Baxter, 1984; Holtgraves & Yang, 1992; Lambert, 1996a; Leichty & Applegate, 1991; Lim & Bowers, 1991; Metts, Cupach, & Imahori, 1992; Wilson & Kunkel, 2000). Others have tested whether persuaders who enact specific superstrategies, such as going off-record, are perceived as polite, appropriate, competent, and/or effective (e.g., Blum-Kulka, 1987; Clark & Schunk, 1980; Fairhurst, Green, & Snavely, 1984; Holtgraves & Yang, 1990; Kline & Floyd, 1990; Metts et al., 1992). In addition to its application in the study of persuasive message production, politeness theory has stimulated research on topics such as children's language acquisition, second-language learning, and cultural universals in the use of honorifics (for a review, see Brown & Levinson, 1987, preface).

Politeness theory has been heuristic for at least two reasons. One is that the theory shows how people's social concerns (i.e., the macro level) both reflect and constrain the linguistic details of their talk (i.e., the micro level). Brown and Levinson (1987) are not the first to suggest that people in all cultures share basic wants (e.g., Maslow, 1943; Schutz, 1971). Politeness theory also is not the first theory to describe and explain linguistic patterns; indeed, CA scholars take this as their primary task. What is unique about politeness theory is that it links the macro and micro levels. Brown and Levinson show how regularities in the wording of speech acts can be explained by the assumptions that conversational participants (a) desire to maintain face, (b) are mutually aware of this desire, and (c) are rational agents (see note 8).

A second reason politeness theory has heuristic value is that it highlights both cross-cultural similarities and differences in influence messages. According to the theory, people in all cultures (a) desire approval and autonomy; (b) have motives to support other people's face; (c) use distance, power, and rank to determine the weightiness of face threat; and (d) have options such as going "on-record" versus "off-record." On the other hand, the theory recognizes that cultures vary in (a) how distance and power are perceived within the "same" relationships (e.g., friendship), (b) how culture members rank the imposition of specific FTAs, (c) which persons culture members view as "significant" and hence as persons whose approval is desirable, and (d) which persons culture members view as having power or status and hence as persons who deserve face protection. Rather than privileging commonality or difference, politeness theory attempts to account for both.

Despite these strengths, politeness theory has been widely criticized (e.g., Coupland, Grainger, & Coupland, 1988; Craig, Tracy, & Spisak, 1986; Goldsmith, 2000; Lim & Bowers, 1991; Tracy & Baratz, 1994; Wilson, 1992; Wilson et al., 1991/1992, 1998; for a response to several criticisms, see Brown & Levinson, 1987, preface). Here I describe four common criticisms. First, Brown and Levinson's (1987) two types of face have been questioned. Lim and Bowers (1991) argue that the concept of positive face compounds two basic human wants: the need to be included (which they term "fellowship face") versus the need to have one's abilities respected (which they term "competence face"). They propose three types of face and three corresponding types of politeness.

Fellowship face is supported by statements of solidarity. Competence face is supported by statements of approbation. Finally, autonomy face is supported by the demonstration of tact. After analyzing written responses to hypothetical compliance-gaining scenarios, Lim and Bowers conclude that (a) message sources match types of politeness to types of face threat (e.g., requests that threaten the target's fellowship face are redressed with solidarity statements), and (b) sources use all three types of politeness independently (e.g., making solidarity statements neither guarantees nor precludes that a source will make statements of approbation). Distinguishing fellowship and competence face seems especially important for cross-cultural research on persuasive message production, because these two types of positive face may vary in salience within individualist versus collectivist cultures (for a discussion of individualism and collectivism, see Chapter 5).

A second criticism is that politeness theory's analysis of how face threats arise is grounded too heavily in the form of speech acts, without sufficient analysis of the context in which acts are performed. Consider a mother who tells her son, "You need to start trying in your math class." This directive constrains the son's options and thus threatens his negative face, but it simultaneously threatens the son's positive face by asserting that, up to this point, he has not been "trying." In contrast, a mother who asks her son to "please pass the salt" places minor constraint on the son's autonomy but, in most cases, communicates no disapproval. When do directives threaten only the message target's negative face, and when do they create multiple threats to the target's face as well as to the source's own face? Brown and Levinson (1987) classify FTAs based only on the constitutive rules for speech acts, irrespective of the contexts in which those acts are performed; thus they have little to say about this issue (Wilson et al., 1991/1992). Aside from the form of speech acts, threats to face also depend on the influence goal underlying an attempt to gain compliance (Wilson et al., 1998). For example, women and men from diverse cultural backgrounds at times worry that they might appear to be "butting into" the affairs of others when they give advice, but they rarely have this concern when asking favors. In contrast, individuals at times worry that they might "owe" their targets big debts in the future when they ask favors, but they rarely have this concern when giving advice (Cai & Wilson, 2000; Wilson, Anastasiou, Kim, Aleman, & Oetzel, 2000; Wilson & Kunkel, 2000). Aside from influence goals that define an interaction, threats to face also vary depending on the unfolding sequence of talk. Thus the degree to which giving advice threatens face varies depending on whether the target has explicitly asked for advice, has disclosed a problem, or has said nothing at all yet about the topic of advice (Goldsmith, 2000).

Third, Brown and Levinson's (1987) claim that positive politeness, negative politeness, and off-record superstrategies are three mutually exclusive options has been criticized. Several studies have shown that, rather than using only one superstrategy, message sources often mix two or three within the same compliance-seeking message (e.g., Craig et al., 1986; Holtgraves & Yang, 1992; Lim & Bowers, 1991). Consider Example 6.12, in which a college student speaks aloud her response to a hypothetical situation that involves making a large request of a friend:

Example 6.12

Hey Milly, uh, I got some great news for you. Uh, I'll be moving to Philadelphia to start a new job and, huh, they want me there on, uh, Monday of next week, uh, I don't have a place to live and, uh, need to take some time to locate at a place. I was wondering, uh, if it would be possible for me to stay with you, uh, at the outside I would guess a couple of weeks, uh, to, uh, give me some time, uh, to find a place. Uh, as you remember I'm a great cat lover and, uh, I'd like to bring my cat with me and I know we'll all get along well. It's an awful big favor to ask and I hesitate but what are friends for, would it be possible for me and my cat to stay with you? (quoted in Craig et al., 1986, p. 450)

Example 6.12 contains numerous positive politeness strategies, including using in-group markers ("we'll" and "friends"), giving reasons ("I don't have a place to live"), assuming that the target is interested in the source's wants ("I've got some great news"), and being optimistic ("I know we'll all get along well"). But the message also contains negative politeness strategies, such as hedging and indirectness ("I was wondering if it would be possible"), minimizing the imposition ("at the outside I would guess a couple of weeks"), and indicating reluctance to impose ("I hesitate"). Rather than choosing between mutually exclusive options, message sources often mix different superstrategies, sequentially or even simultaneously, to redress an FTA.

A fourth criticism targets politeness theory's claim that, regardless of context, the five superstrategies can be rank ordered from least to most polite. Several researchers have found exceptions to Brown and Levinson's (1987) rank ordering, such as on-record strategies being perceived as more polite than off-record strategies and positive politeness being rated as more polite than negative politeness (e.g., Baxter, 1984; Blum-Kulka, 1987; Dillard, Wilson, Tusing, & Kinney, 1997; Holtgraves & Yang, 1990). These exceptions suggest that the perceived politeness of any superstrategy depends heavily on the specific relational, institutional, and cultural context of the situation (Coupland et al., 1988; Dillard et al., 1997; Tracy & Baratz, 1994). Consider the following example, in which a nurse (N1) attempts to convince an elderly hospital patient (M) to take her medication:

EXAMPLE **6.13**

1	N1:	Milly (1.5) Milly (.) come on love (.) wake up (2.0)
2		((4/5 syllables)) (1.0) that's
3		my girl (6.0) come on (.) drink it up (.) Milly it's your
4		medication love (2.0) come
5		on it's your medicine
6	M:	(( ))
7	N1:	here you are (2.0) Linda she won't take it
8	N2:	who? (2.0) what the ((lactose?))
9	N1:	it's for your bowels (.) come on
10	N3:	((she'll take it some time later))
11	N1:	Milly come on love it's for your bowels love you must
12		take it otherwise you'll get
13		a bad stomach (1.5) come on (5.0) ((never mind)) (2.0)
14		((drink some more)) (5.0)
15		not much left (.) come on darling . . .

Although N1 in Example 6.13 issues many bald on-record requests, she also uses several positive politeness strategies (e.g., in-group markers such as "love" and "darling") and negative politeness strategies (e.g., minimizing the FTA in "not much left" and giving reasons such as "bad stomach"). Despite these politeness forms, the nurse's attempts to gain compliance may not be heard as polite. A nurse's addressing an elderly patient as "love" and "darling" may be seen more as her treating the patient like a child than as communicating affection or respect. This impression is reinforced when the nurse (N1) talks about the patient to a colleague (N2) in the patient's presence. Politeness judgments are contextually bound; hence any attempt to rank order the five superstrategies across contexts seems doomed to failure.

In light of these criticisms of politeness theory, scholars typically have taken one of two tacks. Some advocate maintaining the theory's basic concepts (e.g., the intrinsic FTA, the three situational variables that determine weightiness, the five superstrategies) but elaborating or modifying particular assumptions that have proven problematic (e.g., Lim & Bowers, 1991; Wilson et al., 1991/1992, 1998). The challenge for this "conservative" approach is whether it can address the criticisms noted above while maintaining the basic core of politeness theory. A second group of scholars advocate scrapping politeness theory in favor of context-specific analyses of politeness (e.g., Coupland et al., 1988; Tracy & Baratz, 1994). The danger of this more "radical" approach is that context-specific analyses may lose sight of those cross-cultural linguistic regularities that motivated the development of politeness theory in the first place. Regardless of the ultimate outcome, Brown and Levinson's (1987) theory has stimulated a great deal of research about how detailed regularities in influence messages can be understood as attempts to maintain face.

O'KEEFE'S THEORY OF MESSAGE DESIGN LOGICS

Barbara O'Keefe's theory of message design logics emerged from her earlier "goal and behavioral complexity" analysis (see Chapter 5). After sketching the genesis of message design logics below, I describe the theory's key concepts and assumptions, and then evaluate its utility.

Background of the Theory

O'Keefe's (1988, 1990, 1991) theory of message design logics responds to limitations in the earlier "goal and behavioral complexity" account of message production. As you will recall from Chapter 5, O'Keefe and Delia (1982) suggest that a communication situation is complex when its constituent features create multiple "situationally relevant objectives" that appear contradictory and difficult to reconcile. For example, interpersonal arguments in which two parties disagree about a controversial issue are complex because both parties can be expected to present and defend their own positions clearly, but also to show respect for the other party's ideas (i.e., support the other's face). O'Keefe and Delia propose three strategies for managing such goal conflict: (a) selection, or giving priority to one goal (primary or secondary) while ignoring others; (b) separation, or addressing multiple goals one at a time or through different channels; and (c) integration, or reframing the situation so as to pursue multiple goals simultaneously. To investigate these strategies, O'Keefe and Shepherd (1987) paired college students with divergent opinions on a controversial issue, instructed each student to try to convince the other to accept his or her own position on the issue, and then examined the students' use of selection, separation, and integration strategies, turn by turn, throughout the discussions.

Although O'Keefe initially viewed "selection," "separation," and "integration" simply as three different strategies for managing goal conflict, she eventually has come to see them as reflecting three fundamentally different ideas about the nature and possibilities of communication. As O'Keefe (1988) puts it, "These three 'goal management strategies' reflect three different ways of reasoning from goals to messages rather than three alternative message forms derived from the same way of reasoning about communication" (p. 83). To understand her thinking, first consider the strategy of "separation." During an interpersonal argument, a separation strategy might involve directly criticizing the other person's views while also including apologies, disclaimers, qualifiers, and other attempts to offset the criticism. Separation strategies can be interpreted easily within Brown and Levinson's (1987) politeness theory. Criticizing another person's views can be heard as expressing disapproval of that person him- or herself. Given the mutual benefit of supporting face, a speaker who criticizes another person's views should be motivated to redress threats to that person's positive face with just the sort of politeness strategies (e.g., apologies, qualifiers) that O'Keefe and Shepherd (1987) observed in separation strategies.

Both selection and integration strategies, however, make less sense from the perspective of politeness theory. During an interpersonal argument, selection strategies might involve directly criticizing the other person's views with no attempt to qualify or tone down the disagreement (i.e., pursue only the primary goal). Alternatively, selection could involve lying about one's own position and claiming to hold the same view as the other person in order to avoid disagreement (i.e., pursue only the secondary goal). Some of O'Keefe and Shepherd's (1987) participants told exactly such lies, even though both parties were explicitly informed at the start that they were paired together precisely because they held highly divergent opinions. From the perspective of politeness theory, why would an individual choose either to disagree "baldly, on-record" or to tell a detectable lie about his or her own position when other options are available?

Integration strategies also are difficult to comprehend within politeness theory. During an interpersonal argument, integration strategies might involve directly criticizing the other person's views, but doing so within a larger discussion of how considering the strengths and weaknesses of all positions—one's own, the other person's, and other relevant views—allows everyone to make informed choices. Although the speaker still advocates his or her own views, the speaker's actions are reframed from "criticizing the other's view" (an FTA) to "mutually becoming better informed about the issue" (*not* an FTA). Which of Brown and Levinson's (1987) five superstrategies is this (see Table 6.8)? As O'Keefe (1991) explains, reframing is not an instance of the off-record superstrategy: "In indirectness, the FTA is performed but off-record; whereas in this approach, the FTA is not performed at all" (p. 140). It also is not an instance of the "don't do the FTA" strategy, because the speaker does attempt to influence the other party. To summarize, politeness theory presumes that a speaker is limited to using linguistic strategies, within the current context, to redress FTAs, whereas integration strategies presuppose the possibility of redefining the context so as to pursue the primary goal without threatening face at all. Hence O'Keefe (1988) concludes that the three goal management strategies "result from variation in the systems of principles used in reasoning from ends to communicative means, differences in the very definitions of communication that individuals construct and employ" (p. 84).

Key Concepts and Assumptions

Based on the points noted above, O'Keefe (1988) argues for the existence of three message design logics, or systems of means-ends reasoning about communication. A message design logic is "a constellation of related beliefs: a communication constituting concept, a conception of the functional possibilities of communication, unit formation procedures, and principles of coherence" (p. 84). The design logics represent three fundamentally different ideas about what talk is relevant in social situations (Grice, 1975). Key characteristics of each of these three design logics, which O'Keefe labels expressive, conventional, and rhetorical, are shown in Table 6.10.

The fundamental premise of the *expressive* logic is that communication "is a medium for expressing thoughts and feelings" (O'Keefe, 1988, p. 84). Individuals using this logic view "saying what's on one's mind" as the primary function of communication. Expressive individuals communicate directly and literally, and they interpret other people's messages in the same way. They view communication as successful to the degree that it is clear and honest. Messages generated by the expressive logic tend to focus temporally on the past. If an individual using the expressive logic is asked, "Why did you say X now?" the answer typically is "Because some immediately prior event made me think or feel X, and so I said X." Expressive messages often contain "pragmatically pointless" content, in the sense that the speaker says what he or she is thinking even if these thoughts do not help accomplish situationally relevant objectives. When faced with conflicting goals, such as seeking compliance but also supporting the target's face, persons employing the expressive logic see two (and only two) options: Say it or don't say it.

Consider how someone using the expressive design logic might respond to the following "group leader" hypothetical situation:

> You have been assigned to a group project in one of your classes. . . . it is important to you to get a good grade in this class. . . . the instructor . . . designated you to be the leader of your group. . . . Your duties as group leader will include telling the instructor what grade you think each individual in the group deserves based on their individual contributions. One group member (whose name is Ron) . . . seldom makes it to group meetings on time and entirely skipped one meeting without calling anyone in advance. . . . At the next meeting, Ron arrived late but apologized for missing the previous meeting and mentioned something about family problems. Ron did volunteer to do all the background research on one important aspect of the group's topic. . . . the group project is due next week. The

Table 6.10   Characteristics of Three Message Design Logics

Characteristic	Message Design Logic		
	Expressive	Conventional	Rhetorical
Key message function	Self-expression	Secure desired response	Negotiate social consensus
Central dimensions of communication evaluation	Clarity Openness/ honesty Unimpeded signaling	Appropriateness Cooperativeness Control of resources	Flexibility Symbolic sophistication Depth of interpretation
Temporal organization	Reaction to prior event	Response specified by context	Initiate movement toward desired context
Message/context relationship	Little attention to context	Message determined by context	Message creates context
Internal message coherence	Subjective and associative	Intersubjective and rule focused	Intersubjective and style centered
Diagnostic elements	"Pragmatically" pointless content	Mentions of rights and obligations	Explicit context-defining phrases
Method of managing face	Editing	Politeness forms	Context redefinition

SOURCE: From "The Logic of Message Design: Individual Differences in Reasoning About Communication," by B. J. O'Keefe, *Communication Monographs, 55,* p. 85. Copyright 1988 by the Speech Communication Association. Adapted with permission.

group planned to put together the final draft of its report at the meeting scheduled for tomorrow afternoon. Ron calls you up today and says that he doesn't have his library research done and can't get it finished before the meeting. He says he just needs more time. (O'Keefe, 1988, p. 93)

What would you say to Ron? O'Keefe asked 92 undergraduate students to write out what they would say in this situation. One student wrote the following:

Ron, I can't believe you haven't finished your research. You've been inconsiderate to the group all along. Several members even suggested that you be taken out of the group but we decided to give you a chance. Now what are we supposed to do? It was your responsibility and you backed out. I'm afraid I'm going to have to tell the T.A. that you haven't done your share. I will be so mad if we get a bad grade on this—I need an A in this course. (quoted in O'Keefe, 1990, p. 95).

Several characteristics of the expressive logic are evident in this message. Much of the message simply describes and evaluates Ron's past behavior. The message also contains a good deal of pragmatically pointless content. There is still a week before the project is due, and 24 hours before the group's next meeting. Despite this, the student does not attempt to persuade Ron to make progress on his research. Most of the message simply vents the student's frustration with Ron. Being frustrated is an understandable reaction, but that alone does not forward the group's task. Even the threat is noncontingent. The student simply says that he or she is going to tell the T.A. about Ron's failure to contribute, rather than that he or she will do this unless Ron starts doing his part.[9]

The fundamental premise of the *conventional* message design logic is that communication "is a game played cooperatively, according to socially conventional rules and procedures" (O'Keefe, 1988, p. 86). Communication still is viewed as a means of expressing ideas, but these ideas reflect the social effects that the speaker wants to achieve rather than the thoughts that happen to be on the speaker's mind. For example, if an individual using this logic needed assistance, he or she might say something that, given the context, would count as a "request," because making a request is a way of obtaining assistance by calling on the conventional obligations that exist between persons. Individuals applying this logic view communication as successful to the degree to which speakers can achieve their ends while adhering to the norms of appropriateness. They view communicative contexts as "predefined" or "given," meaning that people's roles, rights, and relations are established by the nature of a situation and hence are relatively inflexible.

Messages generated by the conventional logic tend to be focused temporally on the present. If an individual using the conventional logic is asked, "Why did you say X now?" the answer typically is "Because I wanted to accomplish Y, and X is the typical way of doing so," or "Because you just said Z, and X is the relevant response to Z." Conventional messages often include explicit references to constitutive rules that underlie speech acts, rights and obligations that give rise to speech acts, and mitigating conditions that bear on those rights and obligations. When faced with conflicting goals, such as seeking compliance but also supporting face, persons using this logic will employ "conventional" solutions such as politeness strategies. Consider a second student's response to the Ron scenario:

> Well, Ron, I'm sorry you don't have your part of the project done. We have given you several breaks thus far and I don't see how we can give you any more. The whole group is depending on you so I would suggest to you to get it done or at the most bring in what you have got done. If you don't get this done I'm going to have to give you an F for the project. If you can't hold up your responsibility with this

group even under these adverse conditions (family problems), how are you going to make it in life? (quoted in O'Keefe, 1990, p. 96)

Several characteristics of the conventional logic are evident in this message. This student addresses the primary situationally relevant objective explicitly, by "suggesting" that Ron get his research done by the meeting and by following through with a conditional threat. He or she also mentions Ron's obligations: Ron hasn't done his "part" of the project, and he has a "responsibility" to the group. Compared with the expressive message above, this message spends less time berating Ron and more time emphasizing what Ron should be doing at this point in time. This message also briefly acknowledges the mitigating circumstances (family problems) cited by Ron.

The fundamental premise of the *rhetorical* logic is that "communication is the creation and negotiation of social selves and situations" (O'Keefe, 1988, p. 87). Within this logic, selves and social situations are *not* viewed as predefined by a conventional system of rules; rather, selves are enacted in dramas, and social situations are constantly "in flux." From the rhetorical view, communication is the process by which context is created. Rather than being "given" and "fixed," context is interactionally negotiated; speakers can redefine it strategically to accomplish their goals. Individuals applying this logic view communication as successful when participants reach a consensus about the reality in which they want to be engaged (i.e., agreement about "what is going on"). Rhetorical communicators shy away from relying on formal authority based on their roles or positions. Instead, they seek consensus by advocating the benefits of the reality they enact and by listening carefully to determine the drama and perspective being enacted by others.

Messages generated by the rhetorical logic tend to focus temporally on the future. If an individual using the rhetorical logic is asked, "Why did you say X now?" the answer typically is "Because I am trying to accomplish goal Y." Rhetorical messages frequently contain explicit context-describing phrases. Rather than citing rules or sanctions, rhetorical messages often contain "rationale" arguments about why the speaker's definition of the situation is advantageous and makes sense. When faced with conflicting goals, such as seeking compliance and supporting face, persons using this logic look for ways to redefine the situation so as to induce the desired action without threatening face. Consider yet another student's response to the Ron scenario:

Well, Ron, it's due next week, and we have to get it all to the typist. OK, if it's not done it's not. Tell you what. Why don't you jot down your main ideas so that we can include them in the introduction and the conclusion. Also, tell me when you think your section should come in the whole project. Then get it to my apartment by 10:00 the next day because I have to get it to the typist by 2:00. Is this okay? I'll just explain to the group that you'll have it done but not by meeting time. We all want a good grade, so if you need the time to make your part better, go ahead. But if I can't get it to the typist in time, you'll have to type it. Alright, take it easy. (quoted in O'Keefe, 1990, p. 97)

This message illustrates several characteristics of the rhetorical logic. Most of the message is future oriented, proposing a step-by-step plan for getting Ron's work done. The student lays out what Ron needs to do at each point in time and outlines his or her own role as well. He or she avoids threatening Ron and seeks rather than presumes Ron's agreement with the plan ("Is this okay?"). The speaker also redefines what is going on in a face-saving way: Ron is taking time to make his part better so as to assure a good group grade, rather than just completing his part belatedly.

O'Keefe (1988, 1990, 1991) argues that these three message design logics form a natural developmental progression. The first logic an individual must acquire is the expressive, so that he or she understands that words can be used to express internal thoughts and feelings. Should the individual learn that words can be used to perform actions in given contexts, and not just to express thoughts directly, then the conventional logic has subsumed the expressive. Should the individual come to understand that communication conventions and contexts can be redefined, then the rhetorical logic has subsumed the conventional. According to O'Keefe, an individual does not discard one design logic when he or she acquires another: the conventional logic user still employs words to express thoughts as well as to perform other actions, and the rhetorical logic user may choose to play within the situation as currently defined rather than to propose a new situation.

In sum, O'Keefe's (1988) theory presumes that messages "are produced by two conceptually and empirically separable features of the message design process" (p. 96): (a) the message source's goals and (b) the design logic that a message source uses to reason from goals to messages. The people who produced different messages in response to the Ron scenario, for instance, could do so because they formed and pursued different goals: One individual might pursue none of the potential situationally relevant objectives (e.g., convincing Ron to do his part, saving Ron's face), a second might pursue only one of these goals, and a third might pursue multiple goals. Distinct from the number of goals that motivate a message, however, people also might produce different messages in response to the Ron scenario because they rely on different systems of reasoning to move from goals to messages. Although expressive, conventional, and rhetorical communicators all may form multiple goals, each sees fundamentally different options for managing goal conflicts so as to maintain face (see the bottom row in Table 6.10).

Given this conceptualization, O'Keefe (1988, 1990; O'Keefe, Lambert, & Lambert, 1997) argues that people relying on different design logics are most likely to produce different messages, as well as to misunderstand each other, within "complex" communication situations. Simple situations tend to call out the same message from all communicators. In contrast, differences in design logics are most likely to affect the production and interpretation of messages in complex situations where message sources must manage multiple, contradictory situational objectives. In the responses to the Ron scenario presented above, for example, an expressive person might interpret the rhetorical individual's statement that Ron is taking more time to "make [his] part better" as an inaccurate and dishonest description of what is "really" going on. Similarly, the rhetorical person might view the expressive individual as simply wanting to "chew out" Ron, even though this may create more work for other group members who then have to complete Ron's part.

Evaluation of O'Keefe's Theory

O'Keefe's (1988) theory of message design logics incorporates the work of discourse scholars such as Grice (1975) and Searle (1969), as well as the symbolic interactionism of Goffman (1959, 1967), to describe and explain individual differences in the message production process. Parts of the theory have received empirical support. For example, O'Keefe assumes that the expressive, conventional, and rhetorical design logics are developmentally ordered and reflect increasing levels of communicative competence. If this is indeed the case, then people should rate compliance-seeking/resisting messages that display the rhetorical logic as more competent and appropriate than expressive or conventional messages. Data from several studies are consistent with this claim (Bingham & Burleson, 1989; O'Keefe, Lambert, & Lambert, 1993; O'Keefe & McCornack, 1987). O'Keefe and McCornack (1987) had 213 undergraduate students each read a different compliance-seeking message that had been generated in a previous study in response to the Ron scenario. These messages already had been coded for the number of goals pursued by the message source (none, one, multiple) as well as for the design logic evident in the message (scored 1 = expressive, 2 = conventional, 3 = rhetorical). After reading the message, each participant rated the likelihood that it would get Ron to complete his part, the degree to which the message supported Ron's face, and the degree to which they perceived the source of the message as competent and attractive. Participants who evaluated influence messages with more "advanced" design logics, as opposed to messages that displayed the expressive logic, on average perceived the message as more likely to get Ron to do his part and more supportive of Ron's face, and the message source as more competent and attractive.

Although the rhetorical design logic may be more competent, in the sense of providing a broader range of options for managing complicated compliance-gaining situations, O'Keefe et al. (1997) do emphasize that "every design logic provides a logically consistent and potentially satisfactory way for an individual to use language" (p. 49). Rather than training expressives and conventionals to use the rhetorical logic, O'Keefe et al. recommend training everyone "in more general strategies to help them recognize and accommodate to diversity in design logics" (p. 50). For example, people might be taught to appreciate the system of reasoning behind all three sample responses to the Ron scenario (see note 8). This recommendation is consistent with recent evidence indicating that how individuals interpret and evaluate messages displaying the rhetorical design logic depends on the individuals' own particular design logics (O'Keefe et al., 1997; Peterson & Albrecht, 1996).

Although some data support assumptions from O'Keefe's theory, several challenges for the theory remain. First, one might argue that O'Keefe's procedures for measuring design logics and testing the theory have been tautological: A person's design logic is inferred from qualities of his or her compliance-seeking messages, but then design logics are used to "explain" why that person produced that type of message. One might hope for a measure of design logic independent of messages, one that taps more directly into design logics as a "constellation of related beliefs" (O'Keefe, 1988, p. 84) and "type of knowledge organization" (p. 97). Measuring design logics is complicated, however, because design logics are systems of implicit and tacit beliefs; one cannot simply ask a person, "What's your design logic?" O'Keefe and Lambert (1989) have made initial strides in developing a "thought checklist" procedure that measures the types of thoughts typically salient to expressive, conventional, and rhetorical communicators. Much more research is needed to establish the reliability and validity of this newer measure (see Waldron & Cegala, 1992).

Second, one might argue that O'Keefe (1988) should provide more detail about exactly how individuals, using any design logic, go about "reasoning from goals to messages" (p. 83). On what types of prior knowledge do individuals rely when they are deciding what to say as they seek/resist compliance? How is the knowledge composing a design logic integrated with knowledge about particular message targets and influence goals? How are people able to "reason" from goals to messages within the actual time constraints of face-to-face interaction? These questions call for more detail about the psychological processes that underlie message production. I review cognitive theories of message production, including O'Keefe and Lambert's (1995) ideas about psychological processes, in the next chapter. But as O'Keefe (1992) has argued, the theory of design logics provides important insights into persuasive message production, even without a detailed analysis of psychological process.

The theory helps explain why people see different ideas as relevant to express in the "same" compliance-gaining situation, as well as why people draw different interpretations from the "same" compliance-seeking message. By emphasizing how situations are constantly defined through interaction, the theory also shows how individuals, when seeking and/or resisting compliance, have means beyond formal politeness strategies for addressing threats to face.

Summary

Discourse theories of persuasive message production perspectives focus on how people rely on knowledge of linguistic forms and conventions when generating influence messages, and how they design messages in light of the unfolding talk. After using an extended compliance-gaining sequence to illustrate the types of questions raised by discourse scholars, I have reviewed in this chapter some basic concepts from work on conversational maxims, speech acts, and the conversation analysis perspective. Following this background material, I have explored in greater detail two concepts of central relevance to persuasive message production: (a) obstacles, analyzed from the view of speech act and attribution theories; and (b) face, analyzed from the view of politeness and message design logic theories.

Notes

1. As Schiffrin (1994) notes, the field of discourse analysis is "widely recognized as one of the most vast, but also one of the least defined, areas in linguistics" (p. 1). It incorporates works from disciplines in which models and methods for understanding discourse first were developed (e.g., anthropology, linguistics, philosophy, sociology) as well as disciplines that have applied and extended such models given their own concerns (e.g., communication, cognitive science, social psychology). To describe this breadth, Schiffrin compares a "formalist paradigm" of discourse, which looks at the internal structure of language units "above the sentence," with a "functionalist paradigm," which looks at the interdependence of discourse and social life by exploring functions of language external to the linguistic system itself. Some of the theory and research reviewed in this chapter falls outside the bounds of even a broad treatment of discourse such as Schiffrin's. Each work reviewed here, however, speaks to what Schiffrin identifies as the two central goals of discourse analysis: (a) sequential goals, or discovering principles underlying the ordering of utterances; and (b) semantic or pragmatic goals, or discovering how the structure and use of language allow people to convey and interpret meaning (p. 41).

2. The patient's contribution in lines 2-3 still could be interpreted sensibly if the patient was signaling, indirectly, his refusal to cooperate with the physician. If the patient simply is not orienting to the doctor's question, however, then lines 2-3 violate the relevance maxim.

3. Searle (1969, p. 66) also includes an "essential" rule for requests, which states that the speaker's message counts as an attempt to get the target to perform the desired action. For any

speech act, the essential rule spells out the speaker's illocutionary force. The essential rule assumes that the speaker has adhered to each of the other rules listed in Table 6.2.

4. Different people might perceive the same cause as falling at different points on one of the three dimensions; for example, some might perceive Joan's fight with her boyfriend as a stable cause if they fight frequently. The general point, however, is that people use the dimensions of locus, stability, and controllability to describe and compare different causes.

5. Brown and Levinson (1978) originally published their politeness theory in a 250-page book chapter that appeared as part of a collection of essays in volume 8 of the book series Cambridge Papers in Social Anthropology. Almost 10 years later, Cambridge University Press reissued that original chapter, accompanied by a new 50-page introduction and an expanded bibliography, as a book (Brown & Levinson, 1987). Because of its wider availability, I have used the reissued 1987 book for all quotations and materials presented here.

6. Brown and Levinson (1987, pp. 67, 286) do qualify that some acts, such as requests for personal information, intrinsically threaten the target's positive *and* negative face. Unfortunately, they do not provide any guidelines for determining when an act intrinsically threatens multiple types of face, nor do they consider the possibility that some acts may create either one or multiple face threats depending on the context. Brown and Levinson's qualification also is inconsistent with their own formula for determining the magnitude of an FTA. For more on this issue, see Wilson et al. (1991/1992, 1998).

7. Politeness theory recognizes that distance (D), power (P), and rank (R) are context dependent. A bank manager, for instance, typically will have greater power than a bank teller, but perhaps not if the teller represents his or her union in negotiations or sits on a jury that is trying the manager for embezzlement. Thus "situational factors enter into the values of D, P, and R, so that the values assessed hold only for [the speaker] and [the hearer] in a particular context, and for a particular FTA" (Brown & Levinson, 1987, p. 79). Politeness theory also recognizes that values of D, P, and R are socially negotiated. Speakers may use greater or lesser politeness than normally is expected in a situation precisely to affect the perceived values of D, P, and R (Brown & Levinson, 1987, pp. 81-83).

8. Brown and Levinson's (1987, pp. 58-59) claim that people are "rational" often is misunderstood. It is not intended to mean that participants always think a great deal about what to say during influence interactions, or that participants always choose the most effective means for accomplishing their influence and interpersonal goals. Rationality simply implies that people possess knowledge about linguistic means for accomplishing goals, and that their talk can be understood as an attempt to balance their competing desires to avoid threatening face versus to be clear and say no more than is necessary.

9. An expressive communicator might defend this response to the Ron situation by arguing that it is obvious, given the events, that Ron cannot be counted on to complete his part of the project, and that the group would be better off excluding Ron and finishing the work on their own. In this sense, the goal of persuading Ron to do his part may no longer be a sensible "situationally relevant objective."

7

Cognitive Perspectives on Persuasive Message Production

Looking Ahead . . .

This chapter reviews cognitive perspectives on persuasive message production. Cognitive theories explore the mental processes by which people translate knowledge about pursuing interaction goals into influence messages. The chapter opens with an example to illustrate the types of knowledge on which people rely when they are interpreting and producing influence messages. Next, key assumptions underlying cognitive theories are explained. The chapter then describes two specific cognitive perspectives with relevance for an understanding of persuasive message production: theories of plans and planning processes, and action assembly theory.

Background to Example 7.1: My stepdaughter Ashlee is 17 years old at the time of the example. Sheridan is Ashlee's twin sister. Ron, a graduate student in music, has been Ashlee's guitar teacher for 2 years. Bill, a friend of Ron's, is a 23-year-old undergraduate music major. Ashlee met Bill through Ron last year, and Ashlee and Bill dated briefly (Bill and Ron's real names have been changed). Patrice is my partner and Ashlee's mother. Starbusters is a local bar and grill. The conversation took place at our dinner table with all eight family members present.

EXAMPLE 7.1

01	Ashlee:	Uhh, we don't have school this Monday
02	Me:	Why not?
03	Ashlee:	It's Casmir Pulaski's birthday, and we get off. I was
04		wondering—Ron's band is playing at Starbusters
05		Sunday night. Can I go hear him?
06	Patrice:	Would Bill be there?
07	Ashlee:	I don't know
08	Me:	Can you get in?
09	Ashlee:	Yeah, the music starts at 9:00 P.M. Underagers can
10		stay until 11:00 P.M.—they have to leave at 11:00.
11	Me:	Could Sheridan go?
12	Sheridan:	I guess I could
13	Ashlee:	That'd be okay
14	Me:	I don't care
15	Patrice:	I guess you can go since you don't have school
16		Monday.

Although we interpret and produce influence messages with seeming ease in everyday life, in reality we require vast knowledge to accomplish such acts. Let's initially consider what knowledge one needs to make sense of the conversation in Example 7.1. To help clarify the scope of this task, imagine that an alien being from another galaxy is sitting as a guest at my family's dinner table during the conversation. The alien has stored the contents of a dictionary of American English in its photographic-like memory, so it can understand the conventional meanings of the words spoken at our table. Our alien guest, however, has no "world knowledge." That is, the alien has not acquired any of the understandings that come from living on Earth. Given these circumstances, the alien likely would have many questions about what occurred during this conversation, such as the following:

1. Who are Ron and Bill?

2. What is Starbusters?

3. What does it mean to "get off?" (line 03)? What is a birthday, and what does that have to do with getting off?

4. What does it mean to "go hear" a band (line 05)? What's involved in doing so?

5. What does Ashlee's first turn (line 01) have to do with her second turn (lines 03-05)? Is not having school Monday relevant to hearing a band Sunday night?

6. Why does Patrice ask about Bill's being there (line 06)? Is Patrice shifting the topic, or is her question relevant to Ashlee's request in line 05?

7. What does it mean to "get in" (line 08)? What does Ashlee want to get into? Why do I ask her the question about getting in at this point in the conversation?

8. What is an "underager" (line 09)? Is Ashlee shifting the topic, or are the rules for underagers (lines 09-10) relevant to my question about getting in (line 07)?

9. Why do I ask if Sheridan can go (line 11)? What does my question have to do with Ashlee's request in line 05? Toward whom is my question directed? Why does Ashlee comment on Sheridan's willingness to go (line 13)?

Aside from these specific questions, consider more global interpretations of the conversation in Example 7.1. Many readers probably sensed that Patrice and I, as parents, were somewhat reluctant to let Ashlee go hear Ron's band. Given that neither of us said this explicitly, however, would our alien guest sense this reluctance? Did you sense it? If so, what knowledge did you use in doing so? Many readers also might characterize the conversation as one in which Patrice and I reached a "conditional agreement" or "compromise" with Ashlee: She could go hear Ron's band if her sister Sheridan went with her. Given that neither Patrice nor I said, "Ashlee, you may go hear Ron's band if your sister goes along," however, would the alien understand that a deal had been struck? Would you have understood? If so, what allowed you to reach this conclusion?

As Example 7.1 illustrates, one needs vast knowledge to interpret influence interactions. Aside from the literal meanings of words, one needs knowledge about participants (e.g., Bill), settings (e.g., Starbusters), social activities (e.g., hearing a band), and rules/regulations that govern those activities (e.g., the legal drinking age). One needs to know about relationships, such as that adolescent children often desire to make decisions without interference from parents, or that parents might worry about one of their adolescent children dating some-one substantially older. One also needs pragmatic knowledge about conversation, such as that message sources at times refute obstacles to compliance before making requests, that targets often raise obstacles before deciding whether to comply with requests, and that the number of obstacles a target raises may reflect the target's willingness to comply (see Chapter 6).

Aside from interpreting influence interactions, one also needs vast knowledge to produce messages within them. Once I comprehend Ashlee's request in lines 03-05, what must I know in order to decide what to say? Most contemporary theories assume that persuasive message production is a goal-driven process (see Chapter 5); hence it is useful to begin by considering my goals. On the one hand, I want to make sure that Ashlee is safe. Ashlee has used interactions with

Ron to meet Bill in the past, and neither Patrice nor I have been impressed by Bill's character. On the other hand, I want to provide reasonable freedom for Ashlee, given that she is 17 years old. In addition, Ashlee has been cheerful and willing to help around the house for the past several months. I want to acknowledge and reward these qualities rather than seeming to refuse her every request. Finally, I want some say in the decision about Ashlee while also considering and supporting Patrice's reaction.

My interaction goals describe what I hope to achieve, but they themselves do not suggest the means by which my aims can be accomplished. Producing persuasive messages also requires three major sources of knowledge (Clark & Delia, 1977). First, I need *knowledge about other participants* in the conversation. I need to know what makes Ashlee unique from her siblings and I need to be able to predict how she may respond to things I could say (Berger & Calabrese, 1975; Miller & Steinberg, 1975). I also need to anticipate what Patrice will view as a reasonable response to Ashlee's request. Children develop more advanced skills at recognizing and adapting to the perspectives of specific others as they mature. Stable individual differences also exist in children's and adults' abilities to adapt persuasive messages (see the discussion of the "constructivist" research tradition in Chapter 4).

Second, I need *knowledge about rules and expectations* for conversation. For example, I must understand that Ashlee's request implicitly asserts that a certain set of conditions exist in the present situation (e.g., she is old enough to go hear a band at a bar and grill) and that I may (not) agree with her assessment of the situation (see the discussion of speech act theory in Chapter 6). I also should understand implicitly that my saying no is a dispreferred response to Ashlee's request, and hence she and others at the table likely will expect me to give reasons should I choose to refuse her request (see the discussion of conversation analysis in Chapter 6).

Third, I need *procedural knowledge* about potential means for accomplishing my goals. Cognitive theorists draw a distinction between declarative and procedural forms of knowledge (Anderson, 1976; Greene, 1984a; Levelt, 1989). *Declarative knowledge* is "knowing that"; such knowledge involves people, objects, and events. "Casmir Pulaski was a general in the American Revolutionary War," "The legal age for drinking alcoholic beverages in Illinois is 21 years old," "Adolescents often must go to bed earlier on school nights than on weekends," and "Ashlee thinks that musicians are cool" are examples of declarative knowledge. Declarative knowledge becomes easier to recall from memory with practice and repetition (Anderson, 1976). *Procedural knowledge* is "knowing how" to perform activities and solve problems; it pertains to "those things that we have learned to do, and not to do, in order to act efficaciously" (Greene,

1984a, p. 291). Ashlee knows that "requesting permission is one way of getting parents to let me perform a desired activity" and that "refuting an objection that a parent likely will raise can put pressure on that parent to comply with my request." Similarly, I know that "offering a compromise is one way of being responsive to my child's desires while not complying with her original request." Procedural knowledge becomes overlearned with practice and repetition and hence can be difficult to articulate (Anderson, 1976). Without procedural knowledge, I would have had no idea how to go about trying to accomplish my goals as I talked with Ashlee.

Many cognitive theorists agree that people possess procedural knowledge at several levels of abstraction (Berger, 1997; Greene, 1984a, 1990; Levelt, 1989; Parks, 1994). Persuasive message production is complex, in part, because it involves multiple processes operating at several levels of abstraction. We may possess knowledge about abstract "moves" that we might make to achieve a goal (e.g., offer a compromise), but to translate an individual move into an utterance, we also must know about content that could compose the move (e.g., offering to let Ashlee go if her sister Sheridan goes along, as opposed to offering to go along myself). In addition, we must know various speech acts for performing the move (e.g., asking, "Could Sheridan go?" in line 11 rather than saying, "You can go if Sheridan will go"). We must know how to select individual words (e.g., saying, "Could *Sheridan* go?" rather than "Could *she* go?") and how to order the words (e.g., "Could Sheridan go?" rather than "Go could Sheridan?") that make up the move. Finally, we must know how to make the sounds necessary for stating the move aloud as an utterance. Many of these processes operate outside of awareness, yet we must coordinate them in some fashion in order to produce sensible turns at talk (Kellermann, 1992; Greene, 1990, 1994).

Persuasive message production also is complex because individuals often produce messages under time and resource constraints. Ashlee asked to go hear Ron's band for the first time in lines 03-05. The length of time between conversational turns produced by different speakers usually is less than a second (see McLaughlin, 1984, pp. 111). Given Ashlee's expectation that her mother or I would say something, we had very little time to decide how to respond to her request. Aside from time constraints, speakers frequently engage in influence interactions while also devoting their attention to other tasks (e.g., I was helping my 3-year-old daughter cut her food during the conversation) and while they are stressed or fatigued (e.g., the conversation occurred after my partner and I had been at work all day).

The purpose of this example has been to illustrate the complexity of producing persuasive messages. Cognitive theories attempt to model that complexity; that is, they attempt to describe the mental processes by which people translate interaction goals into influence messages. In the next section, I introduce the key concepts and assumptions associated with cognitive theories.

Cognitive Theories: Key Concepts and Assumptions

Cognitive theorists make four important assumptions about people and communication (see Fiske & Taylor, 1991; Hewes, 1995a; Hewes & Planalp, 1987; Greene, 1984b, 1994; Palmer, 1994; Planalp & Hewes, 1982; Wyer & Gruenfeld, 1995). First, cognitive theorists focus on individuals (Greene, 1984b; Hewes & Planalp, 1987; Palmer, 1994). Ultimately, relationships, groups, and societies do not produce messages; individuals do. As Greene (1994) explains:

> The implication of a concern with action is to identify the locus of explanation squarely within the purview of the individual.... Extra-individual factors, such as social prescriptions for behavior, can only influence human action when they are represented in some way within the individual. Of course, this is not to suggest that such social factors are not important, but with respect to human action, the issue becomes one of *how social factors are possessed and used by the individual.* (p. 190)

Second, cognitive theorists assume that individuals actively interpret and respond to their environments (Berger, 1997; Fiske & Taylor, 1991; Greene, 1984b; Hewes & Planalp, 1987); individuals are not robots preprogrammed by their environments. "The capacity to actively use information to accomplish goals is a principal tenet of any cognitive approach and distinguishes it from the behaviorist approach by freeing people from direct environment control" (Planalp & Hewes, 1982, p. 56). In order to reduce uncertainty about others (Berger & Calabrese, 1975) and to feel a sense of personal control (Parks, 1994), individuals actively interpret unfolding situations in light of prior experience and current goals (Hewes & Planalp, 1987; Wyer & Gruenfeld, 1995). Individuals also form goals and develop future plans of action based on their ongoing interpretations of events (Berger, 1997; Greene, 1984b; O'Keefe & Delia, 1982). Thus individuals are not totally predictable based on knowledge of their current environments, because

> the interplay between mental representations and processes may alter the effects of environmental stimuli such that, at least sometimes, one can predict a response only if one knows *both* the stimuli *and* the relevant mental representations and processes that are operating on those stimuli. (Hewes, 1995a, p. 163)

Although cognitive theorists view individuals as active agents, many also assume that individuals possess limited capacity to process information from the environment (e.g., Fiske & Taylor, 1991; Waldron, 1990). Conversation makes heavy demands on people's mental capacities. As Waldron and Cegala (1992, p. 603) argue, participants in conversation often must do several things at once:

1. Process large amounts of information gathered from outside and within themselves

2. Perform multiple mental tasks simultaneously (e.g., listening to a message source's stated reasons for making a request while also making inferences about the source's "real" reasons for requesting)

3. Process ambiguous or conflicting verbal and nonverbal information

4. Process information within restricted time limits (e.g., the length of conversational turns)

5. Select or construct complex behavioral sequences (e.g., plans of action)

Although the demands of these tasks can be reduced with rehearsal or practice (Greene, 1984c; Shiffrin & Schneider, 1977), individuals at times rely on "heuristics," or mental shortcuts, when interpreting and producing persuasive messages (Cialdini, 1993; Eagly & Chaiken, 1993; Wilson, 1995).

Fourth and finally, cognitive theorists assume that explanations of how people produce persuasive messages can be cast quite generally (Anderson, 1976; Greene, 1984b). By focusing on underlying mental processes and limitations, cognitive theorists seek explanations that transcend specific people and contexts. As Greene (1984b) explains: "Cognitive science seeks to develop general, powerful theories that apply across a range of situations and phenomena. . . . an emphasis is placed upon the heuristic function of theory in illustrating the relationships among apparently diverse phenomena by demonstrating common underlying mechanisms" (p. 242). As we will see, cognitive theories focus our attention upon similarities in how people generate persuasive messages across diverse relational/institutional contexts (e.g., parents/children, romantic partners, work associates). Cognitive theories highlight similarities in persuasive message production that otherwise might go unnoticed (see Wilson, 1997, pp. 33-34).

Building on these four assumptions, cognitive theorists typically incorporate three types of concepts within their theories: knowledge structures, cognitive processes, and limits on information processing (Anderson, 1976; Fiske & Taylor, 1991; Greene, 1984b; Hewes & Planalp, 1987; Planalp & Hewes, 1982). *Knowledge structures* are "organized repositories of information about the world, including the social world, that inform experience and action" (Hewes & Planalp, 1987, p. 157). We already have encountered examples of knowledge structures. In Chapter 4, we saw how constructivist scholars have argued that "interpersonal constructs," or bipolar dimensions of judgment, are the basic structures underlying individuals' inferences and judgments about others. In Chapter 5, we saw that the cognitive rules model assumes that individuals represent information about the world in an associative network model of memory (Wilson, 1990, 1995). Within this network, cognitive rules are structures that link nodes representing an interaction goal with nodes representing situational features pertinent to that goal. In the same chapter, I cited several scholars who have proposed that individuals organize their knowledge about compliance gaining in multiple "schemas," such that each schema links a specific influence goal (e.g., giving advice) with situational dimensions, message targets, threats to identity, and emotions relevant to that goal (e.g., Meyer, 1996; Rule, Bisanz, & Kohn, 1985; Smith, 1984). In this chapter, I present additional examples of knowledge structures, including plans, procedural records, and unitized assemblies. In sum, knowledge structures are the ways in which individuals mentally organize information from their external environments. Some theories also make explicit assumptions about how information is represented within knowledge structures (e.g., verbal versus visual form).

Aside from how information is represented, cognitive theories also explore how individuals actively process information. *Cognitive processes* are "operations performed on incoming information, such as focusing on particular aspects, drawing inferences from it, storing it in memory, retrieving it when needed, selecting plans of action based on it, and implementing those plans" (Hewes & Planalp, 1987, p. 157).[1] Although organizing models often include a full range of cognitive processes (e.g., Milner, 1993; Planalp & Hewes, 1982; Wyer & Gruenfeld, 1995), most cognitive theories describe and explain only particular subsets of these processes. Theories of *input processing* deal with how individuals encode, interpret, and organize information from the physical senses; thus theories of perception, attribution, and memory for information fall within the realm of input processing. Theories of *output processing* address how individuals translate goals and prior knowledge into action. Cognitive theories of message production fall within the realm of output processing (see Greene, 1997a, p. 3).

Cognitive processes occur over time (Greene, 1988, 2000). *Serial processes* are those in which each step in the process must be performed in a one-after-another order. *Parallel processes* are those in which multiple steps in a process can be performed simultaneously, such that they take less time than they would if they were performed in serial order (Greene, 1984a). Cognitive processes also are performed with varying levels of awareness. *Automatic processes* can be triggered by environmental cues outside of the person's awareness, unfold without conscious monitoring, make few demands on mental energy, and tend to run to completion once begun (Bargh & Ferguson, 2000; Shiffrin & Schneider, 1977). Highly repetitive behaviors, such as those required to ride a bicycle, often are performed via automatic processing. A good deal of strategic communication also may be learned and performed via automatic processes (Bargh & Ferguson, 2000; Kellermann, 1992). *Controlled processes* require conscious monitoring and make heavier demands on mental energy. Riding a bike for the first time or comprehending a lecture on an unfamiliar topic requires controlled processing. Automatic and controlled processing are better thought of as points on a continuum than as a dichotomy; many complex actions are performed via a combination of automatic and controlled processing.

In addition to structures and processes, cognitive theories often posit *limits on people's ability to process information* (Berger, Knowlton, & Abrahams, 1996; Waldron, 1990). People possess limited attention and capacity for processing information (Kahneman, 1973; Stiff, 1986). Consequently, individuals may not perform up to their optimal capacity when they attempt to pursue multiple interaction goals simultaneously (Waldron, 1990), perform complex actions without sufficient training or rehearsal (Greene, 1984c), or make substantial adjustments to their initial plans within time constraints (Berger et al., 1996). Information-processing limitations help explain the "if only I had said that" phenomenon; that is, the common occurrence of figuring out exactly the "right" thing to say just after an interaction has finished (Greene & Geddes, 1993).

Having reviewed these concepts and assumptions of cognitive theories in general, I now turn to descriptions of two specific cognitive theories with relevance to persuasive message production: (a) plans and planning processes (Berger, 1997; Waldron, 1997) and (b) action assembly theory (Greene, 1984a, 1997b).

Plans and Planning for Communication

Plans and planning processes have been the subject of work by scholars from diverse disciplines, including artificial intelligence, communication, linguistics, philosophy, and psychology (Berger, 1997; Cohen, Morgan, & Pollack, 1990; Friedman & Scholnick, 1997; Levelt, 1989). Rather than generating a single grand theory, scholars have developed concepts and principles that are useful for understanding persuasive message production. Planning perspectives have been applied to how individuals pursue a host of interaction goals, such as asking for dates (e.g., Berger & Bell, 1988), asking favors (e.g., Meyer, 1994b), discussing safe sex (Waldron, Caughlin, & Jackson, 1995), giving advice (e.g., Allen & Honeycutt, 1997), giving directions (e.g., Berger et al., 1996), ingratiating themselves with a new roommate (e.g., Berger & Jordan, 1992), learning personal information about others (Waldron, 1990), persuading others about controversial issues (e.g., Hjelmquist, 1990), regulating perceived child misbehavior (e.g., Beatty, Burant, Dobos, & Rudd, 1996; Wilson, 2000), selling used textbooks (e.g., Roloff & Jordan, 1991), telling lies (e.g., diBattista, 1994), and terminating undesirable behaviors by others (e.g., Meyer, 1994b). In this section, I define the terms *plans* and *planning* prior to exploring their roles during influence interactions.

DEFINING PLANS AND PLANNING

Plans are knowledge structures representing actions necessary for accomplishing goals. This definition should be clarified in four respects. First, plans are not action sequences; rather, plans are mental representations of action sequences (Berger, 1997; Greene, 1990). Thus I distinguish *plans*, which fall in the domain of the mind, from *strategies*, or abstract descriptions of observable behavior (see Chapter 3). Plans represent the procedural knowledge that individuals need to enact behavioral strategies. Second, plans represent knowledge about at least three concepts: one or more goals, actions relevant for achieving those goals, and preconditions for performing relevant actions (Bruce & Newman, 1978; Schank & Abelson, 1977). Third, plans represent more general and less rigidly sequenced actions than do "scripts" (Schank & Abelson, 1977). My plan for persuading one of my high school-age daughters to study more includes multiple actions that can be performed in more or less detail, or in differing order, depending on circumstances. My script for ordering at a fast-food restaurant contains highly specific actions that occur in nearly the same sequence and duration every time. Fourth, plans represent knowledge at multiple levels of abstraction (Berger et al., 1996; Hayes-Roth & Hayes-Roth, 1979; Levelt, 1989). My plan for persuading one of my daughters to study more might include an abstract action such as "regulate her study time more closely," which might spawn ideas for more specific actions, such as "set a minimum time for study each weeknight" and "require that she study outside of her bedroom."

Planning refers to psychological and communicative processes involved in recalling, generating, selecting, implementing, monitoring, modifying, and negotiating plans. Planning occurs in advance of many influence interactions, but a good deal of planning also occurs "on-line"—that is, during interaction (Waldron, 1990, 1997). Like any cognitive process, planning may be performed in a controlled fashion or relatively automatically. When attempting to persuade one of my daughters to study more, I may think carefully about how to approach the topic in a manner different from that I have used in the past (controlled processing). Alternatively, I may recall and implement a frequently used plan from the past with little conscious consideration or adjustment to present circumstances (automatic processing).

Planning can occur in top-down or bottom-up fashion (Berger, 1997; Hayes-Roth & Hayes-Roth, 1979). Top-down planning involves forming an abstract goal (e.g., run errands before suppertime), breaking the goal into a series of chronologically ordered subgoals (e.g., go to the grocery store, then the cleaners), and then formulating precise details for carrying out each subgoal (e.g., take Route 23 to the grocery store). When planning for contract negotiations, union representatives might prioritize all of the issues to be negotiated that year (global planning), decide which issues to mention during the initial negotiating session (regional planning), and then decide what to say in their opening statement during the initial session (local planning; Wilson & Putnam, 1990). Top-down planning assumes that higher-level abstract plans set firm constraints on how lower-level actions are planned. Bottom-up planning occurs when obstacles encountered at lower levels (e.g., Route 23 is closed) cause individuals to modify or reinvent higher-level plans (e.g., go to the cleaners first instead, then to the grocery store). After encountering more opposition than anticipated from management representatives on a specific issue during an initial negotiating session (local/regional plan), union negotiators might rethink their initial goals and targets for several issues (global plan; Wilson & Putnam, 1990).

People engage in a mix of bottom-up and top-down planning. Bratman (1990) argues that individuals typically develop "partial, hierarchical plans" as a balance between the demands of top-down and bottom-up planning:

> On the one hand, we need to coordinate our activities both within our own lives and, socially, between lives. . . . This argues for being planning creatures. On the other hand, the world changes in ways that we are not in a position to anticipate; so highly detailed plans about the far future will often be of little use and not worth bothering with. Partial, hierarchically structured plans for the future provide our compromise solution. (p. 19)

Drawing a slightly different picture, Hayes-Roth and Hayes-Roth (1979) portray individuals as "opportunistic" planners who move up and down levels of abstraction in a rational but by no means completely coordinated fashion:

> The planner's current decisions and observations suggest various opportunities for plan development. The planner's subsequent decisions follow up on selected opportunities. . . . a decision at a given level of abstraction, specifying an action to be taken at a particular point in time, may influence subsequent decisions at higher or lower levels of abstraction, specifying actions to be taken at earlier

or later points in time. This view . . . suggests that planners will produce many coherent decision sequences, but some less coherent sequences as well. (p. 276)

In sum, planning encompasses the processes involved in recalling, generating, selecting, implementing, monitoring, and modifying plans. Scholars studying these processes typically have taken one of three approaches (Bruce & Newman, 1978; Hobbs & Evans, 1980; Waldron, 1997). Studies of *preconversational planning* explore the structure of plans prior to interaction, how preconversational plans are generated, and whether they are translated into action during influence episodes. Research on *conversational planning* investigates how individuals implement, monitor, and modify their plans during influence interactions. Studies of *interactive planning* explore the interdependence between participants' plans, including how message sources and targets make inferences about each other's "real" goals and plans during influence interactions, portray each other's actions as consistent with their own plans, and negotiate mutual plans. In the following subsections, I pose questions about plans and planning from each approach.

QUESTIONS ABOUT PRECONVERSATIONAL PLANS

How Do People Form Preconversational Plans?

Berger and Jordan (1992; Berger, 1995) have employed a "think-aloud" procedure (see Ericsson & Simon, 1984) to investigate the sources of knowledge on which individuals rely when they are forming preconversational goals. The researchers interviewed 72 undergraduate students individually about how they would pursue four goals (requesting a date, ingratiating themselves with a new roommate, persuading another student about a controversial issue, and earning a million dollars). Participants received the description of each goal on an index card. For example, the description of the date request goal read as follows:

Assume that you have met someone to whom you are very attracted for the first time at a party. You would like to ask this person out for the next weekend. How would you go about asking this person for a date? (Berger & Jordan, 1992, pp. 135-136)

After reading the index cards, participants were audiotaped as they explained their plans for the particular situations. Following this, the participants provided verbal protocols in which they described aloud "all they could remember about their thinking while solving the problem" (p. 136). Coders analyzed these verbal protocols to identify sources of planning knowledge.

Berger and Jordan (1992) identified six categories of knowledge their participants used to form plans. Table 7.1 displays examples of these six sources of knowledge taken from participants' verbal protocols. Participants relied on *specific episodes* when they recalled actual situations in which they had attempted to achieve the same goals in the past. Those who relied on *hypothetical episodes* imagined specific situations in which they were trying to accomplish the same goals. Participants who recalled *ensembles of episodes* simultaneously considered several past circumstances in which they had tried to accomplish the same goals. Those who referred to *role models* recalled how other people, real or fictional, had accomplished the same goals. Participants relied on *instructions* by recalling specific directions they had been given on how to accomplish their goals. Finally, those who drew on *previous plans* indicated that they already had developed plans for accomplishing the goals previous to the study. Berger and Jordan also found that participants relied on different sources of knowledge when forming preconversational plans to pursue different goals. For example, participants recalled specific episodes most frequently when planning how to ingratiate themselves with a new roommate, whereas they recalled hypothetical episodes or ensembles of episodes most often when planning how to ask a stranger for a date.

Do People Actually Follow Their Preconversational Plans?

Two studies have explored the degree to which people's actions and thoughts during influence interactions are consistent with their preconversational plans.[2] Hjelmquist (1990) told 20 male Swedish undergraduates that each would be paired with another student with whom he was not acquainted to discuss a specific topic (a recent change of government in Sweden). Prior to meeting his partner, each participant was given a 5-minute planning period during which he was instructed to write down what he "wanted to discuss about the topic during the forthcoming conversation" (p. 281). The participant was then taken to a different room to meet his partner; neither partner was allowed to bring his planning notes with him. Following introductions, each pair of students was instructed to discuss the topic; the researcher then interrupted the conversation after 5 minutes. Transcripts of the conversations were analyzed for idea units spoken by each participant, and written preconversational plans were divided into clauses expressing planned ideas. Coders analyzed the percentage of planned ideas actually expressed during each conversation. For example, a student who wrote, "What significance did it have for the Liberal Party?" in his preconversational plan and who said, "One thing I've also wondered about is what it will mean for the Liberal Party, it must be a . . . it'll be a big thing, advertisement sort of, for them really, they're going to

Table 7.1   Descriptions and Examples of Knowledge Used to Form
Preconversational Plans

Knowledge Source	Description/Example
Specific episodes	Planners recall a specific situation in which they have attempted to achieve the same goal. *Example:* I guess I related this to my roommate this year and tried to realize how I got her to like me. (ingratiate roommate)
Hypothetical episodes	Planners imagine themselves in a specific situation where they are trying to accomplish the goal, but not a situation that they have actually experienced in the past. *Example:* I tried to visualize I was at a party and this person was at some sort of distance away from me and I was picturing the person . . . (date request)
Ensembles of episodes	Planners simultaneously consider a number of similar experiences they have had when trying to reach a goal. *Example:* My thinking was a direct extension of my debate experiences. (persuasion)
Role models	Planners cite people who have accomplished the goal and employ their actions as a planning source. *Example:* I thought of *Wall Street* the movie and the rich people in there. (million dollars)
Instruction	Planners state they have had explicit instructions in how to achieve the goal. *Example:* I was thinking about the public speaking class I had last quarter and how they told us to persuade someone. (persuasion)
Previous plan	Planners state they have developed plans to achieve this goal previously. *Example:* I've thought through it before . . . (date request)

SOURCE: From "Planning Sources, Planning Difficulty, and Verbal Fluency," by
C. R. Berger & J. M. Jordan, 1992, *Communication Monographs, 59,* p. 137. Copyright
1992 by the Speech Communication Association. Adapted with permission.

win a hell of a lot of votes" was scored as having expressed a planned idea
(Hjelmquist, 1990, p. 293).

Hjelmquist (1990) predicted that participants would express many ideas
from their preconversational plans during their conversations, and that those
participants who developed more extensive preconversational plans would
express larger percentages of their planned ideas. Hjelmquist did not expect

total correspondence between preplanned and expressed ideas, however, for several reasons. Aside from forgetting their preplanned ideas, participants also would have new ideas occurring to them during their conversations. Each participant also needed to make contributions relevant to his partner's talk as well as his own preplanned ideas (Grice, 1975), lest the interchange become two unfolding monologues rather than a conversation.

Three findings from Hjelmquist's (1990) study merit note. First, participants on average expressed one-third of the ideas from their preconversational plans during conversation. On average, they included 10.5 ideas in their preconversational plans, of which 3.45 were expressed. Second, participants expressed significantly more of their preplanned ideas during the first half of their conversation compared with the second half. A follow-up analysis revealed that participants, after their conversations, could recall ideas from their preconversational plans with a high degree of accuracy; thus this effect appears to reflect the unfolding and emergent nature of conversation rather than simple forgetting. Third, participants who prepared more extensive preconversational plans also expressed larger percentages of their planned ideas during conversation. Indeed, the correlation between the number of ideas in a preconversational plan and the number of ideas from that plan actually expressed was $r = .72$. This effect was not due simply to loquacity, as the number of words participants spoke during their conversations was not related to the number of ideas in their preconversational plans. This third finding suggests that there may be systematic individual differences in the quality of people's preconversational plans (see below).

In a second study, Jordan (1994) examined correspondence between people's preconversational plans and their on-line thinking during conversational argument. Participants, 35 undergraduates, initially completed a "think-aloud" procedure in which they described aloud what they were thinking as they planned how to accomplish four social goals (requesting a date, ingratiating themselves with a new roommate, persuading another student about whether or not alcohol should be allowed in dormitories, and earning a million dollars). This think-aloud method provided data on participants' preconversational plans.

Two days after completing the think-aloud procedure, participants returned to the lab, where each was told that he or she would be paired with another student (actually a confederate) whose opinion on the alcohol issue was opposite to the participant's own. The participant's task was to persuade the other student to accept the participant's opinion. Participants had not been told, when they had prepared their preconversational plans for this goal two days earlier, that they would actually be involved in conversations on this topic. The confederate was trained to appear unconvinced by each participant's arguments.

Conversations were halted after 7 minutes, at which point the participant was taken to a different room to complete a "stimulated recall" procedure (see Waldron & Cegala, 1992). Each participant watched a videotape of his or her just-completed conversational argument after being instructed to stop the video-tape at any point where he or she remembered exactly what he or she had been thinking or feeling during the conversation. The participant then wrote down his or her thoughts and feelings and noted the time in the conversation at which each occurred. After completing the stimulated recall task, the participant rated how often he or she had taken part in conversational arguments in the past (i.e., interaction experience).

Coders classified each of the recalled thoughts in the stimulated recall data into one of four categories: (a) self-focused units (e.g., thoughts about the participant's own emotions or mental processes), (b) target-focused units (e.g., thoughts about the confederate's appearance or emotions), (c) discourse-centered units (e.g., evaluations of whether goals were being achieved or thoughts about the topic of conversation), and (d) uncodable units (5% of all thoughts). Coders then analyzed the correspondence between on-line thinking and precon-versational plans by taking each thought that occurred to a participant during the stimulated recall task and searching for an exact match in that participant's think-aloud data. For example, a participant who recalled thinking, "Maybe if I let her keep talking, I'll find holes in her argument" while completing the stimulated recall task and who earlier had said, "I would try to find holes in their argument . . . try to attack theirs a little" during the think-aloud proce-dure was scored as having a match (Jordan, 1994, p. 167). Finally, coders made on overall judgment about the degree to which each participant followed his or her preconversational plan in terms of what the participant actually talked about during the argument (1 = *no plan-behavior correspondence;* 7 = *total plan-behavior correspondence*).

Results from Jordan's (1994) study suggest that preconversational plans are one factor that affects what participants think and feel during influence inter-actions. Of the study's participants, 59% exhibited at least one match between their on-line thinking and their preconversational plans. Of the 485 thoughts coded from the stimulated recall data, 9% (54 of these thoughts) had been present in preconversational plans. About one-third of the matches between on-line thinking and preconversational plans involved conversational content (i.e., a student who thought "But these are supposed to be adults" during the conversational argument had written, "You're talking about adults; you're not talking about little kids" in his or her preconversational plan). Slightly more than one-fourth of the matches involved discourse tactics (e.g., a student who thought about how to "find holes in" the confederate's arguments during the conversation had written about "finding holes" in the other person's argument in his or her preconversational plan). Jordan (1994) concludes that although conversations do require

> spontaneous adaptation to the unpredictable behaviors of the partner and some dynamic adjustment to the features of the immediate context, they are also characterized by the performance of actions conceptualized by the participants prior to entering the interaction. Theorists may be well advised not to ignore this [pre]planned aspect of interactions while becoming enamored with the dynamic, situated aspects of discourse. (p. 169)

One other finding from Jordan's study merits note. Students who self-reported more prior experience at conversational argument were judged to have followed their preconversational plans more closely ($r = .33$) even though these same students recalled fewer thoughts from their plans during the conversation itself ($r = -.32$). Students experienced at conversational argument enacted their preconversational plans more closely than did less experienced students, but the experienced students apparently did this in a relatively automatic rather than a controlled fashion.

Does the Structure of People's Preconversational Plans Vary, and Does That Matter?

Differences in persuasive messages reflect, in part, differences in the ways in which people prioritize primary versus secondary goals (see Chapter 5). Verbally aggressive individuals, for example, place greater importance than do less aggressive persons on the cognitive editing standard of "effectiveness" and lesser importance on "person-centered" editing standards (Hample & Dallinger, 1987a). Individuals high in interpersonal construct differentiation are more likely than their less differentiated counterparts to form multiple goals spontaneously when seeking or resisting compliance (Kline & Floyd, 1990; O'Keefe & Shepherd, 1987; but see Wilson, 1990). Aside from differing in how they prioritize goals, however, individuals also may possess differing amounts and types of knowledge about potential means for accomplishing social goals, which in turn may relate to their competence or success at accomplishing goals.

Consistent with this thinking, research has assessed differences in the appropriateness, complexity, and/or effectiveness of people's preconversational plans (see Berger, 1997). For example, Berger and Bell (1988) predicted that loneliness and shyness would be inversely associated with the complexity and effectiveness of people's plans for initiating social relationships. Chronically lonely individuals lack close, satisfying relationships; they have difficulty making friends, initiating social activities, and opening up to others (Peplau & Perlman, 1982). Shy individuals display social inhibitions and anxieties; they display various signs of distress during interaction, such as eye gaze aversion, self-adaptors, speech errors, and bodily tension (Buss, 1984). Lonely and shy persons may have few close, satisfying relationships precisely because they lack complex plans for initiating such relationships.

To test this reasoning, Berger and Bell (1988) had 156 undergraduates (63% female) write their plans for asking a person whom they had just met on a date and for making a good impression with a new dormitory roommate. The researchers scored *plan complexity* by using three indices. *Plan length* refers to the total number of action units in a plan; thus a student who wrote that she would "find out what she likes to do" and "talk about things we have in common" had a more complex plan for making a good impression with a new roommate than someone who planned only the latter action. *Plan diversity* refers to the number of different action units in a plan; thus a student who wrote, "I would find out what she likes to do" and "let her pick which side of the room she'd like to occupy" had planned two different types of actions (asking questions, offering a favor), whereas someone who wrote, "I would find out what she likes to do" and "find out if she's picked a major" has planned only one type of action (asking questions). *Plan contingencies* refers to the percentage of units in the plan that describe alternative actions to be taken should initial attempts to accomplish the goal be thwarted. A student who wrote, "I will find out if she's picked a major, but if not, then I'll ask what kind of music she likes" has considered what to do should her initial plan fail. Aside from scoring plan complexity, Berger and Bell had a group of 10 undergraduates (5 female, 5 male) rate each preconversational plan for "perceived effectiveness." Coders were instructed that an effective plan was one that had a "high probability of being successful in getting a date or in getting the new roommate to like the planner" (Berger & Bell, 1988, p. 223). After writing their plans, participants finished by completing measures of loneliness and shyness.

Berger and Bell (1988) found that complex plans were rated as more effective than simple plans. Plan length and diversity were positively associated with perceived effectiveness in both the dating (rs = .50 and .49) and roommate (rs = .37 and .32) scenarios. Plan contingencies was weakly, albeit significantly, correlated with perceived effectiveness in the dating scenario (r = .16), but not in the roommate scenario.[3] The researchers also discovered that plans written by lonely and shy students were rated as relatively ineffective. In the dating scenario, loneliness and shyness were inversely associated with plan effectiveness for males (rs = −.37 and −.26, respectively) but not for females.[4] In the roommate scenario, loneliness and shyness were inversely associated with plan effectiveness for both males (rs = −.24 and −.42) and females (rs = −.38 and −.40).[5] Finally, plan complexity and effectiveness were found to be domain specific. Neither plan effectiveness ($r = .16$) nor complexity ($rs = .12$ and $.07$ for length and breadth) was strongly associated across the two scenarios. Knowing that a person had a complex or effective preconversational plan for making an impression with a new roommate was not a strong predictor of whether that person had a complex or effective date request plan. Given this finding, individual-difference factors such as loneliness or shyness should predict plan complexity and effectiveness only in those situations where they actually affect a person's experience with a social goal.

Aside from loneliness and shyness, research also has assessed the effects of self-monitoring on preconversational plans. *Self-monitoring* refers to the degree to which actors rely on two sources of information as they decide how to act (Snyder, 1974). High self-monitors rely primarily on situational norms for appropriate behavior, whereas low self-monitors rely primarily on internal states (e.g., attitudes, feelings) to guide action. High self-monitors tend to be more sensitive than low self-monitors to external cues for socially appropriate behavior and are better able to adjust their self-presentation to fit situational demands.

Given this conceptualization of self-monitoring, Jordan and Roloff (1997) expected that self-monitoring would affect people's preconversational plans for negotiation. They expected that high self-monitors would be more committed than low self-monitors to achieving goals for the negotiation that had been set by the parties they represented, because high self-monitors look for external cues to guide their behavior. Jordan and Roloff also expected high self-monitors to be more likely than low self-monitors to plan how to create a desired impression (e.g., someone who was tough but fair) prior to the negotiation. Because high self-monitors attend more to other actors in a situation than do low self-monitors, Jordan and Roloff predicted that high self-monitors would include logrolling, or multiple package issues in which each party trades a low-priority issue for a high-priority one, in their preconversational plans. Given high self-monitors' adaptive ability, the researchers also expected them to develop more complex preconversational plans, such as plans including different potential actions for the negotiation.

To test these predictions, Jordan and Roloff (1997) initially had 60 undergraduate students (68% female) complete a revised version of the Self-Monitoring Scale (Lennox & Wolfe, 1984). Following this, participants completed a negotiation simulation adapted from Pruitt (1981). Students randomly assigned to the role of "seller" were told that a friend had asked them to sell three textbooks back to a store; the friend had specified an amount of money he or she hoped to receive for the three books. Students assigned to the "buyer" role were told that they worked for a store that negotiated buyback prices; they were given a quota from the store on what they needed to receive for the three books. The simulation was structured so that the textbook of most value to the seller was the book with the least profit potential for the buyer (and vice versa), so that both parties could profit if each traded a low-priority book for a high-priority book (see Pruitt, 1981). Participants received information on the value of each book for themselves, but they did not receive information on how much the other party profited on each book.

Prior to completing the simulation, participants wrote out their plans for "how they intended to achieve their profit goals" (Jordan & Roloff, 1997, p. 37). They also rated how committed they were to achieving their prenegotiation goals. Each pair of participants was then given 20 minutes to reach an agreement while being videotaped. Coders placed each element from participants' preconversational plans into one of six categories (examples of each category appear in Table 7.2). The researchers computed an index of plan complexity by calculating the number of different categories mentioned in each prenegotiation plan. Videotapes of the simulations were analyzed for the use of bargaining strategies, and final agreements were scored for the degree to which each participant achieved his or her prenegotiation profit goal.

Analyses of preconversational plans revealed support for most of Jordan and Roloff's (1997) predictions. High, relative to low, self-monitors (a) rated themselves as more committed to their goals prior to the negotiation (especially when those goals were challenging rather than easy to accomplish), (b) included more "impression management" and "logrolling" elements in their preconversational plans, and (c) included a larger number of distinct elements in their preconversational plans. Differences in preconversational plans appeared to affect negotiation processes and outcomes, given that high, in comparison to low, self-monitors (a) used impression management and argument strategies more frequently during the negotiation simulation and (b) achieved a larger percentage of their prenegotiation profit goals.

Results from these and other studies (Beatty et al., 1996; Waldron & Lavitt, 2000) suggest that (a) people vary in the complexity of their preconversational plans for pursuing social goals; (b) personality variables affect persuasive message production, in part, by influencing the complexity of people's preconversational plans; and (c) people with complex preconversational plans, under some conditions, are perceived as more competent as they pursue their goals. Before we conclude that complex preconversational plans always are advantageous, however, we should consider possible cultural and situational limits on such a conclusion.

Are There Cultural Differences in Preconversational Plans?

Most studies of plans for accomplishing social goals have been conducted with participants from the United States, but some researchers have investigated

Table 7.2   Examples of Six Elements From Prenegotiation Plans

Plan Element	Example	Proportion
Logrolling	I'll ask a lot for book three, but give him a lot on the first one.	.30
Impression management	Be friendly so he'll think I'm giving him a good deal.	.23
Argumentation	I will emphasize the quality of the books and what they are worth.	.30
Distributive bargaining	I'll ask for [more than my goal] and then back off to my goal price.	.35
Setting limits	I won't go below [my goal] no matter what they say.	.27
Reactivity	I'll see what they want and then talk about it.	.13

SOURCE: J. M. Jordan & M. E. Roloff, "Planning Skills and Negotiator Goal Accomplishment: The Relationship Between Self-Monitoring and Plan Generation, Plan Enactment, and Plan Consequences," *Communication Research, 24,* p. 49. Copyright © 1997 by Sage Publications, Inc. Adapted by permission of Sage Publications, Inc.

NOTE: Proportion = proportion of participants who included an element from this category in their prenegotiation plans.

cultural differences in such plans. Cai (1998) compared the prenegotiation plans of college students from Taiwan with those of students from the United States. Drawing upon the literature on collectivism and individualism (Triandis, 1993; see Chapter 5), Cai proposed three differences in preconversational plans across cultures. First, members of collectivist cultures value group over individual interests and prefer avoiding in-group disagreement; hence Cai expected that Taiwanese students' prenegotiation plans would include more relational goals than plans by students from the United States. Second, members of collectivist cultures value a long-term perspective and prefer to reach agreements on broad issues before attending to specifics; hence Cai expected that Taiwanese students' prenegotiation plans would focus more on global goals (relevant to the entire negotiation) and less on local goals (relevant to individual acts) compared with plans by U.S. students. And third, because of Taiwanese students' more global, long-term perspective, Cai expected that their prenegotiation plans would be less complex than the prenegotiation plans of U.S. students.

Participants in Cai's (1998) study were 34 Taiwanese students and 50 U.S. students working toward master's degrees at a large U.S. university. Participants were paired into stranger dyads of the same culture and gender to complete a "buyer/seller" negotiation simulation. After receiving instructions but prior to completing the simulation, participants wrote out prenegotiation plans in their native language. Coders identified the number of action units (AUs) in each plan, where an AU is a sentence or clause that describes a single planned act. Each AU then was coded for (a) type (i.e., whether it focused on an instrumental, relational, or identity goal) and (b) level (i.e., whether it focused at the global, regional, or local level of abstraction). Cai (1998) provides the following example of how one plan was coded:

> (AU1) My strategy is to come across as strong willed and difficult to persuade (IDENTITY, REGIONAL). (AU2) I want to make at least 25% profit from each item (INSTRUMENTAL, REGIONAL). (AU3) I want to get $500 profit on the video cameras (INSTRUMENTAL, LOCAL). (AU4) But if I can't make $500, I won't sell them (INSTRUMENTAL, LOCAL). (AU5) Overall, my goal is to establish a relationship that is non-competitive for our stores (RELATIONAL, GLOBAL). (p. 111)

Plan complexity also was scored based on a plan's length (total number of AUs), breadth (number of distinct AUs), and contingencies (number of AUs with the form "If X doesn't work, I'll try Y").

Cai (1998) found no support for her first prediction. Students from both Taiwan and the United States focused primarily on instrumental goals in their prenegotiation plans and did not differ in their attention to relational or identity goals. Taiwanese and U.S. students did differ, however, in level of abstraction in their prenegotiation plans. Mean scores for AUs at three levels of abstraction are shown in Table 7.3. As is apparent, Taiwanese students were about equally likely to plan AUs at local, regional, and global levels of abstraction, whereas U.S. students focused more on local and less on global levels in their prenegotiation plans. Finally, Cai found limited support for her third prediction. Plans by Taiwanese and U.S. students did not differ in length or breadth, but U.S. students did include significantly more contingencies in their plans. In sum, Taiwanese and U.S. students differed primarily in the degree to which they adopted a long-term perspective when developing prenegotiation plans.

Are Complex Preconversational Plans Always Advantageous?

Textbooks on interviewing (Stewart & Cash, 2000) and negotiation (Lewicki, Litterer, Minton, & Saunders, 1999) stress that people are most likely to accomplish their goals when they plan what to say and do before they enter into important interactions. Parents often encourage their children to plan

Table 7.3   Mean Numbers of Action Units at Three Levels of Abstraction

	Level of Abstraction		
Culture	Local	Regional	Global
Taiwan	1.47 (1.39)	1.53 (1.30)	1.22 (1.26)
United States	2.21 (2.32)	1.54 (1.15)	0.56 (0.74)

SOURCE: From "Culture, Plans, and the Pursuit of Negotiation Goals," by D. A. Cai, 1998, *Journal of Asian Pacific Communication, 8*, p. 116. Copyright 1998 by John Benjamins Publishing Company. Reprinted with permission.

NOTE: Numbers outside parentheses are means; numbers within parentheses are standard deviations.

ahead before talking with teachers and peers. Having the ability and motivation to develop complex preconversational plans can be advantageous when one is pursuing a goal such as requesting a date (Berger & Bell, 1988) or obtaining a desired price for a product (Jordan & Roloff, 1997). But are complex preconversational plans always advantageous?

Two factors caution against our assuming that people always benefit from developing complex preconversational plans. First, people may be judged as incompetent when they pursue influence goals that others consider "inappropriate," even if they develop complex plans for accomplishing such goals (Wilson & Sabee, in press). Imagine that a college student, while preparing to give an informative public speech on boa constrictors, asks the course instructor for permission to bring his pet snake into class to capture the audience's attention. Although agreeing that a live snake would be attention getting, the instructor refuses the student's request because some classmates might be frightened of the snake. At this point, the student might remain focused on the goal of doing well on his speech and may thus develop a complex plan that includes several alternative means for capturing the audience's attention (e.g., show color photographs, tell personal stories). Alternatively, the student might reframe his goal to be getting even with his instructor because she refused his request, and then develop a complex plan for accomplishing this new goal (e.g., tell other students that she is unreasonable, give her low teaching evaluation ratings). The student likely will benefit from developing a complex plan in the former case, but will improve neither his public speaking skill nor his course grade by pursuing the latter goal. As noted in Chapter 5, competent communicators are distinguished by the number and types of goals they pursue when seeking/resisting compliance (Adams & Shepherd, 1996; Bingham & Burleson, 1989; Kline & Floyd, 1990; O'Keefe & McCornack,

1987). Thus the effects of plan complexity on perceived outcomes may vary depending on a communicator's goals.[6]

A second reason for caution is that developing highly complex preconversational plans actually can impair a speaker's fluency. According to Berger, Karol, and Jordan (1989), plan complexity and verbal fluency should share an inverted-U-shaped relationship:

> Up to a certain point, persons who have more complex plans are more likely to perform with greater fluency, especially in the face of goal failure. Complex planners have more options from which to choose; thus, when one course of action is thwarted, another course potentially is available to be enacted. However, it is possible that as plans become extremely complex, the uncertainty created by numerous action alternatives might debilitate the fluency of one's performance. (p. 95)

Consistent with this thinking, three studies have shown that preconversational plan complexity can, under some conditions, reduce verbal fluency (Berger et al., 1989, Experiment 1; Knowlton & Berger, 1997, Experiments 2 and 3). Knowlton and Berger (1997, Experiment 3) directly tested the proposition that plan complexity and verbal fluency are related in an inverted-U-shaped fashion. The researchers randomly assigned each of 66 undergraduates to one of four experimental conditions. Participants in the "one," "three," and "six" argument conditions were instructed to plan one, three, or six reasons why student fees at their university should not be raised. Participants in a control condition had no opportunity to plan arguments. Following the planning period, each participant was paired with another student (a confederate) and instructed to try to persuade that person by giving one reason why student fees should not be raised. After hearing the participant's initial reason, confederates in all conditions said, "I do not agree with the argument you just gave me. Could you give me another argument?" (p. 22). Raters measured the length of time that elapsed between when the confederate asked for a second reason and when the participant started speaking again. This measure of speech onset latency served as an indicator of verbal fluency.[7]

Knowlton and Berger (1997) reasoned that participants with moderately complex plans (i.e., those in the "three arguments" condition) would respond most quickly to the confederate's request for an additional reason. Participants with simple plans (i.e., those in the "one argument" and "control" conditions) should be slower than participants with moderately complex plans because the former would be faced with having to generate a second reason to support their position on the spot. Participants with highly complex plans (i.e., those in the "six arguments" condition) also should be slower than participants with moderately complex plans because they would be faced with selecting from

Table 7.4   Speaker Onset Latencies in Four Conditions

Number of Planned Arguments			
One	Three	Six	Control (no planning)
16.63 (4.35)	7.94 (6.10)	13.57 (7.78)	10.30 (4.71)

SOURCE: From "Message Planning, Communication Failure, and Cognitive Load: Further Explorations of the Hierarchy Principle," by S. W. Knowlton & C. R. Berger, 1997, *Human Communication Research, 24,* p. 23. Copyright 1997 by the International Communication Association. Reprinted with permission.

NOTE: Numbers outside parentheses are mean scores in seconds; numbers within parentheses are standard deviations.

many, rather than only a few, preplanned arguments for their second reason. Results for speech onset latencies, which appear in Table 7.4, were consistent with their predictions. The researchers also replicated these findings in a second study in which participants completed the task of giving directions to, rather than trying to persuade, a confederate (Knowlton & Berger, 1997, Experiment 2). In sum, a second reason for being cautious about the benefits of plan complexity is that highly complex plans can be difficult to implement fluently, especially when speakers do not have an opportunity to rehearse how to coordinate and sequence different elements of their complex plans in advance.[8]

Why Do People Fail to Develop Complex Preconversational Plans?

Despite the cautions just expressed, it is clear that developing complex plans often can facilitate people's accomplishing their goals during influence interactions. Given this fact, why do individuals sometimes fail to develop complex preconversational plans? One example of research examining this issue is Adler, Moore, and Tschann's (1997) analysis of why sexually active adolescents fail to plan adequately for the use of contraception. Although Adler et al. focus primarily on young women, many of their findings may be applied to women and men of all ages. Their discussion helps to illustrate the range of factors that affect whether people develop complex preconversational plans.

Given the prevalence of teenage pregnancy and sexually transmitted diseases, developing plans for acquiring and using contraception is a critical task for sexually active adolescents. The use of some forms of contraception, such as condoms, also requires consent from both parties; hence young women may need to plan how to persuade their partners to use condoms (Edgar, Freimuth, Hammond, McDonald, & Fink, 1992). Despite these facts, a range of psychological, social, and cultural factors can impede young women from developing complex plans regarding contraception. Among the cognitive factors at work is that sexually active young women often display an "optimistic bias," meaning that they see themselves as being less likely than other women their age to become pregnant (Adler et al., 1997) or to contract HIV (Edgar et al., 1992). This optimistic bias means that adolescents often perceive themselves as invulnerable to adverse health outcomes, which reduces their motivation to plan (Witte, 1995). Sexually active adolescents also may lack perceived self-efficacy (Bandura, 1977), or the belief that they have the capacity to perform particular behaviors. Young women may lack confidence that they can be assertive with their partners or perform other behaviors necessary for using contraception (Adler et al., 1997; Crowell & Emmers-Sommer, 2000). Even when adolescents perceive themselves as being at risk, low self-efficacy can lead them to engage in defensive avoidance rather than to generate plans for avoiding aversive health outcomes (Witte, 1995).

In addition to psychological factors, social and cultural factors may impede adolescent women from developing complex contraception plans. Adler et al. (1997) note:

> Despite change in some norms in our culture, there is still a widespread view that "good girls" do not have sex, and planning to have sex is associated with being promiscuous. Such beliefs are reinforced within some religious communities in which premarital sex is considered to be a sin and, thus, planning makes it a premeditated sin. (p. 326)

Normative disapproval about adolescent sexual behavior can mean that young women feel guilty or embarrassed about planning contraception, which in turn reduces their chances of using it (Adler et al., 1997). Normative disapproval also may reduce young women's access to family planning services, making it more difficult for them to learn about and acquire contraception. Finally, cultures vary in the degree to which they value planning over spontaneity (Ellis & Siegler, 1997), value long-range versus short-range planning (Cai, 1998), and view contraception as an appropriate topic about which to plan. Culture influences both the degree to which young women view contraception planning as valuable and the circumstances under which young women must develop plans. In sum, this discussion illustrates how people may fail to develop adequately complex preconversational plans due to a variety of psychological, social, and cultural factors.

QUESTIONS ABOUT CONVERSATIONAL PLANNING

Research on conversational planning investigates how individuals implement, monitor, and modify their plans "on-line," as influence interactions unfold. Questions about on-line planning include whether people think about goals and plans during interaction, face situational constraints in on-line planning, differ in the ways they implement plans, and adjust preconversational plans after encountering initial failure to accomplish their goals.

Do People Think About Goals and Plans During Influence Interactions?

As noted at the outset of this chapter, individuals sometimes seek/resist compliance with little conscious awareness of their goals and plans (Kellermann, 1992; Wilson, 1990). But do people devote any conscious attention to planning during influence interactions? Waldron (1990; Waldron et al., 1995) reports two studies that shed some light on this question. Participants in the first, 174 undergraduates, were paired into 87 dyads in order to have "get-acquainted" conversations (Waldron, 1990). Prior to meeting their partners, participants were told that the study was exploring "how people talk to strangers about potentially sensitive topics" (p. 189). Each participant heard that although his or her partner had been instructed simply to "get to know you," he or she had been selected to "obtain three pieces of sensitive information" from the partner (p. 189). In reality, both participants in each dyad were instructed to obtain information about their partners. One student (participant A) was told to find out three specific pieces of information about his or her partner's (participant B's) politics (e.g., how often the partner voted in political elections), whereas the other student (participant B) was instructed to learn three pieces of information about his or her partner's (participant A's) religion. Just before meeting their partners, participants were told, "The other person will not know what your goals are in the conversation. Please do not reveal your goals to the other person" (p. 189).

After receiving these instructions, each pair of participants completed an 8-minute get-acquainted conversation. The participants were separated immediately afterward, at which point each watched a videotape of the just-completed conversation after being instructed:

> As you watch try to relive the conversation. Try to remember what you were thinking or feeling *at that time*. Every time you remember a thought or feeling, stop the tape and describe the thought or feeling in full sentences. The thoughts and feelings might pertain to yourself, your partner, the topic of discussion, your strategy for obtaining your goals or any other aspect of the conversation. . . . Describe only thoughts and feelings you remember experiencing *during* the conversation. (Waldron, 1990, p. 190)

This stimulated recall procedure was used to capture participants' "on-line" cognitions—that is, the thoughts and feelings that participants were aware of during the conversation.

Participants in Waldron's (1990) study recalled a total of 2,273 on-line cognitions, each of which was classified as falling into one of nine categories. Definitions, examples, and percentages for these categories appear in Table 7.5. Three categories reflect thoughts about goals and/or plans. *Plan-oriented* cognitions are future-oriented thoughts about means for accomplishing goals. Such thoughts center on direct or indirect actions designed to acquire information from the partner (instrumental goals) or to avoid embarrassing the partner and create a good impression of oneself (interpersonal goals). *Goal assessment-oriented* cognitions are participants' evaluations of their progress toward achieving a goal; these cognitions differ from plan-oriented thoughts in that they do not focus on specific actions. Results from this analysis showed that almost half (44%) of the thoughts and feelings recalled by participants fell into the plan-oriented or goal assessment-oriented categories. Although participants thought about their partners, themselves, topics of conversation, and so forth, a good deal of their conscious attention during the get-acquainted conversation focused on generating and implementing plans and monitoring progress toward achieving goals.

A more recent study conducted by Waldron et al. (1995) suggests that people think consciously about goals and plans when talking with acquaintances as well as when meeting strangers. The researchers asked each of 120 undergraduates to select a "familiar" same-sex classmate whom "they felt comfortable talking to but did not know well" (p. 256) and then instructed the pairs of participants to discuss the topic of AIDS. Prior to the interaction, 60 of the participants were designated to be discussion "facilitators," whose job was to find out the partner's "knowledge and opinions about people living with AIDS, the behaviors that put individuals at risk of contracting AIDS, and preventative measures" (p. 257). Facilitators were told that they would be required to offer an evaluation of the partner's AIDS knowledge and attitudes after the conversation, but were also cautioned not to press their partners for embarrassing personal details. After finishing an 8-minute conversation, each facilitator completed a stimulated-recall procedure, and all plan-oriented cognitions (i.e., all thoughts and feelings that fall into the first two categories in Table 7.5) were identified. In this second study, 26% of the on-line cognitions reported by discussion facilitators focused on plans. As Waldron et al. (1995, p. 260) note, this figure actually may underestimate the degree to which facilitators consciously thought about goals and plans during conversation, because it does not include goal assessment-oriented thoughts (i.e., the third category in Table 7.5).

Questions can be raised about the generalizability of Waldron's (1990; Waldron et al., 1995) research. Participants in everyday conversation usually are not instructed to learn specific pieces of information about their interactional partners. These studies also focus on attempts to acquire information rather than to seek/resist compliance. Despite these issues, Waldron's work

Table 7.5 Definitions, Examples, and Percentages for Nine Categories of On-Line Cognitions

Definition/Example	Percentage
Plan-oriented units: thoughts indicating a future focus, with the form "I thought about performing Action X to accomplish Goal Y."	
1. Instrumental plan units: units pertaining to the information acquisition task	20.8
A. Direct units: thoughts about undisguised attempts to gain information *Example:* I really needed the information, so why not just ask to find out?	
B. Indirect units: thoughts about less obvious attempts to gain information *Example:* I started a discussion about prayer in schools to find out if she was religious.	
2. Interpersonal plan units: units pertaining to supporting either party's face, creating a positive impression, or maintaining a relationship with the partner *Example:* I am trying to make up for my embarrassing remark by starting to talk about how good I did on the test.	6.3
Assessment-oriented units	
1. Goal related: evaluations of progress in achieving instrumental goals *Example:* I can tell it's working—she's starting to talk about my topic.	17.4
2. Partner: descriptions/evaluations of the interaction partner *Example:* He seems like an interesting person.	18.3
3. Self: descriptions/evaluations of self *Example:* I just feel nervous.	16.4
4. Relational: descriptions/evaluations of the developing relationship *Example:* I think we are getting along pretty well.	7.0
5. Topic: descriptions/evaluations of conversational topics *Example:* I hate this talk about sororities.	9.7
Observer-oriented units: descriptions of an image on the videotape rather than a thought/feeling from the conversation *Example:* I am scratching my nose for some reason.	1.1
Unclassified units: thoughts/feelings not falling into the previous eight categories	2.2

SOURCE: From "Constrained Rationality: Situational Influences on Information Acquisition Plans and Tactics," by V. R. Waldron, 1990, *Communication Monographs, 57*, pp. 191-193. Copyright 1990 by the Speech Communication Association. Adapted with permission.

provides grounds for claiming that individuals plan consciously at some points during compliance-gaining interactions. Individuals are especially likely to think about plans and planning when their expectations are violated (e.g., an unexpected request), their initial attempts to seek/resist compliance are thwarted, or their own goals conflict (Motley, 1986; von Cranach, Kalbermatten, Indermuhle, & Gugler, 1982).

Do Situational Factors Limit People's Ability to Plan On-Line?

Situational factors such as fatigue and the time demands of turn taking set limits on the degree to which individuals can consciously engage in on-line planning during conversation. The number of goals that people attempt to pursue also may constrain, and shape, their on-line planning. In one of the studies just reviewed, Waldron (1990) investigated the effects of goal complexity on people's planning and information-seeking strategies during get-acquainted conversations. Participants were paired into stranger dyads in which each party was instructed to find out three pieces of information about the other's religion or politics. To manipulate "goal complexity," participants in one-half of the dyads were told that, in addition to obtaining potentially sensitive information from their partners, they also had the additional goal of "demonstrating that they were knowledgeable about a topic of their choice" (p. 190).[9] For example, aside from finding out about her partner's religion (or politics), a participant in this condition also might introduce the topic of "basketball" at some point in the conversation and talk knowledgeably about it. Participants in the remaining dyads did not receive this additional instruction. Participants who were assigned two goals constituted the "high goal complexity" condition, whereas those assigned only to acquire information about their partners constituted the "low goal complexity" condition. In addition to coding participants' on-line cognitions during the get-acquainted conversations, Waldron analyzed whether participants tended to use direct, abrupt information-seeking strategies (e.g., "So, what church do you go to?") or more indirect, subtle strategies that eventually steered the conversation to the desired topic.

Goal complexity affected participants' on-line planning as well as their information-seeking strategies during get-acquainted conversations. Participants in the high goal complexity condition, relative to those in the low goal complexity condition, had a smaller percentage of interpersonal plan-oriented cognitions; these participants also used a larger percentage of direct information-seeking strategies. Participants in the high goal complexity condition apparently devoted much of their attention to planning for the two instrumental goals, and thus had less capacity to plan for interpersonal goals. This suggests that seeking or resisting compliance while also attempting to achieve other instrumental goals should set limits on the degree to which a person can plan behaviors (e.g., off-record requests) that also orient to interpersonal (secondary) goals.

Do People Differ in How They Plan On-Line?

Stable individual differences in loneliness, self-monitoring, and verbal aggressiveness are reflected in the complexity of people's preconversational plans. In addition to affecting plans that people bring to influence interactions, individual differences play a role as people recall, generate, implement, and monitor plans during influence interactions. Current research suggests that executive control (cognitive) efficiency and communication competence are associated with differences in on-line planning.

Executive control processes involve a closely interrelated set of higher-order mental activities (Jordan, 1998). These activities include decisions about (a) selection (e.g., which knowledge to access from memory given the current situation), (b) regulation (e.g., how much time/attention to devote to processing information), and (c) monitoring (e.g., whether current conditions warrant a change in processing). As Jordan (1998) explains, executive control processes are assumed by current models of plans and planning because "some knowledge is activated and integrated into the plan and other information is ignored. Executive control processes are entailed as plans are activated for performance, as plans are translated into action, and as plans are monitored during interaction" (p. 6). Executive control processes appear to underlie planning quite generally, as evidenced by the fact that individuals with injuries to parts of the brain thought responsible for these processes often exhibit a broad inability to activate and use social knowledge.

Individuals differ in the efficiency of their executive control processes, with inefficiency being reflected in a propensity for performance errors, slips, and lapses (Reason, 1990). Drawing upon this idea, Jordan (1998) argues that differences in "cognitive efficiency" have implications for how individuals implement and monitor plans. Cognitive efficiency should facilitate preinteraction planning, given that those who lack it may access irrelevant information or lose track of sequences of planned acts. Jordan (1998, Study 2) predicted that cognitive efficiency would be inversely associated with individuals' perceptions of the difficulty of planning to persuade others, and hence also their confidence in their influence plans. To test this reasoning, Jordan asked 144 undergraduates to write out plans for attempting to convince someone to accept their opinion on a controversial issue (banning alcohol in college dormitories), for asking a classmate on a date, and for selling used texts back to a bookstore at a desired price. Participants also rated how difficult it had been to generate each plan and how confident they were that each plan would be successful. Finally, participants completed the Cognitive Failures Questionnaire (CFQ; Broadbent, Cooper, Fitzgerald, & Parkes, 1982), a measure of their executive control efficiency. Instructions and sample items from the CFQ are shown in Table 7.6. For all three influence goals, cognitive efficiency was inversely associated with self-reported difficulty in developing preconversational plans ($rs = -.24$ to $-.28$). Perceived planning difficulty in turn undermined plan confidence ($rs = -.11$ to $-.38$).

One implication of these findings is that cognitively inefficient persons, who lack confidence that their preconversational plans will succeed, may be less likely than cognitively efficient persons actually to implement their plans during influence interactions. Such differences may be especially apparent when individuals are highly motivated to accomplish their goals. To test this reasoning, Jordan (1998, Study 3) had 33 undergraduates complete a think-aloud procedure as they wrote plans for accomplishing four persuasion goals as well as the CFQ measure of executive control efficiency. Two to three days later, participants returned to the lab, and each attempted to persuade another student (actually a confederate) to accept his or her position about banning alcohol in dormitories at their college (one of the four issues for which each had developed a preconversational plan). Participants afterward rated how motivated they had been during the interaction. Coders rated the degree of correspondence between each participant's preconversational planning (i.e., what the participant said during the talk-aloud procedure) and his or her behavior during the influence interaction. For participants who reported being motivated to persuade their partners, cognitive efficiency was positively associated with the degree to which they actually enacted their preconversational plans during their conversations.

Taken together, these two studies suggest that differences in cognitive efficiency can help explain variations in how people implement and monitor plans on-line. More broadly, Jordan's (1998) work suggests that communication competence reflects not only people's goals when they are seeking/resisting compliance (see Chapter 5) and the complexity of their plans for accomplishing goals, but also their ability to generate and deploy plans efficiently during influence interactions.

Along these same lines, Cegala and Waldron (1992) investigated whether differences in perceived communication competence are evident in people's on-line planning. They reanalyzed data from two earlier studies of recalled thoughts and feelings during get-acquainted conversations (Waldron, 1990; Waldron et al., 1990). Coders watched the videotaped conversations and rated each participant's competence at seeking information about his or her partner's religious or political background. Drawing on prior conceptions of communication competence

Table 7.6   Instructions and Sample Items From the Cognitive Failures
Questionnaire

Instructions: The following questions are about minor mistakes that everyone makes
from time to time but some of which happen more often than others. We want to
know how often each of these things have happened to you in the past 6 months,
using the following scale:

0 = Never
1 = Very rarely
2 = Occasionally
3 = Quite often
4 = Very often

1. Do you read something and find you haven't been thinking about it and must
   read it again?
2. Do you find you forgot why you went from one part of the house to the other?
3. Do you fail to notice signposts on the road?
5. Do you bump into people?
13. Do you fail to see what you want in the supermarket (although it's there)?
18. Do you find you accidentally throw away the thing you want and keep what you
    meant to throw away—as in throwing away a matchbox and putting the used
    match in your pocket?
21. Do you start doing one thing at home and get distracted into doing something
    else (unintentionally)?
23. Do you find you forgot what you came to the shops to buy?

SOURCE: From "Executive Cognitive Control in Communication: Extending
Plan-Based Theory," by J. M. Jordan, 1998, *Human Communication Research, 25,*
p. 33. Copyright 1998 by the International Communication Association. Reprinted
with permission.

NOTE: Items are numbered according to their positions in the intact instrument.

(e.g., Spitzberg & Cupach, 1984), the coders analyzed the degree to which
participants used effective and appropriate information-seeking strategies.
Effective strategies were defined as those that actually obtained the required
information, whereas appropriate strategies were defined as those that sought
information using indirect means (e.g., self-disclosure, topic manipulation)
rather than direct, abrupt means (e.g., direct requests for information with no
justification). Based on these two criteria, the researchers subdivided participants
into high-, medium-, and low-competence groups, and then compared on-line
cognitions from these three groups.

Participants rated as highly competent in these studies, compared with
moderate- and low-competence participants, had a larger percentage of instrumental plan-oriented cognitions, and especially more indirect plan-oriented

cognitions (see Table 7.5). In contrast, participants rated as low in competence, relative to moderate- and high-competence participants, had a larger percentage of self-assessment cognitions. High-competence participants spent more time planning indirect information-seeking behaviors on-line, whereas low-competence participants spent more time making negative evaluations of themselves. Cegala and Waldron (1992) speculate that low-competence communicators, due to low self-esteem, experience many conversations as stressful events. Thus "low competence communicators, in general, may be more self-focused than their more competent communicators. This inward orientation probably accounts, in part, for their ineffectiveness at accomplishing task goals" (p. 119).

In sum, results from these and other studies (e.g., Waldron & Applegate, 1994) suggest that individuals vary not only in the complexity of their preinteraction plans for seeking/resisting compliance, but in the focus of their attention and the amount/quality of their on-line planning during compliance-gaining episodes.

Do People Modify Their Preconversational Plans When Faced With Resistance?

Imagine you are part of a group of students assigned to work together on a class presentation. One member of your group, Chris, arrives at your group's first meeting and proposes the idea of having the class perform an exercise. The exercise, if debriefed thoroughly, will take about two-thirds of your group's presentation time. Chris says that the class "will enjoy performing the exercise— it will make the presentation fun." Some group members question whether the exercise will take too much time and prevent your group from covering material that the course instructor believes is important. Upon encountering resistance to his proposal, Chris repeats his argument that "the class will really like the exercise," this time using a somewhat louder voice. Most group members remain skeptical.

Have you ever encountered a situation like this one, in which a message source continues to repeat the same argument over and over when it should be apparent that target individuals are not being persuaded by this argument? Why might this occur? One potential explanation is lack of argumentative skill. Perhaps Chris is not practiced at generating new reasons to defend his proposals on the spot. A second explanation is that negative affect can interfere with a person's ability to monitor and modify plans (Berger, 1997, pp. 38-39). Perhaps Chris feels defensive when his proposal is questioned, and negative arousal interferes with his ability to see that other group members are not being persuaded by his initial argument. Charles Berger (1995, 1997) proposes a "hierarchy principle" that suggests yet a third, and somewhat different, explanation for why sources may not modify their preconversational plans after encountering resistance: Substantial plan revision requires considerable mental effort, and people often are unable or unwilling to devote the cognitive resources necessary to modify plans during influence interactions.

Four assumptions provide groundwork for the hierarchy principle (Berger, 1997, p. 63). First, people are assumed to have limited abilities to process all information available at a given time, a point made at the start of this chapter. Second, people are assumed to rely on less effortful means of processing information (e.g., heuristics) under many conditions (Cialdini, 1993; Eagly & Chaiken, 1993; Fiske & Taylor, 1991). This second assumption recognizes that people will exert considerable effort to process information when their ability and motivation to do so are high, but have a tendency not to do this unless the need is great.

A third assumption is that plans are hierarchically organized knowledge structures, a point made at the start of this section. Chris attended the group's first meeting with the plan of proposing a class exercise and arguing that it would be fun. Upon encountering resistance to this preconversational plan, Chris could simply repeat his argument that "the exercise will be fun" with greater passion and vocal intensity (a low-level plan modification). Alternatively, Chris might continue advocating that the group should do an exercise, but add new arguments, such as that the exercise will not take as long as other members assume (a moderate-level plan modification). Finally, Chris could abandon the specific idea of an exercise altogether and help lead a discussion about alternative ways of involving the class in the group's presentation (a high-level plan modification). A final assumption is that changes in higher levels of a preconversational plan require more cognitive effort than do changes at lower levels. As Berger (1997) explains: "Changes in more abstract units cascade down the plan hierarchy, thus requiring realignment of lower level plan units. By contrast, alterations of low-level units do not necessarily imply changes in more abstract plan units" (p. 63). Building on these four assumptions, Berger postulates the hierarchy principle as follows: "When people experience thwarting internal to the interaction, their first response is likely to involve low-level plan hierarchy alterations. Continued thwarting will tend to produce more abstract alterations to plan hierarchies" (p. 35).[10]

Berger and his colleagues (Berger & diBattista, 1992, 1993; Berger et al., 1996, Studies 1-4) report a series of studies testing the hierarchy principle (for a detailed review, see Berger, 1997, chap. 4). Two studies provide representative evidence regarding the principle. Participants in the first study (Berger & diBattista, 1993), 96 undergraduates, all of whom spoke English as their first language, were brought to a laboratory and assigned the task of giving another person (actually a confederate) directions from the place they were located to a well-known elevated train station near campus. Participants were instructed not to ask the other person questions as they gave directions, and confederates were instructed not to engage participants in conversation. After participants completed giving the directions, confederates immediately indicated that they did not understand and asked the participants to go through the directions again. Berger and diBattista (1993) varied two factors about the confederates. Half of the participants gave directions to a female or a male European American confederate, whereas the other half gave directions to a female or a male Asian confederate (a female student from Taiwan or a male student from Singapore). Nationality was varied to assess whether students changed how they gave their directions depending on whether the confederate appeared to be or might not have been a native English speaker (students could not be sure of the confederate's English fluency initially, because confederates did not speak until after the first set of directions). Aside from nationality, confederates also varied the reasons they provided to justify not understanding. After being given their first set of directions, all confederates told one-half of the participants, "I'm sorry, I don't understand English well. I had trouble following your directions. Could you give me the directions again?" Asian confederates delivered these lines using a heavy native accent, whereas European American confederates were trained to deliver these lines using a heavy Eastern European accent. All confederates told the other half of the participants that they understood English well, but they had difficulty following the specific directions given by the participant.

Berger and diBattista (1993) analyzed videotapes of the two sets of participants for changes at high, medium, and low levels of abstraction. At the highest level, participants would completely reformulate the routes they suggested to the confederates in their second sets of directions. Given the effort involved in devising a completely new route, the researchers expected few participants to suggest different routes spontaneously. At the medium level, participants would describe exactly the same routes but simplify their second sets of directions by mentioning fewer landmarks, such as buildings, along the way. At the lowest level, participants would repeat their directions in a way virtually identical to the first while altering their speech rate and vocal intensity. Based on the hierarchy principle, Berger and diBattista expected participants to make mostly medium- and low-level changes in their second sets of directions, even though some of these changes (e.g., speaking louder to a confederate who had difficulty understanding English) had little chance of solving the likely source of misunderstanding.

Several findings from Berger and diBattista's (1993) study are consistent with the hierarchy principle. Only 5.2% of the 96 participants changed the routes suggested in their second sets of directions. Participants mentioned fewer landmarks (buildings) and spoke louder in their second directions, regardless of the confederate's nationality and stated reason for not understanding. Finally, participants spoke more slowly in their second directions, especially when the confederate was European American and stated that he or she did not understand English well. The researchers attribute this finding to participants' surprise that someone they initially presumed was a native English speaker actually was not. In sum, participants predominantly made moderate and low-level changes to their initial plans across all experimental conditions.

To test more directly the assumption that higher-level plan modifications are cognitively taxing, Berger et al. (1996, Study 3) conducted a field study using the same "direction-giving" paradigm. Experimenter-observer pairs (undergraduate students) approached 78 pedestrians at the corner of a main intersection of a small college town. Experimenters asked directions to either the public library or the university's stadium. After each pedestrian provided directions a first time, the experimenter provided one of three reasons for not understanding the directions. Pedestrians in the "change route" condition were told that their suggested route was difficult to understand; they were asked to provide directions again following a new route. Pedestrians in the "landmarks" condition were told that their directions were difficult to understand because not enough landmarks were included; they were asked to mention more landmarks while giving directions again. Pedestrians in the "change speed" condition were told that their directions were difficult to understand because they had spoken too quickly; they were asked to speak more slowly while giving directions again.

Based on the hierarchy principle, Berger et al. (1996) predicted that pedestrians in the change route condition would be required to expend more cognitive effort than those in the landmarks condition, who in turn would expend more effort than pedestrians in the change speed condition. Cognitive load was assessed in two ways. Using a concealed stopwatch, the observer measured the amount of time that elapsed between the point at which the experimenter stopped explaining why he or she had not understood the first set of directions and the point at which the pedestrian began giving directions again. This "onset latency" measure has been used in prior research as an indicator of difficulty of on-line speech preparation (see Greene, 1988). Second, the observer also noted whether the pedestrian maintained or broke eye contact with the experimenter immediately after being told that the first set of directions was unclear. This eye gaze measure was included based on the idea that pedestrians would be more likely to avert their gaze from the experimenter under conditions of high cognitive load.

Results from the Berger et al. (1996, Study 3) field experiment offer qualified support for the hierarchy principle. As predicted, the pedestrians took significantly longer to begin their second sets of directions ($M = 7.27$ seconds) when asked to provide a new route than when asked to mention more landmarks (M = 4.40 seconds), and in turn when asked to mention more landmarks than when asked to speak more slowly (M = 2.45 seconds). Findings for eye gaze aversion also followed the predicted pattern but did not reach conventional levels of statistical significance.

Taken together, these and other studies provide consistent support for the hierarchy principle. Although Berger and his colleagues have not examined compliance-gaining episodes, their research suggests hypotheses regarding persuasive message production. After encountering target resistance, message sources initially should be prone to make lower-level changes (e.g., raising their voices) rather than higher-level changes (e.g., reframing what they are requesting) to their preconversational plans. This tendency should occur regardless of whether lower-level changes are a sensible way of addressing likely obstacles to compliance in the situation. After encountering persistence from a source, message targets initially should be prone to make lower-level changes (e.g., repeating their initial reason for saying no more slowly) rather than higher-level changes (e.g., suggesting a compromise) to their own preconversational plans. The hierarchy principle illustrates how information-processing limitations can shape and constrain the ways in which people modify their preconversational plans during influence interactions.

To summarize the discussion so far: One research tradition has examined variations in the structure of the plans individuals bring to conversation (questions about preconversational plans), whereas a second has explored how individuals implement, monitor, and modify their plans during conversation (questions about conversational planning). Aside from monitoring their own goals and plans, however, participants in influence interactions make assessments of the other party's goals and plans, reveal or conceal their own goals and plans, and understand the unfolding interaction in light of the perceived relationship between both parties' goals and plans. This suggests yet a third set of questions that can be posed about plans and planning processes.

QUESTIONS ABOUT INTERACTIVE PLANNING

Questions about interactive planning focus on interdependence between a message source's goals and plans and those of the message target as influence interactions unfold. Waldron (1997) describes the focus of interactive planning as follows:

> The *interactive* perspective moves the study of conversational planning to relatively new theoretical ground by considering planning a process of mutual construction and coordination of action plans, rather than simply a process of individual-level

cognition. The verbal and nonverbal messages that allow dyadic partners to coordinate their plans and move through conversational time are the focus of this approach. To some extent, "conversation about planning" rather than "planning about conversation" is what this research tradition seeks to understand. (p. 196)

Although planning theorists recognize the importance of interactive planning (e.g., Berger, 2000; Waldron, 1997), very little communication research has explored these issues to date. Future research in this area might explore at least three questions. First, how do message sources and targets reveal their goals and plans to the other party and make inferences about the other party's goals and plans? Research has explored how people (and computers) understand stories and conversations by making inferences about participants' goals and plans (Haller, 1999), but we know less about the (non)verbal means by which message sources signal their goals and plans (e.g., through presequences such as asking, "Do you have a minute?") or by which targets infer sources' goals and plans as well as reveal their own (Berger, 2000).

A second question is, How do message sources and targets conceal their goals and plans, and make inferences about the other party's "real" as opposed to stated goals and plans? We know that message sources do not always disclose their real reasons for making requests. For example, employees may advocate a change in the way they do their work by stating that it will benefit the larger organization, when in reality their primary motivation is that the change will benefit them personally (Porter, Allen, & Angle, 1981; see Chapter 8). Message targets also do not always disclose their real reasons for resisting requests (see the discussion of obstacles in Chapter 6). We know less about how message sources and targets go about presenting "fabricated" as opposed to real goals and plans (Waldron, 1997), when and how participants "second guess" the other party's stated goals and plans (Hewes, 1995b), and so forth.

Third, planning scholars might investigate when seeking and resisting compliance become the impetus for interactive planning. In their analysis of naturally occurring compliance-gaining episodes, Sanders and Fitch (2001) found that a good deal of the talk beyond the request and response "was directly or indirectly about the practicalities, about what would be workable and sufficient for one or both parties to do that would meet the needs of both compliance seeker and target person" (p. 269). In one of their examples, a request by a young woman to borrow the family car led to questions about both the woman's own and her sister's plans for the day, which in turn led to the incremental construction of a joint plan that accommodated both parties. In other cases, targets may put on public displays of searching for mutually agreeable joint plans when in reality they have no intention of changing their individual plans. Scholars might explore the conversational structure of interactive planning, factors that predict participants' ability and willingness to negotiate joint plans, and so forth.

Along with theories of plans and planning processes, action assembly theory (Greene, 1984a, 1997b) falls within the realm of cognitive theories. Both perspectives explore how speakers utilize procedural knowledge in pursuit of goals. Action assembly theory, however, differs in several respects from the work just reviewed. Although the hierarchy hypothesis has created some awareness of "low-level" plan adjustments, action assembly theory places greater emphasis on the full range of procedural knowledge used to produce messages, including motor commands involved in speaking. Compared with the work of Berger (1997) and Waldron (1990, 1997), action assembly theory also offers more detailed assumptions about the mental structures and processes that underlie message production. Finally, action assembly theory places greater emphasis on how rapidly the mental processes that underlie message production actually occur.

Action Assembly Theory

Greene's presentation of action assembly theory has evolved over time. My description draws heavily on Greene's chapter in his edited volume *Message Production* (1997b), where he introduces a "second-generation" action assembly theory (AAT2). I begin by outlining the theory's key concepts and assumptions, and then describe its application to persuasive message production. The key concepts of action assembly theory include procedural records, activation and assembly processes, coalitions, the output representation, executive processes, and neurophysiological components.

KEY CONCEPTS AND ASSUMPTIONS

From the perspective of AAT2, any communicative behavior is "an inherently creative, multifunctional complex comprised of a very large number of elemental units" (Greene, 1997b, p. 152). AAT2 assumes that the procedural knowledge underlying behavior is stored as part of an associative network model of long-term memory. The basic unit in AAT2 is the procedural record, which is a network structure composed of interconnected nodes representing features of actions, outcomes, and situations. Greene and Geddes (1993) describe them as "modular memory structures which . . . preserve relationships between three types of symbolic elements: (1) behavioral features, (2) outcomes associated with those features, and (3) situational and intrasystematic features that have proven relevant to the action-outcome relationship stored in the record"

(p. 30). Procedural records represent action-relevant information at many levels of abstraction, ranging from knowledge about pursuing goals and performing speech acts to more concrete acts involved in regulating turn taking and maintaining topic coherence, to rules for ordering strings of words, to the most concrete motor commands involved in gesturing and speaking aloud (Greene, 1984a).

Procedural records at any level are formed and strengthened without awareness when nodes representing actions, situational features, and outcomes are activated simultaneously by the environment. They are formed with awareness when persons consciously contemplate meaningful relationships (e.g., temporal, causal) among multiple nodes. Two or more procedural records, or some of the nodes within two records, also may become linked themselves over time via simultaneous activation into "more complex and noisier" structural units that Greene (1997b) terms "unitized assemblies." Alternatively, a lack of simultaneous activation over time weakens the links connecting multiple procedural records.[11]

Given this picture of a long-term memory store with an almost countless number of procedural records, how is the subset of records that constitutes a person's current behavior (what Greene terms the "output representation") actually selected? AAT2 addresses this by specifying an activation process. At any point in time, each node in a procedural record is characterized by some level of activation. Nodes representing situational conditions and desired outcomes are activated when they match a person's perception of the current state of affairs. A node representing a specific behavioral feature (e.g., the speech act of "requesting") thus receives activation through its connection with already activated nodes representing situational features, outcomes, and other behavioral features. One key assumption of AAT2 is that activated nodes decay rapidly with moment-to-moment shifts in a person's perception of the current situation. The theory "assumes a very large decay parameter which rapidly drives the activation of a node back to resting levels" (Greene, 1997b, p. 158).

How are activated procedural records integrated together, before they decay, into an output representation that constitutes a person's behavior at that moment? AAT2 also specifies an assembly process based on the metaphor of "coalition formation." A coalition is "a momentary assemblage of activated behavioral features that could be said to 'fit' together. Thus, a behavioral-feature node representing a syntactic frame with slots for a noun and a verb might coalesce with a particular activated noun and verb" (Greene, 1997b, p. 159). Coalitions have both vertical and horizontal dimensions: They may integrate procedural records that share a temporal relationship (e.g., a string of words) in the same code or in different codes from various levels of abstraction (e.g., the words "I promise" and the motor program for pronouncing those words).

Unlike the initial version of action assembly theory, AAT2 does not assume that assembly is a serial process that makes heavy demands on processing capacities. Instead, the assembly process

> is held to be massively interactive and parallel. Thus, a given behavioral feature may coalesce with any of a number of other activated features represented in either the same code format or in other codes. Further, at any moment, there are likely to be a large number of coalitions, some consisting of a single pair of features while others are comprised of a very large number of action specifications. (Greene, 1997b, p. 160)

Another key assumption of AAT2 is that coalition formation helps offset the rapid decay of activated nodes. Procedural records that are temporarily integrated with others do not decay as rapidly as records that do not find their way into coalitions. Greene (1997b) describes the process as follows:

> The image of behavioral production in AAT2, then, is of a very rapid process of coalition formation where multiple, and potentially competing, coalitions "recruit" activated features, each additional feature resulting in a more extensive output specification and incrementing the activation level of the coalition. A person's behavior at any moment, then, is nothing more nor less than the constellation of coalitions operating at that time. (p. 160)

Along with activation decay and coalition building, executive processes and conscious awareness are important concepts in AAT2. As I have noted above in the section on planning, executive processes are higher-order mental activities such as behavioral rehearsal, editing, and monitoring. Within AAT2, executive processes are assumed to occur through the application of procedural records activated by situational and intraindividual conditions. Becoming momentarily aware of a goal, for example, may activate procedures for planning how to accomplish the goal. Because executive processes are initiated by activated procedural records, these processes help maintain the activation level of coalitions to which they are applied. Conditions that activate procedures for "monitoring" one's behavior, for instance, "allow a person to do just that by keeping the coalitions of features that constitute that behavior highly activated, and, hence, conscious" (Greene, 1997b, p. 163). Because executive processes arise through the same mechanisms as other action-relevant processes, they are subject to the same limitations (e.g., rapid decay in response to changing activating conditions). By enhancing the activation level of specific coalitions, executive processes also may "overwhelm" other coalitions. Put simply, planning or monitoring for one task may impair a person's ability to perform a second task simultaneously (Greene, 1997b, p. 164).

Finally, AAT2 explicitly considers the role of physiological constructs in the production of communicative behavior. Greene (1997a) discusses the effects of momentary changes in arousal levels as well as long-term changes in synaptic density that occur during the later stages of life. Increased physiological arousal, for example, is posited to heighten the activation of all nodes in long-term memory. Up to a point, arousal should further heighten the activation of behavioral features that already match the present situation so that coalitions form around them. Too much arousal, however, also heightens the activation of irrelevant behavioral features to the point that competing or inappropriate coalitions may be formed.

AAT2 portrays people as extremely rapid yet fallible information processors (see Greene, 2000). According to the theory, we are capable of reacting quickly (activation speed) and creatively (coalition formation) in response to a host of activating conditions. Yet we also are prone to lose track of what we are saying or doing (activation decay) and to experience difficulty in integrating our goals, thoughts, words, and movements (problems with coalition formation, executive processes, or arousal). With these assumptions in mind, I turn now to several insights AAT2 can offer about persuasive message production.

AAT2 AND PERSUASIVE MESSAGE PRODUCTION

Producing Multiple-Goal Messages

Researchers have applied action assembly theory to their investigations of a range of phenomena, such as the role of the self in social interaction, cross-situational consistency of behavior, and the nature of social skills deficits (see Greene, 1995a, 1995b). The work most relevant to persuasive message production, however, pertains to the insights AAT2 can provide into the production of multiple-goal messages.

One theme running throughout this book is that speakers often pursue multiple goals as they seek and resist compliance (see Chapter 5). Persuasive message production is complex, in part, due to the relevance of multiple situational objectives (O'Keefe, 1988). It often is difficult to figure out exactly what to say, for example, when trying to convince a friend to stop smoking or drinking excessively without also appearing to be overbearing, or when refusing a request for a favor from a friend while still demonstrating concern for the friend's well-being.

Drawing on action assembly theory, Greene (1995b) proposes two reasons why producing multiple-goal messages is more cognitively taxing than producing messages designed to accomplish only one goal.[12] Forming multiple goals is likely to activate simultaneously procedural records that represent behavioral features relevant to accomplishing each goal. When a speaker pursues multiple goals rather than a single goal, a larger number of records also may be recruited into the coalitions that make up the output representation. Consistent with this idea, compliance-seeking messages done "with politeness" often are longer than those done "baldly, on-record" (Dillard, Wilson, Tusing, & Kinney, 1997). This first line of reasoning suggests that speakers must hold a larger output representation in memory when producing multiple- rather than single-goal messages, and the demands of doing this may be reflected in paralinguistic features such as hesitations and filled pauses (Greene, 1988).

When pursuing multiple goals, speakers often also face goal conflict (O'Keefe & Delia, 1982). Conflicting goals may activate procedural records that represent incompatible or inconsistent behavioral features, which in turn should increase the demands of assembling a coherent output representation in a timely fashion. This second line of reasoning suggests that it is not so much multiple goals as goal conflict that makes the situations in the preceding examples cognitively challenging. This second explanation also suggests that a speaker may be able to reduce the demands of assembling a coherent output representation if he or she has time to plan at least the broad elements of what to say in advance (Greene, 1984c).

Greene and his colleagues report a series of studies that offer some support for both these lines of reasoning (e.g., Greene & Lindsey, 1989; Greene, Lindsey, & Hawn, 1990; Greene, McDaniel, Buska, & Ravizza, 1993; Lindsey, Greene, Parker, & Sassi, 1995). A study by Greene and Lindsey (1989) offers a representative example of the methods and findings from this program of research. Participants in their experiment, 86 undergraduates enrolled in communication courses, initially completed a monologue task that was used to identify and control for stable individual differences in speech fluency. Each participant was given an index card, face down, on which were printed the following instructions: "Your task is to discuss the best and worst aspects of your most recent summer job" (p. 127). On a signal from the experimenter, the participant turned over the card, read the instructions aloud, and then began speaking for as long as he or she wished. Participants were audiotaped while giving their monologues.

After completing this initial task, each participant was randomly assigned to one of four experimental conditions. Participants in each condition were asked to imagine that they were members of a university scholarship committee and that they were evaluating the files of several applicants. They were presented with a single file for a fictitious applicant named Carrie Poole, which contained information about her grades, standardized test scores, and so forth. After reading and returning the file, participants in the multiple-goal condition received the following instructions on an index card:

You must decide against awarding a scholarship to Carrie Poole. Your task will be to record your evaluation and reasons for this decision. Assume that Ms. Poole will hear this recording later. Please be *clear and direct* in your comments, while also *showing concern for her feelings and self-esteem*. (p. 128)

In contrast, participants assigned to the single-goal condition were told:

You must decide against awarding a scholarship to Carrie Poole. Your task will be to record your evaluation and reasons for this decision. Assume that this recording will be heard only by other members of the Scholarship Committee. Please be *clear and direct* in your comments. (p. 128)

The message in the single-goal condition was directed toward a third party, rather than toward Ms. Poole, to avoid spontaneously activating concerns about her face.[13]

In addition to number of goals, opportunity for advance planning also was manipulated. Participants assigned to the "spontaneous message" condition turned over the index card, read the instructions aloud, and then spoke immediately for as long as they wished. Those assigned to the "advance preparation" condition turned over the index card, read the instructions silently, and then were given 60 seconds to plan silently what to say. At the end of this 60-second period, these participants read the instructions aloud and began their monologues.

To assess cognitive demand, Greene and Lindsey (1989) analyzed two paraverbal features. Speech onset latency was measured, using a stopwatch, as the period of time (in hundredths of a second) between when a participant finished reading the instructions aloud and when she or he began speaking again (excluding nonlexical utterances and sociocentric sequences such as "well"). Silent pausing was measured, with a computer program, as the ratio of total duration of silent pauses after the onset of speech to total duration of phonation.[14]

Results for mean speech onset latencies in each condition are shown in Table 7.7. These mean scores are adjusted to control for stable individual differences in onset latencies that existed during the initial monologue. As is apparent from the results shown in the table, participants who were assigned two goals took longer to begin speaking than did those assigned only a single goal. As suggested by AAT2, participants who were able to assemble at least the broad outlines of their output representation in advance also began speaking more quickly than did those who had to assemble an output representation on the spot. This appears to be especially true for participants assigned multiple goals, although the interaction between number of goals and message preparation condition did not reach conventional levels of statistical significance ($p = 0.08$). These findings appear to support the idea that assembling a coherent output

Table 7.7   Speech Onset Latencies in Four Conditions

	Message Preparation	
Number of Goals	Spontaneous	Advance Planning
Single goal	4.04 (2.48)	2.58 (1.40)
Multiple goal	6.26 (3.71)	2.99 (1.07)

SOURCE: From "Encoding Processes in the Production of Multiple-Goal Messages," by J. O. Greene & A. E. Lindsey, 1989, *Human Communication Research, 16,* p. 132. Copyright 1989 by the International Communication Association. Reprinted with permission.

NOTE: Numbers outside parentheses are adjusted mean scores; numbers within parentheses are standard deviations.

representation when pursuing multiple, conflicting goals is taxing and that advance planning can reduce the demands of this task.

Results concerning silent pauses were somewhat different. Participants who were assigned multiple goals (adjusted $M = .490$) had a higher pause/phonation ratio than did those who were assigned only a single goal (adjusted $M = .375$). Neither the main effect for message preparation nor the number of goals × message preparation condition interaction were significant. Once they began speaking, participants pursuing two goals had longer silent pauses than did those pursuing one goal regardless of whether they had planned in advance. These findings appear more consistent with the idea that pursuing multiple goals results in a larger number of procedural records being activated and assembled into the output representation and holding this information in memory while speaking is cognitively taxing.

Greene and his colleagues have replicated and extended these basic findings. For example, participants show greater signs of cognitive demand when pursuing two conflicting goals as opposed to two compatible goals (when onset latencies are measured), but still show greater signs of cognitive demand when pursuing either two conflicting or two compatible goals as opposed to only one goal (when silent pauses are measured; Greene et al., 1993, Study 2).

Although these studies have not examined seeking and resisting compliance per se, they have obvious relevance to several topics discussed in this book. AAT2 provides insight into why compliance-gaining interactions often are experienced as "complex," why speakers may lack fluency when they attempt to seek/resist compliance and also pursue secondary goals, and why speakers may perform differently when they can plan what to say in advance.

AAT2 and Plans/Planning Processes

By emphasizing the fluidity of thought, AAT2 also suggests new questions that can be posed about plans and planning processes. Although influence interactions unfold quickly, Greene (2000) emphasizes that the mental processes underlying talk occur much more rapidly:

> A plan, or perhaps more likely, various of its components, may emerge and fade numerous times as I act to carry out that plan. One moment I have in mind what I intended to do; the next, I'm thinking of my next appointment; then of the mole on the other person's cheek; and then again of my plan, all in the course of the time it takes me to produce a single turn at talk. (p. 145)

Drawing on AAT2, Greene (2000) raises a number of interesting challenges for understanding plans and planning processes. If goals and plans momentarily pass out of conscious awareness, do they continue to exist as cognitive states? If they continue to drive how speakers seek/resist compliance, is the process by which they do so different from that in effect when goals and plans are in conscious awareness? Do people often lose track of their trains of thought (and plans) while seeking or resisting compliance? Are influence messages as coherent as the "planning" metaphor might imply? Planning theorists have emphasized some of these same points, acknowledging that planning involves an opportunistic mix of top-down and bottom-up processes that often are not well coordinated (Hayes-Roth & Hayes-Roth, 1979), and that people may lose track of their plans during interaction due to cognitive inefficiency (Jordan, 1998). Creating more "realistic" characterizations of the processes that give rise to influence messages remains an important challenge for cognitive theories of persuasive message production.

Summary

Cognitive theories of persuasive message production explore the mental processes by which people translate goals and procedural knowledge into influence messages. After presenting an example of the vast range of procedural knowledge that individuals need to produce influence messages, I have described in this chapter the basic assumptions of cognitive theories before going on to explore two cognitive perspectives on persuasive message production: theories of plans and planning processes, and action assembly theory.

Notes

1. Although cognitive models typically distinguish knowledge structures and cognitive processes that operate on those structures, "parallel distributed process" (PDP) models are blurring the distinction between structure and process (Rumelhart, McClelland, & PDP Research Group, 1986). Although PDP models have potential relevance for our understanding of message production (Hewes, 1995a; O'Keefe & Lambert, 1995), they have not generated empirical research on persuasive message production to date, and hence I do not cover them here.

2. Theories of attitude-behavior consistency, such as the theory of reasoned action (Fishbein & Ajzen, 1975) and the theory of planned behavior (Ajzen, 1991), also are potentially relevant to the question of when people will act in ways that are consistent with their preconversational plans. Fishbein and Ajzen's (1975) theory of reasoned action views a person's intention to perform a behavior as the immediate antecedent of behavior. The theory specifies that two factors—attitude toward the act and subjective norms—shape people's behavioral intentions. Research on plans and planning, in contrast, explores how people acquire and utilize the procedural knowledge needed to translate intentions into behavior. Factors that shape intentions also may affect planning processes. For example, shy and lonely individuals may have more negative attitudes or subjective norms than their nonshy/lonely counterparts about date requests. Hence shy/lonely persons may intend to ask people out on dates less frequently than nonshy/lonely persons, but also have less complex date request plans when they do choose to ask for a date (Berger & Bell, 1988). The theory of reasoned action also offers insights into when preconversational plan-behavior consistency is most likely to occur. Specifically, plan-behavior consistency should be highest when preconversational plans and conversational behaviors are measured at the same level of abstraction and in close temporal proximity (Kim & Hunter, 1993).

Ajzen's (1991) theory of planned behavior adds a third factor—perceived control over behavior—to the predictive equation. *Perceived control* refers to a person's judgment about how easy or difficult it will be to perform a behavior. Perceived control can influence behavioral intentions because people who believe that they lack the ability, resources, or opportunity to perform specific behaviors may not form strong intentions to do so. Shy/lonely individuals may be less likely than their nonshy/lonely counterparts to form the intention of making date requests because they doubt whether they can enact any date request plan successfully. Perceived control also can influence behavior directly, independent of intentions. Shy/lonely individuals may be less likely than nonshy/lonely persons actually to make date requests even when they intend to do so. Due to anxiety, shy/lonely individuals may avoid interactions in which date requests could be made. Of course, such anxiety may be caused, in part, by the lack of complex date request plans.

3. Berger and Bell (1988) note that very few people included contingencies in their plans for impressing a new roommate, which may explain why plan contingencies were unrelated to perceived effectiveness in that scenario.

4. Berger and Bell (1988) note that the women in their study reported that they, as a group, were much more likely to be asked than to ask another individual for a date. Thus the lack of significant relationships between loneliness/shyness and perceived plan effectiveness for females in the asking for a date situation may reflect that college-age women, as a group, have limited experience pursuing this social goal.

5. These findings imply that loneliness and shyness should be inversely associated with plan complexity. Although all of the correlations were in the predicted direction, only one of the three negative correlations between shyness and measures of plan complexity in the Berger and Bell (1988) study reached conventional levels of statistical significance, and none of the three correlations between loneliness and plan complexity was significant. At a minimum, these findings suggest that lonely and shy people develop ineffective plans for reasons that go beyond the effects of loneliness and shyness on plan complexity.

6. Cloven and Roloff's (1991) research on "mulling" about conflict can be interpreted as consistent with this first point. *Mulling* means thinking about the nature and causes of an ongoing conflict with another party. Cloven and Roloff asked 97 undergraduates about the degree to which they had mulled over a major conflict with their college roommate. Participants reported on the perceived seriousness of the problem creating the conflict, who was responsible for the problem, how and whether they had talked with their roommate about the problem, what they had thought while mulling, and whether mulling made them feel better. Participants reported that their mulling had included thoughts about the source of the problem, their emotional reaction to the problem, and how the problem might be solved. The latter type of mulling may well have included developing plans for managing the conflict with the roommate. Amount of mulling, in general, was *positively* associated with the degree to which participants thought the problem creating the conflict was serious and the degree to which they blamed the roommate for it. The dysfunctional effects of mulling were especially strong for those participants who reported that they and their roommates had used distributive conflict strategies (e.g., coercion, fault finding) rather than integrative conflict strategies (e.g., cooperation, neutral/positive affect) when discussing the problem. Participants who spent the most time mulling felt the worst about their conflict situation; moreover, they did not believe that mulling had helped them achieve a better understanding of the conflict. Put simply, spending a great deal of time mulling, especially when planning to use distributive conflict strategies, was associated with destructive outcomes.

7. In addition to measuring performance fluency, Knowlton and Berger (1997) treated speech onset latencies as a measure of cognitive load—that is, the degree to which participants had to exert processing capacity to generate/select a second reason on the spot (see Greene, 1988).

8. Although the relationship between preconversational plan complexity and fluency is curvilinear, I suspect that the inflection points in this inverted-U-shaped curve vary depending on prior experience, rehearsal, and task complexity. For example, a speaker who not only plans six arguments but plans the order in which those arguments will be presented may be no less fluent after resistance than a speaker who plans three arguments. People with high levels of prior experience at conversational argument (e.g., academic debaters) also may be no less fluent after preparing six reasons than after preparing three, as they may possess well-learned criteria for choosing among potential reasons that they can apply with little demand on their processing capacity. Berger (1997, p. 41) acknowledges that the magnitude of the inverted-U-shaped relationship between plan complexity and fluency probably varies depending on planning circumstances.

9. Waldron (1990) also manipulated the importance that participants put on the instrumental goal of obtaining information about the partner. Participants in one-half of the dyads were told that they would receive additional extra credit if they obtained the required information from their partners (in reality, all participants received additional extra credit), whereas participants in the remaining dyad did not receive this instruction. Participants in the "high instrumental goal priority" condition, relative to those in the "low goal priority" condition, had a larger percentage of "direct" instrumental plan-oriented cognitions and smaller percentages of "indirect" instrumental and interpersonal plan-oriented cognitions; these participants also used a larger percentage of direct information-seeking strategies during the conversation. Instrumental goal priority did not qualify any of the effects of the "goal complexity" manipulation.

10. As Berger (1997, p. 34) notes, the hierarchy principle assumes that message sources have sufficient motivation to continue pursuing their goals after encountering initial resistance. Berger also recognizes that message sources may make higher-level plan alterations more quickly when their goals are increasingly important to them (p. 35). To date, however, research has focused only on initial plan modifications after resistance has been encountered.

11. This description emphasizes that people's long-term procedural memories change rather than remain static over time. However, this view also creates ambiguities about when multiple nodes have become linked strongly enough to be termed a procedural record, or when multiple records (or some of the nodes within multiple records) have formed unitized assemblies. As

Greene (1997b) acknowledges, one implication of his view is that "the procedural record becomes a memory structure with imprecise boundaries" (p. 156).

12. As Greene (1995b, p. 50) notes, the term *single-goal message* refers to the number of interaction goals that participants were assigned to pursue in an experiment (e.g., "be clear and direct" versus "be clear and direct but also support the other party's face"). A fundamental assumption of action assembly theory is that speakers always pursue a variety of goals, including one or more interaction goals plus discourse goals (e.g., say things relevant to the larger conversation), syntactic goals (e.g., order words in a comprehensible way), and so forth. These latter goals often operate outside of conscious awareness (Kellermann, 1992).

13. After completing this monologue task, participants in both conditions completed questions about their degree of concern with being clear (e.g., "I wanted to make the reasons for my decisions as clear as possible") and with supporting the applicant's face (e.g., "I did not want to hurt the student's feelings"). As expected, participants assigned multiple goals rated supporting the candidate's face as more important than did those assigned only the goal of being clear when communicating with a third party. In addition, six coders, masked to experimental conditions, rated every monologue for the degree to which it showed concern for the applicant's feelings as well as for the degree to which it was direct and clear. Monologues produced by participants in the multiple-goal condition were judged as showing greater concern for the applicant's feelings, but as being no less clear, than monologues produced by those in the single-goal condition.

14. Greene and Lindsey (1989) also measured the proportion of filled pauses ("ah, uh"), by counting the number for each participant and dividing by the length of that participant's monologue. As in other studies, the researchers found no effects for filled pauses. Greene (1995b) argues that filled pauses serve functions other than delaying speech while a message is being assembled.

Part IV

Studying Persuasive Message Production in Context

8

Producing Persuasive Messages in Context

Two Cases

Looking Ahead . . .

People seek and resist compliance as participants in specific relationships, institutions, and cultures. This chapter analyzes how compliance-gaining interactions unfold in two cases, as physically abusive parents respond to perceived misbehavior by their children and as employees seek to influence those at higher levels in their work organizations. For each case, the chapter (a) defines the nature and importance of compliance-gaining interactions in that context, (b) identifies patterns of seeking and resisting compliance that arise in that context, and (c) applies global (i.e., cross-contextual) concepts and theories covered in earlier chapters to explain specific patterns and outcomes. Global theories of persuasive message production offer insights into each case, and particular contexts shape the application and relevance of global theories.

P eople do not seek and resist compliance in a vacuum, but rather as participants in specific relationships embedded within larger institutions and cultures. Yet my primary focus in this volume, up to now, has been on global (i.e., cross-contextual) concepts and theories. My arguments about the significance of message analysis, presented in Chapters 2 and 3, apply broadly. We need to know exactly what we hope to understand about influence interactions in any context of interest, and those message features need to be tied to theories of persuasive message production.

Most of the theories and concepts covered in Chapters 5-7 also are global, in the sense that they offer insights into how people seek and resist compliance across a wide array of age groups, relationships, institutions, and cultures. For example, Dillard's primary and secondary goal framework (Dillard, Segrin, & Harden, 1989; Schrader & Dillard, 1998) assumes that message sources typically are concerned not only about gaining compliance, but, to some degree, about cross-situational concerns such as presenting a positive self-image, maintaining desired relationships, not spending too much time and energy, and keeping arousal within comfortable bounds (see Chapter 5). My colleagues and I have adapted this framework to analyze compliance-gaining interactions involving same- and cross-sex friends as well as romantic partners (Wilson & Kunkel, 2000) in Japan and the United States (Cai & Wilson, 2000). Similarly, Weiner's (1986) attribution theory assumes that message sources, when encountering resistance, make causal judgments about why targets are not willing and/or able to comply with their wishes, and these judgments shape the sources' emotional reactions as well as their motivation to persist in the face of obstacles to compliance (see Chapter 6). Weiner's theory has been applied by researchers seeking to understand, among other things, how students make/ refuse date requests (Folkes, 1982; Paulson & Roloff, 1997), how volunteers attempt to convince others to donate blood (Anderson & Jennings, 1980; Wilson, Levine, Humphreys, & Peters, 1994), and how organizational supervisors respond to poor employee performance (Martinko & Gardner, 1987).

In contrast to these global theories, research on seeking and resisting compliance in a variety of specific contexts has sprung up in many different disciplines. Scholars have developed nominal-level typologies of strategies for seeking and/or resisting compliance in the workplace (Kipnis, Schmidt, & Wilkinson, 1980; Schriesheim & Hinkin, 1990), in the classroom (Kearney & Plax, 1992; Kearney, Plax, Richmond, & McCroskey, 1985), in marriage (Falbo & Peplau, 1980; Witteman & Fitzpatrick, 1986), with prospective sexual partners (Edgar & Fitzpatrick, 1990), and with peers who offer illegal drugs (Alberts, Miller-Rassulo, & Hecht, 1991). Table 8.1 presents examples of research on seeking/ resisting compliance in a wide variety of relationships, institutions, and cultures.

Unfortunately, context-specific literatures typically have developed in isolation from each other. For example, scholars investigating influence strategies in the workplace rarely seem aware of, or at least rarely cite, research on seeking compliance in health care contexts (and vice versa), even though researchers in

Table 8.1   Examples of Research on Seeking/Resisting Compliance in Specific
             Contexts

Relational/Institutional Contexts	Recent Works/Reviews
Families	
How do children's compliance-seeking strategies change as they mature?	Kline & Clinton (1998) Marshall & Levy (1998)
How do physically abusive parents differ from nonmaltreating parents in responding to perceived child misbehavior?	Cerezo (1997) Wilson (1999)
Do husbands and wives use different compliance-seeking strategies?	Sagrestano et al. (1998)
How do satisfied and distressed couples differ in their use of compliance-seeking strategies?	Aida & Falbo (1991) Zvonkovic et al. (1994)
Friendships	
How do adolescents and young adults resist offers from friends to use alcohol and/or illegal drugs?	Harrington (1995) Miller et al. (2000)
Are there ethnic similarities/differences in drug offers and resistance strategies?	Hecht et al. (1997) Miller (1998)
What dilemmas do friends face in giving and receiving advice?	Goldsmith & Fitch (1997)
Romantic relationships	
How do young adults persuade partners to initiate, intensify, or terminate romantic relationships?	Cody et al. (1994)
Are there cultural differences in young adults' use of influence strategies with dating partners?	Belk et al. (1988)
How do young adults persuade sexual partners to use condoms?	Perloff (2001)
How do young adults resist unwanted sexual advances?	Afifi & Lee (2000)
Workplace	
How do employees seek desired changes from coworkers, subordinates, or supervisors?	Barry & Watson (1996) Fairhurst (2001)
Are there cultural and/or gender differences in organizational members' use of influence strategies?	Fu & Yukl (2000) Krone et al. (1994)
How do managers respond to "difficult" employees?	Monroe et al. (1993)
How do employees resist unwanted sexual advances from powerful organizational members?	Jansma (2000)
What compliance-seeking strategies do fund-raisers use?	Abrahams & Bell (1994)

(Continued)

Table 8.1 (Continued)

Relational/Institutional Contexts	Recent Works/Reviews
Health care settings	
What compliance-seeking strategies do physicians use?	Schneider & Beaubien (1996)
What types of requests do patients make of physicians?	Kravitz et al. (1999)
What are the challenges of sustaining compliance for patients coping with chronic illness?	Turk & Rudy (1991)
Do patients expect female and male physicians to use different compliance-seeking strategies?	Klingle & Burgoon (1995)
How do pharmacists confront physicians with concerns about prescribed medications?	Lambert (1996a)
Classroom	
How do elementary, secondary, and college teachers respond to perceived student misbehavior?	Plax & Kearney (1999) Waltman & Burleson (1997a)
How do experienced and novice teachers differ in their use of compliance-seeking strategies?	Plax et al. (1990) Waltman (1995)
How do elementary, secondary, and college students resist teachers' compliance-seeking attempts?	Kearney & Plax (1992)
Are there cultural differences in teachers'/students' use of compliance-seeking/resisting strategies?	Lee et al. (1997) Lu (1997)

both areas are addressing similar issues (e.g., the effects of expert and legitimate power). Many context-specific literatures also have not, until recently, been connected with global theories of persuasive message production. Because of this, many context-specific literatures suffer the same shortcomings as the traditional compliance-gaining literature reviewed in Chapter 4, including a failure to ground typologies theoretically and to develop explanations that account for a wide variety of factors predicting strategy use.

In this chapter, I aim to meld global and context-specific forms of analysis. Rather than providing an abbreviated treatment of every context described in Table 8.1, I offer detailed descriptions of how compliance-gaining interactions unfold in two particular cases. Specifically, I review research on how physically abusive parents respond to perceived misbehavior by their children and on how employees seek to influence those at higher levels in their organizations' hierarchies. I define the nature and importance of compliance-gaining interactions in each case and identify patterns of seeking and resisting compliance that arise in that context. I then apply global theories covered in earlier chapters to account for different patterns and outcomes.

Case 1: Persuasive Message
Production and Child Physical Abuse

CHILD PHYSICAL ABUSE:
DEFINITIONS, PREVALENCE, AND CONSEQUENCES

What Is Child Physical Abuse?

Researchers and policy makers generally recognize four types of child mal-treatment: physical abuse, sexual abuse, neglect of basic needs, and psychological abuse (Barnett, Miller-Perrin, & Perrin, 1997; National Research Council, 1993).[1] Because the etiologies and consequences vary among these types of maltreat-ment, I focus on only one here: child physical abuse, or CPA.

Both legal and research (conceptual) definitions of CPA in the United States have changed over time. The first court case addressing the physical abuse of a child, tried in New York in 1874, had to be prosecuted under laws outlawing cruelty to animals, as no laws prohibited CPA at the time (Barnett et al., 1997). Today there is no uniform law in the United States that defines what constitutes CPA; rather, each state has its own definition. Most definitions emphasize that CPA involves physical injury to a child caused by nonaccidental means. In my home state of Indiana, CPA is said to occur when a "child's physical or mental health is seriously endangered due to injury by the act or omission of the child's parent/guardian/custodian" (Indiana Code, 1997, sec. 31-34-1-2). A child is defined as someone not yet 18 years of age. Most states allow parents to use cor-poral punishment; for example, a subsequent section of the same code states, "This chapter does not . . . limit the right of a parent, guardian, or custodian of a child to use reasonable corporal punishment when disciplining the child" (sec. 31-34-1-15).

Research definitions of CPA often are more inclusive, emphasizing the poten-tial for rather than the actual occurrence of physical injury. In his widely used Conflict Tactics Scales (CTS), Straus (1979; Straus, Hamby, Finkelhor, Moore, & Runyan, 1998) distinguishes between mild and severe forms of violence, where the latter include acts such as "hitting with a fist" or "grabbing around the neck and choking" that have a high potential for injuring a child.[2] Researchers using this measure operationally define CPA as a report by a parent or caretaker of having performed one or more acts of severe violence toward a child in the past year (Straus & Gelles, 1986).

How Common Is CPA?

Estimates of the prevalence of CPA in the United States come from two main sources: reports made to child protective services (CPS) agencies and large-scale surveys of parents. For the past 15 years, the nonprofit organization Prevent

Child Abuse America has conducted an annual survey of rates of reported and substantiated cases of child maltreatment in each of the 50 states. The most recent report indicates that more than 3 million allegations of child maltreatment were made to CPS agencies in 1998 (Wang & Harding, 1998). Upon investigation, approximately one-third of these allegations contained sufficient information to substantiate the reports, resulting in a total of more than 1 million substantiated cases of child maltreatment in 1998, affecting 14 out of every 1,000 children living in the United States. CPA was the second most frequent type of alleged and substantiated type of child maltreatment, with only neglect being more common. In sum, nearly 200,000 cases of physical abuse were substantiated by CPS agencies in 1998.

Data from CPS agencies underestimate the number of physically abused children in the United States, as many episodes are not reported. To address this issue, Straus and his colleagues have conducted a series of nationally representative surveys using the CTS as a measure of parenting practices (Straus & Gelles, 1986; Straus et al., 1998). In the most recent survey, the researchers, in conjunction with the Gallup Organization, conducted a randomly selected telephone survey of 1,000 households, each with at least one child under 18 years of age (Straus et al., 1998). Operationalizing physical abuse as self-reports of one or more acts of severe violence toward a child in the past year, Straus et al. (1998) report a CPA rate of 49 for the 1,000 parents surveyed. This rate, which is 11 times higher than the number of cases substantiated by CPS agencies, produces an estimate of more than 2 million cases of CPA in the United States each year.

What Are the Consequences of CPA?

CPS agencies confirm approximately 1,000 child fatalities due to maltreatment each year, and at least 50% of these deaths are the direct result of physical abuse (Prevent Child Abuse America, 1997; Wang & Harding, 1998). More than three-fourths of the victims each year are under 5 years of age at the time of their deaths. Aside from the immediate risk of injury and death, children who are the victims of physical abuse suffer a host of longer-term psychological and behavioral problems, including low self-esteem, low academic performance, poor interpersonal relationships, and higher risk of aggressive and violent behavior and juvenile delinquency (Kolko, 1992; Malinosky-Rummel & Hansen, 1993).

FACTORS CONTRIBUTING TO CPA

Ecological Perspectives

The etiology of CPA is complex. In a well-known ecological model, Belsky (1980, 1993) argues that factors contributing to CPA reside at multiple levels of analysis, and that factors from different levels interact to determine the occurrence of CPA. At the *individual* level, abusive parents are more likely to have been the victims of abuse during their own childhoods and possess lower self-esteem than do nonmaltreating parents (Milner & Dopke, 1997). At the *family* level, patterns of mother-child interaction differ in physically abusive and nonmaltreating families (see below), and husband-to-wife violence affects how both adults interact with their children (Margolin, John, Ghosh, & Gordis, 1996). At the *community* level, abusive families tend to be more socially isolated than nonmaltreating families (Corse, Schmid, & Trickett, 1990), and rates of CPA covary with rates of violent crime in neighborhoods (Garbarino & Kostelny, 1992). Finally, at the *societal* level, CPA may reflect attitudes about corporal punishment and media portrayals that legitimate violence (Straus, 1994; Tolan & Guerra, 1998).

In the discussion that follows, I focus primarily on individual- and family-level contributors to CPA. Although such a focus does not reveal the total story, it is useful for several reasons. First, episodes of CPA often escalate from parental attempts to correct perceived child misbehavior. Based on an analysis of CPS agency files, Gil (1970) has estimated that 63% of abusive incidents grow out of disciplinary actions by parents or other caretakers. Second, individual- and family-level processes mediate, in part, the effects of factors at the community and societal levels. Factors such as social isolation are associated with parental depression and perceived life stress, which in turn influence parents' emotions and perceptions during parent-child interaction (Milner, 1993, 2000; Wilson & Whipple, 2001). Third, many interventions designed to prevent or treat CPA include parent-education components (Schellenbach, 1998), and research at the individual and family levels may inform such efforts. Given these reasons, I next review research examining interaction between physically abusive mothers and their children.

Mother-Child Interaction

A sizable body of research has explored mother-child communication in families with histories of CPA (see Cerezo, 1997; Wilson, 1999; Wilson & Whipple, 1995). Researchers typically recruit samples of families involved with CPS agencies or treatment programs, as well as comparison families with no documented histories of CPA who are matched sociodemographically (e.g., parent age and education, family structure). Participants in most studies are mothers, along with their children ranging from infancy to adolescence.[3]

This literature can be subdivided into two groups of studies (Wilson & Whipple, 1995). *Microinteraction studies* use observational methods to compare mother-child interaction in abusive and nonmaltreating families. Researchers observe mothers and children, in home or laboratory settings, for periods varying from a single 10-minute session (e.g., Kavanagh, Youngblade, Reid, & Fagot, 1988) to several multiple-hour sessions (e.g., Bousha & Twentyman, 1984). The observers place the mothers' and children's behaviors, every few seconds, into categories describing a range of verbal and nonverbal acts. For example, Reid and his colleagues (Lorber, Felton, & Reid, 1984; Reid, 1978, 1986; Reid, Kavanagh, & Baldwin, 1987) have employed the Family Interaction Coding System, which classifies parent and child behaviors into 29 categories (see Table 8.2). For the purposes of analysis, these categories typically are collapsed into larger groupings, such as the percentages of a mother's and child's overall behaviors that are aversive, neutral, and positive. Sequential analyses, such as a mother's responses to her child's aversive behavior, also are reported in some cases (e.g., Cerezo & D'Ocon, 1999; Lorber et al., 1984).

Studies of parental discipline compare abusive and nonabusive mothers' responses to perceived child misbehavior. Most of these studies analyze mothers' responses based on Hoffman's (1960, 1980) distinction between power-assertive and inductive discipline. *Power assertion* coerces the child into changing his or her behavior, providing no rationale to the child other than the avoidance of punitive consequences. Examples include physical punishment, threats, and verbal aggression. In contrast, *induction* appeals to the child's own internalized standards and judgments. Broadly defined, induction includes any messages in which the parent provides explanations or reasons for requiring behavior change. Examples include providing the child with parent-controlled choices, modeling appropriate behavior, and explaining psychological consequences of the child's actions. Researchers have used several methods in these studies, such as having abusive and comparison mothers provide telephone reports of their discipline practices during the previous 48 hours (e.g., Whipple & Webster-Stratton, 1991) to 12 months (e.g., Straus et al., 1998), keep diaries (e.g., Trickett & Kuczynski, 1986), respond to hypothetical scenarios (e.g., Chilamkurti & Milner, 1993), rate the effectiveness of different practices (e.g., Trickett & Susman, 1988), and interact with their children in the laboratory (e.g., Oldershaw, Walters, & Hall, 1986).

These two sets of studies have revealed several differences in mother-child interactions between families with histories of CPA and those without such histories. Table 8.3 describes and provides examples of eight of these differences. Microinteraction studies show that physically abusive mothers display higher rates of aversive behaviors, lower rates of positive behaviors, and less involvement than do nonmaltreating mothers during interactions with their children. The effect sizes for these differences often are substantial. For example, Bousha and Twentyman (1984) found that abusive mothers on average performed 23 acts of physical aggression and 12 acts of verbal aggression over

Table 8.2   Categories in Reid's Family Interaction Coding Scheme

Aversive Behaviors	Neutral Behaviors	Positive Behaviors
Command negative[a]	Command	Approval
Dependency	Cry	Attention
Destroy	No response	Compliance
Disapproval	Receive	Indulge
High rate	Self-stimulation	Laugh
Humiliate[a]		Normative
Ignore		Physical positive
Negativism		Play
Noncompliance		Talk
Physical negative[a]		Touch
Tease		Work
Whine		
Yell[a]		

SOURCE: From "Social-Interactional Patterns in Families of Abused and Nonabused Children," by J. B. Reid, in C. Zahn-Waxler, E. M. Cummings, & R. Iannotti (Eds.), 1986, *Altruism and Aggression: Biological and Social Origins* (p. 242). Copyright 1986 by Cambridge University Press. Reprinted with permission.

NOTE: For detailed definitions of each behavioral category, see Reid (1978).

a. These four categories are combined into an index of "abusive" parental behavior.

three 90-minute observation periods, whereas nonmaltreating mothers over the same periods performed fewer than 1 act of either type. In contrast, non-maltreating mothers on average performed 18 acts of nonverbal affection and 5 acts of verbal affection, compared with only 5 acts of nonverbal affection and fewer than 1 act of verbal affection by abusive mothers.

Studies of parental discipline paint a similar picture. Physically abusive mothers rely more on power-assertive discipline than do nonmaltreating mothers, who in contrast use inductive discipline more often. In an observational study, Oldershaw et al. (1986) found that abusive mothers on average issued 8 insistent demands and 6 threats per hour, whereas nonmaltreating mothers used fewer than 1 insistent demand or threat during the same time period. Nonmaltreating mothers on average performed 21 acts of reasoning and 3 acts of cooperation (gaining compliance by offering to help) per hour, whereas abusive mothers used fewer than 6 acts of reasoning and 1 act of cooperation.[4]

Aside from differences in behavioral frequency, three studies offer some insights into how abusive mothers differ from nonmaltreating mothers in the duration, pace, and sequencing of their behavior (for definitions of these

Table 8.3   Summary of Differences in Mother-Child Interaction Patterns in Families With and Without Histories of Child Physical Abuse

Interaction Pattern	Behavioral Example	Documenting Studies
1. Abusive mothers engage in less verbal interaction with their children.	Number of speech acts per minute	Burgess & Conger (1978) Schindler & Arkowitz (1986)
2. Abusive mothers display fewer signs of involvement during interaction.	Separate rather than mutual play	Alessandri (1992) Kavanagh et al. (1988)
3. Abusive mothers enact higher rates of aversive behavior.	Humiliation, verbal aggression	Bousha & Twentyman (1984) Herrenkohl et al. (1984)
4. Abusive mothers rely on power-assertive discipline more frequently.	Threats, physical punishment	Oldershaw et al. (1989) Trickett & Kuczynski (1986)
5. Abusive mothers display lower rates of positive behavior.	Praise, approval, nonverbal affection	Bousha & Twentyman (1984) Kavanagh et al. (1988)
6. Abusive mothers adapt less to the situation or type of child misbehavior.	Using power assertion for all misbehaviors	Alessandri (1992) Trickett & Kuczynski (1986)
7. Abusive mothers display noncontingent responses to positive child behavior.	Scolding after a child complies	Cerezo et al. (1996) Oldershaw et al. (1986)
8. Abusive mothers reciprocate others' aversive behavior for longer time periods.	Sequences > 18 seconds	Lorber et al. (1984) Reid (1986)

terms, see Chapter 3). Trickett and Kuczynski (1986) asked physically abusive ($n = 20$) and matched-comparison ($n = 20$) mothers, each of whom had at least one child from 4 to 11 years old, to keep diaries of discipline episodes for five consecutive days. Diary entries were coded for types of child misbehavior (e.g., noncompliance, high arousal behavior), maternal discipline response (power-assertive and inductive techniques), and maternal emotional reaction (e.g., anger, sadness). Physically abusive mothers relied primarily on power-assertive discipline regardless of how their children misbehaved, whereas comparison mothers used power-assertive and inductive techniques in different combinations depending on how their children misbehaved. Abusive, relative to comparison, mothers also were twice as likely to report being angered by child misbehavior, and abusive mothers also reported using more severe forms of physical discipline (e.g., striking a child with an object).

Oldershaw et al. (1986) compared 10 physically abusive and 10 comparison mothers as each completed a 45-minute interaction with one of her children who was from 2 to 4 years old. The researchers analyzed command/control sequences, which began each time a mother issued a request or command and ended when the child complied or the mother stopped seeking compliance. Oldershaw et al. documented several differences in how these episodes unfolded, including the following: (a) Abusive mothers issued a larger percentage (88%) of their initial requests with no accompanying rationale than did comparison mothers (64%); (b) abusive mothers issued most (90%) of their initial requests in a neutral tone of voice, whereas comparison mothers issued the majority (51%) with positive affect; (c) abused children (47%) were less likely than comparison children (72%) to comply immediately with their mothers' requests (see note 4); (d) following child noncompliance, abusive mothers were more likely than comparison mothers to repeat the exact same command and control strategy again; (e) when their children complied, abusive mothers were as likely to criticize (i.e., "It's about time you did that") as to praise their children in the immediate next turn, whereas comparison mothers invariably praised their children; (f) abusive mothers were more likely than comparison mothers to continue seeking compliance even after their children had complied, suggesting that they failed to notice child compliance more often.

Finally, Reid (1986), in a reanalysis of data from three previous studies, compared physically abusive mothers' ($n = 28$) home interactions with those of nonabusive mothers who had children with behavior management problems ($n = 53$) and matched-comparison nonabusive mothers who were not distressed ($n = 48$). Consistent with the findings of previous studies (see Table 8.3), abusive mothers, relative to the other two groups, displayed higher rates of aversive behaviors as well as "abusive" or highly aversive behaviors per minute (see Table 8.2). In addition, Reid analyzed the percentage of episodes in which the duration of a mother's aversive behavior was short (1-11 seconds), medium (12-23 seconds), and long (more than 23 seconds). Although long episodes were infrequent for all three groups, physically abusive mothers as well as mothers with conduct-disordered children were far more likely to enact long episodes relative to nondistressed mothers. When long episodes did occur, physically abusive mothers as well as mothers with conduct-disordered children also escalated the intensity of their aversive behaviors more than did comparison mothers; specifically, 35% of the aversive behaviors performed by physically abusive mothers during long episodes were "abusive," compared with only 23% for nondistressed mothers.

To summarize, research on mother-child interaction has documented clear differences in how physically abusive and nonmaltreating mothers seek their children's compliance. Physically abusive mothers display more aversive behaviors, and the duration and pace of their behaviors also differ from those of nonmaltreating mothers. In particular, abusive mothers seem to have difficulty shutting down escalating cycles of aversive behavior with their children. Physically abusive mothers also rely heavily on power-assertive discipline in most cases, whereas nonmaltreating mothers mix power-assertive and inductive techniques in different ways depending on how their children have misbehaved. Nonmaltreating mothers also consistently reinforce their children's compliance, whereas abusive mothers respond inconsistently to positive child behavior.

Studies of mother-child interaction patterns associated with CPA have avoided many of the pitfalls that befell the traditional compliance-gaining literature (see Chapters 2 and 4). Although researchers have surveyed nationally representative samples of parents about their child-rearing practices during the previous 6 months (e.g., Jackson et al., 1999; Straus et al., 1998) and have asked smaller convenience samples of mothers to keep diaries (e.g., Trickett & Kuczynski, 1986) and respond to hypothetical scenarios (e.g., Chilamkurti & Milner, 1993; Wilson & Whipple, 2001), these self-report methods have been supplemented by a sizable body of studies in which researchers have directly observed mother-child interactions in physically abusive and matched-comparison families. Although researchers often have used nominal-level typologies of mother and child behaviors (e.g., Reid, 1986) or maternal disciplinary responses (e.g., Oldershaw et al., 1986), these typologies have been organized conceptually into larger categories and/or dimensions, such as the frequency, duration, pace, and sequencing of mother's and child's aversive behavior or the degree to which a mother relies on a variety of disciplinary strategies, rather than only power-assertive strategies, over time and/or across varied child misbehavior. Thus these studies allow more straightforward inferences about exactly how physically abusive mothers' behaviors during interactions with their children differ from those of nonmaltreating mothers.

Theories of persuasive message production suggest several potential explanations for these differences. In the subsection that follows, I apply two theories, discussed in Chapters 6 and 7, that can help us understand and explain patterns of seeking and resisting compliance associated with CPA: Weiner's (1986) attributional theory of emotion and motivation, and Berger's (1997) and Waldron's (1997) work on plans and planning processes.

EXPLAINING PATTERNS OF SEEKING/RESISTING
COMPLIANCE ASSOCIATED WITH CPA

Attribution Theories

According to Weiner (1986), message sources make judgments about the degree to which the causes for a target's noncompliance are internal, stable, and controllable, and these judgments in turn affect sources' emotional reactions as well as persistence at seeking compliance (see Chapter 6). Studies have documented several differences in how physically abusive and matched-comparison mothers make attributions about their children and themselves, and these findings have relevance for attempts to understand mothers' discipline responses.

First, physically abusive mothers are more likely than nonmaltreating mothers to attribute their children's negative behaviors, such as noncompliance, to internal and stable causes. Larrance and Twentyman (1983) showed physically abusive, neglectful, and comparison mothers ($n = 10$ per group) pictures of their children performing negative (e.g., drawing on a wall with crayons) and positive (e.g., completing a puzzle) behaviors, and then asked each mother about causes for her child's behavior. Responses were coded for the degree to which causes were internal and stable. Physically abusive mothers, relative to comparison mothers, more often attributed their children's negative behaviors to internal and stable causes, seeing the behaviors as reflective of the children's personalities. Abusive mothers also were more likely to discount their children's positive behaviors by attributing them to external and unstable causes. Dopke and Milner (2000) report similar findings for mothers scoring high versus low on the Child Abuse Potential (CAP) Inventory.[5] After imagining that their children repeatedly had failed to comply, high-risk mothers, in comparison with low-risk mothers, attributed their children's actions more to internal ($p = .065$), stable, and global causes.

Second, physically abusive mothers are more likely to view their children, rather than themselves, as being in control of negative interactions. Bugental and her colleagues (Bugental, Blue, & Cruzcosa, 1989; Bugental & Shennum, 1984) developed the Parent Attribution Test to assess the degree to which parents view themselves and/or their children as having control over interactions. Respondents are given brief scenarios with either positive or negative outcomes and are asked to rate the importance of multiple factors in causing each outcome. Rated factors vary in terms of locus (within the parent or child) and controllability (controllable by the parent or child, not controllable by either). From these ratings, four scores can be computed: (a) high versus low self-control for positive interactions, (b) high versus low self-control for negative interactions, (c) high versus low child-control for positive interactions, and (d) high versus low child-control for negative interactions. Bugental et al.

(1989) show that physically abusive mothers, compared with nonmaltreating mothers, perceive greater child control for interactions with negative outcomes. Bradley and Peters (1991) as well as Dopke and Milner (2000) report that physically abusive and high-risk mothers perceive less self-control for negative interactions with their children than do nonmaltreating and low-risk mothers. Bradley and Peters also found that abusive mothers gave their children less credit for positive interactions than did mothers in two of three different comparison groups.

Third, physically abusive mothers are more likely than nonmaltreating mothers to view negative behaviors by their children as intentional attempts to upset them. Bauer and Twentyman (1985) presented abusive, neglectful, and matched-comparison ($n = 12$ per group) mothers with a series of brief tape-recorded hypothetical scenarios in which their children had misbehaved and/or been injured. The sound of a child crying also was played during each scenario. Mothers rated their level of annoyance continually as they listened. At the end of each scenario, mothers rated the degree to which "the child did that to annoy me." Abusive mothers attributed greater intent to their children than did the other two groups in all scenarios involving misbehavior. Dopke and Milner (2000) report similar findings for mothers scoring high versus low on the CAP Inventory.

These findings regarding how physically abusive and comparison mothers make discrepant attributions suggest several explanations for differences in how mothers in the two groups seek their children's compliance. First, abusive mothers' attributions lead them to experience more intense negative affect. Parents in general are most likely to feel angry when they perceive that their children have control over and intend their negative acts, and hence these acts reflect stable, general features of the children's personalities (Dix, 1991; Weiner, 1986). Abusive mothers tend to make just these sorts of attributions when their children misbehave, which accounts for why they report feeling greater anger (Reid, 1986; Trickett & Kuczynski, 1986) and annoyance (Bauer & Twentyman, 1985). As their anger and annoyance about child misbehavior increase, parents tend to rely more heavily on power-assertive discipline (Dix, 1991; Dix, Ruble, & Zambarano, 1989).

Second, abusive mothers' attributions about themselves may promote feelings of helplessness that lead to violent responses (Wilson & Sabee, in press). Abusive mothers perceive that it is their children, and not themselves, who drive unpleasant mother-child interactions; hence these mothers may come to believe that using inductive discipline (reasoning, bargaining) will have little effect on their children's behavior. Given such feelings of powerlessness, abusive mothers may monitor their children more closely for signs of resistance (Bugental & Lewis, 1999) and then increase the intensity of their own aversive behavior, and use extreme forms of physical discipline, in ill-fated attempts to "regain control" and "show who's the boss" (Reid, 1986).

Third, abusive mothers' attributions reflect life events that make them less sensitive to circumstances surrounding their children's behavior. Abusive mothers consistently report higher levels of depression and perceived life stress than do nonmaltreating mothers matched for socioeconomic status (Milner & Dopke, 1997; Whipple & Webster-Stratton, 1991). Depression and stress are thought to lead abusive mothers to rely more heavily on "automatic" or "theory-driven" processing during mother-child interaction in ways that bias their attributions (Milner, 1993, 2000). Consistent with this reasoning, Milner and Foody (1994) show that women at high risk for child physical abuse are less likely than low-risk women to alter their attributions for child misbehavior in light of mitigating information. In a study of mothers participating in a child abuse prevention program, Wilson and Whipple (2001) found that as depression increased, participants were less likely to alter judgments about whether their children were old enough to know better across different types of misbehavior. Hence abusive mothers, due to depression and/or life stress, may rely primarily on power assertive discipline regardless of how their children misbehave because their attributions fail to take into account circumstances surrounding the children's actions.

Based on these findings, programs designed to prevent the (re)occurrence of child physical abuse often include material on attributional biases and cognitive restructuring in their parent-education curricula (Goddard & Miller, 1993). That said, it is important to remember that child physical abuse arises from multiple causes, and attributions for child noncompliance are unlikely to account for all of the differences in mother-child interaction found between physically abusive and nonmaltreating families. As Bauer and Twentyman (1985) conclude:

> Although the present study highlights the fact that attributional differences occur between groups of mothers, it does not address the question of whether faulty attributional styles need to be combined with deficits in parenting skills, increased impulsivity, or heightened stress levels—to mention just a few variables—before abuse occurs. (p. 342)

Research on plans and planning processes sheds light on other factors that also may help explain patterns of mother-child interaction in families with histories of CPA.

Theories of Plans/Planning

Plans, as you will recall from Chapter 7, are mental representations of actions necessary for overcoming obstacles and achieving goals, whereas planning comprises the psychological and communication processes involved in selecting, implementing, monitoring, and adapting plans. Physically abusive mothers may differ from nonmaltreating mothers both in terms of the plans for regulating perceived child misbehavior that they bring to interaction and in their on-line planning during interaction itself (Wilson, 2000).

Physically abusive parents often are characterized as lacking problem-solving skills (see Milner, 2000), which, in part, may be a reflection of their lack of complex and specific plans for responding to various forms of child misbehavior. To my knowledge, no study has directly compared the preconversational plans of physically abusive and matched-comparison parents, but existing evidence is suggestive. For example, Beatty, Burant, Dobos, and Rudd (1996) have shown that fathers' level of trait verbal aggressiveness is inversely associated with the perceived appropriateness and effectiveness of their reported plans for regulating perceived child misbehavior, especially following child resistance. Trait verbal aggressiveness also has been positively associated with mothers' level of risk for child physical abuse (Wilson et al., 2001) as well with the occurrence of violence between adult partners (Sabourin, Infante, & Rudd, 1993).

Differences in plan complexity and specificity suggest one explanation for some findings about mother-child interaction in families with histories of CPA. Specifically, abusive mothers, relative to nonmaltreating mothers, may issue a larger percentage of requests without any stated rationale, may rely primarily on power-assertion regardless of how their children misbehave, and may be less successful at gaining their children's compliance precisely because they possess simple plans with few alternatives to spanking or threats of punishment. Although this claim seems plausible, it also is clear that differences in preconversational plan complexity cannot fully explain mother-child interaction patterns in families with histories of CPA. How can plan complexity, for instance, explain why physically abusive mothers sometimes criticize their children even though the children have just complied with their requests, or seemingly fail to notice when their children do comply?

In a recent essay, I have suggested three other possible links between planning processes and CPA (Wilson, 2000). First, physically abusive mothers may have less confidence than nonmaltreating mothers that complex plans will lead to goal attainment. More specifically, abusive mothers may not believe that any planned action other than physical discipline will successfully terminate perceived child misbehavior. Physically abusive and high-risk parents believe in the value of physical punishment more than do nonmaltreating and low-risk parents (Crouch & Behl, 2001; Jackson et al., 1999; Wilson & Whipple, 2001) and evaluate power-assertive techniques as more appropriate and inductive techniques as less effective at gaining children's compliance (Chilamkurti & Milner, 1993; Trickett & Susman, 1988). Plan confidence, in turn, has been linked with the likelihood that persons actually will carry out their preconversational plans during interaction (Jordan, 1998; see Chapter 7). Thus physically abusive mothers, even when they do learn alternatives to physical discipline, may not use these new alternatives or may give up on them quickly in the face of child resistance if they lack confidence in either the efficacy of these planned alternatives or their own ability to use them effectively.

Second, physically abusive and nonmaltreating mothers may differ in the focus of their attention during interactions with their children. Physically abusive mothers may spend more time, on a moment-by-moment basis, making negative assessments of themselves and/or their children during everyday interactions, whereas comparison mothers may spend more time thinking about goals and plans. Alternatively, physically abusive and comparison mothers may spend equivalent amounts of time thinking about goals and plans, but the character of their plan-related thoughts (e.g., specificity, valence) may differ. Family violence studies, with rare exception (e.g., Bauer & Twentyman, 1985; Bugental et al., 1993), have not used methods such as stimulated recall to study mothers' on-line thoughts and feelings. Research using college student samples is at least suggestive. Several studies have shown that students who are perceived by others as less competent in achieving social goals report fewer and less specific thoughts about goals and plans during interaction (e.g., Cegala & Waldron, 1992; Waldron, Caughlin, & Jackson, 1995; see Chapter 7). Differences in on-line planning may help explain some patterns of mother-child interaction in abusive families. Physically abusive mothers may display noncontingent thoughts (e.g., scolding a child who has just complied) because their most salient thoughts at the time are negative evaluations of the children rather than ways of pursuing their goals and plans. Abusive mothers also may be less successful than comparison mothers at gaining their children's compliance, in part, because their focus of attention tends to be reactive and evaluative rather than anticipatory and planful.

A third possible link is that physically abusive mothers, upon encountering child resistance, may be less likely than comparison mothers to alter their preconversational plans. As you will recall, Berger (1997) has proposed the hierarchy principle, which states that when people encounter obstacles to their goals, their first response is likely to be low-level rather than high-level alterations to their preconversational plans. High-level changes are cognitively taxing and hence, left to their own devices, people often initially make low-level changes (e.g., speaking louder) even in cases where it should be apparent that higher-level changes are needed (Berger & diBattista, 1993). My suggestion here is that physically abusive mothers, perhaps due to anger and/or perceived life stress, may be especially susceptible to the hierarchy principle; that is, they may continue making only low-level plan adjustments even when it should be apparent that their current plans are unlikely to succeed. Nonmaltreating mothers, in contrast, may interpret continued child resistance as a sign that they need to "try something different." The idea that abusive mothers are more susceptible to the hierarchy principle may explain why it is that they are more likely than comparison mothers to repeat the exact same command and control strategies again after encountering child resistance (Oldershaw et al., 1986). The same idea also may help explain why abusive mothers have difficulty breaking out of escalating cycles of reciprocated aversive behaviors with their children (Reid, 1986).

To summarize the discussion of this first case: Studies of mother-child interaction reveal many differences in how physically abusive versus nonmaltreating mothers seek their children's compliance. Specifically, compared with nonmaltreating mothers, abusive mothers (a) display more aversive and fewer positive behaviors, (b) rely primarily on power-assertive discipline rather than on a mix of power assertion and induction depending on how their children misbehave, (c) fail to notice and reinforce child compliance consistently, and (d) escalate the intensity of their aversive behaviors more when faced with repeated child noncompliance. I have explored how attribution and planning theories help account for such findings. To date, more research has been concerned with attributions in families with histories of CPA than has examined plans and planning processes in such families, but both theories can help us understand, and hopefully respond to, CPA.

In a second set of context-specific studies, researchers have investigated the strategies that employees use to seek compliance from their supervisors or superiors in the workplace. Although this work is far removed from that just reviewed, the sizable literature on upward influence in organizations also can be informed by general theories of persuasive message production.

Case 2: Persuasive Message Production and Upward Influence in Organizations

UPWARD INFLUENCE: DEFINITION, FREQUENCY, AND CONSEQUENCES

Influence is an inevitable and important part of organizational life. Organizational members exert influence in upward, lateral, and downward directions in pursuit of personal and organizational goals (Kipnis et al., 1980; Yukl, Guinan, & Sottolano, 1995). For example, managers may attempt to convince those at higher levels to support new work projects or procedures, cajole managers from other units to share resources needed for important assignments, and persuade the employees they supervise to take on new responsibilities.

My focus in this section is upward influence, or "attempts to influence someone higher in the formal hierarchy of authority in the organization" (Porter, Allen, & Angle, 1981, p. 111). Several reviews of research on how leaders and managers seek compliance in a "downward direction" have been published (e.g., Barry & Watson, 1996; Fairhurst, 2001; Hellweg, Geist, Jorgensen, & White-Mills, 1990); I will discuss such work only when it sheds comparative light on upward influence.

Studies of upward influence were relatively few until about 20 years ago, but since that time there has been an explosion of research on how "followers, members, and protégés" seek compliance from those at higher levels in their organizations (Waldron, 1999). Scholarly interest in the topic has grown, in part, due to organizational and societal trends that have created greater opportunities for upward influence. According to Waldron (1999), such trends include a shift toward decentralized, team-based organizing as well as changing conceptions of leadership that emphasize the essential role of followers.

Waldron (1999) argues that societal trends also have made upward influence more important for individuals and organizations. Corporate downsizing in the United States, as well as the changing nature of social contracts between organizations and their employees (Buzzanell, 2000), have made strategic communication such as upward influence vital to employee success. Employees' use of upward influence strategies predicts their salary attainment and job stress, as well as affects their superiors' performance evaluations and promotability assessments of them, even after factors such as length of employment and type of organization are statistically controlled (e.g., Dreher, Dougherty, & Whitely, 1989; Kipnis & Schmidt, 1988; Wayne, Liden, Graf, & Ferris, 1997).

Despite the importance of upward influence in contemporary organizations, attempting it still can be a risky undertaking. Upward influence involves seeking compliance from a target who has greater formal authority, and often greater power of several different types (e.g., expertise, connections to powerful others), than oneself. Porter et al. (1981) explain, "When considering upward influence, it is critical to note that this salient feature—the fact that the person attempting to exercise influence cannot rely on formal authority—results in a situation that is distinctly different from that of downward influence" (p. 111).

Power differences affect both how upward influence attempts are interpreted as well as the consequences of such interpretations. According to Brown and Levinson's (1987) politeness theory, seeking a target's compliance always creates some degree of constraint on the target's autonomy (or "negative face"), but this threat is magnified in cases such as upward influence, where the target possesses greater power than the message source (see Chapter 6). Seeking compliance also creates other potential threats to both the source's and the target's desire for approval (or "positive face"), depending on the reason or goal underlying the request (Cai & Wilson, 2000; Wilson, Aleman, & Leatham, 1998; Wilson, Anastasiou, Kim, Aleman, & Oetzel, 2000; Wilson & Kunkel, 2000). Because of this, the potential exists for the more powerful target, and/or other actors within the organization, to perceive that an employee is exerting upward influence for inappropriate reasons or via inappropriate means. Such perceptions may result not only in resistance, but in long-term costs to the employee (Porter et al., 1981). In other words, "The exertion of influence by followers remains a strategic, complicated, and sometimes threatening activity" (Waldron, 1999, p. 252).

Having defined and described the importance of upward influence in organizations, I now turn to a description and evaluation of the existing literature. The majority of studies to date have addressed one of two issues: (a) How should upward influence behaviors by employees be described? and (b) What factors predict an employee's choice of upward influence behaviors?

TYPOLOGIES OF UPWARD INFLUENCE STRATEGIES

Upward influence behaviors can be described in multiple ways. For example, we might look at the strategies employees use when attempting to exert upward influence, the themes that pervade their talk during such episodes, the dimensions along which their upward influence behaviors vary, and the sequential patterns that occur during such episodes (see Chapters 2 and 3). Similar to the traditional compliance-gaining literature (see Chapter 4), the most common approach has been to conceptualize upward influence behaviors as "strategies" that are grouped into nominal-level typologies.[6] Studies by Kipnis et al. (1980), Schriesheim and Hinkin (1990), and Yukl and Falbe (1990; Yukl, Falbe, & Youn, 1993) have been important in this regard.

In a groundbreaking article, Kipnis et al. (1980) reported two studies investigating "the [strategies] of influence used by people at work when attempting to change the behavior of their superiors, co-workers, and subordinates" (p. 441). Participants in the first study, 165 managers in engineering, technical, and professional occupations who also were enrolled part-time in graduate business school courses, described episodes in which they had succeeded in getting their bosses, coworkers, or subordinates to do something that they wanted. In the description of each episode, the participant recounted what he or she wanted from the target, what the participant did or said, whether or not the target resisted, and how the participant responded if resistance occurred. Kipnis et al. analyzed the goal being sought from the target person as well as the strategies used to achieve this goal.

Drawing on these open-ended data, Kipnis et al. wrote 58 questionnaire items describing various upward influence behaviors. Sample items included "Demanded that he or she do what I requested," "Acted very humbly to him or her while making the request," "Wrote a detailed plan that justified my ideas," and "Reminded him or her of past favors that I did for them." They administered this questionnaire to a new sample of 754 employees enrolled part-time in graduate business classes. Participants described "how frequently during the past six months they had used each item" to influence their bosses, coworkers, or subordinates, using a scale ranging from 1 = *never use this tactic to influence him/her* to 5 = *usually use this tactic to influence him/her* (p. 443). Participants also rated how frequently each of five goals identified in Study 1 had motivated them to seek compliance from the same target person.

Kipnis et al. (1980) conducted a factor analysis on reports of how frequently the behavior in each item had been used, both for the entire sample and separately for each direction of influence. They then grouped the 58 items into eight organizational influence strategies:[7]

1. *Rationality* (4 items): for example, explaining reasons for request, writing a detailed plan to justify ideas

2. *Assertiveness* (5 items): for example, demanding, ordering, setting deadlines, having a showdown

3. *Ingratiation* (6 items): for example, acting humble, making target feel important, praising target

4. *Exchange* (5 items): for example, offering reciprocal favors, reminding the target of past favors, offering to help if target will comply

5. *Coalitions* (2 items): obtaining the support of coworkers or subordinates, having target come to a formal conference where request is made

6. *Upward appeal* (4 items): for example, making a formal appeal to others at higher levels in the organization, obtaining informal support of "higher-ups"

7. *Sanctions* (5 items): for example, giving target no pay raise, threatening target's job security

8. *Blocking* (3 items): for example, threatening to notify an outside agency or to engage in a work slowdown if target doesn't comply

Kipnis et al.'s (1980) findings regarding how frequently each influence strategy had been used over the past 6 months, broken out by whether participants were reporting on upward, lateral, or downward influence, are shown in Table 8.4. Reported use for every strategy except coalitions varied significantly depending on direction of influence.[8] A comparison of rank orderings for the strategies, however, reveals a good deal of similarity across the three directions. Rationality is the most frequently reported influence strategy for upward, lateral, and downward influence attempts, and assertiveness is the only strategy for which rank orderings appear to vary substantially across the three directions of influence (see Table 8.4).

Table 8.4   Rated Frequency of Use for Kipnis et al.'s (1980) Organizational
                  Influence Strategies

| Influence Strategy[a] | Direction of Influence | | |
	Upward (n = 225)	Lateral (n = 285)	Downward (n = 244)
Rationality	3.68 (1)	3.44 (1)	3.51 (1)
Assertiveness	1.39 (5)	1.61 (6)	2.41 (3)
Ingratiation	2.42 (2)	2.68 (2)	2.65 (2)
Exchange	1.71 (4)	2.02 (4)	1.88 (5)
Coalitions	2.27 (3)	2.15 (3)	2.19 (4)
Upward appeal	1.36 (6)	1.71 (5)	1.76 (6)
Blocking	1.10 (7)	1.17 (7)	1.10 (7)
Sanctions	1.03 (8)	1.05 (8)	1.28 (8)

SOURCE: From "Intraorganizational Influence Tactics: Explorations in Getting One's Way," by D. Kipnis, S. M. Schmidt, & I. Wilkinson, 1980, *Journal of Applied Psychology, 65,* p. 449. Copyright 1980 by the American Psychological Association. Adapted with permission.

NOTE: Numbers outside parentheses are mean frequency scores (divided by the number of items tapping each strategy); numbers within parentheses are rank orderings for strategy usage.

a. Respondents rated how frequently they had used each strategy to influence their bosses, coworkers, or subordinates during the past 6 months (1 = *never use this tactic to influence him/her;* 5 = *usually use this tactic to influence him/her*).

Focusing specifically on upward influence, Schriesheim and Hinkin (1990) identified several problems with Kipnis et al.'s (1980) influence strategy scale, including that (a) several items appear to lack content validity (e.g., they are worded in such a way that they plausibly illustrate two different strategies), (b) subsequent factor analyses (e.g., Erez & Rim, 1982; Erez, Rim, & Keider, 1986) failed to replicate the finding of eight strategies, and (c) two strategies (blocking, sanctions) appear to be used infrequently to exert upward influence.[9] Schriesheim and Hinkin thus undertook four studies "to explore the quality of the Kipnis et al. scales and to improve on them" (p. 248). Across these four studies, undergraduate business and graduate MBA students were asked either to (a) rate the degree to which each of the Kipnis et al. items were clear examples of the intended strategy (and only the intended strategy) or (b) report how frequently they had used the behavior in each item with their bosses during the past 6 months. Frequency-of-use data were subjected to several types of factor analysis (exploratory and confirmatory) with multiple samples. Schriesheim and Hinkin discarded items lacking content validity in these tests and wrote new items for strategies with few valid items. Based on these analyses, they

Table 8.5   Schriesheim and Hinkin's (1990) Upward Influence Scale

---

Ingratiation strategies

   1. Acted very humbly to him or her while making the request.

   2. Acted in a friendly manner prior to asking for what I wanted.

   3. Made him or her feel good about me before making my request.

Exchange strategies

   4. Reminded him or her of past favors that I did for him or her.

   5. Offered an exchange (e.g., if you do this for me, I will do something for you).

   6. Offered to make a personal sacrifice if he or she would do what I wanted (e.g., work late, work harder, do his or her share of the work, etc.).

Rationality strategies

   7. Used logic to convince him or her.

   8. Explained the reasons for my request.

   9. Presented him or her with information in support of my point of view.

Assertiveness strategies

   10. Had a showdown in which I confronted him or her face-to-face.

   11. Expressed my anger verbally.

   12. Used a forceful manner; tried such things as demands, the setting of deadlines, and the expression of strong emotion.

Upward appeal strategies

   13. Obtained the informal support of higher-ups.

   14. Made a formal appeal to higher levels to back up my request.

   15. Relied on the chain of command—on people higher up in the organization who have power over him or her.

Coalition strategies

   16. Obtained the support of coworkers to back up my request.

   17. Obtained the support of my subordinates to back up my request.

   18. Mobilized other people in the organization to help me in influencing him or her.

SOURCE: From "Influence Tactics Used by Subordinates: A Theoretical and Empirical Analysis and Refinement of the Kipnis, Schmidt, and Wilkinson Subscales," by C. A. Schriesheim & T. R. Hinkin, 1990, *Journal of Applied Psychology, 75*, pp. 250, 255. Copyright 1990 by the American Psychological Association. Adapted with permission.

NOTE: Respondents rated how frequently they had used each strategy to influence their bosses, coworkers, or subordinates during the past 6 months (1 = *never use this tactic to influence him/her;* 5 = *usually use this tactic to influence him/her*).

settled on an 18-item upward influence scale, with 3 items each measuring ingratiation strategies, exchange strategies, rationality strategies, assertiveness strategies, upward appeal strategies, and coalition strategies (see Table 8.5).

Yukl and his colleagues also have made important adjustments and extensions to Kipnis et al.'s (1980) typology (Fu & Yukl, 2000; Yukl & Falbe, 1990; Yukl et al., 1993, 1995). Specifically, these researchers have (a) supplemented Kipnis et al.'s list of influence strategies, (b) assessed message targets' as well as sources' perceptions of strategy use, and (c) employed a variety of methods to assess strategy use.

In their initial work, Yukl and Falbe (1990) highlighted several potential problems with Kipnis et al.'s (1980) scales, including that Kipnis et al.'s typology does not include several options suggested by recent leadership theories such as transformational leadership (see Fairhurst, 2001) and that their measure of influence goals does not include several objectives suggested by studies on the nature of managerial work. Yukl and Falbe retained six of the eight Kipnis et al. strategies (dropping blocking and sanctions) and added two new strategies (consultation and inspirational appeals; see Table 8.6 for definitions). They created four or five items to assess each of the two new influence strategies and rewrote many items Kipnis et al. originally had developed to measure the other six strategies. They also expanded Kipnis et al.'s list of influence goals from five to eight objectives.

Yukl and Falbe (1990) conducted two studies comparing reports of organizational influence goals and strategies by message sources (agents) and targets. In the first study, each of 197 evening MBA students rated how frequently he or she had used each of the eight organizational influence strategies during the preceding year with his or her boss, a coworker, or a subordinate with whom the participant interacted regularly. Each also rated how frequently he or she had pursued each of the eight influence goals with the same target. In the second study, each participant in a different sample of 237 evening MBA students rated how frequently his or her boss, a coworker, or a subordinate had used each of the eight influence strategies and pursued each of the eight influence goals with the participant. Rank orderings for rated use of the eight influence strategies, broken out by perspective (message source versus target) and direction of influence (upward, lateral, and downward) are shown in Table 8.7.

Several of the findings displayed in Table 8.7 merit note. First, the two new strategies (consultation and inspirational appeals) were rated as being used frequently by both message sources and targets. Second, the strategy of "rational persuasion" also was rated as being used frequently, as it was in the Kipnis et al. (1980) study. Third, and more generally, reports of strategy use by both message sources and targets corresponded highly across all three directions of influence. Although direction of the influence attempt had some effect on ratings of strategy use (especially for assertiveness), Yukl and Falbe (1990) conclude, "The big story is not directional differences but rather the discovery that some [strategies] are used more than others, regardless of whether the target is a subordinate, peer, or superior" (p. 139).

Table 8.6   Yukl and Falbe's (1990) Typology of Organizational Influence
             Strategies

Strategy	Definition
Pressure (assertiveness)	The person uses demands, threats, or intimidation to convince you to comply with a request or to support a proposal.
Upward appeal	The person seeks to persuade you that the request is approved by higher management, or appeals to higher management for assistance in gaining your compliance with the request.
Exchange	The person makes an explicit or implicit promise that you will receive rewards or tangible benefits if you comply with a request or support a proposal, or reminds you of a prior favor to be reciprocated.
Coalition	The person seeks the aid of others to persuade you to do something or uses the support of others as an argument for you to agree also.
Ingratiation	The person seeks to get you in a good mood or to think favorably of him or her before asking you to do something.
Rational persuasion (rationality)	The person uses logical arguments and factual evidence to persuade you that a proposal or request is viable and likely to result in the attainment of task objectives.
Inspirational appeals	The person makes an emotional request or proposal that arouses enthusiasm by appealing to your values and ideals, or by increasing your confidence that you can do it.
Consultation	The person seeks your participation in making a decision or planning how to implement a proposed policy, strategy, or change.

SOURCE: From "Influence Tactics and Objectives in Upward, Downward, and Lateral Influence Attempts," by G. Yukl & C. M. Falbe, 1990, *Journal of Applied Psychology*, 75, p. 133. Copyright 1990 by the American Psychological Association. Reprinted with permission.

In a follow-up study, Yukl et al. (1993) employed a critical incident method to investigate the use of organizational influence strategies. Yukl et al. asserted that the technique of asking employees to rate their use of influence strategies in the recent past (6 months or year) by responding to a preformulated list, as Kipnis et al. (1980) and many subsequent researchers had done, has several potential limitations. Reminiscent of concerns about "item desirability bias" raised in regard to traditional compliance-gaining research (see Chapter 4), Yukl et al. (1993) note, "It is possible that both agents (sources) and targets

Table 8.7   Rank Orderings for Rated Use of Yukl and Falbe's (1990)
              Organizational Influence Strategies

Influence Strategy[a]	Upward		Lateral		Downward	
	Sources	Targets	Sources	Targets	Sources	Targets
Consultation	1	1	1	1	2	1
Rational persuasion	2	2	2	2	1	2
Inspirational appeals	3	3	3	4	3	3
Ingratiating	4	4	4	3	5	4
Coalitions	5	6	5	5	4	5
Pressure	6	5	7	7	7	6
Upward appeals	7	7	6	6	6	7
Exchange	8	8	8	8	8	8

SOURCE: From "Influence Tactics and Objectives in Upward, Downward, and Lateral Influence Attempts," by G. Yukl & C. M. Falbe, 1990, *Journal of Applied Psychology, 75*, p. 139. Copyright 1990 by the American Psychological Association. Reprinted with permission.

a. Sources rated how frequently they had used each strategy with their bosses, coworkers, or subordinates during the previous year (1 = *never use this strategy under any circumstances;* 5 = *use this strategy very often–almost every week*). Targets rated how frequently their bosses, coworkers, or subordinates had used this strategy with them during the previous year.

report more agent use of socially desirable [strategies] such as rational persuasion, as compared to "undesirable" [strategies], such as pressure (assertiveness)" (p. 6). In addition, ratings of preformulated strategies provide no information about how employees mix strategies within their initial upward influence attempts, or how they respond to resistance either immediately or over repeated interactions with the message target.[10]

To address such concerns, Yukl et al. (1993) gathered critical incident data in two ways. Students in evening MBA courses (*n* = 145) each described separate influence episodes at work that had resulted in commitment (i.e., the target had complied willingly and with strong enthusiasm), compliance (i.e., the target had complied, but with minimum enthusiasm or commitment), and resistance (i.e., the target had opposed the request and tried to avoid complying). Each student described upward, lateral, and downward influence episodes in which he or she had participated as either the message source or the target. In addition, 16 MBA students each conducted interviews with 18 managers in the student's work organization, gathering data on episodes involving various directions of influence and outcomes. Of this group, 10 students had interviewees recall episodes in which they were targets; the other 6 had interviewees recall episodes in which they were message sources.

For each critical incident, the participant described the direction of influence, initial and final outcome of the influence attempt, what the message source said initially, how the target reacted, and whether the incident occurred during a single conversation or over several conversations. A total of 646 usable target incidents and 238 source incidents were gathered. Of these 884 critical incidents, 42% (370) involved both initial and follow-up (immediate or delayed) influence attempts. Two coders independently identified strategies used during each influence attempt, using a typology of strategies slightly modified from Yukl and Falbe (1990).[11] When an initial attempt involved only a simple request, strategies were analyzed in only the follow-up attempt, which resulted in the analysis of a total of 1,094 influence attempts (initial and follow-up).

Yukl et. al.'s (1993) findings regarding frequency of use and rank ordering for influence strategies are shown in Table 8.8.[12] A careful comparison of these data with those from Kipnis et al. (1980) and Yukl and Falbe (1990) reveals both similarities and differences. One similarity is the frequent use of rational persuasion. Participants in both Kipnis et al.'s and Yukl and Falbe's studies reported that rational persuasion had been used frequently in upward, lateral, and downward influence. Rational persuasion was ranked either first or second among all influence strategies used in the recent past (either 6 months or year; see Tables 8.4 and 8.7). In a similar vein, Yukl et al.'s (1993) participants recalled frequent use of rational persuasion during incidents of upward, lateral, and downward influence. Indeed, 77% (275 of 358) of the initial and follow-up upward attempts included rational persuasion, as did more than half of the episodes of lateral and downward attempts. These percentages far exceed those for any other strategy (see Table 8.8).

On the other hand, Yukl et al. (1993) found greater recalled use of some "undesirable" strategies and less use of some socially desirable strategies than did prior studies that relied on ratings of preformulated strategies. Consider Yukl et al.'s data on recalled upward influence strategies (i.e., the second column in Table 8.8). The "undesirable" strategy of pressure (assertiveness) tied as the second most frequent strategy (out of nine) when participants recalled upward influence episodes. In contrast, assertiveness was ranked fifth out of eight upward influence strategies by message sources in the Kipnis et al. (1980) study (see Table 8.4), and sixth by message sources and fifth by targets among eight upward influence strategies in the Yukl and Falbe (1990) study (see Table 8.7). As a second example, the "desirable" strategy of consultation was recalled infrequently (ranks = seventh-ninth out of nine strategies) by participants recalling upward, lateral, and downward influence attempts in the Yukl et al. (1993) study, whereas it was ranked either first or second when rated by Yukl and Falbe's (1990) participants for frequency of use across a variety of conditions. Findings such as these suggest that asking employees to rate how frequently they use preformulated lists of upward influence strategies, or how

Table 8.8   Reported Frequency of Use for Yukl et al.'s (1993) Organizational
             Influence Strategies

| Influence Strategy | Direction of Influence Attempt | | |
	Upward (n = 358)	Lateral (n = 289)	Downward (n = 447)
Rational persuasion	275 (1)	161 (1)	234 (1)
Inspirational appeals	7 (8)	15 (9)	50 (5)
Consultation	4 (9)	19 (8)	30 (7)
Ingratiation	12 (6)	32 (6)	68 (3)
Personal appeals	20 (4)	52 (2)	17 (8)
Exchange	13 (5)	35 (4)	62 (4)
Coalition	55 (2)	38 (3)	17 (8)
Legitimating	9 (7)	20 (7)	45 (6)
Pressure (assertiveness)	55 (2)	33 (5)	97 (2)

SOURCE: G. Yukl, C. M. Falbe, & J. Y. Youn, "Patterns of Influence Behavior for Managers," *Group & Organization Management, 18,* p. 19. Copyright © 1993 by Sage Publications, Inc. Adapted by permission of Sage Publications, Inc.

NOTE: n = the number of influence attempts (initial and follow-up) in each direction. Numbers outside parentheses are the number of influence attempts in a specific direction containing each strategy; numbers within parentheses are rank orderings for reported use of strategies in each direction of influence.

frequently they are the targets of such strategies, creates an overly "rosy" picture of upward influence in organizations (for additional evidence on this point, see the discussion of item desirability bias in Chapter 4).

In sum, research by Kipnis et al. (1980), Schriesheim and Hinkin (1990), and Yukl and Falbe (1990; Yukl et al., 1993) presents a fairly consistent description of upward influence strategies. Although the typologies differ from one another slightly, rational persuasion, assertiveness (pressure), coalitions, exchange, and ingratiation appear in every case. Rational persuasion consistently is reported as the most common upward influence strategy, but (depending on the data collection method) the other four strategies also appear with some frequency.

THE SEARCH FOR FACTORS THAT PREDICT
CHOICE OF UPWARD INFLUENCE STRATEGIES

Building on the research reviewed so far, a sizable number of studies have sought to identify factors that predict employees' choice of upward influence strategies. In the majority of these studies, employees have rated how frequently they have used Kipnis et al.'s (1980; Schriesheim & Hinkin, 1990;

Yukl & Falbe, 1990) upward influence strategies with their supervisors during the past 6 months (e.g., Deluga, 1988; Deluga & Perry, 1991; Erez & Rim, 1982; Erez et al., 1986; Farmer, Maslyn, Fedor, & Goodman, 1997; Kipnis & Schmidt, 1983; Kipnis, Schmidt, Swaffin-Smith, & Wilkinson, 1984; Rao, Schmidt, & Murray, 1995; Schmidt & Kipnis, 1984). In other studies, researchers have asked employees to (a) rate their likelihood of using Kipnis et al.'s upward influence strategies in response to specific hypothetical scenarios (e.g., Ansari & Kapoor, 1987; Schermerhorn & Bond, 1991) or (b) recall their use of an expanded version of Kipnis et al.'s strategies during actual upward influence episodes with their supervisors (e.g., Case, Dosier, Murkison, & Keys, 1988; Schilit & Locke, 1982; Yukl et al., 1993). Only a few studies have departed substantially from the Kipnis et al. (1980) typology.[13]

Similar to researchers seeking to develop ecological models of child physical abuse, upward influence researchers have searched for factors that predict strategy choice at several levels of analysis. Four different levels, along with representative topics and studies, are shown in Table 8.9. Research on *characteristics of the message source* has explored whether an employee's personality (e.g., locus of control), sociodemographic qualities (e.g., years of education), and/or job characteristics (e.g., middle- versus upper-level management) predict his or her use of upward influence strategies. Studies focusing on *target and relationship characteristics* have assessed whether an employee's perceptions of the supervisor (e.g., power bases) and his or her own relationship with the supervisor (e.g., level of leader-member exchange) predict the employee's use of upward influence strategies. Research on *characteristics of influence episodes* has investigated whether an employee's use of upward influence strategies depends on specific features of the episode(s) that he or she recalls or imagines. Relevant factors at this third level include whether employees pursue particular influence goals, report on episodes in which they participated as the message source or target, recall their initial strategies or strategies used following resistance, and report on episodes in which ultimately they succeeded or failed at gaining their supervisors' compliance. Finally, studies focusing on *macro-organizational characteristics* have explored whether features of the organization in which upward influence occurs, such as the organization's size or perceived norms regarding innovation, predict an employee's choice of strategies. Most studies at each level have treated individual strategies from the Kipnis et al. (1980) typology as dependent variables, but a few (e.g., Farmer et al., 1997) have grouped the strategies into larger clusters such as "hard," "soft," and "rational" upward influence strategies (see below). Some researchers have investigated predictor variables from only one of these four levels, but others (e.g., Farmer et al., 1997; Krone, 1992; Maslyn, Farmer, & Fedor, 1996) have assessed predictors from several levels simultaneously.

Table 8.9 Categories of Predictor Variables Studied in the Upward Influence Literature

Type of Predictor Variable	Representative Studies
Characteristics of message source	
1. Personality: locus of control, Machiavellianism, need for achievement/power, self-monitoring	Chacko (1990), Farmer et al. (1997), Lamude et al. (1987), Mowday (1978)
2. Sociodemographics: age, formal education, biological sex, culture	Deluga & Perry (1991), Farmer et al. (1997), Offermann & Kearney (1988), Schermerhorn & Bond (1991)
3. Job characteristics: different vs. same workplace as supervisor, length of employment, middle vs. upper-level manager, number of subordinates, staff vs. line manager	Kipnis et al. (1984), Farmer et al. (1997), Erez & Rim (1982), Erez et al. (1986), Maslyn et al. (1996)
Target and relationship characteristics	
1. Sociodemographics (e.g., biological sex of supervisor)	Offermann & Kearney (1988)
2. Perceptions of supervisor: global evaluation, leadership style, power bases	Ansari & Kapoor (1987), Cheng (1983), Deluga (1988), Garko (1992)
3. Perceptions of leader-member exchange	Deluga & Perry (1991), Krone (1992), Waldron et al. (1993)
Characteristics of influence episode	
1. Influence goal: type of goal, importance of goal	Maslyn et al. (1996), Schmidt & Kipnis (1984), Yukl et al. (1995)
2. Role: whether participant reports as message source vs. target	Erez et al. (1986), Yukl & Falbe (1990), Schilit & Locke (1982)
3. Resistance: whether recall initial vs. follow-up influence attempt	Maslyn et al. (1996), Yukl et al. (1993)
4. Outcome: whether employee was successful or not in gaining superior's compliance	Case et al. (1988), Schilit & Locke (1982)
Macro-organizational characteristics	
1. Size (number of employees)/type (public/private)	Erez & Rim (1982), Krone (1992)
2. Perceived norms about formalization/innovation	Rao et al. (1995)

How much have we learned after 20 years of research on what predicts an employee's choice of upward influence strategies? A comprehensive review of the studies listed in Table 8.9 is beyond the scope of this chapter. My own assessment of the upward influence literature is similar to my view of the traditional compliance-gaining literature (see Chapter 4). In both cases, scholars have accumulated a large body of studies, yet upward influence scholars, like those associated with the compliance-gaining tradition, have identified few strong predictors of strategy choice. As Barry and Watson (1996) claim in their review of influence strategies in organizations: "Empirical findings often run counter to expectations, and effect sizes are usually modest. This adds up to a tenuous empirical foundation for understanding dyadic influence" (p. 285).

Farmer et al. (1997) report one of the most ambitious studies to date investigating predictors of upward influence strategy use. These researchers assessed whether Kipnis et al.'s (1980) strategies can be grouped into a smaller number of clusters and attempted to identify factors that predict the use of strategies in each cluster. Farmer et al. mailed a survey about upward influence to employees at 53 branch locations of a national nonprofit organization. A total of 285 employees at all organizational levels received the survey, of which 225 employees (87%) returned usable data. The sample was largely female (89%). Respondents on average were 39 years old and had worked in their present jobs 4.5 years. About two-thirds worked at the same physical locations as their immediate supervisors. Respondents completed Schriesheim and Hinkin's (1990) upward influence scale (see Table 8.5), assessing the frequency with which they had used each of six upward influence strategies with their supervisors during the past 6 months. Respondents also completed measures of eight predictor variables, including information about (a) their sociodemographic characteristics (years of education), (b) their personality traits (Machiavellianism, locus of control, and self-monitoring), (c) their supervisors (perceptions of their supervisors' reward and coercive power bases, perceived level of leader-member exchange), and (d) the characteristics of their jobs (whether they worked at the same locations as their supervisors or at different locations).

Farmer et al. (1997) report results for upward influence strategies as well as for strategy clusters. As in earlier studies, rationality was rated as the most frequently used strategy ($M = 4.38$ on a 5-point scale), whereas assertiveness ($M = 1.63$), coalitions ($M = 1.78$), exchange ($M = 1.38$), ingratiation ($M = 2.54$), and upward appeals ($M = 1.26$) were rated as being used less often. Of the 54 separate correlations between the eight predictor variables and these six upward influence strategies, nearly half (22 of 54) were statistically significant. Only 1 of the 54 correlations, however, was even modest in size ($r = .30$). None of the individual predictor variables was a strong predictor of an employee's choice of upward influence strategies.

Results were more promising when Farmer et al. (1997) grouped strategies into clusters and examined predictor variables as a set. Based on a second-order factor analysis,[14] they grouped the six upward influence strategies into three clusters based loosely on Kelman's (1958, 1961) three processes of attitude change:

1. *Hard strategies:* An employee attempts to gain his or her supervisor's compliance through the direct control of rewards or punishments—via assertiveness, coalitions, and upward appeals (similar to Kelman's process of compliance).[15]

2. *Soft strategies:* An employee attempts to gain his or her supervisor's compliance by reinforcing desired role relationships—via exchange and ingratiation (similar to Kelman's process of identification).

3. *Rational strategies:* An employee attempts to gain his or her supervisor's compliance by using rational persuasion to show how complying would be consistent with organizational goals valued by supervisor (similar to Kelman's process of internalization).

Farmer et al. then explored how well the predictor variables, as a group, accounted for variance in these three strategy clusters. After correcting for measurement error, they found that the eight predictors, as a set, accounted for 22% of the variance in employees' reported use of hard strategies and 29% of the variance for soft strategies, but only 9% of the variance in rational strategies.

LIMITATIONS OF THE UPWARD INFLUENCE LITERATURE

Upward influence scholars have recognized some of the pitfalls that befell traditional compliance-gaining researchers, but they have not yet seriously addressed other limitations of the upward influence literature. Farmer et al.'s (1997) study is instructive in this regard; hence I analyze it here to make several points about the upward influence literature more generally.

There is much to commend in Farmer et al.'s (1997) research. Most of the studies listed in Table 8.9 analyzed upward influence using nominal-level typologies composed of categories that vary from each other in countless unspecified ways. As Kellermann and Cole (1994) explain, the Kipnis et al. (1980) typology "includes strategies defined by form (e.g., sanctions), content (e.g., rationality), presentation (e.g., ingratiation, assertiveness), context (e.g., upward appeal, coalitions), and interactive use (e.g., exchange)" (p. 27). As we saw in Chapter 2, relying on an atheoretical typology of upward influence strategies makes it nearly impossible to interpret the meaning of research findings even when significant predictors are identified. To their credit, Farmer et al.

grouped upward influence strategies, albeit after the fact, into theoretically meaningful clusters. Their study also assessed the message source's perceptions of both participants (employee and supervisor) in upward influence episodes.

Despite these strengths, Farmer et al.'s (1997) study also reveals several conceptual and methodological weaknesses of the upward influence literature. One problem involves how upward influence behaviors have been described. By describing upward influence behaviors using abstract clusters such as hard, soft, and rational, upward influence scholars ignore theoretically relevant variation in the concrete utterances that enact strategies in each cluster. Consider rational persuasion strategies. Research studying message sources and targets, relying on multiple methods and cultures, indicates that "rationality" is the most frequently reported upward influence strategy during both successful and unsuccessful initial and follow-up attempts (e.g., Ansari & Kapoor, 1987; Case et al., 1988; Kipnis et al., 1980; Schermerhorn & Bond, 1991; Schilit & Locke, 1982; Yukl & Falbe, 1990; Yukl et al., 1993; see Tables 8.4, 8.7, and 8.8). The pervasiveness of rationality may explain why Farmer et al. (1997) were largely unsuccessful at predicting its use. Rational persuasion, however, varies in many ways. For example, employees vary how much they elaborate claims and evidence to support their requests. In their analysis of critical incidents, Yukl et al. (1993) comment on how employees varied how much they elaborated rational persuasion depending on its sequential placement:

> An initial influence attempt often involved a weak form of rational persuasion (e.g., a brief explanation, an assertion without supporting evidence), whereas follow-up influence attempts usually involved a stronger form of rational persuasion (e.g., a detailed proposal, elaborate documentation, a convincing reply to concerns raised by the target). (p. 21)

Rational persuasion also varies in the degree to which claims and evidence focus on the employee, the supervisor, or the larger organization (Wilson & Kunkel, 2000), as well as how it is mixed with other strategies within the same upward influence episode (Barry & Shapiro, 1992; Falbe & Yukl, 1992; Yukl, Kim, & Falbe, 1996). Although upward influence scholars are now paying attention to how rational persuasion is elaborated, mixed, and sequenced, theoretical analyses of why this might occur have lagged behind. And the method used by Farmer et al. (1997) and most other upward influence scholars offers little insight into these issues. Asking employees about their upward influence behaviors over the previous 6 months "tends to obscure how [a strategy] may be combined with other strategies, may vary across situations, or may function within a sequence of reciprocal moves" (Fairhurst, 2001, p. 389).

Tremendous variability also exists within the concrete utterances that enact hard and soft strategies. *Assertiveness* or *persistence*, for example, often may be perceived as a hard strategy, but the degree to which this is true varies substantially depending on how and when the strategy is enacted. Based on a qualitative analysis of how pressure was enacted differently depending on its sequential position, Yukl et al. (1993) observe:

> A relatively weak form of pressure (e.g., insistent demand, sarcasm, vague threat) was more likely to be used in an initial influence attempt or an immediate follow-up attempt, whereas in a delayed follow-up attempt a strong form of pressure was more likely to be used (e.g., explicit threat or warning). . . . Persistent reminders, checking, or nagging were other (weak) forms of pressure unique to delayed follow-up attempts. (p. 21)

Whether upward influence behaviors are perceived as hard or soft thus depends not only on what strategy is employed but also on exactly what is said and done, how and when it is said, and what else also is said.

To summarize, when upward influence scholars such as Farmer et al. (1997) have attempted to organize strategies in theoretically meaningful ways, they often have done so by creating clusters that contain tremendous within-category variation. As Fairhurst (2001) explains: "Survey studies tend to paint influence strategies in such broad strokes that the details of their instantiation are often lost. Yet the inconsistency across studies regarding [strategy] use and associated variables . . . reminds us that the devil is in the details" (p. 393).

A second problem with the upward influence literature involves how predictor variables have been selected and organized. Most upward influence studies have not been guided by any theoretical framework that could suggest why some characteristics of the message source, target, episode, or larger organization, as opposed to others, would be especially important in predicting and explaining specific variations in upward influence behaviors. Farmer et al.'s (1997) study also is illustrative in this regard. These researchers organize upward influence behaviors into clusters loosely corresponding to Kelman's (1958, 1961) processes of attitude change. Kelman's framework, however, is a theory of message effects; that is, it postulates three processes by which message targets adopt (or express) new attitudes. Because of this, the theory has less to say about why an employee (message source) might produce upward influence messages (e.g., soft strategies) that attempt to elicit particular processes in his or her supervisor (e.g., identification). Thus Farmer et al. are left with having to formulate separate rationales for why each of their eight predictor variables might be associated with the use of hard, soft, or rational strategies. The various rationales include organizational norms regarding appropriate upward influence behaviors, power differences and contextual features that limit or enable strategic options, personality predispositions, and political or intellectual skills needed to enact particular strategies. It also is not clear why Farmer et al. considered their eight predictor variables, as opposed to others (see Table 8.9), to be especially relevant for predicting choice of hard, soft, or rational strategies.

What is missing from Farmer et al.'s analysis are global theories of persuasive message production that could suggest which features or dimensions of upward influence behaviors merit attention as well as which factors are most important in predicting and explaining variations in those features. Although scholars occasionally have argued that some of the message production theories reviewed earlier in this book, such as attribution (Case et al., 1988; Erez et al., 1986; Porter et al., 1981; Schilit & Locke, 1982) and politeness (Drake & Moberg, 1986; Fairhurst, 1993; Morand, 2000; Waldron et al., 1993) theories, could inform upward influence research, the studies listed in Table 8.9 for the most part have proceeded without recourse to such theories. The result, as Barry and Watson (1996) note, is that our understanding of the determinants of upward influence is "disjointed and isolated, rather than incremental and integrative" (p. 285).

In the subsection that follows, I show how one theory of persuasive message production—a theory of the identity implications of influence goals (Wilson et al., 1998)—can be used to reframe current research on upward influence goals in organizations. Although the theory, to date, has been applied only within the context of young adults' personal relationships, it also suggests new questions about how employees exert upward influence at work.

EXPLAINING PATTERNS OF UPWARD INFLUENCE: IDENTITY IMPLICATIONS OF INFLUENCE GOALS

Current Research on Upward Influence Goals

Several studies have investigated upward influence goals, or specific reasons why employees seek compliance from those at higher levels in their organizations (Ansari & Kapoor, 1987; Erez & Rim, 1982; Kipnis et al., 1980; Rao et al., 1995; Schmidt & Kipnis, 1984; Waldron et al., 1993; Yukl & Falbe, 1990; Yukl et al., 1995; see Chapter 5). This research clarifies what goals commonly motivate upward influence, but offers less insight into how employees vary their compliance-seeking messages when pursuing different goals.

In their initial research, Kipnis et al. (1980) investigated not only organizational influence strategies but influence goals. They identified five goals in open-ended descriptions of organizational influence episodes (Study 1). The two goals motivating most *upward* influence attempts ($n = 62$ episodes) were "obtaining personal benefits" (e.g., a salary increase, promotion, or improved work schedule; 58% of episodes) and "initiating a change in work" (e.g., proposing a new product or work procedure; 26% of episodes). Reanalyzing data originally reported by Yukl et al. (1993; Falbe & Yukl, 1992), Yukl et al. (1995) reached a similar conclusion. In a sample of 288 critical incidents gathered from both message sources and targets, Yukl et al. (1995) found that the two goals most commonly motivating upward influence were "getting support for a proposed organizational change or innovation" (52%) and "obtaining personal benefits" (33%).[16]

Proposing a change in work and seeking personal benefits both are common upward influence goals, but they differ in important respects (Porter et al., 1981; Schmidt & Kipnis, 1984). Proposing a new product or procedure is an example of an "organizational" goal, that is, a goal that arises primarily from an employee's role and responsibilities in the organization. Suggesting that a scheduling procedure be changed so as to improve coordination among multiple work units, for instance, benefits not only the employee but also the larger organization. Seeking a raise, promotion, or favorable work schedule is more clearly a "personal" goal, that is, a goal that arises primarily from the employee's needs and self-interest.

Analyzing the politics of upward influence, Porter et al. (1981) suggest that employees will attempt to influence superiors differently depending on whether their attempts are likely to be perceived as motivated primarily by organizational or personal goals. According to Porter et al., upward influence attempts are "political" when they are motivated primarily by an employee's or group's self-interest and when the desired change threatens the self-interests of other organizational actors or groups. An employee seeking to be selected for promotion from among a pool of candidates is engaging in political behavior, as is an employee promoting a new work procedure because it will benefit his or her unit at the expense of other organizational units. Porter et al. claim that employees are more likely to exert upward influence covertly when it is politically motivated, because pursuing personal goals at the expense of others could create "attributional problems" for an employee as well as generate opposition by other actors.

Building on Porter et al.'s (1981) analysis, five studies have investigated whether employees use different upward influence strategies depending on whether their requests are motivated by personal or organizational goals. In three studies, Schmidt and his colleagues (Kipnis et al., 1980; Rao et al., 1995; Schmidt & Kipnis, 1984) have asked employees to rate how frequently they have used strategies from the Kipnis et al. typology with their bosses during the past 6 months, and also how frequently each of five to seven goals "had been the cause of their trying to influence their immediate superior" (Schmidt & Kipnis,

1984, p. 783). Findings regarding specific influence goals differ somewhat across the three studies, but in general employees report greater use of rational persuasion and coalitions when "convincing their boss to support a new product or procedure" has been a frequent reason for exerting upward influence, whereas they report greater use of exchange and ingratiation when "obtaining personal benefits" has been a frequent reason for exerting upward influence. Schmidt and Kipnis (1984) also report correlations ranging from $r = .15$ to $.34$ between how frequently employees recall having pursued six different organizational and personal goals with their bosses, indicating that "managers who attempted to influence their superiors for organizational reasons also tended to influence for individual reasons" (p. 789).

Two studies have compared the use of upward influence strategies in situations defined by organizational versus personal goals. Ansari and Kapoor (1987) asked male college undergraduates in India to read scenarios in which each was asked to imagine that he wanted to convince his manager that the manager needed to hire additional personnel to help meet an upcoming company deadline (organizational goal) and that the participant should be selected for promotion (personal goal). Each student rated how frequently he would use four strategies from the Kipnis et al. (1980) typology in each scenario. Although the students relied heavily on rationality in both scenarios, they rated rationality, upward appeal, and blocking as significantly more likely to be used in pursuit of the organizational goal than in pursuit of the personal goal, and ingratiation as more likely to be used in pursuit of the goal of seeking personal benefits (i.e., a promotion).

Yukl et al. (1995) used multiple methods to compare the strategies employees relied on to pursue five different influence goals. Reanalyzing earlier data (Yukl et al., 1993), the researchers looked at both goals and strategies reported in 878 critical incidents involving upward, lateral, and downward influence. A new sample of 168 evening MBA students also rated how often they pursued each of five goals during upward, lateral, and downward influence attempts, and then how often they used each strategy from Yukl and Falbe's (1990) typology (see Table 8.6) when pursuing each goal with their supervisors, coworkers, or subordinates (1 = *never use this strategy with my boss for this type of request;* 4 = *usually use this strategy with my boss for this type of request*). Many findings regarding goals and strategies differed depending on the method employed. However, rational persuasion and coalition both were more likely to be mentioned in critical incidents that involved the goal of getting support for a proposed change (68% and 13%, respectively) than in incidents that involved seeking personal benefits (48% and 6%), and these same two strategies were rated as more likely to have been used when seeking support for a proposed change in work than when seeking personal benefits. Ingratiation and personal appeals were more likely to be mentioned in critical incidents that involved the goal of seeking personal benefits (5% and 12%, respectively) than in incidents that involved getting support for a proposed change in work (1% and 1%), and these same two strategies were rated as more likely to have been used when seeking personal benefits than when seeking support for a proposed change.

In sum, research to date offers some support for Porter et al.'s (1981) claim that employees will exert upward influence differently depending on whether they are perceived as being motivated by organizational or personal goals. Employees report greater use of reasoning and coalitions when proposing a new product or work procedure, and greater ingratiation when seeking personal benefits from the boss. Yet the effect sizes in these studies typically have been modest, and relationships between goals and other strategies (e.g., assertiveness, exchange, upward appeal) have differed across studies. Yukl et al. (1995) themselves conclude:

> Even though some [strategies] were used more often for particular objectives, the relationship between [strategies] and objectives was not a strong one. An important finding in our study was that most of the [strategies] could be used for any of the objectives. (p. 294)

Why have Porter et al.'s (1981) predictions about differences in pursuing organizational versus personal goals not received stronger support to date? There are several possible reasons. First, Porter et al. claim that specific features of upward influence attempts will differ depending on the degree to which upward influence is political, and these features are not tapped cleanly by existing nominal-level typologies. According to Porter et al., political upward influence is more likely to occur through "manipulative persuasion" (i.e., an employee overtly tries to persuade his or her supervisor, but conceals his or her real reasons for doing so) than through "open persuasion." Asking employees how frequently they have "used logic" or "presented information to support their views" ignores this distinction. Second, the distinction between organizational and personal goals itself is not a sharp one; for example, employees may propose a new product or work procedure either because they genuinely believe it will benefit the larger organization or because they believe it will benefit their own unit but not the larger organization. Third, Porter et al.'s framework highlights only some potential threats to the message source's and target's "face" that can arise during upward influence attempts (see Chapter 6). Proposing a new product or procedure and seeking a promotion both have the potential to threaten the employee's and the supervisor's face, albeit in different ways. This third point suggests that what may be needed is a broader analysis of the identity implications of upward influence goals.

Identity Implications of Upward Influence Goals

As I have noted in discussing politeness theory (see Chapter 6), seeking compliance can threaten both parties' desires for autonomy (negative face) and approval (positive face). How do message sources and targets anticipate threats to their own and the other party's face during compliance-gaining interactions? My colleagues and I argue that individuals typically rely on two widely shared types of tacit knowledge to do so (Cai & Wilson, 2000; Wilson, Kim, & Meischke, 1991/1992; Wilson et al., 1998; Wilson, Anastasiou, et al., 2000; Wilson & Kunkel, 2000). The first type is knowledge of the defining conditions for directives (e.g., requests, recommendations), the class of speech acts that lies at the heart of any attempt to seek compliance (see Chapter 6). By seeking compliance, message sources inevitably make claims, even if only implicitly, about the current situation—a need for action exists, the target would not have acted without being requested, the target plausibly may be willing/obligated and able to comply, and so forth (see Table 6.2). Message targets may object to defining the current situation in this way. The second type is knowledge of influence goals, or common reasons why persons seek compliance (see Chapter 5). Our research to date has focused on three influence goals that young adults commonly pursue in their personal relationships: asking favors, giving advice, and enforcing unfulfilled obligations. Situations defined by these influence goals differ in terms of who will benefit from compliance as well as each party's rights and obligations (Cody, Canary, & Smith, 1994; Dillard, 1989), and such differences in turn create distinct potential threats to each party's face.

In a nutshell, we argue that individuals anticipate potential face threats by overlaying their knowledge of the defining conditions for seeking compliance onto their understandings of the influence goal currently being pursued. When a message source utters the prerequest "Can I ask you a favor?" we expect one type of interaction to unfold, whereas when a source says, "Can I give you some advice?" we expect another. The latter utterance presumes that the message source has the right to give advice, and a source who makes this presumption too liberally risks being seen as someone who is "nosy" and who "butts into" the affairs of others. Thus appearing nosy is "relevant" to situations defined by the goal of giving advice in a way that it is not in situations defined by the goal of asking a favor (Wilson & Kunkel, 2000).

Using multiple methods (e.g., scenarios, critical incidents), we have shown that young adults associate distinct potential threats to identity with different influence goals. Specifically:

1. When asking favors, students perceive potential threats to the target's desire to be autonomous, as well as to their own desires not to appear lazy or to feel indebted.

2. When giving advice, students perceive potential threats to the target's desires to be autonomous and to appear competent, as well as to their own desire not to appear nosy.

3. When enforcing obligations, students perceive potential threats to the target's desires to be autonomous and to appear responsible. (Wilson et al., 1998)

These differences have been replicated for both female and male students as they sought compliance from same-sex friends, cross-sex friends, and romantic partners (Wilson & Kunkel, 2000) and with students from a variety of ethnic backgrounds in the United States (Wilson, Anastasiou, et al., 2000) as well as from Japan (Cai & Wilson, 2000). Because they associate different potential threats to face with different influence goals, young adults also vary the importance they place on primary and secondary goals—as well as the degree to which they express approval, exert pressure, and give reasons in their compliance-seeking messages—when asking favors, giving advice, and enforcing obligations. In some studies, reasons have been subdivided into two types: explanations why the message source is making a request/recommendation (self-focused) versus explanations why the message target should comply with the request/recommendation (other-focused) (Wilson, Anastasiou, et al., 2000; Wilson & Kunkel, 2000). As would be expected in light of the distinct potential threats associated with each goal, we found in one study that "participants who recalled giving advice included more than three times the number of other-focused reasons than did those who recalled asking favors . . . participants who recalled asking favors included over 50% more self-focused reasons than did those who recalled giving advice" (Wilson & Kunkel, 2000, pp. 212-213).

Although my colleagues and I have not applied this analysis to organizational contexts, it certainly has relevance for an understanding of how employees might alter their upward influence attempts when pursuing organizational versus personal goals. To illustrate this point, Table 8.10 shows how a number of potential threats to both an employee's and a supervisor's face can be identified when the defining conditions for seeking compliance (i.e., the rules for directives) are overlaid onto the goals of "proposing a new product or procedure" versus "seeking personal benefits." Keep in mind that the threats to identity summarized in Table 8.10 are *potential* threats, that is, threats to the employee's or supervisor's face that plausibly could, but not necessarily will, arise in any situation defined by that goal (Wilson et al., 1991/1992, 1998). Employees do not always appear to "overstep their bounds" (e.g., by making proposals about which they lack adequate knowledge, or about which they should have consulted others first) when they propose new products or work procedures, but what it means to "overstep the bounds" seems different in such situations than when an employee seeks personal resources. Put differently, questions such as whether an employee should have sought the input of others

Table 8.10   Potential Face Threats Associated With Two Upward Influence Goals

	Influence Goals	
Rules for Directives	Proposing New Product/Procedure	Seeking Personal Benefits
Need for action	Do circumstances really warrant a new product/procedure? Does the employee (or supervisor) accurately understand this?	Do circumstances really warrant a raise/promotion/schedule change? Does the employee (or supervisor) accurately understand this?
Need for directive	Why hasn't the supervisor (or other actors) already responded to the exigent circumstances (i.e., implemented this/other proposals)?	Why hasn't the supervisor (or other actors) already responded to the exigent circumstances (i.e., given raises, modified work schedules)?
Ability	Does the supervisor have the expertise/resources/connections to implement the proposal?	Does the supervisor have the resources/connections to obtain the desired benefits?
Willingness	Is the supervisor willing to give the proposal a fair hearing? Is resistance motivated by factors extraneous to the merits of the proposal (e.g., disliking the employee, jealousy)?	Is the supervisor willing to give the request a fair hearing? Is resistance motivated by factors extraneous to the merits of the request (e.g., favoring other employees)?
Rights	Does the employee have the right to make this proposal? Should it have come from others, or should others have been consulted first?	Does the employee have the right to seek these personal benefits? Does he or she typically have organizational, and not just personal, goals in mind?
Sincerity	Is the employee truly motivated by organizational goals, or will the proposal simply benefit the employee (or close others)?	Is the employee truly sincere about how much he or she needs/wants the requested benefits? Does the supervisor understand this? What will the employee owe the supervisor/organization if he or she receives the benefits?

first before approaching the supervisor seem relevant to situations defined by the goal of proposing a change in work in ways that they do not when the employee's goal is seeking personal benefits.[17]

An analysis of the identity implications of upward influence goals suggests explanations for prior findings and highlights additional features of upward influence appeals that should be analyzed. Consider the finding that employees report using rationality more frequently when proposing a new product or procedure than when seeking personal benefits. Table 8.10 suggests several reasons why employees would rely heavily on rational persuasion when proposing a change in work. First, an employee must demonstrate that a need for action exists: Why does the organization need a new product, service, program, or procedure? What currently is missing, and would the new product or procedure really fill this void? By making claims and referring to data, the employee demonstrates that he or she understands the current situation accurately and attempts to build willingness on the part of the supervisor. Second, the employee needs to demonstrate that she or he sincerely is motivated by what will benefit the organization as a whole (or at least plausibly appear this way), rather than appearing to be motivated only by self-interest (Porter et al., 1981). By providing reasons why the proposal actually will benefit the larger organization, the employee can manage this potential threat to his or her identity.

Employees also have motives to provide reasons when seeking personal benefits, which explains why rationality is common with both goals. There are several reasons, however, why employees may rely less heavily on rational persuasion when seeking personal benefits as opposed to when proposing work changes. By providing too many reasons why he or she deserves a raise or promotion (e.g., writing multiple detailed memos about how he or she is wonderful), an employee runs the risk of appearing to have an overinflated view of his or her own contributions and also seems immodest. In addition, an employee may feel that he or she already has "earned" the raise or promotion, and hence the supervisor should be willing to grant the request due to the employee's prior contributions, without the employee's having to create long persuasive arguments.

This discussion suggests that, in addition to measuring the frequency of rationality, upward influence scholars would benefit from analyzing its focus. When proposing changes in work, employees should spend most of their time making claims and providing data about their larger work units and/or organizations, whereas when seeking personal benefits, employees should spend most of their time making claims and providing data about their own contributions to the organization or their personal/family needs outside of the organization. Based on a similar distinction, Wilson and Kunkel (2000) found that influence goals (advice versus favors) accounted for 20% of the variance in whether the reasons undergraduates provided when seeking a friend's or romantic partner's compliance were self- or other-focused.

Table 8.10 also offers insight into why employees would use coalitions more frequently when proposing changes in work than when seeking personal benefits. Proposing a new procedure for manufacturing a product, for example, affects not only the employee him- or herself but others involved in making the product, and perhaps also those responsible for distribution, marketing, quality control, and human resources. In order to demonstrate that he or she has thought about a proposal seriously (need for action) and considered the reactions of others (rights), an employee might well have informal discussions with others before approaching his or her supervisor with a proposal, and may even approach the supervisor with a group (initially or in a follow-up attempt). In contrast, an employee's seeking personal benefits (e.g., asking for a raise) often will not directly affect how other employees do their jobs, and hence the employee may have less need to consult with others beforehand when pursuing this goal than when proposing a work change.

Coalitions, however, are risky (Olufowote, 2001), which may explain why they co-occur with other upward influence strategies that are both soft and hard (Farmer et al., 1997).[18] A supervisor may be pleased that an employee has considered how others would be affected by a proposed work change, and may interpret coalitions as a sign that the employee has thought carefully about the proposal's consequences and sought needed information. On the other hand, a supervisor may be displeased that an employee has consulted with others first if the supervisor perceives that the employee is trying to make an "end run" around him or her or to apply undue pressure without properly respecting the supervisor's freedom to make decisions (i.e., the supervisor's negative face). By making the upward influence attempt more "public," coalitions likely heighten the supervisor's awareness of and concern about maintaining his or her own face (Wilson, 1992).

This discussion suggests that, in addition to measuring the frequency of coalitions, upward influence scholars would benefit from analyzing the forms that coalitions take (see the distinction between rhetorical and strategic coalitions drawn by Olufowote, 2001) as well as the types of facework that employees use when enacting coalitions (Wilson, 1992). In some cases, such as when employees feel that a supervisor is not giving their proposal a fair hearing (see Table 8.10) and when the level of leader-member exchange is low (Fairhurst, 1993, 2001; Waldron et al., 1993), employees may enact coalitions with little regard for the supervisor's face (in which case coalitions likely will be perceived as a hard strategy). In other cases, however, employees may offer face-saving accounts (Scott & Lyman, 1968) for why they themselves consulted with others beforehand, or create face-saving stories (e.g., suggesting that the supervisor no doubt already had considered the proposal anyway) that allow the supervisor to comply with the employees' request without appearing to "cave in" to the coalition (in which case coalitions might be perceived as a softer strategy).

To summarize my discussion of this second case: Upward influence in organizations is increasingly common and important, yet still potentially risky. The current literature identifies common strategies that employees use when trying to influence their bosses as well as a variety of personal, relational, episodic, and organizational factors that predict employees' choice of strategies. Although upward influence scholars have avoided some of the limitations that befell traditional compliance-gaining researchers (e.g., there is widespread recognition that upward influence does not always occur in one-shot episodes), they have not seriously addressed other limitations (e.g., the need for theoretically informed message analysis). As a result, researchers have identified few strong predictors of upward influence strategy choice, and their work lacks theoretical frameworks that can account for those predictors that have been identified. I have argued that a more in-depth analysis of the identity implications of influence goals would help explain several existing findings and highlight new ways of analyzing upward influence appeals. More generally, I have shown how the upward influence literature can be informed by global (i.e., cross-contextual) theories of persuasive message production.

Summary

In this chapter I have reviewed research on seeking and resisting compliance in two specific contexts, as (a) physically abusive parents regulate perceived misbehavior by their children (Case 1), and (b) employees exert upward influence with those at higher levels in their organizations (Case 2). I have addressed what is known about patterns of seeking and resisting compliance in each context and applied global (i.e., cross-contextual) theories of persuasive message production from Chapters 5-7 to help explain those patterns. By doing so, I have attempted to show how compelling explanations of persuasive message production can be developed through the integration of general theories of psychological and interactional processes with analyses of seeking and resisting compliance in particular relational, institutional, and cultural contexts.

Notes

1. Virtually every U.S. state recognizes physical abuse, sexual abuse, and neglect of basic needs as forms of child maltreatment; however, states vary in whether they recognize psychological maltreatment or emotional abuse as a unique problem. Legal definitions tend to emphasize the tangible consequences of child maltreatment (e.g., injury, failure to thrive), whereas the consequences of psychological maltreatment often are not visible and may not be apparent for years. For further discussion, see Brassard and Hardy (1997) and Morgan (2001).

2. Violence in turn is defined as "an act carried out with the intention or perceived intention of causing physical pain or injury to another person" (Gelles, 1997, p. 14). This definition includes the mild sting of a slap as well as the severe pain of a burn or broken bone. Critics charge that the line between mild and severe violent acts is blurry and cannot be defined out of context. An act such as "slapped" may not create serious risk of injury when it occurs between young siblings, but the same act may create a high risk of injury when a parent repeatedly slaps a child in the head. The most recent version of the CTS (Straus et al., 1998) attempts to draw finer-grained distinctions regarding intensity of behavior. In the end, Straus and his colleagues argue that behaviors and their consequences should be assessed separately, rather than behavior being defined as abusive only post hoc, based on consequences. Behaviors such as grabbing a child around the neck and choking are dangerous enough to be defined as abusive regardless of whether the child is injured the first time they occur. For more discussion, see Barnett et al. (1997) and Gelles (1997).

3. The vast majority of studies on parent-child interaction and CPA have focused on mothers; only a few observational studies have also included data on fathers (e.g., Burgess & Conger, 1978; Herrenkohl et al., 1984). Researchers have focused on mothers for several reasons, including that mothers often still are presumed to be primarily responsible for child rearing and that single-parent families, which in most cases are headed by mothers, are overrepresented among families with CPS involvement (Gelles, 1997; National Research Council, 1993).

4. Some readers may wonder whether the findings reviewed so far indicate that physically abused children are more challenging interaction partners, and hence bring about more aversive behavior and power-assertive discipline from their mothers. Abusive, relative to nonmaltreating, mothers do perceive their children to be more aggressive, conduct disordered, and hyperactive (Reid et al., 1987; Whipple & Webster-Stratton, 1991), and abused children do display higher rates of noncompliance and verbal aggression than comparison children (Bousha & Twentyman, 1984; Oldershaw et al., 1986). However, physically abusive parents hold exaggerated perceptions of their children. Reid et al. (1987) found that both abusive mothers and fathers had much more negative perceptions of their children than did nonmaltreating parents, even though trained observers, masked to condition, could not distinguish the same two groups of children during multiple home observations. As the following discussion shows, physically abusive mothers, through incompetent discipline practices, also help create the very behavioral problems they perceive in their children.

5. The CAP Inventory is a 160-item scale initially designed to be used as an initial screen during investigations of child maltreatment (Milner, 1994). The primary scale is made up of 77 items that assess the degree to which respondents endorse six characteristics thought to typify physically abusive parents: distress (e.g., "I often feel frustrated"), rigidity (e.g., "Children should always be neat"), unhappiness (e.g., "I am a happy person"), problems with child and self (e.g., "I have a child who is slow"), problems with family (e.g., "My family fights a lot"), and problems with others (e.g., "Other people have made my life hard"). Milner (1994) provides extensive evidence supporting the CAP Inventory's reliability and construct validity.

6. In the upward influence literature, abstract categories of behavior used to influence those at higher levels in the organization (e.g., ingratiation, coalition) typically are referred to as *tactics* rather than *strategies* (although the terms *tactic* and *strategy* have been used inconsistently in the upward influence literature, just as in the traditional compliance-gaining literature; see Waldron, 1999, p. 256). To maintain consistency with the definitions presented in Chapter 2, however, I will refer to abstract categories of upward influence behaviors as *strategies*, and distinguish them from *utterances*, or the concrete words and nonverbal behaviors used to enact a strategy. Strategies also can be grouped together at higher levels of abstraction; I will refer to these groups as *strategy clusters*. For example, the strategies of assertiveness, coalition, and upward appeal have been grouped together into a cluster of "hard" upward influence strategies (Farmer, Maslyn, Fedor, & Goodman, 1997).

7. Of Kipnis et al.'s (1980) original 58 items, 6 did not load cleanly (i.e., did not have a factor loading of .40 or higher) on any of the eight influence strategy factors. An additional 18 items

cross-loaded; that is, these items had loadings of .25 or higher on two or more strategy factors. Kipnis et al. cut these 24 items from their final upward influence scales.

8. Although these directional differences were statistically significant, Kipnis et al. (1980) do not report estimates of effect size. With the exception of assertiveness, differences in how often participants used each strategy with a boss, coworker, or subordinate appear to be small.

9. Kipnis and Schmidt (1982) themselves have developed a slightly modified version of their original organizational influence scale, called the Profile of Organizational Influence Strategies (POIS). The POIS is a streamlined version of the 1980 Kipnis et al. scale in which strategies have been relabeled (e.g., "rationality" is called "reason," "ingratiation" is called "friendliness") and the strategy of "blocking" is omitted. Different versions of the POIS assess the influence strategies a manager tends to use with his or her superiors (form M), coworkers (form C), and subordinates (form S). The POIS is a copyrighted instrument, and hence it has been used more frequently in training and consulting than in scholarly research (Schriesheim & Hinkin, 1990). For more information about the POIS, see Hellweg et al. (1990).

10. Kipnis and Schmidt (1983, 1988; Kipnis et al., 1984) performed cluster analyses on managers' responses to the POIS, form M, measure (see note 9) to identify three "styles" of upward influence. "Shotgun" managers report frequent use for most influence strategies, including assertiveness, with their superiors. "Tactician" managers report average use for most influence strategies and high use of rationality. "Bystander" managers report little use of any influence strategies with their superiors. This work bears a resemblance to Hunter and Boster's (1987) empathy model (see Chapter 4), in the sense that shotgun and bystander managers appear to have low and high thresholds, respectively, for selecting influence strategies. Although interesting, this work on upward influence styles does not offer any insight into how managers actually mix or sequence strategies within the same upward influence episodes.

11. For incidents containing only an initial influence attempt, Yukl et al. (1993, p. 15) report that the two coders independently identified the same strategies as being present in 85% of the cases. They do not report any measure of strategy categorizing reliability for incidents involving follow-up influence attempts, nor do they report any measure of how often the coders agreed on whether an incident included a follow-up attempt (immediate or delayed). Yukl et al. used a nominal-level typology containing nine strategies. Specifically, they combined the strategies of coalitions and upward appeals into a single strategy (labeled "coalitions"), and added two new strategies: (a) "legitimating strategies," which seek "to establish the legitimacy of a request by claiming the authority or right to make it or by verifying that it is consistent with organizational policies"; and (b) "personal appeals," which appeal to "target feelings of loyalty and friendship toward [the source] when asking for something" (p. 7).

12. Yukl et al. (1993) do not report their data in a manner that allows readers to compare upward, lateral, and downward influence attempts separately for message sources versus targets (as was done in Yukl & Falbe, 1990; see Table 8.7). However, a comparison of critical incidents reported by sources versus targets, collapsed across direction of influence, reveals more similarities than differences. For example, message sources and targets both recall that "rational persuasion" was the most frequently used organizational influence strategy, both alone and in combination with other strategies. In addition, sources and targets both recall that inspirational appeals, consultation, ingratiation, and legitimating strategies were more likely to be used in combination with other strategies than by themselves.

13. Krone (1992) classified upward influence strategies into the clusters of "open," "strategic," or "political" based on Porter et al.'s (1981) analysis of upward influence as political activity. Offermann and Kearney (1988) relied on an eight-category typology adapted from Falbo's (1977; Falbo & Peplau, 1980) two-dimensional model of direct/indirect and unilateral/bilateral power strategies. Finally, Waldron, Hunt, and Dsilva (1993) organized upward influence strategies into four clusters—direct, compensation, avoidance, and redefinition strategies—based on Brown and Levinson's (1987) politeness theory.

14. Second-order factor analysis is a procedure in which multiple factors underlying a scale (e.g., the six upward influence strategies in Schriesheim & Hinkin's, 1990, upward influence scale) themselves are treated as "items" and then factored in search of higher-level groupings. Different proposed groupings of first-order factors also can be compared for goodness of fit. For additional explanation, see Levine and McCroskey (1990).

15. See note 2 in Chapter 1 for a description of how Kelman's (1958, 1961) use of the term *compliance* differs from its meaning in the compliance-gaining literature.

16. Similar, but not identical, results are obtained when employees rate how frequently their upward influence attempts are motivated by specific goals included on preformulated lists (Kipnis et al., 1980, Study 2; Schmidt & Kipnis, 1984; Yukl & Falbe, 1990). When given a list of 5-6 goals, employees consistently rate "seeking support for organizational change" as the most frequent reason why they try to influence their bosses. Employees rate "seeking personal benefits" as a less common influence goal, although they report it as a goal pursued almost exclusively with superiors (as opposed to coworkers or subordinates). Seeking personal benefits can be politically risky (Porter et al., 1981), so it is possible that employees may underreport how often they pursue this goal when they are asked to rate it explicitly among a list of possible influence goals.

17. Our analysis attempts to predict "potential" rather than "actual" threats to face (see Wilson & Kunkel, 2000, pp. 216-217). Whether an employee actually would appear to be "overstepping the bounds" by proposing a new product or procedure no doubt depends on a host of factors, including the exact nature of the proposal, the employee's knowledge and experience with regard to the proposal, how the employee actually presents the proposal, the employee's relationship with his or her supervisor, the employee's prior history of proposing changes, and the larger organization's norms about innovation. The point is that the question of whether an employee should have consulted others first seems relevant to the goal of "proposing a new product or procedure" in a way that it does not to "seeking personal benefits," and hence competent employees are likely to orient to this possibility when proposing changes in work.

18. Although Farmer et al. (1997) treat coalition as a hard strategy, their own second-order factor analysis reveals that frequency-of-use ratings for coalition load equally well with strategies that compose the hard and soft clusters.

9

The Future of Theory and Research on Persuasive Message Production

Looking Ahead . . .

This concluding chapter poses three challenges for theory and research on persuasive message production. Specifically, can current perspectives (a) offer useful insights into seeking and resisting compliance as interactive phenomena, (b) offer insights into seeking and resisting compliance in particular contexts, and (c) help us to understand the role of emotion during message production? Implications for future work on persuasive message production are considered.

The overarching question addressed in this book is posed in the subtitle: Why do people say what they do when trying to influence others? As I have shown, theory and research addressing this question have coalesced, over time, around two metaphors. An initial generation of scholarship, guided by a metaphor of strategy selection, implicitly assumed that participants in compliance-gaining interactions define what is going on in similar fashion, possess sizable repertoires of strategies for seeking and resisting compliance, make conscious decisions about the relative benefits and costs of various strategies, and possess the knowledge and skill necessary to enact various strategies (see Chapter 4). A newer generation of scholarship, guided by the metaphor of goal pursuit, assumes that participants in compliance-gaining interactions create individual, and potentially different, understandings of what is (or should be) going on; form multiple, conflicting goals that change quickly as interaction unfolds; develop plans of varying complexity for pursuing and coordinating goals; possess differing abilities to enact those plans; and maintain only limited, momentary, and shifting awareness of their goals and plans (see Chapter 5).

In looking to the future, several questions arise. How will theories of persuasive message production based on the goal-pursuit metaphor fare? If "strategy selection" and "goal pursuit" have defined two generations of research, what metaphor might define a third generation? I do not propose direct answers to these questions, because my ill-fated predictions would be especially apparent to future readers. Rather, I conclude by posing three challenges for current theory and research on persuasive message production. Throughout the discussion, I highlight several themes running throughout this book. I pose each challenge as a question.

Persuasive Message Production: Three Challenges

CAN CURRENT WORK OFFER IMPORTANT INSIGHTS INTO INFLUENCE INTERACTIONS?

Seeking and resisting compliance are interactive phenomena (see Chapter 1), and this has two important implications for theories of persuasive message production. First, *descriptions of how people seek and resist compliance should be grounded in interaction.* Participants in most traditional compliance-gaining studies either selected strategies or wrote responses to hypothetical scenarios (see Chapter 4), whereas participants in the majority of upward influence studies have rated how frequently they have used various upward influence strategies in the recent past (see Chapter 8). These data collection methods are useful for addressing many questions, but researchers who rely too heavily on such methods risk developing overly simplistic pictures of seeking and resisting compliance.

Based on the strategy-selection metaphor, one might assume that most interpersonal influence episodes would unfold as follows: A message source makes a request and possibly supplements it with other compliance-seeking strategies in the same turn, a target individual says either yes or no and uses one or more compliance-resisting strategies, the message source either desists or persists with one or more compliance-seeking strategies, and so forth. Observational research, however, has documented more varied patterns. Consider the study discussed in Chapter 6, in which college students volunteering on behalf of the American Red Cross telephoned prior blood donors and asked them to donate again (Wilson, Levine, Humphreys, & Peters, 1994).

When confronted with a request for a repeat donation, some prior donors did immediately say yes (16%) or no (56%, most of whom also included a reason for refusing in the same turn). Other donors (12%), however, responded with a "conditional yes," indicating that they would be willing to comply if a stated obstacle (e.g., busy schedule) could be overcome. These donors responded with elements of both agreement and resistance. The final 16% of prior donors did not respond immediately with either yes or no, but instead asked questions, such as where/when they would donate (see the discussion of insertion sequences in Chapter 6). Some donors in this last group used the message sources' answers as grounds for subsequently saying no, but others eventually agreed to donate.

Put simply, patterns of seeking and resisting compliance are more varied than is implied by the strategy-selection metaphor. Message targets do not necessarily choose between "complying" and "using resistance strategies" when responding to requests, and their initial responses may not be either. A message source may not even begin with the desired request itself, but rather with "prerequests" designed to assess the target's ability and willingness to comply (see Chapter 6). Both participants often proceed incrementally, assessing the other's agreeableness and adapting incrementally (Sanders & Fitch, 2001). By supplementing hypothetical scenarios and self-report surveys with actual observation of compliance-gaining interactions, we will have a better understanding of the phenomena that theories of persuasive message production actually need to explain.

In addition to explaining interaction, *cognitive theories of persuasive message production also need to work within the constraints of interaction.* Message sources often seek compliance without prior planning, in which case they have to recall/adapt/implement plans on-line, within the time constraints of turn taking, while producing responses that are relevant to the targets' reactions even when those reactions were not anticipated (see Chapter 7). Message targets also are expected to produce timely, relevant responses to sources' appeals, even though they may not have anticipated the sources' requests or expected particular inducements to be offered. Message sources and targets typically do all this while coordinating influence and secondary goals, often under less-than-optimal conditions (e.g., fatigue). Much of the research testing cognitive theories (see Chapter 7), as well as my own cognitive rules model of interaction goals (see Chapter 5), however, has been conducted in conditions far removed from the demands of everyday interaction, such as in laboratory settings with monologue tasks. Waldron (1995) raises legitimate concerns about whether theories developed under such conditions can explain how people actually produce influence messages during interaction. At the least, cognitive theories of persuasive message production are most compelling when data bearing on their claims include studies that employ interactive tasks (e.g., Berger, Knowlton, & Abrahams, 1996).

Because theories of persuasive message production need to work within interactive constraints, Waldron and Cegala (1992) have argued that cognitive scholars should rely primarily on methods tapping the content of conversational thought on-line. I do not agree. Although stimulated recall (e.g., Waldron & Applegate, 1994) and think-aloud protocols (e.g., Berger, 1995) have provided useful insights, they offer only a partial picture of persuasive message production. Producing a message involves numerous psychological processes, some of which at times are subject to consciousness and others of which almost always occur outside of awareness (see Chapter 7). Although we often are aware of at least some interaction goals, processes that underlie goal formation are affected by stimuli occurring completely outside of awareness (e.g., "priming" effects; see Chapter 5). Given the complexity of understanding persuasive message production, we need to apply a variety of methods to gain useful insights.

CAN CURRENT WORK OFFER
IMPORTANT INSIGHTS INTO SPECIFIC CONTEXTS?

People seek and resist compliance as members of particular relationships embedded within larger institutional and cultural contexts. The traditional compliance-gaining literature, however, paid little attention to how influence interactions are shaped by particular contexts. Miller, Boster, Roloff, and Seibold (1977) explored which strategies students selected to seek compliance from a used car dealer, a neighbor, and a long-term romantic partner, yet they did not analyze what rights and obligations typically are associated with each relationship (see Chapter 4). In contrast, I have argued throughout this book that the most compelling explanations of persuasive message production integrate global (i.e., cross-contextual) theories of interactional and psychological processes, analyses of specific message functions such as seeking and resisting compliance, and analyses of particular relational, institutional, and cultural contexts. But do the global concepts and theories reviewed in Chapters 5-7 really offer important insights about specific contexts?

My attempt to understand child physical abuse and upward influence in organizations by integrating global and context-specific analyses certainly highlights the importance of the latter (see Chapter 8). Consider the issue of which features of influence messages and interactions need to be explained in each case. Whether a message source provides "reasons" to support his or her request appears to be an important feature in both cases, perhaps reflecting that the degree to which explicit reasons are offered is a dimension of influence messages salient in many contexts (see Chapter 3). The ways in which message sources vary in giving reasons, however, differ in the two cases. Physically abusive mothers differ from nonmaltreating mothers based on their limited use of inductive discipline (i.e., reasons that appeal to the child's internalized standards). Abusive mothers tend to rely primarily on power-assertive rather than inductive discipline regardless of how their children misbehave, whereas nonmaltreating mothers mix various forms of power assertion and inductive reasoning in response to different child misbehaviors (Trickett & Kuczynski, 1986; see Chapter 8). In contrast, employees and their supervisors both report that "rational persuasion" is the most frequently used upward influence strategy (Yukl & Falbe, 1990; Yukl, Falbe, & Youn, 1993). Employees are distinguished not by whether they give reasons when seeking their bosses' compliance, but rather by how much they elaborate the reasons they do give, mix those reasons with "hard" or "soft" strategies, and so forth (see Chapter 8).

Given the importance of context-specific analyses, some scholars advocate abandoning global theories such as politeness theory altogether (e.g., Tracy & Baratz, 1994). I think this position is too strong. Global theories highlight similarities across contexts that otherwise might be missed. Berger's (1997) hierarchy hypothesis, for instance, suggests why parents who are regulating perceived child misbehavior and faculty who are debating academic curricula both might engage in repetitive argument (see Chapter 7). Brown and Levinson's (1987) politeness theory posits that giving reasons can communicate positive and negative politeness (see Chapter 6) and suggests that this is particularly important when requests are made within relationships involving differential power (something that is true in both of the cases analyzed in Chapter 8). Although context-specific analyses are vital, we will best understand persuasive message production by melding global and specific analyses.

CAN CURRENT THEORIES INCORPORATE EMOTION?

It seems self-evident that emotions are an important part of why people say what they do when trying to influence others. Emotion and message production are intertwined in many ways:

Emotion may be associated with specific influence goals and hence define situations; emotions may motivate attempts to seek/resist compliance; emotions may be an activating condition for procedural knowledge; emotions may affect criteria for using/suppressing arguments; emotions may be aroused by success/ failure at gaining/resisting compliance; and regulating emotions may be a secondary goal during influence interactions. . . . Felt emotions may be expressed verbally/nonverbally during influence interactions; emotional displays may reinforce/complement compliance-seeking/resisting strategies; norms for displaying emotions may be associated with exerting influence within particular roles; and display rules for emotions during influence episodes may vary across culture. (Wilson, 1997, pp. 35-36)

Despite the sensibility of these claims, theories of persuasive message production have, until quite recently, virtually ignored the role of emotion (Burleson & Planalp, 2000).

Analyzing the role of emotion during message production is challenging, in part, because of complexities involved in defining emotion. Scholars typically distinguish emotions from other affective states such as moods; thus Dillard (1998) states that emotions are "affect as phasic" whereas moods are "affect as tonic." Burleson and Planalp (2000) note that as forms of affect, emotions and moods both "are feelings that have some valence (typically on a good-bad or positive-negative continuum) and some level of intensity (mild to strong)" (pp. 222-223). Despite this similarity, they argue,

emotions typically have definite or specific object (they are provoked by some particular circumstance), exhibit a relatively brief duration (in most cases lasting only a few moments), and are comparatively intense. Moods . . . are more global and diffuse in character, tend to be less intense states than emotions, and are comparatively enduring (often lasting many minutes, even hours), and usually are not tied to any particular provoking incidents. (pp. 223)

According to Burleson and Planalp, emotions have relatively direct effects on goals and planning process, whereas moods have more indirect and subtle effects on persuasive message production.

Emotions themselves also represent a complex of physiological, psychological, and behavioral tendencies (Burleson & Planalp, 2000; Metts & Bowers, 1994). Different levels of physiological arousal characterize different emotions; for example, anger, fear, and joy typically are associated with greater arousal than are sadness and sympathy. Different emotions arise from different appraisals of the current situation (Dillard, Kinney, & Cruz, 1996; Weiner, 1986). Although anger and fear both are arousing and negatively valenced, they arise from different appraisals of the relevance, cause, power, and legitimacy of environmental stimuli (Dillard et. al., 1996). Anger and fear also are associated with different action tendencies (e.g., the impulse to attack versus flee; Burleson & Planalp, 2000; Metts & Bowers, 1994). In sum, people's emotions are reflected in their arousal, appraisals, and action tendencies.

Despite the complexity of emotion, scholars recently have theorized multiple links between emotion and persuasive message production. First, message sources and target may be motivated to seek and resist compliance by emotion. Message sources experience different emotions depending on their attributions for targets' resistance, and these emotions in turn affect their own goals during subsequent interaction (MacGeorge, 2001; Weiner, 1986). For example, physically abusive mothers make more internal and stable attributions than do nonmaltreating mothers when their children misbehave, which leads abusive mothers to experience greater anger and thus to rely more heavily on power-assertive discipline (Dix, 1991; see Chapter 8). Burleson and Planalp (2000) label this first link "emotional messages," whereas Dillard (1998) refers to it as "emotion-motivated communication."

Second, message sources and targets sometimes alter their own emotional displays to gain or resist another's compliance (e.g., Sutton, 1991). In the upward influence literature, the strategy of "ingratiation" frequently involves exaggerated or feigned displays of emotion, such as when employees "act in a friendly manner towards my supervisor before making my request," "sympathize with my supervisor about the added problems that my request could cause," "agree with my immediate supervisor's opinions outwardly even when I disagree inwardly," and "take an interest in my immediate supervisor's personal life" (Deluga & Perry, 1994; Wayne & Ferris, 1990). Burleson and Planalp (2000) refer to this second link as "messages of emotion," whereas Dillard (1998) labels it "emotion-manifesting communication."

Third, message sources and targets may attempt to influence how the other party appraises a situation, and thus experiences emotion, as a way of seeking or resisting compliance. In the area of health communication, patients who suffer chronic pain (e.g., back pain) often experience feelings of helplessness and depression (Turk & Rudy, 1991). Chronic pain is a condition to be managed rather than cured, and relapses sometimes occur even when a patient has been compliant with recommendations about exercise, medication, and surgery. One of the challenges that health care providers face, then, is how to help patients develop "realistic yet optimistic" appraisals of their life circumstances that afford them some feeling of control with regard to managing their pain (Turk & Rudy, 1991; Wilson & Sabee, in press). Burleson and Planalp (2000) refer to this third link as "emotion-focused messages," whereas Dillard (1998) refers to it as "emotion-inducing communication."

In sum, scholars have proposed several links between emotion and persuasive message production. Much work remains to be done, however, in fleshing out the role of emotion within the many specific theories discussed in Chapters 5-7 of this book.

Summary

In this concluding chapter I have posed three challenges for current theory and research on persuasive message production. By posing these challenges, I do not intend to close this book on a pessimistic note. Persuasive message production is an exciting, interdisciplinary area of research. Communication scholars are at the forefront in developing original, insightful theories, and their work has pragmatic implications for important issues that confront our world today. These three challenges simultaneously highlight avenues for future research. Whether these challenges can be addressed within theories guided by a goal-pursuit metaphor or whether they will lead to a new generation of theories is a question that only time will answer.

References

Abrahams, M. F., & Bell, R. A. (1994). Encouraging charitable contributions: An examination of three models of door-in-the-face compliance. *Communication Research, 21,* 131-153.

Adams, C. H., & Shepherd, G. J. (1996). Managing volunteer performance: Face support and situational features as predictors of volunteers' evaluations of regulative messages. *Management Communication Quarterly, 9,* 363-388.

Adler, N. E., Moore, P. J., & Tschann, J. M. (1997). Planning skills in adolescence: The case of contraceptive use and non-use. In S. L. Friedman & E. K. Scholnick (Eds.), *The developmental psychology of planning: Why, how, and when do we plan?* (pp. 321-336). Mahwah, NJ: Lawrence Erlbaum.

Afifi, W. A., & Lee, J. W. (2000). Balancing instrumental and identity goals in relationships: The role of request directness and request persistence in the selection of sexual resistance strategies. *Communication Monographs, 67,* 284-305.

Aida, Y., & Falbo, T. (1991). Relationships between marital satisfaction, resources, and power strategies. *Sex Roles, 24,* 43-56.

Ajzen, I. (1991). The theory of planned behavior. *Organizational Behavior and Human Decision Processes, 50,* 179-210.

Alberts, J. K., Miller-Rassulo, M. A., & Hecht, M. L. (1991). A typology of drug resistance strategies. *Journal of Applied Communication Research, 19,* 129-151.

Alessandri, S. M. (1992). Mother-child interactional correlates of maltreated and nonmaltreated children's play behavior. *Development and Psychopathology, 4,* 257-270.

Allen, M., Mabry, E., Banski, M., & Preiss, R. (1991). Valid and constructive thoughts: Continuing the dialog about the RCQ. *Communication Reports, 4,* 120-125.

Allen, T. H., & Honeycutt, J. M. (1997). Planning, imagined interaction, and the nonverbal display of anxiety. *Communication Research, 24,* 64-82.

American Red Cross. (1989). *A history of helping others.* Washington, DC: Author.

Anderson, C. A. (1983). Motivational and performance deficits in interpersonal settings: The effects of attributional style. *Journal of Personality and Social Psychology, 45,* 1136-1147.

Anderson, C. A., & Jennings, D. L. (1980). When experiences of failure promote expectations of success: The impact of attributing failure to ineffective strategies. *Journal of Personality, 48,* 393-407.

Anderson, J. R. (1976). *Language, memory, and thought.* Hillsdale, NJ: Lawrence Erlbaum.

Anderson, J. R. (1983). *The architecture of cognition.* Cambridge, MA: Harvard University Press.

Anderson, J. R. (1984). Spreading activation. In J. R. Anderson & S. M. Kosslyn (Eds.), *Essays in learning and memory* (pp. 61-89). New York: Freeman.

Anderson, J. R. (1985). *Cognitive psychology and its implications* (2nd ed.). New York: Freeman.

Ansari, M. A., & Kapoor, A. (1987). Organizational context and upward influence tactics. *Organizational Behavior and Human Decision Processes, 40,* 39-49.

Applegate, J. L. (1980a). Adaptive communication in educational contexts: A study of teachers' communicative strategies. *Communication Education, 29,* 158-170.

Applegate, J. L. (1980b). Person- and position-centered communication in the day-care center. In N. K. Denzin (Ed.), *Studies in symbolic interaction* (Vol. 3, pp. 59-96). Greenwich, CT: JAI.

Applegate, J. L. (1982). The impact of construct system development on communication and impression formation in persuasive contexts. *Communication Monographs, 49,* 277-289.

Applegate, J. L., Burke, J. A., Burleson, B. R., Delia, J. G., & Kline, S. L. (1985). Reflection-enhancing parental communication. In I. E. Sigel (Ed.), *Parental belief systems: The psychological conse-quences for children* (pp. 107-142). Hillsdale, NJ: Lawrence Erlbaum.

Applegate, J. L., & Woods, E. (1991). Construct system development and attention to face wants in persuasive situations. *Southern Communication Journal, 56,* 194-204.

Austin, J. L. (1962). *How to do things with words.* Oxford: Clarendon.

Baglan, T., Lalumia, J., & Bayless, O. (1986). Utilization of compliance-gaining strategies: A research note. *Communication Monographs, 53,* 289-293.

Bandura, A. (1977). Self-efficacy: Towards a unifying theory of behavior change. *Psychological Review, 84,* 191-215.

Bargh, J. A., & Ferguson, M. J. (2000). Beyond behaviorism: On the automaticity of higher mental processes. *Psychological Bulletin, 126,* 925-945.

Barnett, O. W., Miller-Perrin, C. L., & Perrin, R. D. (1997). *Family violence across the lifespan: An introduction.* Thousand Oaks, CA: Sage.

Barry, B., & Shapiro, D. L. (1992). Influence tactics in combination: The interactive effects of soft versus hard tactics and rational exchange. *Human Relations, 65,* 555-574.

Barry, B., & Watson, M. R. (1996). Communication aspects of dyadic social influence in organ-izations: A review and integration of conceptual and empirical developments. In B. R. Burleson (Ed.), *Communication yearbook 19* (pp. 269-317). Thousand Oaks, CA: Sage.

Bauer, W. D., & Twentyman, C. T. (1985). Abusing, neglectful, and comparison mothers' responses to child-related and non-child-related stressors. *Journal of Consulting and Clinical Psychology, 53,* 335-343.

Bavelas, J. B. (1991). Some problems with linking goals to discourse. In K. Tracy (Ed.), *Under-standing face-to-face interaction: Issues linking goals and discourse* (pp. 119-130). Hillsdale, NJ: Lawrence Erlbaum.

Bavelas, J. B., Black, A., Chovil, N., & Mullett, J. (1990). *Equivocal communication.* Newbury Park, CA: Sage.

Baxter, L. A. (1984). An investigation of compliance-gaining as politeness. *Human Communication Research, 10,* 427-456.

Baxter, L. A., & Montgomery, B. M. (1996). *Relating: Dialogues and dialectics.* New York: Guilford.

Beach, W. A., & Dunning, D. G. (1982). Pre-indexing and conversational organization. *Quarterly Journal of Speech, 68,* 170-185.

Beatty, M. J. (1987). Erroneous assumptions underlying Burleson's critique. *Communication Quarterly, 35,* 329-333.

Beatty, M. J., Burant, P. A., Dobos, J. A., & Rudd, J. E. (1996). Trait verbal aggressiveness and the appropriateness and effectiveness of fathers' interaction plans. *Communication Quarterly, 44,* 1-15.

Beatty, M. J., & Payne, S. (1984). Loquacity and quantity of constructs as predictors of social perspective-taking. *Communication Quarterly, 32,* 207-210.

Beatty, M. J., & Payne, S. (1985). Is construct differentiation loquacity? A motivational perspective. *Human Communication Research, 11,* 605-612.

Belk, S. S., Snell, W. E., Jr., Garcia-Falconi, R., Hernandez-Sanchez, J. E., Hargrove, L., & Holtzman, W. H., Jr. (1988). Power strategy use in the intimate relationships of women and men from Mexico and the United States. *Personality and Social Psychology Bulletin, 14,* 439-447.

Belsky, J. (1980). Child maltreatment: An ecological integration. *American Psychologist, 35,* 320-335.

Belsky, J. (1993). Etiology of child maltreatment: A developmental-ecological analysis. *Psychological Bulletin, 114,* 413-434.

Bem, S. (1993). *The lenses of gender: Transforming the debate on sexual inequality.* New Haven, CT: Yale University Press.

Benoit, P. J. (1990). The structure of interaction goals. In J. A. Anderson (Ed.), *Communication yearbook 13* (pp. 407-416). Newbury Park, CA: Sage.

Berger, C. R. (1994). Power, dominance, and social interaction. In M. L. Knapp & G. R. Miller (Eds.), *Handbook of interpersonal communication* (2nd ed., pp. 450-507). Thousand Oaks, CA: Sage.

Berger, C. R. (1995). A plan-based approach to strategic communication. In D. E. Hewes (Ed.), *The cognitive bases of interpersonal communication* (pp. 141-180). Hillsdale, NJ: Lawrence Erlbaum.

Berger, C. R. (1997). *Planning strategic interaction: Attaining goals through communicative action.* Mahwah, NJ: Lawrence Erlbaum.

Berger, C. R. (2000). Goal detection and efficiency: Neglected aspects of message production. *Communication Theory, 10,* 156-166.

Berger, C. R. (in press). Goals and knowledge structures in social interaction. In M. L. Knapp & J. A. Daly (Eds.), *Handbook of interpersonal communication* (3rd ed.). Thousand Oaks, CA: Sage.

Berger, C. R., & Bell, R. A. (1988). Plans and the initiation of social relationships. *Human Communication Research, 15,* 217-235.

Berger, C. R., & Calabrese, R. J. (1975). Some explorations in initial interaction and beyond: Toward a developmental theory of interpersonal communication. *Human Communication Research, 1,* 99-112.

Berger, C. R., & diBattista, P. (1992). Information seeking and plan elaboration: What do you need to know to know what to do? *Communication Monographs, 59,* 368-387.

Berger, C. R., & diBattista, P. (1993). Communication failure and plan adaptation: If at first you don't succeed, say it louder and slower. *Communication Monographs, 60,* 220-238.

Berger, C. R., & Jordan, J. M. (1992). Planning sources, planning difficulty, and verbal fluency. *Communication Monographs, 59,* 130-149.

Berger, C. R., Karol, S. H., & Jordan, J. M. (1989). When a lot of knowledge is a dangerous thing: The debilitating effects of plan complexity on verbal fluency. *Human Communication Research, 16,* 91-119.

Berger, C. R., Knowlton, S. W., & Abrahams, M. F. (1996). The hierarchy principle in strategic communication. *Communication Theory, 6,* 111-142.

Bingham, S. G., & Burleson, B. R. (1989). Multiple effects of messages with multiple goals: Some perceived outcomes of responses to sexual harassment. *Human Communication Research, 16,* 184-286.

Bisanz, G. L., & Rule, B. G. (1989). Gender and the persuasion schema: A search for cognitive invariants. *Personality and Social Psychology Bulletin, 15,* 4-18.

Bisanz, G. L., & Rule, B. G. (1990). Children's and adults' comprehension of narratives about persuasion. In M. J. Cody & M. L. McLaughlin (Eds.), *The psychology of tactical communication* (pp. 48-69). Clevendon, Eng.: Multilingual Matters.

Biskin, D. S., & Crano, W. (1977). Structural organization of impressions derived from inconsistent information: A developmental study. *Genetic Psychology Monographs, 95,* 331-348.

Blum-Kulka, S. (1987). Indirectness and politeness in requests: Same or different? *Journal of Pragmatics, 11,* 131-145.

Blum-Kulka, S., House, J., & Kasper, G. (Eds.). (1989). *Cross-cultural pragmatics: Requests and apologies.* Norwood, NJ: Ablex.

Bochner, A. P. (1984). The functions of human communication in interpersonal bonding. In C. C. Arnold & J. W. Bowers (Eds.), *Handbook of rhetorical and communication theory* (pp. 544-621). Boston: Allyn & Bacon.

Bonito, J. A. (2001). An information-processing approach to participation in small groups. *Communication Research, 28,* 275-303.

Boster, F. J. (1988). Comments on the utility of compliance-gaining message selection tasks. *Human Communication Research, 15,* 169-177.

Boster, F. J. (1990). An examination of the state of compliance-gaining message production behavior research. In J. P. Dillard (Ed.), *Seeking compliance: The production of interpersonal influence messages* (pp. 7-17). Scottsdale, AZ: Gorsuch Scarisbrick.

Boster, F. J. (1995). Commentary on compliance-gaining message production research. In C. R. Berger & M. Burgoon (Eds.), *Communication and social influence processes* (pp. 91-114). East Lansing: Michigan State University Press.

Boster, F. J., Kazoleas, D., Levine, T., Rogan, R. G., & Kang, K. H. (1995). The impact of power on communicative persistence, strategic diversity and bargaining outcomes. *Communication Reports, 8,* 136-144.

Boster, F. J., & Levine, T. (1988). Individual differences and compliance-gaining message selection: The effects of verbal aggressiveness, argumentativeness, dogmatism, and negativism. *Communication Research Reports, 5,* 114-119.

Boster, F. J., Levine, T., & Kazoleas, D. C. (1993). The impact of argumentativeness and verbal aggressiveness on strategic diversity and persistence in compliance gaining behavior. *Communication Quarterly, 41,* 405-414.

Boster, F. J., & Stiff, J. B. (1984). Compliance-gaining message selection behavior. *Human Communication Research, 10,* 539-556.

Boster, F. J., Stiff, J. B., & Reynolds, R. A. (1985). Do persons respond differently to inductively-derived and deductively-derived lists of compliance gaining message strategies? A reply to Wiseman and Schenck-Hamlin. *Western Journal of Speech Communication, 49,* 177-187.

Bowers, J. W., Elliot, N. D., & Desmond, R. J. (1977). Exploiting pragmatic rules: Devious messages. *Human Communication Research, 3,* 235-242.

Bousha, D. M., & Twentyman, C. T. (1984). Mother-child interactional style in abuse, neglect, and control groups: Naturalistic observations in the home. *Journal of Abnormal Psychology, 93,* 106-114.

Bradley, E. J., & Peters, R. D. (1991). Physically abusive and nonabusive mothers' perceptions of parenting and child behavior. *American Journal of Orthopsychiatry, 61,* 455-460.

Brassard, M. R., & Hardy, D. B. (1997). Psychological maltreatment. In M. E. Helfer, R. S. Kempe, & R. D. Krugman (Eds.), *The battered child* (5th ed., pp. 392-412). Chicago: University of Chicago Press.

Bratman, M. E. (1990). What is intention? In P. R. Cohen, J. Morgan, & M. E. Pollack (Eds.), *Intentions in communication* (pp. 15-31). Cambridge: MIT Press.

Bresnahan, M., Cai, D. A., & Rivers, A. (1994). Saying no in Chinese and English: Cultural similarities and differences in strategies of refusal. *Asian Journal of Communication, 4,* 52-76.

Brewer, W. F., & Nakamura, G. (1984). The nature and functions of schemas. In R. S. Wyer & T. K. Srull (Eds.), *Handbook of social cognition* (Vol. 1, pp. 119-160). Hillsdale, NJ: Lawrence Erlbaum.

Broadbent, D. E., Cooper, P. F., Fitzgerald, P., & Parkes, K. R. (1982). The Cognitive Failures Questionnaire (CFQ) and its correlates. *British Journal of Clinical Psychology, 21,* 1-16.

Brown, P., & Levinson, S. C. (1978). Universals in language usage: Politeness phenomena. In E. Goody (Ed.), *Questions and politeness: Strategies in social interaction* (pp. 56-289). Cambridge: Cambridge University Press.

Brown, P., & Levinson, S. C. (1987). *Politeness: Some universals in language usage.* Cambridge: Cambridge University Press.

Bruce, B. C., & Newman, D. (1978). Interacting plans. *Cognitive Science, 2,* 196-233.

Bugental, D. B., Blue, J., Cortez, V., Fleck, K., Kopeikin, H., Lewis, J. C., & Lyon, J. (1993). Social cognitions as organizers of autonomic and affective responses to social challenge. *Journal of Personality and Social Psychology, 64,* 94-103.

Bugental, D. B., Blue, J., & Cruzcosa, M. (1989). Perceived control over caregiving outcomes: Implications for child abuse. *Developmental Psychology, 25*, 532-539.

Bugental, D. B., & Lewis, J. C. (1999). The paradoxical misuses of power by those who see themselves as powerless: How does it happen? *Journal of Social Issues, 55*, 51-64.

Bugental, D. B., & Shennum, W. A. (1984). "Difficult" children as elicitors and targets of adult communication patterns: An attributional-behavioral transactional analysis. *Monographs of the Society for Research in Child Development, 49*, 1-81.

Burgess, R. L., & Conger, R. D. (1978). Family interaction in abusive, neglectful, and normal families. *Child Development, 49*, 1163-1173.

Burgoon, J., & Hale, J. L. (1984). The fundamental *topoi* of relational communication. *Communication Monographs, 51*, 193-214.

Burgoon, M. (1994). Paths II: The garden variety. *Communication Theory, 4*, 81-92.

Burgoon, M., Birk, T. S., & Hall, J. R. (1991). Compliance and satisfaction with physician-patient communication: An expectancy theory interpretation of gender differences. *Human Communication Research, 18*, 177-208.

Burgoon, M., & Burgoon, J. K. (1990). Compliance-gaining and health care. In J. P. Dillard (Ed.), *Seeking compliance: The production of interpersonal influence messages* (pp. 161-188). Scottsdale, AZ: Gorsuch Scarisbrick.

Burgoon, M., Dillard, J. P., & Doran, N. (1984). Friendly and unfriendly persuasion: The effects of violations of expectations by males and females. *Human Communication Research, 10*, 283-294.

Burgoon, M., Dillard, J. P., Doran, N., & Miller, M. D. (1982). Cultural and situational influences on the process of persuasive strategy selection. *International Journal of Intercultural Relations, 6*, 85-100.

Burgoon, M., Dillard, J. P., Koper, R., & Doran, N. (1984). The impact of communication context and persuader gender on persuasive message selection. *Women's Studies in Communication, 7*, 1-12.

Burgoon, M., Parrott, R., Burgoon, J. K., Coker, R., Pfau, M., & Birk, T. (1990). Patients' severity of illness, noncompliance, and locus of control and physicians' compliance-gaining messages. *Health Communication, 2*, 29-46.

Burke, J. A. (1989). A comparison of methods for eliciting persuasive strategies: Strategy selection versus message construction. *Communication Reports, 2*, 72-82.

Burke, J. A., & Clark, R. A. (1982). An assessment of methodological options for investigating the development of persuasive skills across childhood. *Central States Speech Journal, 33*, 437-445.

Burleson, B. R. (1982). The affective perspective-taking process: A test of Turiel's role-taking model. In M. Burgoon (Ed.), *Communication yearbook 6* (pp. 473-488). Beverly Hills, CA: Sage.

Burleson, B. R. (1985). The production of comforting messages: Social-cognitive foundations. *Journal of Language and Social Psychology, 4*, 253-274.

Burleson, B. R. (1987). Cognitive complexity. In J. C. McCroskey & J. A. Daly (Eds.), *Personality and interpersonal communication* (pp. 305-349). Newbury Park, CA: Sage.

Burleson, B. R. (1989). The constructivist approach to person-centered communication: Analysis of a research exemplar. In B. Dervin, L. Grossberg, B. J. O'Keefe, & E. Wartella (Eds.), *Rethinking communication: Vol. 2. Paradigm exemplars* (pp. 29-46). Newbury Park, CA: Sage.

Burleson, B. R., Applegate, J. L., & Delia, J. G. (1991). On validly assessing the validity of the Role Category Questionnaire: A reply to Allen et al. *Communication Reports, 4*, 113-119.

Burleson, B. R., Applegate, J. L., & Neuwirth, C. M. (1981). Is complexity loquacity? A reply to Powers, Jordan, and Street. *Human Communication Research, 7*, 212-225.

Burleson, B. R., & Caplan, S. E. (1998). Cognitive complexity. In J. C. McCroskey, J. A. Daly, & M. M. Martin (Eds.), *Communication and personality: Trait perspectives* (pp. 230-286). Cresskill, NJ: Hampton.

Burleson, B. R., & Planalp, S. (2000). Producing emotion(al) messages. *Communication Theory, 10*, 221-250.

Burleson, B. R., & Waltman, M. S. (1988). Cognitive complexity: Using the Role Category Questionnaire measure. In C. H. Tardy (Ed.), *A handbook for the study of human communication: Methods and instruments for observing, measuring, and assessing communication processes* (pp. 1-35). Norwood, NJ: Ablex.

Burleson, B. R., Waltman, M. S., & Samter, W. (1987). More evidence that cognitive complexity is *not* loquacity: A reply to Beatty and Payne. *Communication Quarterly, 35,* 317-328.

Burleson, B. R., & Wilson, S. R. (1988). On the continued undesirability of item desirability: A reply to Boster, Hunter, and Seibold. *Human Communication Research, 15,* 178-191.

Burleson, B. R., Wilson, S. R., Waltman, M. S., Goering, E. M., Ely, T. K., & Whaley, B. B. (1988). Item desirability effects in compliance-gaining research: Seven studies documenting artifacts in the strategy selection procedure. *Human Communication Research, 14,* 429-486.

Buss, A. H. (1984). A conception of shyness. In J. A. Daly & J. C. McCroskey (Eds.), *Avoiding communication: Shyness, reticence, and communication apprehension* (pp. 39-49). Beverly Hills, CA: Sage.

Buzzanell, P. M. (1994). Gaining a voice: Feminist perspectives in organizational communication. *Management Communication Quarterly, 7,* 339-383.

Buzzanell, P. M. (2000). The promise and practice of the new career and social contract: Illusions exposed and suggestions for reform. In P. M. Buzzanell (Ed.), *Rethinking organizational and managerial communication from feminist perspectives* (pp. 209-235). Thousand Oaks, CA: Sage.

Buzzanell, P. M., & Burrell, N. A. (1997). Family and workplace conflict: Examining metaphorical conflict schemas and expressions across context and sex. *Human Communication Research, 24,* 109-146.

Buzzanell, P. M., Burrell, N. A., Stafford, R. S., & Berkowitz, S. (1996). When I call you up and you're not there: Application of communication accommodation theory to telephone answering machine messages. *Western Journal of Communication, 60,* 310-336.

Cai, D. A. (1994). *Planning in negotiation: A comparison of U.S. and Taiwanese cultures.* Unpublished doctoral dissertation, Michigan State University.

Cai, D. A. (1998). Culture, plans, and the pursuit of negotiation goals. *Journal of Asian Pacific Communication, 8,* 103-123.

Cai, D. A., & Wilson, S. R. (2000). Identity implications of influence goals: A cross-cultural comparison of interaction goals and facework. *Communication Studies, 51,* 307-328.

Canary, D. J., Cody, M. J., & Marston, P. (1986). Goal types, compliance-gaining, and locus of control. *Journal of Language and Social Psychology, 5,* 249-269.

Carli, L. L. (1999). Gender, interpersonal power, and social influence. *Journal of Social Issues, 55,* 81-99.

Case, T., Dosier, L., Murkison, G., & Keys, B. (1988). How managers influence superiors: A study of upward influence tactics. *Leadership and Organizational Development Journal, 9,* 25-31.

Cegala, D. J., & Waldron, V. R. (1992). A study of the relationship between communicative performance and conversation participants' thoughts. *Communication Studies, 43,* 105-123.

Cerezo, M. A. (1997). Abusive family interaction: A review. *Aggression and Violent Behavior, 2,* 215-240.

Cerezo, M. A., & D'Ocon, A. (1999). Sequential analyses in coercive mother-child interaction: The predictability hypothesis in abusive versus nonabusive dyads. *Child Abuse & Neglect, 23,* 99-113.

Cerezo, M. A., D'Ocon, A., & Dolz, L. (1996). Mother-child interactive patterns in abusive families versus nonabusive families: An observational study. *Child Abuse & Neglect, 20,* 573-587.

Chacko, H. E. (1990). Methods of upward influence, motivational needs, and administrators' perceptions of their supervisors' leadership styles. *Group & Organization Studies, 15,* 253-265.

Chilamkurti, C., & Milner, J. S. (1993). Perceptions and evaluations of child transgressions and disciplinary techniques in high- and low-risk mothers and their children. *Child Development, 64,* 1801-1814.

Chaffee, S. H. (1991). *Explication.* Newbury Park, CA: Sage.

Cheng, J. L. C. (1983). Organizational context and upward influence: An experimental study of the use of power tactics. *Group & Organization Studies, 8,* 337-355.

Cialdini, R. (1993). *Influence: Science and practice* (3rd ed.). Glenview, IL: Scott Foresman.

Clark, H. H., & Schunk, D. H. (1980). Polite responses to polite requests. *Cognition, 8,* 111-143.

Clark, R. A. (1979). The impact of self interest and desire for liking on the selection of communicative strategies. *Communication Monographs, 46,* 257-273.

Clark, R. A., & Delia, J. G. (1976). The development of functional persuasive skills in childhood and early adolescence. *Child Development, 47,* 1008-1014.

Clark, R. A., & Delia, J. G. (1977). Cognitive complexity, social perspective-taking, and functional persuasive skills in second- to ninth-grade children. *Human Communication Research, 3,* 128-134.

Clark, R. A., & Delia, J. G. (1979). Topoi and rhetorical competence. *Quarterly Journal of Speech, 65,* 187-206.

Cloven, D. H., & Roloff, M. E. (1991). Sense-making activities and interpersonal conflicts: Communicative cures for the mulling blues. *Western Journal of Speech Communication, 55,* 134-158.

Cody, M. J., Canary, D. J., & Smith, S. W. (1994). Compliance-gaining goals: An inductive analysis of actors' goal types, strategies, and successes. In J. A. Daly & J. M. Wiemann (Eds.), *Strategic interpersonal communication* (pp. 33-90). Hillsdale, NJ: Lawrence Erlbaum.

Cody, M. J., & Greene, J. O. (Eds.). (1985). Cognition in social interaction: Production principles [Special issue]. *Journal of Language and Social Psychology, 4*(3-4).

Cody, M. J., Greene, J. O., Marston, P. J., O'Hair, H. D., Baaske, K. T., & Schneider, M. J. (1986). Situation perception and message strategy selection. In M. L. McLaughlin (Ed.), *Communication yearbook 9* (pp. 390-420). Beverly Hills, CA: Sage.

Cody, M. J., & McLaughlin, M. L. (1980). Perceptions of compliance-gaining situations: A dimensional analysis. *Communication Monographs, 47,* 132-148.

Cody, M. J., & McLaughlin, M. L. (Eds.). (1990). *The psychology of tactical communication.* Clevendon, Eng.: Multilingual Matters.

Cody, M. J., McLaughlin, M. L., & Jordan, W. J. (1980). A multidimensional scaling of three sets of compliance-gaining strategies. *Communication Quarterly, 28,* 34-46.

Cody, M. J., McLaughlin, M. L., & Schneider, M. J. (1981). The impact of intimacy and relational consequences on the selection of interpersonal persuasive messages: A reanalysis. *Communication Quarterly, 29,* 91-106.

Cody, M. J., Woelfel, M. L., & Jordan, W. J. (1983). Dimensions of compliance-gaining situations. *Human Communication Research, 9,* 99-113.

Cognition in message processing and production [Special issue]. (1989). *Human Communication Research, 16*(1).

Cohen, P. R., Morgan, J., & Pollack, M. E. (Eds.). (1990). *Intentions in communication.* Cambridge: MIT Press.

Colloquy on generalization [Special issue]. (1988). *Human Communication Research, 15*(1).

Corse, S., Schmid, K., & Trickett, P. (1990). Social network characteristics of mothers in abusing and nonabusing families and their relationships to parenting beliefs. *Journal of Community Psychology, 18,* 44-59.

Coupland, N., Grainger, K., & Coupland, J. (1988). Politeness in context: Intergenerational issues. *Language and Society, 17,* 252-262.

Craig, R. T. (1986). Goals in discourse. In D. G. Ellis & W. A. Donohue (Eds.), *Contemporary issues in language and discourse processes* (pp. 257-274). Hillsdale, NJ: Lawrence Erlbaum.

Craig, R. T., Tracy, K., & Spisak, F. (1986). The discourse of requests: Assessment of a politeness approach. *Human Communication Research, 12,* 437-468.

Crockett, W. H. (1965). Cognitive complexity and impression formation. In B. A. Maher (Ed.), *Progress in experimental personality research* (Vol. 2, pp. 47-90). New York: Academic Press.

Cronen, V. E., Pearce, W. B., & Snavely, L. M. (1979). A theory of rule-structure and types of episodes and a study of perceived enmeshment in undesired repetitive patterns. In D. Nimmo (Ed.), *Communication yearbook 3* (pp. 225-240). New Brunswick, NJ: Transaction.

Crouch, J. L., & Behl, L. E. (2001). Relationships among parental beliefs in corporal punishment, reported stress, and physical child abuse potential. *Child Abuse & Neglect, 25,* 413-419.

Crowell, T. L., & Emmers-Sommer, T. M. (2000). Examining condom use self-efficacy and coping in sexual situations. *Communication Research Reports, 17,* 191-202.

Dallinger, J. M., & Hample, D. (1989). Biological and psychological gender effects upon cognitive editing of arguments. In B. E. Gronbeck (Ed.), *Spheres of argument* (pp. 563-568). Annandale, VA: Speech Communication Association.

Dallinger, J. M., & Hample, D. (1991). Cognitive editing of arguments and interpersonal construct differentiation: Redefining the relationship. In F. H. van Eemeren, R. Grootendorst, J. A. Blair, & C. A. Willard (Eds.), *Proceedings of the second international conference on argumentation* (pp. 567-574). Amsterdam: SICSAT.

Dallinger, J. M., & Hample, D. (1994). The effects of gender on compliance gaining strategy endorsement and suppression. *Communication Reports, 7,* 43-49.

Daly, J. A., Weber, D. J., Vangelisti, A. L., Maxwell, M., & Neel, H. (1989). Concurrent cognitions during conversations: Protocol analysis as a means of exploring conversations. *Discourse Processes, 12,* 227-244.

Daly, J. A., & Wiemann, J. M. (Eds.). (1994). *Strategic interpersonal communication.* Hillsdale, NJ: Lawrence Erlbaum.

Delia, J. G., & Clark, R. A. (1977). Cognitive complexity, social perception, and the development of listener-adapted communication in six-, eight-, ten-, and twelve-year old boys. *Communication Monographs, 44,* 326-345.

Delia, J. G., Kline, S. L., & Burleson, B. R. (1979). The development of persuasive communication strategies in kindergartners through twelfth-graders. *Communication Monographs, 46,* 241-256.

Delia, J. G., O'Keefe, B. J., & O'Keefe, D. J. (1982). The constructivist approach to communication. In F. E. X. Dance (Ed.), *Human communication theory* (pp. 147-191). New York: Harper & Row.

Deluga, R. J. (1988). Relationship of transformation and transactional leadership with employee influence strategies. *Group & Organization Studies, 13,* 456-467.

Deluga, R. J., & Perry, J. T. (1991). The relationship of subordinate upward influencing behavior, satisfaction, and perceived superior effectiveness with leader-member exchanges. *Journal of Occupational Psychology, 64,* 239-252.

Deluga, R. J., & Perry, J. T. (1994). The role of subordinate performance and ingratiation in leader-member exchanges. *Group & Organization Management, 19,* 67-86.

deTurck, M. A. (1985). A transactional analysis of compliance-gaining behavior: Effects of noncompliance, relational contexts, and actors' gender. *Human Communication Research, 12,* 54-78.

deTurck, M. A. (1987). When communication fails: Physical aggression as a compliance-gaining strategy. *Communication Monographs, 54,* 106-112.

deTurck, M. A., & Miller, G. R. (1983). Adolescent perceptions of parental persuasive message strategies. *Journal of Marriage and the Family, 45,* 543-552.

diBattista, P. (1994). Effects of planning on performance of trust-violating versus tactful, white lies: How are familiar speech acts cognitively represented? *Communication Studies, 45,* 174-186.

Dillard, J. P. (1988). Compliance-gaining message selection: What is our dependent variable? *Communication Monographs, 55,* 162-183.

Dillard, J. P. (1989). Types of influence goals in personal relationships. *Journal of Social and Personal Relationships, 6,* 293-308.

Dillard, J. P. (1990a). A goal-driven model of interpersonal influence. In J. P. Dillard (Ed.), *Seeking compliance: The production of interpersonal influence messages* (pp. 41-56). Scottsdale, AZ: Gorsuch Scarisbrick.

Dillard, J. P. (Ed.). (1990b). *Seeking compliance: The production of interpersonal influence messages.* Scottsdale, AZ: Gorsuch Scarisbrick.

Dillard, J. P. (1997a). Explicating the goal construct: Tools for theorists. In J. O. Greene (Ed.), *Message production: Advances in communication theory* (pp. 47-69). Mahwah, NJ: Lawrence Erlbaum.

Dillard, J. P. (1998). Foreword: The role of affect in communication, biology, and social relationships. In P. A. Anderson & L. K. Guerrero (Eds.), *Handbook of communication and emotion: Theory, research, application, and contexts* (pp. xvii-xxxii). San Diego, CA: Academic Press.

Dillard, J. P., & Burgoon, M. (1985). Situational influences on the selection of compliance-gaining messages: Two tests of the predictive utility of the Cody-McLaughlin typology. *Communication Monographs, 52,* 289-304.

Dillard, J. P., & Fitzpatrick, M. A. (1985). Compliance-gaining in marital interaction. *Personality and Social Psychology Bulletin, 11,* 419-433.

Dillard, J. P., Kinney, T. A., & Cruz, M. G. (1996). Influence, appraisals, and emotions in close relationships. *Communication Monographs, 63,* 105-130.

Dillard, J. P., & Schrader, D. C. (1998). On the utility of the goals-plans-action sequence. *Communication Studies, 49,* 300-304.

Dillard, J. P., Segrin, C., & Harden, J. M. (1989). Primary and secondary goals in the production of interpersonal influence messages. *Communication Monographs, 56,* 19-38.

Dillard, J. P., & Solomon, D. H. (2000). Conceptualizing context in message production research. *Communication Theory, 10,* 167-175.

Dillard, J. P., Wilson, S. R., Tusing, K. J., & Kinney, T. A. (1997). Politeness judgments in personal relationships. *Journal of Language and Social Psychology, 16,* 297-325.

Dix, T. (1991). The affective organization of parenting: Adaptive and maladaptive processes. *Psychological Bulletin, 110,* 3-25.

Dix, T., Ruble, D. N., & Zambarano, R. J. (1989). Mothers' implicit theories of discipline: Child effects, parent effects, and the attribution process. *Child Development, 60,* 1373-1391.

Donohue, W. A. (1990). Interaction goals in negotiation: A critique. In J. A. Anderson (Ed.), *Communication yearbook 13* (pp. 417-427). Newbury Park, CA: Sage.

Dopke, C. A., & Milner, J. S. (2000). Impact of child noncompliance on stress appraisals, attributions, and disciplinary choices in mothers at high and low risk for child physical abuse. *Child Abuse & Neglect, 24,* 493-504.

Drake, B. H., & Moberg, D. J. (1986). Communicating influence attempts in dyads: Linguistic sedatives and palliatives. *Academy of Management Review, 11,* 567-584.

Dreher, G. F., Dougherty, T. W., & Whitely, W. (1989). Influence tactics and salary attainment: A gender-specific analysis. *Sex Roles, 20,* 535-550.

Dweck, C. S. (1999). *Self-theories: Their role in motivation, personality, and development.* Philadelphia: Psychology Press/Taylor & Francis.

Eagly, A. H., & Chaiken, S. (1993). *The psychology of attitudes.* Fort Worth, TX: Harcourt Brace Jovanovich.

Edgar, T., & Fitzpatrick, M. A. (1990). Communicating sexual desire: Message tactics for having and avoiding intercourse. In J. P. Dillard (Ed.), *Seeking compliance: The production of interpersonal influence messages* (pp. 107-122). Scottsdale, AZ: Gorsuch Scarisbrick.

Edgar, T., Freimuth, V. S., Hammond, S. L., McDonald, D. A., & Fink, E. L. (1992). Strategic sexual communication: Condom use and resistance. *Health Communication, 4,* 83-104.

Ellis, S., & Siegler, R. S. (1997). Planning as a strategic choice, or why don't children plan when they should? In S. L. Friedman & E. K. Scholnick (Eds.), *The developmental psychology of planning: Why, how, and when do we plan?* (pp. 183-208). Mahwah, NJ: Lawrence Erlbaum.

Erez, M., & Rim, Y. (1982). The relationship between goals, influence tactics, and personal and organizational variables. *Human Relations, 35,* 871-878.

Erez, M., Rim, Y., & Keider, I. (1986). The two sides of the tactics of influence: Agent vs. target. *Journal of Occupational Psychology, 59,* 25-39.

Ericsson, K. A., & Simon, H. A. (1984). *Protocol analysis: Verbal reports as data*. Cambridge: MIT Press.

Fairhurst, G. T. (1993). The leader-member exchange patterns of women leaders in industry: A discourse analysis. *Communication Monographs, 60,* 321-351.

Fairhurst, G. T. (2001). Dualisms in leadership research. In F. M. Jablin & L. L. Putnam (Eds.), *The new handbook of organizational communication: Advances in theory, research, and methods* (pp. 379-439). Thousand Oaks, CA: Sage.

Fairhurst, G. T., Green, S. G., & Snavely, B. K. (1984). Face support in controlling poor performance. *Human Communication Research, 11,* 272-295.

Falbe, C. M., & Yukl, G. (1992). Consequences for managers of using single influence tactics and combinations of tactics. *Academy of Management Journal, 35,* 638-652.

Falbo, T. (1977). Multidimensional scaling of power strategies. *Journal of Personality and Social Psychology, 35,* 537-547.

Falbo, T., & Peplau, L. A. (1980). Power strategies in intimate relationships. *Journal of Personality and Social Psychology, 38,* 618-628.

Farmer, S. M., Maslyn, J. M., Fedor, D. B., & Goodman, J. S. (1997). Putting upward influence strategies into context. *Journal of Organizational Behavior, 18,* 17-42.

Fazio, R. H., Sanbonmatsu, D., Powell, M. C., & Kardes, F. R. (1986). On the automatic activation of attitudes. *Journal of Personality and Social Psychology, 50,* 229-238.

Fishbein, M., & Ajzen, I. (1975). *Belief, attitude, intention, and behavior: An introduction to theory and research*. Reading, MA: Addison-Wesley.

Fiske, S. T., & Taylor, S. E. (1991). *Social cognition* (2nd ed.). Reading, MA: Addison-Wesley.

Fitch, K. L. (1994). A cross-cultural study of directive sequences and some implications for compliance-gaining research. *Communication Monographs, 61,* 185-209.

Folkes, V. S. (1982). Communicating the reasons for social rejection. *Journal of Experimental Social Psychology, 18,* 235-252.

Foss, S. K., & Griffin, C. L. (1995). Beyond persuasion: A proposal for an invitational rhetoric. *Communication Monographs, 62,* 2-18.

Francik, E. P., & Clark, H. H. (1985). How to make requests that overcome obstacles to compliance. *Journal of Memory and Language, 24,* 560-584.

Friedman, S. L., & Scholnick, E. K. (Eds.). (1997). *The developmental psychology of planning: Why, how, and when do we plan?* Mahwah, NJ: Lawrence Erlbaum.

Fu, P. D., & Yukl, G. (2000). Perceived effectiveness of influence tactics in the United States and China. *Leadership Quarterly, 11,* 251-266.

Garbarino, J., & Kostelny, K. (1992). Child maltreatment as a community problem. *Child Abuse & Neglect, 16,* 455-464.

Garko, M. G. (1992). Physician-executives' use of influence strategies: Gaining compliance from superiors who communicate in attractive and unattractive styles. *Health Communication, 4,* 137-154.

Gastil, J. (1995). An appraisal and revision of the constructivist research program. In B. R. Burleson (Ed.), *Communication yearbook 18* (pp. 83-104). Thousand Oaks, CA: Sage.

Gelles, R. J. (1997). *Intimate violence in families* (3rd ed.). Thousand Oaks, CA: Sage.

Gibbs, R. W. (1986). What makes some indirect speech acts conventional? *Journal of Memory and Language, 25,* 181-196.

Gibbs, R. W., & Mueller, R. A. G. (1988). Conversational sequences and preference for indirect speech acts. *Discourse Processes, 11,* 101-116.

Gil, D. G. (1970). *Violence against children: Physical child abuse in the United States*. Cambridge, MA: Harvard University Press.

Goddard, H. W., & Miller, B. C. (1993). Adding attribution to parenting programs. *Families in Society, 74,* 84-92.

Goffman, E. (1959). *The presentation of self in everyday life*. New York: Doubleday.

Goffman, E. (1967). *Interaction ritual: Essays on face-to-face behavior.* Chicago: Aldine.

Goldsmith, D. J. (2000). Soliciting advice: The role of sequential placement in mitigating face threat. *Communication Monographs, 67,* 1-19.

Goldsmith, D. J., & Fitch, K. (1997). The normative context of advice as social support. *Human Communication Research, 23,* 454-476.

Graham, J. L., & Sano, Y. (1989). *Smart bargaining: Doing business with the Japanese* (Rev. ed.). New York: Harper Business.

Greene, J. O. (1984a). A cognitive approach to human communication: An action assembly theory. *Communication Monographs, 51,* 289-306.

Greene, J. O. (1984b). Evaluating cognitive explanations of communicative phenomena. *Quarterly Journal of Speech, 70,* 241-254.

Greene, J. O. (1984c). Speech preparation processes and verbal fluency. *Human Communication Research, 11,* 61-84.

Greene, J. O. (1988). Cognitive processes: Methods for probing the black box. In C. H. Tardy (Eds.), *A handbook for the study of human communication: Methods and instruments for observing, measuring, and assessing communication processes* (pp. 37-66). Norwood, NJ: Ablex.

Greene, J. O. (1990). Tactical social action: Towards some strategies for theory. In M. J. Cody & M. L. McLaughlin (Eds.), *The psychology of tactical communication* (pp. 31-47). Clevendon, Eng.: Multilingual Matters.

Greene, J. O. (1994). What sort of terms ought theories of human action incorporate? *Communication Studies, 45,* 187-211.

Greene, J. O. (1995a). An action-assembly perspective on verbal and nonverbal message production: A dancer's message unveiled. In D. E. Hewes (Ed.), *The cognitive bases of interpersonal communication* (pp. 51-85). Hillsdale, NJ: Lawrence Erlbaum.

Greene, J. O. (1995b). Production of messages in pursuit of multiple social goals: Action assembly theory contributions to the study of cognitive encoding processes. In B. R. Burleson (Ed.), *Communication yearbook 18* (pp. 26-53). Thousand Oaks, CA: Sage.

Greene, J. O. (Ed.). (1997a). *Message production: Advances in communication theory.* Mahwah, NJ: Lawrence Erlbaum.

Greene, J. O. (1997b). A second generation action assembly theory. In J. O. Greene (Ed.), *Message production: Advances in communication theory* (pp. 151-170). Mahwah, NJ: Lawrence Erlbaum.

Greene, J. O. (2000). Evanescent mentation: An ameliorative conceptual foundation for research and theory on message production. *Communication Theory, 10,* 139-155.

Greene, J. O., & Geddes, D. (1993). An action assembly perspective on social skill. *Communication Theory, 3,* 26-49.

Greene, J. O., & Lindsey, A. E. (1989). Encoding processes in the production of multiple-goal messages. *Human Communication Research, 16,* 120-140.

Greene, J. O., Lindsey, A. E., & Hawn, J. J. (1990). Social goals and speech production: Effects of multiple goals on pausal phenomena. *Journal of Language and Social Psychology, 9,* 119-134.

Greene, J. O., McDaniel, T. L., Buska, K., & Ravizza, S. M. (1993). Cognitive processes in the production of multiple goal messages: Evidence from the temporal characteristics of speech. *Western Journal of Communication, 57,* 65-86.

Grice, H. P. (1975). Logic and conversation. In P. Cole & J. L. Morgan (Eds.), *Syntax and semantics: Vol. 3. Speech acts* (pp. 41-58). New York: Academic Press.

Gudykunst, W. B., Gao, G., Schmidt, K. L., Nishida, T., Bond, M. H., Leung, K., Wang, G., & Barraclough, R. A. (1992). The influence of individualism: Collectivism, self-monitoring, and predicted outcome value on communication in ingroup and outgroup relationships. *Journal of Cross-Cultural Psychology, 23,* 196-213.

Hale, C. L. (1986). Impact of cognitive complexity on message structure in a face-threatening context. *Journal of Language and Social Psychology, 5,* 135-144.

Hale, C. L., & Delia, J. G. (1976). Cognitive complexity and social perspective-taking. *Communication Monographs, 43,* 195-203.

Haller, S. (1999). An introduction to interactive discourse processing from the perspective of plan recognition and text planning. *Artificial Intelligence Review, 13,* 259-311.

Hample, D., & Dallinger, J. M. (1985, November). *Cognitive editing of argument strategies.* Paper presented at the annual meeting of the Speech Communication Association, Denver.

Hample, D., & Dallinger, J. M. (1987a). Individual differences in cognitive editing standards. *Human Communication Research, 14,* 123-144.

Hample, D., & Dallinger, J. M. (1987b). Self monitoring and the cognitive editing of arguments. *Central States Speech Journal, 38,* 152-165.

Hample, D., & Dallinger, J. M. (1990). Arguers as editors. *Argumentation, 4,* 153-169.

Hample, D., & Dallinger, J. M. (1998). On the etiology of the rebuff phenomenon: Why are persuasive messages less polite after rebuffs? *Communication Studies, 49,* 305-321.

Hample, D., Dallinger, J. M., & Meyers, K. A. (1989). *Marital argument.* Paper presented at the annual meeting of the Speech Communication Association, San Francisco.

Harper, N. L., & Hirokawa, R. Y. (1988). A comparison of persuasive strategies used by female and male managers I: An examination of downward influence. *Communication Quarterly, 36,* 157-168.

Harrington, N. G. (1995). The effects of college students' alcohol resistance strategies. *Health Communication, 7,* 371-391.

Hayes-Roth, B., & Hayes-Roth, F. (1979). A cognitive model of planning. *Cognitive Science, 3,* 275-310.

Hecht, M. L., Boster, F. J., & LaMer, S. (1989). The effect of extroversion and differentiation on listener-adapted communication. *Communication Reports, 2,* 1-8.

Hecht, M. L., Trost, M. R., Bator, R. J., & MacKinnon, D. (1997). Ethnicity and sex similarities and differences in drug resistance. *Journal of Applied Communication Research, 25,* 75-97.

Heider, F. (1958). *The psychology of interpersonal relations.* New York: John Wiley.

Hellweg, S. A., Geist, P., Jorgensen, P. F., & White-Mills, K. (1990). An analysis of compliance-gaining instrumentation in the organizational communication literature. *Management Communication Quarterly, 4,* 244-271.

Heritage, J. (1984). A change-of-state token and aspects of its sequential placement. In J. M. Atkinson & J. Heritage (Eds.), *Structures of social action: Studies in conversation analysis* (pp. 299-346). Cambridge: Cambridge University Press.

Herrenkohl, E. C., Herrenkohl, R. C., Toedter, L., & Yanushefski, A. M. (1984). Parent-child interactions in abusive and nonabusive families. *Journal of the American Academy of Child Psychiatry, 23,* 641-648.

Hertzog, R. L., & Bradac, J. J. (1984). Perceptions of compliance-gaining situations: An extended analysis. *Communication Research, 11,* 363-391.

Hewes, D. E. (1995a). Cognitive interpersonal communication research: Some thoughts on criteria. In B. R. Burleson (Ed.), *Communication yearbook 18* (pp. 162-179). Thousand Oaks, CA: Sage.

Hewes, D. E. (1995b). Cognitive processing of problematic messages: Reinterpreting to "unbias" texts. In D. E. Hewes (Ed.), *The cognitive bases of interpersonal communication* (pp. 113-140). Hillsdale, NJ: Lawrence Erlbaum.

Hewes, D. E., & Planalp, S. (1987). The individual's place in communication science. In C. R. Berger & S. H. Chaffee (Eds.), *Handbook of communication science* (pp. 146-183). Newbury Park, CA: Sage.

Higgins, E. T., Bargh, J. A., & Lombardi, W. (1985). Nature of priming effects on categorization. *Journal of Experimental Psychology: Learning, Memory, and Cognition, 11,* 59-69.

Higgins, E. T., King, G. A., & Marvin, G. H. (1982). Individual construct accessibility and subjective impressions of recall. *Journal of Personality and Social Psychology, 43,* 35-47.

Hirokawa, R. Y., Kodama, R. A., & Harper, N. L. (1990). Impact of managerial power on persuasive strategy selection by female and male managers. *Management Communication Quarterly, 4,* 322-333.

Hirokawa, R. Y., Mickey, J., & Miura, S. (1991). Effects of request legitimacy on the compliance-gaining tactics of male and female managers. *Communication Monographs, 58,* 421-436.

Hirokawa, R. Y., & Miyahara, A. (1986). A comparison of influence strategies utilized by managers in American and Japanese organizations. *Communication Quarterly, 34,* 250-265.

Hjelmquist, E. (1990). Planning and execution of discourse in conversation. *Communication & Cognition, 23,* 277-293.

Hobbs, J. R., & Evans, D. A. (1980). Conversation as planned behavior. *Cognitive Science, 4,* 349-377.

Hoffman, M. L. (1960). Power assertion by the parent and its impact on the child. *Child Development, 31,* 129-143.

Hoffman, M. L. (1980). Moral development in adolescence. In J. Adelson (Ed.), *Handbook of adolescent psychology* (pp. 295-343). New York: John Wiley.

Hofstede, G. (1980). *Culture's consequences: International differences in work-related values.* Beverly Hills, CA: Sage.

Hofstede, G. (2001). *Culture's consequences: Comparing values, behaviors, institutions, and organizations across nations* (2nd ed.). Thousand Oaks, CA: Sage.

Holtgraves, T. (1992). The linguistic realization of face management: Implications for language production and comprehension, person perception, and cross-cultural communication. *Social Psychology Quarterly, 55,* 141-159.

Holtgraves, T., & Yang, J. N. (1990). Politeness as universal: Cross-cultural perceptions of request strategies and inferences based on their use. *Journal of Personality and Social Psychology, 59,* 719-729.

Holtgraves, T., & Yang, J. N. (1992). Interpersonal underpinnings of request strategies: General principles and differences due to culture and gender. *Journal of Personality and Social Psychology, 62,* 246-256.

Hopper, R., Koch, S., & Mandelbaum, J. (1986). Conversation analysis methods. In D. G. Ellis & W. A. Donohue (Eds.), *Contemporary issues in language and discourse processes* (pp. 169-186). Hillsdale, NJ: Lawrence Erlbaum.

Howard, J. A., Blumstein, P., & Schwartz, P. (1986). Sex, power, and influence tactics in intimate relationships. *Journal of Personality and Social Psychology, 51,* 102-109.

Hui, C. H., & Triandis, H. C. (1986). Individualism-collectivism: A study of cross-cultural researchers. *Journal of Cross-Cultural Psychology, 13,* 43-59.

Humphreys, L., & Wilson, S. R. (1996, May). *The role of argumentativeness and verbal aggressiveness in compliance-gaining: Predicting persistence, obstacle focus, and strategy use in telephone requests for blood donation.* Paper presented at the annual meeting of the International Communication Association, Chicago.

Hunter, J. E. (1988). Failure of the social desirability response set hypothesis. *Human Communication Research, 15,* 162-168.

Hunter, J. E., & Boster, F. (1978). *An empathy model of compliance-gaining message strategy selection.* Paper presented at the annual meeting of the Speech Communication Association, Minneapolis.

Hunter, J. E., & Boster, F. (1987). A model of compliance-gaining message selection. *Communication Monographs, 54,* 63-84.

Hunter, J. E., Schmidt, F. L., & Jackson, G. B. (1982). *Meta-analysis: Cumulating research findings across studies.* Beverly Hills, CA: Sage.

Ifert, D. E., & Roloff, M. E. (1994). Anticipated obstacles to compliance: Predictors of their presence and expression. *Communication Studies, 45,* 120-130.

Ifert, D. E., & Roloff, M. E. (1996). Responding to rejected requests: Persistence and response type as functions of obstacles to compliance. *Journal of Language and Social Psychology, 15,* 40-58.

Indiana Code. (1997). *Article 34. Juvenile law: Children in need of services.* Retrieved from http://www.in.gov/fssa/servicemental/pub/law/title31.pdf

Infante, D. A., & Wigley, C. J. (1986). Verbal aggressiveness: An interpersonal model and measure. *Communication Monographs, 53,* 61-69.

Instone, D., Major, B., & Bunker, B. B. (1983). Gender, self-confidence, and social influence strategies: An organizational simulation. *Journal of Personality and Social Psychology, 44*, 322-333.

Jackson, S., & Backus, D. (1982). Are compliance-gaining strategies dependent on situational variables? *Central States Speech Journal, 33*, 469-479.

Jackson, S., & Jacobs, S. (1980). Structure of conversational argument: Pragmatic bases for the enthymeme. *Quarterly Journal of Speech, 66*, 251-265.

Jackson, S., & Jacobs, S. (1983). Generalizing about messages: Suggestions for design and analysis of experiments. *Human Communication Research, 9*, 169-181.

Jackson, S., Thompson, R. A., Christiansen, E. H., Colman, R. A., Wyatt, J., Buckendahl, C. W., et al. (1999). Predicting abuse-prone parental attitudes and discipline practices in a nationally representative sample. *Child Abuse & Neglect, 23*, 15-29.

Jacobs, S. (1994). Language and interpersonal communication. In M. L. Knapp & G. R. Miller (Eds.), *Handbook of interpersonal communication* (2nd ed., pp. 199-228). Thousand Oaks, CA: Sage.

Jacobs, S., & Jackson, S. (1983). Strategy and structure in conversational influence attempts. *Communication Monographs, 50*, 285-304.

Jansma, L. L. (2000). Sexual harassment research: Integration, reformulation, and implications for mitigation efforts. In M. E. Roloff (Ed.), *Communication yearbook 23* (pp. 163-225). Thousand Oaks, CA: Sage.

Javidi, M. N., Jordan, W. J., & Carlone, D. (1994). Situational influences on the selection or avoidance of compliance-gaining strategies: A test of motivation to communicate. *Communication Research Reports, 11*, 127-134.

Jefferson, G. (1979). A technique for inviting laughter and its subsequent acceptance/declination. In G. Psathas (Ed.), *Everyday language: Studies in ethnomethodology* (pp. 79-96). New York: Irvington.

Johannesen, R. L. (1995). Perspectives on ethics in persuasion. In C. U. Larson (Ed.), *Persuasion: Reception and responsibility* (7th ed., pp. 27-54). Belmont, CA: Wadsworth.

Johannesen, R. L. (1996). *Ethics in human communication* (4th ed.). Prospect Heights, IL: Waveland.

Jones, E. E., & Nisbett, R. E. (1972). The actor and the observer: Divergent perceptions on the causes of behavior. In E. E. Jones, D. E. Kanouse, H. H. Kelley, R. E. Nisbett, S. Valins, & B. Weiner (Eds.), *Attribution: Perceiving the causes of behavior* (pp. 79-94). Morristown, NJ: General Learning.

Jordan, J. M. (1994). Plan monitoring in conversations: An exploration of on-line cognitive activity. *Communication Studies, 45*, 159-173.

Jordan, J. M. (1998). Executive cognitive control in communication: Extending plan-based theory. *Human Communication Research, 25*, 5-38.

Jordan, J. M., & Roloff, M. E. (1997). Planning skills and negotiator goal accomplishment: The relationship between self-monitoring and plan generation, plan enactment, and plan consequences. *Communication Research, 24*, 31-63.

Kahneman, D. (1973). *Attention and effort.* Englewood Cliffs, NJ: Prentice Hall.

Kavanagh, K. A., Youngblade, L., Reid, J. B., & Fagot, B. I. (1988). Interactions between children and abusive versus control parents. *Journal of Clinical Child Psychology, 17*, 137-142.

Kearney, P., & Plax, T. G. (1992). Student resistance to control. In V. P. Richmond & J. C. McCroskey (Eds.), *Power in the classroom: Communication, control, and concern* (pp. 67-84). Hillsdale, NJ: Lawrence Erlbaum.

Kearney, P., & Plax, T. G. (1997). Item desirability bias and the BAT checklist: A reply to Waltman and Burleson. *Communication Education, 46*, 95-99.

Kearney, P., Plax, T. G., Richmond, V. P., & McCroskey, J. C. (1985). Power in the classroom III: Teacher communication techniques and messages. *Communication Education, 34*, 19-28.

Kellermann, K. (1992). Communication: Inherently strategic and primarily automatic. *Communication Monographs, 59*, 288-300.

Kellermann, K., & Cole, T. (1994). Classifying compliance-gaining messages: Taxonomic disorder and strategic confusion. *Communication Theory, 4*, 3-60.

Kellermann, K., & Kim, M.-S. (1991, May). *Working within constraints: Tactical choices in the pursuit of social goals.* Paper presented at the annual meeting of the International Communication Association, Miami, FL.

Kellermann, K., & Park, H. S. (2001). Situational urgency and conversational retreat: When politeness and efficiency matter. *Communication Research, 28,* 3-47.

Kellermann, K., & Shea, B. C. (1996). Threats, suggestions, hints, and promises: Gaining compliance efficiently and politely. *Communication Quarterly, 44,* 145-165.

Kelley, H. H., Berscheid, E., Christensen, A., Harvey, J. H., Huston, T. L., Levinger, G., et al. (1983). Analyzing close relationships. In H. H. Kelley, E. Berscheid, A. Christensen, J. H. Harvey, T. L. Huston, G. Levinger, et al. (Eds.), *Close relationships* (pp. 20-67). New York: W. H. Freeman.

Kelly, G. A. (1955). *The psychology of personal constructs.* New York: W. W. Norton.

Kelman, H. C. (1958). Compliance, identification, and internalization: Three processes of attitude change. *Journal of Conflict Resolution, 2,* 51-60.

Kelman, H. C. (1961). Processes of opinion change. *Public Opinion Quarterly, 25,* 57-78.

Kendall, P. C., & Fischler, G. L. (1984). Behavioral and adjustment correlates of problem solving: Validational analyses of interpersonal cognitive problem-solving measures. *Child Development, 55,* 879-892.

Kerlinger, F. N. (1973). *Foundations of behavioral research* (2nd ed.). New York: Holt, Rinehart & Winston.

Kim, M.-S. (1994). Cross-cultural comparisons of the perceived importance of conversational constraints. *Human Communication Research, 21,* 128-151.

Kim, M.-S., & Bresnahan, M. (1994). A process model of request tactic evaluation. *Discourse Processes, 18,* 317-344.

Kim, M.-S., & Bresnahan, M. (1996). Cognitive bases of gender communication: A cross-cultural investigation of perceived constraints in requesting. *Communication Quarterly, 44,* 53-69.

Kim, M.-S., & Hunter, J. E. (1993). Attitude-behavior relations: A meta-analysis of attitudinal relevance and topic. *Journal of Communication, 43,* 101-142.

Kim, M.-S., Hunter, J. E., Miyahara, A., Horvath, A. M., Bresnahan, M., & Joon, H. J. (1996). Individual- vs. cultural-level dimensions of individualism and collectivism: Effects on preferred conversational styles. *Communication Monographs, 63,* 28-49.

Kim, M.-S., & Sharkey, W. F. (1995). Independent and interdependent construals of self: Explaining cultural patterns of interpersonal communication in multi-cultural organizational settings. *Communication Quarterly, 43,* 20-38.

Kim, M.-S., Sharkey, W. F., & Singelis, T. M. (1994). The relationship between individuals' self-construals and perceived importance of interactive constraints. *International Journal of Intercultural Relations, 18,* 117-140.

Kim, M.-S., Shin, H. C., & Cai, D. A. (1998). Cultural influences on the preferred forms of requesting and re-requesting. *Communication Monographs, 65,* 47-66.

Kim, M.-S., & Wilson, S. R. (1994). A cross-cultural comparison of implicit theories of requesting. *Communication Monographs, 61,* 210-235.

Kipnis, D., & Schmidt, S. M. (1982). *Profiles of organizational influence strategies (POIS).* San Diego, CA: University Associates.

Kipnis, D., & Schmidt, S. M. (1983). An influence perspective on bargaining within organizations. In M. Bazerman & R. Lewicki (Eds.), *Negotiating in organizations* (pp. 309-319). Beverly Hills, CA: Sage.

Kipnis, D., & Schmidt, S. M. (1988). Upward influence styles: Relationships with performance evaluations, salary, and stress. *Administrative Science Quarterly, 33,* 528-542.

Kipnis, D., Schmidt, S. M., Swaffin-Smith, C., & Wilkinson, I. (1984). Patterns of managerial influence: Shotgun managers, tacticians, and bystanders. *Organizational Dynamics, 12,* 58-67.

Kipnis, D., Schmidt, S. M., & Wilkinson, I. (1980). Intraorganizational influence tactics: Explorations in getting one's way. *Journal of Applied Psychology, 65,* 440-452.

Kitayama, S., Markus, H. R., Matsumoto, H., & Norasakkunkit, V. (1997). Individual and collective processes in the construction of the self: Self enhancement in the United States and self criticism in Japan. *Journal of Personality and Social Psychology, 72,* 1245-1267.

Kline, S. L. (1979). Toward a contemporary linguistic interpretation of the concept of *stasis. Journal of the American Forensic Association, 16,* 95-103.

Kline, S. L. (1991). Construct differentiation and person-centered regulative messages. *Journal of Language and Social Psychology, 10,* 1-27.

Kline, S. L., & Ceropski, J. M. (1984). Person-centered communication in medical practice. In J. T. Wood & G. M. Phillips (Eds.), *Human decision making* (pp. 120-141). Carbondale: Southern Illinois University Press.

Kline, S. L., & Clinton, B. L. (1998). Developments in children's persuasive message practices. *Communication Education, 47,* 120-136.

Kline, S. L., & Floyd, C. H. (1990). On the art of saying no: The influence of social cognitive development of messages of refusal. *Western Journal of Speech Communication, 54,* 454-472.

Klingle, R. S., & Burgoon, M. (1995). Patient compliance and satisfaction with physician influence attempts: A reinforcement expectancy approach to compliance-gaining over time. *Communication Research, 22,* 148-187.

Knowlton, S. W., & Berger, C. R. (1997). Message planning, cognitive failure, and cognitive load: Further explorations of the hierarchy principle. *Human Communication Research, 24,* 4-30.

Kolko, D. J. (1992). Characteristics of child victims of physical violence: Research findings and clinical implications. *Journal of Interpersonal Violence, 8,* 169-192.

Kosloski, D. L., Hinck, S. S., & Dailey, W. O. (1991, May). *An investigation of the impact of situation on the cognitive editing of argument strategies.* Paper presented at the annual meeting of the International Communication Association, Miami, FL.

Kravitz, R. L., Bell, R. A., & Franz, C. E. (1999). A taxonomy of requests by patients (TORP): A new system for understanding clinical negotiation in office practice. *Journal of Family Practice, 48,* 872-878.

Krippendorff, K. (1980). *Content analysis: An introduction to its methodology.* Beverly Hills, CA: Sage.

Krone, K. J. (1992). A comparison of organizational, structural, and relationship effects on subordinates' upward influence choices. *Communication Quarterly, 40,* 1-15.

Krone, K. J., Allen, M., & Ludlum, J. (1994). A meta-analysis of gender research in managerial influence. In L. Turner & H. Sterk (Eds.), *Differences that make a difference: Examining the assumptions in gender research* (pp. 73-84). Westport, CT: Bergin & Garvey.

Kuczynski, L., & Kochanska, G. (1990). Development of children's noncompliance strategies from toddlerhood to age 5. *Developmental Psychology, 26,* 398-408.

Labov, W., & Fanshel, D. (1977). *Therapeutic discourse: Psychotherapy as conversation.* New York: Academic Press.

Lambert, B. L. (1996a). Face and politeness in pharmacist-physician interaction. *Social Science and Medicine, 43,* 1189-1198.

Lambert, B. L. (1996b, May). *The theme machine: Theoretical foundation and summary of methods.* Paper presented at the annual meeting of the International Communication Association, Chicago.

Lambert, B. L., & Gillespie, J. L. (1994). Patient perceptions of pharmacy students' hypertension compliance-gaining messages: Effects of message design logic and content themes. *Health Communication, 6,* 311-325.

Lamude, K. G., Daniels, T. D., & White, K. (1987). Managing the boss: Locus of control and subordinates' selection of compliance-gaining strategies in upward communication. *Management Communication Quarterly, 1,* 232-259.

Lamude, K. G., & Scudder, J. (1993). Compliance-gaining techniques of Type-A managers. *Journal of Business Communication, 30,* 63-80.

Lannamann, J. W. (1991). Interpersonal communication as ideological practice. *Communication Theory, 1,* 179-203.

Larrance, D. T., & Twentyman, C. T. (1983). Maternal attributions and child abuse. *Journal of Abnormal Psychology, 92,* 449-457.

Lee, C. R., Levine, T. R., & Cambra, R. (1997). Resisting compliance in the multicultural classroom. *Communication Education, 46,* 29-43.

Leichty, T. S., & Applegate, J. L. (1991). Social-cognitive and situational influences on the use of face-saving persuasive strategies. *Human Communication Research, 17,* 451-484.

Lennox, R. D., & Wolfe, R. N. (1984). Revision of the Self-Monitoring Scale. *Journal of Personality and Social Psychology, 46,* 1349-1364.

Levelt, W. J. M. (1989). *Speaking: From intention to articulation.* Cambridge: MIT Press.

Levine, T. R., & McCroskey, J. C. (1990). Measuring trait communication apprehension: A test of rival measurement models for the PRCA-24. *Communication Monographs, 57,* 62-72.

Levine, T. R., & Wheeless, L. R. (1990). Cross-situational consistency and use/nonuse tendencies in compliance-gaining tactic selection. *Southern Communication Journal, 56,* 1-11.

Levinson, S. C. (1983). *Pragmatics.* Cambridge: Cambridge University Press.

Lewicki, R. J., Litterer, J. A., Minton, J. W., & Saunders, D. M. (1999). *Negotiation* (3rd ed.). Burr Ridge, IL: Irwin.

Lim, T. S. (1990). The influence of receivers' resistance on persuaders' verbal aggressiveness. *Communication Quarterly, 38,* 170-188.

Lim, T. S., & Bowers, J. W. (1991). Facework: Solidarity, approbation, and tact. *Human Communication Research, 17,* 415-450.

Lindsey, A. E., Greene, J. O., Parker, R. G., & Sassi, M. (1995). Effects of advance message formulation on message encoding: Evidence of cognitively based hesitations in the production of multiple-goal messages. *Communication Quarterly, 43,* 320-331.

Littlejohn, S. W. (1992). *Theories of human communication* (4th ed.). Belmont, CA: Wadsworth.

Littlejohn, S. W. (2002). *Theories of human communication* (7th ed.). Belmont, CA: Wadsworth.

Lorber, R., Felton, D., & Reid, J. B. (1984). A social learning approach to the reduction of coercive processes in child abuse families: A molecular analysis. *Advances in Behavior Research and Therapy, 6,* 29-45.

Lu, S. (1997). Culture and compliance gaining in the classroom: A preliminary investigation of Chinese college teachers' use of behavioral alteration techniques. *Communication Education, 46,* 10-28.

Lustig, M., & King, S. (1980). The effects of communication apprehension and situation on communication strategy choices. *Human Communication Research, 7,* 74-82.

Ma, R. (1996). Saying "yes" for "no" and "no" for "yes": A Chinese rule. *Journal of Pragmatics, 25,* 257-266.

MacGeorge, E. L. (2001). Support providers' interaction goals: The influence of attributions and emotions. *Communication Monographs, 68,* 72-97.

Malinosky-Rummel, R., & Hansen, D. J. (1993). Long-term consequences of childhood physical abuse. *Psychological Bulletin, 114,* 68-79.

Mandelbaum, J., & Pomerantz, A. (1991). What drives social action? In K. Tracy (Ed.), *Understanding face-to-face interaction: Issues linking goals and discourse* (pp. 151-166). Hillsdale, NJ: Lawrence Erlbaum.

Margolin, G., John, R. S., Ghosh, C. M., & Gordis, E. B. (1996). Family interaction process: An essential tool for exploring abusive relationships. In D. D. Cahn & S. A. Lloyd (Eds.), *Family violence from a communication perspective* (pp. 37-58). Thousand Oaks, CA: Sage.

Markus, H. R., & Kitayama, S. (1991). Culture and the self: Implications for cognition, emotion, and motivation. *Psychological Review, 98,* 224-253.

Marshall, L. L., & Levy, V. M., Jr. (1998). The development of children's perceptions of obstacles in compliance-gaining interactions. *Communication Studies, 49,* 342-357.

Martinko, M. J., & Gardner, W. L. (1987). The leader/member attribution process. *Academy of Management Review, 12*, 235-247.

Marwell, G., & Schmitt, D. R. (1967). Dimensions of compliance-gaining behavior: An empirical analysis. *Sociometry, 30*, 350-364.

Maslow, A. H. (1943). A theory of motivation. *Psychological Review, 50*, 370-396.

Maslyn, J. M., Farmer, S. M., & Fedor, D. D. (1996). Failed upward influence attempts: Predicting the nature of subordinate persistence in pursuit of organizational goals. *Group & Organization Management, 21*, 461-480.

McLaughlin, M. L. (1984). *Conversation: How talk is organized.* Beverly Hills, CA: Sage.

McLaughlin, M. L., Cody, M. J., & Robey, C. S. (1980). Situational influences on the selection of strategies to resist compliance-gaining attempts. *Human Communication Research, 7*, 14-36.

McQuillen, J. S. (1984). *An investigation of compliance-resisting behaviors in first-, fourth-, and tenth-grade children.* Unpublished doctoral dissertation, University of Oklahoma.

McQuillen, J. S. (1986). The development of listener-adapted compliance-resisting strategies. *Human Communication Research, 12*, 359-375.

McQuillen, J. S., Higginbotham, D. C., & Cummings, M. C. (1984). Compliance-resisting behaviors: The effects of age, agent, and type of request. In R. N. Bostrom (Ed.), *Communication yearbook 8* (pp. 747-763). Beverly Hills, CA: Sage.

Merritt, M. (1976). On questions following questions (in service encounters). *Language in Society, 5*, 315-357.

Metts, S. (1992). The language of disengagement: A face-management perspective. In T. L. Orbuch (Ed.), *Close relationship loss: Theoretical perspectives* (pp. 111-127). New York: Springer-Verlag.

Metts, S., & Bowers, J. W. (1994). Emotion in interpersonal communication. In M. L. Knapp & G. R. Miller (Eds.), *Handbook of interpersonal communication* (2nd ed., pp. 508-541). Thousand Oaks, CA: Sage.

Metts, S., Cupach, W. R., & Imahori, T. T. (1992). Perceptions of sexual compliance-resisting messages in three types of cross-sex relationships. *Western Journal of Communication, 56*, 1-17.

Meyer, J. R. (1992). Fluency in the production of requests: Effects of degree of imposition, schematicity and instruction set. *Journal of Language and Social Psychology, 11*, 232-251.

Meyer, J. R. (1994a). Effects of situational features on the likelihood of addressing face needs in requests. *Southern Communication Journal, 59*, 240-254.

Meyer, J. R. (1994b). Formulating plans for requests: An investigation of retrieval processes. *Communication Studies, 45*, 131-144.

Meyer, J. R. (1996). Retrieving knowledge in social situations: A test of the implicit rules model. *Communication Research, 23*, 342-351.

Meyer, J. R. (2000). Cognitive models of message production: Unanswered questions. *Communication Theory, 10*, 176-187.

Miller, G. R. (1990). Final considerations. In J. P. Dillard (Ed.), *Seeking compliance: The production of interpersonal influence messages* (pp. 189-200). Scottsdale, AZ: Gorsuch Scarisbrick.

Miller, G. R., Boster, F. J., Roloff, M. E., & Seibold, D. (1977). Compliance-gaining message strategies: A typology and some findings concerning effects of situational differences. *Communication Monographs, 44*, 37-51.

Miller, G. R., Boster, F. J., Roloff, M. E., & Seibold, D. (1987). MBRS rekindled: Some thoughts on compliance-gaining in interpersonal settings. In M. E. Roloff & G. R. Miller (Eds.), *Interpersonal processes: New directions in communication research* (pp. 89-116). Newbury Park, CA: Sage.

Miller, G. R., & Burgoon, M. (1978). Persuasion research: Review and commentary. In B. D. Ruben (Ed.), *Communication yearbook 2* (pp. 29-47). New Brunswick, NJ: Transaction.

Miller, G. R., & Parks, M. R. (1982). Communication in dissolving relationships. In S. Duck (Ed.), *Personal relationships 4: Dissolving personal relationships* (pp. 127-154). Orlando, FL: Academic Press.

Miller, G. R., & Steinberg, M. (1975). *Between people: A new analysis of interpersonal communication.* Chicago: Science Research Associates.

Miller, L. C., Cody, M. J., & McLaughlin, M. L. (1994). Situations and goals as fundamental constructs in interpersonal communication research. In M. L. Knapp & G. R. Miller (Eds.), *Handbook of interpersonal communication* (2nd ed., pp. 162-198). Thousand Oaks, CA: Sage.

Miller, M. (1982). Friendship, power, and the language of compliance-gaining. *Journal of Language and Social Psychology, 1,* 111-121.

Miller, M. A. (1998). The social process of drug resistance in a relational context. *Communication Studies, 49,* 358-375.

Miller, M. A., Alberts, J. K., Hecht, M. L., Trost, M. R., & Krizek, R. L. (2000). *Adolescent relationships and drug use.* Mahwah, NJ: Lawrence Erlbaum.

Milner, J. S. (1993). Social information processing and physical child abuse. *Clinical Psychology Review, 13,* 275-294.

Milner, J. S. (1994). Assessing physical child abuse risk: The Child Abuse Potential Inventory. *Clinical Psychology Review, 14,* 547-583.

Milner, J. S. (2000). Social information processing and child physical abuse: Theory and research. In D. J. Hersen (Ed.), *Nebraska Symposium on Motivation: Vol. 45. Motivation and child maltreatment* (pp. 39-84). Lincoln: University of Nebraska Press.

Milner, J. S., & Dopke, C. A. (1997). Child physical abuse: Review of offender characteristics. In D. A. Wolfe, R. J. McMahon, & R. D. Peters (Eds.), *Child abuse: New directions in prevention and treatment across the lifespan* (pp. 25-52). Thousand Oaks, CA: Sage.

Milner, J. S., & Foody, R. (1994). The impact of mitigating information on attributions for positive and negative child behavior by adults at low and high risk for child-abusive behaviors. *Journal of Social and Clinical Psychology, 13,* 335-351.

Monroe, C., Borzi, M. G., & DiSalvo, V. S. (1993). Managerial strategies for dealing with difficult subordinates. *Southern Communication Journal, 58,* 247-254.

Morand, D. A. (2000). Language and power: An empirical analysis of linguistic strategies used in superior-subordinate communication. *Journal of Organizational Behavior, 21,* 235-248.

Morgan, W. (2001, November). *Verbal abuse by any other name . . . : A look at definitional issues across existing constructs.* Paper presented at the annual meeting of the National Communication Association, Atlanta.

Motley, M. T. (1986). Consciousness and intentionality in communication: A preliminary model and methodological approaches. *Western Journal of Speech Communication, 50,* 3-23.

Mowday, R. T. (1978). The exercise of upward influence in organizations. *Administrative Science Quarterly, 23,* 137-156.

National Research Council. (1993). *Understanding child abuse and neglect.* Washington, DC: National Academy Press.

Neuliep, J. W. (1986). Self-report vs. actual use of persuasive messages by high and low dogmatics. *Journal of Social Behavior and Personality, 1,* 213-222.

Neuliep, J. W. (1989). A naturalistic transactional approach to compliance-gaining behavior. *Communication Research Reports, 6,* 119-124.

Newton, D. A., & Burgoon, J. K. (1990). The use and consequences of verbal influence strategies during interpersonal disagreements. *Human Communication Research, 16,* 477-518.

Nidorf, L. J., & Crockett, W. H. (1965). Cognitive complexity and the integration of conflicting information in written impressions. *Journal of Social Psychology, 66,* 165-169.

Nofsinger, R. E. (1991). *Everyday conversation.* Newbury Park, CA: Sage.

Nunnally, J. C. (1967). *Psychometric theory.* New York: McGraw-Hill.

Offermann, L. R., & Kearney, C. T. (1988). Supervisor sex and subordinate influence strategies. *Personality and Social Psychology Bulletin, 14,* 360-367.

Offermann, L. R., & Schrier, P. E. (1985). Social influence strategies: The impact of sex, role, and attitudes toward power. *Personality and Social Psychology Bulletin, 11,* 286-300.

O'Hair, M. J., Cody, M. J., & O'Hair, D. (1991). The impact of situational dimensions on compliance-resisting strategies: A comparison of methods. *Communication Quarterly, 39,* 226-240.

O'Keefe, B. J. (1988). The logic of message design: Individual differences in reasoning about communication. *Communication Monographs, 55,* 80-103.

O'Keefe, B. J. (1990). The logic of regulative communication: Understanding rationality in message designs. In J. P. Dillard (Ed.), *Seeking compliance: The production of interpersonal influence messages* (pp. 87-106). Scottsdale, AZ: Gorsuch Scarisbrick.

O'Keefe, B. J. (1991). Message design logic and the management of multiple goals. In K. Tracy (Ed.), *Understanding face-to-face interaction: Issues linking goals and discourse* (pp. 131-150). Hillsdale, NJ: Lawrence Erlbaum.

O'Keefe, B. J. (1992). Developing and testing models of message design. *Human Communication Research, 18,* 637-649.

O'Keefe, B. J. (1996, May). *Automated content analysis: Issues of reliability and validity.* Paper presented at the annual meeting of the International Communication Association, Chicago.

O'Keefe, B. J., & Delia, J. G. (1979). Construct comprehensiveness and cognitive complexity as predictors of the number and strategic adaptation of arguments and appeals in a persuasive message. *Communication Monographs, 46,* 231-240.

O'Keefe, B. J., & Delia, J. G. (1982). Impression formation and message production. In M. E. Roloff & C. R. Berger (Eds.), *Social cognition and communication* (pp. 33-72). Beverly Hills, CA: Sage.

O'Keefe, B. J., & Lambert, B. L. (1989, November). *Effects of message design logic on the communication of intention.* Paper presented at the annual meeting of the Speech Communication Association, San Francisco.

O'Keefe, B. J., & Lambert, B. L. (1995). Managing the flow of ideas: A local management approach to message design. In B. R. Burleson (Ed.), *Communication yearbook 18* (pp. 54-82). Thousand Oaks, CA: Sage.

O'Keefe, B. J., Lambert, B. L., & Lambert, C. A. (1993, May). *Effects of message design logic on perceived communication effectiveness in supervisory relationships.* Paper presented at the annual meeting of the International Communication Association, Washington, DC.

O'Keefe, B. J., Lambert, B. L., & Lambert, C. A. (1997). Conflict and communication in a research and development unit. In B. D. Sypher (Ed.), *Case studies in organizational communication 2: Perspectives on contemporary work life* (pp. 31-52). New York: Guilford.

O'Keefe, B. J., & McCornack, S. A. (1987). Message design logic and message goal structure: Effects on perceptions of message quality in regulative communication situations. *Human Communication Research, 14,* 68-92.

O'Keefe, B. J., Murphy, M. A., Meyers, R. A., & Babrow, A. S. (1989). The development of persuasive communication skills: The influence of developments in interpersonal constructs on the ability to generate communication-relevant beliefs and level of persuasive strategy. *Communication Studies, 40,* 29-40.

O'Keefe, B. J., & Shepherd, G. J. (1987). The pursuit of multiple objectives in face-to-face persuasive interaction: Effects of construct differentiation. *Communication Monographs, 54,* 396-419.

O'Keefe, B. J., & Shepherd, G. J. (1989). The communication of identity during face-to-face persuasive interactions: Effects of perceiver's construct differentiation and target's message strategies. *Communication Research, 16,* 375-404.

O'Keefe, D. J. (1990). *Persuasion: Theory and research.* Newbury Park, CA: Sage.

O'Keefe, D. J. (1993). Understanding social influence: Relations between lay and technical perspectives. *Communication Studies, 44,* 228-238.

Oldershaw, L., Walters, G. C., & Hall, D. K. (1986). Control strategies and noncompliance in abusive mother-child dyads: An observational study. *Child Development, 57,* 722-732.

Oldershaw, L., Walters, G. C., & Hall, D. K. (1989). A behavioral approach to the classification of different types of physically abusive mother-child dyads. *Merrill-Palmer Quarterly, 35,* 255-279.

Olufowote, J. (2001). *Reconceptualizing subordinate coalition influence in organizations: Linguistically managing multiple interaction goals.* Unpublished manuscript, Purdue University.

Owen, W. F. (1984). Interpretive themes in relational communication. *Quarterly Journal of Speech, 70,* 274-286.

Owen, W. F. (1989). Image metaphors of women and men in personal relationships. *Women's Studies in Communication, 12,* 37-57.

Palmer, M. T. (1994). Introduction to the special edition on cognition and interpersonal communication. *Communication Studies, 45,* 113-119.

Parks, M. R. (1982). Ideology in interpersonal communication: Off the couch and into the world. In M. Burgoon (Ed.), *Communication yearbook 5* (pp. 79-107). New Brunswick, NJ: Transaction.

Parks, M. R. (1994). Communication competence and interpersonal control. In M. L. Knapp & G. R. Miller (Eds.), *Handbook of interpersonal communication* (2nd ed., pp. 589-618). Thousand Oaks, CA: Sage.

Parks, M. R. (1995). Ideology in interpersonal communication: Beyond the couches, talk shows, and bunkers. In B. R. Burleson (Ed.), *Communication yearbook 18* (pp. 480-497). Thousand Oaks, CA: Sage.

Paulson, G. D., & Roloff, M. E. (1997). The effect of request form and content on constructing obstacles to compliance. *Communication Research, 24,* 261-290.

Peplau, L. A., & Perlman, D. (Eds.). (1982). *Loneliness: A sourcebook of current theory, research, and therapy.* New York: John Wiley.

Perloff, R. M. (1993). *The dynamics of persuasion.* Hillsdale, NJ: Lawrence Erlbaum.

Perloff, R. M. (2001). *Persuading people to have safer sex: Applications of social science to the AIDS crisis.* Mahwah, NJ: Lawrence Erlbaum.

Peterson, L. W., & Albrecht, T. L. (1996). Message design logics, social support, and mixed-status relationships. *Western Journal of Communication, 60,* 291-309.

Piliavin, J. A. (1990). Why do they give the gift of life? A review of research on blood donors since 1977. *Transfusion, 30,* 444-459.

Planalp, S., & Hewes, D. E. (1982). A cognitive approach to communication theory: *Cogito ergo dico?* In M. Burgoon (Ed.), *Communication yearbook 5* (pp. 49-77). New Brunswick, NJ: Transaction.

Plax, T. G., & Kearney, P. (1999). Classroom management: Contending with college student discipline. In A. L. Vangelisti, J. A. Daly, & G. W. Friedrich (Eds.), *Teaching communication: Theory, research, and methods* (2nd ed., pp. 269-285). Mahwah, NJ: Lawrence Erlbaum.

Plax, T. G., Kearney, P., & Sorenson, G. (1990). The strategy selection-construction controversy II: Comparing pre- and experienced teachers' compliance-gaining message constructions. *Communication Education, 39,* 128-141.

Porter, L. W., Allen, R. W., & Angle, H. L. (1981). The politics of upward influence in organizations. In L. L. Cummings & B. M. Staw (Eds.), *Research in organizational behavior* (Vol. 3, pp. 109-149). Greenwich, CT: JAI.

Powers, W. G., Jordan, W. J., & Street, R. L. (1979). Language indices in the measurement of cognitive complexity: Is complexity loquacity? *Human Communication Research, 6,* 69-73.

Prevent Child Abuse America. (1997). *Child abuse and neglect statistics.* Retrieved from http://www.preventchildabuse.org/facts97.html

Pruitt, D. G. (1981). *Negotiation behavior.* New York: Academic Press.

Pruitt, D. G., Parker, J. C., & Mikolic, J. M. (1997). Escalation as a reaction to persistent annoyance. *International Journal of Conflict Management, 8,* 252-270.

Psathas, G. (1995). *Conversation analysis: The study of talk-in-interaction.* Thousand Oaks, CA: Sage.

Pudlinski, C. (1998). Giving advice on a consumer-run warm line: Implicit and dilemmatic practices. *Communication Studies, 49,* 322-341.

Rao, A., Schmidt, S. M., & Murray, L. H. (1995). Upward impression management: Goals, influence strategies, and consequences. *Human Relations, 48,* 147-167.

Rao, N., Singhal, A., Ren, L., & Zhang, J. (2001). Is the Chinese self-construal in transition? *Asian Journal of Communication, 11,* 68-95.

Rawlins, W. K. (1992). *Friendship matters: Communication, dialectics, and the life course.* New York: Aldine de Gruyter.

Reason, J. T. (1990). *Human error.* Cambridge: Cambridge University Press.

Reid, J. B. (1978). *A social learning approach to family intervention: II. Observations in home settings.* Eugene, OR: Castalia.

Reid, J. B. (1986). Social-interactional patterns in families of abused and nonabused children. In C. Zahn-Waxler, E. M. Cummings, & R. Iannotti (Eds.), *Altruism and aggression: Biological and social origins* (pp. 238-255). New York: Cambridge University Press.

Reid, J. B., Kavanagh, K., & Baldwin, D. V. (1987). Abusive parents' perceptions of child problems: An example of parental bias. *Journal of Abnormal Child Psychology, 15,* 457-466.

Ritter, E. M. (1979). Social perspective-taking ability, cognitive complexity, and listener-adapted communication in early and late adolescence. *Communication Monographs, 46,* 40-51.

Rogers, C. R. (1957). The necessary and sufficient conditions for therapeutic personality change. *Journal of Consulting Psychology, 21,* 95-103.

Rogers, C. R. (1975). Empathetic: An unappreciated way of being. *Counseling Psychology, 5,* 2-10.

Rogers, C. R. (1980). *A way of being.* Boston: Houghton Mifflin.

Roloff, M. E. (1976). Communication strategies, relationships, and relationship change. In G. R. Miller (Ed.), *Explorations in interpersonal communication* (pp. 173-196). Beverly Hills, CA: Sage.

Roloff, M. E., & Barnicott, E. (1978). The situational use of pro- and anti-social compliance-gaining strategies by high and low Machiavellians. In B. D. Ruben (Ed.), *Communication yearbook 2* (pp. 193-208). New Brunswick, NJ: Transaction.

Roloff, M. E., & Barnicott, E. (1979). The influence of dogmatism on the situational use of pro- and anti-social compliance-gaining strategies. *Southern Speech Communication Journal, 45,* 37-54.

Roloff, M. E., & Janiszewski, C. A. (1989). Overcoming obstacles to interpersonal compliance: A principle of message construction. *Human Communication Research, 16,* 33-61.

Roloff, M. E., Janiszewski, C. A., McGrath, M. A., Burns, C. S., & Manrai, L.A. (1988). Acquiring resources from intimates: When obligation substitutes for persuasion. *Human Communication Research, 14,* 364-396.

Roloff, M. E., & Jordan, J. M. (1991). The influence of effort, experience, and persistence on the elements of bargaining plans. *Communication Research, 18,* 306-322.

Rule, B. G., & Bisanz, G. L. (1987). Goals and strategies of persuasion: A cognitive schema for understanding social events. In M. P. Zanna, J. M. Olson, & C. P. Herman (Eds.), *The Ontario Symposium: Vol. 5. Social influence* (pp. 185-206). Hillsdale, NJ: Lawrence Erlbaum.

Rule, B. G., Bisanz, G. L., & Kohn, M. (1985). Anatomy of a persuasion schema: Targets, goals, and strategies. *Journal of Personality and Social Psychology, 48,* 1127-1140.

Rumelhart, D. E., McClelland, J. L., & PDP Research Group. (Eds.). (1986). *Parallel distributed processing: Explorations in the microstructure of cognition: Vol. 1. Foundations.* Cambridge: MIT Press.

Sabourin, T. C., Infante, D. C., & Rudd, J. E. (1993). Verbal aggression in marriages: A comparison of violent, distressed but nonviolent, and nondistressed couples. *Human Communication Research, 20,* 245-267.

Sacks, H., Schegloff, E. A., & Jefferson, G. (1974). A simplest systematics for the organization of turn taking in conversation. *Language, 50,* 696-735.

Saeki, M., & O'Keefe, B. J. (1994). Refusals and rejections: Designing messages to serve multiple goals. *Human Communication Research, 21,* 67-102.

Sagrestano, L. M., Christensen, A., & Heavy, C. L. (1998). Social influence techniques during marital conflict. *Personal Relationships, 5,* 75-90.

Samter, W., & Burleson, B. R. (1984). Cognitive and motivational influences on spontaneous comforting behavior. *Human Communication Research, 11,* 231-260.

Sanders, R. E. (1991). The two-way relationship between talk in social interaction and actors' goals and plans. In K. Tracy (Ed.), *Understanding face-to-face interaction: Issues linking goals and discourse* (pp. 167-188). Hillsdale, NJ: Lawrence Erlbaum.

Sanders, R. E., & Fitch, K. L. (2001). The actual practice of compliance-seeking. *Communication Theory, 11,* 263-289.

Scarlett, H. H., Press, A. N., & Crockett, W. H. (1971). Children's descriptions of peers: A Wernerian developmental analysis. *Child Development, 42,* 439-453.

Schank, R. C., & Abelson, R. P. (1977). *Scripts, plans, goals, and understanding: An inquiry into human knowledge structures.* Hillsdale, NJ: Lawrence Erlbaum.

Schegloff, E. A., & Sacks, H. (1973). Opening up closings. *Semiotica, 7,* 289-327.

Schellenbach, C. J. (1998). Child maltreatment: A critical review of research on treatment for physically abusive parents. In P. K. Trickett & C. J. Schellenbach (Eds.), *Violence against children in the family and the community* (pp. 251-268). Washington, DC: American Psychological Association.

Schenck-Hamlin, W. J., Wiseman, R. L., & Georgacarakos, G. N. (1982). A model of properties of compliance-gaining strategies. *Communication Quarterly, 30,* 92-100.

Schermerhorn, J. R., & Bond, M. H. (1991). Upward and downward influence tactics in managerial networks: A comparative study of Hong Kong Chinese and Americans. *Asian Pacific Journal of Management, 8,* 147-158.

Schiffrin, D. (1994). *Approaches to discourse.* Cambridge, MA: Blackwell.

Schilit, W. K., & Locke, E. A. (1982). A study of upward influence in organizations. *Administrative Science Quarterly, 27,* 304-316.

Schindler, F., & Arkowitz, H. (1986). The assessment of mother-child interactions in physically abusive and nonabusive families. *Journal of Family Violence, 1,* 247-257.

Schlueter, D. W., Barge, J. K., & Blankenship, D. (1990). A comparative analysis of influence strategies used by upper- and lower-level male and female managers. *Western Journal of Speech Communication, 54,* 42-65.

Schmidt, S. M., & Kipnis, D. (1984). Managers' pursuit of individual and organizational goals. *Human Relations, 37,* 781-794.

Schneider, D. A., & Beaubien, A. (1996). A naturalistic investigation of compliance-gaining strategies employed by doctors in medical interviews. *Southern Communication Journal, 61,* 332-341.

Schrader, D. C., & Dillard, J. P. (1998). Goal structures and interpersonal influence. *Communication Studies, 49,* 276-293.

Schriesheim, C. A., & Hinkin, T. R. (1990). Influence tactics used by subordinates: A theoretical and empirical analysis and refinement of the Kipnis, Schmidt, and Wilkinson subscales. *Journal of Applied Psychology, 75,* 246-257.

Schutz, W. C. (1971). *Here comes everybody: Bodymind and encounter culture.* New York: Harper & Row.

Schwartz, S. H. (1990). Individualism-collectivism: Critique and proposed refinements. *Journal of Cross-Cultural Psychology, 21,* 139-157.

Scott, M., & Lyman, S. (1968). Accounts. *American Sociological Review, 33,* 46-62.

Scudder, J. N., & Andrews, P. H. (1995). A test of two alternative models of powerful speech: The impact of power and gender on threat use. *Communication Research Reports, 12,* 24-34.

Searle, J. R. (1969). *Speech acts: An essay in the philosophy of language.* Cambridge: Cambridge University Press.

Searle, J. R. (1975). Indirect speech acts. In P. Cole & J. L. Morgan (Eds.), *Syntax and semantics: Vol. 3. Speech acts* (pp. 59-82). New York: Academic Press.

Searle, J. R. (1976). A classification of illocutionary acts. *Language in Society, 5,* 1-25.

Seibold, D. R. (1988). A response to "Item desirability in compliance-gaining research." *Human Communication Research, 15,* 152-161.

Seibold, D. R., Cantrill, J. G., & Meyers, R. A. (1985). Communication and interpersonal influence. In M. L. Knapp & G. R. Miller (Eds.), *Handbook of interpersonal communication* (pp. 551-611). Beverly Hills, CA: Sage.

Seibold, D. R., Cantrill, J. G., & Meyers, R. A. (1994). Communication and interpersonal influence. In M. L. Knapp & G. R. Miller (Eds.), *Handbook of interpersonal communication* (2nd ed., pp. 542-588). Thousand Oaks, CA: Sage.

Selman, R. L., Schorin, M. Z., Stone, C. R., & Phelps, E. (1983). A naturalistic study of children's social understanding. *Developmental Psychology, 19,* 82-102.

Shepherd, G. J. (1992). Communication as influence: Definitional exclusion. *Communication Studies, 43,* 203-219.

Shepherd, G. J. (1998). The trouble with goals. *Communication Studies, 49,* 294-299.

Shepherd, G. J., & Condra, M. B. (1988). Anxiety, construct differentiation, and message production. *Central States Speech Journal, 39,* 177-189.

Shiffrin, R. M., & Schneider, W. (1977). Controlled and automatic human information processing: II. Perception learning, automatic attending, and a general theory. *Psychological Review, 84,* 127-190.

Sillars, A. L. (1980). The stranger and spouse as target persons for compliance-gaining strategies: A subjective utility model. *Human Communication Research, 6,* 265-279.

Sillars, A. L., Weisberg, J., Burggraf, C. S., & Wilson, E. A. (1987). Content themes in marital communication. *Human Communication Research, 13,* 495-528.

Simons, H. W. (1974). The carrot and the stick as handmaidens of persuasion in conflict situations. In G. R. Miller & H. W. Simons (Eds.), *Perspectives on communication in social conflict* (pp. 172-205). Englewood Cliffs, NJ: Prentice Hall.

Smith, M. J. (1982). Cognitive schemata and persuasive communication: Toward a contingency rules theory. In M. Burgoon (Ed.), *Communication yearbook 6* (pp. 330-362). Beverly Hills, CA: Sage.

Smith, M. J. (1984). Contingency rules theory, context, and compliance behaviors. *Human Communication Research, 4,* 489-512.

Smith, S. J., Cody, M. J., LoVette, S., & Canary, D. J. (1990). Self-monitoring, gender and compliance-gaining goals. In M. J. Cody & M. L. McLaughlin (Eds.), *The psychology of tactical communication* (pp. 91-135). Clevendon, Eng.: Multilingual Matters.

Smith, S. J., & Wilson, S. R. (1996). Using social knowledge in communication. In W. A. Donohue & D. A. Cai (Eds.), *Communicating and connecting: The functions of human communication* (pp. 63-82). Fort Worth, TX: Harcourt Brace.

Snyder, M. (1974). Self-monitoring of expressive behavior. *Journal of Personality and Social Psychology, 30,* 526-537.

Sorenson, G., Plax, T. G., & Kearney, P. (1989). The strategy selection-construction controversy: A coding scheme for analyzing teacher compliance-gaining constructions. *Communication Education, 38,* 102-118.

Spitzberg, B. H., & Cupach, W. R. (1984). *Interpersonal communication competence.* Beverly Hills, CA: Sage.

Sprowl, J. P. (1986). Sales communication: An analysis of sex differences in compliance-gaining strategy use. *Communication Research Reports, 3,* 90-93.

Srull, T. K., & Wyer, R. S. (1979). The role of category accessibility in the interpretation of information about persons: Some determinants and implications. *Journal of Personality and Social Psychology, 37,* 1660-1672.

Stewart, C. J., & Cash, W. B. (2000). *Interviewing: Principles and practices* (9th ed.). New York: McGraw-Hill.

Stiff, J. B. (1986). Cognitive processing of persuasive message cues: A meta-analytic review of the effects of supporting information on attitudes. *Communication Monographs, 53,* 75-89.

Stiff, J. B. (1994). *Persuasive communication.* New York: Guilford.

Straus, M. A. (1979). Measuring intrafamily conflict and violence: The Conflict Tactics Scales. *Journal of Marriage and the Family, 41,* 75-88.

Straus, M. A. (1994). *Beating the devil out of them: Corporal punishment in American families.* Lexington, MA: Lexington.

Straus, M. A., & Gelles, R. J. (1986). Societal change and change in family violence from 1975 to 1985 as revealed by two national surveys. *Journal of Marriage and the Family, 48,* 465-479.

Straus, M. A., Hamby, S. L., Finkelhor, D., Moore, D. W., & Runyan, D. (1998). Identification of child maltreatment with the parent-child Conflict Tactics Scales: Development and psychometric data for a national sample of American families. *Child Abuse & Neglect, 22,* 249-270.

Streeck, J. (1980). Speech acts in interaction: A critique of Searle. *Discourse Processes, 3,* 133-154.

Sullivan, J. J., Albrecht, T. L., & Taylor, S. (1990). Process, organizational, relational, and personal determinants of managerial compliance-gaining communication strategies. *Journal of Business Communication, 27,* 331-355.

Sutton, R. L. (1991). Maintaining norms about expressed emotions: The case of bill collectors. *Administrative Science Quarterly, 36,* 245-268.

Tabachnick, B. G., & Fidell, L. S. (1989). *Using multivariate statistics.* New York: Harper & Row.

Tannen, D. (1981). Indirectness in discourse: Ethnicity as conversational style. *Discourse Processes, 3,* 221-238.

Tolan, P. H., & Guerra, N. (1998). Societal causes of violence against children. In. P. K. Trickett & C. J. Schellenbach (Eds.), *Violence against children in the family and the community* (pp. 195-210). Washington, DC: American Psychological Association.

Tracy, K. (1984). The effects of multiple goals on conversational relevance and topic coherence. *Communication Monographs, 51,* 274-287.

Tracy, K. (1989). Conversational dilemmas and the naturalistic experiment. In B. Dervin, L. Grossberg, B. J. O'Keefe, & E. Wartella (Eds.), *Rethinking communication: Vol. 2. Paradigm exemplars* (pp. 411-423). Newbury Park, CA: Sage.

Tracy, K. (1991a). Introduction: Linking communicator goals with discourse. In K. Tracy (Ed.), *Understanding face-to-face interaction: Issues linking goals and discourse* (pp. 1-20). Hillsdale, NJ: Lawrence Erlbaum.

Tracy, K. (Ed.). (1991b). *Understanding face-to-face interaction: Issues linking goals and discourse.* Hillsdale, NJ: Lawrence Erlbaum.

Tracy, K., & Baratz, S. (1994). The case for case studies of facework. In S. Ting-Toomey (Ed.), *The challenge of facework: Cross-cultural and interpersonal issues* (pp. 287-306). Albany: State University of New York Press.

Tracy, K., & Coupland, N. (Eds.). (1990). Multiple goals in discourse [Special issue]. *Journal of Language and Social Psychology, 9*(1-2).

Tracy, K., Craig, R. T., Smith, M., & Spisak, F. (1984). The discourse of requests: Assessment of a compliance-gaining approach. *Human Communication Research, 10,* 513-538.

Trapp, R., & Hoff, N. (1985). A model of serial arguments in interpersonal relationships. *Journal of the American Forensic Association, 22,* 1-11.

Triandis, H. C. (1993). Collectivism and individualism as cultural syndromes. *Cross-Cultural Research, 27,* 155-180.

Triandis, H. C., Bontempo, M. J., Villareal, M., Asia, M., & Lucca, N. (1988). Individualism and collectivism: Cross-cultural perspectives on self-ingroup relationships. *Journal of Personality and Social Psychology, 54,* 323-338.

Trickett, P. K., & Kuczynski, L. (1986). Children's misbehaviors and parental discipline strategies in abusive and non-abusive families. *Developmental Psychology, 22,* 115-123.

Trickett, P. K., & Susman, E. J. (1988). Parental perceptions of child-rearing practices in physically abusive and nonabusive families. *Developmental Psychology, 24,* 270-276.

Turk, D. C., & Rudy, T. E. (1991). Neglected topics in the treatment of chronic pain patients—relapse, noncompliance, and adherence enhancement. *Pain, 44,* 5-28.

Vinson, L. R., & Biggers, J. T. (1993). Emotional responses as a predictor of compliance-gaining message selection. *Southern Communication Journal, 58,* 192-206.

von Cranach, M., Kalbermatten, U., Indermuhle, K., & Gugler, B. (1982). *Goal-directed action.* New York: Academic Press.

Waldron, V. R. (1990). Constrained rationality: Situational influences on information acquisition plans and tactics. *Communication Monographs, 57,* 184-201.

Waldron, V. R. (1995). Is the "golden age of cognition" losing its luster? Toward a requirement-centered perspective. In B. R. Burleson (Ed.), *Communication yearbook 18* (pp. 180-197). Thousand Oaks, CA: Sage.

Waldron, V. R. (1997). Toward a theory of interactive conversational planning. In J. O. Greene (Eds.), *Message production: Advances in communication theory* (pp. 195-220). Mahwah, NJ: Lawrence Erlbaum.

Waldron, V. R. (1999). Communication practices of leaders, members, and protégés: The case of upward influence tactics. In M. E. Roloff (Ed.), *Communication yearbook 22* (pp. 251-299). Thousand Oaks, CA: Sage.

Waldron, V. R., & Applegate, J. L. (1994). Interpersonal construct differentiation and conversational planning: An examination of two cognitive accounts for the production of competent verbal disagreement tactics. *Human Communication Research, 21,* 3-35.

Waldron, V. R., & Applegate, J. L. (1998). Person-centered tactics during verbal disagreements: Effects on student perceptions of persuasiveness and social attractiveness. *Communication Education, 47,* 53-66.

Waldron, V. R., Caughlin, J., & Jackson, D. (1995). Talking specifics: Facilitating effects of planning on AIDS talk in peer dyads. *Health Communication, 7,* 249-266.

Waldron, V. R., & Cegala, D. J. (1992). Assessing conversational cognitions: Levels of cognitive theory and associated methodological requirements. *Human Communication Research, 18,* 599-622.

Waldron, V. R., Cegala, D. J., Sharkey, W. F., & Teboul, B. (1990). Cognitive and tactical dimensions of goal management. *Journal of Language and Social Psychology, 9,* 101-118.

Waldron, V. R., Hunt, M. D., & Dsilva, M. (1993). Towards a threat management model of upward communication: A study of influence and maintenance tactics in the leader-member dyad. *Communication Studies, 44,* 254-272.

Waldron, V. R., & Lavitt, M. R. (2000). "Welfare-to-work": Assessing communication competencies and client outcomes in a job training program. *Southern Communication Journal, 66,* 1-15.

Waltman, M. S. (1994). An assessment of the convergent validity of the Checklist of Behavior Alteration Techniques: The association between teachers' likelihood-of-use ratings and informants' frequency-of-use ratings. *Journal of Applied Communication Research, 22,* 295-308.

Waltman, M. S. (1995). An assessment of the discriminant validity of the Checklist of Behavior Alteration Techniques: A test of the item desirability bias in prospective and experienced teachers' likelihood-of-use ratings. *Journal of Applied Communication Research, 23,* 201-211.

Waltman, M. S., & Burleson, B. R. (1997a). Explaining bias in teacher ratings of behavior alteration techniques: An experimental test of the heuristic processing account. *Communication Education, 46,* 75-94.

Waltman, M. S., & Burleson, B. R. (1997b). The reality of item desirability bias and heuristic processing in BAT ratings: Respecting the data. *Communication Education, 46,* 100-103.

Wang, C. T., & Harding, K. (1998). *Current trends in child abuse reporting and fatalities: The results of the 1998 annual fifty state survey.* Retrieved from http://www.preventchildabuse.org/survey98.htm

Wayne, S. J., & Ferris, G. R. (1990). Influence tactics, affect, and exchange quality in supervisor-subordinate interactions: A laboratory experiment and field study. *Journal of Applied Psychology, 75,* 487-499.

Wayne, S. J., Liden, R. C., Graf, I. K., & Ferris, G. R. (1997). The role of upward influence tactics in human resource decisions. *Personnel Psychology, 50,* 979-1006.

Weiner, B. (1986). *An attributional theory of motivation and emotion.* New York: Springer-Verlag.

Weiner, B., Amirkhan, J., Folkes, V. S., & Verette, J. A. (1987). An attributional analysis of excuse giving: Studies of a naive theory of emotion. *Journal of Personality and Social Psychology, 52,* 316-324.

Weiner, B., Figueroa-Muñoz, A., & Kakihara, C. (1991). The goals of excuses and communication strategies related to causal perceptions. *Personality and Social Psychology Bulletin, 17,* 4-13.

Werner, B. (1957). The concept of development from a comparative and organismic point of view. In D. B. Harris (Ed.), *The concept of development* (pp. 125-146). Minneapolis: University of Minnesota Press.

Werner, C. M., & Baxter, L. A. (1994). Temporal qualities of relationships: Organismic, transactional, and dialectical views. In M. L. Knapp & G. R. Miller (Eds.), *Handbook of interpersonal communication* (2nd ed., pp. 323-379). Thousand Oaks, CA: Sage.

Wheeless, L. R., Barraclough, R., & Stewart, R. (1983). Compliance-gaining and power in persuasion. In R. Bostrom (Ed.), *Communication yearbook 7* (pp. 105-145). Beverly Hills, CA: Sage.

Whipple, E. E., & Webster-Stratton, C. (1991). The role of parental stress in physically abusive families. *Child Abuse & Neglect, 15,* 279-291.

Wilson, S. R. (1990). Development and test of a cognitive rules model of interaction goals. *Communication Monographs, 57,* 81-103.

Wilson, S. R. (1992). Face and facework in negotiation. In L. L. Putnam & M. E. Roloff (Eds.), *Communication and negotiation* (pp. 176-205). Newbury Park, CA: Sage.

Wilson, S. R. (1995). Elaborating the cognitive rules model of interaction goals: The problem of accounting for individual differences in goal formation. In B. R. Burleson (Ed.), *Communication yearbook 18* (pp. 3-25). Thousand Oaks, CA: Sage.

Wilson, S. R. (1997). Developing theories of persuasive message production: The next generation. In J. O. Greene (Ed.), *Message production: Advances in communication theory* (pp. 15-43). Mahwah, NJ: Lawrence Erlbaum.

Wilson, S. R. (1999). Child physical abuse: The relevance of language and social interaction research. *Research on Language and Social Interaction, 32,* 173-184.

Wilson, S. R. (2000). Developing planning perspectives to explain parent-child interaction patterns in physically abusive families. *Communication Theory, 10,* 210-220.

Wilson, S. R., Aleman, C. G., & Leatham, G. B. (1998). Identity implications of influence goals: A revised analysis of face-threatening acts and application to seeking compliance with same-sex friends. *Human Communication Research, 25,* 64-96.

Wilson, S. R., Anastasiou, L., Kim, M.-S., Aleman, C. G., & Oetzel, J. (2000, June). *Identity implications of influence goals: Ethnicity and facework among same-sex friends.* Paper presented at the annual meeting of the International Communication Association, Acapulco.

Wilson, S. R., Brown, V., Bylund, C., Hayes, J., Herman, A., & Behl, L. E. (2001, April). *Mothers' trait verbal aggressiveness and child abuse potential.* Paper presented at the annual meeting of the Central States Communication Association, Cincinnati, OH.

Wilson, S. R., Cameron, K., & Whipple, E. E. (1997). Regulative communication strategies in mother-child interactions: Implications for the study of reflection-enhancing parental communication. *Research on Language and Social Interaction, 30,* 73-92.

Wilson, S. R., Cruz, M. G., & Kang, K. H. (1992). Is it always a matter of perspective? Construct differentiation and variability in attributions about compliance-gaining. *Communication Monographs, 59,* 350-367.

Wilson, S. R., Cruz, M. G., Marshall, L. J., & Rao, N. (1993). An attributional analysis of compliance-gaining interactions. *Communication Monographs, 60,* 352-372.

Wilson, S. R., Greene, J. O., & Dillard, J. P. (Eds.). (2000). Message production: Progress, challenges, and prospects [Special issue]. *Communication Theory, 10*(2).

Wilson, S. R., & Kang, K. H. (1991). Communication and unfulfilled obligations: Individual differences in causal judgments. *Communication Research, 18,* 799-824.

Wilson, S. R., Kim, M.-S., & Meischke, H. (1991/1992). Evaluating Brown and Levinson's politeness theory: A revised analysis of directives and face. *Research on Language and Social Interaction, 25,* 215-252.

Wilson, S. R., & Kunkel, A. W. (2000). Identity implications of influence goals: Similarities in face threats and facework across sex and close relationships. *Journal of Language and Social Psychology, 19,* 195-221.

Wilson, S. R., Levine, K. J., Cruz, M. G., & Rao, N. (1997). Attribution complexity and actor-observer bias. *Journal of Social Behavior and Personality, 12,* 709-728.

Wilson, S. R., Levine, K., J. Humphreys, L., & Peters, H. (1994, November). *Seeking and resisting compliance: Strategies and sequences in telephone solicitations for blood donation.* Paper presented at the annual meeting of the Speech Communication Association, New Orleans.

Wilson, S. R., & Putnam, L. L. (1990). Interaction goals in negotiation. In J. A. Anderson (Ed.), *Communication yearbook 13* (pp. 374-406). Newbury Park, CA: Sage.

Wilson, S. R., & Sabee, C. (in press). Explicating communicative competence as a theoretical term. In B. R. Burleson & J. O. Greene (Eds.), *Handbook of communication and social interaction skills.* Mahwah, NJ: Lawrence Erlbaum.

Wilson, S. R., & Whipple, E. E. (1995). Communication, discipline, and physical child abuse. In T. J. Socha & G. H. Stamp (Eds.), *Parents, children, and communication: Frontiers of theory and research* (pp. 299-318). Mahwah, NJ: Lawrence Erlbaum.

Wilson, S. R., & Whipple, E. E. (2001). Attributions and regulative communication by parents participating in a child abuse prevention program. In V. Manusov & J. H. Harvey (Eds.), *Attributions, communication behavior, and close relationships* (pp. 227-247). New York: Cambridge University Press.

Wilson, S. R., Whipple, E. E., & Grau, J. (1996). Reflection-enhancing regulative communication: How do parents vary across misbehavior types and child resistance? *Journal of Social and Personal Relationships, 13,* 553-569.

Wiseman, R. L., & Schenck-Hamlin, W. (1981). A multidimensional scaling validation of an inductively-derived set of compliance-gaining strategies. *Communication Monographs, 48,* 251-270.

Witte, K. (1995). Generating effective risk messages: How scary should your risk communication be? In B. R. Burleson (Ed.), *Communication yearbook 18* (pp. 229-254). Thousand Oaks, CA: Sage.

Witteman, H., & Fitzpatrick, M. A. (1986). Compliance-gaining in marital interaction: Power bases, processes, and outcomes. *Communication Monographs, 53,* 130-143.

Wood, J. T. (1999). *Gendered lives: Communication, gender, and culture* (3rd ed.). Belmont, CA: Wadsworth.

Wyer, R. S., & Gruenfeld, D. H. (1995). Information processing in interpersonal communication. In D. E. Hewes (Ed.), *The cognitive bases of interpersonal communication* (pp. 7-50). Hillsdale, NJ: Lawrence Erlbaum.

Yukl, G., & Falbe, C. M. (1990). Influence tactics and objectives in upward, downward, and lateral influence attempts. *Journal of Applied Psychology, 75,* 132-140.

Yukl, G., Falbe, C. M., & Youn, J. Y. (1993). Patterns of influence behavior for managers. *Group & Organization Management, 18,* 5-28.

Yukl, G., Guinan, P. J., & Sottolano, D. (1995). Influence tactics used for different objectives with subordinates, peers, and superiors. *Group & Organization Management, 20,* 272-296.

Yukl, G., Kim, H., & Falbe, C. M. (1996). Antecedents of influence outcomes. *Journal of Applied Psychology, 81,* 309-317.

Zimmerman, D. H. (1988). On conversation: The conversation analytic perspective. In J. A. Anderson (Ed.), *Communication yearbook 11* (pp. 406-432). Newbury Park, CA: Sage.

Zvonkovic, A. M., Schmiege, C. J., & Hall, L. D. (1994). Influence strategies used when couples make work-family decisions and their importance for marital satisfaction. *Family Relations, 43,* 182-188.

Author Index

Abelson, R. P., 250
Abrahams, M. F., 249, 250, 275, 277, 295, 344
Adams, C. H., 166, 263
Adler, N. E., 265, 266
Afifi, W. A., 295
Aida, Y., 295
Alberts, J. K., 39, 294, 295
Albrecht, T. L., 102, 238
Aleman, C. G., 1, 136, 143, 144, 152, 167, 176,
     218, 226, 227, 229, 312, 327, 331, 332
Alessandri, S. M., 302
Allen, M., 103, 125, 295
Allen, R. W., 279, 311, 312, 327, 328, 330, 334
Allen, T. H., 250
Amirkhan, J., 211
Anastasiou, L., 144, 227, 312, 331, 332
Anderson, C. A., 73, 216, 294
Anderson, J. R., 168, 169, 177, 244, 245, 247
Andrews, P. H., 44
Angle, H. L., 279, 311, 312, 327, 328, 330, 334
Ansari, M. A., 321, 322, 325, 327, 329
Applegate, J. L., 44, 67, 113, 120, 121, 122, 125,
     127, 163, 165, 166, 225, 274, 344
Arkowitz, H., 302
Asia, M., 154
Austin, J. L., 192, 202

Baaske, K. T., 97, 98, 99, 141
Babrow, A. S., 120
Backus, D., 112
Baglan, T., 32, 41
Baldwin, D. V., 300
Bandura, A., 266
Banski, M., 125
Baratz, S., 226, 228, 229, 345
Barge, J. K., 102, 104
Bargh, J. A., 169, 170, 249

Barnett, O. W., 297
Barnicott, E., 32, 94, 99, 112
Barraclough, R. A., 41, 91, 154
Barry, B., 295, 311, 323, 325, 327
Bator, R. J., 295
Bauer, W. D., 306, 307, 309
Bavelas, J. B., 9, 16, 178
Baxter, L. A., 11, 225, 228
Bayless, O., 32, 41
Beach, W. A., 75, 76, 200
Beatty, M. J., 125, 250, 260, 308
Beaubien, A., 296
Behl, L. E., 308
Belk, S. S., 102, 295
Bell, R. A., 257, 258, 263, 295, 296
Belsky, J., 298
Bem, S., 175
Benoit, P. J., 135
Berger, C. R., 14, 29, 74, 115, 133, 134, 137,
     177, 244, 245, 246, 249, 250, 251, 252,
     253, 254, 257, 258, 263, 264, 265, 274,
     275, 276, 277, 279, 280, 304, 309,
     344, 345
Berkowitz, S., 191
Berr, R. A., 249
Berscheid, E., 7, 12, 97
Bingham, S. G., 67, 114, 165, 166, 237, 263
Birk, T. S., 32, 67, 104, 152
Bisanz, G. L., 74, 102, 139, 140, 142, 143, 248
Biskin, D. S., 116
Black, A., 9
Blankenship, D., 102, 104
Blue, J., 305, 309
Blum-Kulka, S., 43, 56, 226, 228
Blumstein, P., 102
Bochner, A. P., 9, 12
Bond, M. H., 154, 321, 322, 325

377

Bonito, J. A., 52, 54
Bontempo, M. J., 154
Borzi, M. G., 295
Boster, F. J., 32, 33, 41, 44, 67, 71, 73, 86, 87,
    88, 89, 90, 91, 93, 94, 97, 99, 100, 101,
    102, 104, 105, 106, 109, 113, 114, 126,
    127, 130, 147, 212, 344
Bousha, D. M., 300, 302
Bowers, J. W., 67, 225, 226, 228,
    229, 346, 347
Bradley, E. J., 306
Bratman, M. E., 251
Bresnahan, M., 43, 67, 97, 102, 153, 154, 155,
    157, 159, 218
Brewer, W. F., 143
Broadbent, D. E., 272
Brown, P., 60, 187, 191, 197, 209, 218-230, 231,
    311, 345
Brown, V., 308
Bruce, B. C., 250, 252
Buckendahl, C. W., 304, 308
Bugental, D. B., 305, 306, 309
Bunker, B. B., 103
Burant, P. A., 250, 260, 308
Burgess, R. L., 302
Burggraf, C. S., 48, 55
Burgoon, J. K., 32, 44, 67, 97, 153
Burgoon, M., 6, 32, 43, 67, 91, 97, 98, 99, 100,
    102, 104, 109, 113, 115, 152, 153, 296
Burke, J. A., 107, 116, 120, 121, 123, 126
Burleson, B. R., 15, 36, 41, 62-64, 67, 101, 107,
    108, 109, 114, 116, 117, 119, 120, 121,
    124, 125, 126, 127, 163, 165, 166, 237,
    263, 296, 346, 347
Burns, C. S., 9, 67, 73, 74, 75, 124,
    191, 195, 217
Burrell, N. A., 48, 191
Buska, K., 284
Buss, A. H., 258
Buzzanell, P. M., 48, 175, 191, 311
Bylund, C., 308

Cai, D. A., 28, 43, 67, 97, 102, 137, 143, 144,
    155, 157, 167, 227, 261, 262, 266, 294,
    312, 331, 332
Calabrese, R. J., 244, 246
Cambra, R., 296
Cameron, k., 114
Canary, D. J., 71, 72, 73, 100, 101, 102, 113,
    129, 139, 140, 141, 142, 143, 144, 152,
    168, 215, 295, 331
Cantrill, J. G., 15, 86, 91, 129, 134, 179

Caplan, S. E., 67, 127
Carli, L. L., 102, 104
Carlone, D., 100, 102
Case, T., 321, 322, 325, 327
Cash, W. B., 262
Caughlin, J., 249, 267, 268, 309
Cegala, D. J., 28, 137, 166, 238, 247, 256, 272,
    274, 309, 344
Cerezo, M. A., 7, 295, 299, 300, 302
Ceropski, J. M., 120, 127, 163
Chacko, H. E., 322
Chaffee, S. H., 26, 27
Chaiken, S., 7, 247, 275
Cheng, J. L. C., 322
Chilamburti, C., 300, 304, 308
Chovil, N., 9
Christensen, A., 7, 12, 97, 295
Christiansen, E. H., 304, 308
Cialdini, R., 7, 247, 275
Clark, H. H., 206, 207, 208, 210, 226
Clark, R. A., 32, 60-62, 66, 67, 68, 97, 107, 114,
    116, 117-119, 120, 121, 123, 124, 125,
    126, 127, 130, 134, 202, 244
Clinton, B. L., 295
Cody, M. J., 14, 28, 36-39, 40, 42, 43,
    44, 45, 57, 58, 59, 71, 72, 73, 91,
    95-97, 98, 99, 100, 101, 102, 105,
    107, 108, 113, 124, 126, 129, 134,
    139, 140, 141, 142, 143, 144, 147,
    152, 168, 215, 295, 331
Cohen, P. R., 249
Coker, R., 32
Cole, T., 28, 39, 67, 68, 324
Colman, R. A., 304, 308
Condra, M. B., 120
Conger, R. D., 302
Cooper, P. F., 272
Corse, S., 299
Cortez, V., 309
Coupland, J., 226, 228, 229
Coupland, N., 134, 226, 228, 229
Craig, R. T., 8, 36, 97, 106, 135, 137, 162, 202,
    226, 228
Crano, W., 116
Crockett, W. H., 116, 117, 163, 171
Cronen, V. E., 72
Crouch, J. L., 308
Crowell, T. L., 266
Cruz, M. G., 23, 44, 67, 68, 71, 73, 75, 79, 113,
    117, 126, 169, 173, 204, 205, 207, 215,
    346, 347
Cruzcosa, M., 305

Cummings, E. M., 301
Cummings, M. C., 39, 97
Cupach, W. R., 152, 162, 225, 226, 273

Dailey, W. O., 147, 148
Dallinger, J. M., 13, 32, 74, 102, 103, 105, 112,
    125, 137, 144-148, 152, 160, 167, 215,
    218, 257
Daly, J. A., 28, 137
Daniels, T. D., 32, 100, 102, 322
Delia, J. G., vii, 14, 32, 60-64, 66, 68, 86, 114,
    115, 116, 117-119, 120, 121, 123, 124,
    125, 126, 127, 129, 130, 134, 160, 161,
    162, 163, 165, 166, 167, 202, 230, 244,
    246, 284
Deluga, R. J., 321, 322, 347
DeTurck, M. A., 32, 74, 102, 215
diBattista, P., 250, 275, 276, 309
Dillard, J. P., 7, 12, 14, 15, 28, 36, 43, 44, 58, 59,
    67, 97, 98, 99, 100, 102, 105, 106, 109,
    110-112, 113, 127, 129, 134, 137, 138,
    140, 141, 142, 144, 148-151, 152, 160,
    166, 167, 176, 178, 212, 218, 228, 284,
    294, 331, 346, 347
DiSalvo, V. S., 295
Dix, T., 306, 347
Dobos, J. A., 250, 260, 308
D'Ocon, A., 300, 302
Dolz, L., 302
Donohue, W. A., 13, 16, 135
Dopke, C. A., 299, 305, 306, 307
Doran, N., 43, 102, 109, 152
Dosier, L., 321, 322, 325, 327
Dougherty, T. W., 311
Drake, B. H., 327
Dreher, G. F., 311
Dsilva, M., 322, 327, 335
Dunning, D. G., 75, 76, 200
Dweck, c. S., 216

Eagly, A. H., 7, 247, 275
Edgar, T., 114, 265, 266, 294
Ellis, S., 266
Ely, T. K., 36, 41, 101, 107, 108, 109, 126, 127
Emmers-Sommer, T. M., 266
Erez, M., 140, 314, 321, 322, 327

Fagot, B. I., 300, 302
Fairhurst, G. T., 67, 226, 295, 311, 316, 325,
    326, 327, 335
Falbe, C. M., 139, 140, 312, 316-321, 321, 322,
    325, 326, 327, 328, 329, 345

Falbo, T., 57, 58, 59, 294, 295
Fanshel, D., 193, 194
Farmer, S. M., 321, 322, 323, 324, 325, 326, 335
Fazio, R. H., 170
Fedor, D. D., 321, 322, 323, 324, 325, 326, 335
Felton, D., 300, 302
Ferguson, M. J., 249
Ferris, G. R., 311, 347
Figueroa-Muñoz, A., 211, 212
Fink, E. L., 265, 266
Finkelhor, D., 297, 298, 300, 304
Fischler, G. L., 127
Fiske, S. T., 143, 246, 247, 275
Fitch, K. L., ix, 12, 43, 113, 114, 162, 168, 198,
    279, 295, 343
Fitzgerald, P., 272
Fitzpatrick, M. A., 44, 114, 294
Fleck, K., 309
Floyd, C. H., 67, 119, 137, 162, 163, 166, 226,
    257, 263
Folkes, V. S., 201, 206, 211, 212, 294
Foody, R., 307
Foss, S. K., 10, 11, 12, 13
Francik, E. P., 206, 207, 208, 210
Franz, C. E., 296
Freimuth, V. S., 265, 266
Friedman, S. L., 249
Fu, P. D., 295, 316

Gao, G., 154
Garbarino, J., 299
Garcia-Falconi, R., 102, 295
Gardner, W. L., 294
Garko, M. G., 322
Gastil, J., 125, 126
Geddes, D., 249, 280
Geist, P., 311
Gelles, R. J., 297, 298
Georgacarakos, G. N., 28, 32-36, 39, 43, 44, 45,
    57, 70, 71, 91, 108, 110
Gibbs, R. W., 108, 203, 207, 210
Gil, D. G., 299
Gillespie, J. L., 48, 49, 51, 52, 54, 55, 161
Goddard, H. W., 307
Goering, E. M., 36, 41, 101, 107, 108,
    109, 126, 127
Goffman, E., 138, 203, 218, 219, 237
Goldsmith, D. J., 162, 168, 226,
    227, 295
Goodman, J. S., 321, 322, 323, 324, 325,
    326, 335
Gordis, E. B., 299

Graf, I. K., 311
Graham, J. L., 44
Grainger, K., 226, 228, 229
Grau, J., 9, 71, 73, 74, 114, 215
Green, S. G., 67, 226
Greene, J. O., 14, 15, 26, 74, 97, 98, 99, 133,
        136, 137, 141, 169, 177, 244, 245, 246,
        247, 248, 249, 250, 277, 280-283, 284,
        285, 287
Grice, H. P., 188-192, 223, 232, 237, 255
Griffin, C. L., 10, 11, 12, 13
Gruenfeld, D. H., 246, 248
Gudykunst, W. B., 154
Guerra, N., 299
Gugler, B., 136
Guinan, P. J., 140, 142, 144, 310, 316,
        322, 328, 329, 330

Hale, C. L., 117, 125, 163
Hale, J. L., 97
Hall, D. K., 71, 72, 300, 301, 302, 303, 304, 310
Hall, J. R., 67, 104, 152
Hall, L. D., 295
Hamby, S. L., 297, 298, 300, 304
Hammond, S. L., 265, 266
Hample, D., 13, 32, 74, 102, 103, 105, 106, 112,
        125, 137, 144-148, 152, 160, 167, 215,
        218, 257
Hansen, D. J., 298
Harden, J. M., 7, 28, 36, 67, 105, 106, 137, 138,
        148-151, 152, 160, 167, 178, 218, 294
Harding, K., 298
Hargrove, L., 102, 295
Harper, N. L., 102, 103, 104
Harrington, N. G., 295
Harvey, J. H., 7, 12, 97
Hawn, J. J., 284
Hayes, J., 308
Hayes-Roth, B., 250, 251, 287
Hayes-Roth, F., 250, 251, 287
Heavy, C. L., 295
Hecht, M. L., 39, 294, 295
Heider, F., 202, 203
Hellweg, S. A., 311
Heritage, J., 197
Hernandez-Sanchez, J. E., 102, 295
Herrenkohl, E. C., 302
Herrenkohl, R. C., 302
Hewes, D. E., 175, 178, 246, 247, 248, 279
Higginbotham, D. C., 39, 97
Higgins, E. T., 169, 170

Hinck, S. S., 147, 148
Hinkin, T. R., 43, 294, 312, 314, 315, 320, 323
Hirokawa, R. Y., 43, 102, 103, 104
Hjelmquist, E., 250, 253, 254, 255
Hoffman, M. L., 300
Hoff, N., 72
Hofstede, G., 154
Holtgraves, T., 43, 201, 225, 226, 228
Holtzman, W. H., Jr., 102, 295
Honeycutt, J. M., 250
Hopper, R., 198
Horvath, A. M., 153, 154, 155, 159
House, J., 43, 56
Howard, J. A., 102
Hui, C. H., 154
Humphreys, L., 44, 71, 73, 74, 113, 114, 185,
        200, 201, 343
Hunt, M. D., 322, 327, 335
Hunter, J. E., 13, 41, 93, 94, 106, 109, 127, 153,
        154, 155, 159, 218
Huston, T. L., 7, 12, 97

Iannotti, R., 301
Ifert, D. E., 75, 203, 212, 217
Imahori, T. T., 152, 162, 225, 226
Indermuhle, K., 136, 270
Infante, D. A., 147
Infante, D. C., 308
Instone, D., 103

Jackson, D., 249, 267, 268, 309
Jackson, S., 75, 76, 112, 113, 191, 200, 203,
        304, 308
Jacobs, S., 75, 76, 112, 113, 191, 198, 199,
        200, 203
Janiszewski, C. A., 9, 20, 67, 73, 74, 75, 124,
        144, 191, 195, 207, 208, 209, 210, 217
Jansma, L. L., 295
Javidi, M. N., 100, 102
Jefferson, G., 197
Jennings, D. L., 73, 216, 294
Jerman, A., 308
Johannesen, R. L., 8, 9
John, R. S., 299
Jones, E. E., 204
Joon, H. J., 153, 154, 155, 159, 218
Jordan, J. M., 74, 91, 137, 250, 252, 253, 254,
        255, 256, 257, 259, 260, 261, 263, 264,
        271, 272, 273, 287, 309
Jordan, W. J., 57, 58, 59, 95, 100, 102, 125
Jorgensen, P. F., 311

Kahneman, D., 249
Kakihara, C., 211, 212
Kalbermatten, U., 136, 270
Kang, K. H., 44, 71, 72, 73, 113, 117, 126, 168, 173, 204
Kapoor, A., 321, 322, 325, 327, 329
Kardes, F. R., 170
Karol, S. H., 74, 264
Kasper, G., 43, 56
Kavanagh, K. A., 300, 302
Kazoleas, D. C., 44, 67, 71, 73, 100, 101, 102, 113
Kearney, C. T., 102, 322
Kearney, P., 41, 43, 109, 126, 294, 296
Keider, I., 314, 321, 322, 327
Kellermann, K., 28, 39, 67, 68, 135, 136, 151-153, 155, 210, 245, 249, 257, 267, 324
Kelley, H. H., 7, 12, 97
Kelly, G. A., 115
Kelman, H. C., 324, 326
Kendall, P. C., 127
Kerlinger, F. N., 29
Keys, B., 321, 322, 325, 327
Kim, M. -S., 42, 43, 56, 67, 105, 144, 152, 153, 154, 155-160, 167, 175, 203, 218, 226, 227, 229, 312, 325, 331, 332
King, G. A., 170
King, S., 32, 97, 100, 109, 112
Kinney, T. A., 58, 59, 228, 284, 346, 347
Kipnis, D., 43, 139, 140, 144, 176, 294, 310-317, 320, 321, 322, 323, 324, 325, 327, 328, 329
Kitayama, S., 12, 154
Kline, S. L., 62-64, 67, 116, 119, 120, 121, 124, 127, 136, 137, 162, 163, 166, 203, 226, 257, 263, 295
Klingle, R. S., 296
Knowlton, S. W., 249, 250, 264, 265, 275, 277, 344
Kochancka, G., 43
Koch, S., 198
Kodama, R. A., 102
Kohn, M., 139, 140, 142, 143, 248
Kolko, D. J., 298
Kopeikin, H., 309
Koper, R., 102, 109
Kosloski, D. L., 147, 148
Kostelny, K., 299
Kravitz, R. L., 296
Krippendorff, K., 29
Krizek, R. L., 295

Krone, K. J., 103, 295, 321, 322
Kuczynski, L., 43, 300, 302, 304, 306, 345
Kunkel, A. W., 7, 143, 144, 225, 227, 294, 312, 325, 331, 332, 334

Labov, W., 193, 194
Lalumia, J., 32, 41
Lambert, B. L., 48, 49, 51, 52, 53, 54, 55, 127, 161, 225, 237, 238, 296
Lambert, C. A., 237, 238
Lamude, K. G., 32, 100, 102, 113, 322
Lannamann, J. W., 16, 174, 175
Larrance, D. T., 305
Lavitt, M. R., 260
Leatham, G. B., 1, 136, 143, 144, 152, 167, 176, 218, 226, 227, 229, 312, 327, 331, 332
Lee, C. R., 296
Lee, J. W., 295
Leichty, T. S., 67, 163, 166, 225
Lennox, R. D., 259
Leung, K., 154
Levelt, W. J. M., 244, 245, 249, 250
Levine, K. J., 44, 71, 73, 74, 113, 114, 185, 200, 201, 204, 343
Levine, T. R., 44, 67, 71, 73, 99, 102, 105, 113, 147, 296
Levinger, G., 7, 12, 97
Levinson, S. C., 60, 187, 190, 191, 196, 197, 199, 200, 201, 209, 218-230, 231, 311, 345
Levy, V. M., Jr., 295
Lewicki, R. J., 262
Lewis, J. C., 306, 309
Liden, R. C., 311
Lim, T. S., 44, 67, 75, 76, 77, 78, 113, 127, 225, 226, 228, 229
Lindsey, A. E., 15, 74, 133, 137, 284, 285
Litterer, J. A., 262
Littlejohn, S. W., 14
Locke, E. A., 321, 322, 325, 327
Lombardi, W., 169, 170
Lorber, R., 300, 302
LoVette, S., 101, 102, 144
Lucca, N., 154
Ludlum, J., 103, 295
Lu, S., 296
Lustig, M., 32, 97, 100, 109, 112
Lyman, S., 335
Lyon, J., 309

Ma, R., 43, 160
Mabry, E., 125
MacGeorge, E. L., 347
MacKinnon, D., 295
Major, B., 103
Malinosky-Rummel, R., 298
Mandelbaum, J., 198
Manrai, L. A., 9, 67, 73, 74, 75, 124,
    191, 195, 217
Margolin, G., 299
Markus, H. R., 12, 154
Marshall, L. J., 23, 44, 67, 68, 71, 73, 75, 79,
    113, 169, 205, 207, 215
Marshall, L. L., 295
Marston, P. J., 97, 98, 99, 100, 129, 141, 143,
    144, 152
Martinko, M. J., 294
Marvin, G. H., 170
Marwell, G., 29-32, 36, 39, 40, 41, 43, 44, 45,
    79, 88, 90, 92, 94, 97, 98, 102, 107, 108,
    109, 110, 113, 145
Maslow, A. H., 226
Maslyn, J. M., 321, 322, 323, 324, 325, 326, 335
Matsumoto, H., 154
Maxwell, M., 137
McCornack, S. A., 71, 165, 166, 237, 263
McCroskey, J. C., 294
McDaniel, T. L., 284
McDonald, D. A., 265, 266
McGrath, M. A., 9, 67, 73, 74, 75, 124, 191,
    195, 217
McLaughlin, M. L., 28, 35-39, 39, 40, 42, 43,
    44, 45, 57, 58, 59, 91, 95-97, 99, 105,
    124, 134, 147, 245
McQuillen, J. S., 39, 64-66, 97, 119, 124
Meischke, H., 203, 218, 226, 227, 229, 331, 332
Metts, S., 152, 162, 225, 226, 346, 347
Meyer, J. R., 74, 136, 143, 167, 248, 249, 250
Meyers, K. A., 148
Meyers, R. A., 15, 86, 91, 120, 129, 134, 179
Mickey, J., 102, 104
Mikolic, J. M., 74
Miller, B. C., 307
Miller, G. R., vii, 6, 32, 41, 86, 87, 88, 89, 90,
    91, 94, 104, 105, 106, 109, 114, 115, 130,
    244, 344
Miller, L. C., 134
Miller, M., 97, 105
Miller, M. A., 295
Miller, M. D., 43
Miller-Perrin, C. L., 297

Miller-Rassulo, M. A., 39, 294
Milner, J. S., 248, 299, 300, 304, 305, 306,
    307, 308
Minton, J. W., 262
Miura, S., 102, 104
Miyahara, A., 43, 153, 154, 155, 159, 218
Moberg, D. J., 327
Monroe, C., 295
Montgomery, B. M., 11
Moore, D. W., 297, 298, 300, 304
Moore, P. J., 265, 266
Morand, D. A., 327
Morgan, J., 249
Motley, M. T., 136, 270
Mowday, R. T., 322
Mueller, R. A. G., 207
Mullett, J., 9
Murkison, G., 321, 322, 325, 327
Murphy, M. A., 120
Murray, L. H., 321, 322, 327, 328

Nakamura, G., 143
Neel, H., 137
Neuliep, J. W., 36, 107, 109, 113, 126
Neuwirth, C. M., 125
Newman, D., 250, 252
Newton, D. A., 44, 67
Nidorf, L. J., 117
Nisbett, r. E., 204
Nishida, T., 154
Nofsinger, R. E., 75, 197, 201
Norasakkunkit, V., 154
Nunnally, J. C., 29, 56

Oetzel, J., 144, 227, 312, 331, 332
Offermann, L. R., 102, 103, 322
O'Hair, D., 37, 39, 42, 97, 107, 126
O'Hair, H. D., 97, 98, 99, 107, 126, 141
O'Hair, M. J., 37, 39, 42, 97
O'Keefe, B. J., 14, 48, 49, 51, 52, 53, 54,
    55, 67, 70, 71, 79, 86, 105, 106, 114,
    115, 116, 120, 121, 123, 124, 127, 129,
    136, 137, 160, 161, 162, 163, 164, 165,
    166, 167, 177, 187, 230-239, 246, 257,
    263, 284
O'Keefe, D. J., 7, 40, 41, 67, 104, 106,
    113, 115, 116
Oldershaw, L., 71, 72, 300, 301, 302, 303,
    304, 310
Olufowote, J., 335
Owen, W. F., 48

Palmer, M. T., 246
Park, H. S., 152
Parker, J. C., 74
Parker, R. G., 284
Parkes, K. R., 272
Parks, M. R., 9, 41, 166, 174, 245, 246
Parrott, R., 32
Paulson, G. D., 213, 214, 294
Payne, S., 125
Pearce, W. B., 72
Peplau, L. A., 57, 58, 59, 102, 257, 294
Perlman, D., 257
Perloff, R. M., 7, 295
Perrin, R. D., 297
Perry, J. T., 321, 322, 347
Peters, H., 44, 71, 73, 74, 113, 114, 185, 200,
        201, 343
Peters, R. D., 306
Peterson, L. W., 238
Pfau, M., 32
Phelps, E., 127
Piliavin, J. A., 185
Planalp, S., 175, 178, 246, 247, 248, 346, 347
Plax, T. G., 41, 43, 109, 126, 294, 296
Pollack, M. E., 249
Pomernatz, A., 198
Porter, L. W., 279, 311, 312, 324, 327, 328, 334
Powell, M. C., 170
Powers, W. G., 125
Preiss, R., 125
Press, A. N., 116
Pruitt, D. G., 74, 259, 260
Psathas, G., 197
Putnam, L. L., 135, 136, 137, 179, 251

Rao, N., 23, 44, 67, 68, 71, 73, 75, 79, 113,
        169, 175, 204, 205, 207, 215, 321, 322,
        327, 328
Ravizza, S. M., 284
Rawlins, W. K., 11, 12, 168, 175
Reason, J. T., 271
Reid, J. B., 300, 301, 302, 306, 307, 310
Ren, L., 175
Reynolds, R. A., 33, 91, 101
Richmond, V. P., 294
Rim, Y., 140, 314, 321, 322, 327
Ritter, E. M., 120, 124
Rivers, A., 43, 67, 97, 102
Robey, C. S., 36-39, 39, 40, 42, 43, 44,
        45, 91, 97
Roedter, L., 302

Rogan, R. G., 44, 73
Rogers, C. R., 10, 12, 13
Roloff, M. E., 9, 32, 41, 67, 73, 74, 75, 87,
        88, 89, 90, 91, 94, 99, 100, 101, 104,
        105, 106, 109, 112, 114, 124, 130, 144,
        191, 195, 203, 207, 208, 209, 210, 212,
        213, 214, 217, 250, 259, 260, 261, 263,
        294, 344
Ruble, D. N., 306
Rudd, J. E., 250, 260, 308
Rudy, T. E., 296, 347
Rule, B. G., 74, 102, 139, 140, 142, 143, 248
Runyan, D., 297, 298, 300, 304

Sabee, C., 166, 263, 306, 347
Sabourin, T. C., 308
Sacks, H., 197, 198
Saeki, M., 49, 51, 52, 53, 54, 55, 137, 162
Sagrestano, L. M., 295
Samter, W., 125, 126
Sanbonmatsu, D., 170
Sanders, R. E., ix, 113, 114, 179, 198, 279, 343
Sano, Y., 44
Sassi, M., 284
Saunders, D. M., 262
Scarlett, H. H., 116
Schank, R. C., 250
Schegloff, E. A., 197, 198, 199
Schellenbach, C. J., 299
Schenck-Hamlin, W. J., 28, 32-36, 39, 43, 44,
        45, 57, 58, 59, 70, 71, 91, 108, 110
Schermerhorn, J. R., 321, 322, 325
Schilit, W. K., 321, 322, 325, 327
Schindler, F., 302
Schleuter, D. W., 1-4, 102
Schmid, K.., 299
Schmidt, K. L., 154
Schmidt, S. M., 43, 139, 140, 144, 294,
        310-317, 320, 321, 322, 323, 324,
        325, 327, 328, 329
Schmiege, C. J., 295
Schmitt, D. R., 29-32, 36, 39, 40, 41, 43, 44, 45,
        79, 88, 90, 92, 94, 97, 98, 102, 107, 108,
        110, 113, 145
Schneider, D. A., 296
Schneider, M. J., 97, 98, 99, 105
Schneider, W., 247, 249
Scholnick, E. K., 249
Schorin, M. Z., 127
Schrader, D. C., 137, 166, 176, 294
Schrier, P. E., 10, 102, 103

Schriesheim, C. A., 43, 294, 312, 314, 315, 320, 323
Schunk, D. H., 226
Schutz, W. C., 226
Schwartz, P., 102
Schwartz, S. H., 154
Scott, M., 335
Scudder, J. N., 44, 113
Searle, J. R., 187, 193, 194, 195, 196, 202, 219, 237
Segrin, C., 7, 28, 36, 67, 105, 106, 137, 138, 148-151, 152, 160, 167, 178, 218, 294
Seibold, D. R., 15, 32, 86, 87, 88, 89, 90, 91, 94, 104, 105, 106, 109, 110, 114, 129, 130, 134, 179, 344
Selman, R. L., 127
Shapiro, D. L., 325
Sharkey, W. F., 137, 155, 157, 158, 159, 272
Shea, B. C., 152, 153, 157
Shennum, W. A., 305
Shepherd, G. J., 16, 67, 105, 106, 120, 136, 139, 163, 164, 165, 166, 167, 175, 176, 230, 231, 257, 263
Shiffrin, R. M., 247, 249
Shin, H. C., 155, 157
Shosh, C. M., 299
Siegler, R. S., 266
Sillars, A. L., 32, 40, 48, 55, 79, 91-93, 97, 105, 109, 112
Simons, H. W., 9
Singelis, T. M., 155, 157, 159
Singhal, A., 175
Smith, M., 36, 106, 162, 202
Smith, M. J., 105, 143, 167, 248
Smith, S. J., 101, 102, 143, 144
Smith, S. W., 71, 72, 73, 113, 129, 139, 140, 141, 142, 144, 168, 215, 295, 331
Snavely, B. K., 67, 226
Snavely, L. M., 72
Snell, W. E., Jr., 102, 295
Snyder, M., 259
Solomon, D. H., 166, 167
Sorenson, G., 41, 109, 126, 296
Sottolano, D., 140, 142, 144, 310, 316, 322, 328, 329, 330
Spisak, F., 8, 36, 97, 106, 162, 202, 226, 228
Spitzberg, B. H., 273
Sprowl, J. P., 102
Srull, T. K., 170
Stafford, R. S., 191
Steinberg, M., 87, 244

Stewart, C. J., 262
Stewart, R., 41, 91
Stiff, J. B., 7, 33, 44, 91, 97, 99, 100, 101, 113
Stone, C. R., 127
Straus, M. A., 297, 298, 299, 300, 304
Streeck, J., 196
Street, R. L., 125
Sullivan, J. J., 102
Susman, E. J., 300, 308
Sutton, R. L., 347
Swaffin-Smith, C., 321, 322

Tannen, D., 43, 160
Taylor, S. E., 102, 143, 246, 247, 275
Teboul, B., 137, 272
Thompson, R. A., 304, 308
Tischann, J. M., 265, 266
Tolan, P. H., 299
Tracy, K., 8, 36, 97, 106, 133, 134, 135, 136, 137, 162, 166, 167, 202, 226, 228, 229, 345
Trapp, R., 72
Triandis, H. C., 154, 175, 261
Trickett, P. K., 299, 300, 302, 304, 306, 308, 345
Trost, M. R., 295
Turk, D. C., 296, 347
Tusing, K. J., 58, 59, 228, 284
Twentyman, C. T., 300, 302, 305, 306, 307, 309

Vangelisti, A. L., 137
Verette, J. A., 211
Villareal, M., 154
von Cranach, M., 136, 270

Waldron, V. R., 3, 9, 15, 28, 127, 137, 165, 166, 178, 238, 247, 249, 250, 256, 260, 267, 268, 269, 270, 272, 274, 278, 279, 280, 304, 309, 311, 312, 322, 327, 335, 344
Walters, G. C., 71, 72, 300, 301, 302, 303, 304, 310
Waltman, M. S., 36, 41, 67, 101, 107, 108, 109, 113, 116, 125, 126, 127, 296
Wang, C. T., 298
Wang, G., 154
Watson, M. R., 295, 311, 323, 327
Wayne, S. J., 311, 347
Weber, D. J., 137
Webster-Stratton, C., 300, 307
Weiner, B., 187, 202, 204, 211, 212, 215, 217, 304, 305, 306, 346, 347
Weisberg, J., 48, 55

Werner, B., 115
Whaley, B. B., 36, 41, 101, 107, 108, 109, 126, 127
Wheeless, L. R., 41, 91, 105
Whipple, E. E., 9, 71, 73, 74, 114, 215, 299, 300, 304, 307, 308
White, K., 32, 100, 102, 322
White-Mills, K., 311
Whitely, W., 311
Wiemann, J. M., 28
Wigley, C. J., 147
Wilkinson, I., 43, 139, 140, 144, 294, 310-317, 320, 321, 322, 323, 324, 325, 327, 328, 329
Wilson, E. A., 48, 55
Wilson, S. R., 1, 2, 7, 9, 14, 16, 23, 36, 41, 42, 43, 44, 56, 58, 59, 67, 68, 71, 72, 73, 74, 75, 79, 91, 101, 105, 107, 108, 109, 113, 114, 115, 117, 126, 127, 134, 135, 136, 137, 143, 144, 152, 153, 155, 156, 157, 158, 160, 162, 166, 167, 168, 169, 170, 172, 173, 175, 176, 179, 185, 200, 201, 203, 204, 205, 207, 215, 218, 225, 226, 227, 229, 247, 248, 251, 257, 263, 267, 284, 294, 295, 299, 304, 306, 307, 308, 312, 325, 327, 331, 332, 334, 335, 343, 346, 347

Wiseman, R. L., 28, 32-36, 39, 43, 44, 45, 57, 58, 59, 70, 71, 91, 108, 110
Witte, K., 266
Witteman, H., 44, 294
Woelfel, M. L., 95
Wolfe, R. N., 259
Wood, J. T., 102
Woods, E., 120, 163
Wyatt, J., 304, 308
Wyer, R. S., 170, 246, 248

Yang, J. N., 43, 225, 226, 228
Yanushefski, A. M., 302
Youn, J. Y., 312, 316-321, 322, 325, 326, 327, 328, 329, 345
Youngblade, L., 300, 302
Yukl, G., 139, 140, 142, 144, 295, 310, 312, 316-321, 322, 325, 326, 327, 328, 329, 330, 345

Zahn-Waxler, E. M., 301
Zambarano, R. J., 306
Zhang, J., 175
Zimmerman, D. H., 197
Zvonkovic, A. M., 295

Subject Index

Action assembly theory, 280
  activation process, 281
  coalition formation, 281-282
  communication behavior, physiological
    constructs and, 283
  executive processes in, 282
  multiple-goal message production,
    283-286, 286 (table)
  planning processes and, 287
  procedural record, network
    structure of, 280-281
Age factor, 60-62, 62 (table), 115-116
Argument:
  cognitive editing standards and, 144-148,
    146 (table)
  conceptual dimension of, 59-60, 59 (table)
  goal pursuit and, 164-165
  one-sided vs. two-sided, 7
Attribution theory, viii, 203-205, 305-307,
    345-348

Behaviors:
  compliance-gaining, 110-112
  goal/behavior complexity, 160-166
  strategy construction and, 127
  See also Listener adaptation

Child physical abuse, 7, 72, 297
  attribution theories and, 305-307
  compliance seeking-resisting patterns
    and, 305-310
  consequences of, 298
  ecological perspectives and, 298-299
  hierarchy principle and, 309-310
  mother-child interaction, 299-304,
    301-302 (tables)
  planning theories and, 307-310
  prevalence of, 297-298

Coercion, 8
Cognitive editing standards, 13, 144-148,
    146 (table)
Cognitive Failures Questionnaire (CFQ),
    272, 273 (table)
Cognitive perspectives, 241-243
  assumptions in, 246-247
  cognitive processes in, 248-249
  conceptual structure of, 247-249
  information processing, limits on, 249
  knowledge structures in, 243-245,
    247-248
  message production, complexity in,
    245-246
  See also Action assembly theory;
    Conversational planning;
    Pre-conversational plans
Cognitive rules (CR) model, 168, 169 (table)
  associative memory network, activation
    process of, 168-169
  predictive accuracy of, 172-173
  situational fit/ambiguity and, 169-171,
    172 (table)
  strength/recency criteria in, 170-171
Communication. See Goal pursuit; Message
    design logic theories
Communication theory, 27, 133-134
  conversational constraints, 151-160, 156
    (table), 158 (table)
  See also Action assembly theory;
    Conversational planning
Compliance-gaining interactions,
    vii, ix, 3-4
  behaviors in, 110-112
  conceptual criticisms, studies and, 104-106
  dimensions of, 58-60, 59 (table), 95-97,
    96 (table)
  directives and, 203

face, threats to, 220
  interpersonal influence contexts, 6-7
  message production and, 128-129
  message sources, 6
  message strategies, 7, 112-114
  methodological criticisms, studies and,
    106-114
  obstacle typology and, 215-218
  study of, 7-8
  See also Discourse perspective; Persuasive
    message production; Strategy
    selection
Compliance seeking/resisting:
  ethical issues in, 8-13
  example of, 4-6
  goal of, 9-13
  listener adaptation and, 62-66,
    63-65 (tables)
  means of, 8-9
  request messages and, 211-213
  strategies of, 28
  See also Cognitive editing; Contextual
    factors; Ethical-threshold model;
    Message analysis
Computer-assisted analysis, 54
Conceptual dimensions, 56-57, 67 (table)
  deductive derivation of, 60-66,
    62-65 (tables)
  evaluation of, 66-69
  inductive derivation of, 57-60, 59 (table)
  influence strategies and, 56-57
  See also Cognitive perspectives
Conflict Tactics Scales (CTS), 297
Constructivist perspective, vii, 60
  abstractness in, 116-117, 121
  conceptual criticisms of, 123-124
  construct system development, 116,
    119-123, 122 (table)
  listener adaptation, analysis of, 60-66,
    62-64 (tables), 117-119, 119 (table)
  message production and, 128-129
  methodological criticisms, 124-128
  role category questionnaire and, 125-126
  social-perception processes, 117, 118
  strategy-construction procedure, 126-128
  theoretical/methodological foundations
    of, 115-117
  See also Strategy selection
Content theme analysis, 48
  computer-assisted analysis system, 54
  evaluation of, 52-55

exhaustiveness criterion and, 54
  thematic analysis, 48-52, 50-51(table),
    53 (table)
  theoretical structure and, 54-55
Contextual factors, 43-44, 293-296,
    295-296 (table)
  child physical abuse, 297-310
  interactive contexts, viii, ix, 3-4, 16
  research on, 344-345
  upward influence strategies, 310-336
Conversation. See Discourse perspectives;
    Pre-conversational plans
Conversation analysis (CA), 197
  analytic concepts in, 198-201
  conditional relevance, 199-200
  goals/assumptions of, 197-198
  insertion sequences, 200
  preference organization, 200-201
Conversational implicative
    theory, 188-192
Conversational planning, 249-252
Cognitive Failures Questionnaire, 272,
    273 (table)
  communication competence, perception
    of, 272-274
  executive control processes and,
    271-272
  interactive planning and, 278-280
  on-line cognitions and, 267-270,
    269 (table)
  physically abusive mothers and, 307-310
  plans in, 250
  situational factors, on-line planning and,
    270-271
  top-down/bottom-up approaches,
    251-252
  See also Pre-conversational plans
Cross-cultural comparisons, 43-44
Cultural issues, 12-13
  cross-cultural comparisons, 43-44
  individualist vs. collectivist cultures,
    154-160, 156 (table), 158 (table)
  intercultural interactions, 154-160, 156
    (table), 158 (table)
  pre-conversational plans and, 260-262,
    263 (table)

Data collection, 113-114
Deception, 8-9
Developmental theory. See Constructivist
    perspective

Discourse perspectives:
  case study, 183-185
  compliance-seeking strategies and,
     215-218
  conversational maxims, 187-192
  conversation analysis, 197-201
  obstacle construct and, 201-205
  questioning strategies in, 185-187
  request messages, obstacles and,
       205-210, 206-207 (tables),
       209 (table), 213-215
  resistance, motivation/truth and, 211-213
  speech act theory, 192-197
  See also Cognitive perspectives; Face;
     Message design logic theories;
     Politeness theory
Dominance, 11-12, 58-60, 59 (table)

Emotion. *See* Attribution theory
Emotional appeal strategy, 37, 93-94, 106,
   345-348
Ethical issues:
  domination, 11-12
  goal of compliance, 9-13
  individual selfhood, 12-13
  means to compliance, 8-9
  positive regard, 10
  self-determination, right of, 10-11
Ethical threshold model, 13, 93-94, 106
Explicitness, 58-60, 59 (table)

Face, viii, 218
  compliance-gaining and, 220
  face-threatening acts, 219-225, 221-222
     (table), 224 (table), 227
  maintenance of, 219
  message design logic theories
     and, 230-239
  politeness theory and, 218-230
  redressive action and, 223
  upward influence goals and, 331-336,
     333 (table)
Family Interaction Coding System, 300, 301
   (table)
Fear appeals, 7, 8
Feminist values, 10-11

Gender differences, 13
  compliance-seeking/resisting strategies
     and, 102-104
  goal pursuit and, 175-177

Goal pursuit, viii, 15-16, 133-134
  argument strategies, 164-165
  cognitive editing standards and, 144-148,
     146 (table)
  cognitive rules model and, 168-173, 169
     (table), 172 (table)
  complexity, goal/behavioral, 160-166
  construct differentiation and, 163,
     165-166, 171
  conversational constraints and,
     151-160
  cultural influences on, 154-160, 156
     (table), 158 (table)
  gender differences and, 175-177
  goal measurement and, 136-137
  goals perspective, utility of, 173-179
  ideological assumptions in, 174-177
  influence goals, research summary,
     139-144, 140 (table), 166-168
  interaction goals, 134-137, 168-173
  outcomes of, 177-179
  primary goals, 137-139, 150
  schema development, 142-144
  secondary goals, 139, 148-150, 149 (table),
     151 (table)
  situationally relevant objectives, 161-162
  See also Cognitive perspectives; Discourse
     perspectives; Message design logic
     theories

Hierarchy principle, 274-278, 309-310
Hypothetical scenarios, 113-114, 127

Identity management strategies, 36-37,
   38 (table)
Influence goals, 139-144, 140 (table)
  cognitive editing standards and, 144-148,
     146 (table)
  goal/behavior complexity and, 160-166
Influence interactions, viii, ix, 3-4, 16
  knowledge requirements in, 243-245
  research in, 342-344
  sequencing in, 75-76
  strategy-construction procedures and,
     127-128
  transactional nature of, 78
  See also Interpersonal influence episodes;
     Message analysis; Upward influence
     strategies
Institutional contexts.
    See Contextual factors

Interactions:
    contexts of, viii, ix, 3-4, 16
    goals of, 134-137
    intercultural, 154-160, 156 (table),
        158 (table)
    See also Influence interactions
Interpersonal communication.
    See Goal pursuit
Interpersonal construct systems, 116-117,
    120-121
Interpersonal influence episodes, viii-ix, 7
    hypothetical vs. naturalistic interactions,
        113-114
    positive regard and, 10
    See also Compliance-gaining interactions;
        Message analysis
Invitational rhetoric, 11

Justification strategies, 37, 38 (table)

Knowledge. See Cognitive perspectives;
    Pre-conversational plans

Likelihood-of-use ratings, 106-112, 109 (table)
Listener adaptation:
    age factor in, 60-62, 62(table), 117-119,
        119 (table)
    compliance-resisting appeals and, 64-66,
        65 (table)
    compliance-seeking appeals and, 62-64,
        63-64 (table)
    construct system development and,
        119-123, 122 (table)
Locus of control, 58

Mass communication, 6-7, 91
Maxims. See Discourse perspective
MBRS Study, 86-88
    findings of, 88-91, 89-90 (tables)
    likelihood-of-use ratings and, 108
    strategy choice and, 88, 112-113
Message analysis:
    case study, 21-24
    conceptual dimensions, 56-69, 59 (table),
        62-65 (tables), 67 (table)
    content themes, 48-55, 50-51 (table),
        53 (table)
    hypothetical scenarios, 113-114
    influence interactions, description
        of, 24-26
    significance of, 26-27

temporal characteristics, 69-79, 71 (table)
    See also Listener adaptation; Nominal-level
        typologies
Message design logic theories, viii, 70
    background, communication strategies,
        230-232
    concepts/assumptions in, 232-237,
        233 (table)
    conventional logic, 234-235
    developmental progression and, 236
    evaluation of, 237-239
    expressive logic, 232-234
    message production, 236-237
    rhetorical logic, 235-236
Metaphors. See Discourse perspectives
Motivation. See Attribution theory

Naturalistic interactions, 114
Negotiation strategies, 37, 38 (table)
Nominal-level typologies, 27, 105
    coding scheme, exhaustiveness of, 42-44
    compliance-resisting strategies, 36-39,
        38 (table)
    compliance-seeking strategies, 29-36,
        30-31 (table), 34-36 (tables)
    evaluation of, 39-44
    strategy typology and, 28-29
    theoretical grounding of, 39-42
Nonnegotiation strategies, 36, 38 (table)

Obstacle construct, 201-202
attribution theory and, 203-205
    compliance-seeking and, 215-218
    directives and, 203
    motivation/emotion, dimensions of,
        204-205, 206-207 (tables)
    obstacle hypothesis, 206-210
    request messages and, 205-210,
        209 (table), 213-215, 214 (table)
    resistance, reasons for, 211-213
    speech act theories and, 202-203
On-line cognition. See Conversational
    planning
Organizations. See upward
    influence strategies
Orthogenic principle, 115-116

Personal construct psychology. See
    Constructivist perspective
Personality attributes, 99-102, 100-101 (table),
    105, 147

Persuasive message production, vii, 6-7
    compliance seeking/resisting and, 4-6
    examples of, 1-4
    goal-oriented activity of, 15-16
    interactive contexts and, 16
    research in, 13-14
    See also Compliance seeking/resisting;
        Goal pursuit; Influence interactions;
        Message analysis; Strategy selection
Planning. *See* Conversational planning
Politeness theory, viii, 60
    assumptions of, 218-225
    context-specific analysis and, 229-230
    criticisms of, 226-230
    face, maintenance of, 219
    face-threatening acts, 219-225,
        221-222 (tables), 224 (table), 227
    heuristic value of, 225-226
    linguistic strategies in, 223-225,
        224 (table)
    power and, 220-221
Positive regard, 10, 13
Pre-conversational plans:
    analysis of, 260, 261 (table)
    complexity in, 258-259, 262-266,
        265 (table)
    cultural differences in, 260-262,
        263 (table)
    formation of, 252-253
    knowledge sources in, 253, 254 (table)
    resistance, hierarchy principle and,
        274-278
    self-monitoring, effects
        of, 259-260
    structural variability in, 257-260
    utilization of, 253-257
    verbal fluency and, 264-265,
        265 (table)
Punishment-based strategies, 58
    See also Child physical abuse

Rebuff hypothesis, 74-75
Reciprocity norm, 78
Relationships. *See* Contextual factors
Request messages, 205
    assistance requests, 208
    clause typology within, 209-210,
        209 (table)
    indirect requests, 208
    initial request, compliance and, 213-215,
        214 (table)

obstacle hypothesis and, 206-210
    resistance, true reasons for, 211-213
Reward-based strategies, 58
Role Category Questionnaire (RCQ), 116, 118,
    125-126, 163, 171

Self-determination, 10-11
Selfhood, 12-13
Sex/gender differences, 13, 102-104
Situated talk. *See* Conversation analysis (CA)
Situationally relevant objectives, 161-162
Social contexts, 43-44
Socially acceptable/unacceptable
        strategies, 90, 93
    conversational constraints and, 152-153
    likelihood-of-use and, 107, 108-109,
        109 (table)
Social-perception processes, 117, 118,
    119 (table)
Social Perspectives Task, 125
Speech act theories, viii, 192
    constitutive rules, 193-197, 194 (table)
    illocutionary level of, 192-193
    indirect speech acts, 195-196
    obstacle construct and, 202-203
    persuasive message production and,
        196-197
    preparatory rules, 194-195
    propositional content rule, 193-194
    regulative rules, 193
    sincerity rule, 195
    See also Politeness theory
Strategies, 27-28
    construction procedure, 126-128
    nominal-level typologies, 28-39
    Strategy selection, vii, 3-4,
        15, 85-86
    compliance-gaining tradition and,
        86-115
    constructivist tradition, 115-128
    ethical threshold model, 93-94, 106
    gender/sex differences, 102-104
    MBRS study, 86-91, 89-90 (tables)
    personality attributes and, 99-102,
        100-101 (table)
    predictors of, 97-104, 106-112,
        109 (table), 126-127
    role category questionnaire and, 116,
        118, 125-126
    situational dimensions and,
        95-99, 96 (table)

subjective expected utility model and,
    91-93, 105
theoretical foundations, criticisms of,
    104-114, 123-128
Structural developmental theory. *See*
    Constructivist perspective
Subjective expected utility (SEU) model,
    91-93, 105

Temporal characteristics, 69
    duration of episodes, 73-74
    evaluation of, 78-79
    frequency data, 72-73
    pace, 76-78
    research on, 71 (table)

salience, message design logic and, 70-71
sequencing, interaction events, 74-76
Thematic analysis. *See* Content theme analysis
Threats, 8

Upward influence strategies, 310-312
    goals, identity implications of, 331-336,
        333 (table)
    goals, research on, 327-330
    literature limitations, 324-327
    power differences and, 311-312
    predictor variables, ecological perspectives,
        320-324, 322 (table)
    typologies of, 312-320, 314-315 (tables),
        317-318 (tables), 320 (table)

About the Author

Steven R. Wilson is Associate Professor and Director of Graduate Studies in the Department of Communication at Purdue University. He is one of five associate editors for the interdisciplinary journal *Personal Relationships* and past chair of the International Communication Association's Interpersonal Communication Division. His research and teaching focus on interpersonal influence and message production in a variety of contexts, from parent-child interaction in abusive families to intercultural business negotiations. He has published nearly 40 articles and book chapters on these topics.